It has been said, in regard to computer network communities, that no community is worthy of the name until it has had a wedding and a funeral. We, in the computer virus research tribe, have had both. We will not embarrass the newlyweds here. We wish, however, to dedicate this book to the memory of Ysrael Radai and Harold Joseph Highland. Their contributions to our field, and to so many others, are appreciated, and they will be sorely missed.

To the Meeter Machine, and its viral output.

—Robert Slade

To my daughter Katie, my constant reminder that computer security should not be confused with real life. Now, perhaps, we'll have time to play Monopoly.
Also to my mother, Gwendoline Harley, for being an honorary parent to Katie when I had to find time for Baby Book.

—David Harley

Dedicated to my friends Inger Marie, Melanie, Lars, Rainer, Stefano, and all my current and past students who continue in keeping me going when obstacles seem insurmountable.

—Urs Gattiker

Viruses Revealed

David Harley, Robert Slade, Urs Gattiker

Osborne/**McGraw-Hill**

New York Chicago San Francisco
Lisbon London Madrid Mexico City Milan
New Delhi San Juan Seoul Singapore Sydney Toronto

Osborne/**McGraw-Hill**
2600 Tenth Street
Berkeley, California 94710
U.S.A.

To arrange bulk purchase discounts for sales promotions, premiums, or fund-raisers, please contact Osborne/**McGraw-Hill** at the above address. For information on translations or book distributors outside the U.S.A., please see the International Contact Information page immediately following the index of this book.

Viruses Revealed

1234567890 CUS CUS 01987654321

ISBN 0-07-213090-3

Publisher	Brandon Nordin
Vice President & Associate Publisher	Scott Rogers
Acquisitions Editor	Jim Schachterle
Project Editor	Jody McKenzie
Acquisitions Coordinator	Timothy Madrid
Technical Editor	Christine M. Orshesky
Copy Editors	Andy Carroll, Andy Saff
Proofreader	Nancy McLaughlin
Indexer	Irv Hershman
Computer Designers	Roberta Steele, Jim Kussow, George T. Charbak
Illustrators	Michael Mueller, Lyssa Wald
Series Design	Roberta Steele
Cover Design	Greg Scott
Cover Illustration	Victor Stabin

This book was composed with Corel VENTURA™ Publisher.

Information has been obtained by Osborne/**McGraw-Hill** from sources believed to be reliable. However, because of the possibility of human or mechanical error by our sources, Osborne/**McGraw-Hill**, or others, Osborne/**McGraw-Hill** does not guarantee the accuracy, adequacy, or completeness of any information and is not responsible for any errors or omissions or the results obtained from use of such information.

Table of Contents

III Case Studies: What Went Wrong, What Went Right, What Can We Learn?

Foreword

David and Rob asked me to write a foreword to this new book. I've corresponded with both over the years, and their work with viruses has been of great value to many of us. After browsing a draft of their comprehensive effort, I am pleased at the amount of useful information they present in such an accessible manner (although, as an academic, I wish they provided more specific references to their sources—something to look forward to in the second edition). In fact, their book is so comprehensive, I wondered what I could address that they had not already covered. However, as I thought more about it, I realized that they haven't completely addressed what is yet to come. To understand the future, it helps to consider the past as context. Thus, I will reflect some on the past and how it relates to the present. After that, I challenge you to read this book with thoughts of what the present portends for the future—and how your awareness and action may have an effect. As George Santayana wrote, "Those who forget the past are condemned to fulfill it". (Yes, that is the correct quote. Many people cite it incorrectly.)

Twelve years ago, I coauthored the first general, English-language technical reference on computer viruses ("Computer Viruses: Dealing with Electronic Vandalism and Programmed Threats," by E. H. Spafford, K. A. Heaphy, and D. J. Ferbrache, ADAPSO (now ITAA), 1989). At that time, there were fewer than 100 viruses in general circulation—about 75 for DOS/Windows, 20 for the Apple Macintosh, and a few dozen for other platforms, including the Amiga. This had grown from the first virus in the wild, the Elk Cloner virus for Apple II computers in 1982, through a half-dozen new viruses for the Intel-based platform in 1986–1988, to the IBM Christmas Tree EXEC worm/virus, and then to the Morris Internet and WANK worms.

As of mid-2001, there are thousands of computer viruses—perhaps as many as 75,000. Some vendors claim to receive reports of as many as 20 new viruses a week. In fact, with the ease of creating macro viruses for popular email and word processing software, the rate at which new viruses are being reported appears to be increasing. Throw the various worms, Trojan horses, backdoors, and other malware into the mix, and the numbers grow even larger.

If you do a little analysis of the historical data, you can project the trends of the past two decades forward with some statistical tools. Within a few short years, we will be seeing a new worm or virus released more frequently than once every hour. How is anyone going to keep up with that rate of attack? What defences can we possibly employ? And how much of our processing power will we need to employ to gain reasonable protection?

It really didn't have to be like this.

Fred Cohen wrote extensively about computer viruses in the 1980s, but only a few people seemed to pay attention. The late Harold Highland focused attention on viruses in his editorials in *Computers & Security,* along with publishing articles on viruses. The book I coauthored, along with other references of the time, warned about good computer hygiene and the potential for future problems. At many conferences and workshops, we discussed the future of computer viruses and malware. In 1990 and 1991, both Harold and I made presentations at the NYC DPMA Virus conferences (the premier virus research meetings of the time) on macro viruses, and their potential—long before the emergence of the Concept virus.

However, several of the major software vendors failed to send anyone to those meetings, nor did they appear to read any of the security publications. The vendors told researchers that viruses weren't their concern, because only a few of their customers had problems with them at the time.

One major company in particular was notably absent from the scene, and the results are painfully obvious today. For instance, that company designed features into its software that helped viruses spread more easily, despite warnings to the contrary. That same software company labelled the first major macro virus a "prank", and apparently never tried to find or discipline the employee who wrote it. Can you guess which company that might be? Here's a hint: more than 99 percent of all known computer viruses and worms run solely on its products, out of proportion to its actual share of the market. Here's another hint: the Melissa and LoveBug incidents affecting its software and causing billions of dollars of damage were almost identical in overall nature to the extensively documented Christmas Tree EXEC incident in 1987. Today's problems should surprise only those who forgot the past—or never bothered to learn it.

Unfortunately, the dominant software architecture that runs our national defences, underlies our public utilities, powers our government agencies, and supports our banks, medical establishments, and educational organizations is also from this same company. Our whole computing infrastructure is highly vulnerable to malware as a result. And in addition to being susceptible to computer viruses, those products seem to be subject to a never-ending stream of critical security patches, many as a result of sloppy coding (for example, buffer overflows) that have been known for decades to present security problems. We are now operating in a world where a 12-year-old with a web browser and a text editor can run self-duplicating software to execute network attack scripts—software that can disrupt a government agency or multinational corporation. If some attack software isn't on a WWW site this week, then all an attacker needs to do is wait a few weeks for a few more vulnerabilities and attacks to be discovered and posted.

Remember the Aztecs? They ruled a mighty empire until exposure to a few hundred Spaniards with smallpox and measles incapacitated or killed 90 percent of their population and left them too weak to resist conquest. With no immunity, they were easy pickings for a vastly smaller (and weaker) force. Do you think we might have something to learn from the past?

Of course, the fault is not solely that of the software vendors. Consumers are not demanding better quality, are not making informed choices, and are not holding vendors accountable for shoddy goods. Thus, vendors are providing what the consumers seem to want to buy without complaint, and it is hard to fault them (completely) for that. Many computer users today accept computer viruses, crashes, and security flaws as a standard part of their everyday computing existence. They don't understand other alternatives, or they think the cost of switching to something else will be too high. However, before long, the cost of anti-virus and security software, recovery efforts, incident response, and Help Desks will overwhelm the cost of the systems to which they are so attached. Then what?

We also have a real problem with effective deterrence by way of penalizing the authors of malware. Since 1980, I am aware of fewer than 10 people who have been charged and convicted in a criminal court for writing malware. I am aware of only two civil suits for damages. Given the attitudes expressed by authors of viruses (see Chapter 15), what is being done to deter them? Without some credible threat of exposure and penalty, it seems unlikely we will reduce the population of virus writers. In fact, as more computers come online, the tools become more accessible, and the attitude continues that viruses are a part of "business as usual", we should expect the number of authors to increase, perhaps even faster than it already has.

So, we have an environment that is very susceptible to viruses, vendors to whom security has historically seemed to be a secondary concern (if it has been a concern at all), consumers who accept the pitiful status quo as normal, and perpetrators who have no credible fear of reprisal. Is it any wonder that the anti-virus vendors are profiting....and are necessary?

Despite all that has happened, I do not believe that the future needs to be like the past. Each of us can make a difference. We can start by modifying our own behavior:

▶ If even 10 percent of people would stop accepting email attachments in formats that can carry malware (macro-related or otherwise), then perhaps people would stop sending them. That would eliminate or at least curtail one common method of transmission.

▶ If each time a new threat appeared we all referred to it with a more precise name than "computer virus", perhaps users would develop a little more awareness. In most cases, "Microsoft virus" would be a far more accurate term.

▶ If we all stopped using the same three or four applications for *everything,* perhaps we wouldn't see malware that would threaten the majority of users on the planet when the next vulnerability is found or virus released.

▶ If one out of every five users would evaluate alternative platforms for reasons of safety rather than cost, then perhaps we would eventually have more credible choices available with security as a design goal.

Armies that stuck with cavalry because of their investment in saddles, stables, and training received a rude awakening in the first half of the 20th century, when the tank and machine gun were widely deployed. Having a platform immune to common security threats is a competitive advantage in any arena, even if it costs more and requires some additional training to employ.

So, as you read through all the history and advice compiled in this book by these accomplished researchers, keep your eyes and mind open for hints on how to design your own protection and shape the future. Resolve to make a new future as one who remembers the past, and actually learns from the experiences of others.

Safe computing, all.

—spaf

July 2001

Eugene H. Spafford is a professor of computer sciences at Purdue University, a professor of philosophy, and is director of the Center for Education Research Information Assurance and Security (CERIAS). CERIAS is a campuswide multidisciplinary centre, with a broadly focused mission to explore issues related to protecting information and information resources. Spaf has written extensively about information security, software engineering, and professional ethics.

Spafford is a fellow of the Association for Computing Machinery (ACM), fellow of the American Association for the Advancement of Science (AAAS), fellow of the Institute of Electrical and Electronics Engineers (IEEE), and is a charter recipient of the Computer Society's Golden Core Award. In 2000, he was named as a CISSP, honoris causa. Among his many activities, he is co-chair of the ACM's US Public Policy Committee, a member of the board of directors of the Computing Research Association, and a member of the US Air Force Scientific Advisory Board. He was the year 2000 recipient of the National Institute of Standards and Technology/ National Center for Standards and Certification (NIST/NCSC) National Computer Systems Security Award, generally regarded as the field's most significant honour in information security research. In 2001, he was named as one of the recipients of the Charles B. Murphy Awards, Purdue University's highest award for outstanding undergraduate teaching. In 2001, he was elected to the Information Systems Security Association (ISSA) Hall of Fame, and he was awarded the William Hugh Murray medal of the National Colloquium for Information Systems Security Education (NCISSE) for his contributions to research and education in infosec.

About the Authors

Robert Slade

Rob Slade is a data communications and security specialist from North Vancouver, British Columbia, Canada.

His research into computer viral programs began when they first appeared as a major problem "in the wild". Acting initially as the unofficial archivist for the budding research community, he has since become known for "Mr. Slade's lists". One of the working group for the VIRUS-L FAQ, he has produced a series of review and tutorial articles that have been published as *Robert Slade's Guide to Computer Viruses*. He is the founder of the DECUS Canada Security SIG. He still considers data security to be a minor sideline, and was astounded to hear himself referred to recently as a "leader" in the security community.

Rob is more widely known for his series of technical book reviews. If you would rather not have to scour USENET looking for them, you can now place yourself on a mailing list to receive new ones either by sending any message to techbooks-subscribe@egroups.com or by visiting the eGroups web site at www.egroups.com/list/techbooks/, which also has an archive of recent postings. Full archives of the book reviews are kindly hosted by both Victoria Telecommunity Net at http://victoria.tc.ca/techrev/mnbk.htm and the Computer Underground Digest at Northern Illinois University (http://sun.soci.niu.edu/~rslade/mnbk.htm). The reviews form the basis of a column in *TeleManagement* (www.angustel.ca/teleman/tm.html).

At present, he takes every available opportunity to teach operating systems to his grandchildren. He is married to the world's best executive secretary, which is probably the only reason he actually got the book finished. His next book will be a computer security glossary. It is next to impossible to get him to take "bio" writing seriously.

Rob Slade can be reached as rslade@sprint.ca or rslade@vcn.bc.ca.

David Harley

David Harley has a work history more chequered than most chessboards, embracing music, nursing, various aspects of the building trade, computing, and administration. He worked from 1989 to 2001 at the Imperial Cancer Research Fund in London, originally as an administrator and programmer, then as a network engineer and support analyst, latterly as a security specialist. He now works for the United Kingdom's NHS Information Authority as Support Services Manager, where he still specializes in security, but is now allowed to express himself more pompously.

He is an active member of EICAR (the European Institute for Computer Anti-Virus Research) and a charter member of AVIEN (the Anti-Virus Information Exchange Network), where he is participating in projects concerned with certification of anti-virus personnel and virus analysis, not to mention the Disciplinary Committee, which is much less exciting than it sounds.

His other affiliations include the WildList Organization and ICSA Labs, where he is working on Apple Macintosh-related security projects. He has something of a reputation as an expert in the Mac arena, largely because no one else actually cares about Macs except those who don't own an Umbrella. He maintains a number of security-focused web sites (when time allows), including Mac Virus II.

His previous security-related writing includes several Internet FAQs, a curious assortment of conference papers, magazine articles, chapters on viruses and Trojan horses for the third edition of *Maximum Security,* and a chapter on security and healthcare for the fourth edition of the *Computer Security Handbook* (with Paul Brusil).

His hobbies include parenting, flippancy, blues guitar, not getting to the opera, and spending money he doesn't have on software he doesn't have time to use. His ambitions include getting a life and returning to some nontechnical writing.

David Harley can be reached as macvirus@dircon.co.uk.

Urs E. Gattiker

Urs Gattiker is Obel Family Foundation Professor of Innovation and Technology Management at the University of Aalborg. His previous positions include Stanford Center for Organization Research, the Melbourne Business School, the University of Lethbridge, the University of the German Federal Armed Forces at Hamburg, and the Aarhus School of Business. He is a member of the supervisory board of KonNet GmbH (Germany), and a member of Bankinvest's Advisory Board for its BI Technology A/S' IT Venture Fund (http://www.BankInvest.dk). He also is a board member of various organizations, including B2B Agro Scandinavia A/S, Naventi A/S, Vigilante Inc. (USA), and Vupti A/S.

His books include *Technology Management and Organizations* (Sage, 1990), and *The Internet as a Diverse Community: Cultural, Organizational and Political Issues* (Lawrence Erlbaum, 2001); he is currently writing *Electronic Patient Records, Internet and Data Security* with Inger Marie Giversen and Christine Orshesky (Lawrence Erlbaum). He has recently edited a book with Laurie Larwood, *Impact Analysis: How Research Can Enter Application and Make a Difference* (Lawrence Erlbaum, 1999) and is currently writing on a book about entrepreneurship and start-ups.

Gattiker served as Chair for the Technology & Innovation and Research Method divisions of the U.S. Academy of Management (the leading association for academics and consultants in management in the United States). He is one of the founders and was an executive member of the Canadian Association for the Management of Technology (CANMOT), now the Innovation Management Association of Canada (IMAC) and the Technology Management Division of the Administrative Sciences Association of Canada (ASAC). Gattiker also chairs the Task Force for Trust and e-Commerce of the European Institute for Computer Anti-Virus Research (EICAR) and is a member of EICAR's Scientific Advisory Board as well as the EICAR Board.

He is currently spearheading the efforts of a virtual research organization on e-commerce, new media, and technology policy. Research and white papers can be found at http://Papers.WebUrb.net.

Urs Gattiker can be reached as WebUrs@WebUrb.net.

About the Technical Editor

Christine M. Orshesky, with more than ten years of information security experience, has supported information security efforts, including malware protection and incident response at various government and corporate organizations. Her most notable responsibility included managing malware response initiatives for the Department of Defense at the Pentagon. After her experiences there, Orshesky founded i-secure Corporation to provide vendor-neutral malware-protection strategies and education. She has participated in numerous information security and other industry conferences, and maintains her professional certifications in information security and quality assurance.

Acknowledgments

We owe too much to too many people to list them all. In particular, we must mention our families, for their patience and support through a long and demanding project.

We acknowledge the work of many people at *Virus Bulletin*, AVIEN, EICAR, ICSA Labs, the WildList Organization, the Universities of Hamburg, Tampere, and Magdeburg, and the anti-virus (AV) companies. Thank you for your expertise, for your help, and just for holding the line. We can't possibly list everyone who deserves a mention, but any such list would have to include a number of people who may not have contributed directly to this book, but without whose hard work and generosity in sharing information, our work would have been even harder. We list just a few here, and in no particular order: Alan Solomon, Paul Ducklin, Vesselin Bontchev, Jimmy Kuo, Sarah Gordon, Robert Vibert, Henri Delger, Joe Wells, Larry Bridwell, Bruce Burrell, Shane Coursen, Nick FitzGerald, and Graham Cluley. We also thank Rob Rosenberger and George Smith, for not letting anyone get away with anything; those virus writers and former virus writers who felt it was worth maintaining a dialogue and discussing the issues; and the volunteers of VIRUS-L, alt.comp.virus, alt.comp.antivirus, security-focus, and elsewhere, who continue to provide help and advice because so many people seem to need it. We don't always agree with them, but their public-spiritedness makes a real difference.

A book is almost always a team effort. This one is no exception—fortunately, given the difficulties that arose during the production stage. Many people deserve credit: Urs, for kicking the project off in the first place; David, for attempting to keep the thing in some sort of order; Rob, for holding it together when family illness and a drastic change of career and location nearly knocked David off the project altogether; Christine, whose contributions went far beyond technical review; Spaf, for saying what needed to be said (as always); the long-suffering production team at Osborne, for their never-ending struggle to keep an overstretched and sometimes irascible team of authors focused; and Gloria, for copyediting services beyond the call of marital duty.

Introduction

Why Did We Write This Book?

We intend to make available high-quality and broadly useful information about malicious software (malware) in general, viruses in particular, and about anti-virus/anti-malware technology and its application in the real world and in the context of general security. We also want to ensure that we cover the most contemporary trends in regard to viruses and malware, which have diverged significantly in recent years from traditional forms. Finally, while we are particularly addressing systems administrators and IT managers, we want to make sure that this material is available for any computer user, and not just those who have made a special study of the field.

Perhaps even more urgently, we mean to counter the extremely poor information that bedevils the security field in general and the virus field in particular. To this end, we include not only analysis of threats and countermeasures, but also information on sources of further information with some indication as to our assessment of their reliability.

We also hope to be the first authors ever to make a million out of a book on computer viruses, but we're not counting on it.

Why This Book Is Different

This book isn't quite like the majority of works on security. Many security volumes are good sources of information on other areas of security, yet inaccurate on virus specifics.

General security books are also often inclined to a full-disclosure mode, which isn't altogether appropriate for a virus book. Not that we necessarily advocate the paternalist, "Gods and Ants" mindset that characterizes some sectors of the anti-virus industry, who usually lean towards the nondisclosure end of the continuum. We hope that you will, as far as possible, test what we tell you and make up your own mind. But the greatest disclosure problem in virus literature concerns actual virus code.

The indiscriminate inclusion of virus code (existing or new) in previous books and elsewhere has, in our opinion, been of more use to the aspiring virus writer than to the hard-pressed systems administrator. As Gene Spafford has famously said, showing people how to pour sugar into the gas tank doesn't teach them much about auto mechanics. You have to know a bit about how viruses operate in order to protect against them, but the finer details of virus coding are completely irrelevant. So we won't publish virus code (let alone original virus code).

Roll-your-own viruses are generally the opposite of helpful, except in very carefully controlled circumstances. We can't say that no bona fide researcher ever modified or created a virus to test a concept (though some highly capable individuals will not do so under any circumstances, and some companies flatly forbid it). However, publishing viable virus code is not where we want to go.

Dissecting individual viruses doesn't give you the means of defending against all viruses. You can't implement countermeasures to their maximum effect without knowing more than a little about the attacks. However, most readers will rely heavily on commercial solutions, although we hope you won't put this book down convinced that anti-virus is always enough. We consider it generally more useful to concentrate on the details of evaluation and implementation of solutions than the minutiae of a few of the tens of thousands of viruses and variants. Where we do focus on particular viruses, we will be more concerned with their significance in terms of social impact and the defensive measures they necessitate than with the fine detail of their code.

However, we will tell you more than enough about virus mechanisms to understand what the threat is, and, more importantly, how commercial anti-virus software protects against it. Furthermore, unlike most vendor manuals and web sites, we'll tell you about some cracks that anti-virus software can't paste over. Virus authors are already exploiting these, directly or indirectly, and you'll need to know about them too if you're to maximize your own security.

Roll-your-own anti-virus software is a pretty limited option: systems administrators and home users may be able to block certain classes of threat, but can't compete with the professionals at detecting and disinfecting the tens of thousands of distinct known viruses. We are aware of attempts to sell books on the premise that "If you read this, you can write your own anti-virus software, and the security vendors will be lining up to give you a job". This premise is based on the mother of all fallacies. You can fill in some of the gaps left by commercial anti-virus products. You can sometimes bypass the need for commercial products by avoiding vulnerable operating systems, applications and utilities, or configurations. You can (at a price) use generic defences, such as change detection software, rather than distribute definitions updates as new viruses are discovered. What you can't do is compete with the industry on its own terms on detecting known viruses. The chances are you don't have the time or access to every new virus.

Isn't virus management a security issue? Of course it is, and it's best implemented within the context of a holistic security strategy, when it's done right by people who know viruses as well as or better than they do other areas of security. Unfortunately, people who are competent in some areas of security sometimes overestimate their own competence in other areas, and viruses seem to attract a particularly virulent brand of ultracrepidarianism ("acting or speaking outside one's ability or knowledge"). (A tip of the hat here to Rob Rosenberger, whose article on "False Authority Syndrome" first introduced at least one of us to the word; you can find the article at www.vmyths.com/fas/fas1.cfm.) Of course, this principle also works the other way. For instance, only the bravest, most nervous, or least experienced systems administrator is likely to let an anti-virus vendor write his or her firewall policy, however good the product may be.

Ultracrepidarianism

The term derives from the Latin *ultra crepidem* (beyond the sole of the shoe). The story goes that a cobbler criticized Apelles, a painter in ancient Greece, for his representation of a human figure in a painting. Apelles accepted the criticism as applied to the figure's slipper, but not *ultra crepidem,* regarding the representation of the leg as beyond the cobbler's specialist expertise. Why he did so in Latin rather than Greek is not altogether clear.

This book also differs a little from other virus books. After all, aren't there enough virus books already? Well, there are good virus books, and there are recent virus books, and at the time of starting this project, these are disjoint sets. Unfortunately, the most accurate books aren't usually current, so that they miss out on some of the issues that have come to concern us all since. Meanwhile, most of the current books aren't accurate. One or two exceptions are noted in the book, but not here, since we want to keep you focused on buying this one....

Neither do we think that we've included everything you'll ever need to know, but this book is as up-to-date, accurate, and comprehensive as we can make it, and that in itself makes it somewhat unique. Just to make sure we don't have to eat those words, we include at the end of Chapter 19 information on hot issues that started to warm up as we were completing the last few chapters. Mind your fingers.

Who Should Use This Book?

This book is also somewhat different as regards its target audience. There is a notable absence of books in this area that are aimed specifically at the information-technology (IT) professional with a "need to know" about virus management. This group might include systems and network administrators, security analysts and specialist anti-virus engineers, other support engineers, power users, management, the computing press, and even students of computer science. We aim to redress that deficit. However, this book makes few assumptions about levels of technical knowledge (though it rather assumes that you use computers). Home computer users or non-specialists within corporate organizations will also be able to follow this book and benefit according to their needs. Education is a vital component in the fight against virus infestations. We expect that technical managers should be able to hand this book (marked as to appropriate chapters) to the ordinary office worker or executive, and raise his or her awareness of specific topics.

The book isn't intended for anti-virus professionals within the industry: full-time, competent researchers, virus analysts, and such will not need us to fill them in on the technical detail of their own jobs. On the other hand, much time spent in conversation with anti-virus sales staff and marketroids has convinced us that knowledge of one product is no substitute for knowledge of product-nonspecific virus/anti-virus technology. Often, these people aren't even aware that they're selling you what they have, not what you need, and that their sales pitches are based on fallacies as much as facts. (Q: What's the difference between a computer salesperson and a used-car salesperson? A: A car salesperson can usually drive, and knows when he or she is lying to you.) Furthermore, we can think of some high-powered anti-virus researchers who have yet to learn that knowledge of that technology is only part of virus management. If we can't rely on the vendor information providers to get it right, we can at least hope that you'll be better equipped to evaluate their expertise once you've read this book.

The clarion calls "Trust me: I'm a vendor" or "Trust me: I'm a consultant", or even "Trust me: I'm an Instant Expert" make no more sense than "Trust me: I'm a virus writer". We don't want you to trust anyone (even us) because of who that person claims to be, or what he or she claims to know. Too many people are already willing to relieve you of all responsibility for your virus problems. We aim to empower you to make at least one decision about virus management yourself. If that decision is to hire others to deal with the problem, at least make that decision on the basis of your own knowledge, not on wishful thinking (yours or theirs).

Clearly, this isn't a book for virus writers, either. We've already explained our reluctance to demonstrate or reproduce certain types of code, so the book will be of little use to the kind of virus writer who makes trivial modifications to existing code to make his or her own variant. Yes, we know that lots of legitimate and useful code is based on other people's code. In our experience, though:

▶   Virus code isn't generally legitimate or useful.

▶   Many virus variants are changes so trivial (such as the modification of a nonessential text string) that they can only be intended to allow the writer to claim authorship without more than the barest minimum of effort.

Perhaps a virus writer will catch a passing idea from something mentioned here and develop it into something startlingly novel, and possibly malevolent. This is one of the risks taken by all writers in the security field. We can take a stand on not publishing what is useful only to the bad guys, but most technical information is value-free. If it's useful to you, it might be useful to your enemy too. We take each case on its own merits.

Sometimes, anti-virus researchers play off-duty games (usually at security conferences), such as testing each other's help lines or swapping nightmare scenarios. In general, we intend to keep our nightmares to ourselves unless there is something you can do about them right now.

How This Book Is Organized

The book is divided into five main parts, as described in the following sections.

Part I: The Problem

Malware takes many forms, and we'll deal with nearly all of them. However, single instances of malware are not necessarily or even usually dealt with individually. Although we will sometimes suggest a specific approach to a specific type of problem, usually we explore general classes of malware, then (in Part II) the general classes of anti-malware technology that can be used to deal with them.

We intend this book to be useful to a wide range of computer users, including (indeed, especially) the highly computer-literate. However, experience indicates that it's unsafe to assume that expertise in one field of computer use, including security (or systems administration and security), necessarily indicates expertise in anti-virus issues. We therefore start with some baseline definitions, just to ensure that we all understand approximately the same thing when we talk of key concepts like Trojan horses, viruses, worms, damage, and infection. If you are familiar with older books and other resources on the subject, not all this material will be new to you. However, Part I does reflect recent trends in the way we think about older threats, which may be of interest in its own right. We will of course focus on current threats and classes of threat. These are likely to be of particular interest given that they have appeared since the first wave of classic texts, and are therefore not covered there, while recent books have generally demonstrated a poor grasp of the technology and its implications. A detailed analysis of classes and subclasses of malware follows in later chapters, while malware meriting individual attention is examined in detail in Part III.

Part II: System Solutions

Part II considers anti-virus and anti-malware technology in detail, then goes on to discuss their real-world application within the enterprise.

Part III: Case Studies

In Part III we provide a detailed look at some specific virus/malware incidents—what makes them noteworthy, and what lessons can we learn from them.

Part IV: Social Aspects

Part IV looks at social issues. We believe that viruses are a social problem, and social problems cannot be solved by purely technological means. Sadly, it will take more than this book to solve the social problems of which computer vandalism is a small component. Certainly, though, the virus management professional cannot afford to ignore the human dimension, whether it concerns the vandals themselves or their victims. Part IV also contains the summary of summaries and the "stop press" chapter.

Part V: Appendixes and Glossary

The final part includes a detailed glossary and some extra material donated by the authors and others.

Where to Go from Here

There is a fair amount of reading in this book, and some suggestions for hands-on work on systems protection. The book won't turn you into a top-flight anti-virus expert, but if that's your ambition, reading the book straight through will certainly give you a reasonable grounding and links to enough further information to keep you going for years. You may be accustomed to books like this coming with a CD full of free software and documentation. This doesn't work very well with anti-virus software, since by the time the book hits the bookshelves, many programs will already be out of date. Our experience suggests that making anti-virus software available for evaluation can actually become counterproductive as it gets increasingly past the software's sell-by date. Furthermore, while there is some freeware and shareware that we have no hesitation in recommending, it's probably better to give you pointers to current versions and information. We can do this better from a dynamic information source—that is, the web site—than we can from a CD, which may go out of date between the date of press and the publication of the book. We specifically mention free software in Chapter 8, and on web pages at the following sites:

> http://victoria.tc.ca/techrev/vrfresft.htm
> http://sun.soci.niu.edu/~rslade/vrfresft.htm

You can also check for updated web links at these sites:

> http://www.osborne.com/errata/errata.shtml
> http://www.viruses-revealed.org.uk/

We hope these sites will keep you safe enough to read the rest of the book.

The Problem

Baseline Definitions

IN THIS CHAPTER:

Computer Virus Fact and Fantasy

Definitions

Instant Guide to Anti-Virus Software

You might call this the executive summary of the whole book, or the two-minute guide to viruses and related problems. This chapter may not tell you anything you do not already know, but bear with us. The computer security field is over-populated by "instant experts" who "know everything" about security in general and viruses in particular, without actually having done the research. We therefore prefer to level the playing field a little with some basic definitions to ensure that you are not "infected" with some of the misconceptions perpetuated by some sectors of the press and other undependable resources.

NOTE

This may sound anti-journalist. In fact, we all know responsible, capable journalists. We even know computer journalists who could reasonably be described as virus experts (and we turn in the occasional article ourselves). However, a journalist without specific expertise in a particular area is highly reliant upon the quality of information received from others, and some have been very unfortunate in their choice of expert informants on anti-virus issues. In this way, misinformation from individuals who should have known better has become widely distributed.

This chapter does not go into full details of virus and other mechanisms, but is restricted to broad principles. Malicious software (malware) is an area where there are very few indisputable definitions, and misconceptions are rife, so we prefer to start with a few simple baseline definitions. We will proceed to the heavy-duty jargon and hair-splitting later.

Some examples in Chapter 2 will give you an idea of how viruses can work, and more details are given on actual viral operations in Chapters 3, 4, and 5. Part III includes detailed case studies.

Computer Virus Fact and Fantasy

We already have said, and will in the future say, unkind things about other virus "experts", the media, various software companies, other virus book authors, and a few other people as well. Are we a bunch of arrogant twits who think we alone have the secret knowledge? Not at all. (Well, we would say that, wouldn't we?) We know dozens of legitimate virus experts, some of whom have quite literally forgotten more about specific technical fields than we will ever know.

The problem is that the computer virus field has generated an enormous amount of misinformation and myth. In fact, one entire subject of research is that of the "virus hoax", which we'll discuss in more detail later in the book. Frankly, we aren't completely certain why legends and lies have become so prevalent in the discussion of viruses. (We'll give you some more thoughts on that later.) The plain fact is that the vast majority of articles in the general media and even computer trade media (better than 97 percent according to one of our collections) contain significant and substantial fallacies. We are not talking about trivial errors such as the wrong date for the discovery of a virus or a slight mistake in the wording of a message. We are talking about the central thesis of essays that are not only flatly wrong, but that recommend to computer users that they take steps more detrimental to computer operation than the viruses themselves.

Some people who buy this book may be real virus experts. (And to our colleagues, we say hello again, and be kind in your reviews, OK?) Some of you may sincerely regard yourselves as experts in this field, having worked hard to gain knowledge and experience. In such a case, you might take offence at some of what we say and at being put in the same box as those instant experts whose expertise is based on misapprehension and guesswork. To those of you who are feeling offended at this point, we hope that you will keep an open mind and stay with us. Bear in mind that we have, between us, somewhere near 30 years of full-time research. That's not just X years since we first saw a virus. That's full-time, serious study, often in addition to our regular jobs. As we say, we have met, along the way and in that time, dozens of virus experts. However, we have also met thousands of "instant experts" with just enough experience behind them to illustrate the truth of the saying that a *little* knowledge is a dangerous thing.

Even between us, we don't know everything about viruses. We are going to be as careful as we can, but there are going to be some errors in this book. (We hope they are small enough not to cause you trouble.) Yet, we're willing to bet that you've been told some unbelievable things about viruses—we certainly have. Please be patient while we challenge some of those common and misplaced assumptions.

Definitions

A major problem with viruses, as we shall try to make clear in this and the next chapter, lies in the fact they are not automatically identifiable. Viruses, or any kind of self-reproducing programs, only use functions that are used by other programs and that are necessary for other operations. Admittedly, the use of certain functions can suggest viral (self-replicating) activity. Indeed, detecting such functionality is one of the ways in which some anti-virus software attempts to detect new, hitherto unknown viruses.

However, the fact that this comes under the umbrella term "heuristic analysis" indicates a basic problem. *Heuristic* means a "rule of thumb", or proof by trial and error. *Heuristic analysis* is in part a scoring system. We define criteria, then we note that the suspect program meets or exceeds a threshold score, suggesting that it is viral. What those criteria are, and how a scanner establishes conformity or non-conformity with those criteria, will be explored in due course. However, it has been demonstrated that it is impossible to write a program that can analyse a file and state with 100 percent certainty that it is or isn't viral. (This demonstration actually bears closer examination, but we'll save that for Chapter 4.)

Furthermore, there is no absolute test for malice, making it effectively impossible to detect hitherto unknown non-viral malicious software (such as Trojan horses) automatically. We can't say that a given program is malicious just by analysing the code, even if we can say it replicates, and we can sometimes only confirm replication by testing.

By *malware*, we mean (primarily) viruses, worms, and Trojan horses, and those are the main types considered in this chapter. However, other subclasses will also be considered in Chapters 3, 4, and 5.

Viruses and Virus Mechanisms

By *virus,* we mean a program meeting the much-used definition included by Dr. Frederick Cohen in *A Short Course on Computer Viruses*: "...a program that can 'infect' other programs by modifying them to include a, possibly evolved, copy of itself".

By *infect*, we mean that a virus inserts itself into the chain of command, so that attempting to execute a legitimate program results in the execution of the virus as well as (or instead of) the program.

We do not define every program that destroys or steals data as a virus. A virus need not have any sort of payload (malicious or otherwise). That is, it doesn't have to do anything explicitly or deliberately damaging; it doesn't even have to operate covertly (though most of them do); all it has to do is replicate. We will not, therefore, call programs that cause damage "viruses" if they don't replicate. We might call them Trojan horses, but that's a discussion for later. We will not assume that a virus causes any intentional damage (though it can be argued that all viruses do some collateral damage).

Virus Structure

We are assuming here a common tripartite model of virus structure; that is, we assume up to three main component mechanisms:

- ▶ **Infection**   The *infection* mechanism may be defined as the way or ways in which the virus spreads.
- ▶ **Payload**   The *payload* mechanism is defined as what (if anything) the virus does apart from replicate.
- ▶ **Trigger**   The *trigger* mechanism is defined as the routine that decides whether now is the time to deliver the payload (if there is a payload).

As previously indicated, only the presence of the infection mechanism is mandatory if the program is to be defined as viral: payload and trigger are optional. Be aware, though, that this is a somewhat simplified model: in some circumstances the dissemination of the viral program itself may be described as the payload. Some worms (and we'll get to defining worms shortly) have been described in this way. Furthermore, if the virus is at all selective about the circumstances under which it will attempt to infect, the infection mechanism may also be said to incorporate a trigger.

Damage

By virus *damage*, we mean, primarily, one or more of the following:

- ▶ Deliberate damage inflicted by the virus payload mechanism, if it exists, such as the trashing or intentional corruption of files.
- ▶ Accidental damage caused when the virus attempts to install itself on the victim system (the newly infected host), such as corruption of system areas preventing the victim system from booting.
- ▶ Incidental damage that may not be obvious or severe but is nevertheless inherent in the fact of infection. Nearly all viruses entail damage in this category, since their presence involves loss of performance due to theft of memory, disk space, clock cycles, system modification, or a combination of two or more of these.

Attempts to conceal the presence of the virus (or other malware) may also entail a measure of intentional or accidental damage as the environment is manipulated or reconfigured. Examples include the following:

▶ The disappearance of Word menu options relating to the presence of macros

▶ Encryption or displacement of system areas, such as the Master Boot Record

▶ Manipulation of the Windows Registry

▶ The trashing or corruption of legitimate macros as part of the installation of a macro virus

However, the physical manifestations of a virus are often trivial. Viruses certainly exist that inflict savage, intentional damage on the victim system, and they are in some cases widely distributed. However, many exemplify the maxim that by not killing its host, a parasite tends to enhance its own chances of long-term survival. The most damaging aspects of viruses, in general, are social rather than technical. Social damage includes such phenomena as:

▶ The scapegoating of virus victims

▶ Secondary damage to systems caused by inappropriate responses to a perceived virus threat (low-level formatting of the hard disk to eradicate a macro virus, for instance)

▶ Legal or quasi-legal issues, such as failure to comply with data-protection legislation and policies

Hold that thought: we'll have much more to say on social implications in Part IV.

Damage Versus Infection

We are particularly anxious to avoid the common confusion between infection and damage. Virus incidents are often reported in terms of damage, where infection would be a more appropriate term. We would also prefer to distinguish between the presence of a virus on a system and an actual infection. A computer user may have dozens of infected attachments sitting within his or her mail Inbox. However, as long as none of the infected programs are actually run (that is, the infective code is not executed), the system is not said to be infected. Infective objects in this state of dormancy are sometimes described as *latent viruses*.

Use of the term *latency* in this context may invite confusion, since it is sometimes used in networking (especially in the context of firewalls) to indicate delay rather than inactivity. In the networking context, the usage probably derives from the use of the term "latency period" in neurology to refer to the delay between the moment a nerve impulse reaches a muscle fibre and the moment that fibre starts to contract. In fact, the notion of latency as entailing delay has its uses in discussion of virus issues, so *dormancy* may be a better term.

A special case of dormancy occurs when a virus is found on a system on which it cannot be executed. For example, a PC-specific program infected by a PC-specific file virus cannot normally be executed on a UNIX server or a Macintosh, but may nevertheless be found in an FTP directory or as a mail attachment. The risk here is that such a virus might later be passed on to a system on which the viral code *could* be executed, even though the replicative code is not executed at this stage of its dissemination. This mechanism is sometimes referred to as *heterogeneous* virus transmission, though it closely parallels the mechanism that drives the dissemination of other malware.

NOTE

A number of papers and presentations by Peter Radatti have alluded to this phenomenon, including the 1992 paper "Heterogeneous computer viruses in a networked UNIX environment" (Proceedings of the First International Virus Prevention Conference and Exhibition (NCSA), Washington, DC).

Stealth Mechanisms

Viruses that use concealment mechanisms are often described as *stealth* viruses. This term has become so popularly debased as to include virtually any virus that neither asks permission to infect nor announces its presence by a characteristic message, graphic, sound effect, and so on. Stealth methods and classification are discussed in Chapter 3.

Despite the tendency of the media and instant experts to scream "Arggghhh!!! It's a stealth virus!", stealth and stealth classification are, while technically interesting, of little consequence to the everyday user of anti-virus software. Once a virus has been analysed by an anti-virus vendor's researchers, circumvention of any novel stealth techniques it uses is incorporated into the process of adding recognition of that virus to a scanner's capabilities. Nonetheless, the tricks used by viruses to conceal their presence can have implications for their victims that disinfection by an anti-virus program may not address. Viruses and worms may introduce changes into the environment, such as modification of Word menus or the Windows Registry, that anti-virus software cannot (or in some instances chooses not to) reverse as part of the disinfection process.

Polymorphism

Another word that inspires panic in the press is *polymorphism*, a concept poorly understood by instant experts and generally overestimated in its long-term impact on the malware problem in general. A polymorphic ("many shaped") virus attempts to make detection of its presence more difficult by changing its "shape" from one infection to another. (The mechanisms for achieving such shape-shifting will be considered later.) This is often mistaken (not only by the press, but by writers of low-grade books on security and/or viruses) as meaning that the virus becomes a different virus or virus variant at each infection. This is not the case. A polymorphic remains the same virus but cannot be detected by looking for a characteristic scan string within the possibly infected file (or other infectable object). The code remains essentially the same, but the expression is different, so that the same program is represented by a different sequence of bytes.

   This by no means indicates, however, that polymorphic viruses are undetectable, though the first examples contributed to the disappearance of a number of early anti-virus products published by vendors who couldn't handle the problem. It does mean, of course, that the anti-virus programmer has to think beyond *grep*-like scanning of infectable objects using pattern matching with regular expressions.

> ### NOTE
>
> grep, egrep, and fgrep *are a group of UNIX tools used to search text files for lines that match regular expressions, as defined in the next section of this chapter. Similar (and similarly named) tools have been created to run under DOS, Windows, and other operating systems. The scripting language* awk *(also found as* nawk *and* gawk*) and editing tools such as* sed *and* vi *also support regular expressions. The* perl *language combines the functionality (and in some cases the syntax) of these and other tools, and is available for many platforms. We should make it clear that these tools do not all use the same sets of regular expressions, still less in exactly the same way.*

What Is This, a UNIX Textbook?

No, although UNIX has its issues with viruses too, whatever the Linux zealots may say, and we'll consider those too, in the fullness of time. Indeed, we've already discussed one of them: the question of heterogeneous virus transmission. However, the UNIX shell programmer's obsession with regular expression parsing can also help us to understand how scanner technology works on platforms other than UNIX.

Simple scanning for fixed strings (sequences of text or binary characters) is Stone-Age technology, and no competent modern virus scanner relies exclusively on it. UNIX-like regular expressions involve applying search or filtering criteria that mix normal characters with special metacharacters to find not only fixed strings, but also relevant variations, thus allowing a far more flexible approach to pattern matching. Tools like *grep*, *awk*, and *perl* allow you to search for a character by string using criteria such as:

```
^.fruitcake[^0-9]\.$
```

This expression would be Really Useful for searching a text file for lines consisting of

- ▶ Any single character;
- ▶ Immediately followed by the fixed string literal "fruitcake";
- ▶ Immediately followed by any non-numeric character;
- ▶ Immediately followed by a literal period (full stop) character;
- ▶ Immediately followed by the end of the line.

The metacharacters used here include "^" (beginning of line), "." (any single character), "[^0-9]" (any character not included in the set of characters 0, 1, 2, 3, 4, 5, 6, 7, 8, or 9), "\" (treat the next character as a literal period character, not a metacharacter denoting any character), and "$" (end of line). Thus, either of the following lines will match:

```
%fruitcake&.
```

```
XfruitcakeX.
```

The following lines will not match:

```
%fruitcake&. Plus any other text whatsoever.
```

(No line break after the period character.)

```
%FRUITCAKE&.
```

(Literal string "FRUITCAKE" is not the same as the string "fruitcake".)

```
Xfruitcake7.
```

(Character following literal string is numeric.)

Finding a set of circumstances under which looking for this particular expression would ever be useful (let alone in the context of virus detection) is left as an exercise for the reader. Furthermore, *grepping* a text file for a string isn't exactly the same as scanning a binary file for a search string. In fact, looking for a text string (even where the virus author is considerate enough to provide one) inside a (possibly) infected binary file is, more often than not, neither efficient nor dependable. However, it may not surprise you that we can find uses for tools like *grep* in virus management to fill in some of the corners that commercial anti-virus products don't quite reach, such as the management of log files.

Diet of Worms

By *worm*, we mean a self-replicating program that may or may not be a virus. We'll discuss the finer distinctions later. For the moment, we'll use the following rough-and-ready definition: a program that usually spreads across networks and doesn't attach itself parasitically to another program. (However, it can be said to "infect" an operating system, a mail application, or a network, if you really want to make your life complicated.) Be aware, though, that many anti-virus researchers regard worms as a special case of virus, not a completely different class of malware. In fact, we'd go so far as to say that an insistence on maintaining an artificial and unspecified distinction between the two species often suggests the sort of instant expert whose (self-)perceived authority exceeds his or her actual knowledge. Furthermore, many of the current malicious programs described popularly as worms may be more properly regarded as viruses or as worm/virus hybrids: Melissa or MTX, for example. (Both Melissa and MTX are considered at length in Part III.) Certainly, most experts consider the Internet Worm of 1988 and today's email worms to be beasts of quite a different colour, both in concept and in execution.

Trojan Horses

When we refer to a *Trojan horse* (or a *Trojan,* for short), we mean something that probably isn't a virus, or a worm, because it doesn't self-replicate. That is, it can only move from system to system if someone is persuaded to move it deliberately, since it doesn't include a programmed infection routine. However, worms are sometimes described by vendors as Trojans, and some people regard viruses as a special case of Trojan. Both these arguments are defensible, but such usage confuses the issue somewhat. Certainly, if we ever use a term like "Trojan horse virus" in this book, we'll probably be quoting a hoax rather than using it in all seriousness. If not, you'll be entitled to ask for your money back (though you probably won't get it).

Trojan horses are often defined as "programs that claim to do something useful or desirable, and may do so, but also perform actions that the victim wouldn't expect or want". These actions may include payloads such as password stealing or out-and-out destruction.

However, this presumption of malice is not common to all researchers. Some use the term "accidental Trojan" to describe programs that include an undesirable effect the programmer did not intend to include. Such a problem may be differentiated from other software bugs by their severity, such as a situation that results in the destruction of data, for example. A particularly notorious (and apt) illustration of this idea is documented in Vesselin Bontchev's *"Vircing" the InVircible*, a highly critical analysis of InVircible, a generic anti-virus product. Bontchev reported that running some of the tools in this product suite during testing resulted in the deletion of a legitimate data file with the filename SOFIA. This problem appears to have arisen because of the undocumented use of a temporary file of the same name by InVircible. The effect caused Dr. Bontchev to classify it "as a Trojan Horse destroying data" without going so far as to accuse the program's author of deliberate malice.

NOTE

InVircible is a product that stands somewhat outside the mainstream of anti-virus technology. Its author, Zvi Netiv, has a forceful personality and an aggressive approach to marketing that has resulted in fierce controversy. The war between Mr. Netiv and the rest of the industry is interesting, but a little beyond the scope of this chapter. In later chapters we will consider in more depth the ideological and technical differences between generic and virus-specific approaches to virus management. We will, however, avoid dwelling on the flame wars and personality clashes associated with specific products.

In the Wild

How many viruses are there? Well, it depends on what and how you measure, of course. This may be a good point at which to note that many of the objects detected by anti-virus software are not actually viruses at all. We'll come back to what else they may be in the next chapter.

Of those objects that really are bona fide viruses, most will never be seen on your desktop or anywhere else within your organization, unless someone goes out of his or her way to collect them. At the time of writing, anti-virus vendors are claiming to detect between 50,000 and 60,000 PC viruses. This is a somewhat spurious claim, incidentally, but we'll take that particular diversion further down the line. However, the WildList Organization's report for July 2001 lists 698, including the Supplemental List as well as the WildList proper, which lists only 214. Who is correct?

NOTE

The WildList Organization is a volunteer group consisting of a number of anti-virus researchers who are well-placed and well-qualified to contribute information concerning viruses currently seen in the field. We will look more closely at this organization in Chapter 8.

Actually, neither total is (nor can be) strictly correct, but the WildList is a much better guide than vendor marketing as to which viruses seriously threaten your organization. The vendor's packaging massively overstates the problem (in a sense) by claiming detection of all the viruses that are known to exist (and some variants and non-viruses that shouldn't be quoted, from a purist point of view). The WildList and Supplemental List include viruses that have been reported by businesses and other computer users as spreading on their systems, and that have been verified by the highly qualified anti-virus professionals who report to the WildList Organization. By definition, these lists understate the problem, because there are always viruses that are "out there" in the field but that haven't made the list yet. However, the difference between the viruses that constitute the WildList and those that are out there but not included in the WildList is usually assumed to be measurable in hundreds rather than in tens of thousands. This does not mean that the vendors are purposely misleading you, by the way (at least, not always). It simply means that the problem is too complex to be served well in the context of this introduction. If you want to know more right now, you'll have to skip ahead to Chapter 3 (on virus epidemiology in general) and Chapter 8 (on information gathering and risk assessment).

So let's go back to the question we asked at the beginning of this section. How many viruses are there? Answer: tens of thousands, by almost anyone's reckoning. How many should you be concerned about? All of them, since you can't tell whether one of them might get lucky and escape into "the wild". However, it makes sense to worry more about those that are known to be in the field now, especially those conspicuous enough to have made the WildList. What do we mean by _in the wild_? To quote Paul Ducklin (of Sophos, the UK anti-virus company), we mean viruses that are "spreading as a result of normal day-to-day operations on and between the computers of unsuspecting users". (See the WildList Organization's FAQ (Frequently Asked Questions) document at http://www.wildlist.org/faq.htm). Viruses found only in collections, e-zines, or VX (Virus eXchange) web sites are not considered to be in the wild. Such viruses are sometimes described as "zoo viruses" or even "in the zoo".

The terms "in the wild", "In the Wild", and "ItW" lead to a certain amount of confusion, and we should try to clarify our usage of these terms:

▶ By "in the wild" (without capitals), we mean "in the field", or conforming to Ducklin's definition without particular reference to the WildList. In other words, viruses that are out there on everyday computer users' desktops but not necessarily on the current (or an earlier) WildList. In fact, we will usually use the term "in the field" rather than "in the wild" in this more general sense, in the hope of reducing confusion.

▶ Use of the term "In the Wild" is restricted here to the context of "included on the WildList or possibly on the Supplemental List". However, this restriction is not, by any means, adhered to by all researchers. The eccentrically capitalized abbreviation ItW will be avoided in this book but is frequently found where anti-virus (AV) and pro-virus (VX) people gather and exchange email.

Instant Guide to Anti-Virus Software

Finally, here's a brief summary of what anti-virus programs are and how they work. We're keeping the details in reserve for Part II, but a cursory scan of almost any anti-virus software comparative review indicates that we can't assume that you already have a realistic broad understanding of anti-virus technology. We don't mean you personally, of course, but the guy next to you reading over your shoulder. (Especially if he happens to be a journalist.)

There are two main streams of anti-virus thinking: virus-specific and generic. By *virus-specific,* we mean what is sometimes referred to as Known Virus Scanning (KVS). This means that every time a new virus or variant is discovered, it is analysed and a suitable identifying pattern is extracted. Virus-specific scanners are then (if necessary) modified so that they will detect and identify that specific virus or variant using that pattern. *Generic* scanners detect viruses (hopefully), but don't identify them (at least, not exactly). Whereas a virus-specific scanner says "Object X is infected with the Y virus", a generic scanner says "Object X is (or may be) infected with an unidentified virus". Clearly, it's easier for a virus-specific scanner to disinfect, where disinfection is possible. A generic scanner is more likely to suggest that you discard or replace the (possibly) infected object X, or else that you check it with a virus-specific scanner.

However, some (most, these days) virus-specific scanners can also use a generic technique called heuristic analysis to detect new (unknown) viruses. Simplistically, they look for indications of virus infection in object X by seeing what the code actually does. This is closely allied to behaviour monitoring and behaviour blocking. The differences and resemblances between these techniques are beyond the scope of this introductory chapter, but we'll have lots to say on the subject later.

> ### NOTE
>
> *There is an important distinction here between disinfection and detection. Some products don't disinfect all classes of viruses, and commercial virus-specific scanners can't usually disinfect all the viruses they detect—some types of infection are not repairable. The word* disinfection *implies that the virus code has been removed from the infected object. However, this does not necessarily indicate that the object has been returned to its pre-infection state. Nor does it mean that the object will necessarily function as it did before it was infected, although it will in many cases. It does not mean that the environment in which the infected object exists is restored to its former state, either, nor that all the damage caused by the infection or the payload is reversed.*

Scanners are broadly divided into two main types: on-access (real-time) scanners, and on-demand scanners. *Real-time* scanners are memory-resident: they check infectable objects (files, diskettes, system areas) as they are accessed. *On-demand* scanners may also check one or more files, disks or other media, or whole systems, but they aren't memory-resident. Either the user calls them as needed (when you want to verify that a CD you just received is virus-free, for instance), or else they're called by scheduling software at predetermined times. They may also be called by the operating system at fixed times, by an entry in AUTOEXEC.BAT, for instance.

Summary

We know of many people in management positions (including security managers) who would know a great deal more than they do now if they were to read this chapter. However, we've probably said enough to indicate that the virus-management problem is far too complex to allow the anti-virus professional to hope that clicking on the Anti-Virus icon will solve all his or her problems. Certainly, if you have the deep joy to be a systems administrator or security professional, we have a lot more to share with you. In Chapter 2, we take a look at some historical background.

Historical Overview

IN THIS CHAPTER:

Virus Prehistory: Jurassic Park to Xerox PARC

Real Viruses: Early Days

The Internet Age

And So It Goes...

17

A major problem in providing a history of viruses lies in knowing where to start. Some people have insisted that they were writing viral programs as far back as 1956. Since computers then had very little similarity to computers now, and since the methods of use were so different, these claims have to be taken with a very large grain of salt. There are some operations that could have been considered viral, such as the opcode in early machines that simply copied itself into the next memory location. (This was used to overwrite the entire memory space, leaving it in a known state.) However, only by the most strained definition of "virus" can these functions be seen as similar to modern viruses.

NOTE

An opcode in assembly language is the part of an instruction or directive that identifies the specific operation to be performed. (An instruction is a statement to be translated into machine language; a directive is a statement that gives directions to the assembler.)

On the other hand, as we shall also see, computer viruses have changed radically in the 15 years that they have been widely known. Certain patterns do, though, tend to recur.

Much of this chapter will concentrate on the MS-DOS and Windows platforms. Viruses have been written for just about every major, full-blown computer operating system (with the possible exception of CP/M). However, as you will see, the basic viral ideas remain the same. In addition, the prevalence of viruses has little to do with questions of operating system design or even security. Viruses are, in general, most frequent in those operating systems that are most widely used. The Wintel platform (Windows running on a PC driven by an Intel processor or equivalent) has the dubious honour of having the greatest number of viral examples.

With this history, we intend to give you a very basic overview of fundamental virus concepts. Although the technology is changing constantly, the underlying ideas never change very much at all. The story starts before viruses were known, or even contemplated, at least under that name.

Virus Prehistory: Jurassic Park to Xerox PARC

While there is no proof that true viruses existed in the early days of computing, it is important to note certain programs and activities that did. These exercises and studies probably did not presage the development of viruses themselves, but they did influence opinions and later examinations.

Wormholes

As computer technology advanced, it became possible to run more than one program at a time on a single machine. In even the most rudimentary multitasking environment, it was important that each program be contained within certain bounds, known as *partitions*. Programs would perform inappropriate operations on the data, or on other programs belonging to different procedures, or would transfer control to random areas and try to execute data as program instructions.

> **NOTE**
>
> *Because the design of most computers is based on what is known as von Neumann architecture, there is no inherent difference between data and programs. Thus, there is no way to tell the difference between a scrap of data and a section of program without trying either to run it or to make sense of it.*

Programs that encroach upon another program's personal space in this way tend to generate random operations and damage. (Even now, we can see all the Windows support engineers out there nodding and muttering "protection fault" and wincing.) Attempts to trace the "path" of damage or operation would show random patterns of memory locations. Plotting these on a printout map of the memory made irregular curving traces, which began and ended suddenly. Since these looked like holes in worm-eaten wood, the model became known as a "wormhole" pattern, and the rogue programs were sometimes known as "worms".

Nowadays, the term *worm* is often used for viral programs that spread by some method other than attachment to, or association with, other program files. However, this use of the word probably derives from the Shoch and Hupp experiment that resulted in the Xerox worm, which we discuss later in this chapter. Rogue programs that created wormhole damage were haphazard mistakes, and very little like today's premeditated viral programs, except that they wreaked havoc where they shouldn't have.

Core Wars

Programmers being the individuals they are, the development of such rogue programs became a subject of contests, specifically the game of "Core Wars". In this game, program is run to set up an environment like the core memory of older computers. A standard set of computer opcodes, known as *Redstone Code* (because the simulator version was developed at the Redstone missile development or testing facility of the US military) or just *Redcode*, is used to build programs that which then do battle with each other within the simulated environment. The program's objective is survival, rather than reproduction and spread. However, virus researchers have an interest in the use of such tactics as attack, avoidance, and replication, as well as the trade-off between complexity of design and chance of destruction.

For example, a very simple, but effective, Core Wars program is one referred to as an Imp. An *Imp* simply tries to run through the memory, overwriting locations as it goes. Since it is very small, an Imp is hard to find and kill. Larger programs may have more sophisticated means of detecting other programs, or of defending against attacks, but, because of their size, are more likely to have part of the program destroyed by an Imp. In the same way, small and simple viruses have sometimes been more successful at surviving and reproducing than more complicated programs.

Core Wars is most widely known due to a series of articles done by A. K. Dewdney in his "Computer Recreations" column in *Scientific American*. The first of these articles was printed in the March 1984 issue. Images of these articles can be found at http://www.koth.org/info/sciam/. More details on Core Wars can be found at these sites:

- ▶ http://www.koth.org/info.html
- ▶ http://www.sci.fi/~iltzu/corewar/guide.html
- ▶ http://www.cs.ucla.edu/~jperry/corewars.html
- ▶ http://kuoi.asui.uidaho.edu/~kamikaze/documents/corewar-faq.html

The Xerox Worm (Shoch/Hupp Segmented Worm)

We have given one possible derivation of the term "worm". There is another, and this is the one that is more likely the source of the current definition of the word in the field of computer virology. It is interesting that two completely separate routes should give rise to the same term and that the meanings should complement so well. It is also interesting, given the ongoing debate as to whether viruses can ever be useful, that this story arises from an early attempt to use viral programming for beneficial purposes.

> **NOTE**
>
> Vesselin Bontchev has written a useful paper on the non-usefulness of "good" viruses. You can find it at a number of sites:
> ftp://ftp.informatik.uni-hamburg.de/pub/virus/texts/viruses/goodvir.zip
> http://www.virusbtn.com/OtherPapers/GoodVir/
> Fred Cohen, to whom we'll introduce you shortly, has taken an opposite view in books such as
> A Short Course on Computer Viruses.

John Shoch and Jon Hupp were researchers at Xerox PARC in Palo Alto, California, where one of the earliest examples of a local area network (LAN) had been set up. They were interested in the concept of *distributed processing*, the ability of computers to work cooperatively on single or related tasks. Specifically, they were testing an experimental program whose function was to check other computers on the network to see if they were active.

If a computer were idle after normal working hours, for example, the program would submit a copy of itself to the idle machine. In this way, the original program would spawn multiple copies of itself to idle machines in order to make use of the CPU time, which would otherwise go to waste. This system was a precursor of systems that have now become very popular on the Internet and have already made significant contributions in fields such as encryption and decryption. A problem can be broken down into small chunks, and if each sub-problem can be addressed and resolved on one of the machines on a network, this is functionally equivalent to running a single, large program. However, the actual processing is done by small program segments working on individual machines, rather than by sharing a single processor. Since biological worms are defined by the fact that they have segmented bodies, Shoch and Hupp called this new type of program a "worm". In many references, you will also find mention of John Brunner's novel, *Shockwave Rider*. This book refers to a "tapeworm" program that could be said to have some resemblance to the cumulative computing effort.

Alas, the experiment, at that time, was not an altogether unqualified success. One night, a programming error was made. This glitch caused the computers running the worm program to hang, and since the program had been sent to many computers over the course of the night, the researchers arrived in the morning to find an institution full of dead computers. This program became known as the Xerox worm or, in many references, the "infamous Xerox worm". Shoch and Hupp detailed their experiences in a paper published in the March 1982 issue of the *Communications of the ACM* ("The Worm Programs—Early Experience with a Distributed Computation").

As noted, the Shoch and Hupp worm program *did* reproduce by submitting itself to other computers, but it was written as part of research in the field of distributed computing. The program had no malicious or security-breaking intent. Nor did it attempt to hide its presence or operation. On the other hand, as we pointed out in Chapter 1, neither malicious intent, nor covert operation, constitute defining characteristics of a virus (or worm).

NOTE

Some abstract notes are available at http://ftp.unina.it/pub/docs/rfc/ien/ien159.txt. A German account is available at http://www.cert.dfn.de/tutorial/wuermer/kap211.html, and can be roughly translated by AltaVista's Babelfish (http://world.altavista.com/).

Real Viruses: Early Days

The earliest case of a virus, as we know them to today, that actually succeeded in the wild, goes back to late 1981. In fairness, this activity does not appear to have been noted by many until long after the fact. Those who have followed Apple's "Think different" advertising campaign may not be surprised that an earlier generation of Apple hardware "gave birth" to this novel concept.

1981: Early Apple II Viruses

We have reports of two very similar programs with almost identical features and histories. Here, for the sake of simplicity, we will discuss the first one that was related on the Internet. The other instance was startlingly similar, even to the state in which it took place.

The idea was sparked by a speculation regarding "evolution" and "natural selection" in pirated copies of games at Texas A&M: the "reproduction" of preferred games and the "extinction" of poor ones. This led to considerations of programs that reproduced on their own, and the term "computer virus" was apparently used in the context of that idea. There is no obvious reason to doubt the author's contention that there was no malice involved. At the time, it was one originator's belief that a virus had to be relatively "benign" in order to survive. Indeed, there is some truth in that assertion, though it can't be described as an absolute. Viruses with no destructive payload do tend to survive better over the long haul.

Apple II computer diskettes of that time, when formatted in the normal way, always contained the disk operating system.

The programmer attempted to find the minimum change that would make a viral version of the operating system, and then tried to find an "optimal" viral DOS. A group came up with the first version of such a virus in early 1982, but didn't let it spread because of side-effects. The second version was allowed to "spread" to a limited extent through the disks of group members.

Eventually, the virus escaped into the general Apple user population. It was only then observed that the additional code length caused some programs, and one computer game in particular, to crash. A third version was written, and the developers made strenuous efforts to avoid the memory problems. This version was subsequently found to have spread into disk populations previously considered to be uninfected, but no adverse reactions were ever reported.

1983: Elk Cloner

This virus seems to have been written around 1983. It became well known in the Apple community, probably because of the message (in doggerel verse) that it presented. It also created nuisances in the computer, such as displaying the wrong file type, inverting the video, and clicking the speaker. The virus worked only under AppleDOS 3.3; any other disks, such as those based on HackerDos, DiversiDos, and ProDOS, tended to be rendered unusable. The author is known, and his claims to have intended no real harm appear credible. All damage generated by the virus seems due to simple carelessness.

By way of an epilogue, in 1989 a virus appeared for the then-current Apple IIGS and ProDOS. Apple users were used to rebooting in order to change operating systems or boot special disks. Load Runner trapped the reset command (holding down the CONTROL key plus the COMMAND (Apple) key plus the RESET key) and, when it was issued, wrote itself to the diskette in the drive, thus surviving a reset.

1984: Fred Cohen, Computer Viruses—Theory and Experiments

Fred Cohen first presented his ideas to a graduate class in information security in 1983, and history credits his seminar advisor, Len Adleman, with the assignment of the term "virus" to Cohen's concept. Of course, this isn't Adleman's only claim to fame. The RSA encryption algorithm derives its name from those of its inventors: Rivest, Shamir, and Adleman. Cohen did extensive theoretical research, and he also set up and performed numerous practical experiments regarding viral-type programs. Cohen's first virus paper was published in 1984, and his dissertation was presented in 1986 as part of the requirements for a doctorate in electrical engineering from the University of Southern California. This work is foundational, and any serious student of viral programs disregards it at his or her own risk. Cohen's major contributions lie in the foundations of basic theory and analysis in virus research, and the development of the defensive techniques that have historically been most effective and are now the most widely implemented. His work experimentally demonstrated and theoretically resolved vital issues. He outlined every basic antiviral concept that is now in use; despite what vendors may tell you, nobody has ever found any other way to deal with viruses.

1984: Fred Cohen, Computer Viruses—Theory and Experiments *(continued)*

Dr. Cohen's definition of a computer virus as "a program that can 'infect' other programs by modifying them to include a, possibly evolved, copy of itself" is generally accepted as a standard. Indeed, we couldn't get through Chapter 1 without quoting it. Occasionally, it is unclear as to whether it can include, say, boot-sector viral programs, or entities such as the Internet/UNIX/Morris Worm. It is not, however, fair to Dr. Cohen to hold him responsible for the misuse of his work by others. The definition given above was an attempt, in the 1984 paper, to express a mathematical concept in English. The English version is only an approximation.

Fred Cohen's work was never given the credit or value it deserved. From the very beginning, systems administrators and the security community have seen his work as either negative or as an academic curiosity. In addition, viruses have advanced the plot of many a book or movie, and Cohen has never received a royalty check from Hollywood. Viruses even save the world on occasion, but no one phones Fred to thank him. This situation is decidedly odd, but it may have been aggravated by the perception of Cohen as a bit of a grouch. Fred's friends, however, argue against the negative characterization, noting that he has a very keen sense of humour. This last is amply demonstrated in *A Short Course on Computer Viruses*, a book that goes a long way towards bridging the gap between the practicalities of virus and anti-virus technology, and their theoretical, mathematical basis.

This overview is the merest introduction to his work. Indeed, computer virology plays little part in his more recent writing. The most important aspects of his early work are the demonstration of the universality of risk and the limitations of protection. His practical work proved the technical feasibility of a viral attack in any computing environment more complex and interactive than a pocket calculator. (This feat was achieved within a closed environment and could not, by its nature, have predicted the social and psychological factors that have contributed to the pandemic spread of viral programs in the wild.) Equally important, his theoretical study proved that the "universal" and purely automatic detection of a virus is impractical. Although monitoring and analytical programs have a place in the antiviral pantheon, this fact means that they, and all other antiviral software, can never give 100 percent guaranteed protection.

You can find out more about Dr. Cohen and his more recent work in other areas of security at http://www.all.net/.

1986: © BRAIN

1986 was not only the year in which Fred Cohen presented his dissertation, it was also the year in which Ralf Burger demonstrated VIRDEM, a .COM infector. Over the next few years, many more .COM and .EXE infectors would be written than boot-sector infectors, but parasitic file viruses were comparatively unsuccessful at spreading in the wild (with some very notable exceptions, including Jerusalem, discussed later in this chapter). This trend has changed course in recent years, however, with the advance of the email worm/virus juggernaut.

The Brain virus is probably the earliest PC virus, and at one time, it was the most widespread of PC viral programs. Extensive study has been done on the Brain family. In spite of this, and in spite of the existence of address and phone number information for the supposed author, we still have only second-hand reports of the production of the virus. Consequently, little can be said with absolute certainty about its origins.

Brain is a boot-sector infector (BSI), somewhat longer than some more recent BSIs. Brain occupies three sectors itself, and, as is usual with BSIs, repositions the normal boot sector in order to mimic the boot process. As the boot sector is only a single sector, Brain, in infecting a disk, reserves two additional sectors on the disk for the remainder of itself, plus a third for the original boot sector. This is done by occupying unused space on the diskette and then marking those sectors as "bad" so that they will not be used and overwritten. The "original" Brain virus is relatively harmless. It does not infect hard disks or disks with formats other than 360K. (Other variants are less careful and can overlay FAT and data areas.)

The Brain family is prolific, although less so than Jerusalem, for instance.

NOTE

Seemingly, any successful virus spawns a plague of copies if virus-writer wannabes use it as a template. This has become more so as macro viruses and other script viruses have made virus coding easier. The code requires less programming knowledge and no specialized development tools. In addition, when and if interpreted viruses go wild, they tend to spread faster and farther, and the actual code is often freely available (including to people who aren't actually looking for it).

Again, like the Jerusalem virus, it seems that one of the lesser variants of Brain might be the "original". The Ashar version appears to be somewhat less sophisticated than the most common Brain, but Brain contains text that makes no sense unless Brain is derived from ashar. Brain contains other timing information: a "copyright" date of 1986 and an apparent "version" number of 9.0.

1987: Goodnight Vienna, Hello Lehigh

By 1987, the virus scene was heating up. Bernt Fix's disassembly of the Vienna virus was included in Ralph Burger's book *Computer Viruses: A High Tech Disease*, published in that year, though the code for Burger's own VIRDEM was not included. VIRDEM did spawn a number of variants, but was never any real threat or of major importance in the wild, unlike the widely copied Vienna.

The Lehigh virus, on the other hand, was described in the book, although its real impact outside Lehigh University was virtually non-existent. Lehigh was the first file infector that came to public attention, but the virus only infected the COMMAND.COM file, which rather restricted its capacity to spread. After infecting four disks, Lehigh would erase all data on all disks in the machine at the time.

This immediate, and fairly devastating, payload ensured that Lehigh would be noticed. The same factors guaranteed that the virus would be actively pursued and eliminated. It received a great deal of publicity, and had a direct impact on the anti-virus scene. Ken van Wyk, who was working at Lehigh at the time, and later went on to join CERT (the Computer Emergency Response Team), set up the VIRUS-L/comp.virus mailing list and newsgroup. Moderated by Ken, and then by Nick FitzGerald, later an editor of *Virus Bulletin*, VIRUS-L became an extremely useful resource for the exchange of anti-virus information, but it hasn't been consistently active for some years.

Stoned/New Zealand, one of the most successful boot-sector viruses ever, was written at the University of Wellington. (The other main contender for most common boot-sector virus is Form, which appeared a little later.) Written by a student, and apparently let loose by the author's brother, the virus had no damaging payload, and a minimal display payload. The infection mechanism was sturdy, and the code had few incompatibilities with normal computer operations. All of these factors contributed to the success of the virus in the wild, and also meant that it was used as a model for many other variants. Stoned and its derivatives are considered at length in Part III.

Cascade was the first encrypted virus. The encryption was an early and very simple form of polymorphism. Only the decryptor stub was detectable by "signature scanning". The self-encryption idea was developed subsequently (mostly by Mark Washburn, author of the V2P polymorphic virus family) into the use of variable encryption as a polymorphic mechanism. However, Cascade is probably best remembered for the visual effect it displays (letters "falling" out of their proper place on the screen into a heap at the bottom of the screen).

Rob Slade started to collect some messages about an intriguing new idea in operating system function: that of programs which copied themselves. By making this compilation available to interested security mavens, he accidentally became the unofficial archivist of what eventually became the international virus research community.

CHRISTMA EXEC, an email worm specific to IBM mainframes, was a precursor of the Windows scripting viruses of the late 1990s. It promised a Christmas card for the user, and did actually draw a vaguely coniferous shape on the terminal screen, using a scripting language called REXX. This screen display meant that the virus was sometimes known as "The Christmas Tree", but there is also an MS-DOS virus called "Christmas Tree", which appears to have been written in homage to the original.

Characteristics CHRISTMA had in common with the later scripting viruses included the use of social engineering in the subject header (to stop the victim from reading the REXX code), self-mailing to everyone in the victim's address book, and exploitation of the trusted source fallacy.

NOTE

To this day, we hear of people puzzled to find that they're infected by an email worm, despite opening only attachments received from people they know. Moral: trusting the person doesn't mean you have to trust the object. In general, people receive viruses and similar threats from other victims, not directly from the virus creator: that's one of the major weaknesses exploited by self-replicating malware. You have to trust not only the intentions of everyone you deal with, but also their ability to protect themselves from infection.

The attempt to fool the user distinguishes CHRISTMA EXEC from the Internet Worm that appeared almost a year later. The Internet Worm and other related beasts, as well as some of the more recent Linux viruses, tried to use system functions and programming bugs in order to avoid alerting or involving the user at all.

The first Amiga virus seems to have appeared in late 1987. It was essentially a boot-sector infector (boot-block, for the Amiga—it actually uses two sectors). It employs a form of stealth, and so may well be modelled after the MS-DOS Brain virus. The virus had message text that was displayed on occasion, and probably referred to the movie "2010", which had been released in 1984: "Something wonderful has happened Your AMIGA is alive !!!"

1988: The Worm Turns

Scores, a Macintosh system virus, was apparently intended to target a specific company (EDS, in Dallas, Texas). This incident is discussed at some length in Part III.

The first instances of the Jerusalem virus were discovered in the wild late in 1987. It was known variously as "Israeli" (because of the initial discovery in Israel by Yisrael Radai), "PLO" (because of supposed terrorist intentions), "1813" (for the infective length), "suMsDos" (after a text string found in the body of virus code), and a variety of other names (for other reasons). Jerusalem had a destructive payload programmed into it, but it also had an unintended bug which led to early detection: Jerusalem would infect the same file again and again, leading to a noticeable increase in file size for some programs. This led to the common assertion that viruses can be detected by changes in file size, even though most other file infectors are tiny scraps of code in comparison to their targets. Of course, even a few bytes difference between file sizes *might* denote virus infection. Indeed, an increased size is one of the heuristics used by some generic anti-virus software, but only one, and by no means the most important.

While Lehigh did infect program files, it was limited to only one specific file, COMMAND.COM, because of both targeting and the infection mechanism. Jerusalem was the first MS-DOS virus to infect the full range of program files, including both COM and EXE formats. In addition, the basic infective code in Jerusalem is remarkably clear and straightforward, and three early versions—sURIV 1, sURIV 2, and sURIV 3, respectively—demonstrate how to infect .COM files, .EXE files, and both. Therefore, Jerusalem has become the precursor to a whole family of viruses. Initially, copycat virus writers merely changed trigger dates for the destructive payload, but eventually the infection module was found in a variety of other viruses with other payloads. Jerusalem itself spread worldwide, but also lives on in many other file-infecting viruses.

NOTE

In fact, most of the viruses in the late 1980s did spawn such virus families, and did pioneer various virus technologies. Therefore, we have covered more of the details in the chapters dealing with case studies in Part III. For the remainder of Chapter 2, we will only be touching on highlights, and following broad trends, particularly for standard file and boot-sector infectors.

Jerusalem is thus an important milestone on the virus road, and will be considered in greater length with the case studies in Chapter 12.

The MacMag Macintosh virus was the first major infection for that platform. MacMag earned several other firsts, such as the first time a virus was written on commission, the first use of a non-viral "dropper", and the first time a perceived data file was used for transmission. It also infected several thousand release copies of Aldus Freehand—probably the first instance of commercial software being infected before it left the pressing plant.

The virus was instigated, though not written, by the editor of *MacMag* magazine, probably as a publicity stunt. Internal evidence in the code does seem to suggest the name of someone else as the author. No damaging payload was included with the program, although it did have a message designed to trigger on a certain date.

Part of the spread of MacMag was facilitated by a file that purported to contain information about new Macintosh models that were due to be released near to that time. The file was a HyperCard stack, a type of free-form database with graphical and other features. ("Stack" is the term for a HyperCard data file, a reference to a stack of cards.) Most users saw HyperCard stacks only as data, but it was possible to associate programming functions with and in the stacks. The MacMag virus is said to be the first example of a HyperCard virus, but HyperCard was only used to "drop" the virus into a system; the infective mechanism did not use HyperCard, and MacMag did not infect other HyperCard stacks.

One interesting vector was traced from a game, to a party, to a consultant, and then to the companies using the consultant. One of those companies was Aldus, and the master copy of the disks containing the Freehand program became infected. The infected disk was duplicated and distributed to dealers. Fortunately, the company, very responsibly, admitted to the problem as soon as it was discovered, and so further spread was minimized. Few companies in similar situations have acted with the same degree of integrity.

IBM entered the research field when their site at Lehulpe in Belgium was infected with Cascade. While IBM's anti-virus technology is now channelled through Symantec, the impact of their research has been and continues to be considerable.

Utility software guru Peter Norton was quoted in *Insight* as saying that computer viruses were an urban myth, like the alligators said to inhabit the sewers of New York. Later, however, he lent his name to what became one of the top-selling anti-virus programs.

The Internet Worm, also known as the Morris Worm (after the author) and the UNIX Worm (after the targeted operating system) swept through UNIX-based systems and brought the Internet to a near-halt in the early part of November. This was probably the first mention most people ever heard of the computer virus phenomenon. News stories about the event appeared in the general media, and, for many years afterward, no news story about viruses failed to mention the Internet Worm, regardless of the fact that it used technologies radically different from the other, more common, viruses.

The Internet Worm exploited a number of known weaknesses and loopholes in the networking and email software common to UNIX systems connected to the Internet. It used these vulnerabilities to transmit itself to new systems and to start running new copies of itself. Other parts of the program would then try to guess at common passwords and try to increase the level of privilege on the new target. In contrast to most viruses, the Internet Worm did not rely on any user actions at all, except for laziness on the part of managers who did not patch known problems, and account holders who chose bad passwords.

Using many of the same ideas, the WANK.COM and HI.COM worms spread through DEC (Digital Equipment Corporation) VAX model computers running an operating system known as VMS.

On the Atari ST computer, most disks were not bootable. (Hard disks were common by this time, and usually the system would be booted from the hard drive.) However, Atari disks had a boot sector, and it was read in order to obtain information about the format of the disk. If the first byte of the boot sector had a value of 60H, then the boot sector was marked as executable, and the contents would be run. In early 1988, an Atari ST virus appeared. It used the boot sector, and it only infected floppy disks. However, if a disk was present in the floppy drive when the computer booted up, the virus was executed before the system loaded from the hard drive. (Because bootable disks were few, leaving a floppy in the drive seems to have been a common practice.) The virus would copy itself to each uninfected floppy disk, and would add this infection to a counter. When the counter reached a certain number, the virus would trigger a payload that overwrote the system areas of the disk.

The Internet Age

The late 1980s and early 1990s saw the development of many technologies within the basic virus model that had been laid down in earlier years.

1989: Worms, Dark Avenger, and AIDS

Eugene Spafford's "Crisis and Aftermath" and Rochlis and Eichin's "With Microscope and Tweezers: the Worm from MIT's Perspective" (both in *Communications of the ACM*) analysed the Morris Worm of the previous year. A number of CHRISTMA EXEC knockoff worms appeared. The WANK worm infected VMS systems using techniques synthesized from the Morris Worm and HI.COM.

Jerusalem panic struck as the virus's next trigger date (Friday, 13th January, 1989) approached. Indeed, every Friday the 13th became Jerusalem panic day for years afterwards. Datacrime (or Columbus Day) became one of the first media viruses (a virus that is mostly significant because of the media attention it attracts) later in the year. Datacrime was a minor variant of Jerusalem, and, like its ancestor, triggered on Friday the 13th. In October, Friday the 13th fell near the Columbus Day weekend, and this fact seemed to capture media attention. There was no other reason to pay particular attention to the Datacrime virus.

Virus Bulletin, still the most significant publication in the anti-virus field, was launched.

Dark Avenger's eponymous virus, better known among the research community as Eddie, introduced the concept of slow random damage as a virus payload. Thus, scrupulous backup procedures ceased to be a universal cure for virus damage, if they ever had been. The program stayed resident in memory once it had been run, and not only infected programs that were invoked, but also files as they were opened or copied. The Bulgarian author included programming targeting the Bulgarian virus researcher, Vesselin Bontchev.

NOTE

Dark Avenger was ugly, but innovative (the virus, that is): it also introduced the concept of fast infection. A memory-resident virus that infects files as they are opened for reading can spread quickly across a PC's hard disk (or, under the right circumstances, a network). Later viruses used modifications of this technique, such as infecting all executables in the current directory, or in all directories listed by the DOS PATH variable.

Frodo, the first full-stealth parasitic (file) virus, was detected in Israel. Also known as 4096 or 4K because of the length of the code, it attempted to hide the increase in the length of files from the user. While the virus was active in memory, any directory listing of files, as well as certain other utilities, would only show the original file size. However, because this was not consistent with the number of sectors being used to store the files, cross-linking of infected files would occur in the system areas of the disk. In addition, because of the way the virus chose targets, data files would sometimes be corrupted. Frodo contained a message payload, but all known versions contain bugs, and it is unlikely that it ever successfully displayed the message without hanging the host machine.

Dr. Popp distributed his AIDS information diskette, which used a Trojan mechanism in an attempt to extort money for the recovery of the victim's data. The disk, purporting to be information on the user's risk of AIDS, did present a quiz in the foreground, but would also encrypt the contents of the hard disk. A message would then pop up saying that the free trial period was over, and that in order to recover your information, you would have to pay a licence fee to obtain the key. The AIDS Trojan is the subject of a case study in Part III.

In October of 1989, an interesting virus was demonstrated at an Amiga Users Group meeting. Referred to as the 2608 virus, after the length of the code, this program would associate itself with the first program in the start-up sequence. However, the file did not simply append itself to the original file, as most viruses did at that time. Instead, it copied the first program into the devs directory, and copied itself into the old position in the C directory. When the computer was started, the virus would run, and would then call the real command. Some subsequent Amiga viruses, such as Smiley, worked the same way. This technique is similar to a function later used in an MS-DOS virus family called DIR, which caused file directory entries to point to the virus, which in turn pointed to the original file. More recently, some malware has varied the technique further by changing the Windows Registry to point to the virus code, which then passes control to the legitimate program.

Commodore's reaction to the news of early Amiga malware was to dismiss the whole subject as a hoax. Later, they moved on to ignoring the issue altogether. The Amiga has also been more or less ignored by commercial anti-virus vendors, but the number of Amiga viruses is surprisingly high (higher than the number of native Macintosh viruses, for example).

NOTE

Doesn't this contradict our earlier assertion that the frequency with which viruses are found on a given platform is related to how widely used that platform is? First, we didn't state it as an immutable law: after all, someone with the time, programming skills, and inclination to swamp a relatively little-used platform might do so with the express intention of disproving such a "law". Second, the total of viruses to which the Macintosh is subject far exceeds the number associated with the Amiga. The Amiga does not support Microsoft Word, and so has not been subject to the flood of Word and other macro viruses that have appeared since 1995. Macintosh versions of Word, however, have supported first WordBasic and later Visual Basic for Applications since version 6.0. While macro virus payloads are usually PC-specific, many (even most) macro viruses can and do infect irrespective of whether they are executed on a Macintosh. Since 1995, unprotected Macs (or machines on which protection has not been consistently updated) have been a major channel for the dissemination of Office macro viruses. This issue is explored in much greater depth in Appendix B.

1990: Polymorphs and Multipartites

In 1990, polymorphic viruses started to make serious waves, using technologies more complex than simple self-encryption. Without a definite decryption stub, these more advanced forms were slightly harder to detect. This had a number of consequences: vendors who couldn't handle variable decryption started to look for alternative careers, and false alarms began to be a serious problem.

One of the first of the new breed was Whale: a virus so complex and unwieldy that it was practically impossible to get it to replicate, so it never really made it into the wild. However, as an exercise in making a virus difficult to analyse, it became somewhat notorious. The virus was also one of the longest found up to that time, with over nine thousand bytes of code. In spite of the size of the program, it only produced some thirty different forms.

Bulgaria gave the world what may have been the first virus-exchange bulletin board.

Flip/Omicron became, arguably, the first successful multipartite virus, infecting .COM and .EXE files, as well as the Master Boot Record. However, the infection could only spread further via .EXE files. In addition to a poor infective mechanism, Flip had a number of other coding errors, and infected systems generally developed errors with cross-linking of files. The name Flip came from the payload of the virus: at a certain time and day of the month, the monitor display on infected systems would flip horizontally.

EICAR (European Institute for Computer Anti-virus Research) was founded in Hamburg and became a forum for cooperation between vendors, academics, and corporate customers.

Peter Norton got over his disbelief in viruses enough to lend his name to Symantec's new anti-virus program—Norton Anti Virus.

Harold Highland's *Computer Virus Handbook* was published. Although dated in certain specifics, the book contains a wealth of research and opinion that is still valid today. It was a compilation work, as were, oddly enough, both Peter Denning's *Computers Under Attack* and Lance Hoffman's *Rogue Programs*, published the same year.

In 1990, as now, there were myriad requests for information as to which current anti-virus program was "the best". Since no one else seemed to be responding, Rob Slade started his longstanding series of reviews of anti-virus programs.

1991: Renaissance Virus, Tequila Sunrise

Michelangelo, a seriously destructive boot sector virus, was first identified in February of 1991. Based on the solid infection mechanism of the Stoned virus, it carried a destructive payload that would use random information to overwrite the first 256 tracks of the disk used to boot the computer. Usually this would be the hard disk, and these areas contained most of the system information for the computer.

The name "Michelangelo" was assigned solely based on the trigger date of 6th March, which was the birthday of the Renaissance artist. No formal identification has been made of the author, although there are strong indications that the virus was written and released in Taiwan.

The total number of known viruses climbed towards a thousand. More and more anti-virus programs appeared, as did more VX (Virus eXchange) bulletin boards.

Tequila, the first widespread polymorphic virus, seems to have been based on the earlier Flip. Tequila contained a number of viral technologies, including multipartite form, stealth, and variable encryption polymorphism. Like its predecessor, Flip, Tequila could result in cross-linking. File corruption often resulted from attempts to deal with the problem.

At about the same time, another virus to use variable encryption was Maltese Amoeba. It was a standard file infector, but carried a somewhat destructive payload, overwriting the first sector of available disks on two days a year. Slightly before work began on the first version of the VIRUS-L FAQ (to which he became a contributor), Rob Slade began to publish a weekly series of computer virus tutorials on the Internet and on FidoNet.

NOTE

Before the popularization of the Internet, bulletin board systems (BBSs) were the most popular means of mass communication. FidoNet was a means of communication between BBS users, somewhat similar to the way that the Internet links networks. This communication included not only mail, but echomail, which extends the availability of local discussion topics to anyone on FidoNet. By the time the World Wide Web started to take off, there were tens of thousands of bulletin boards connected in this way, but interest has declined as Internet take-up has accelerated. A number of FidoNet discussion echoes have dealt specifically with pro-virus and anti-virus issues.

The Saddam virus used the Commodore Amiga's validation function (run on new disks) for reproduction and infection. It would place itself on a disk, identified as the validator program. When an infected disk was inserted, the system would, for some reason, use the validator program on the disk, and thus infect itself. The computer was infected simply by putting an infected disk in the drive, without the operator running any programs. This virus seems to have appeared in the spring of 1991. The operation of the virus was very similar to the earlier WDEF virus on the Mac, and it included a form of stealth, to hide its existence.

Interestingly, there was also a Saddam (or SADAM) virus for MS-DOS at the same time. Although the virus contained numerous bugs (including egregious spelling errors in the message payload), it was never a major problem.

1992: Revenge of the Turtle

The VCL (Virus Creation Laboratory) virus authoring package allowed virus generation capability to those with no programming skills at all. VCL didn't exhibit much coding proficiency, and generic detection of VCL viruses presented no problems. Virus creation or authoring "kits" can create thousands of different viruses, but the base code modules used are all the same. The infective code for any virus created by such a kit is generally identical to every other virus produced by the same "laboratory", and detection of one can generally detect all of them. We must note, however, that the recent VBSWG virus generator is something of an exception. Some products are more successful than others at detecting new viruses generated from that particular kit.

Michelangelo

Michelangelo became something of an epidemic (see the case study in Part III), although it didn't quite live up to its advance publicity. Nevertheless, thousands of systems went down on the day it triggered, and perhaps there would have been many more if the publicity hadn't been so widespread before the trigger date. Michelangelo became another media virus, and this led to a very strange denouement. Since the media played up the story, many people were encouraged to check for viruses, in some cases for the first time. When cases of Michelangelo were detected, they were, of course, eliminated. Therefore, while millions of instances of the virus were found, only a few (possibly less than a million) triggered on what the media saw as "Michelangelo Day": 6th March, 1992. When the world did not end, the media, oddly disappointed, did an about-face, and decided that Michelangelo was some type of hoax.

NOTE

In fact, Michelangelo was present and active in the wild for many years thereafter. In the mid-1990s it constituted the major infection in some countries. Michelangelo still survives to this day, although, because of changing computer patterns, in greatly reduced numbers.

One PC company in the UK distributed a number of brand-new PCs with this particular shard of "added value" (one of which ended up on David Harley's desk). A couple of anti-virus companies caused a certain amount of distress by issuing free Michelangelo "special editions" of their software without making it clear that Michelangelo was the only virus they could detect.

Dark Avenger

Dark Avenger (or one of a number of virus authors who may have used this "handle") released the Self Mutating Engine (MtE): not a virus itself, but a means of adding polymorphism to a virus with a minimum of coding. Fortunately, the MtE left a signature, and therefore became a generic means of identifying a suspected virus.

The same author's Commander Bomber made the job of virus detection harder by forcing the scanner either to scan the whole file or to "step through" the code. Instead of inserting code or a pointer at the beginning or end (referred to in the research community as the "top and tail") of the infected program, the virus body was inserted, as fragments, in the middle of the file. The pieces were connected to each other by a complicated series of links. This was a nuisance at the time, but a useful addition to the scanner's armoury as technology advanced on both sides of the AV/VX divide. The virus itself was rather simple, despite its enormous code size, infecting only .COM files.

Altair

In the summer of 1992, another Atari boot-sector virus appeared, carrying a message indicating that it was an antiviral program. It is possible that the code was intended to be a kind of (incompetent) anti-virus, since it would overwrite any existing boot-sector virus. However, since the common Atari boot-sector viruses of the time only wrote to disks that were not already executable, it was more virulent than most viruses on that platform. As with other attempts at antiviral viruses, this was a failure. (It's not uncommon, either, for virus-infected files or virus droppers to masquerade as anti-virus software.)

1993: Polymorphism Rules

Trident Polymorphic Engine (TPE), Nuke Encryption Device (NED), and Dark Angel's Multiple Encryption (DAME) built on the work started by Dark Avenger in MtE. None caused the end of virus signature scanning as we know it.

MS-DOS version 6 was released, incorporating the not-very-good Microsoft Anti-Virus (MSAV), based on a not-very-good product owned by Central Point, which was acquired and eventually dropped by Symantec. The package contained an extremely weak "on-access" component, which has become famous primarily because it encouraged virus writers to include a short section of code that turned off the target system's antiviral protection.

NOTE

Yisrael Radai's review of MSAV is reprinted in Pamela Kane's book PC Security and Virus Protection Handbook *(M&T Press, 1994). His essay is a textbook example of a solid product review, and is an amusing read even if you have no responsibility for antiviral protection.*

Joe Wells posted the first WildList, an attempt to list and track the activity of viruses known to be out in the field and causing problems. The WildList Organization, which grew out of this list, was discussed in Chapter 1, and we will return to it in Part II.

Computers and Epidemiology

IBM researchers Jeffrey Kephart, Stephen White, and David Chess published their paper on "Computers and Epidemiology". Anti-virus researchers have always been attracted by the application of an epidemiological model based on biological infection mechanisms. In biological life, a body invaded by pathogenic organisms from outside identifies and reacts against these assaults automatically. The use of this model has led to the introduction of models of virus management based on biological immune systems. Recently, some have wondered whether a model based on metastasis (the spread of a malignant growth from its point of origin) might be a more appropriate model for recent malware than the traditional pathogenic infection model. In fact, both models have their uses, the former being more generic, and the latter reacting more quickly.

Amiga Obscene

In June of 1993, Fuck, an extremely malicious Amiga virus, was released.

> **NOTE**
>
> *Look, it's not our fault. That's what the darned thing was called. Actually, a number of viruses have been blessed with this unattractive name, including a formerly widespread Macintosh virus. In addition to finding names in this book that some might find offensive, you will also notice, as we provide more details of specific viruses, that many messages and text inclusions in the body of the virus contain errors in grammar and spelling. In the interests of accuracy, and because the specific strings can be used to identify the presence of a virus, we have left the messages as they are, warts and all. In all quotations, any mistakes you see are deliberate.*

It was initially spread by a Trojan dropper program that was advertised as a program to check your modem. The virus would replace a system file called loadWB. The viral code would be run when the computer started, and it would then call the real system file. The virus would wait out a time period determined by the screen refresh rate, and would then start overwriting the disk with the titular obscenity, eventually trashing everything.

Like other viruses of that general era, this one checked for the presence of a popular antiviral program and, if found, turned it off.

1994: Smoke Me a Kipper

Black Baron's Smeg.Pathogen and Smeg.Queeg caused real (albeit overstated) damage to some corporates. If Pathogen's payload was triggered, a message was displayed that included the words "'Smoke me a kipper, I'll be back for breakfast...' Unfortunately some of your data won't!!!!!!" and then the first 256 cylinders of the hard disk were trashed.

Kaos4 was posted to a newsgroup specializing in erotic pictures. This was not the last time this particular vector was exploited, of course. Indeed, some victims of the later Hare virus were caused additional embarrassment. Not understanding how quickly a virus can be passed on by secondary infection, people assumed that they were infected as a result of haunting unsavoury newsgroups.

Virus hoaxes, by no means new, became a serious problem with the rise and rise and rise of the Good Times alert, followed by a wave of copycat hoaxes. In fact, most current hoaxes can still be said to belong to this group, conforming as they do to a stereotyped pattern. "Don't open email with such and such a title: it contains a virus that will perform sundry devastating acts. Send this on to everyone you know." Virus hoaxes have been somewhat neglected by the anti-virus community in the last couple of years, but continue to be a major problem. We will consider that problem at some length in Chapter 16.

The first edition of *Robert Slade's Guide to Computer Viruses* was published. (And the title was not his idea.)

1995: Microsoft Office Macro Viruses

Christopher Pile (the Black Baron, see 1994) was convicted and imprisoned under the UK's Computer Misuse Act. (Did ever a virus writer have a more appropriate surname?) Somewhat depressingly, the next highly publicized arraignment of a virus author was not until that of the author of Melissa in 1999.

FAQs and Figures

The Good Times FAQ (Frequently Asked Questions) document was released, as was Version 2 of the VIRUS-L FAQ (see Appendix A). At this time, many former inhabitants of comp.virus had migrated during a period of dormancy to the altogether wilder (unmoderated) newsgroup alt.comp.virus. At about this time also, at the suggestion of Dr. Alan Solomon, work started on the alt.comp.virus FAQ. (The FAQ was drafted, edited, and maintained by David Harley, but, like the VIRUS-L FAQ, included material contributed by some major names in anti-virus research.)

Proof of Concept

Wm.Concept, the "first" macro virus, was closely followed by several more MS Word (and MS Excel) viruses. Arguably, the first macro viruses in the wild were earlier Macintosh HyperCard infectors. There had also been unpublicized test viruses using macro languages such as Lotus 123, but Microsoft Office viruses changed the whole profile of the industry, which took a fair while to weather the change. Concept appears to have originated within Microsoft, which for a while referred to it as a "prank macro" rather than a virus. (No-one else was willing to accept the Microsoft assessment.)

The original version of Concept carried a comment, "That's enough to prove my point", buried in its code, instead of a payload. It became the most widespread virus in the world for a while, and spawned a major virus subclass that continues to trouble PC and Macintosh users.

Protection against the very first Word viruses was relatively easy to achieve by disabling automacros, which took only a line or two of WordBasic, and several experts quickly published appropriate code. Eugene Kaspersky, a prominent anti-virus researcher, published a Microsoft Word template containing protective macros: dishearteningly, a subverted version of this file appeared soon afterwards on a web site, infected with the then unknown Nuclear macro virus. Of course, virus authors soon found other methods of infection.

Introducing proper detection of macro viruses into scanner technology, however, proved a major, time-consuming undertaking: indeed, changes to Office file formats and the macro language technology that underpins MS Office applications continue to provide researchers with interesting little puzzles.

NOTE

Proof-of-concept viruses have become something of a growth industry in their own right. Viruses have been written simply to prove that a specific loophole exists. However, the author gets the "glory" of being the first to exploit the vulnerability, irrespective of the likelihood of having a virus achieve widespread dissemination. Thus, viruses have been written for applications, such as MS PowerPoint or MS Access, that support Visual Basic for Applications (VBA) or related macro languages such as CorelScript, even though they are not normally associated with the routine exchange of macro-infected documents.

1996: Macs, Macros, the Universe, and Everything

More macro viruses appeared, inevitably. Boza, a mediocre file virus, materialized. Its only real importance was that it was the first Windows 95 virus using the new PE-EXE format, rather than the earlier MS-DOS .EXE structure. Hare was also launched via USENET, and was probably more significant as a media virus than for its actual impact. Laroux became the first MS Excel infector to be a real problem in the wild.

The second NCSA/ICSA survey was conducted in 1996, and from this year on, it became a yearly event.

PC users began to become accustomed to the idea that macro viruses are here to stay: Mac users, and others, acclimated to the idea that viruses were mostly a PC problem, continued to put their trust in Disinfectant and Gatekeeper. However, since neither program detected Microsoft Word or Excel macro viruses, macro epidemics started to build up across the Mac/PC divide. David Harley began work on the "Viruses and the Mac" FAQ, in the hope of addressing this problem.

Some people still have trouble understanding that a macro virus can be problem on any hardware platform supporting applications that themselves support the relevant macro language. In other words, macro viruses aren't necessarily specific to a single hardware architecture or operating system. In fact, as more applications (including some not published by Microsoft) offer support for Visual Basic for Applications (VBA), it may even be a little misleading to say that macro viruses are application-specific.

1997: Hoaxes and Chain Letters

Good Times and a number of related hoaxes continued to resonate, and the 1997 Virus Bulletin conference included several related papers (as well as a presentation on Mac issues by David Harley).

"Stormbringer", an ex-virus writer, delivered a presentation to the assembled industry representatives on why they should give him a job as an anti-virus developer. In vain—it seems no company thought his (genuine) programming skills were worth the bad publicity they were likely to reap by employing someone from the Dark Side.

Away from the conference circuit, "Red Team" started to blur the borders between hoaxes, spam, and real viruses. It exploited the fear inspired by Good Times, and offered an alleged anti-virus program that was actually a virus dropper.

AOL trojans became a growth industry. Worm revival began slowly with mIRC worms, using the automated functions in that particular Internet Relay Chat client, and email-aware macro viruses.

Most experts regard the second wave of worms as qualitatively different from the first wave (such as the Internet Worm), in that they don't usually spread independently of any action on the part of the user. That is, they must persuade the victim in some way to "invite them in" by running an infective program. Older worms were more likely to exploit programmatic loopholes, and they infected vulnerable systems autonomously.

1998: It's No Joke

Esperanto was a PC virus widely hyped as a cross-platform virus (that is, it was alleged to infect Macs too). Some virus encyclopaedias continue to compound this error, derived from the writer's boastful and wishful thinking.

Joke/prank programs were becoming a serious nuisance: less because of their alleged destructive or replicative properties than because anti-virus products insist on flagging them as viruses.

The AutoStart worm/virus became the first significant Macintosh-specific threat in many years. It was first noticed on the Pacific Rim, but quickly spread to the US and Europe. Several variants were seen, some of them severely destructive. SevenDust and a handful of other Mac viruses were discovered shortly afterwards, suggesting a short-lived revival of interest in the creation of Macintosh malware.

CIH (Spacefiller, Chernobyl) was first reported in June. It was most noticeable for the ugliness of the payload carried by some variants. On its trigger date, it would attempt to rewrite the flash BIOS. (If it succeeded, the PC would become unbootable.) Since the BIOS chip cannot economically be replaced on some motherboards, it was sometimes necessary to replace the entire motherboard. For many years, there have been discussions about viruses destroying hardware. Technically, CIH trashes firmware, not hardware, but the distinction was, for many victims, completely academic. The virus would also trash the victim's hard disk.

Network Associates acquired Dr. Solomon's, and many users of the Dr. Solomon's product range started to vote with their feet. This was probably due to widespread distrust of the McAfee brand name, which already belonged to NAI.

1999: Here Comes Your 19th Server Meltdown

The first edition of Back Orifice was released in early 1999, or possibly late in 1998. Back Orifice is a curious program. It is definitely not a virus, though anti-virus software usually identifies it as such. Its creators don't even want it to be seen as a Trojan, and a later edition, BO2K (Back Orifice 2000), was promoted as legitimate commercial software. To clarify the situation requires some deliberation.

Commercial "remote-access" programs, such as PC Anywhere, have been available for many years. These programs make it possible to connect home and office computers in such a way that your office computer can be run from your keyboard and screen at home. This gives you access to all the programs and files on your office machine. In fact, the programs that you run are executing on your office computer—only the interface information is being communicated between the two systems. In addition, of course, network functions like RAS (Remote Access Service) on Microsoft Windows computers allow access to information on one computer from another, even over the Internet.

Back Orifice permits similar functions, except that the access can be achieved without the user of the computer being aware of the situation. The program is designed such that once Back Orifice is run on a computer, it installs itself as a service and alerts some remote user that the computer is accessible. Therefore, it is only necessary to get someone to run an unknown program, once, and their computer is open to you. In network support situations, "some remote user" is defined as the technical support worker, and "someone" is the user having difficulty. But in security breaking circumstances, "some remote user" is the attacker, and "someone" is the victim. A similar function was used to gain access to Microsoft's own computer network in late 2000.

Back Orifice is not a virus, but it can certainly be defined as a Trojan, and in the most classic sense. Once you have run a copy of Back Orifice on your computer, the enemy is inside, controlling operations, and can even turn off anti-penetration systems.

Melissa, a macro virus/worm hybrid, was perhaps the first of the modern "fast burners": viruses/worms that go global in hours, or less, spreading quickly enough to cause mail-server "meltdown" on some sites. Melissa achieved this effect by mailing itself to the first 50 entries in each victim's address book. It spawned many imitators and variants, due both to the publicity and to the fact that, like a macro virus, it carried its own source code. Its impact can be compared to that of the CHRISTMA EXEC and Morris worms. These, too, spread within hours, although they infected a specific subset of users. (The same could be said of Melissa, except that the subset was rather larger.) The impact of the earlier worms was similar to that of Melissa, although not as widespread since the 'Net wasn't as big in those days. We should reiterate, however, that researchers differentiate between first-generation worms like the Morris worm, many of which are self-launching, and the current generation, most of which can't execute if the victim is cautious.

Happy99 (Ska) took a firm hold on the world's email. Spanska, its author, likes to give good value, so when the virus is launched it displays a graphic representation of a fireworks display and a Happy New Year 1999 message. It replaces WSOCK32.DLL with itself in order to make use of email functions. Fortunately, the original library is kept under the name WSOCK32.SKA, so recovery is generally fairly simple. Each time the victim sends email, a second message including the virus as an attachment is sent to the same recipient. Happy99 is also compatible with USENET news, so when you send a message to a newsgroup, a second posting will also be made in your name and with the same subject, but containing the virus.

PrettyPark spreads via the victim's address book, but also via IRC (Internet Relay Chat). If it is able to spread this way, the virus author is able to use the program's back-door functionality to harvest information about the victim's system. One of PrettyPark's unpleasant side-effects was that Registry changes introduced by the virus impeded its removal with anti-virus software, once the antiviral was updated to recognize the virus. In some cases, once the update had been applied, the memory-resident scanner blocked an on-demand scanner from loading (and therefore from removing the virus), since the latter was perceived as being infected—the nature of the Registry modification made it seem as though all .EXE files were infected, since the virus was executed before the .EXE.

Script viruses started to creep out from under rocks. BubbleBoy fulfilled the Good Times dream of a virus that can infect just by mail being read. (But this happened only if you used Outlook, and Microsoft issued patches to repair that particular security hole.)

In the fall, trinoo (or tr1n00), one of the first pre-programmed distributed denial of service (DDoS) packages, became available on malware distribution sites. DDoS systems are not viruses, but we'll talk more about them in relation to the year 2000 at the end of this chapter.

ExploreZip was notable for a number of reasons. It masqueraded as a self-extracting zip file and piggy-backed valid messages by using a subject line that made it look like a reply to legitimate mail. It also looked for shared network drives, installing itself on shares giving access to other computers in a local or wide area network.

Shared volumes have long been a vector for virus infection. However, the fact that ExploreZip uses the function means that it is able to evade the commonplace precautions of mail hygiene, such as avoiding opening attachments. It does not matter how paranoid A is about opening attachments: if A grants B significant write access to his workstation or server through a shared volume, B's lack of similar caution can render A just as vulnerable (albeit indirectly) to an initially email-borne attack.

ExploreZip also carries a damaging payload, erasing the data contained in certain types of files. Shared drives, even if uninfected, can also have files truncated. This virus enjoyed a return to the charts later in the year when variants packed with diverse compression packages appeared, requiring anti-virus vendors to update their detection.

Everyone covered their heads in anticipation of the breakdown of civilization as we know it on New Year's Day, 2000. Consultants and other Instant Experts described (sometimes in absurd detail) an incoming wave of Millennium viruses, despite the protests of anti-virus experts who expected no such deluge. There were minor indications that some virus writers tried to instigate a massive flood of viruses and other malware. Some companies chose to hibernate for days or even weeks in the hope that things would still work when they were switched back on.

2000: Year of the VBScript Virus/Worm

No millennium virus worth mentioning appeared, despite the hyperbole. A handful of minor viruses, Trojans, and hoaxes spread, however, by taking advantage of the prevailing panic.

REVS (Rapid Exchange of Virus Samples) was launched in an attempt to improve industry response time to "fast burner" viruses/worms, such as Melissa.

Wireless application protocol (WAP) malware started to look like a real possibility, and personal digital assistant (PDA) malware appeared. Palm/Phage, though rare, was capable of infecting the Palm OS, while the (also rare) Trojan horse Palm/Liberty-A deleted Palm OS applications. While there is no known virus that uses Psion's EPOC operating system at the time of this writing, anti-virus products for wireless devices and WAP gateways were already being announced as the year drew towards an end.

DDoS and DDon'ts

In February of 2000, the general public first became aware of DDoS (distributed denial of service) attacks when a number of major commercial servers were affected. Denial of service (DoS) has long been known as a risk in computer security circles, but has not been the subject of much public discussion. News reports and marketroids have referred to them as viruses, but DDoS systems and attacks are not viral, and, so far, have not involved viruses. DDoS attacks are considered in detail in Chapter 3, which deals with malware technology.

> ### NOTE
>
> *Occasionally, there is confusion between the acronyms DOS and DoS—note the capitalization. DOS normally stands for disk operating system. The acronym is often used as shorthand for MS-DOS, Microsoft's venerable operating system. It has no etymological connection with denial of service (DoS) attacks.*

KAKworm

VBS/KAKworm took the BubbleBoy concept (a virus that could infect on reading email, and that didn't need an attachment) into the wild (it was one of the most commonly reported viruses of the year). Like BubbleBoy, it exploits a vulnerability (Scriptlet. Typelib) in Internet Explorer that can be fixed by downloading and applying a software patch described in Microsoft's Security Bulletin MS99-032. In pre-patch versions of Internet Explorer, it was possible for the infective code to be executed just by opening or previewing an infected message. The infective script is contained in the signature, but isn't seen by the victim, as no displayable text is present. The script is, however, very noticeable in other mail clients. KAKworm is considered in detail in Part III.

Curiously enough, KAKworm corresponds more closely to the old-style Morris-type worm than most recent worms or viruses since it doesn't have to trick the victim into executing it.

How Was It for You?

In spring, a virus author's fancy lightly turns to thoughts of love. The Love Bug (LoveLetter) virus appeared on 4th May and spread faster and further than Melissa. Several variants appeared almost immediately, due in part to the wide availability of the original VBScript code. The first widespread version mailed itself out to everyone in a victim's address book, attached to a message with the subject line ILOVEYOU. The message body read "kindly check the attached LOVELETTER coming from me". The attachment itself used the file name LOVE-LETTER-FOR-YOU.TXT.vbs. The trick of giving an attachment two extensions has grown very common. In this instance, the first extension suggests a harmless, non-executable text file, in the hope that the second extension (indicating the real nature of the file) won't be seen by the victim.

All charges against Onel de Guzman, suspected of having released and possibly written the virus, were dropped by the Manila Department of Justice several months later. Phillipine authorities said that, under the laws in force at the time of the incident, sufficient evidence could not be produced to successfully prosecute the case.

LoveLetter uses Outlook to spread and, like other Visual Basic Script (VBScript) viruses, can only execute if the Windows Script Host is active and enabled. LoveLetter and its many variants will be examined at some length in Part III.

Social Engineering

Since worms have to work harder to persuade the victim to execute the malicious program, the term "social engineering" was bandied about a lot. There's a paradox here. As we've previously mentioned, the first generation of worms tended to be more autonomous. Yet conventional viruses don't usually need social engineering in this sense, since they (mostly) piggyback legitimate code, and are executed as a result of an attempt to execute legitimate code. In some respects, most of the current generation of worms resembles Trojan horses in needing to trick victims into colluding in their own downfall. In fact, many vendors and general security discussion lists nowadays are often referring to what we would call worms when they use the term Trojan horses.

NOTE

Social engineering *is a term that has attracted a wide range of definitions, some of them mutually exclusive. In this context, we offer a definition from David Harley's Social Engineering FAQ: "Psychological manipulation of an individual or set of individuals to produce a desired effect on their behaviour." A summarized version of the Social Engineering FAQ is included in the resources section of this book, and the subject is also discussed in depth in Chapter 16.*

Stages of Life

Stages of Life introduced a mild polymorphic twist. Many sites had noted that LoveLetter variants could be blocked at the mail gateway by discarding mail with a characteristic subject field, without the use of specialized filtering software. Stages varied the subject line by using one of 12 possible permutations, some of which were general enough to result in the discarding of legitimate messages if filtering wasn't carefully set. The attachment, a shell scrap file called LIFE_STAGES.TXT.SHS, introduced an additional complication in that the SHS extension can remain hidden in Windows even if Windows Explorer is set to show file extensions. If executed, the virus created a number of randomly named SHS files, the number of possible names being in the thousands.

Test Match

CNET, the sprawling information technology product portal, published an anti-virus product review in September that plumbed new depths in incompetence. Inept reviews are nothing new, of course, but this one triggered a concerted response from the anti-virus community. Joe Wells, founder of the WildList Organization and editor of *WarLab Journal*, wrote an open letter to CNET's editorial staff, to which a number of anti-virus professionals added their signatures. The letter contended that the review "did antivirus product users a major disservice" and argued that case at some length.

NOTE

You can find out more about both the review and the open letter at http://www.warlabs.org/portal/ advisories.html. Some signatories of the letter also carry copies of the letter on their web sites, including one of the authors of this book (http://www.sherpasoft.org.uk/).

We will consider some of the problems and issues of comparative testing at length in Chapter 9. Naturally, we'd like you to have the best possible information on testing: you wouldn't believe how deleterious an incompetent review is to an expert's blood pressure.

W95/MTX (Matrix, Apology)

This virus/worm hybrid first came to light around the end of August, but chose the end of September, when most of the big guns of anti-virus research were at the annual Virus Bulletin conference, to "get lucky". MTX also made some use of the "double extension" trick: when it mailed itself out from a victim's account, the attachment was given a number of potentially misleading names. In many cases, a first extension suggested a JPEG or a text file, but the second extension was .PIF, indicating an executable file. While the actual file format was that of an EXE, not a PIF, this did not, of course, stop the program from being executed. Files with the .PIF extension can include many objects, including executable code. MTX was notable for the fact that it blocked browser access to some anti-virus vendor web sites, infected some files with the virus component, and replaced others with files with the worm component (necessitating replacement from the Windows installation CD). The author had gone to some lengths to make its removal difficult.

Navidad

Feliz Navidad ("Happy Christmas") was in some respects a very lame virus, a brilliant example of a virus author who couldn't be bothered to test his creation. If the victim was rash enough to execute the infective mail attachment, the Windows Registry was tweaked so that any time an .EXE file was run, the virus was executed first. However, the file name referenced in the Registry was not the name given to the file actually dropped by NAVIDAD.EXE, so after the PC was rebooted, it became virtually unusable, since no .EXE file could be executed (including virus scanners). You might think that this would restrict the spread of the virus, but since the virus managed to fire itself off as soon as it infected, this was not necessarily so.

Unfortunately, the author proved abler at social engineering than at Quality Assurance. The worm mailed itself out as if it were a reply to mail previously received by the victim. Since it homed in on received messages that included an attachment, normally cautious recipients were primed to expect an attachment in the "reply". Happily, the virus proved rather simple to remove with a little Registry editing and the manual removal of a couple of files. Less happily, an "improved" version followed in due course.

Prolin/Shockwave/Creative

W32.Prolin caused a certain amount of confusion when one anti-virus vendor chose to call it Shockwave. It is not a "Shockwave virus", but is distributed as an .EXE file that claimed to be a "great Shockwave flash movie". Its author seems to have intended some social engineering in a traditional sense, as well as in terms of manipulating the victim into executing the program in the first place. .Zip, .MP3, and .JPG files are moved to the root directory and renamed by having the string "change at least now to LINUX" appended to the existing extension. It also generates a text file with a hectoring message:

> Hi, guess you have got the message. I have kept a list of files that I
> have infected under this. If you are smart enough just reverse back
> the process. I could have done far better damage, I could have even
> completely wiped your harddisk. Remember this is a warning & get
> it sound and clear... - The Penguin

What would we do without the superior intellects of virus writers to remind us of the need to take precautions against—er, virus writers?

Update Viruses

Several viruses that emerged in 2000 suggested a movement towards a new type of functionality. A number of recent viruses include in their code the ability to make calls to a specific web or ftp site in order to download files. (Probably the most widely known example is the Love Bug, which attempted to fetch a file from a site in the Philippines.) In some cases, the file to be downloaded is an additional payload for the virus, made available separately in order to reduce the size of the virus itself, thereby making it less conspicuous. In other cases, the file may be an updated version of the virus, so that the author can continue to "improve" his (or her) creation while it is out in the wild.

Late in the year, Hybris demonstrated an additional use of this technique. The virus appears to be built in a very modular fashion, and the downloading function can be used to replace missing or damaged modules. The modular construction also makes updating quite simple, and new features can very easily be plugged into the virus. W32.Music attempted to call updates somewhat similarly, but from specific sites.

Fortunately, it is easy to detect the operation of such downloading functions, and to determine the sites and files being called. Once these facts are known, requests to site administrators to remove the files, or to remove access to the sites, are generally honoured quite quickly. Once the sites or files have been removed, the danger of updating is eliminated. Sadly, the danger of updating viruses cannot be completely disregarded.

There are other, less easily identifiable means of communication over the Internet. Hybris already uses USENET news postings for some of its downloads. Other viruses have called on the functions of IRC (Internet Relay Chat) with a range of automated "bot" technologies little known to casual users. Anonymizing remailers can be used in various ways. (Lest this seem a slap at the cypherpunk movement, please note that commercial "free email" servers like Hotmail have already been variously misused.)

Opening a channel of communication between an infected system and a remote system outside the control of the victim offers possibilities beyond allowing the virus author to track the progress of his or her creation, updating modules, or transferring confidential data. The very fact that the victim system uses that channel announces its vulnerability and reveals host information, not only to the controlling system, but to other software probing for open ports (for example). This, in turn, can inspire and enable other directed attacks using the vulnerabilities detected.

And So It Goes...

History continues, but chapters and books have to end at some point. New viruses, and new virus technologies, are constantly evolving. As this book is in preparation, a virus has been seen that advertises and spreads itself using one of the popular peer-to-peer file-sharing systems. Some new Linux viruses have appeared, using network vulnerabilities in a manner similar to that of the old Internet/Morris/UNIX Worm. There has even been a file-infecting virus compatible with both the Microsoft Windows and Linux executable file types.

But publishing deadlines beckon, so we must leave you with one final exhortation. Keep watching.

Summary

It does not take much familiarity with Internet technology to see where some of these trends are leading. Virus writing is heading for a convergence with other forms of electronic vandalism. Email viruses such as Melissa and Love Bug (only slower, and thus less noticeable) can be used to launch self-updating viruses, incorporating some form of polymorphism from a modular updating capability. Payloads can include backdoor programs, such as that carried by Back Orifice (which can be used to take remote control of any net-connected computer), or client-side "zombie" programs for large-scale distributed denial of service attacks. In fact, viruses with some sort of backdoor functionality, such as "calling home" to send back data about the victim system and its owner, have become increasingly common over recent years. (W97M/Marker and W32/Babylonia are high-profile examples.)

Thus, anti-virus technology is no longer simply about keeping your own computers safe. (It never was, actually, and we'll explore this thought further when we consider that technology at length in Chapter 6.) Anti-virus practices now have a larger role to play in the security of the connected computing environment as a whole.

To understand anti-virus technology, we must first examine virus technology more closely.

CHAPTER 3

Malware Defined

IN THIS CHAPTER:

What Computers Do

Virus Functionality

In-the-Wild Versus Absolute Big Numbers

What Do Anti-Virus Programs Actually Detect?

The term *malware* covers a wide range of threats, most of them addressed, to some degree, by anti-virus software. In fact, the software we generically describe as "anti-virus software" delivers both more and less than it promises. Most antiviral software detects more than just viruses. Even single-shot anti-virus programs that recognize only one virus need to distinguish between uninfected and infected objects. On the other hand, no anti-virus program consistently detects all known malware. Strictly speaking, no anti-virus software can even detect all known *viruses* (if only because of the time lag between encountering a new threat and adding detection to the program).

What about programs that claim to detect all known and unknown viruses? (Such programs were memorably characterized by Padgett Peterson with the acronym TOAST, from a product advertised as "The Only Antivirus Software That Won't Be Obsolete By The Time You Finish Reading This Ad".) We need to clarify terms a little at this point, by jumping ahead to the topic of anti-virus technology, covered in much more detail in Part II of this book. In particular, we must distinguish between *detection* and *identification*. Virus-specific scanners detect and identify known viruses, and, where appropriate, remove them. Some products may be able to detect *some* unknown viruses, but they don't detect the presence of *all* unknown viruses. Generic products may detect (or block without detecting) all viruses (known and unknown), or at least all viruses in a certain class. However, they don't identify them. This has two major implications. Firstly, 100 percent correct detection of all unknown viruses is not compatible with zero percent incorrect identification of all non-viruses: that is, some non-viruses will be incorrectly identified as viruses. Secondly, what you can disinfect is limited by what you can identify. If you conclude from this that detecting viruses is only part of the solution of virus management, we will not disagree. But more of that later.

What Computers Do

First, we must look at what computers are and what they do—briefly, and at a level of abstraction that most computer users don't normally need to consider. The functions that we ask of computers tend to fall into a number of general categories, including copying, automatic operation, and "decision" making.

Computers are great at copying. This makes them useful for storing and communicating data and for much of the "information processing" that we ask them to do, such as word processing. Computers are also great for the automation of repetitive tasks. Programming allows computers to perform the same tasks, in the same way, with only one initiating call. Indeed, we can, on occasion, eliminate the need for the call to be initiated by the computer user, as programs can be designed to use available data to make "decisions" without user intervention. Finally, computer processors need not be specially built for each task assigned to them: computers are multipurpose tools that can do as many jobs as there are programs available to them.

All computer operations and programs are comprised of these main components. All computer operations and programs, in various combinations, can also fulfil many more specific functions. It is no coincidence that it is these same functions that allow computer viral programs to operate.

Virus Functionality

The first and defining function of a viral program is to reproduce—in other words, to copy. This copying operation must be automatic, since the operator is not an actively informed party to the function. In most cases, the viral program must come to some decision about when and whether to infect a program or disk, or when to deliver a payload. All of these operations must be performed regardless of the intended purpose of the specific computer.

It should thus be clear that computer viral programs use the most basic of computer functions and operations. It should also be clear that no additional, unique functions are necessary for the operation of viral programs. Not only is it extremely difficult to differentiate computer viral programs from valid programs, but there can be no single identifying feature that can be used for such distinction. Without running the program, or simulating its operation, there is no way to say that this program is viral and that one is valid.

Application Functionality Versus Security

These difficulties in identification also indicate that it is very hard to defend against intrusion by viral programs. If you want *guaranteed* protection, you can follow Jeff Richards' Laws of Data Security:

1. Don't buy a computer.
2. If you do buy a computer, don't turn it on.

On the other hand, as is often said, "a ship in a harbour is safe, but that is not what ships are built for". A completely protected computer is safe, but it is not useful. A computer in operation is a useful device, but it is vulnerable. The prudent operator will learn the reality and extent of the dangers and will take appropriate precautions, while still taking advantage of the uses of the machine. Tools such as Word and Outlook are very attractive to users because of the wide range of functionality they offer. However, the security community has had to accept, grudgingly, the axiom that "if the choice is between functionality and security, functionality will win out". Unfortunately, the way in which functionality is extended in these products has the negative side-effect of reducing security.

Furthermore, as we have noted in Chapter 2, Fred Cohen proved that there is no absolute means of identifying an unknown virus on sight. Don't look for the Holy Grail or Silver Bullet of anti-virus protection. You, and your customers, are going to have to keep your eyes open.

However, if you pay due attention to where and how viruses act, you stand a far better chance of spotting a possibly malicious anomaly.

In-the-Wild Versus Absolute Big Numbers

We must address the technical definition of the difference between viruses. Because it is so very hard to determine even what a virus is, researchers have agreed that two viruses are different if, when infecting the same object under the same circumstances, they differ by as much as a single bit.

NOTE

An exact definition runs along the lines of "two viruses are different if they differ, even by a single bit, in their constant code and data areas" (Vesselin Bontchev, Methodology of Computer Anti-Virus Research; University of Hamburg, 1998). However, researchers also generally agree that this definition isn't entirely useful under all circumstances. The change of a single bit may create a serious difference between the behaviour of two viruses, whereas major changes to the content of the viral code may entail no behavioural changes. (Some viral programs use this fact as a means of concealment.) Nor does differentiation between two samples necessarily affect the way in which they are detected or even disinfected by a known-virus scanner.

Under this definition, there are generally agreed to be tens of thousands of computer viruses: around 60,000 as this book was written, and possibly close to 100,000 by the time it is published. If we didn't include the proviso about infecting under the same circumstances, the number would range into the billions, since polymorphic viruses present themselves in many different ways, depending upon such circumstances as encoding keys. However, subsequent instances of a polymorphic (shape-changing) virus are not variants, since they originate from exactly the same program.

It is also agreed that most viruses can be grouped into families, and that they have major similarities within families. In some cases, all that is changed between one variant and another is some text message, which has no bearing on how the virus is programmed or operates. One virus, for example, contains the text "Legalise Marijuana" buried within it. A variant in the same family has simply had the spelling changed to read "Legalize". Other changes can be more significant, of course. Nonetheless, experienced researchers can point out similarities between different viruses. In some cases, they may be able to say when one virus derives directly from another, which was the original and which the derivative version, and whether the changes were made by the original programmer.

As we hinted in Chapter 1, the number of detected viruses claimed by anti-virus vendors is seriously suspect. Apart from the difficulties previously described, this number reflects a difference in the way virus variants have been counted by anti-virus vendors playing the "numbers game". In 1998, anti-virus researchers received a CD containing around 14,000 "new" viruses. However, they were kit viruses, generated by a construction program. Previously, kit viruses were not counted as individual viruses, since they can be detected by a "generic" driver or definition, and don't require individual detection for each created virus. However, one vendor chose to claim them as 14,000 new viruses. Other vendors protested, but followed suit, anticipating loss of market share if they were perceived as less successful at detecting overall numbers of viruses. Moral: the number of viruses claimed by a given product is mostly a marketing issue, not statistical.

NOTE

Peter Morley's article "The Biggie" (Virus Bulletin, November 1998) gives more information on this incident of inflated claims. Paul Ducklin's conference paper "Counting Viruses" explores the issues that complicate attempts to standardize virus-counting metrics (Virus Bulletin 1999 Conference Proceedings). We describe kit viruses in more detail later in this chapter, in the "Generators" section.

Of greater significance is the fact that not all viruses are equally successful in spreading, or even reproduce as intended. Therefore, the tens of thousands of viruses that exist reduce to a few hundred that have actually made an impact in the real world of computers and users. These viruses are said to be "in the wild", in the same sense that animals in the wild run free and unchecked. As we've already indicated in Chapter 2, however, the question of "wildness" is far less straightforward than is implied by that simple definition.

Distinctions must be made between different animals (and viruses) that are in the wild. In the animal kingdom, there are thousands of viable species (that is, species that aren't on the verge of extinction, although, as human beings, we seem to be trying to reduce that total on an ongoing basis). Some are regularly seen even in cities (pigeons, rats, cockroaches); some are only seen by people who visit zoos or spend time in the native habitats of those species; some are never seen except, perhaps, by their Creator. The virus situation is somewhat similar.

A comparatively small number of viruses is known to be commonly found wild, though not necessarily in all parts of the globe. These are carefully classified, and sightings are confirmed by the WildList Organization.

There are viruses known to be wild, according to Paul Ducklin's definition in Chapter 1 ("spreading as a result of normal day-to-day operations on and between the computers of unsuspecting users"), but not so carefully classified or reported. The WildList is not a complete list of all viruses in the wild, for geographical and chronological reasons—not all regions are well served by WildList reporters, and viruses are in the wild before they are verified and make the WildList. At the other end of the chronological scale, viruses become, in some sense, extinct. Sometimes the virus is, in itself, time-limited and ceases to spread and/or trigger accordingly. Sometimes the environment that enables it to spread declines in popularity, or is modified so that it becomes more hostile to a given virus or class of viruses. Nonetheless, viruses that are no longer formally in the wild may still exist somewhere, on an unchecked floppy disk or a VX web site.

Finally, there are viruses in zoos (viruses that exist as source code, or as samples in electronic magazines, or on web sites, or in collections, but that are never seen spreading between the desktops of unknowing computer users), and their number exceeds that of feral viruses by tens of thousands (unlike animal species, which are much more numerous in the wild).

It is possible, perhaps, that the number of zoo viruses represents the tip of a much larger iceberg. Given that replication is the whole point of a virus's existence, though, this seems unlikely. No doubt there are viruses that are known only to their creators. However, given the vanity and craving for attention that characterizes so many virus writers, we doubt that such viral programs exist in large quantities. Does this mean that you only need to worry about a handful of viruses? Unfortunately, the answer is no. Unlike extinct species of animals, computer viruses can be resurrected at any time. Even time-limited examples can be given a new lease on life simply by turning back the system clock. In addition, many successful viruses target, and can turn off, anti-virus protection. Once that happens, you are subject to attack by many of the less-successful programs, should they somehow find their way onto such a system. The most usual justification for including detection of all known viruses, though, is that we never know when a zoo virus might "get lucky" and find its way into the wild. We will discuss this more fully in Part II.

NOTE

Increasingly, anti-virus researchers are coming round to the idea that adding detection for every virus as it appears may be counter-productive. Joe Wells's paper on the subject, found at http://www.warlabs.com/journal/v1_i1/oldschool.html, may seem an extreme statement at present. Its assertion that "the more viruses an anti-virus product detects the worse it is" is somewhat against the flow, but rather persuasive. Less contentiously, David Harley has suggested a number of times that an anti-virus product that offered scanning for zoo viruses as an option, rather than as a default, might make itself quite a few friends. However, that's an argument we'll consider when we discuss the evaluation of anti-virus software in Chapter 9.

What Do Anti-Virus Programs Actually Detect?

You will note that we have already spoken of viruses, worms, Trojan horses, and other forms of malware. Researchers frequently use *malware* as the term for all classes of malicious software, or programs that are designed with a malicious intent, as opposed to merely being poor implementations of legitimate software.

Vendors of anti-virus software do not always agree on what should be detected and reported to the user.

Most anti-virus programs of the scanning type detect both viruses and worms. After all, even those who don't consider worms to be a special case of virus consider both classes of malware to be primarily self-reproducing programs. However, some anti-virus programs are unable to examine all the types of objects that worms can affect but that viruses cannot. In this case, the decision to exclude certain types of malware depends on a technicality.

In other cases, the decision is made on a psychological basis. Should anti-virus programs, intended to detect programs that reproduce, report the existence of Trojans, which cannot?

NOTE

Sometimes modern worm/virus hybrids are defined as Trojans because they rely on tricking the recipient of infected email into opening an attachment. We understand this viewpoint, but prefer to define such programs according to their replicative function. Indeed, Ian Whalley ("Talking Trojan", Virus Bulletin, June 1998) has suggested abandoning the term Trojan altogether in favour of the less catchy (but also less ambiguous) non-replicative malware. The term malware is sometimes used specifically in the context of non-replicative malicious software, especially Trojans. We prefer to avoid this usage: if we do use the term in this sense, we will qualify it as "non-replicative" in accordance with Whalley's suggestion.

There is already enough confusion between the different types of malicious software: should an anti-virus program add to the problem, on the basis that it should try to report on any security problem? And, if that is the case, should anti-virus software try to report on intrusion detection, and other tenuously connected security issues? In general, anti-virus software reports (more or less) all viruses known to it and a selection of known Trojans. Many programs also report some ambiguous objects, such as remote-access tools and DDoS agents (both of which we will consider at length later in this chapter, but which could be described as Trojans or Trojan-like).

An even more difficult decision arises in the case of *prank* or *joke* programs. If a user is running an anti-virus program and suddenly crabs start running around the windows and "eating" the screen, will the user lose faith in the anti-virus software and stop using it? Obviously some vendors think so, since they alert on joke programs, such as CokeGift (Geschenk), which does nothing more sinister than offer the "victim" the computer's CD tray as a holder for canned soft drinks. On the other hand, if anti-virus software reports the existence of a joke program, will the user panic, even when the message clearly states that the file is only a prank? Probably we will only know the answer to this when scanners stop reporting jokes with confusing messages such as "!!!File myjoke.exe is infected with the virus W95.Joke.MyJoke", or "Virus Myjoke.exe is not a virus". These examples are fictitious, but they are no sillier than messages put up by real anti-virus software. Anti-virus scanners detect joke programs because corporate customers wish to detect time-wasting, and because some jokes mislead the victim into believing that they are real Trojans or viruses. However, other vendors choose not to detect such programs.

Nonetheless, jokes are no joke. While working on this chapter, David Harley became aware of email with the Bearded Trojan attached sent to one of his customers. Bearded does no intentional damage to files or file systems: it changes the Windows desktop to a graphic of a female nude. Potentially offensive or embarrassing, but not, you might think, exactly dangerous. However, in the environment in which the mail was received, a policy is in force forbidding the use of company resources for non-business use, especially where there is a suggestion of pornography. Damage to file systems is by no means the only possible destructive consequence of malware.

Viruses

Computer viral programs are not a "natural" occurrence. Viruses are programs written by programmers. They do not just appear through some kind of electronic evolution. Viral programs are written, deliberately, by people. (Having studied the beasts almost from their inception, Rob Slade was rather startled when a young, intelligent, well-educated executive proposed to him that viruses had somehow "just grown" like their biological counterparts.)

> **NOTE**
>
> *There are, for instance, many hundreds of variants of some Word 6.0 macro infectors that are all "spontaneous" mutations of the original code, which in no sense came into being "accidentally". It is widely accepted, however, that macro viruses have proven to be highly susceptible to mutation and corruption by such factors as the accidental capture of legitimate macros and unrelated viral macros, and incomplete disinfection by anti-virus products.*

Most people are now aware of the term "computer virus" even if they don't use computers. However, it is often the case that those who are otherwise technically literate do not understand some of the implications of the name. A *virus* is an entity that uses the resources of the host to spread and reproduce itself, usually without informed operator action. Let us stress here the word "informed". A virus cannot run completely of its own volition. The computer user must always take some action, even if it is only to turn the computer on. This is the major strength of a virus: it uses *normal* computer operations to do its dirty work, and so there is no single unique characteristic that can be used to identify a previously unknown viral program.

> **NOTE**
>
> *We have stated that covert action is not a defining characteristic of a virus. A few viruses have asked permission before infecting. (They don't seem to have been particularly successful in terms of widespread propagation.)*

Fred Cohen was the first to formally define the virus phenomenon. His original definition covers only those sections of code that, when active, attach themselves to other programs. This definition is sometimes thought to neglect many of the programs that have been most successful in the wild, such as boot-sector infecting viruses and macro viruses. Some people still insist on a strict interpretation of Cohen's definition and use other terms, such as *worm* and *bacterium*, for those viral programs that do not attach themselves directly to programs (though Cohen himself described worms as a "special case" of virus). Most, however, agree that a virus is any program that attaches in some way to an object that contains, or has the reasonable potential to contain, other programming. This definition allows us to include boot-sector viruses (since boot sectors generally do contain a program), but also macro viruses, which infect an object that at the time of infection often contains no code.

The term *worm* has become more widely used (not always correctly) in relation to network and email related programs. Do you think we overstate the problem of getting people to agree on a definition of what a virus is? If you have a few spare years, you can have some fun by getting together a group of academically oriented computer people, and asking them to agree on a formal definition of what a "program" is.

Virii and Octopii

If one program is a virus, what are two of them called? Given that the term is still in the realm of slang, this debate has been the longest, silliest, and most bitter debate in the whole field of computer virus research. Various linguistic "experts" have called for *virae*, *vira*, *viri*, *virii*, *viren*, and *virides*. The correct plural in biology for virus has always been *viruses*, and that is, in fact, the most common usage among computer virus researchers. Virus authors, distributors, and collectors tend to prefer *virii*, though there is no etymological basis for that particular plural form. Although the word *virus* was normally used in the singular in Latin (as a mass noun meaning poison), the plural *viri* seems to have been used occasionally, though inviting confusion with the plural of *vir* (man). We are not aware that this usage has ever been found in biology. *Viren* is probably imported from the German. Robert Slade's personal favourite, however, is the suggestion that it is one *virus*, two *virii*, three *viriii*, four *viriv*... *Viriiii* might be more appropriate for computer-using clockmakers, who usually use IIII rather than IV on clock faces. A tip of the hat goes to Ed Fenton for drawing our attention to that horological quirk.

Viral programs cannot be considered a joke. Many may have been written as pranks, but even those that were not intended to do any damage have had bugs. The original author of Stoned knew nothing of certain drive specifications, and yet the virus causes unintended damage to some disk formats. It appears that the trashing of data by the Ogre/Disk Killer virus, one of the most damaging viruses, was originally intended to be reversible, but is not, thanks to an error on the part of the programmer. Any program that makes changes to the computer system without the knowledge of the user can cause problems, the more so when the program is designed to keep spreading those changes to other systems. Form is a fairly trivial boot-sector virus that caused no significant damage to systems when it was written, a fact that no doubt has a bearing on its continued survival in the field, many years after. However, because it infects the DOS boot record rather than the partition sector, it can, unlike most boot-sector infectors, prevent a PC running Windows NT—an operating system that didn't exist at that time—from booting.

NOTE

This doesn't let the author of Form off any hooks, though. Even at the end of the 1980s, not all PCs were running versions of MS-DOS or PC-DOS. Any virus writer who says, "I don't know what the effects of this virus will be on all the systems it might infect..." is also saying "...and I don't care". Of course, no programmer can claim to know that their program will work properly on every possible system, but honourable programmers offer support when trouble occurs. In fairness, it's not unknown for a virus author to offer some help to someone accidentally infected or sustaining unanticipated damage as a result of infection.

Worms

As noted in Chapter 2, there are many variant meanings proposed for the term *worm*. However, most virus researchers now accept (sometimes reluctantly) the term as applied to a viral or reproductive program that copies and spreads itself without associating with a particular host program. More specifically, a worm usually spreads over network links from one machine to another.

Worms have been around since the beginning of the virus plague in the wild. CHRISTMA EXEC and the Morris Internet Worm are two examples. More recently, there have been the mail storms associated with Melissa and the Love Bug. Note that there are technical differences between some first-generation worms, not all of which require user intervention to spread, and more recent worms, which usually rely on some form of social engineering to trick the victim into running them.

Worms generally spread extremely rapidly, and the modern examples are challenging the traditional models of virus spread. Because of the explosive nature of worms, they have caught the attention and imagination of the news media. Therefore, when non-specialists think of viruses, they are often thinking in terms of what may be better described as worms.

Carey Nachenberg has suggested a classification scheme for worms along the following lines ("Computer Parasitology", *Ninth International Virus Bulletin Conference Proceedings*, 1999).

By transport mechanism:

► Email Worms spread via email.

► Arbitrary Protocol Worms spread via protocols other than email protocols, such as TCP/IP sockets.

By launching mechanism:

▶ Self-launching Worms, such as the Morris or Internet Worm, require no interaction with the victim. These are currently rare; however, KAK, BubbleBoy, and other script viruses that exploit a security hole in Microsoft Outlook's default (unpatched) environment to execute without user interaction would certainly qualify as such.

▶ User-launched Worms must be executed by the user, and therefore incorporate a degree of social engineering.

▶ Hybrid-launch Worms use both mechanisms.

Aside from the rapidity of their spread and some specifics about detection (many worms are easily detected at the mail gateway even without virus-specific software), the differences between worms and viruses are slightly academic. From the perspective of the average user or systems administrator, worms and viruses can generally be considered together.

Intendeds

When speaking publicly on the virus problem, we are frequently asked what our favourite viruses are. (From our perspective, this is a curious question, along the lines of "What way would you most like to be tortured to death?") When Rob Slade first encountered the question, he replied that his favourite virus was Pentagon. Why Pentagon? Simple. It doesn't reproduce. It doesn't work. Many programs were intended to be viruses, but fail to qualify. All virus collections contain programs that were obviously supposed to reproduce, but don't. Some researchers carefully weed them out of their collections, but most vendors feel they have to detect non-viruses because they are in other collections. Since software reviewers often use badly maintained collections to test anti-virus software, vendors are obliged to detect objects they know to be harmless. The alternative is to be penalized while less scrupulously constructed products earn the Editor's Choice awards.

Virus programmers include some of the sloppiest coders in the world (and, given the state of many legitimate programs we've had to use, review, or support, that is saying a great deal). In some viruses, the payload never triggers, although failure of the payload doesn't disqualify them as viruses. In some attempted viruses, the reproductive function never triggers. Sometimes the infective mechanism triggers but fails to attach the infective code to the host program. In other cases, the virus may attach to the host program, but in such a way that the code is never executed.

Programs that match this last case are normally categorized as *intended viruses*, or just as *intendeds* (much to the irritation of the authors' spellcheckers). We must distinguish here between attempted viruses that fail to reproduce unto the third and fourth generation, and viruses that fail to reproduce under *some* circumstances. For example, a VBA virus that flourishes on PCs running Office 97 but fails to replicate beyond the global template on a Mac running Office 98 is not an intended. It is a virus, but one that is not viable on all of the same platforms as its host application.

On occasion, of course, the code is so badly messed up that you simply have no idea what the author was trying to do. Usually, though, it is not difficult to see what was intended, and where it went wrong. In one virus, it is readily apparent that the programmer wanted the damaging payload to trigger on Sundays. The virus waits for the seventh day of the week. And waits. And waits. Computers start counting at zero (unless they're told otherwise), and DOS's *Get Date* function returns a value between 0 and 6, not 1 and 7. Furthermore, it returns a value of 0 for Sunday, not 6. Do you still believe that virus writers are programming geniuses?

Of course, sometimes the errors don't work out to anyone's advantage. Some mistakes create more serious problems. The Michelangelo destructive payload may have been intended to overwrite the whole hard disk. Instead, it reportedly sticks in an infinite loop (not to be confused with the "nth complexity binary loop" associated with the Good Times hoax): however, that doesn't work to anyone's advantage, either. The Morris Worm was obviously intended to be a slow infector, except that Morris inverted two factors. Instead of sending out a copy of itself every once in a while, it exploded, and drew attention to itself by bringing down systems with sheer overload.

Corruptions

Intendeds may be a failure to meet the programmer's actual purpose, but it is common for a viable virus to become corrupted as it spreads from system to system. In this instance, the virus is modified under circumstances the virus author didn't or couldn't anticipate, or didn't bother to allow for. Since such modifications are accidental, they rarely offer a Darwinian "improvement" to the viability of the virus, but they don't always prevent it from replicating either. This is particularly (not exclusively) characteristic of macro viruses. The original virus (or rather, a later instance of the virus) is modified by some transient system glitch. Causes may include inadequate disinfection (this happened frequently in the early days of macro-virus detection), picking up legitimate macros from an infected machine, or losing one or more component macros. Anti-virus programs normally detect known instances of corrupted viruses, just as they do intended viruses.

Corrupted non-viral programs may also find their way into poorly maintained virus collections, perhaps because someone assumed that they were corrupt because they'd been infected by an unknown virus. Anti-virus programs may detect corrupted non-viral programs and other non-viral objects (even text files) known to exist in widely available virus collections, for the reasons already discussed. That is, to avoid being penalized by incompetent testers in comparative reviews.

Germs

This is a rarely used term for an infrequently met phenomenon. A *germ* is a first-generation virus—an instance of a virus that hasn't yet infected anything—and it is not generated by the normal process of infection. A germ is, that is, the original infective object (or an exact copy) created by the virus author, or by someone with access to the original source code. For instance, a file virus that has not yet infected a program may exist as only the virus code. Again, we must distinguish between *germs* and *droppers* (discussed next), both of which are different from worms that "infect" by spreading copies of the original, which don't attach to a host file. Germs are most likely to be found in collections and are detected by anti-virus software for that reason. A germ cannot meaningfully be described as being in the wild.

Droppers

A *dropper* is not itself a virus, but a program written expressly to install a virus, especially a boot-sector virus. We do not describe a virus-infected program as a dropper, since the program was not written specifically for the purpose. What if a dropper program is infected with another virus? The answer depends on the context. If the program was written to install virus A and only virus A, then it remains a dropper, even when infected with virus B. However, it is still not a dropper for virus B. Confused? You should be.

A dropper may be designed as a sort of Trojan, though in this case the term *injector* is sometimes preferred. The victim is tricked into running a program that does not, itself, replicate, but that has a malicious payload. Red Team has been described in these terms. However, droppers have often been intended as a convenient means of transport, most commonly of boot-sector viruses, rather than as a means of covert introduction to a system.

It's often said that boot sector viruses cannot *infect* across networks, which is more-or-less accurate. However, they can be *transported* across networks, either by a dropper or as a binary image of an infected disk. BSIs (boot-sector infectors) are examined in more detail later in Chapter 5. Initially a dropper would have been used to spread boot-sector viruses via online systems. A BSI dropper would place the virus in active memory, thus allowing it to infect the hard disk, and subsequently spread via disk sharing.

Anti-virus software detects known germs, droppers, and injectors because of their possible use as Trojans, and, of course, because they're found in collections.

Test Viruses

Quite early on in the development of anti-virus technology, customers wanted to test whether their anti-virus programs were installed and working properly. Some vendors introduced detection of *test "viruses"* into their software. Such programs were not viruses (they didn't replicate), but they contained an arbitrary string (sequence of characters) that triggered an alert similar (but not always identical) to that triggered by real viruses. Originally, each vendor who adopted this approach used a product-specific test string and instructed customers on how to use it in a test file. This was considered preferable to supplying the test virus as a ready-made file that would trigger an alert at inconvenient times. Later, this approach was consolidated into the EICAR test-string. This is a sequence of ASCII characters that can be typed into a file with a text editor, but that constitutes a stand-alone DOS program that will be recognized by most anti-virus products as a "test virus". The EICAR test string is:

```
X5O!P%@AP[4\PZX54(P^)7CC)7}$EICAR-STANDARD-ANTIVIRUS-TEST-FILE!$H+H*
```

Running the file displays the text

```
EICAR-STANDARD-ANTIVIRUS-TEST-FILE!
```

In the meantime, some individuals produced "neutered" versions of real viruses, or even "harmless" real viruses, for similar purposes; however, most virus experts loathe this approach, and we'll explore the reasons for that in some detail in Chapter 9. (We'll also examine the use of the EICAR test string more closely.) Nonetheless, simulated viruses are often detected by anti-virus programs, since the vendors are aware that their products are liable to be tested against such simulations.

Generators

In the early 1990s, some virus writers started producing *virus creation kits*, or *generators*. These programs allow you to create viruses, simply by selecting the functions you want from a menu. No programming skills needed. Now you, too, can create a destructive menace. Equal-opportunity vandalism.

In reality, of course, all that was happening was that certain pre-programmed modules were being added together. No new virus could be produced by the generators, since the user was simply connecting existing bits together. For example, the Virus Creation Laboratory (VCL) could not create a macro virus because macro viruses hadn't been invented when this generator was developed. (There have been macro-virus kits since, but they have made little real impact.) In fact, VCL wasn't that good at creating file viruses: many of the attempted viruses it created were not viable.

A number of virus kits exist, especially for the creation of DOS file infectors and macro infectors, but they have never made much of a splash. Given a finite set of modules, the kit could only produce a finite set of viruses. In fact, it was rather easy to detect any virus produced from the generators, since every module was detectable by scanning for a search string. Therefore, even "new" viruses generated from the lab could be detected before they were created. For example, some scanners detected the Kournikova virus at first sight, using a generic driver or advanced heuristics, though it took others a little while to catch up. In short, even the competent generators don't merit the superstitious fear they sometimes inspire.

Trojans

At an EICAR conference in 1999, a vendor representative was heard to whimper, "This is anti-virus software, not anti-Trojan software". Anti-virus vendors have good reason for wishing they'd kept out of the Trojan arena from the beginning: the species presents considerable difficulties, not least of definition.

Trojan horses are often described as programs that pretend to do one thing while performing another unadvertised and unwanted action. Common modern usage is to describe them as non-replicating malware, or as programs with a payload but no automatic replication mechanism.

This description is useful for distinguishing between viruses and Trojans, but it depends on an implicit assumption of malicious intent. How do we detect an unknown virus? We can't say for sure that a program is replicative algorithmically, but we can do a test run, as heuristic engines do. How do we detect an unknown Trojan? Not by trial and failure. If we know that a program formats a hard disk, that tells us nothing about the author's intent, malicious or otherwise—it could be a Trojan, or it could be a systems utility. It could even be a systems utility that has been *trojanized* (the term *trojaned* is sometimes used) by describing it as doing something quite different from disk formatting. However, examining the file or stepping through the code only tells us that it formats a disk. It doesn't tell us anything about the author's intent, the supplier's intent, or the recipient's expectations.

NOTE

Trojans are sometimes defined, according to the action they perform, as destructive or password-stealing. However, it's common for the same program to attempt both actions. Indeed, an attack intended to gain unauthorized access or disclosure might well cause some destruction with the intention of covering the intruder's tracks. Destructive Trojans range from simple batch files, shell scripts, IRC scripts, and the like, that call a system command such as rm or format, to more sophisticated compiled programs. Their basic modus operandi, however, tends to be simple and immediate destruction. Password stealers are more accurately regarded as a subset of a whole range of privacy-invasive threats, concerned with stealing access rather than direct destruction. They include AOL password stealers, backdoor Trojans, Remote Access Tools, and rootkits, all of which are considered in the following sections.

Viruses and worms are sometimes described as "special cases" of Trojans. This is defensible: you can describe a virus-infected object as being in some sense trojanized. However, we prefer to distinguish between viruses and Trojans according to their ability to replicate, as it seems less confusing. Worms still constitute a problem: self-launching worms might be considered truly auto-replicative, but most modern worms rely on tricking a victim into running a program that installs the worm or virus and triggers the mechanism for mailing it on. Some sources, including anti-virus vendors, therefore equate worms and Trojans. Even worse, some malware can be described as being in some sense multipartite, combining a virus, a worm, and a Trojan (MTX has been described in these terms). We suspect that most readers will be less concerned with these niceties than with the practical issues of defending against all these threats, so we will observe that the terminological problem exists, rather than try to solve it.

We don't consider Easter Eggs (harmless code concealed in production software by the original production team) as Trojans here. This is not necessarily because we like the idea of having a flight simulator concealed in our spreadsheet applications, but because anti-virus software doesn't usually target such things.

Joke programs are considered separately in this and the following chapters. Installation routines and other programs that pass back information to the manufacturer without the knowledge of the user might be considered Trojans, and we sometimes see security alerts concerning such phenomena, but they aren't usually detected by anti-virus software. Accidental Trojans were touched upon in Chapter 1, and the concept is not explored further here (mainly because anti-virus software doesn't usually detect them).

Trojan programs used to be spread almost entirely via public-access electronic bulletin board systems (BBSs). Obviously, a damaging program that can be identified

Forget Solitaire

Did you know that there is a flight simulator concealed in Microsoft Excel 97?
To access this game use the following (presented by Larry Werring in the
RISKS-FORUM Digest mailing list, edition 19.53 on 5th January, 1998):

1. Open Excel 97.
2. Open a new worksheet and press F5.
3. Type **X97:L97** and press ENTER.
4. Press TAB.
5. Hold CTRL-SHIFT and click the Chart Wizard button on the toolbar.
6. Once the Easter Egg is activated, use the mouse to fly around: right button
   for forward, left for reverse. There are also keyboard controls.

We're not going to go into detail about how to run the game. If you want, you
can play with it yourself. The point is, what is a game doing inside the spreadsheet
program? There is no reason for the inclusion of this code, even granted the
opinion that software bloat is not always a bad thing. But this game, the code for
it, the graphics, and other extraneous pieces, are taking up space on millions of
computers. Most users of those computers have no idea the function is there.

This says something about quality control at Microsoft. Here is an undocumented
feature, and a rather large one, coming out of a widely used office product.
However, Microsoft is not the only company at fault. You can find a large
number of such concealed functions at various web sites, including the following:

▶   http://geocities.com/ant_hill11/Eastereggs1.html
▶   http://www.anu.edu.au/mail-archives/link/link9804/0262.html
▶   http://www.jokingaround.com/eggs/
▶   http://www.microseconds.com/easter.htm
▶   http://www.logolinks.co.uk/computer/coegg.htm
▶   http://www.suite101.com/article.cfm/computer_security/36424

Forget Solitaire *(continued)*

However, this also says something about security. Take another look at those instructions. Think anybody would be likely to do all this in the course of a day's work? But with millions of curious computer users out there, even this type of sequence is going to be found out. Which means that any kind of security bug, no matter how deeply buried, is eventually going to be found. Probably by the wrong people first.

is unlikely to be distributed through a medium in which the donor can be held to account. Some BBSs were hangouts for software pirates, and acted as distribution points for security-breaking tips and utilities. Pirate BBS systems have now been replaced by a variety of (generally short-lived) web sites and FTP download archives ("warez servers"). These sites are usually killed as soon as system managers find them, but given the ease of establishing personal web pages, a few dozen may be in operation on any given day.

The original tie-in of Trojan and pirate software has led to confusion between Trojan programs, viral programs, and system crackers, and this false association has proven extremely resistant to correction. It has also led to a view of BBSs, and, by extension, all download sites, as distribution points for viral programs. (One paper's computer columnist, normally better versed than this, dismissed the availability of anti-virus software to combat Michelangelo by saying that no self-respecting company would ever use a BBS.) This bias continued to survive for many years, in spite of the fact that the most successful viral programs at the time, boot-sector viruses, could not be transmitted over BBS systems in normal use.

We have suggested that Trojans normally include an element of pretence, or social engineering. The extent of the pretence may vary greatly. Many of the early PC Trojans relied merely on a deceptive filename and description on a bulletin board. *Login* Trojans, popular among university students in mainframe days, mimicked the screen display and the prompts of the normal login program. They often passed the username and password along to the valid login program at the same time as they captured the user data. Other Trojans may or may not contain actual code that does what the Trojan is supposed to do, while performing additional and unpleasant acts that the victim does not expect. Many distinguish between Trojans and joke or prank programs on the basis that Trojans are always malicious. As we shall see, however, this distinction is sometimes rather fuzzy.

One oft-quoted example of a Trojan is 1989's AIDS Information Diskette, often incorrectly identified in both the general and computer-trade press as a virus. Not to be confused with the fairly rare AIDS I and II computer viruses, the AIDS trojan program appears to have been part of a well-organized extortion attempt, as discussed in Chapter 2. The "evaluation disks" were shipped to medical organizations in England and Europe with covers, documentation, and licence agreements, just like any real commercial product. When installed and run, the program did give information and an evaluation of the subject's risk of getting AIDS. However, it also modified the boot sequence so that after 90 reboots of the computer, all files on the disk were encrypted. The user was informed that, in order to get the decryption key, a "licence fee" had to be paid.

Trojan horse programs, especially destructive Trojans, are sometimes referred to as *Arf, Arf* or *Gotcha* programs. The phrases are taken from the screen messages presented by one of the first examples, distributed as a program that would enable graphics on early TTL monitors. This would have been quite a feat, if it had actually been possible. Instead, it presented its message and erased the contents of the hard drive.

Password Stealers and Backdoors

While a Trojan without a payload would be a sorry piece of malware, that payload doesn't have to include sheer destruction. It might, for instance, entail data leakage without direct harm to the original data.

Versions have been written for microcomputers as well, appearing to be network login screens. A number of these have also been designed for the World Wide Web, pretending to be a popular web site in order to steal passwords for that site. In recent years, it has become common to distinguish *password stealers* as a separate class of malware so that some software is specified as detecting both Trojans (that is, destructive Trojans) and password stealers.

Not all password stealers use fake login screens: some use simple social engineering. The most prominent examples of this group are AOL password stealers, many hundreds of which have been reported. Some anti-virus software detects these routinely, not only by signature recognition, but also heuristically. However, the simplest heuristic works well in this context. If anyone from any company or system that you legitimately use sends an email message asking for a username and password, they almost certainly are not entitled to it. System administrators normally have privileges beyond those accorded to other system users, and they are able to do any work they need to do on another user's account without needing to know that user's password.

Mind Games

One of the factors involved in the success of malicious programs is a study of the mindset of the user—a study of the psychology or sociology of the computer community. Since the spread of viral programs usually requires some activity, however innocent in appearance, from the operator, looking at the security-breaking aspects of other programs can give us some insights.

Password stealers simulating a login program may send back a message to the user that the login has been denied. Most users will accept this as an indication that they have either made a mistake in entering the login data or that there is some unknown fault in the system. Few users question the message, even after repeated refusals. Some programs are sophisticated enough to pass the login information on to another spawned process: few users know to check the level of nesting of processes.

Up and ATM

This type of activity has recently been repeated in less innocuous fashion. Criminals have been known to build false fronts for automated teller machines at banks. These devices fit over the regular machines and are similar in appearance. The false fronts will accept cards, prompt for the holder's personal identity number (PIN), and then give a message about some problem and a suggestion to contact the bank in the morning. After a few hours, the crooks collect the device, remove the cards, read the stored PINs, and spend a few hours extracting as much cash as possible at legitimate bank machines using the cards and access codes thus collected. Clearly, this isn't a problem that anti-virus vendors can be expected to do much about.

Backdoor Man

Backdoor or *trapdoor* are terms normally used to describe a means of accessing a system with privileges higher than those normally granted to ordinary users. It's not uncommon, for example, to use such a privileged account during system or program development: sometimes it is left in production software, deliberately or otherwise. It would be unusual for anti-virus software to detect such a security breach. More recently, however, the term has been used in the context of *backdoor Trojans*, which we consider at length in the "Remote-Access Tools (RATs)" section later in this chapter.

Jokes

A famous, if relatively harmless, prank in earlier computers was the *cookie* program which ran on PDP series computers. This program would halt the operation in progress and present a message requesting a cookie.

Despite the fact that this program became rather widely known as a joke, it is often reported in security books as a virus. The original cookie program had no reproductive functions, however. It barely even qualifies as a Trojan, although it could certainly be regarded as a nuisance.

NOTE

The cookies in this case were strictly virtual and had nothing to do with the "cookies" used by web sites to track visitors. The latter type of cookie is accused from time to time of being a security risk. In fact, such cookies are little globs of data rather than code: even if they contained a program (malicious or otherwise), it is hard to see how that program could actually be executed. There are, certainly, privacy issues associated with web cookies; however, these are not really in the scope of this chapter.

There were consistent reports of viral programs following this pattern, including a very detailed report of a Spanish Cookie virus. None of us has ever seen this virus, although one of us has been assured that it really exists. There have been commercially produced joke packages offering "Stupid Mac (or PC) Tricks". There are countless pranks available as shareware or freeware. Some make the computer appear to insult the user; some use sound effects or voices; some use special visual effects. A common characteristic of such pranks is that the computer is, in some way, apparently non-functional. Many pretend to have detected some kind of fault in the computer (and some pretend to rectify such faults, of course making things worse). One such program in our own field was PARASCAN, the paranoid scanner. This reported large numbers of very strange viral programs, none of which, oddly, have ever appeared on the WildList.

It can be argued that, aside from temporary aberrations of heart rate and blood pressure, pranks do no damage, and that they can be distinguished from Trojans on that basis. However, some researchers refer to *accidental* Trojans, whose intent is non-malicious but whose effect is destructive.

At the same time, some joke programs are clearly meant to do psychological damage. Some use "gotcha" messages to trick the victim into believing that they have lost all their files. Furthermore, a victim may be prompted by such a message to take ill-advised action in an attempt to recover "lost" data or to stop data from being lost in the first place, resulting in actual damage. For instance, a panicking victim might lose data or even access to the system by hitting the reset button while the joke displays its symptoms. Most joke programs (and non-programs, such as virus hoaxes) are plainly meant to humiliate the victim when they realize that they've been duped, thus asserting the superiority of the joker or hoaxer.

UltraCool, for example, claims that "A LOW level Hard Disk format will procede [sic] in 27 seconds if cancel button is not pressed", but keeps moving the Cancel button away from the mouse cursor until the countdown reaches zero. (It then displays a "Just kidding…" message.)

Pranks have, in various ways, entered the realm of virus mythology. The PDP-series cookie prank, as noted, has given rise to all manner of reports of a cookie virus. There is also the crabs program. This initially ran on the Xerox Star system and was later ported to Apple and Atari systems. More of a screen saver than anything else, it was sometimes reported by careless security writers as a class of viral programs that attack video displays. A similar program in the MS-DOS world was BUGRES, which was reported as a virus by a major commercial anti-virus program. This is how pranks do most damage: in addition to causing time to be spent getting rid of a prank on a system, they tend to generate calls to researchers, and waste not only time, but bandwidth.

Joke programs have become a major cause of annoyance, even where there is no apparent malice intended. Thus arises the difficulty of deciding whether to alert the user to prank programs on the computer. A program like this doesn't do any harm, and so generating a warning might be considered a false alarm. On the other hand, anti-virus developers don't want to have to contend with a bunch of calls about a new virus every time somebody rediscovers BUGRES. Yet CokeGift probably holds the world record for protests to the industry from consultants and systems administrators who are called out to remove an essentially harmless program from PCs when anti-virus software has reported infection by the "Joke/CokeGift Virus" or some similarly misleading message.

Some vendors decline to detect jokes like this as a matter of policy. Others detect jokes because "they may frighten victims" or "to discourage the promiscuous exchange of executable programs". A few offer a choice, and some are even considering modifying their alert messages, by not describing non-viruses as viruses, in order to reduce the Panic Factor. We recommend that you find out, before you deploy anti-virus software, whether the package detects pranks or not. Alert users to the fact that scanners can find joke software, and tell them to read the screen messages carefully.

Anti-virus vendor web sites are seriously inconsistent about the information they offer on jokes, and there is no standard nomenclature or reporting mechanism for such software. If you feel the need to research this topic further, here are some resources:

- ▶ http://hamptonroads.about.com/citiestowns/southeastus/hamptonroads/libr
- ▶ http://www.supershareware.com/Apps/4072.asp
- ▶ http://www.btsunlimited.com/shareware_nopass/shareware_prank.htm
- ▶ http://members.tripod.com/~wiseguysinc/joke.htm
- ▶ http://www.geocities.com/netsur24/gags.html
- ▶ http://www.sidor.ru/sick/index1.html
- ▶ http://looneytunes.acmecity.com/tune/213/

WARNING

Use at your own risk! Apart from the annoyance caused by the way in which they are reported by some scanners, pranks have been used to spread Trojans or viruses in the past.

Remote-Access Tools (RATs)

A difficult subject to pin down is that of *remote-control software*. Some people would like to refer to the programs as remote-access Trojans, while the "developers" would rather have them called remote-access (or remote-administration) tools (RATs). A moment of thought will make the problem plain: all networking software can, in a sense, be considered to be remote-access tools. We have file transfer sites and clients, web servers and browsers, and terminal-emulation software that allows a microcomputer user to log on to a distant computer and use it as if he or she were on site.

Many remote-access programs are available commercially, ranging from simple file-copying utilities, such as LapLink, to full remote-operation packages, like PC Anywhere. The RATs considered to be in the malware camp tend to fall somewhere in the middle of the spectrum. Once a client, such as Back Orifice, is installed on the target computer, the controlling computer is able to obtain information about the victim system, such as which programs and processes are currently running, and what files and directories it contains. The master computer will be able to download files from, and upload files to, the target. The control computer will also be able to submit commands to the victim, allowing the distant operator to control a range of activities. This activity goes on without any alert being received by the owner or operator of the targeted system.

NOTE

The authors of some RAT programs assert that the software is not malicious. As "proof", they point out that such packages have valid uses. This is quite true. RAT programs can be used to support computers over a LAN and even over the Internet. When a user rings technical support, the support person can connect to the actual machine, and then gather information and diagnose and treat problems without having to rely on questionable data and actions from customers who may have very little computer knowledge. However, RAT programs are not necessarily configurable to prevent misuse of the remote-access capability, and they are designed in such a way that the malicious use of the software is quite easy and transparent to the victim. The authors of such programs have also been known to attempt to legitimize them by introducing a charge for the software. This reassures potential victims. It also allows the authors to complain about monopolistic security vendors impeding legitimate business interests if they advertise detection of such programs.

When a RAT program has been executed on a computer, it can install itself in such a way as to be active every time the computer is subsequently turned on. Information is sent back to the controlling computer noting that the system is active. The user of the command computer is then able to explore the target, escalate access to other resources requiring a higher level of privilege, and install other software, such as DDoS zombies, if so desired.

Once more, it should be noted that remote-access tools are not viral. When the software is active, though, the master computer can submit commands to send the installation program on, via network transfer or email, to other machines. These programs must be executed on the other machines, but a little social engineering via email can be enough to accomplish this.

DDoS Agents

A *denial of service* (DoS) attack generally does not attempt to crack security on a computer system or network. It tries to use up some resource, and thus deny that service to legitimate functions or users. For example, a massive spam (unsolicited email) or mail bomb attack might be considered a denial of service attack, because it ties up the network connection and also uses up great amounts of disk space for the mail queue. No security is broken, and no data are corrupted, but the computer system cannot be used for its intended purpose.

Other types of denial of service attacks might entail trying to log on to the target computer, thus using up processing time as the host tries to validate the requests. The most sophisticated of such attacks send network-control messages that request the host to contact some other machine to verify information. These requests must be honoured, because they are part of the dynamic configuration process of the Internet, but the DoS attacks use fake addresses, and therefore the host computers make repeated attempts to connect to computers that don't exist.

A *distributed denial of service* (DDoS) attack goes one step further. By sending out Trojan programs, crackers try to gain at least partial control of a number (possibly thousands) of computers. At the designated time, the master computer sends a very short command message to those computers running the Trojan server or agent software. Thus one computer starts and controls hundreds, thousands, or tens of thousands of computers, all sending some kind of DoS attack to a given target. One computer sending DoS packets to a huge site like Yahoo is nothing more than a nuisance. But with hundreds of computers participating, the effect is greatly magnified.

DDoS programs do not conform to commonly accepted definitions of the term *virus*, but anti-virus packages often detect them. At one point, DDoS was called a *flood network* attack, from the name given to the second program to employ the concept. The structure of a DDoS attack requires a master computer to control the attack, a target of the attack, and a number of computers in the middle that the master computer uses to generate the attack. These computers in between the master and the target are variously called agents or clients, but are usually referred to as running *zombie* programs.

So, do the attackers own hundreds of computers? By no means: however, by distributing Trojan programs, crackers try to gain at least partial control of many computers, which may number in the thousands or even tens of thousands. The zombie software is generally only a single program, which can be emailed to potential suckers or, preferably, is posted on USENET newsgroups with names such as Sheila_gets_undressed.exe. The zombie program, when run, installs itself on the computer and then notifies the master computer that another agent is in place. It usually also generates a spurious error message so that the user doesn't suspect anything when Sheila fails to perform as expected.

DDoS programs are not viral, and managing them is a systems issue, not just a desktop issue. Nevertheless, checking for zombie software not only helps to protect you and your system, but lowers the risk of attacks on others, as well. It is your responsibility and it is in your best interest to ensure that no zombie programs are active on any of your machines. If your computers are used to launch an assault on some other system, you could be liable for damages. In addition, although it is a very bad idea, some people talk about launching retaliatory strikes in the case of a DDoS attack.

Why is retaliation a bad idea? All of the DoS attack packets are being launched by zombie computers. The master computer never sends a packet directly to the target. Therefore, striking back will only ever hit zombie machines, which, aside from a little negligence, are probably all owned by completely innocent victims. In any case, computer security reprisals are generally a bad idea. Attacking anyone is likely to render you liable to prosecution or a lawsuit. Floods of mail storms, spam, and attack packets only use up bandwidth, reduce cooperation, and ultimately damage the networks that you are trying to use in the first place.

For more information on DDoS attacks and programs, you can look up information at any of these sites:

► staff.washington.edu/dittrich/talks/cert/

► staff.washington.edu/dittrich/misc/stacheldraht.analysis

► staff.washington.edu/dittrich/misc/tfn.analysis

► staff.washington.edu/dittrich/misc/trinoo.analysis

> ► staff.washington.edu/dittrich/misc/ddos_scan.tar

> ► staff.washington.edu/dittrich/misc/sickenscan.tar

> ► www.cert.org/advisories/CA-2000-01.html

> ► www.cert.org/reports/dsit_workshop.pdf

> ► www.cisco.com/warp/public/707/newsflash.html

> ► www.fbi.gov/nipc/trinoo.htm

Rootkits

A *rootkit* is a suite of trojanized system applications that might be substituted for the untrojanized originals. Such programs can include monitoring utilities and system processes gimmicked so that they don't draw attention to illegitimate processes. They can also include utilities modified to enable an intruder to escalate account privileges or to hide other component files. They are mostly associated with UNIX, but examples have been reported for Windows NT. Anti-virus programs have not, until recently, routinely detected such programs (in general) but there's no absolute reason why they shouldn't. The recent upsurge of Linux worms that use social engineering and other techniques to persuade users to execute a program that installs a rootkit has ensured that vendors with a Linux product have begun to lead the way in the detection of such programs.

False Alarms

No, these aren't the virus hoaxes that we talked about in Chapter 2. The false alarms we are talking about here are programming and implementation bugs. We know it will come as a shock, but we have to tell you: anti-virus software is not perfect. When we discuss the evaluation of anti-virus software in Chapter 9, we will go into more detail about the two major problems: false positives and false negatives. For the moment, false positive alerts are what are commonly known as false alarms. That is, a virus is reported where none exists. A false negative is an instance of a virus not being reported where one does exist.

Known-virus scanners are the most popular type of anti-virus software, and they generally identify viruses by name and specific variant, although the latter is not always reported. Unfortunately, the only way to be absolutely sure that you have a specific virus is to have a complete copy of each of the tens of thousands of known viruses in a database that is accessed by the scanning program. (This is sometimes called *exact identification*.) Given the number of viruses and a rough estimate of the average size, such a database would probably require many hundreds of megabytes of disk space. Even that wouldn't be sufficient, though, since there are small changes to viruses depending on the object that they are infecting, which would entail multiple database entries. Polymorphic viruses might require thousands, even billions, of entries for each, just to be sure of finding every single match. Even for a large corporation, having this volume of data for anti-virus protection is unrealistic, and the processing overhead would be gigantic.

Developers of anti-virus software therefore take shortcuts. Or, to put it a little more kindly, all known-virus scanning is to some extent heuristic. Anti-virus researchers look for a reasonably short scan string that is unique to the virus and that does not appear in other software. Careful vendors will try to find more than one such string, and will also calculate a digital signature of the whole virus. However, every once in a while, some arithmetic fluke is going to identify an oddball self-booting game floppy disk as the Stoned virus.

Of course, some developers take more shortcuts than others. If a vendor just looks for the first relatively complicated string, it won't necessarily be unique. In one infamous case, a major anti-virus vendor found a nice, seemingly arbitrary, string in a virus that was written in a high-level language. The string was quite arbitrary, since it didn't do much: it was an identifier routinely included by a particular compiler. The scanner concerned suddenly started flagging all kinds of innocent programs as being infected. All these programs had been put together using the same compiler.

Once we move beyond the virus-specific scanning into generic anti-virus programs, the problem becomes more acute. Activity monitors, change-detection software, and heuristic scanners (all of which we will discuss in more detail in Part II of this book) look for what might be termed *circumstantial evidence* of viruses. Although these procedures can find new viruses that are not yet known in terms of scan strings, they aren't perfect. They are vulnerable both to false positives and to false negatives.

Therefore, any anti-virus program is, sooner or later, likely to give a false alarm. Be aware, then, that not every alert you get will be valid. On the various virus-discussion mailing lists and newsgroups, we are quite used to questions of the form "I have the X virus, but it is supposed to do/be Y, and I don't have that on my system. How come?" The standard answer you will receive to all such questions is, "Have you tried another scanner?" Using a second anti-virus program to confirm the report of the first is standard practice.

Summary

It is, perhaps, inevitable that we have been obliged from time to time to jump ahead to consider elements of anti-virus technology. Indeed, almost the whole of this chapter has been based on the implicit assumption that malicious software is what anti-virus software detects. This is, of course, an extraordinarily naive assumption, and not universally held, even among non-experts. Looking at a recent comparative review of anti-virus products in a non-specialist magazine, we find in the features table, under "Type of software", that a variety of software types and functions are listed:

- ▶ Detection of viruses of various types
- ▶ Tracking of suspicious behaviour and unusual file changes
- ▶ "Protection against hackers"
- ▶ Privacy protection
- ▶ Child surfing protection
- ▶ Blocking of hackers and unwanted banner ads
- ▶ Workstation and network-directory locking
- ▶ Cookie management
- ▶ Filtering of "inappropriate content", which may mean spam (unsolicited bulk email and/or newsgroup postings), hoax virus alerts and other chain letters, or pornographic material

Elsewhere, we often see virus scanners, Trojan detectors, personal firewalls, intrusion-detection software, and anti-spam software stuffed into the same bag. There is some justification for describing some of the packages associated with spam generation as malware, and it is possible to regard virus scanning as a special case of content filtering. However, we have not felt it appropriate to discuss the more social and less technological elements of content analysis in detail in this chapter: instead, we shall consider them further in Part IV, when we turn to social issues. It is misleading and short-sighted to consider perimeter protection in isolation from viruses and Trojans, and we will discuss the integration of anti-virus technology with other security software in due course. Before we even discuss core anti-virus technology, however, we must take a closer look at virus technology, which is, after all, the main subject of the book.

Virus Activity and Operation

IN THIS CHAPTER:

We now come to some specifics of virus operation and activity. This section of the book may appear to be rather intricate, particularly for those who have not previously studied the inner functions of operating systems. However, it provides a background for understanding how, exactly, viruses do what they do. This, in turn, shows where computers are vulnerable to virus attacks, and where viruses are vulnerable to detection and prevention or removal.

For any of you who are expecting to learn how to program a virus in this or the following chapter: you bought the wrong book (and we did warn you in the introduction!). To make a virus requires some knowledge about programming and operating system (or possibly Microsoft Word or Outlook) internals. Having that knowledge, however, doesn't protect you against viruses, any more than being a gunsmith gives you an edge in making flak jackets.

NOTE

The truth is that most virus writers are less accurately compared to gunsmiths than to amateur hit-men: their skill level is just about sufficient to fire a sawn-off shotgun. While many virus writers play up to the image of the misunderstood or diabolical genius running rings around the men in suits, most viruses are trivial modifications of someone else's code, and may or may not work. We have a rich store of anecdotes concerning "kOOl dOOds" posting to alt.comp.virus and other traditional hangouts of the ethically challenged, who needed help to compile or assemble a virus. This doesn't mean that virus writers are never capable of competent code, or better. Nor does it mean that virus writers are never capable of useful input into ethical or technical discussions of anti-virus matters, and even corporate virus management. However, the notion that the people who write viruses know the most about them is a complete myth.

Unfortunately, the converse happens to be true: knowing how to protect against viruses can help a programmer build a better virus. The information in this chapter might assist those who know how to make viruses to design "better" ones. We feel that the risk is worth it, since we hope to support more system administrators than virus writers. We also consider that many people in the virus-writing game are there because they don't understand the consequence of their actions, and that some wouldn't consider themselves virus-writers, as such. We have in mind "white hat" virus writers such as system administrators and product reviewers who are compiling or otherwise modifying existing viruses for purposes of experimentation.

NOTE

Sarah Gordon's paper "The Generic Virus Writer II" (Virus Bulletin Conference Proceedings, September 1996) addresses some of the issues associated with virus writers who diverge from the "spotty adolescent" stereotype. We will return to this subject in Part IV of this book, and we will particularly point out the problems with inappropriate virus modification for experimental purposes. The paper is also available at http://www.research.ibm.com/antivirus/SciPapers/ Gordon/GVWII.html and is referenced at Sarah's own site at http://www.badguys.org/.

Our objective in this chapter is to present enough information about virus components and functions to enable you to make smart decisions about getting protection for your computer, system, or network. While we use pseudo-code from time to time to illustrate a point, that's as far as we go.

While we hope that any computer user should be able to understand this chapter, a background with computer internals will be a big help in putting this information to practical use. For example, knowing the structure of program files will give you a clearer picture of the differences between viruses and worms. Knowing how the operating system handles a call for an executable file will help you comprehend the different ways a companion virus can work. For obvious reasons, we are not going to include a full discussion of all the internal operations of all the operating systems that are available. We will try to provide some examples, mostly from the Wintel world, in order to explain the basic ideas for those without a serious technical background. Those who do know the inside details, for whatever operating system they use, should be able to extrapolate from the information given to their own environments.

How Do You Write a Virus?

How do you write a virus? And what language do you use? These are standard questions on alt.comp.virus, and they rarely earn a friendly answer from either side of the black hat/white hat divide. However, while this is not intended to be a programming text (far less a virus-writing primer), we need to make sure that you understand some basics (no pun intended).

Human beings don't generally write programs in raw machine code any more. Programs are written in a higher-level computer language, ranging from the inscrutable abbreviations of assembler language to those that attempt to emulate "natural language" as spoken by human beings. Clearly, there has to be some sort of translation process into the binary code that a computer can understand.

An *assembler* translates assembly language programs into machine-readable code. Assembly language is as near "to the metal" (low level) as most people go. High-level languages (HLLs) use two basic approaches to translation. A *compiler* evaluates the syntactical correctness of a whole program and outputs it as machine language, whereas an *interpreter* scans and executes a program one statement at a time. In the land of PCs, we tend to think in terms of compiled stand-alone programs (.COM and .EXE files), drivers (.VxD files), or support files such as overlay files, and link libraries such as .DLL files.

> **NOTE**
>
> *On no account should the preceding be taken as implying that only a handful of traditional file-type extensions (.DOC, .COM, .EXE, .OVL, and so on) are vulnerable to virus attack. Many files with quite different name extensions have the same format as .EXE files (.SCR screensavers, for instance), and are just as vulnerable. Many people are now aware that .VBS denotes a Visual Basic script file. Fewer people are equally wary of files with a .VB, .VBE, or .VBX extension. In fact, Robert Vibert lists nearly 200 types of infectable objects in* The Enterprise Anti-Virus Book *(Segura Solutions, 2000) and doesn't claim that list to be all-inclusive.*

Most early PC viruses were written in PC assembler, with a few compiled in high-level languages such as C or Turbo Pascal. In fact, even now many virus writers regard proficiency in assembler as a necessary qualification for admittance to the Worshipful Order of Computer Vandals, and don't talk to people who are presumed not to qualify (especially anti-virus people). The following snippet of assembler language code illustrates a simple variation of the traditional Hello World program. As well as giving you a feel for what an assembly language program looks like, if it is assembled to a .COM file and executed, it displays a suitable response to assembler zealots.

```
code segment
;   define a code segment (one stack only) for a .COM
;   for an .EXE we'd have more work to do here.
assume CS:code, DS:code
;   set code and data segment registers to this segment
org 100h
;   because it's a .COM file we have to reserve
;   100 bytes for the PSP (Program Segment Prefix)
start: ; 'just' a label
mov ah,9 ; load AH with value 9h
;   INT 21H Function 9H writes a character string
;   to standard output
mov dx, offset message ; load character string
int 21h ; go ahead and do it
mov ah,4ch ; INT 21H Function 4C terminates process
int 21h ; do it
message DB 'Get a life.$'
;   this is our character string. It may seem
```

```
;    counter-intuitive to declare a constant
;    at the end, but it shortens the code. In a more
;    complex program, we'd have to be more careful
;    with forward references.
code ends ; end of segment
end start ; all done.
```

By contrast, the following Turbo Pascal code compiles to a program that displays the same message.

```
program raspberry;
const
  BiteMe = 'Get a life'; {declare string constant}
begin
  writeln(BiteMe); {Display string}
end.
```

Clearly, this is much easier to read (and to write—it's one of the few programs in our repertoire to compile correctly the first time). However, assembler (assembly language) has its advantages. It can be used to perform tasks not easily achieved in high level languages. Turbo Pascal would not be the language of choice for writing a boot-sector virus, for instance, and assembler is potentially much more compact. The previous assembly language program weighs in at 30 bytes when assembled and linked, whereas the Pascal version compiles to 1,920 bytes. A compiled (Turbo) BASIC version runs to 34,992 bytes!

In real life, this is less dramatic than it sounds. DOS allocates disk space to each file in clusters (allocation units), and a cluster is one or more sectors. On a FAT16, 32MB hard disk (hard though it is to find such a thing nowadays), a cluster is equivalent to four sectors or 2,048 bytes. Thus, our assembly language program and Pascal program would essentially take up the same amount of space, despite the disparity in file length. On a 32GB FAT32 partition, the cluster size is 32,768 bytes, so our BASIC version is just a little too large for a single cluster. It therefore occupies two clusters, so that it is effectively only twice as long as the 30 byte assembler program.

In the context of parasitic programs, however, file length can make a serious difference. Most computer users nowadays don't take much notice of file length details, even in a purely DOS environment. Recent versions of the Windows environment go to some lengths to shield the user from such minutiae (not to mention other trivia, such as filename extensions, much to the virus writer's advantage). However, in the early days of PC viruses (when a 10MB hard disk cost several hundred dollars and a directory listing was, by default, ridiculously detailed), small file changes could be quite noticeable in directory listings.

```
C:\WINDOWS>dir \*.com

 Volume in drive C is PC DISK
 Volume Serial Number is 3AF1-41A7
 Directory of C:\

COMMAND   COM        93,812  08-24-96 11:11a COMMAND.COM
          1 file(s)          93,812 bytes
          0 dir(s)       61,571,072 bytes free
C:\WINDOWS>
```

In this context, the compactness of an assembly language program could be advantageous in reducing the size discrepancy between an infected object and the same object in its uninfected state, compared to a virus that added several kilobytes or more to an infected program. By the end of the millennium, however, 10GB hard drives were considered entry-level, even UNIX had become an almost exclusively GUI environment, and uninfected Word documents quickly grew to sizes that ten years before would have been considered gross for a major word-processing application. Second-generation worms, distributed as stand-alone programs, exploited social-engineering techniques to trick victims into running malicious software masquerading as legitimate software, so that size became virtually irrelevant. Thus, compiled high-level languages such as C++ and Delphi became increasingly popular among virus and worm authors.

Of course, not all high-level languages are compiled. It's perfectly possible to write a virus in an interpreted language such as MSBASIC or QBasic, for instance. Indeed, it's possible to call a program from the command line or a batch file almost as if it were a stand-alone, compiled program. Visual Basic programs can be run quasi-independently as long as the run-time module is available on the system.

It's possible to write a virus in just about any language with minimal file input/output capabilities, though the likelihood of such a virus spreading far is another matter. Trojans written in Visual Basic, especially password stealers, became common in the latter half of the 1990s. As we write this book, WordBasic and Visual Basic for Applications, the native languages of most macro viruses, have become the most popular interpreted languages among virus writers, followed shortly by VBScript.

Tripartite Structure

As noted in Chapter 1, computer viruses are considered to have three parts to their structure: the infection mechanism, the trigger, and the payload. We will not go into elaborate detail on the constituent parts, since this is a book on protection against viruses, rather than a treatise on how to build them. However, keeping the model in mind will help you to read and understand virus warnings.

Infection Mechanism

The first, and only necessary, part of the structure is the *infection mechanism*. This is the code that allows the virus to reproduce, and thus to be a virus. The infection mechanism itself has a number of parts to it.

The first function is to search for, or detect, an appropriate object to infect. The search may be active, as in the case of some file infectors that take directory listings in order to find programs of appropriate size and format. Alternatively, the search may be passive, as in the case of macro viruses that infect each document as it is saved.

There may be additional decisions taken once such an object is found. Some viruses (sparse infectors) actually may try to slow the rate of infection in order to avoid detection. Fast infectors, on the other hand, aim to infect as many objects as possible, in as short a time as possible. Most viruses will check to see if the object has already been infected with a test like the following pseudo-code (multiple infections tend to be rather conspicuous):

```
BEGIN
    IF (infectable_object_found)
    AND (object_not_already_infected)
    THEN (infect_object)
END
```

The next action will be the installation of a copy of the virus code into the infectable object itself. This may entail one or more of a number of operations, depending on the virus or worm type:

▶ The writing of a new section of code to the boot sector

▶ The addition of code to a program file

▶ The addition of macro code to the Microsoft Word NORMAL.DOT file

▶ The addition of code to standard system programs to intercept network services so as to send an infected file attachment to harvested email addresses

There are additional sub-functions at this step as well, such as the movement of the original boot sector to a new location, or the addition of jump codes in an infected program file to point to the virus code. There may also be changes to system files, to try to ensure that the virus will be run every time the computer is turned on.

At the time of infection, a number of steps may be taken to try to keep the virus safe from detection. The original file-creation date may be conserved and used to reset the directory listing, in order to avoid a change in date. The virus may have its form changed, in some kind of polymorphism. The active portion of the virus may take charge of certain system interrupts, in order to make false reports when someone tries to look for a change to the system. There may also be prompts or alerts generated, in an attempt to make any odd behaviour noticed by the user appear to be part of a normal, or at least innocent, computer error.

Trigger

The second major component of a virus is the payload *trigger*. The virus may look for a certain number of infections, a certain date and/or time, a certain piece of text, or may simply blow up the first time it is used. (For obvious reasons, these latter viruses are not widespread.) As noted, a virus does not necessarily need to have either a trigger or a payload. A virus with a trigger and payload but no replication mechanism is not, in fact, a virus, but may well be described as a Trojan. A simple trigger mechanism might work like this:

```
BEGIN
    IF (date_is_Friday_13ᵗʰ)
    THEN (set_trigger_status_to_yes)
END
```

Payload

The *payload* mechanism is similarly simple in conception:

```
BEGIN
    IF (trigger_status_is_yes)
    THEN (execute_payload)
END
```

If a virus does have a trigger, then it usually has a payload (the term *warhead* is sometimes preferred). The payload can be anything, from a simple, one-time message, to a complicated graphical display, to reformatting of the hard disk, to mailing a copy of the virus to addresses in the victim's address book. However, the bigger the payload, the more likely it is that the virus will be noticed. You may have seen lists of symptoms to watch for. Some signs often quoted include text messages, ambulances running across the screen, and letters falling down to the bottom of the screen.

NOTE

We admit that the virus-fighter's use of the terms warhead *and* payload *to describe what a virus actually does is somewhat imprecise. After all, we differentiate between a bomb, a flare, and a firework: we don't usually describe them all as bombs with different types of warhead. The term* payload *differs significantly from the way it is normally used in the transport context: it would be nonsensical to talk of the total weight of viruses carried. However, this usage is well established, and we make no apology for following it.*

Nonetheless, checking for payloads isn't a very good way to detect (let alone keep free of) viruses. The most successful viruses are generally far less conspicuous. Sometimes the only time a characteristic display is observed is when the virus first infects (as with WM/Concept, for instance). Most times, there is no display at all, and it's only when anti-virus software sounds an alert that a problem is noticed, thus inspiring the Berkeleyesque thought that sometimes there is only a virus problem because anti-virus software perceives the presence of a virus.

NOTE

Bishop Berkeley (1685–1753) denied the existence of matter, maintaining that material objects exist only because they are perceived.

Some of the most successful viruses are sub-clinical in their effects: they have no payload, and their presence causes no significant effect on the health of the victim system, except the psychological damage to the system's owner who is then identified as a Typhoid Mary. Many viruses have less impact on victim systems than the common cold does on human beings.

NOTE

Typhoid Mary was the popular nickname for Mary Mallon, a cook who carried typhoid without showing any of the symptoms herself. She died in 1938 under permanent detention, having refused to give up serving food.

We have to wonder whether it's helpful that all viruses are regarded as if they were the computer equivalent of Ebola or Marburg. The panic that results from routine detection of unremarkable viruses may be more damaging (at least psychologically) than the presence of the virus on the infected system could ever be. We don't suggest completely abandoning attempts to detect and remove viruses, of course, but less disinformation about the nature of the threat would remove much of its sting.

Replication

Why are viral programs special? What is it about the simple fact that they reproduce that puts them in a class by themselves? There is no shortage of malware (malicious software) out there. Trojans and logic bombs were known long before viral programs existed, and they continue to flourish. Why can we not simply classify viral programs as another form of Trojan?

A Trojan program relies upon other programs to do the copying necessary for it to spread beyond an initial target. The dangers (and the results) are self-limiting. If a friend gives you a Trojan and it triggers, you lose trust in that friend. It is very seldom that you will be hit from the same source twice. Trojan writers like to use bulletin boards, web sites, or file archives, but even those methods of transmission are limited. A non-anonymous posting of a Trojan program will usually get an individual barred from archive sites.

These types of malware, therefore, can generally present an attack from a single point. As any military strategist can tell you, defence against such an attack is straightforward. Intelligence, in the form of advice from other users, can help to eliminate the attack before it starts.

In theory, at any rate, the closely-related worm problem is easy to address. If you don't allow any unverified program received by email to execute, irrespective of how well you know and trust the sender, most worms can't become established. The fact that worms continue to be effective only demonstrates the continued success of social engineering in overriding common sense.

NOTE

We must stress that the activation or execution of the virus is not the same as the activation of the payload that a virus may carry. For example, the payload of the original Stoned virus was a message, which appeared on the screen saying "Your PC is now Stoned!" This message only appeared when the PC was rebooted, and even then only one in eight times. The virus, however, was active and infectious all the time, once the hard disk had been infected.

The virus has three main possibilities for the moment of infection: direct action (*one-shot*), during program run (*while-called*), or from then on (*memory-resident*). A resident virus may remain in memory but be actively infecting only when a disk is accessed. A while-called virus may infect a new program only when a directory is changed, for example.

Non-Resident Viruses

One-shot (direct-action) viral programs get only one chance to propagate on each run of the infected program. The viral code will seek out and infect a target program. The viruses then pass control to the original program and perform no further actions. These are, of course, the simplest of the viral programs. Mainframe mail viruses are generally of this type.

Memory-Resident Viruses

Resident viral programs (often, and somewhat misleadingly, referred to as *terminate-and-stay-resident*, or TSR, viruses) become active when an infected program is run (at boot time for BSIs), and remain active until the computer is rebooted or turned off. Note that some viral programs (Joshi, for example) trap the rebooting sequence, which is normally called when you press CTRL-ALT-DEL on an MS-DOS PC, and are thus able to survive a warm boot.

The most successful of pre-Windows file infectors, the Jerusalem virus, was memory-resident, as are all boot-sector viruses. (The boot sector is never called in normal operation once the boot process is completed, so the virus can only be called if it stays in memory.)

If a DOS virus is active in memory, it can be difficult to disinfect a file or disk. (In fact, file disinfection is a contentious issue at the best of times, but we'll get back to that in Part II of this book.) No sooner is the file cleaned than it becomes a suitable target for reinfection, unless there is an anti-virus product already in memory preventing further execution of the infective code. Attempts to disinfect a hard disk may be as extreme as performing a low-level format. Even if this were ever necessary, it's perfectly possible that when a high-level format was executed subsequently, the disk might be infected all over again. Nonetheless, many products are capable of detecting and cleaning some viruses while still in memory, even in DOS.

The term *TSR* is applied to DOS programs that pop up when a "hot key" is pressed (Borland Sidekick, for example) while another application is running, or that execute in the background, like the PRINT command. Such programs use the MS-DOS TSR function (INT 21h Function 31h or INT 27h) to leave a portion of their own code in memory. Hardware interrupts (INT stands for *interrupt*), such as INT 9h (the keyboard handler), are intercepted by pop-up TSRs so that the program "knows" when its presence is required. The application of this idea to viral software has obvious advantages. Joshi, for instance, intercepts 9h to trap the CTRL-ALT-DEL reboot sequence and survive a warm boot. File viruses intercept various sub-functions of INT 21h for purposes of infection and/or concealment. Boot-sector viruses tend to hook INT 13h, which handles low-level disk access.

NOTE

DOS TSR programming is beyond the scope of this book. Two useful resources are Undocumented DOS, *by Andrew Schulman et al. (Addison Wesley), which has pointers to further in-depth information, and Ray Duncan's* Advanced MS-DOS Programming *(Microsoft Press). (Neither of these books makes the smallest reference to virus programming, by the way.)*

In a modern, Windows-based environment, the mechanisms of memory-resident viruses are different, though the principles are similar. A Windows-savvy file infector is not constrained by the same limitations of available space as a DOS TSR program, and it doesn't have to worry about the niceties of directly accessing DOS services. It may be implemented as a VxD (virtual device driver) or NT service.

Calls to the Windows application programming interface (API) are handled with varying degrees of transparency by a high-level language rather than raw assembly language, since compact, fast code is less of an issue now than in the days of DOS. (The assumption that assembler is necessarily faster than compiled code is not altogether well founded, but that's a discussion for a completely different book.) Mail-borne viruses and worms often use Windows scripting and messaging services to scan and parasitize email, and Internet traffic may be directly or indirectly monitored to harvest mail addresses not in the victim's address book. (Hybris does something like this.)

Hybrid Viruses

A hybrid or while-called virus will activate when the infected program is called. It will then pass partial control to the original program. The virus, however, will remain operational during the time that the infected program is running. It is only a slight "progression" from residence while an infected program is running to a fully memory-resident virus, independent of the original infective file.

Macro viruses may be considered somewhat similarly. A Word macro virus is effectively memory-resident by virtue of having infected the global template, which is normally resident and referenced as long as Word is active. In an unprotected environment, this allows the virus to infect documents as they are created or opened for editing, and also to implement stealth measures, such as substituting its own code for standard menu options.

Generality, Extent, Persistence

Fred Cohen described the virus threat in terms of three characteristics:

▶ **Generality**   Whereas most threats before viruses were specific to a particular application or operating environment, viruses are generally far from specialized and may be able to replicate through an entire system or network.

▶ **Extent**   Viruses tend to be long range: once they start to replicate, they may spread fast and far.

▶ **Persistence**   Viruses can keep coming back.

It is usually considered a truism in virus research that viruses are prevalent in those operating systems that are used by the most people. There are more Wintel viruses than Mac viruses because more people have and use Wintel machines. In the same way, even within a particular operating system, a virus that uses general functions is more successful than one with special requirements.

For example, one of the earliest viruses is called Lehigh, since it was discovered at Lehigh University. The Lehigh virus only infects the COMMAND.COM file, which exists on bootable DOS disks. Even at the time Lehigh was written, hard disks were becoming common, and bootable DOS disks were becoming less so. This factor, along with Lehigh's extremely dangerous and visible payload, ensured that the virus was never discovered in the field outside of the university campus.

Generality is not limited to operating systems, and in virus research, the term *platform* has a greater range than in any other computer field. Word macro viruses have been enormously successful, partly because they operate in Microsoft Office on both Windows and Mac systems. The recent spates of email viruses are not, strictly speaking, Windows scripts, but rather Windows/Outlook scripts. If you use, for example, the Pegasus email program, your system might be damaged, but you will not send forth any more copies of the worms.

Other factors can limit the extent of a virus. Boot-sector infectors can only spread via infected disks. Therefore, it was rather interesting, in the early 1990s, to note that the Stoned virus was far and away the most common virus in North America, while Form held a commanding lead in the UK. Throughout the history of virus research, similar geographic pools of infection have been noted. At the same time, the Michelangelo virus, probably starting from a base in Taiwan, spread worldwide in little over six months.

It is interesting to note that the model of virus infection is starting to change. Viruses of the Stoned family, including Michelangelo and Monkey, persisted for years. Indeed, they can still be found in the field. Melissa and the Love Bug spread worldwide within hours, but aside from variants, it is comparatively rare to find them today in the field; hence, the frequent contemporary use of the term *fast burner*.

Viruses can also "die" for other reasons. At one point, the Macintosh WDEF virus was extremely infective, since any disk, inserted at any time, into a running Mac would have the WDEF resource read and run. This behaviour was changed in Mac OS 7, and the WDEF virus, deprived of its main entry point, is now considered a mild historical curiosity. (On the other hand, since modern commercial anti-virus software needs a comparatively recent version of the operating system to run, who knows what old-time system viruses are still lurking on obsolete systems?)

Out in the PC mainstream, though, things may be changing further. Traditional boot-sector viruses have become rarer—or at least reported instances of them have. New BSIs are rarely seen, and older ones have a rapidly decreasing "market share". Newer operating systems (OS/2, Windows NT, Windows 2000) can be damaged by boot-sector infectors, but don't generally allow them to replicate.

Payload Versus Reproduction

Network and mail viral programs carry, in a sense, their own payloads. The reproduction of the programs themselves uses the resources of the hosts affected and, in the cases of both the Morris Internet and CHRISTMA worms, went so far as to deny service by using all available computing or communications resources.

Most other viral programs seem to be written "for their own sake"—a kind of electronic, self-writing, self-replicating graffiti. However, even these can do unintended damage. Of those viral programs that do include a payload mechanism, relatively few carry a deliberately damaging payload. Those that *do* attempt to erase infected programs or disks are, fortunately, self-limiting, though the more successful examples give themselves time to fan out to other systems before trashing the currently infected system.

The most iniquitous form of payload is, perhaps, the gradual corruption over time of the environment or of data. The term *data diddling* is sometimes used in this context, not altogether appropriately. The term is also used when data are modified for fraudulent purposes. However, slow corruption from a virus is generally just destructive: the author derives no benefit except the kick of knowing that damage has been done. Dark Avenger gets much of the "credit" for this innovation: the Dark Avenger viruses and Nomenklatura specifically target those careful souls who back up data regularly. In this case, data files are corrupted, not infected, and the damage is more-or-less random, so anti-virus software can neither detect nor repair affected files, even after the presence of the virus is known. Any backup subsequent to the initial infection is unreliable at best, useless at worst. And, of course, it's often impossible for the victim to ascertain which backups predate the infection, even if exist.

Characteristically, macro viruses modify data within infected files, so identification of the infection gives some indication of the integrity status of the infected file. Clearly, it's unsafe to trust the integrity of the data contained in a file infected by a virus that makes random modifications, and anti-virus software can't usually be expected to reverse random changes. Of course, many macro viruses don't make any modifications to actual data, so removal of infected or corrupted macros is often sufficient to reverse the effects of the virus. However, this isn't always the case. Removal of viral macros isn't enough to restore menu options such as Tools | Macro (removed by WM/Cap, for instance), or to reverse the effects of a virus that passwords Word files. Furthermore, it would be unsafe to assume that a currently uninfected document has never been infected or otherwise touched by malicious software. A disinfected document may have been left with unnoticed modifications, or even fragments of viral code.

NOTE

This, incidentally, is one of the disadvantages of the (understandable) urge to deal with virus infections as transparently as possible. If infected data files are "transparently" detected and cleaned by anti-virus software (whether at the perimeter or the desktop), can you trust the product to completely reverse the effects of the infection? We will return to that thought in Part II of this book, but will just point out now that if you can't, you might be better off going against the flow and discarding infected files instead of disinfecting them.

Damage

We have spoken of damaging payloads in viruses, and should probably address that topic more carefully. Viruses can do any kind of damage that software can do. This includes overwriting data, erasing files, scrambling system information, reformatting disks, disabling security systems, corrupting software, or killing program processes.

> **NOTE**
>
> *In principle, a virus can do anything that other software can do: hence the persistent idea of "useful" viruses, such as the maintenance viruses described by Cohen. It's a sad reflection of human nature, however, that most authors of viruses and other malware prefer payloads that are at best trivial, at worst damaging.*

Primary damage is normally associated with viruses and other malicious code not identified and prevented from executing at the point of entry, and can be defined as damage to systems and data caused when the computing environment is modified by virus or Trojan attack.

A virus can cause significant damage simply by being installed, independently of delivering any payload. This type of primary damage frequently arises from boundary conditions not taken into account by the virus author.

Viruses that don't normally cause visible damage on older DOS or Windows systems can suddenly cause difficulties if it becomes necessary to remove them from a FAT32 system. They may damage an executable file by modifying it in such a way that the operating environment will no longer run it, or they may bring down a PC running Windows NT by displacement or encryption of system areas.

Impact of Viral Infection on the Computing Environment

Irrespective of payload, just the presence of the virus may be enough to cause damage. Theft of memory may result in loss of functionality and performance: some code may no longer run. A spectacular example is that of the first version of the Navidad worm. After an infected system was rebooted, a combination of a logical error in the code and the use of a change in the Registry meant that no file with the filename extension .EXE could be run.

Theft of disk space may have the same effects. Data, application files, or system areas may be partly or totally overwritten, and infected files may no longer function properly.

Theft of clock cycles may result in a noticeable slowing of processes, time-critical processes may behave unpredictably, and resource-intensive software may lose functionality and performance.

General incompatibility and destabilization may give rise to the following symptoms:

▶ System software, applications, or utilities display unpredictable behaviour.

▶ General Protection Faults (GPFs) and similar conflicts and errors are encountered.

▶ Parity and checksum errors are observed.

▶ Loss of performance due to loss of (for example) 32-bit access may be observed.

▶ Overwritten disk-management software may result in loss of availability.

▶ Loss of access to system areas may be observed, possibly entailing lost access to normally mounted volumes and the subsequent unavailability of data and/or applications.

NOTE

Any "real" virus entails some form of "damage": that is, impact on performance in one or more of the classes of impact described in the preceding list. Both real and imagined viruses (the latter including those described in hoax alerts) can also have psychosocial consequences. Assessing the real impact of a perceived threat can be a serious drain on systems administrators, the Help Desk, management, and users or clients. Damage due to inappropriate reaction to a perceived threat is better considered as secondary damage.

Direct Damage from Virus and Trojan Payloads

Direct damage can be considered in terms of the classic tripartite security model (Availability, Integrity, Confidentiality). Viruses and malware have an impact across all three areas described by this model, as well as other areas, such as accountability. The type of damage that might be caused includes the following:

Attacks on Availability

▶ Deletion of files and subdirectories

▶ Renaming of files

- ▶ Encryption of files, disks, or system areas
- ▶ Unauthorized calls to system software, such as FORMAT, FDISK, and so on

Attacks on Integrity

- ▶ Corruption of system files and system areas (for example, the DOS and Master Boot Records, the File Allocation Table, and so on), by random or non-random disk writes, including displacement of system areas
- ▶ Data diddling—modification of targeted data files, such as garbling of spreadsheet formulas
- ▶ Corruption of application files and data files by unauthorized file writes

Attacks on Confidentiality

- ▶ Capture and forwarding of passwords
- ▶ Forwarding of personal and confidential files to newsgroups and elsewhere

Viruses, in particular, often have a more trivial payload, such as a visual or audio effect or message, which in itself may not merit classification as primary damage.

Psychological and Social Damage

Malware may also do damage that might be better considered as psychological. All viruses can be described in these terms, since discovering that one's system is infected is potentially frightening. If one is perceived by others to be a virus carrier, the consequences are at least embarrassing. This phenomenon is further explored in the next section ("Secondary Damage"). However, some malware is specifically designed to have a psychological effect (fear, amusement, titillation, and so on). Malware displaying a message announcing its intention to reformat the hard drive could thus be described as doing direct psychological damage. In general, this is characteristic of Trojans and jokes rather than viruses.

Secondary Damage

Unfortunately, a computer user faced with some visible symptom may react inappropriately and cause more damage than the virus itself does. This is a manifestation of what might be called secondary damage, which can be defined as:

▶   A fan-out of direct damage, as defined above, to other PC systems as a result
    of secondary infection.

▶   Damage caused by misunderstanding and inappropriate response to problems,
    such as scrapping of systems or system components, unnecessary reformatting,
    inappropriate use of disk-recovery utilities.

▶   Indirect damage as a result of secondary infection, including psychosocial
    risks, such as damage to morale through insecurity and scapegoating. Other
    potential damage includes business risks, such as loss of confidence, reputation,
    and credibility; legal risks, such as litigation resulting from infection, and
    possible damage sustained by peer organizations; and punitive action for
    breach of prescribed standards and policies, contracts, and so on (penalty
    clauses, withdrawal of previous agreements, penalties associated with
    non-compliance with Data Protection legislation).

▶   Damage as a result of attempts at concealment of an incident, including
    inappropriate physical measures, and secondary infection due to the
    concealment of relevant information.

▶   Traumatic costs, such as time spent on checking, restoring, or repairing
    operating environments, programs, and data; or the cost of implementing
    or upgrading anti-malware defences.

Hardware Damage

There is one type of damage missing from the previous lists. Software does not usually
damage hardware, though it remains a possibility. The myth of viral programs damaging
hardware seems to be one of the more enduring. No viral program yet found has been
designed to damage hardware. However, it *is* possible for certain pieces of hardware to
be damaged by programming.

Certain older types of display monitors (notably early IBM monochrome graphics
adapters) could be made to "freeze" the sweep of the electron beam, and thus burn
in a section of the screen phosphors. No one has ever burned a hole in a monitor, nor
have they ever caused one to overheat and blow up because of software.

Except for some very specific and limited functions dealing with powering down
in advanced computers, power supplies cannot be addressed by software. No one has
ever "melted down" a power supply with software.

As with any physical or mechanical devices, printers can be damaged by getting
them to do any one thing for too long. This, of course, depends upon the machine
running unattended for a long time. Some disk drives can be damaged by "pushing"

the heads beyond normal limits. Some IDE controllers and drives do not allow for the calls used to generate a low-level format of earlier types of hard drive. If such a call is made on a system with an IDE controller, the results are uncertain. The drive will not be formatted, but it may not be left in a usable state. IDE drive manufacturers have not always shipped programs for low-level formatting, and so a call for a low-level format on an IDE drive appears, to the normal user, no different from hardware damage. As this has become known in the user community, more IDE manufacturers have made such formatting software generally available.

The CIH/Spacefiller virus, while it doesn't literally destroy hardware, can effectively render some PCs unusable by writing garbage to a flashable BIOS chip. In some cases, it may be cheaper to discard a flashtrashed motherboard than to replace a soldered BIOS, and in this case the distinction between hardware and firmware damage starts to look pretty academic. Furthermore, BIOS chips are only one instance of the use of flash EPROMs.

In fact, CIH was by no means the first virus capable of conning the victim into discarding apparently dysfunctional hardware. However, no useful statistics exist as to how many serviceable hard disks have been dumped as a result of virus action.

Ban the Bomb

A number of security-related phenomena have been described as various types of bombs, with varying degrees of justification and relevance to this chapter and to the anatomy of malware in general. We have included several in the hope of reducing confusion.

Logic Bombs

A logic bomb is a routine or set of routines that are activated when a particular set of conditions is met (for example, the nth time the program is executed), and may be a component of a virus or Trojan. A logic bomb might also be inserted into a legitimate program as a precursor to blackmail, or pre-emptive revenge in anticipation of dismissal, or with some sort of backdoor functionality. (Backdoors are described in Chapter 3.) Clearly, anti-virus software is unlikely to be useful in the context of such one-off programs.

Time Bombs

Time bombs are a special case of logic bomb, where the trigger condition is a particular time and/or date.

ANSI Bombs

ANSI bombs are not viral, in that they do not reproduce, and have never been particularly common. They may be considered Trojans or logic bombs. An ANSI bomb is a sequence of characters that is interpreted by ANSI.SYS as redefining a key, or keys, on the keyboard. Thereafter, these keys will not send the normally assigned characters, but rather the redefined string. This string may contain any ASCII characters, including <RETURN> and multiple commands. Therefore, the space bar, for example, can be redefined to:

```
"DEL *.*<cr>Y<cr>"
```

This sequence would, in an MS-DOS environment, delete all files in the current directory.

ANSI bombs can be carried in normal text files or messages. They are triggered when text is sent to the "console" device while ANSI emulation is active, normally by reading the file with the *TYPE* command. Reading a text file with a word processor generally does not port the data to the console, since the text is interpreted by the word processor before it is displayed to the screen. Only a very few older word processors use the ANSI.SYS program for screen control. However, reading an email message with a terminal program that uses ANSI.SYS could have the same effect, as could extraction of an archived file that contains the ANSI sequence in the text comment header.

Reading all text files with an editor, a file viewer such as *list*, or a word processor is a protection against ANSI bombs, but it still leaves the possibility of being affected. The best protection is to remove ANSI.SYS from the system and not to use terminal emulators or other programs that require it. You can also replace ANSI.SYS with shareware versions that do not have the key-binding mechanism. In fact, very few programs still in use require ANSI.SYS to be present, which is fortunate, as anti-virus software rarely offers any protection against this particular, albeit uncommon, threat.

ANSI bombs apart, ANSI.SYS is not intended for use with modern versions of Windows, though it continues to be supplied.

> **NOTE**
>
> In the RISKS-FORUM Digest (March 1988: 6–42), there was a story about the use of the intelligent features of Wyse 75 terminals. This was a specific instance of the use of peripherals for security cracking. The Wyse terminal in question had a feature that allowed keys to be remapped from the host system, and another feature that permitted the keys to be called for from the host. Thus, the subject lines in email messages could present commands that would remap a key to correspond to a command, and then have the command submitted by the terminal. With only a little thought, an email virus could be written taking advantage of this fact. This is quite similar to the phenomena of ANSI bombs on MS-DOS machines that, while not viral, use the ANSI.SYS key remapping facility to assign deletion or formatting commands to specific keys.

Mail Bombs and Subscription Bombs

These are mail abuses that anti-virus software cannot realistically address. A mail bomb is a denial of service attack performed by bombarding the victim's mailbox with email messages. A subscription bomb achieves a similar effect by subscribing victims to a multiplicity of mailing lists so that they receive an avalanche of mail from the lists. These threats are mentioned here for completeness, and in the hope of reducing confusion.

Summary

While some of the content of this chapter has been fairly low-level, we have so far focused on the effects of infection rather than on the internal mechanisms of malicious software. Next, we complete our survey of the virus problem with a closer look at virus anatomy.

Virus Mechanisms

W e have considered in some depth the effects of virus infection, and given an overview of virus structures. We must now move from basic anatomy to physiology. It is no more possible to understand viruses fully by a study of their basic structure than it is to understand human biology by the study of the skeleton.

We have pointed out several times that covert operation is not a defining characteristic of computer viruses. However, it is an almost universal characteristic, for the compelling reason that covert operation is generally a prerequisite for the dissemination of malicious software. (Though we sometimes suspect that if a malicious program arrived as an attachment that said "Danger! Do not execute this program: it will trash your system!!!" a number of people would still try to run it, just to see if it really did.) Since self-concealment is a major contributing factor to the size of the virus problem, it occupies a considerable proportion of this chapter. First, however, we must look in more detail at virus types and infection mechanisms.

Hardware-Specific Viruses

We have noted that operating platforms for viruses don't have to be linked to operating systems. Microsoft Office, whether running on Wintel or Mac, can spread macro viruses. At the other end of the hardware/software spectrum, some viruses thought to be DOS viruses are not. Most boot-sector infectors aren't DOS viruses, but BIOS viruses, specific to hardware rather than the operating system.

A boot-sector virus runs when the boot sector is executed, and this is before DOS, or any other operating system, gets a chance to start. (We'll get to the details of that in a moment.) A BSI runs before any program on the disk, and, therefore, the only programming that starts earlier is the ROM (read-only memory) BIOS (basic input/output system) programming required by all ISA machines. (ISA—Industry Standard Architecture—is the rather pretentious title for the basic design of IBM PC compatibility.)

NOTE

There are, of course, other operating systems that use this same architecture, such as Windows, OS/2, and Linux. We have seen boot-sector viruses happily infect OS/2 and NT machines. However, if the infected machine's operating system does not use the interrupts trapped by the virus, the BSI won't proceed to infect diskettes accessed subsequently by the PC. This doesn't mean that there are no NT virus problems, as we are sometimes told. File viruses and macro viruses can often execute and infect just as well on an NT platform as on a Windows 95 PC.

Boot-Sector Infectors

Most people think of viral programs in terms of a variation on Cohen's definition:
that is, a virus is a program that always "attaches" to another program. This has
given rise to misconceptions concerning boot-sector infectors.

Boot-sector infecting viral programs *do* (in a sense) attach to another program.
Most people are unaware of the fact that there is a program on every disk, even those
that are blank (that is, contain no files). Every formatted disk has a boot sector,
located at the first physical sector (or logical sector, in the case of a hard drive).
When the computer is booted, the BIOS programming looks for a disk, and then runs
whatever happens to be in the boot sector of that disk as a program.

In most cases, with non-bootable disks, the program placed there by the formatting
process simply displays a message informing the user that the disk is not bootable.
However, any viral program that places itself in that boot-sector position on the disk
will be the first thing, other than BIOS code, to be executed when the computer
starts up. Once installed onto a system, BSIs will copy themselves onto floppy disks
and infect a new host computer when the "target" machine is booted (usually
inadvertently) with one of the infected diskettes in the A: drive.

BSI terminology is derived from MS-DOS systems, and this leads to some additional
confusion. The first *physical sector* on a hard drive is not the operating-system boot
sector. The hard drive's boot sector is the first *logical sector*. The number one position
on a hard drive is the Master Boot Record (MBR). The MBR contains the partition
table—the data specifying the type of hard disk and the partitioning information.
The terms "Master Boot Record", "partition table", and "partition boot record" are
often used interchangeably, although they are not exactly the same thing. Some viral
programs, such as the Stoned virus, always attack the physical first sector: the boot
sector on floppy disks and the Master Boot Record on hard disks. Thus, viral programs
that always attack the boot sector might be termed "pure" BSIs, whereas programs like
Stoned might be referred to as an "MBR type" of BSI. The term *boot-sector infector* is
used for all of them, though, since all of them infect the boot sector on floppy disks.

In saying that every disk has a boot sector, we are using the term "boot sector" in
its most generic sense. In the MS-DOS environment, "boot sector" has a more limited
technical definition, and a hard disk actually starts with a Master Boot Record rather
than a boot sector. In either case, however, one system area gives the computer some
definition of the disk and information about the next step in the boot sequence.

In most cases, the boot sector does *not* point to the next step in the boot sequence,
because system files are not available on most diskettes. In the case of a *bootable
disk*, the "bootable" sector points to the location of files containing both the
programming necessary for input and output activity and a program for the interpretation

of operating-system commands. A *data*, or *non-bootable*, *disk* may simply contain information on the disk specification, and a small program informing the system, or operator, that the disk is "not a system disk".

The important points, however, are that there is a program in every boot sector, and that the boot program isn't visible in normal operation. There is no entry for it in the directory listing of the disk, and therefore most people are not aware that it exists.

The existence of a boot sector on every disk is the major strength of boot-sector infecting viral programs, and it is a psychological, rather than a technical, advantage. Because a "data disk" does not contain any recognizable "programming", it is often seen as safe. However, there is, in fact, a "hidden" program on the disk, and it *can* be infected.

NOTE

We should clarify the fact that in the MS-DOS world, "hidden" also has a technical meaning as a file attribute. Files with that attribute are invisible to the casual observer, and are also a little more difficult to modify. However, this should not be taken as offering significant protection against viruses: most virus authors have learned by now how to modify file attributes.

Boot-sector infectors either displace or replace the existing boot sector. Usually they move it to another location on the disk. This means that the viral program gets first crack at control of the computer before most protective measures have a chance to kick in. It installs itself in memory and then passes control to the original boot sector. Thus, the disk appears to behave normally unless the virus carries some noticeable payload.

A BSI, to be effective at all, must be memory-resident. However, because BSIs modify the environment pre-emptively when the PC powers up, and make changes to system areas that are not normally seen, their changes are often undetected in normal operation.

When the machine is first powered up, there is a certain amount of programming contained in boot ROM. The amount varies greatly between different types of machines, but this programming describes the most central devices, such as the screen and keyboard, and points to the location of disk drives. These operations allow the system to make use of those peripherals.

The boot record (or boot sector) contains further information about the structure of the disk and the location of subsequent operating system files. Because this information is in the form of a program rather than data, and because this sector is writable, in order to allow for different structures, the boot record is vulnerable to attack or change. BSIs may overwrite either the boot record or the boot sector, and may or may not move the original boot sector or record to another location on the disk. The repositioning of the original sector's program allows the viral program to "pretend" that everything is as it was by presenting the original sector code for inspection rather than the infected code.

This pretence is not absolute. A computer with an active viral program will differ in some way from the normal environment. The original sector position will contain different information than is normally located at that address. The viral program will need to "hook" certain vectors for its own use in order to monitor activity in the computer and to execute its infection and payload mechanisms. The virus occupies a certain portion of memory, and its presence may be deduced from the unavailability of that memory.

These indicators are not conclusive, though. There may be various reasons why the top-of-memory marker is set to indicate less than 640KB on a DOS machine. Each different type of disk drive, and each drive of the same type that is partitioned differently, will have a different boot record. As operating systems or versions change, so will the boot sector.

It is possible, however, to compare any machine with itself in a "known clean" state. Indeed, this is the foundation of change detection or integrity checking as an antiviral measure and technology. By saving information about the environment after a minimal clean boot and comparing this with subsequent boots, changes can be detected and the user alerted to a potential problem. The boot record can also be replaced with a program that will check the state of the disk, memory, and interrupt table in order to detect the changes that a virus must make. (A program like this can also function as the foundation of a security system that cannot be avoided by "escaping" out of the boot sequence.)

Obtaining the state of the environment immediately after the boot sector code has been run is not as easy as it might sound at first. The computer, while functional, does not have all the parts of the operating system installed at this point, and it is the "higher" levels of the operating system with which users generally interact. Even low-level code may not be able to access information on programs not yet executed.

There are some interesting variations in the boot process with implications for security on other platforms. Macintosh-specific system viruses are rarely reported today, with a few notable exceptions (AutoStart, SevenDust, MacSimpsons), and they are not considered further in this chapter. This isn't to say that there is no virus problem on Macs: Microsoft Office macro viruses continue to constitute a major Mac problem, although it's not the same problem as we see in the PC world.

NOTE

The whole issue of virus management on Macintosh computers is examined in depth by David Harley in the "Viruses & the Macintosh" FAQ, which is included as Appendix B in this book. The subject is also examined in more detail in the 1997 Virus Bulletin Conference paper "Macs and Macros", available at http://www.sherpasoft.org.uk/MacSupporters/macvir.html.

The Atari computer may reserve up to six sectors for the boot sector: only one is ever used in the normal course of events. This, of course, provides an excellent hiding place for a virus. The additional five sectors can contain a reasonably capable virus, and there is no danger of overwriting other files, nor any need for the virus to try to avoid detection from file size changes.

However, most Atari programs, and even boot disks, do not require any executable code in the boot sector. Start-up files, including system accessories, are placed in a standard directory, and all such files found in the directory are run at boot time. Many Atari anti-virus programs do nothing more than overwrite executable boot sectors. The overwriting action will eliminate any boot-sector viruses (although it will not provide protection against any that may be installed in the start directory). Since Atari computers are able to read MS-DOS formatted disks, some of these antiviral utilities may corrupt DOS disks.

We have already pointed out that an Intel-based PC running UNIX (for example, Linux, 386BSD, SCO UNIX, and so on) can also be infected by a boot-sector virus if booted from an infected disk. The same goes for PCs hosting other operating systems, such as NetWare and Windows NT, of course. Such systems are not usually associated with secondary infection (that is, viruses won't fan out to other systems), since the viruses are not usually able to infect floppy disks (although systems with multiple operating systems open up interesting possibilities). However, infection of the boot sector may be enough to cause noticeable damage.

NOTE

There are very few non-experimental UNIX viruses at present, although this situation is beginning to change with the massive increase of interest in the operating system among corporate and home users. In the past, UNIX viruses tended to be shell scripts rather than binary executables, since scripts are far more portable—UNIX runs on a wide range of system architectures. There have been some UNIX-specific worm incidents, most notably the Morris Worm (a.k.a. the Internet Worm) of 1988. Some Linux viruses exist (as binary executables, rather than shell scripts), but they are not widespread. As this chapter is being written, the Ramen worm, which infects Red Hat Linux 6.2 and 7.0 installations, is known to be in the wild. UNIX servers running as web servers and FTP servers are still considered a major potential source of files infected with viruses specific to other platforms, even if they are not directly infectable themselves. This problem is sometimes referred to as the "latent virus" problem, or "heterogeneous virus transmission".

On MS-DOS computers with extended partitioning of the hard disk, the Master Boot Record may be read while accessing a different logical drive. It is therefore possible, even if the computer has been booted from a clean floppy disk, for an infection on a drive to show up in memory. Although there is almost no chance that a virus will become active in this way, such partitioning will often trigger a "virus in memory" alert from scanning programs.

BSIs were the most "successful" of traditional viral programs in terms of the number of copies made and the number of systems infected. This may seem odd, given that BSIs can only make, at most, one copy per disk.

On the other hand, once they are "installed" on a hard drive or boot disk, BSIs are always active, since they start at boot time and remain in memory, if the operating system allows for that type of activity. Unless the system is booted from a clean disk, the virus will continuously infect any and all disks that are proper targets for it.

It is sometimes possible for more than one boot virus to infect a disk. This scenario is sometimes referred to as a *cocktail*. Some cocktails conflict in their use of the same areas of the disk. Some combinations (such as Stoned and Michelangelo) can render the system unbootable, and thus alert the user to a problem.

NOTE

Some sources advocate the use of the DOS command FDISK with the /MBR switch, thereby rewriting part of the MBR but leaving the partition table intact, as a generic means of dealing with boot-sector viruses. This actually works much of the time, but we cannot recommend it. First, it doesn't help with pure BSIs (such as Form) that don't infect the boot sector. Second, if it's done with the wrong virus in memory (Monkey, for instance), the system can become inaccessible. We'll return to this issue in Part II of this book.

The Boot Zone

Let's consider the continuation of the boot sequence that we started earlier. When setting up antiviral defences, it is important to know the sequence of events in the boot process in order to know which programs will protect to which level. The MS-DOS sequence provides the clearest example, and those knowledgeable in other systems can use the illustrations it provides to analyse the specific details of their own systems. This becomes a bit of a grey area, since we are no longer dealing with hardware-specific boot sectors but aren't yet into ordinary files, which are the subject of the next section.

The last part of the boot-sector program points to the files or areas on the disk containing the next step in the start-up sequence. At this point, of course, the specific files and steps begin to diverge greatly from one operating system to another. However, it is common for operating systems to have hidden files along this route that may be subject to viral attack. Given that these files are not evident to the user, they are even more vulnerable—not to attack, but to an undetected change.

After the Master Boot Record and boot sector have been read and executed, MS-DOS normally runs two additional programs that set up input/output routines and the most basic operating system. (As these programs are called by the boot sector, it is possible to reroute this process to call specialized driver programs first or at the same time. Some esoteric disk drives use such a process.) After they have run, the system has sufficient information to interpret a text file (CONFIG.SYS) that contains listings of various additional programming that the user wishes to have in order to run specialized hardware.

After the programs listed in CONFIG.SYS are run, the command interpreter is invoked. The standard MS-DOS interpreter is COMMAND.COM, but this may be changed by an entry in the CONFIG.SYS file. After COMMAND.COM is run, the AUTOEXEC.BAT batch file is run, if it exists. AUTOEXEC.BAT is the most commonly created and modified boot file, and many users and antiviral program authors see this as the point at which to intervene. It should be clear by now, however, that many possible points of intervention are open to the virus before AUTOEXEC.BAT is run.

In spite of the greater number of entry points, viruses that attack the programs of the boot sequence are rare and not very successful. For one thing, while every disk has a boot sector, not every disk has a full boot sequence. For another, different versions of a given operating system may have different files in this sequence. (For example, the hidden files have different names in MS-DOS, PC-DOS, and DR-DOS.) Finally, viral programs that can infect ordinary program files may not work on boot-sequence files, and vice versa.

Even though Windows 95, 98, NT, and 2000 use some of the same filenames as MS-DOS, their functionality and importance to the operating system's start-up sequence have been drastically modified. The DOS sequence is described here as an example, not as a definitive description. It is, however, a sequence assumed by many older viruses. A more generic summary of the PC boot sequence is given in the "Typical PC Boot Sequence" sidebar.

Typical PC Boot Sequence

In general, PCs boot up according to the following sequence of events:

1. The user powers up the computer.

2. The computer runs a power supply self-test.

3. ROM BIOS code is executed.

4. ROM BIOS performs a test of central hardware.

5. The computer runs a video test.

6. The computer runs a memory test.

7. On a cold boot, the full POST (Power On Self Test) would be run here—it is skipped on a warm boot.

8. The computer tests for the partition boot record at the first sector of the default boot drive. (The default is usually specified in the BIOS set-up menu.)

9. The partition boot record is executed.

10. The computer initializes specified system files, or displays a message if these are not available. In DOS, the specified files are IO.SYS and MSDOS.SYS. (Other names may be used by related operating systems, such as PC-DOS.) Under Windows 9*x*, most of the functionality of the original MSDOS.SYS file is transferred to IO.SYS. Under NT and Windows 2000, the operating system loader is NTLDR; NTDETECT .COM is responsible for checking hardware; NTOSKRNL.EXE initializes the operating system.

11. The base device drivers are initialized and device status is checked.

12. The computer reads configuration files (CONFIG.SYS, SYSTEM.DAT, USER.DAT and so on, according to operating system).

13. The command shell (COMMAND.COM, for instance) is loaded.

14. The shell's start-up command files (AUTOEXEC.BAT, for instance) are executed.

File Infectors

File-infecting viral programs are variously known as *file viruses* or *parasitic viruses*.

> **NOTE**
>
> The term link virus *is sometimes used in the context of platforms other than PCs. We prefer to avoid this usage, however, since the term* link virus *or* linking virus *is also sometimes used by PC-centric researchers to refer to viruses (most notably DIR-II) that are more often described as cluster viruses.*

File viruses link, or attach, to their program file targets in many different ways. There are, in fact, four main ways to attach code to an existing program.

▶ Overwrite existing program code

▶ Add code to the beginning of the program

▶ Add code to the end of the program

▶ Insert viral code into the chain of command so that it is run when the legitimate code is executed.

File- or program-infecting viral programs, while possibly not as numerous as BSIs in terms of actual infections, represent the greatest number of known viral strains, at least in the PC world. This may be due to the fact that file infectors are not as constrained in size as BSIs or that file infectors do not require the detailed knowledge of system internals that may be necessary for effective boot-sector viral programs. As "easier" routes to malware programming are discovered (Microsoft Office macro viruses, AOL password stealers, VBScript viruses), there are fewer viruses that require extensive knowledge and industry on the part of virus writers.

File-infecting viruses spread by adding code to, or associating code with, existing executable files. (It can be argued that macro viruses are a special case of file infector, but we consider them separately later in this chapter.) File infectors become active when an infected program is run. Whereas BSIs must be memory-resident in order to spread, file-infecting programs have more options in terms of infection. This means that there is greater scope for writing file-infecting viral programs, but it also means that there may be fewer opportunities for a given virus to reproduce itself.

With two exceptions, file-infecting viral programs must, of necessity, make some kind of change in the target file. If normal DOS calls are used to write to the target file, the file-creation date will be changed. If code is added to it, the file size will change. Even if areas of the file are overwritten in such a way that the file length remains unchanged, a parity, checksum, cyclic redundancy, or Hamming code check should be able to detect the fact that there has been some change. The Lehigh and Jerusalem viral programs, the first to become widely known to the research community on the Internet, were both initially identified by changes they made to target files (Jerusalem being widely known by its length—1813). Change detection, therefore, remains a viable means of virus detection on the part of antiviral software producers, though it is not often used currently.

Because change detection does not require sophisticated programming (in some cases, no programming at all), virus writers have attempted to camouflage changes where they can. It is not a difficult task to avoid making changes to the file creation date, or to return the date to its original value. It is also possible to overlay the original code of the program so that the file is not increased in size. Many virus authors have also been using stealth programming to bypass the operating system and return only the original, unchanged, values when a request for information is made.

In DOS there are three main types of executable programs that can be called directly from the command-line prompt: files with .BAT, .COM, and .EXE filename extensions. Even in DOS there are many other types of files that can contain executable code; Windows environments however, not only increase the range of files that can contain code, but the range of ways in which such files can be called.

Executable files with .BAT filename extensions are referred to as *batch files*, although they have little in common with the batch processing of mainframe computers. Batch files are text files with collections of DOS commands, and are thus restricted to the operations that are possible with those commands. They are similar in concept to shell scripts, which are widely used on some multi-user operating systems (especially UNIX), but are comparatively limited in functionality. .BAT file viruses have been written, but they are generally regarded only as curiosities.

.COM and .EXE files are the "real" programs. They are structures of machine instructions, or opcodes. Of the two, .COM files are much more basic. A .COM file is a fairly straightforward list of opcodes with no reference to outside files and few jumps from one section of code to another. .COM files are therefore much simpler to infect, not least because they always start from the same address.

An .EXE program has a more complicated structure. For example, it starts out with a section of data describing the structure of the program. This data section has a length that can vary, but only in multiples of a specific size. Viruses that infect .EXE programs have to make changes to this data section and, depending on the original size, have to increase its length. Therefore, virus-infected .EXE files do not increase by a specific length related to the virus, as is the case with .COM files, but have an increase that partly depends upon the structure of the original program.

Windows 1, 2, and 3.*x* generally ran DOS programs without too much problem, and the program structures for Windows-specific programs were only marginally more complex. However, with Windows 32-bit versions (Windows 95, 98, NT, Me, and 2000) the programs began to use a new format, called PE-EXE (Portable Executables). DOS viruses could usually infect Windows 1, 2, and 3 version programs, though the functionality of those programs was often impaired. PE-EXE files are sufficiently different that the techniques used by old .COM and .EXE infectors no longer work, although there are viruses that can infect all types of .EXE files.

Prependers and Appenders

Most file viruses place the bulk of the viral code towards the end of the program file, with a jump sequence at the beginning of the file that points to the main body of the virus. Some viral code attaches to the beginning of the file—this is simpler in concept, but actually more difficult in execution. These two techniques are known as *appending* and *prepending*, respectively, but these terms are used less now than in years past.

Adding code at the beginning of the original program ensures that the viral code is run whenever the program is run. (This also ensures that the virus is run before the program runs, giving the virus priority in terms of operation, possible conflicts, and detection.) By adding code to the beginning of the program, it is possible to avoid any change to the original code. It *is*, however, necessary to alter at least the file/disk allocation table to ensure that the program call starts with the viral code, and that the viral code is not overwritten by other changes to the disk or files. Also, while the original code may be left unchanged, the file will nevertheless be altered, and unless techniques are used to disguise this, the file will show a different creation date, size, and image.

It is also possible to add viral code to the end of the original program and still ensure that the viral code is run before that of the original program. All that is necessary is to alter the file header information to reflect the fact that you want to start executing the file towards the end, rather than at the normal location. At the end of the viral code, another jump returns operation to the original program.

This kind of operation is not as odd as it may sound. It is not even uncommon. A legacy from the days of mainframe "paging" of memory, it is used in a great many MS-DOS executables, either in single .EXE files or in overlays. It is, therefore, not a coding indication that can be used to identify viral type programs or infected files.

Appending, or prepending, viral code to an existing program avoids the problems of damage and potential failure to run, which plague the overwriting type of viral programs. Even these viral programs, however, are not foolproof. Programs that load in very non-standard ways use the header information that the viral programs alter. Although not originally designed for virus detection, the "Program abort—invalid file header" message thus generated is an indication of viral infection, though not a very reliable one. In a complex operating environment such as Windows, there are all too many possible non-viral reasons why a program may stop functioning properly.

Overwriting Viruses

Some viral programs do not attach to the beginning or end of the file, but write their code into the target program itself. Most often this is done by simply overwriting whatever is there already. Most of the time, the virus will also make a modification to the beginning of the program that points to the virus, but on occasion the virus will rely on chance for a computer operation to stumble upon the code and run it.

Of course, if a virus has overwritten existing code, the original target program is damaged, and there is little or no possibility of recovery other than by deleting the infected file and restoring from a clean backup copy. However, some overwriting viruses are known to look for strings of null (or NUL) characters that may provide a space to overwrite. If such a string can be identified, the viral code can be removed and replaced with nulls again. (The Lehigh virus, for example, attaches "behind" the COMMAND.COM file, in a sense, but overwrites slack space at the end of the file so as not to change the file size. The details of this virus will be explained in Chapter 12.)

Overwriting existing code is a very simplistic answer to the problem of adding code to an existing program without changing the file size. By simply overlaying code that is already on the disk, the original size remains unchanged. There are a few problems with this approach. The most obvious is that preserving file size is an ineffective means of avoiding detection. Probably no competent anti-virus program using generic techniques would check file size alone, without checking content, if only by a simple checksum.

Then there is the problem of how to make sure the virus is called when the infected program is run. If the code is just inserted anywhere, it may not be in a part of the program that is used every time the program is run. (Every programmer is aware of the Pareto Principle's application here: 20 percent of the code does 80 percent of the work. Some code never gets called at all.) It is possible, by an analysis of the target program's code, to find an entry point that is used extensively. It is also possible, and a lot easier, to place a jump at the beginning of the program that points to the viral code.

The second problem is much more difficult to deal with. If the virus code overwrites existing portions of the program code, how do you know whether the loss of that program code is fatal to the target program? Analysis of this type, on the original code, is very difficult indeed. Successful overwriting viral programs tend to be short and to look for extensive strings of NUL characters to replace (ZeroHunt is an example). The NUL characters tend to be used to reserve stack space, and thus are not vital to the program. However, even if the original code is not vital to the program, it may cause the program to exhibit strange behaviours if replaced, and thus lead to detection of the viral infection.

We should also mention the Nina virus, which overwrites the beginning of a file, and the Phoenix family, which overwrites a random section of a file. Both Nina and Phoenix append the overwritten part to the end of the infected file. The Number of the Beast/512 virus and 1963 both overwrite the beginning of the file and then move the contents of the overwritten section beyond the *physical* end of the file into a portion of the last cluster that the file occupies. The clusters are always of a fixed size, and because it is very unusual for a file to exactly match a multiple of the cluster size, there is generally some space past the "end" of the file that is, essentially, invisible to the operating system.

While overwriting viral programs solve the (trivial and often irrelevant) problem of maintaining file size, they bring with them some inherent problems, which appear, at this time, to severely limit their effectiveness. To this date, while many overwriting viruses have been written, none have enjoyed great success nor have they become major, widespread problems.

There is still one class of overwriting virus that we have not yet considered, and this is perhaps the lowest form of virus writing. Some virus authors bypass the comparative complexities of the overwriting techniques just described by using code like this:

```
If (infectable_object_exists)
then
(replace_object_with_self)
```

Such code makes it easier to guarantee that the infected program is viable. However, the fact that no attempt is made to preserve the functionality of the target program drastically restricts the chances that such a virus will survive. The non-functioning program draws attention to the presence of a problem, even if the implication of a viral program is overlooked. In fact, it can happen that the infected file can be replaced by a fresh copy without the victim ever realizing what the problem actually was, though in such a case the possibility of reinfection remains. Where such an overwriter is detected by conventional anti-virus software, it's normally only possible to erase the infected file. It can be replaced, but not repaired.

Recent worms have modified this approach by targeting and overwriting specific program files (characteristically, .DLL files associated with email). The replacement file has the functionality of the file it replaces, but is modified (subverted) to suit the purpose of the worm (that is, to propagate itself). We must distinguish here between this type of overwriting (as performed by MTX) and that performed by LoveLetter.A, which replaces graphics files with VBScripts but doesn't attempt to maintain the original content of the graphics files.

In the world of prependers, the Rat virus uses a technique similar to overwriting. .EXE file headers are always multiples of 512 bytes in size, so there is often an unused block of space in the header, itself, that the Rat assumes to be available. The sURIV 2.01 works a bit harder: it moves the body of the file and inserts itself between the header and original file, and then changes the relocation information in the header.

Misdirection

DIR-II, often referred to as a cluster virus, takes a different approach. The viral code is written to one section of the disk, the last available cluster (even if the cluster is already in use). Directory and file-allocation information is altered in such a way that all programs seem to start in that one section of the disk, enabling the viral code to be executed without its being directly attached to any of those programs. Because of the convoluted way this virus works, it is possible to "lose" all the programs on the disk by attempting to "repair" them.

> ### NOTE
> This doesn't mean it isn't possible to repair infected files, by the way. In spite of the fearsome reputation that DIR-II originally acquired, it is actually rather easy to detect and remove—it doesn't even require anti-virus software—as long as you know how it works.

At one time, this type of operation was referred to as a FAT virus, because of the change made to the File Allocation Table (FAT). However, this usage is confusing, since it can be misinterpreted as meaning that the FAT itself becomes infected.

The most successful and current variation on this theme involves modifying the Registry so that when a given file type is called (characteristically, any .EXE file), the virus is also executed. This trick has been used by a number of recent viruses and worms. Time and again in computer virology, we encounter this principle of misdirection. Like an illusionist, the virus writer attempts to distract us with smoke and mirrors from the real mechanism at work. Companion viruses provide a particularly interesting example of misdirection.

Companion (Spawning) Viruses

The simplest way for a viral program to avoid the detection that results from modifying the code of an existing program is to *not* modify the original program. The virus must then find another way to insert itself into the chain of command so that it will still be called when the (unmodified) original file is called. Companion viruses take advantage of a feature of the MS-DOS operating system. As we've previously indicated, three types of executable file are recognized at the MS-DOS command line, denoted by the .COM, .EXE, and .BAT filename extensions.

Because the different extensions provide an additional means to distinguish a file, three different executable files under MS-DOS can exist in the same directory with the same filename, but different filename extensions: for example, MYFILE.COM, MYFILE.EXE, and MYFILE.BAT. Normally, a program is only invoked by calling the filename; the extension is "filled in" by the operating system.

How, then, does the computer decide which of these three to run? It uses the following rules of precedence. First, a search is made for an "internal" command listed in the command interpreter. If that succeeds, that command is run. Thus, under MS-DOS, when you give the command *DIR*, the system generally runs the directory-listing subroutine provided by COMMAND.COM, even if a file named DIR.COM exists. If the search for an internal command does not succeed, the computer looks for a file with that filename and a .COM extension, then an .EXE extension, and then a .BAT extension. At each stage, if the search succeeds, the file is run; if it fails, it goes to the next level. Thus, in MS-DOS, .COM takes precedence over .EXE, which takes precedence over .BAT. A companion virus can thus "infect" a MYFILE.EXE file by making a copy of itself called MYFILE.COM. MYFILE.COM file will take precedence, and typing **MYFILE** at the DOS prompt will always call the virus first. In order to avoid detection, the viral file will generally end with a call to the original program, and the viral program's file attribute is set to "hidden" so that the program is invisible to a cursory directory listing. Variations on this scenario include renaming the original file and giving the virus file the name of the original file.

Fortunately, companion viral programs are by no means perfect. For one thing, they are limited to acting on those programs that are lower in the order of precedence. For another, the hidden attribute is relatively easy to overcome (particularly in MS-DOS), and an alphabetical listing of files will quickly turn up the anomaly of identical names. (Oddly, antiviral packages generally do little to alert the user to duplicate filenames. Often the user will be asked to validate a file without any suggestion that something might be amiss if the file has not just been added to the system.)

There is a valid argument that says that *companion* (or *spawning*) viral programs are not viral at all. Companion viral programs certainly do not link to existing program code, at least not in a physical way. They use a certain provision of the system to trick you into running them rather than the program you meant to run. Thus, they might be said to be closer in definition to a Trojan.

On the other hand, companion viruses do reproduce. They also form, in a sense, a logical link with existing programs. They certainly behave in a viral fashion by inserting themselves into the chain of command.

In GUI operating systems, it is possible for a virus to take precedence by overlaying an existing icon with another that is either transparent or identical to the first. Windows provides some additional means for companion viruses to operate, since it has a rather complicated sequence for searching directories when an executable program is called, and some of the "early" directories are almost completely unused.

Multipartite Viruses

At first glance, file infectors have many advantages over BSIs. There are many more program files on a given system than boot sectors and, therefore, more opportunities or targets for infection. Also, multiple copies of a given virus can reside on any system. While some viral programs may conflict in the use of memory or interrupts, multiple viral programs can often quite happily infect the same program file. Files can also be transferred via bulletin boards, web sites, and networks. On the other hand, a virus that has infected a file must still wait until that file is executed in order to be successful.

Most people trade data far more readily than they do programs, and, in the olden days, that meant they passed around diskettes, which could be infected by boot-sector infectors. (In trading Microsoft Office documents, of course, they may be trading both data and viruses. However, the perception of Word documents and Excel spreadsheets as data rather than as potential hosts for programs means that they are freely traded, whether by email, between networked machines, or on removable media such as diskettes.)

Removable media provide a better vector for BSIs (except that BSIs are restricted to diskette exchange), than for file infectors. Also, program files tend to be passed in "archived" form, usually as zip files, and even if the program becomes infected on one system, the original archive, itself, is unaffected. Usually the original archive is passed along, rather than a re-archived copy that might have become infected. Unless the original archive was infected, it will likely not become a vector, even if it passes through an infected system.

BSIs, therefore, have certain advantages, while file infectors have others. To get the greatest "spread", a virus writer wants to build a virus that will infect both files and boot sectors—a *multipartite* virus. In practice, these programs have had some success, but they have not spread as widely as you might expect. Multipartite, or *dual-infection*, viral programs have the potential to infect both program files and boot sectors, which expands the range of possible vectors. Dual infections can theoretically travel on any disk, and multiple copies may travel on a disk if program files are present. Multipartite infectors can also usually travel on networks and via files passed over bulletin board systems and other communications channels.

Are multipartite infectors a terrible new threat? Well, no. They've been around for a few years now. Why haven't they taken over the world?

There are disadvantages, as well as advantages, to multipartite viral programs. One of the major disadvantages is complexity. A number of file infectors infect only one type of program file, an MS-DOS .COM file, for example. A virus that infects both .COM and .EXE files generally has more than twice the code of one that infects .COM files alone. The virus must not only know how to deal with both file types, but also how to distinguish between the target files. The same logic holds true for multipartite infectors. The virus must carry with it the means to infect two radically different types of targets, as well as the means to identify two very different types of potential hosts. The necessary size of the program is much larger, as is the requirement for processing. The multipartite virus can be reduced in size, but this generally means a reduction in function as well.

Classic "file and boot" infectors are not actually the only multipartite viruses. There have long been examples, for instance, of macro viruses that install DOS file viruses. The current generation of worms illustrates a disturbing trend towards multipartite configurations. MTX, for example, spreads both as a non-parasitic worm and as a file virus. Multipartite worms are likely to survive better than the previous multipartite generation, because they work in an environment where file size matters less. Recent versions of Windows demand generous resources (disk space, main memory, processor speed). The truism that programs expand to fill the available workspace is as true of malware (and anti-virus software) as it is of office applications.

The choice of targets might seem to be an easy matter, but the reality is slightly more complex. The most effective means of spreading would be a "get-everything" policy, but this might also lead to conflicts and detection. Some programs might choose to alternate: a program infector would infect boot sectors, and a boot-sector infector would infect program files. This seems reasonable, until you realize that it merely makes the virus sequentially a BSI *or* a file infector in alternating generations. Statistically, this means that it will be slightly less effective than a boot-sector virus, rather than more.

Interpreted Viruses

Macro viruses dominated the mid-1990s (since the emergence of WM/Concept in 1995, though Concept was not, strictly speaking, the first macro virus). As the decade came to an end, virus writers turned their attention to other scripting environments, especially VBScript.

Macro Viruses

Macro viruses are currently, as they have been since their inception, restricted primarily to Microsoft Office applications. Many are associated with Word, most of the rest with Excel. There are a handful of viruses for other Office applications (proof-of-concept viruses, mostly). A few other proof-of-concept viruses are associated with non-Microsoft products using licensed versions of Visual Basic for Applications (AutoCAD) or a similar macro language (CorelSCRIPT, for instance). Some examples of unrelated macro malware (Lotus 123 Trojans, and HyperCard infectors, for instance) exist. Not all Office-based malware is viral: there are Trojans and virus generators, too. We will start off with some general discussion of macro viruses, and then move into specifics of the Microsoft technology.

Macros were originally intended to be small items of user-defined (or definable) programming that automated routine tasks. In fact, older applications often had no way of writing or editing macro code directly. The only way to create a macro was to record a series of actions (keystrokes and mouse movements) that could be played back as required later, but not edited.

While some people make distinctions between macros, scripts, and programs, the differences are largely matters of degree in terms of breadth of functionality, ease of use, and connection to a given application. Macros and scripts are supposed to be small, simple, easy to use, and they are generally interpreted, rather than compiled, so they carry their own source code. However, Visual Basic for Applications (VBA) and similar languages are full-blown programming languages whose functionality exceeds that of many older compiled or interpreted languages.

NOTE

The fact that macro viruses carry their own source code doesn't necessarily make them easier to spot. Like QBasic and GW-BASIC before them, VBA and most of its siblings have the ability to save code in an encrypted format (what GW-BASIC used to call "protected" files, and WordBasic called "execute-only" macros). Microsoft Office viruses generally go to some lengths to "hide" their presence (though to the practised eye, the absence of macro-related menu options can be something of a giveaway). Furthermore, they take advantage of an execute-only macro's ability to prevent the VBA editor from loading it for examination.

Macros or scripts, in order to be run, have to be executed by an appropriate application. They are (in principle) application-specific rather than specific to a particular hardware platform, operating system, or operating environment. In practice, though, they are restricted to platforms that support the host application. In some cases, the virus may be a stand-alone program, as in the case of Microsoft Windows shell scrap objects or Windows Script Host (WSH) files. However, in most cases, it is an advantage to be able to associate the macro with a data file or object. Thus, you can hide a JavaScript program in an HTML email, or a Word macro in a Word document file.

Actually, you can't put a Word macro into a document file in older versions of Word. However, you can put data into a macro template file. A template file should have a .DOT extension in DOS or Windows, but Microsoft doesn't want to bother you with those details. As a result, it is quite possible to create a file with a macro and some data in it, call it a document, and have Word figure out that there is executable content. And run it. In more recent versions of Word, documents containing macros are legitimate and distinct from templates.

You can create names for macros in Word, and some names are better than others. If a macro is named "AutoOpen", for example, it will run every time the associated file is opened. If you called it "FileSaveAs", it will perform the action specified every time the Save As item is chosen from the File menu. Therefore, virus writers can create files that appear, to the user, to be documents, but which can automatically perform some operation when read in the Word program, and which can change the functions of Word itself.

Macros can also be persistent. The global template file (called NORMAL.DOT in DOS and Windows versions—on the Macintosh, where filename extensions are less significant, it's just called NORMAL) contains those macros that you want to use in different documents. It is quite possible for a macro to copy itself into that global template file, thus sticking around long after the original infective document has been deleted.

VBA is a very functional language. Some purists would insist that it no longer qualifies as a macro language: certainly it no longer allows you the quick and dirty operations that macros were intended for, before the advent of programming Wizards. However, it is definitely capable of producing some of the most damaging viral programming on the planet.

Scripting Viruses

As noted earlier, the difference between macros and scripts is one of degree. The difference between macro viruses and script viruses generally lies in the details of the virus itself. As noted earlier, the difference between macros and scripts is one of degree. The difference between macro viruses and script viruses likewise generally lies in the details of the virus itself. Certainly, the difference between a VBA macro and a VBA script, both contained in an ostensible document, is definitely one for the internals books.

At the moment, the difference between what is considered a script virus and what is considered a macro virus generally turns on the association with a data file. If it is buried in a .DOC or .XLS file, it is a macro; if it comes as a .VBS attachment in an email, it is a script.

Concealment Mechanisms

Viral programs have almost no defence at all against disinfection. Ninety-nine percent of viral programs are almost trivially simple to get rid of—simply replace the infected file (or boot sector) with an original copy. Some more recent boot-sector and system viruses require slightly more knowledge in order to perform effective disinfection, but few require drastic measures. The same is not, unfortunately, true of worms. Some recent worms (MTX springs to mind) are awkward to remove, and it is unsafe to rely upon anti-virus software to do the whole job. Note that disinfection is not the same as complete recovery from the changes made by a virus.

NOTE

Far from their image as the predators of the computer world, viral programs behave much more like prey. Their survival is dependent upon two primary factors: reproductive ability and avoidance of detection. Viruses are more like the rabbits of the computer kingdom, except that stopping them can be as simple as basic computer hygiene. Exercising caution with disks and files from outside and keeping anti-virus software up-to-date is easier than culling virus authors with myxomatosis. If only life were really so simple.

Using the standard system calls to modify a file leaves very definite traces. The change in a file's creation or last-modified date is probably more noticeable than a growth in file size. File size is rather meaningless, whereas dates and times do have significance for users. Changing the date back to its original value, however, is not a major programming challenge. Adding code while avoiding a change in file size is more difficult, but not impossible. Overwriting existing code and adding code to "unused" portions of the file or disk are two possible methods discussed in the "File Infectors" section of this chapter.

Some viral programs, or rather, virus authors, rely on psychological factors. There are a number of examples of viral programs that will not infect program files under a certain minimum size, knowing that an additional 2KB is much more noticeable on a 5KB utility than on a 300KB spreadsheet. Not only because in the former case 2KB represents a 40 percent increase and in the latter case less than 1 percent, but because it's normal for data files to increase their size, whereas it is not for system utilities or applications.

In a sense these are all *stealth* technologies, but this term is most often used for programs that attempt to avoid detection by trapping calls to read the disk and "lying" to the interrogating program. By so doing, they avoid any kind of detection that relies upon perusal of the disk. The disk gives back only that information regarding file dates, sizes, and makeup appropriate to the original situation, providing, of course, that the virus is active at the time of checking. Although this stealth method avoids any kind of "disk" detection, including checksumming and signature scanning, it leaves traces in the computer's memory that can be detected. (Some viral programs also try to "cover their tracks" by watching for any analysis of the area they occupy in memory and crashing the system if it occurs, but this tends to be rather noticeable behaviour.)

Although the majority of viral programs spread via disk boot sectors, the infection of programs, Word documents, and email attachments, it is possible (and nowadays increasingly common) to use other means of replication. The important factor is the ability of a system component to submit information, which is then run as a program. It is, therefore, possible for terminals, peripherals, and network devices to operate as viral vectors.

NOTE

To quote Fred Cohen, "Three basic things allow viruses to spread: sharing, programming, and changes. All we have to do is eliminate those three things and we will be perfectly free of viruses". (A Short Course on Computer Viruses, *second edition*.)

In order to function as a viral vector, a peripheral device needs three features (or components):

▶ The computers using the peripheral must be able to submit information or programs to the peripheral.

▶ The peripheral must have access to a certain minimum amount of memory or storage and must be able to perform certain levels of automated processing.

▶ The peripheral must be able to communicate with other computers making use of that peripheral, and the information communicated must be accepted by those computers as executable code with access to at least a minimum level of resources.

Once those conditions are met, any peripheral, be it printer, modem, disk pack, or terminal, can act as a means of replication and spread.

However, as with hardware damage, there is a major weakness in the use of peripherals as viral vectors. Peripheral command sets, particularly those dealing with the more powerful functions, tend to be very hardware-specific. In the case of the programmable function keys mentioned in Chapter 4, one command set was used for Teleray terminals, for example, while another was used for Wyse terminals. The commands for these terminals are not interchangeable, although the functions are almost identical. This is an advantage of the current incoherent computing environment. However, as open-systems initiatives gain strength, many new viral vectors may become possible.

Peripherals are not the only unusual vectors for viral programs. Consider the common boot sector. A knowledge of the structure of the boot (and Master Boot) sectors and boot sequence is practically a prerequisite for any serious viral study. However, the VIRUS-L mailing list and FidoNet discussion echoes (the equivalent to a bulletin board) were formerly inundated with frequent postings by users claiming to have contracted Stoned (or Michelangelo, or Monkey, or...), to have deleted all the files on the disk, and yet to still be infected! To the vast majority of users, the fact that a program can be located at a *physical* position on the disk but *not* be referenced by the file directory list is a foreign concept. This confusion may contribute to the longstanding success of boot-sector infectors. (Some boot-sector viruses still in the wild date back to the 1980s.)

The boot sector on any write-enabled disk, and the partition boot record on a hard disk, are accessible to dedicated amateurs armed with utility software. However, there are other places to hide code or data on a disk, and these are not as easily examined. It is quite possible to format an additional track outside the normal range, for example. In order to avoid problems between drives with variations in tolerance, the software does not push the limits of the hardware. There are various programs for MS-DOS and other operating systems that provide greater storage on the same-sized disks.

In addition to tracks outside of and between normal formats, there is substantial space between the sectors on a disk (slack space), and there are programs that can increase the number of sectors so as to increase the space on disk. However, it is also possible to use the additional space without formatting additional sectors by writing information to slack space. Commercial software sometimes uses this technique for copy protection purposes. Both of these hiding places are so well concealed that viral programs infecting them never have a chance to become active. Viral code using these techniques has to provide the means to access the extra tracks or extra sector space, and then use the hiding space in order to store additional code.

Some hiding places are definitely a part of the system, while not being necessarily obvious. The Mac OS, for example, associates a number of *resources* with each program and data file. Most of these resources can have code associated with them, and therefore provide a number of additional hooks for viral access. It is interesting to note that undocumented features in the 32-bit versions of Windows are starting to allow the same type of function and are being identified as potential security risks.

Stealth

A virus usually contains some kind of identifiable string or code that can be used to identify it. Even if the virus is new or polymorphic, it still adds its code to the infected program, thus adding to the size of the program. If the virus overwrites original code so that it does not add to the length of the file and even tries to match a "checksum" calculated on the code overwritten, a sophisticated cyclic redundancy check (CRC) will still find a change. So how can a virus hide from all of these detection mechanisms? By tricking the operating system into concealing the virus's "footprint", the changes it has made in the environment.

Stealth technology, as applied to computer viral programs, most broadly refers to all the various means that viral programs use to hide themselves. Specifically, however, it refers to the trapping mechanisms that viral programs use to avoid detection. These mechanisms are only effective once the virus is active in the computer (active in memory). The virus will trap calls intended to read the data on the disk and in response return only the information that the original, uninfected, program would have returned.

Viral programs can trap all functions that perform disk access in order to hide the fact that the virus is copying itself to the disk under the cover of a directory listing. Viral programs can also trap system calls in order to evade detection. Some viral programs will sense an effort to read the section of memory that they occupy and will cause the system to hang. Others trap all reading of disk information and will return only the original information for a file or disk.

Because of possible differences in hardware, and also because these functions are generally fairly standard, the manipulation of the disk (whether by a virus or a legitimate application) is accomplished by calls to the operating system and underlying software and hardware, rather than being performed directly by applications. The operating system provides standard system calls and hooks to the required functions. When a program wishes to read data from the disk, it asks the operating system to do it by calling a standard operating system function.

However, since the function is standard, virus writers know it as well. Code inserted at the standard address can redirect the call to code provided by the virus. This stealth code may indeed use the original programming provided by the operating system, but it filters the data returned to the calling program. If an infected file is being read, the infection simply does not appear in the information that the calling program receives.

Stealth is a technology, not a virus per se, though the name Stealth has been applied to individual viruses from time to time. Most viral programs implement stealth in one form or another. Stealth is not, in fact, limited to viral programs. Antiviral software, and even utilities, use similar means to avoid compatibility problems with the wide range of computers and programs now operating (though the preferred term in this case is *transparency*). Stealth mechanisms have sometimes been classified as follows:

▶ **Negative (level -1)**   These are usually overwriting viruses, discussed in the "Overwriting Viruses" section earlier in this chapter. Not only is there no attempt at concealment, but the virus author didn't care whether the infected program file would function or not after infection, and coded the virus accordingly. Viruses that accidentally stop an infected program from running because of a programming error, or because of an unanticipated environmental condition, are not included in this category. There is a potential problem with this classification, because, to some extent, it depends on assumptions about the virus author's state of mind. It's not always easy to tell whether the author was indifferent as to whether the virus would be detected, or simply failed to anticipate some of the consequences of infection.

▶ **Non-stealth (level 0)**   The targeted program is expected to run more-or-less normally after infection, but no specific measures are taken to avoid detection. These viruses may even put up characteristic graphic displays and text messages.

▶ **Elementary (level 1)**   These viruses don't draw the victim's attention to themselves by any characteristic display. Basic anti-detection steps are taken, such as preserving an infected file's time and date stamp.

▶ **Intermediate (level 2)**   These viruses use more sophisticated stealth measures. Characteristically, an image or a partial image is retained of an object in its uninfected state—the original boot sector, for instance. If information is required by the system, the image is shown rather than the real (infected) object. Sometimes the image is a complete copy, but it may be as basic as a record of the size of an infected file before it was infected. This approach may involve modifying the environment as well as the infected object.

▶ **Advanced (level 3)**   These viruses use concealment methods intended to hide them from anti-virus software. Viruses that attempt to protect themselves from specific anti-virus software using known loopholes are sometimes referred to as *retroviruses*, using a slightly forced biological analogy.

Tunnelling

Somewhat related to stealth technology is the concept of *tunnelling*. Again, this is a technology, not a virus per se, and one that is used in both viral and antiviral programs.

Before there were viral programs, there were Trojans. Anti-Trojan software was (and is) largely based on change detection, or else on activity monitoring and the restriction of operations (activity blocking), much as is done by a number of antiviral programs today. Activity monitors do not really monitor activity: they place traps and interrupts at certain points in the operating system. Certain system calls are either potentially dangerous themselves (such as the function that formats a disk) or are precursors to dangerous activities. Therefore, when a program calls one of these functions, the activity monitor is triggered. Again, this relies upon the fact that operating-system functions *must* be made available in a known location so that valid programs can use them. The activity monitor can then alert the user, and the user can choose to stop the action or to allow the action, in which case the original operating-system code is run.

Since the state of the system is generally well known, a virus can be written to examine these system entry points, and it can *tunnel* or trace back along the programming associated with the system call. If an activity-monitoring program is found (and this generally means anything other than the original operating-system code), the trap can be reset to point to the original system call. The activity-monitor program is now bypassed, and will *not* trigger—at least, not for that particular function.

This same type of activity can be used against viral programs. Viruses often trap certain system calls in order to trigger infection activities. Antiviral software can tunnel along the various interrupts, looking for changes. Viral programs can thus be disarmed.

Anyone who has ever tried to manage accounts on mainframes or local area networks (LANs) will recognize that there is a constant battle between the aspects of security and user friendliness in computer use. This tension arises from the definition of the two functions. If a computer is easy to use, it is easy to misuse. If a password is hard to guess, it is hard to remember. If access to information is simple for the owner, it is simple for the cracker.

NOTE

This axiom often gives rise to two false corollaries. First, the reverse—that those systems that are difficult to use must therefore be more secure—does not hold. Second, many people assume that restricting the availability of information about a system will make that system secure. While this application of the STO (Security Through Obscurity) strategy may work in the short term, its effectiveness as protection is limited. Indeed, it often has the unfortunate side effect of making information less accessible to those who should have it, such as systems managers, while slowing the attackers only marginally.

User-friendly programs and operating systems tend to hide information from the user. There are two reasons for this. In order to reduce clutter and the amount of information that a user needs to operate a given system, it is necessary to remove options and, to a certain extent, functionality. A user-friendly system is also more complex in terms of its own programming. In order for the computer to behave intuitively, it must be able to accommodate the many counter-intuitive ways that people work. Therefore, the most basic levels of a graphical user interface system tend to be more complex than the corresponding levels of a command-line interface system. These levels are hidden from the user by additional intervening layers, which also add more complexity. (Hence the rule of thumb that the easier an operating system is to use, the harder it is to program.)

The additional layers in an operating system, and the fact that a great deal of management takes place automatically, without the user's awareness, furnish the ideal environment for a viral program. Since many legitimate and necessary operations and changes are performed without the user's knowledge, viral operations can also proceed at a level completely hidden from the user. Also, because the user is largely unaware of the structure and operations of the computer, changes to that structure and operation are difficult to detect.

Polymorphism

Virus-specific or known-virus scanning software is, for all of its limitations, still the most widely used type of antiviral software. The idea behind this software is that you can identify a virus by a unique *scan string* or (less correctly) *signature* within the virus that will not be found in any other program. There is an art to the choice of a scan string. Code is preferable to text, which may easily be altered—some variants differ only by trivial modifications of text messages from the original virus. The code should also be integral to the operation of the virus. Ideally, you want a string that may identify future mutations of this virus, as well as the current infection. Once you have a suitable signature, you can identify the virus.

Unless, that is, the virus changes in some way so that it doesn't contain a constant pattern that can always be used for identification.

This is the idea behind *polymorphism*. There are a number of ways to change the "shape" of a virus. One way is to start with a simple "random" number, such as the value of the seconds field of the system time when the infection occurs. Then perform a simple encryption on the value of each byte in the viral code. Only a short chunk is left at the beginning to decrypt the rest of the virus when the time comes to activate it. Encryption can be used in other ways: encrypting a regular, but arbitrary, number of bytes, or encrypting most of the code as a whole, rather than on a per-byte basis. From a scanning point of view, this isn't too much of a problem. Extracting an identifiable string from the code of the decryptor/loader stub is quite possible. This signature can be used to check for the presence of the virus.

In programming, there are always at least half a dozen means to the same end. Many programming functions are commutative—it doesn't matter in what order certain operations are performed. This means that very small chunks of code, pieces too small to be used in isolation as scan strings, can be rearranged in a different order each time the virus infects a new object. Meaningful instructions can be randomly interspersed with instructions that perform some non-essential task, or do nothing at all (a NOP, or null operation). Single instructions or subroutines can be replaced with different but functionally identical instructions or subroutines. These approaches may be combined with one or more encryption routines to produce a variable decryptor/loader that can't easily be scanned by using a fixed scan string.

A distinction tends to be made between the first, and limited, self-encrypting viral programs, and the later, more sophisticated, polymorphs. Earlier, self-encrypting viral programs had limited numbers of variants: even the enormous Whale virus had fewer than 40 distinct forms. However, it was noticeable for the layers of obfuscation put in the way of anyone trying to analyse it in detail. (It isn't actually necessary to analyse Whale to that level of detail in order to detect it, of course.) Later polymorphic viruses have been more prolific: Tremor is calculated to have almost 6,000,000,000 forms.

An even later development was the polymorphic "engine". This is not a virus as such, but code that can be added to *any* virus in order to make it polymorphic. The most widely known of these is the Mutating Engine, known as MtE, written by one

of the virus writers who used the "handle" Dark Avenger. There *is* no MtE (or
DAME: Dark Avenger's Mutating Engine) virus—only other viral programs that
have had the code attached. MtE is not the only such program around; many others
have been developed, such as TPE (Trident Polymorphic Engine).

Polymorphic engines are sometimes confused with virus kits, or generators, which
we dealt with in Chapter 3. The *polymorphic engine*, if properly attached to the
original virus, will re-form the viral code on each new infection. A *virus kit* is a
program to automate the actual writing of a virus—the user picks characteristics
from a menu of choices, and the kit program sticks together pre-programmed pieces
of code to make a virus. A polymorphic engine, then, is code added to a virus to
make the same virus change its appearance each time it reproduces. A virus kit is
a non-replicating, non-viral program that automates the process of generating viral
programs, each with different characteristics. Unless polymorphism is one of the
available options, viral programs produced by a kit will retain their signatures from
that point on.

Fortunately, polymorphism in any form and at any level has not been that great a
threat, despite the superstitious dread that the term arouses in non-experts. Polymorphs
are as easily detected by change-detection and activity-monitoring software as any
other viruses. Even virus-specific scanners have not (in the long term) had great difficulty
dealing with polymorphic programs, though some scanners that were unable to adapt
to early polymorphic threats have become (deservedly) extinct. The early self-encrypting
programs usually provided readily identifiable signatures, since the decryptor stub
had to be left unencrypted. Even those programs that performed significant encryption
or used variable encryption routines generally had only a few forms, which could all
be recognized. Later polymorphs are sometimes more difficult to analyse and identify
initially, but algorithmic analysis, as opposed to pure signature scanning, is generally
successful. Indeed, in the case of the polymorphic engines, the use of these encryption
techniques has sometimes been advantageous to the antiviral researcher. When you
can identify the MtE code, you can also identify, as a virus, every new virus to
which it is attached.

Recently, a less sophisticated form of polymorphism has been seen in the worm
arena. One of the side effects of the Love Bug epidemic was that system administrators
were encouraged to block at the mail gateway email attachments that had particular
filenames associated with particular email Subject headers. Inevitably, malware
authors were inspired to introduce a measure of polymorphism into worm creation.
Some subsequent worms have been characterized by variable Subject headers and
filenames. It is likely that some malware authors will continue to develop this theme.

Social Engineering and Malware

Social engineering refers to breaking security through non-technical means. In fact, social engineering has always been a very effective computer-cracking tool, and is used extensively in all manner of viruses and Trojans. Despite the fancy name, social engineering refers to plain, old-fashioned, garden-variety fraud and psychological manipulation. Social engineers are con men (and women), and deceit is the oldest (remember talking snakes in gardens?) and most banal form of crime that exists. There is absolutely nothing novel about computer crime: only the tools have changed.

> **NOTE**
>
> The original Trojan horse, as recounted in Virgil's Aeneid, was a great piece of social engineering. Can't get through the walls? Pretend to go away and leave a jolly great trophy outside the walls of your enemy. If they are stupid enough to drag your troops into the city, you're laughing. Trojan programs do the same thing. Would anybody run a program labelled "Erase the whole disk immediately?" Of course not. So you call it "Greatest sexxx scenes" instead. Gets 'em every time.

Old-style viruses don't need extensive social engineering, since they are designed to spread without needing to trick the victim into executing a program they would not otherwise execute. Most of the programs we currently refer to (with varying degrees of accuracy) as worms, however, would not usually be executed unless some means of deception was employed. In Nachenberg's terminology, they are not self-launching. Another way of looking at the whole virus issue is to regard social engineering as integral to the ability of a virus to spread promiscuously without the knowledge of the victims who pass it on, since the trickery depends on the ability of the malicious program to infect legitimate code. Most people don't receive viruses from a computer vandal with a black eye patch and a cutlass between his teeth, but from a friend or colleague. They trust the infective object because they trust the sender.

Boot-sector infectors relied on the fact that most people had hard disks, and most diskettes were not bootable. Most computer users did not know that all DOS disks, including diskettes, contained a program in the boot sector. Nobody bothered about whether you put a diskette in the drive before the computer was turned on. There was no possible problem: if the computer told you "Non-system disk", you just ejected it and hit any key—except that, by that time, the virus on an infected diskette had already taken hold on your computer.

By the time Word macro viruses came along, the virus community had been telling people for many years that you couldn't get a virus from data, only from programs. Microsoft, however, found a way to include executable content in what was supposedly a data file. Thus, macro viruses took off like a rocket. (After all, you didn't have to check .DOC files, since they were just data.)

NOTE

Other word processors have macro languages, so why is it that only Word and Excel get successful macro viruses? One reason is the huge functionality built into WordBasic and Visual Basic for Applications: more features than any sane person would ever use in a word processor. The other factor, however, is that Word can have both macros and data in the same file. A WordPerfect macro is stored in a separate file, and you'd tend to notice if someone tried to get you to run this macro when you were supposedly just trying to read the document. To be fair, Microsoft didn't invent the concept of combining programs and data in the same file: PostScript and spreadsheets have done something similar for years, and experimental spreadsheet viruses had been known for some time previously.

Email viruses and worms use social engineering extensively. The original CHRISTMA EXEC worm displayed all its code clearly, if people only looked at it. However, the accompanying message stated that browsing the code was no fun at all, and suggested that the victim just run it. And most people did just that.

More recently, Melissa used extensive social engineering. For starters, it was posted on alt.sex, a great place to find a lot of people with, shall we say, a lack of discrimination. It was posted as a document supposedly containing passwords for pay sex sites. (Oh, good, sex *and* something for free.) When active, it mailed itself from your email program to people in your address book. In other words, it would always come from someone you knew: someone you could probably trust. The subject line is "Important Message From: [name of sender]" with the name taken from the registration settings, so the message is 1) generic, 2) important, and 3) again, from someone you know. The text of the body states "Here is that document you asked for ... don't show anyone else ;-)". The document obviously has to do with some prior conversation (that you have, for the moment, forgotten), and it is confidential. This makes it irresistible.

Love Bug used much the same features (who can resist a love letter from an unknown admirer?) with one addition: the filename of the attachment was LOVE_LETTER_FOR_YOU.TXT.vbs. Obviously you were supposed to notice the .TXT extension. Text files are harmless. The fact that the last extension, in spite of its lowercase unimportance, is the "real" extension was generally ignored. Again, the code was clearly visible to anyone who cared to look at it (and the fact that it contained a routine called InfectFiles was, one would think, something of a giveaway).

NOTE

But what if you really can't even program well enough to modify an easy worm like Melissa? One possibility is to warn people about the virus you wish you could write. Tell them there is a terrible virus on the loose, and it is just going to destroy everything. Tell them to tell everybody they know to stop reading email and avoid this horrible plague. Be sure to give your virus a good name, though. Maybe something like "Good Times". We will have much more to say about Good Times and other hoaxes in Part IV of this book.

The most recent example of a social-engineering virus is unlikely to do anybody any harm, but it replicates nicely. In the wake of Melissa and the Love Bug, an email joke started doing the rounds. Most variants note that it is the "honour system" virus. If you feel left out of the latest email virus furor, you are invited to randomly delete half the files on your computer, and send the joke message off to everyone you know. (While computer virology is not a suitable pastime for the humorously disadvantaged, we feel we have been delighted enough by this particular example of gallows humour. And it's still a chain letter. Please don't send us any more.)

Summary

It may seem odd that we have not offered a technical section dealing specifically with worm technology in this chapter, especially in view of the fact that email viruses and worms constitute one of the major current threats. However, the class "worm" is at a higher level of abstraction than the subclasses addressed here, such as file viruses and macro viruses. The term *worm* may be applied to particular examples of a wide range of malware, including script viruses, macro viruses, file viruses, overwriters, and even Trojans. In fact, worms exemplify the trend towards convergence to which we have alluded previously. It seems to us to be more useful to examine particular examples of the breed in more detail than to attempt to impose a contextual straitjacket onto viral programs that may or may not meet a particular definition.

There are all kinds of subtle variations on the themes covered in this chapter, and some less-subtle ploys that will only become obvious after some virus writer explores techniques not yet used. However, it is important to note that the most successful viral programs, in terms of numbers of infections, are not necessarily the new models, but the older and often less-sophisticated versions. On the one hand, this indicates that novelty is not necessarily a viral survival factor. On the other hand, it points out, in a rather depressing manner, that most computer users are still not employing even the most basic forms of antiviral protection.

This has been a long introduction to a complex subject. Now that we have considered the technological basis on which current malicious software is based, it is time to look at the technology for countering it, and see how best to use it.

PART

II

System Solutions

Anti-Malware
Technology Overview

W hat is anti-virus software? Better, what do you want (or expect) your anti-virus software to do? When we ask this question in a seminar context, the first answer is almost inevitably, "To stop viruses". Here comes the first disappointment: anti-virus software can't "stop" viruses, any more than a police station can "stop" crime. In a perfect world, a global social engineering programme (as social scientists understand it, rather than hackers) might attempt to educate computer users of all ages and persuasions in the mysteries of "ethical" computing. However, it is not realistic to expect the application of a purely technological approach to individual systems to solve what is essentially a special case of a worldwide social problem.

Great Expectations

If we take this discussion a little further, we generally find that what the respondent to our question actually means is "to stop viruses on my desktop or on the desktops of my users". Well, we can't all be altruists. Most people just don't want to be bothered with malware at all; they want anti-virus software (and maybe other defensive measures) to take care of all virus protection totally transparently. Such solutions might work for some individuals, but really would not work at all for corporate institutions, even if they were technically feasible. In real life, of course, they are not at all feasible. It can be proved formally that it is not possible to detect all viruses, let alone block them.

Total transparency is approximately equal to a process like this:

1. *A* sends an infected or otherwise dangerous object to *B*.

2. *B*'s defences kick in and discard the dangerous object.

3. *B* gets on with his or her life, blissfully unaware.

A moment's thought suggests that this process might not be the optimal strategy. It's probably based on the assumption that *A* is an evil malware author sending malicious programs to *B*, a potential victim. Viruses and worms *are* sometimes injected into the mainstream (into the wild, if not Into the Wild) this way. However, most people who receive worms and viruses get them from people they trust— colleagues, friends and relatives—people who are indeed fellow victims, not villains. If *A* is an innocent party, it may damage a social or commercial relationship if communications are bounced back with no explanation or a curt automatic message, or simply not acknowledged. Wouldn't *B* want to let *A* know that *A* has a problem (and, if possible, what it is, and even how to deal with it)? Wouldn't *B* want to know that a trusted party has become (knowingly or unknowingly) a vector for incoming malware? You may recall that we said in Chapter 2 that anti-virus technology is not all about keeping your own computer safe. Alerting other people to the fact that they're virus victims is not an act of altruism (or not exclusively); it can benefit you too, in the following ways:

▶   If you handle the situation diplomatically, you score brownie points.

▶   If the victims improve their defences, the warning reduces the risk of your receiving other viruses from them. In a sense, you extend your perimeter defences.

▶   The victims are encouraged to act maturely and responsibly when they, in turn, receive infected objects from others. The beneficial effects ripple outwards, peace gets given a chance, the Age of Aquarius begins in earnest, and virus writers give up and take up gardening.

Perhaps we have been asking the wrong question here. We need to broaden it from "What do you want anti-virus/anti-malware software to do for you?" to "How do you want to manage virus incidents?" When we ask this, we often find that what people really want is based on unrealistic expectations of the software available to them. We usually find that what they really, really want is a combination of some or all of the following goals:

▶   To detect known viruses

▶   To detect other known malware

▶   To detect stuff that isn't really malware (some organizations would like their anti-virus vendors to block spam, for instance)

▶   To detect unknown viruses (preferably *all* unknown viruses) and other malicious software

▶   To stop viral and other malware from being executed, so that it can't infect or deliver a malicious payload

▶   To repair legitimate but infected incoming objects

▶   To discard illegitimate objects

▶   To advise the sender of the unwanted object that he or she has a problem

▶ To block loopholes brought to light by virus incidents

▶ To record the incident and/or advise the appropriate person. Recording is essential to monitor the performance of the measures implemented, if only to justify ongoing licensing of security products. It also helps to keep track of whether an organization is catching "friendly fire" from a peer organization who may have failed to apply "due diligence".

The question then becomes, how realistic are these expectations? While some are attainable, they are not attainable by *all* anti-virus software, they are not necessarily *fully* attainable by anti-virus software, and they are not necessarily reconcilable with the desire for complete transparency.

The degree to which customer expectations are at variance with the technology available deserves more attention than we can give it here. The European Institute for Computer Anti-virus Research (EICAR) has undertaken an initiative to improve information security by a closer binding of customer needs (and expectations) and actual functionality. The first stage of the EICAR Anti-Virus Enhancement Program (EAVEP) is a survey, presented to the EICAR conference in March 2001, of the views of network and system administrators, security officers, and other technical decision makers on what weaknesses they perceive in current technology. Similarly, the Anti-Virus Information Exchange Network (AVIEN) is increasingly drawing attention to the shortfall between what vendors are happy to offer and what customers really want.

Virus management is often seen as exclusively (or primarily) a desktop issue. Indeed, for a home user, this perspective offers probably the only way of looking at the problem that makes sense. In the corporate environment, virus management may be seen as (primarily) a networks/systems issue. However, the virus/malware problem ranges across desktop management, LAN management, and Internet/ intranet/extranet management, as well as less obvious areas such as human resources management. Only by defining the problem globally is it possible to work towards holistic solutions that cross boundaries within the organization, rather than relying on piecemeal relief of individual symptoms. To this end, anti-malware technology and the functionality behind it are considered in some detail in this chapter. We will also consider how anti-virus technology might be better mapped to the client organization's needs. The chapter generally considers anti-malware technology in terms of functional specification rather than in terms of detailed implementation. After all, anti-virus vendors are unusually secretive about some aspects of the ways in which their products work. They are concerned not only with keeping proprietary code hidden from potential rivals, but also with staying a step or two ahead of the virus writers.

How Do We Deal with Viruses and Related Threats?

Management of viruses and other malicious software is sometimes divided into two main areas: proactive anti-virus measures and reactive incident management (sometimes referred to as "playing first" and "playing second"). Strictly speaking, this distinction is illusory. All anti-virus software is essentially reactive—that is, it exists only because viruses and other programmed threats existed first. That somewhat academic point aside, it is common to distinguish between virus-specific scanning or Known Virus Scanning (KVS) on the one hand and generic measures on the other, as if they were on opposite sides of the proactive/reactive divide. This distinction is also illusory. For example, change detection, the most commonly used generic approach, can be considered more reactive than a virus-specific scanner that denies entry proactively to a recognized virus by discarding it at the mail gateway.

The essential distinction here is between detection of viruses at (or before) the point of entry and identification of viruses *after* they have entered the protected environment. However, anti-virus software leans towards the reactive. The most popular technology is based on the identification and disinfection of a virus either at the point of entry or after it has entered the system. We prefer to consider the technological aspects of anti-virus software in terms of three main approaches: pre-emptive measures, virus-specific measures or KVS, and generic detection:

► *Pre-emptive measures* are those that do not attempt to identify specific viruses or deduce the presence of an unknown virus. Rather, they simply attempt to render the environment so inhospitable to viruses that they cannot enter that environment or cannot be executed if they do. Many of these measures barely qualify as anti-virus technology, but implement commonsense precautions along the same lines as the "Safe Hex" guidelines included in Chapter 11. However, the implementation of these precautions involves rather different strategies and tools for a systems administrator in a complex environment than it does for a single home computer user.

► *Virus-specific software* takes the approach, "I have identified virus X. Do you want me to sort it out for you?" Such scanners look for search strings whose presence are characteristic of a known virus, and usually can remove the virus from an infected object. However, some objects cannot be repaired. Even where an object can be repaired, it is often held to be preferable (in fact, safer) to replace the object rather than repair it, and some scanners are very selective about which objects they repair. (Boot sectors and Microsoft Office documents are usually easily repairable; binary executables are much more difficult.)

▶ *Generic detection software* deduces the presence of a virus from environmental anomalies. It doesn't identify a specific virus by name. This approach might be defined as "You might have a virus. Message ends". Usually it is much easier to replace an infected object than to repair it, even where the virus is known. Repairing an object (especially a binary executable) infected with an unknown virus is far harder.

Pre-emptive Measures

Creating policies or educating users in safe practices can reduce the risk of becoming infected, even when a virus enters the organization. There are many possible pre-emptive measures:

▶ Avoiding the use of applications that are vulnerable to macro viruses, such as the constituents of the Microsoft Office suite.

▶ Disabling PC floppy booting to block the entry of boot sector infectors.

▶ Disabling or removing floppy drives to block the entry of all disk-borne viruses.

▶ Denying entry to mail attachments that are likely to be vectors for inbound viruses. These can include program files such as those with .EXE, .COM, .SCR, and other filename extensions indicating binary executables, files carrying double filename extensions such as in badfile.txt.vbs, Word and Excel documents, and others.

Such measures can be very effective at addressing aspects of anti-virus damage that reactive anti-virus software doesn't deal with very well, and we'll return to them in due course. However, they have two major drawbacks. First, they may impair productivity. Second, we should recall the latent virus problem. In this scenario, the virus is inactive in the protected environment. However, since the virus has not been detected or known, it may become active again if that environment is modified or if an infected file or disk is transferred to a vulnerable environment. (Such a transfer of infected material via an uninfectable environment is sometimes referred to as *heterogeneous virus transmission*.)

Some measures are similar in intent but less effective in practice. For example, it's possible to reduce the risk of macro virus infection in Word 6 and above by disabling auto macros and using built-in or add-in measures to block all macro execution unless explicitly permitted by the user (or authenticated by digital certificate, for instance). However, it is not possible to eliminate the risk entirely. The binding of the underlying macro language to the application interface and infrastructure precludes the complete "turning off" of the macro language that would be necessary for full security.

Access Control and Anti-Virus

You can use access-control software suites to minimize the possibility of a virus or Trojan gaining entry, by enforcing authentication of program files, disks, users, or any combination of the three. (By program files, incidentally, we imply not only unequivocal applications but also data objects, such as Word documents, that can also contain program code in the form of macros.) This approach is sometimes combined with virus-specific or generic scanning. Applying such a "moat and wall," or multilayered strategy, can be much more effective than using only one of these approaches, but the strategy's success in avoiding threats has to be balanced against the probable impairment of performance that multilayering entails.

One formerly popular scenario works like this: individual workstations belong to a domain or group of machines on which access-control software is installed. The software blocks the use of unvalidated diskettes on standard workstations. To be validated, a diskette must be authenticated on a "gateway" machine, which checks and modifies the diskette and its contents so that it can be used on workstations within that group. This series of checks may include scanning with one or more anti-virus scanners (or other anti-malware measures), in which case the operation is hybrid rather than purely proactive. This scenario can be regarded as an instance of what is sometimes referred to as *integrity management.* This is a more systems-based approach to managing malicious code that is not entirely focussed on specialized virus-specific software, even though it is likely to involve the deployment of such software.

We should, however, note a significant difference between access control as it is used in this example and access control as it is sometimes understood by systems administrators. Access-control systems determine the appropriate allocation of access privileges to individuals, and grant systems access to authenticated individuals. In other words, if the system recognizes an individual, he or she is allowed to use that system to the extent that the user's privileges allow. However, as by now we hope to have convinced you, authenticating the individual is not enough in the virus/malware arena, since viruses and worms are usually spread (unwittingly) by trusted individuals. Confirming the identity of the individual doesn't tell us anything about his or her good intentions, though we would usually hope that the human resources department has applied the appropriate checks. It tells us still less about the individual's competence at following security guidelines, or the currency and acuity of his or her anti-virus measures.

In short, trusting the individual is not necessarily sufficient justification for trusting modifications in the local environment introduced by that individual. Organizations are aware of this principle in other contexts; for example, a group with a change management policy will not authorize a privileged individual to make changes in a "live" environment without the appropriate checks and balances. However, many administrators (or their managers) lack sufficient knowledge of the virus field to enable them to apply the same principles in the area of code integrity management. Like most computer users, they fall into the trap of trusting the object because they trust the individual. "I don't open attachments from people I don't know", usually means, "I do open attachments from people I do know". The problem here is that much of the difficulty of managing current worms and viruses lies in the fact that most people will not receive infected material from strangers with malicious intentions. Rather, they will receive them from people they know and trust, and who are unaware that they are being used as a channel for transmission of malicious code.

Firmware Settings

There are a number of ways specific to the hardware by which to secure a PC. Most of these involve the so-called CMOS (Complementary Metal Oxide Semiconductor) settings, pieces of information stored in CMOS memory that govern how your computer runs at a basic level.

The first, and easiest, is the boot order sequence. On older computers, the default CMOS setting would be to check for a bootable disk in the first floppy drive (A) of the machine, and then, if no diskette was found, to boot from the hard disk. This method, of course, allowed boot sector viruses to infect machines if an infected floppy had been left in the drive of the machine when it shut down or rebooted. Later, it became possible to configure a setting to change the boot order so that the hard drive was always accessed first. It was even possible to force the computer to boot only from the hard drive, regardless of whether there was a diskette in the first floppy drive and whether it was bootable. Nowadays there are other selectable settings, including booting from a CD-ROM or over a network.

An additional security feature is password protection. This feature is of little use in antiviral protection. In some cases, it is of little use at all. We recall one computer where the password protection didn't appear to protect anything except the password. However, in most cases, modern CMOS passwords prevent anyone else from booting up your computer and using it in your absence.

NOTE

This CMOS password protection is by no means absolute. It is relatively simple for a knowledgeable person to remove the password protection from even the best of systems, and ways of doing so are widely documented. The DISKSECURE anti-virus program has a password protection feature that is much harder to get around, as do other programs that encrypt some or all of the hard disk.

Hardware Solutions

It is often held in the security field that whatever software can do, software can undo. Therefore, any anti-virus software can be circumvented by a virus that targets vulnerabilities in the software. Viruses that target weaknesses in specific anti-virus software are sometimes called retroviruses, although this mechanism is not an altogether appropriate analogy for the biological model from which it is borrowed.

NOTE

In biology, a retrovirus contains RNA (ribonucleic acid). Genetic material from the virus is inserted into the host's DNA (deoxyribonucleic acid). Computer retroviruses, however, conceal their presence from antiviral agents in ways that are product-specific. They might be described as anti-virus-specific.

The converse also holds: no virus is impossible to remove from an infected system, although removal is not always cost-effective and does not always restore the system to full functionality.

There are some hardware antiviral measures. Indeed, the simplest one is the write-protect tab on floppy disks and certain types of removeable cartridge drives. Virus researchers have long wanted someone to make hard drives (or CD-RW drives) with write-protect switches, but this approach has not found favour. There are also some specific examples of antiviral hardware. Most are activity blocking systems—very fancy forms of write protection. One involved a very specific configuration of the motherboard and the system support chips. Various "secure" computers have also been built. None of these systems has had much success.

Chipaway was a simple antiviral system designed by Trend, makers of the PC-cillin antiviral packages. Chipaway, as the name suggests, was intended to be included with the BIOS programming in the ROM chip. It primarily addressed some basic types of boot-sector viruses. Someone at Trend, though, had either an unfortunate sense of humour or a lack of facility with the English language. When active, the Chipaway system would tell the user that his or her computer had the Chipaway virus. Other antiviral companies had many calls asking about the Chipaway virus—which, of course, did not actually exist.

A more recent device uses a hardware/software hybrid approach to the problem of worms and viruses. StopIT consists of an internal PC card and a hardware device that sits between the modem and the Internet. Network traffic is scanned against an automatically updated internal database of definitions. Whether this product offers improved security and/or performance over an on-access scanner is a debatable question, and one that doesn't seem to have been taken up.

Secure Software

It is frequently suggested (with a variable degree of flippancy) that the easiest way to render an environment virus proof is to avoid Microsoft operating systems or applications. While there is enough truth in this assertion so as to be embarrassing to Microsoft, this solution is rather like reducing fire risks by removing all oxygen from the atmosphere. Right now, most of the market for desktop and laptop operating systems and network file servers seems to belong to Microsoft. Even in more rarified atmospheres, such as those occupied by firewall servers and web servers, Microsoft has a substantial presence. In environments where Microsoft's presence is less obvious, such as the Macintosh world—Macs probably still constitute the nearest thing to a competitive operating system—Microsoft applications (including Word, Excel, Outlook, and Internet Explorer) are almost as predominant as they are on PCs. Even the Linux success story owes something to the availability of a Microsoft-compatible Office suite (StarOffice).

> ### NOTE
>
> *You might have noted certain statements in this book that indicate a lack of enthusiasm for Microsoft software. Are we saying these things because we are fanatical Mac, Linux, VMS, OS/400, or CP/M devotees, and we seek to trash the evil empire? No. We say these things because they are true. And because we have been paid enormous sums to spearhead a return to dominance of the Commodore Pet.*

There is some software, the use of which places you at higher risk of virus infection. This is a simple fact. As we have noted, the more widely an operating system is used, the more likely it is that someone has written a virus for it. The same is true for application platforms, such as email programs and word processors. But there are other factors that can increase or decrease risk. What you choose to use is, of course, up to you. But we would be remiss in our responsibility if we did not point out that certain software designs are more dangerous than others.

Microsoft Windows is the most widely used desktop operating system by a considerable margin. It is, therefore, the one currently most subject to attack, in terms of the number of people attempting to produce malware. However, specific strategic factors render Windows more vulnerable than it needs to be. It may be necessary to point out that the assumption of the overriding importance of security is far from universal, except possibly among security specialists. Financial analysts are inclined to resent the restrictions that a highly secure environment imposes on the pursuit of business aims. Management often pays lip service to the importance of security in meetings and reports, but cuts corners on implementation. Computer users frequently resent the obtrusiveness of most security measures.

Windows continues to stress ease of use above any consideration of security, despite having outgrown its origins on single-user systems, where security is rarely a primary consideration. Windows 95, 98, and Me are less secure than MS-DOS, in that they can give the user a sense of false security. Time and again, people tirelessly type in their Windows password, unaware that simply pressing the ESCAPE key would be just as effective for many systems. This lack of intrinsic security is less acute with Windows NT and 2000, which have the same basic security features as older multi-user systems, though an "out-of-the-box" configuration is not noticeably secure. However, this was often true of older systems, too.

Windows also tries, as much as possible, to hide system information from the user. In most cases, users can obtain information about the system and ongoing processes easily enough—if they know where to look. By default, the system automates many processes that allow access to the system. For example, network access and resource sharing are generally enabled by default, and must be turned off if the user does not want to make access available. This makes it very easy to set up networks, but it also means that access can be permitted over dedicated Internet links without the user even being aware of the fact.

Microsoft holds the source code for the operating system closed (as opposed to open-source systems) and has consistently refused to document a great many functions of the package. This is, of course, the corporation's right as a business with proprietary information, but it does mean that finding security holes is a matter of hit-and-miss testing rather than direct analysis of code.

Microsoft is trying to tighten the links between its operating system and its applications. This interrelation between platform and programs is behind a number of the recent email viruses. Outlook and Internet Explorer cannot be easily secured, since they use programming that is also foundational to the operating system. Making a change to the operating system can affect applications and computer operations in a variety of ways, and therefore patches for security bugs have to be made very tentatively and tested extensively before being released. More than once Microsoft has released a patch for one problem, only to create another. Microsoft also tries (not altogether unreasonably) to make the minimum change necessary to fix the current problem, often leaving related loopholes still open in the software. Where Microsoft offers a major fix, it may be either a fix to the wrong problem or so extreme as to reduce drastically the functionality of the product. The latter occurred with a security patch for Outlook, which turned a highly relaxed mail client into a monster that refused to allow access to any attachment with an .EXE filename extension.

Microsoft is not the only company in the world with software subject to security weaknesses, and it isn't even the worst. In fact, anti-virus software is often subject to analogous problems, for some of the same reasons. Vendors are aware that customers often value transparency above security, and may be tempted to set unsafe defaults so that an out-of-the box installation is fast and unobtrusive, but not very good at detecting viruses. For instance, the Novell version of a highly rated scanner (now extinct) by default checked only the standard system directories on a server. While it is reasonable to check files that are accessed by all users (such as LOGIN.EXE), it has to be remembered that on a competent server installation, everyday users don't have write permission to such files. In general, they can write only to directories they own or of which they share ownership, and these are the directories in which infected games, Word documents, and so on are most likely to be found.

There are some general guidelines of which you should be aware. The more automated a system is, the more it does for you without asking, and the greater the possibility of a security problem, particularly one involving viruses. The more difficult it is to look at the internals of a system, the less secure it is. The more flash and glitz on the surface, the less solid the underlying structure may be—although, the history of programming offers many examples of programs that are neither flashy nor stable.

In general, you can use Windows and reduce your risk of virus infection by using other software. Microsoft Word is almost the only platform susceptible to macro viruses; WordPerfect is largely free of them. If you want something that looks like Word, there is the StarOffice package, which is also less expensive than Word. Outlook is the major platform for email viruses, but other email programs are available. For example, Pegasus is a highly functional product available for free. Internet Explorer appears to have the greatest problem with active content; Netscape, Opera, Mosaic, and many others are safer.

Some of the problems with Windows do not allow for an easy solution. One of the recent email viruses used the shell scrap object file format. This format can contain just about anything: the Windows system will execute text, binary data, programming, and any active content in this format. In addition, Windows does *not* display the file extensions for shell scrap object files, even if you request that Windows display all file extensions. The icon for a shell scrap file differs very subtly from that for a text file; most users would not notice the difference.

NOTE

To see the difference for yourself, open Notepad. Type in some text (a word or two is fine) and then save the file in the C:\TEMP directory. Save the file under the names "test1.ini", "test2.txt", and "test3.txt.shs". Remember that you will have to put quotation marks around the filename or Notepad will just add .TXT to each filename. Now look at the directory with Windows Explorer. Note that the icons are superficially similar, although the Type column identifies them correctly. (You will have to select Details under the View menu in order to see the Type column: by default it is not displayed.) Note also that, regardless of your settings, the "test3.txt.shs" file will display as "test3.txt". You can force Windows to display the scrap object extension, but only by making a change to the Registry. (Edit the Registry entry HKEY_CLASSES_ROOT\ShellScrap from NeverShowExt to AlwaysShowExt. Remember to back up your Registry before doing any work on it: editing the Registry can get you in a lot of trouble.)

Microsoft's attitude regarding these security issues is interesting. In the late 1990s, the company was taken to task about the number of security problems associated with its product line. In one particular speech, Steve Ballmer reportedly admitted that the products were insecure. He said that Microsoft made insecure products because Microsoft made what the market wanted, and the market didn't want security. Ballmer went on to say that he could prove his assertion, given that Microsoft wasn't broke; if people wanted secure products, they would buy other products that were secure, and Microsoft would go broke.

What Does Anti-Virus Software Do?

All antiviral software fits into one or more of three main categories. *Scanners* read information on disk and in memory, looking for recognizable patterns characteristic of a known virus. *Activity monitors* examine operations as they occur in the computer, sounding the alarm when a possibly dangerous event happens. *Change-detection software* takes a snapshot of the details of the system, alerting the user when some modification has been made. In general, anti-virus software performs one or more of the following functions, according to the class of software to which it belongs and how it is configured:

▶ Identification of known viruses (virus-specific detection). This is the core function of most contemporary anti-virus software, and the main advantage, flawed though it is, to this approach is its conceptual simplicity: as a virus comes to light, the vendor adds detection to its product. However, the main disadvantage of this approach is that it is essentially reactive.

- ▶ Detection of suspected viruses not yet known to virus-specific software (generic detection).

- ▶ Blocking of possible viruses, implying generic detection.

- ▶ Disinfection of infected objects (usually associated with virus-specific products).

- ▶ Deletion, overwriting, and/or replacement of infected objects. This function is common to both generic and virus-specific products, where disinfection is technically impossible or considered unsafe.

What does *disinfection* mean? It certainly doesn't mean that everything is put back to exactly the same state it was in before the virus infected the host object. Some effects of infection or triggering of a payload can't be reversed, and others, such as Registry changes, while reversible, are not characteristically addressed by anti-virus software. A few vendors offer "single-shot" tools to remove well-entrenched viruses such as these rather than attempting to incorporate removal of such recalcitrant viruses into their main scanner.

Checksum disinfectors are unsuitable in environments where a virus infection is known to be present, suspected of being present, or could be present. This type of software uses checksum, CRC, hamming, or image calculations that *must* be done while the software is clean, since this software only tries to return the disk, drive, or program files to an "original" state. Even then, checksum disinfectors have a very low success rate and would undoubtedly fail any test created to measure a set of "cleaning" programs. Heuristic disinfectors are even worse; they sometimes harm "good" programs. While disinfection is often not recommended, in some situations you want to keep an existing program rather than replace it with an original copy, which may not contain setup information. In this case, you may need the services of a disinfection program that does not rely on a database of known viral programs. The chance of this situation happening is slight, but should it arise, "generic" disinfectors could be useful when ordinary disinfectors fail.

These basic types of anti-virus programs have a great many variations. You can run antiviral software as manual utilities (on demand) or set them up to be memory-resident and to scan automatically as potentially infected objects are accessed (*on-access* or *real-time* scanning). Some systems cover the entire computer and network in depth; others check only the likeliest areas in order to avoid requiring more processing overhead than the virus risk merits. The vital point to keep in mind is that *no* single antiviral program is the best for all situations. Software that is great for the data entry pool may be useless in the development office. You must understand both anti-malware technology and your own work environment in order to find the best fit. Many people are interested only in the "best protection program they can get" and do not want to endure any talk about what a virus is or how it works. They want to buy something that enables them to forget about the whole virus situation.

This attitude ignores three vitally important points. The first is that "the best" may not be good enough by itself. No security force would ever pick "the best" guard and then leave him to guard an entire refinery by himself. There is a trade-off between security and cost, but it often makes sense to use multiple antiviral programs—different products, of different classes, and at different operational levels.

Second, even within the limited realm of antiviral programs, data security software operates in many different ways. Thus, one type of security may be better in one situation while another may be better in a different environment.

The final point is that security, of every type, is always a "moving target," and the virus world moves faster than most. Not only are new viral programs being written every day, but new types of viral functions are being coded all the time (albeit at a much slower rate than the run-of-the-mill copycat viruses). Any developer who claims that its antiviral program "guarantees" protection against "all known and unknown" viral programs simply does not comprehend the reality of the situation.

Generic Solutions

There are two main sub-branches of the generic approach to virus detection: behaviour monitoring/blocking and integrity checking. Monitors and behaviour blockers remain memory-resident throughout a computing session and watch for suspicious processes. If they observe one, they sound an alert. They may, for example, check for any calls to format a disk or attempts to alter or delete a program file while a program other than the operating system is in control. They may be more sophisticated and check for any program that performs "direct" activities with hardware, without using the standard system calls.

Although the analogy should not be stretched too far, behaviour or activity monitors do suggest some characteristics, though not functions, of medical vaccines, being memory-resident and preventive in nature. In addition, blockers actually prevent the execution of the suspicious process. Unfortunately, legitimate programs often perform operations that might look very suspicious, such as writing directly to disk, modifying system areas, deleting files, and so on.

Activity monitors can detect "unknown" (that is, not previously identified) viral programs, and do not require a database of signatures of known viruses. They generally require less frequent updates than do scanners. Activity monitors do not require the same level of setup as do authentication or change-detection systems, and they may be able to function on already infected systems.

Despite some recent announcements, activity monitors represent some of the oldest examples of antiviral software. Generally, such programs followed in the footsteps of the earlier anti-Trojan software, such as BOMBSQAD and WORMCHEK in the MS-DOS arena, which used the same "check what the program tries to do" approach. This tactic can be startlingly effective, particularly given the fact that so much malware is slavishly derivative and tends to use the same functions over and over again. However, activity monitors demand more of the user. Because there is no absolute difference between a legitimate and illegitimate operation, these programs need constant reassurance that operations are legitimate. When they do detect a genuine malicious program, the decision as to what action to take generally remains with the user, who would much rather have the activity monitor deal with the problem automatically.

Also, viral programs that do low-level programming rather than use the standard operating system calls, or those programs that actually replace the standard system calls with viral triggers, may bypass activity monitors. In addition, while viral technologies such as stealth and polymorphism have little effect on activity monitoring, new approaches in viral spread require that new checks be added to monitors.

Activity monitors have a good chance to detect viral activity of new and unknown viral strains, but it would be very difficult to agree with those that claim to be able to detect "all current and future" viral programs. Unfortunately, activity monitors tend to encourage a set-and-forget mentality toward viral protection. You should avoid adopting this attitude at all costs. If activity-monitoring software is your protection method of choice, continue to keep up to date with viral methods and to test your software regularly. We suggest that you use it as a complement to other means of protection rather than as a substitute.

As with mainframe security "permission" systems, operation-restricting packages allow you to restrict the activities that programs can perform, sometimes on a file-by-file basis. However, the more options these programs allow, the more time they will take to set up. You must modify the program each time that you make a valid change to the system, and, as with activity monitors, some viral programs may be able to evade the protection by using low-level programming.

"Sandbox" products, such as SAFETNET, monitor Internet protocols (for example, SMTP, HTTP, and FTP) and/or applications (such as the Office suite), scanning code not for virus signatures, but for conformance with a security policy database. These products do not permit code from a monitored channel to run outside of them unless the code complies with corporate policy. Such applications have advantages in restricting the user's ability to subvert security, but require careful preconfiguration.

Integrity checkers (change detectors) look for changes in system areas and files compared to what one product calls a "baseline snapshot". A change detector examines system and/or program files and configuration, stores the information, and compares it to the actual configuration at a later time. Most of these programs perform a checksum or cyclic redundancy check (CRC) that will detect changes to a file even if the length is unchanged. Some programs will even use sophisticated encryption techniques to generate an authentication signature that is, if not absolutely immune to malicious attack, prohibitively expensive in processing terms, from the point of view of a virus. If a sufficiently broad overview of the system is taken, this signature will provide 100 percent effective detection of a viral infection, but it also may raise a number of false alarms.

NOTE

Strictly speaking, "100 percent effective detection" applies only if you can guarantee that the "day zero" baseline snapshot is of a genuinely clean system, that no malicious code is executed while the database is set up, and that the authentication mechanism can't be spoofed. In other words, it's not quite 100 percent effective.

The integrity-checking approach is fine for monitoring changes to static code such as system utilities, but hopeless for monitoring most Word documents, for instance. Furthermore, this approach works only if you can be sure that the system was clean when you took the "snapshot". Absolute certainty is not usually a possibility; in theory, even a day zero (brand-new) installation of the operating system might have been compromised before delivery. In the end, all generic measures *either* assume that you've blocked all the entry points *or* alert you to a possibility that you have malicious code on your system. The decision on how to react to the alert is generally up to you.

Authentication refers to strong encryption systems which both guarantee that a program is unaltered and identify its source. Change detection can be seen as a weaker version of authentication.

A sufficiently advanced change-detection system, which takes into account all factors including system areas of the disk and the computer memory, has the best chance of detecting all current and future viral strains. Even with the most esoteric stealth technology, a virus must change *something* in the system. Therefore, adequately broadly based change detection is the best bet for absolute detection of all viral programs—if you can put up with the false alarms.

NOTE

Some vendors have a problem with the term "false alarm", pointing out, quite reasonably, that change-detection software is simply doing its job when it flags a change, irrespective of whether the change really is due to malicious code. In this context, an alert could be reasonably described as a false alarm only if it flagged a change where none had been made. Nonetheless, you must investigate each alert and take appropriate action. The increase in security (arguably, the software will detect all viruses) is offset by the probable increase in incident-management overhead.

Change detection has the highest probability of false alerts, since it will not know whether a change is viral or valid. Additional thought put into the installation of change-detection software will go a long way towards reducing the level of false-positive results. As always with security systems, there is a trade-off between the easy and the effective. The addition of intelligent analysis of the changes detected may mitigate this shortcoming.

Retail Viruses

Rob Slade frequently (all *too* frequently) receives a certain type of call from people who think their systems are infected. After some questioning, it generally turns out that they are correct, and they start wondering about how they got the virus, prompting Rob to ask about the last change they made to the system. "But that's just it," they say, "I just got the computer an hour ago!" Then it was infected when you got it: you'd better contact the store and tell them that they are selling infected computers.

This type of call is inevitably followed up 45 minutes later by another from the same, now totally bewildered user. "I called the shop," the user will say, in a mild state of shock. "They said that, yeah, they'd had the virus around and didn't know what to do about it."

We do not mean to leave the impression that all computer retailers are malevolent and ignorant oafs who don't care whether they infect you. But the plain fact is that knowing how to put a computer together and take it apart does not automatically give you the skills to identify and deal with computer virus infections. Most computer retailers or repair shops take some precautions, but few of them have any security expertise.

And, unfortunately, some truly don't care.

Change-detection software provides no protection, but only after-the-fact notification of an infection. It is, therefore, quite possible to install an infected program on your system and have it continue to infect other programs. The change-detection software will (or should) detect the subsequent infections, but will not identify the original culprit. However, deductive reasoning, along with the software's assistance, may help.

You must inform the software of any changes *you* make to the system; otherwise the change-detection software will generate a false positive. This means that you must have sufficient knowledge of the system to know *when* you are making changes. Each invocation of the DOS SETVER program, for example, changes the program file, whereas setup changes made to an older version of WordPerfect sometimes alter the program file and/or change an external data file.

The increasing complexity of graphical operating systems with extensive networking capabilities implies that simply opening and closing windows may make significant changes to log files, system files, configuration files, or the Windows Registry (or its equivalent). Opening a Word document and then closing it again may result in the creation of temporary files, adjustment to the global template and other templates, and calls and changes to macros and customizations associated with the menu structure. It is not practical for an external program to assess the "legitimacy" of such transactions. In fact, it is often impractical for the operating system or a vulnerable application itself to distinguish generically between legitimate and illegitimate code. The only long-term solution—short of reengineering operating environments and applications—is to conform to a model whereby code and data are properly separated and users' access and modification privileges are properly defined.

As with scanning software, change-detection software may not see changes made and hidden by stealth viral programs if the software inspects file sizes alone.

There are numerous implementations of change-detection software. Some versions of this software run only at boot time; others check each program as it is run. Some of these systems attach a small piece of code to the files they are protecting, and this may cause programs that have their own change-detection features, or nonstandard internal structures, to fail. Some packages protect only system software; others protect only application files. Some change detectors keep the signature file in the root directory, others in the "local" directories. Some allow you the option of keeping the file on a diskette offline and out of the reach of viruses that might try to damage the file.

An approach sometimes used to reduce the processing overhead associated with virus-specific scanning is to use a hybrid scanning approach, where a change detector is used in conjunction with a virus-specific scanner. An object is first checked for changes; if the software observes no change since it last scanned the object, or since the scanner was last updated, no further action is necessary. However, if the object has changed, the scanner has been updated, or the object has not been scanned previously, the software invokes the virus-specific scanner.

Virus-Specific Scanning

Virus-specific software is effective as long as Virus X (or something closely enough related to it to be detectable by the same scan string) is in the product's current virus definitions database. If you're hit by a virus that your scanner doesn't recognize, you may find that it's a very dumb piece of software indeed. In fact, although we have distinguished between known-virus scanning and generic scanning, all KVS programs are actually hybrid, since all scanning requires a degree of heuristic analysis to work in real time.

Scanners, particularly signature scanners, are currently the most popular of antiviral software. This popularity is probably due to three factors: the fact that viral programs are specifically identified, because disinfecting software is included with most scanners, and because it's easy to play numbers games with signature-scanning programs.

Scanners can find infections only after they occur, but this does not mean that scanners cannot play a preventive role in protecting the system. If you use properly maintained scanning software consistently to check each disk or file that enters a system (as should happen with an on-access scanner), you greatly reduce the chance of allowing a viral infection to enter your system.

Scanners look for known viral scan strings. Because of this, scanning software usually will detect only known viruses and must be updated regularly. Most commercial scanners now have provisions for online updating on a weekly, or even daily, basis. Some scanners will alert users to programs that are "close" to a given signature. (The MS-DOS scanner F-PROT uses at least two signatures to identify a given virus and has always been particularly good at identifying "new" variants.)

There are tens of thousands of PC viruses and variants known at the time of writing (depending on what measurement criteria are used). When a scanner checks for all those viruses and variants, checking for every byte of viral code each time would impose a huge processing overhead. To keep this overhead to a minimum, scanners check for the shortest search strings they can afford and deduce the presence of a given virus accordingly. Scanners may apply a number of heuristics according to virus type, including simple virus string scanning (a long search string in a known location) and complex wildcard searches. In fact, as we've pointed out previously, virus-specific scanning as it is currently implemented is essentially heuristic. The processing overhead of comprehensive checking makes exact identification too resource-intensive for general scanning. Virus-specific scanning is most useful for confirming a possible infection flagged by heuristic scanning, or in support of file disinfection, where the aim is to restore the file to its pre-infected state.

However, the term *heuristic analysis* is also applied to the process of stepping through a program before it is executed and searching for suspicious code. In fact, an on-access scanner in heuristic mode is very nearly a cross between a known-virus scanner and a monitor. If such a scanner is configured to disallow execution of suspicious code (as is normal), it is for all intents and purposes a behaviour blocker as well. In this mode, a scanner effectively leaves the question of what you do about the suspicious program up to you. That is, you can remove it, take whatever steps are necessary to verify the presumed infection, assume that it's a false alarm and exclude the object from scanning, or reconfigure the scanner so that the offending program is not flagged or blocked from execution.

Heuristic scanning, an analysis of suspect code or files based upon possible activities rather than specific patterns, is nowhere near being a dependable form of viral detection. A great many programs, including antiviral software and other powerful utilities, have been accused (falsely) of being "suspicious" when checked by an aggressively heuristic scanner. At the same time, such scanners may fail to catch a number of other malicious programs. Thus heuristic scanning would fail miserably at the sort of evaluation criteria used to judge KVS software.

It would, though, be a great pity to inhibit the development of heuristic scanning software. This field is really the application of "expert systems" to antiviral software. Using a heuristic scanner is a little like having an "expert" antiviral disassembler check the code for you. Along with hoped-for advances in change detection, this field's development bodes well for the future of antiviral software. Indeed, not only does a heuristic scanner identify suspect viral programs, but it may also, with only minor additions, detect some Trojans and other malware too. A heuristic scanner looks for covert file modifications, unusual calls to the system or to networking software such as the WSOCK32.DLL library and email clients, or other activities associated with virus attacks. When the number and type of such activities exceed a "threshold of tolerance", the software flags the program under examination as being infected. In general, scanners are not either KVS or heuristic; most scanners are virus-specific by default, but can perform heuristic analysis too, as an option. This default mode is probably inevitable, given the additional processing overhead that heuristic scanning software entails.

On-Demand Scanning   On-demand KVS scanners run a scan on one or more mounted disks (or individual files or folders) when the user runs them. They can also scan more or less automatically at set times using scheduling software. A primitive implementation of this approach is to run a scan at bootup by calling the scanner from AUTOEXEC.BAT (on DOS-based machines) or using an equivalent script-based approach. Many modern scanners have built-in scheduling and scan in the background by default at set times or when the system is comparatively idle.

On-demand scanners vary widely in their functionality. The fine points will be considered in much more detail when we evaluate anti-virus software.

On-Access Scanning   On-access scanning, as the name suggests, tests for the presence of a virus every time an object is accessed. This may occur when a file is read or when a program is executed. On-access scanners are also referred to as *resident* or *TSR* (Terminate and Stay Resident) scanners, since in the DOS world the programs had to stay resident in the background in order to operate. Usually the terms *on-access* and *memory-resident* are applied only to known-virus-scanning programs. Activity monitors must, by their nature, be resident at all times. Some change-detection software systems also check "on-access", but usually aren't seen as a separate class of software. However, the hybrid change-detector/virus-specific scanner model described earlier suggests that such scanners may be much more useful than their comparative rarity suggests.

In the days of DOS, slower processors, and the 640KB memory limit, resident scanners were sometimes seen as more trouble than they were worth. These programs must, after all, consume memory space and processor cycles every time the system accesses a program or file. In these days of bloatware, and the attendant necessity of huge memories and fast processors, on-access scanners are not so often perceived as significantly draining resources, perhaps because their performance in this respect is not consistently benchmarked.

On-access scanners are often seen as the best form of antiviral software. After all, they operate all the time and do not require any intervention by the user. Nobody has to remember to scan the disk every Monday morning, and a virus infection on Tuesday doesn't have most of a week to spread before the next scanning run. In addition, many modern on-access antiviral programs add capabilities to check automatically any material that comes in via the Internet and Web. On-access or real-time virus-specific scanners don't have to be executed as a conscious act by the user: they're implemented as DOS TSRs, Windows VxDs, Macintosh control panels, and so on, and sit in memory. Such scanners don't usually (by default) scan whole volumes (though they might check floppies as they hit the drive); they scan individual files as they're accessed. This makes them useful for keeping a clean system clean (as long as they're updated regularly), but not very suitable for performing batch disinfection of a heavily infected system.

DOS TSR (memory-resident) scanners are generally rather restricted, mostly due to processing overheads and memory limitations. They are rarely aware of macro viruses (which is reasonable, since some macro viruses cannot normally be executed in a DOS environment). Such scanners are usually unable to detect complex polymorphic viruses, and in modern GUI environments such as the various flavours of Windows, are of secondary importance. Windows-hosted on-access scanners normally remain resident even when a DOS shell process (DOS box) is spawned within the Windows environment. They do still have a use on Windows 9*x*/Me PCs when booting directly into DOS—for instance, they can be used to disinfect viruses, recover data, or aid in reconfiguration. It's unusual however, for a TSR scanner to remove viruses as well as detect them.

NOTE

TSR stands for Terminate and Stay Resident, *referring to a DOS-specific system call (INT 21h, Function 31h). Characteristically, the call is used to load a utility or driver into memory so that it can be reentered through a hardware or software interrupt.*

Windows 16-bit and 32-bit VxD (virtual device driver) scanners are also memory-resident, but are not subject to the same limitations as DOS TSRs. They usually detect (almost) the same range of viruses as an associated on-demand scanner (and often use the same virus definitions file). Some VxD scanners can remove viruses on the fly as well as detect them. They may also be capable of enhanced detection similar to that offered by advanced on-demand scanners. Unsurprisingly, these capabilities may entail a noticeable processing overhead. Scanners implemented as Macintosh control panels, system extensions, and so on are approximately equivalent to Windows 95/98/Me VxD scanners. In Windows NT and 2000, on-access scanners are implemented as system services.

However, some serious limitations are ascribed to resident scanners. On-access scanners have sometimes had poorer detection capabilities than their on-demand, or manual, counterparts. The memory resident and on-demand components of a modern anti-virus suite may use the same definitions database and still not score identical results with the identical test set. This is particularly true in respect to encoded and archived file formats. These formats are the very ones that are used to transfer material over the Internet, and therefore there is a rather cruel irony: the antiviral systems that are supposed to provide protection against material from the Internet may perform very poorly in doing so. On the other hand, some modern memory-resident scanners, freed from the tyranny of DOS, *may* be configurable to include all the functionality of an on-demand scanner. For example, such scanners may be configured to perform heuristic analysis, recursive scanning of archived files (nested zip files, for example), macro and polymorphic detection, disinfection, and on-the-fly decryption of files using low-grade encryption algorithms. Clearly, accepting all these options will have a processing overhead.

Another point in regard to on-access scanners is that, as with any scanning software, the system is only as good as the definitions (scan strings) database.

The fact that resident scanners operate all the time does not mean that they update themselves. Indeed, it is important to update on-access scanners more frequently than on-demand scanners, since users tend to rely more on them and dismiss other indications of virus infection.

Beyond the Desktop

All of the preceding types of antiviral programs are available in desktop, or stand-alone, versions. Indeed, for many years, stand-alone antiviral software was the only real choice, and network versions merely added some frills to ease updating of files.

LAN Servers

Back when LANs (local area networks) and viral programs were both fairly esoteric phenomena, people used to ask if viral programs would work on a network. "Why should they?" would be the reply. "Nothing else does".

Well, times and technologies have changed. Incompatibility is no longer an issue, and therefore no longer any protection. Within limits, viral programs will work, and infect, on networks as well as on stand-alone machines. Indeed, stand-alone machines are the minority in most corporate organizations. All modern operating systems are to some extent multi-user, and the distinction between workstation and server is no longer absolute.

LANs do have certain advantages. Boot-sector infectors, for one thing, will *not* infect across networks. (Note, however, that we are not claiming that they cannot be transported across networks.) Since LANs have cut down on diskette exchange and "sneakernet", the risk of infection from what was once the most successful class of virus is vastly reduced. However, the risk has only been reduced, not eliminated. And this reduction has little impact on the spread of file infectors and macro viruses.

Novell has been the target of a number of accusations in regard to antiviral security. Understandably, the corporation has been a bit touchy in response. Let it be said, then, that no known virus has successfully been able to subvert Novell's security attributes—when they have been properly implemented.

That said, it must be admitted that very few LAN administrators know how to set up proper security. The establishment of appropriate rights, privileges, and attributes is a task that not all mainframe systems operators understand, and few network managers take the time to ground themselves thoroughly in security concepts. Microsoft does no better; some security experts have opined that the reason it is so hard to understand the Microsoft networking security model is that Microsoft networking does not actually have a security model.

Network security, over the years, has also received some knocks from deliberate attacks. A group of Dutch hackers wrote a program that would look for passwords on the network traffic. Another program exploited an unusual bug in the LOGIN program in an attempt to gain SUPERVISOR access. Both of these programs, however, required physical access to a node on the network for a length of time. Neither was in any way viral.

One Novell-specific virus is known. The GP-1 virus is rather old. It does *not* manage to break Novell's security and infect properly protected programs. It is designed, however, to reside on workstations and collect passwords as network users log in. These passwords are then broadcast on the 'Net, supposedly to a receiver program. The receiver program has never been found. (This circuitous means of stealing passwords seems to be an unnecessary bit of overkill: it is quite easy to write a program to obtain any passwords transmitted over an Ethernet backbone.)

Most microcomputers in the business environment nowadays are connected to some form of LAN, and the majority of these are also connected to the Internet. You may have noted that the discussion of antiviral software so far has not addressed the use of local area networks. There are two reasons for this. The first is, basically, that any antiviral program can work in a microcomputer attached to a LAN almost as easily as in a microcomputer that is not attached. The second is that LAN-specific antiviral programs follow the same basic operating principles as their desktop counterparts. Indeed, on Microsoft networks, the server and the workstation might be running essentially the same operating system and the same anti-virus program. The same does not apply to Novell networks, by the way. Server-side scanning in such an environment is done with a Novell native executable (a NetWare Loadable Module, or NLM). In principle, though, any server that can be mounted as a virtual drive (irrespective of its native operating system) can be scanned with workstation software from an account with appropriate privileges. Indeed, this strategy was at one time the only way of scanning most servers.

Many LAN functions do not vary among systems. For example, email is almost universal these days. Some of the specialized LAN anti-virus programs use email, text paging, and SMS (Short Messaging System) messaging to alert the administrator to a security breach or possible infection. This is an admirable feature—and one that, with a minimum of time and batch or script programming skills, can be duplicated on many networks. (The more homogenous the network environment, the easier it is in general to introduce such technologies reliably.) The same can be said of centralized logging of scanning and audit reports, updating of scanners from a central resource, and a number of other supposedly advanced features. One need not accept an inferior antiviral product simply because it has LAN capabilities. In fact, since most developers assume a Microsoft network when designing specialized network anti-virus distribution and remote management software, organizations that haven't wholeheartedly embraced Windows as a server operating system are often forced to introduce home-brewed substitutes.

The network administrator can find many uses for LAN features and functions. These do not necessarily require specialized programs for LAN antiviral protection, although small utility programs might assist an administrator for some uses. Each function requires some level of programming skills, and some features and functions may tax the limits of intermediate-level computer users. However, LAN administration is not for the faint of heart anyway.

So you want to make sure that all copies of your antiviral programs are kept up to date? Well, why not just have one copy? It may be possible to call the antiviral program from the server with a memory-resident program on the workstation. Unfortunately, this approach can be network-intensive.

If you really do need copies on each machine, there are a number of ways to ensure regular updates. A solution could be as simple as invoking a copying process when a user signs on to a client-server LAN. In fact, administrators routinely use such techniques as a fallback for sophisticated self-updating mechanisms that don't always work. Small utility programs could compare file dates, or a copy program might only copy a source to a destination if the destination is older than the source.

If you want to collect all audit or report logs to one location, nothing could be simpler. Invoke the antiviral program from a batch file. The batch file will also create a file noting the workstation, date, and time. You can easily append both the identification file and the report file to a master report file in a central location or server. Generally, this appending requires a simple copy function. If you have any problem creating a master file, you can collect separate files in one directory, or in subdirectories for each workstation.

Many antiviral programs will return one code or error level if they find a virus and another if they don't. You can use these codes to decide whether or not to send a mail message. Voilà! We have an automated virus-alert reporting system that can send a warning to the LAN administrator or to the security specialist. The message can be a simple, "Come look at Larry's machine". Alternatively, the report log generated by the anti-virus program could be written to disk and sent as well. Most LAN email systems write messages as a text file in the first place. The log file can simply be sent as a message every time it is run (similar to the collecting of reports at a central location), or, since you really only want the exception reports, sent only if the "found something" flag has been set.

It may be desirable to check for the presence or activity of resident activity monitors or scanners. The better antiviral packages, which contain resident program components, also contain programs that will check for the background program. You can run these checking programs during login on a client-server network—and log out the workstation user if the checks fail.

Intranet Servers

Generally, an intranet is simply a local or wide area network that makes extensive use of Internet (TCP/IP, Transmission Control Protocol/Internet Protocol) and particularly Web (HTTP, HyperText Transfer Protocol) technologies. Most of the points relating to LANs apply also to intranets.

One additional point should be made: TCP/IP is a layered protocol. For example, web pages may contain many different types of content, transferred by HTTP standards. The HTTP-formatted material may be sent over the network within TCP packets. The TCP packets are probably physically transmitted inside Ethernet packets.

This means that different types of data may be encapsulated inside other types. Therefore, antiviral programs have to be able to analyse material in some depth, particularly if a program is examining material on the fly. As we noted with on-access scanners, the more layered the system, the more likely it is that scanner developers will take shortcuts to avoid slowing down and blocking network traffic.

The most obvious point about an intranet server, though, is that like any other file server, it can contain infective and infected files, irrespective of whether the server itself (or its operating system) is vulnerable to the malware in question. You therefore must protect the server with much the same anti-virus measures as you would a LAN server. The most common intranet platforms are addressed by anti-virus vendors as regards server-hosted solutions.

WAN Protection

LANs and intranets usually are controlled by a single organization. As one progresses into the world of wide area networks (WANs), that control may lessen. WAN links are generally provided by an outside utility, and may in fact be shared among a number of enterprises. Therefore, WANs may entail additional security considerations.

Most of these security vulnerabilities do not relate to virus infection or risk. However, to the extent that outside users communicate with the network, there are additional sources of infected files or objects, and administrators are obliged to take appropriate measures.

Internet Servers

Aside from the problems of a layered network environment, there are few special considerations in protecting an Internet server from virus infection. Arguably, if you have vulnerabilities that allow someone to submit a virus infection to your server, you have far greater security problems than virus infections. But virus infections do happen.

However, you should bear in mind one factor when considering virus protection for your Internet servers. A server will be distributing files and objects to users both within and without your organization. As with any other file server, an Internet server may carry material infected with latent viruses—code to which the server itself may not be susceptible. When you are implementing server-side protection, detection of native viruses is unlikely to be enough. Distributing an infected file can lose you a lot of goodwill. Servers deserve extra protection on the basis that, by providing infected files to outside users and customers, you are advertising that you are not competent to protect yourself and others, and are therefore to be avoided.

Gateway Scanning

The theory is an obvious, and even logical, one: if you want to keep viruses away from the desktop, examine everything before it gets to the desktop. Therefore, if you scan all materials as they come through your gateway to the Internet, you can keep yourself clear of all known viruses.

The idea is certainly attractive. You only have to install antiviral software at a single chokepoint, and it will deal with everything—file viruses, macro viruses, email viruses, and malicious web pages—before anything ever reaches your users. Updating desktop machines becomes less important as long as the scanner at the main entry point is up to date.

Unfortunately, the theory has a couple of problems. Diskettes, while not as important as they used to be, still exist. Viruses can come into the organization on CD-ROMs. And email viruses usually spread so fast that they have run around the world 17 times before anybody has updated a scanner. (For this reason, the question of the location of the scanner to be updated actually becomes academic. But it's still easier to update one gateway scanner than a whole bunch of workstations.) Still, the argument holds that the best single point to protect is the desktop, since it is the intended target of almost all viruses (including boot-sector viruses, which are difficult to detect anywhere else). On the other hand, the stricture against putting all the eggs in one basket also applies. A single-point solution is a single point of failure, so it's best not to think of this as an "either/or" proposition. Two layers are better than one, especially if you use different products at the gateway and at the desktop.

Still, gateway scanning can catch *most* carriers of infection. Nevertheless, you should check a few points before you sign up. Be sure that you know what the system will do when it finds an infection, and be prepared to deal with it. Does the software just alert the administrator? Alert the user? Quarantine the file? Delete it? Just stop working?

Real-time gateway scanners, like all real-time or on-access scanners, take shortcuts in order to increase scanning speed. Remember that detection is a weakness in all such products. Also note the performance itself. Gateway scanners have to check everything that is coming into your LAN or WAN, and you need a box that is big enough and sufficiently powerful to handle the task.

In addition, remember that Internet traffic is encoded, and therefore in a sense encrypted, in a variety of ways. Make sure that scanning accuracy and performance speed remain high when scanning encoded, archived, and compressed materials. The software also needs to handle layers of encoding and nested compressed files. Unless the package can deal with 8-to-7-bit conversions, uuencoding, xxencoding, MIME, base64, zip, arc, arj, lha, and all the other possible file format complications, you need to make stern decisions about quarantining or discarding files that can't be scanned. Otherwise, use your second-line defence at the desktop to plug the gaps.

Firewall Scanning

Firewalls have become the magic word in Internet security to many people. While they are valuable and useful tools, they are not silver bullets. Firewalls are complex and poorly understood utilities (or suites of utilities), requiring constant tuning in order for them to remain effective. Like virus-scanning software, they only protect against known attacks, and not all of those. Like a gateway scanner, they don't protect all vectors.

At its simplest, a firewall looks at where a packet is coming from, where it is going, and what type it is, and then makes a send/trash decision. This type of firewall is generally known as a filtering router. At a higher level, some firewalls examine the packet type and then do additional analysis and negotiation on behalf of the user. This activity is usually referred to as *proxy* or a*pplication service*; the proxy server is interposed between the client and the remote application server. However, the same firewall can maintain both filtering and proxy services.

There are plenty of books on firewalls. The classic is generally thought to be *Firewalls and Internet Security* by William R. Cheswick and Steven M. Bellovin (Addison-Wesley, 1994), but the second edition of *Building Internet Firewalls* by Elizabeth D. Zwicky, Simon Cooper, and D. Brent Chapman (O'Reilly and Associates, 2000), is more thorough and addresses today's technology. In any case, we will not try to write another firewalls text here. We will, however, make two points.

Firewalls, especially proxy firewalls, do perform somewhat the same function as virus scanners (both types of program are essentially filters), so adding the functionality to a firewall does make some sense. However, the analysis done by a firewall is not really the same as the full, byte-by-byte reading of an incoming stream that a scanner does. In principle, a firewall is concerned with scanning packets for source addresses, destination addresses, and port numbers rather than the details of the whole stream. Even simple signature scanning requires that the data stream is identified as a program and that the signature be found in the right place (which implies assumptions about the form of the program). Therefore, adding virus scanning to a firewall may seriously slow performance of the network connection as a whole (this drag on performance is sometimes called *latency*).

In addition, note that firewall scanners are subject to all the same problems and limitations discussed for gateway scanners. Some firewalls (Firewall-1 is a well-known example) can be used with virus scanner plug-ins. Since anti-virus technology at the perimeter works best with store-and-forward technologies (especially email) where the user doesn't notice reasonable latency, some vendors have found it easier to separate the firewall and virus-scanning functions onto separate servers. Sometimes the term *viruswall* is used to describe a firewall-like server that focuses on real-time virus scanning rather than packet filtering, though the term is often associated with one particular vendor's product (Trend Micro). It's also increasingly common to find a third type of server somewhere near the DMZ (de-militarized zone) doing content filtering (for spam, pornographic material, and so on). Generally, an anti-virus product will be plugged in to such a product (MIMEsweeper, for example) rather than the firewall. Recently, we have been encountering the hideous term *contentwall* to describe such products. The complementary functionality of these three types of product enhances security, as long as the servers are sufficiently well specified and the network bandwidth is available.

In recent years, personal firewalls have become popular. These sometimes include some intrusion detection capabilities, as well as packet filtering and filtering by source port. This combination provides some potential defence against backdoor Trojans such as NetBus, Sub7, and similar programs. However, for (fairly) complete protection, most home users use such programs as complements to anti-virus programs, not as substitutes.

Intrusion Detection Systems

The latest hot topic in security is intrusion detection. As with any "next great thing", there are a few good (and some really bad) books on the subject, in this case many with pretty much the same title. Edward G. Amoroso's *Intrusion Detection* (Intrusion.Net Books, 1999) and Rebecca Gurley Bace's *Intrusion Detection* (Pearson Higher Education, 1999) are both excellent, while *Intrusion Detection,* by Terry Escamilla (John Wiley & Sons, 1998), is merely a promotional pamphlet for one commercial product. You might also be interested in some research by SRI International posted at http://www.sdl.sri.com/intrusion/index.html and the IDS FAQ at http://www.sans.org.

Intrusion detection is not firmly nailed down yet as a subject or specialty. However, it shares many of the functional characteristics of activity-monitoring software. It involves collection of data concerning activities, a comparison against known dangerous activities in the past, and some analysis of vulnerability. Still, activity monitors look at files on disk, whereas intrusion detection systems (IDS) are concerned with entire networked systems, so the analysis is considerably different. DDoS attacks and some types of worms/Trojans are often effectively detected in this manner. However, consumers and even IDS specialists are sometimes misled by the use of the term *signature scanning* in IDS and in virus detection into assuming that the technologies are more similar than is actually the case. While further convergence is likely, these are complementary technologies, not alternatives.

Outsourcing

Some Internet service providers are now offering scanning services, (or buying them from third parties) such as MessageLabs. These services are essentially gateway, firewall, or content scanners that operate offsite. Note that everything that applies to the previous sections also applies to these scanners, but there is an extra consideration. You don't get to choose how serious the service providers are about your protection.

Outsourcing is less a matter of an alternative technology than of alternative implementation. However, such attempts to extend virus protection beyond the organizational perimeter, and graft such technologies onto the infrastructure of the Internet itself, are having a noticeable impact on the tracking and detection of viral threats, especially through email.

In addition to outsourcing email security, you can also outsource your complete security requirements. Some companies will do a security analysis for you, and then will undertake all the necessary management to take care of normal security activities.

On the one hand, outsourcing such security elements is a terrifying prospect. Your entire business is in the hands of strangers. They will control you completely. The most basic of management tasks will be completely controlled by an outside firm, and taking that control back, if you find you don't like how the firm manages these tasks, will be extremely difficult, and perhaps impossible.

On the other hand, most companies do not need serious security protection, as evidenced by the fact that most firms currently have almost no security. Hiring security can be very expensive, and it is difficult to judge the expertise of professionals. An outside firm probably has more experience in more areas than you can hope to hire. Nonetheless, we've talked to (and been patronized by) consulting firms whose staff would clearly be more at home with a six-gun and branding iron than a full suite of anti-virus software.

One thing to do before signing a contract with an outsourcing firm is to ensure that you have developed your own security policy. This serves two purposes. First, it ensures that you have decided what level and types of security you want. Second, it will greatly assist in ensuring that you get what you want from the contract you eventually sign, which should make reference to your policy.

Having a policy also helps you to evaluate security firms. If they try to take things out of your policy or sell you on additional points, go back and do the policy process over again, yourself. Under no circumstances should you let the firm that is bidding for the security contract also define the policy.

Summary

By now you should have a clear idea of the basic mechanisms of malicious software technology and of the technology available to counter them. However, knowing what a word processor does is not, in itself, sufficient qualification to write a best-selling novel. Anti-virus software is an essential tool, but doesn't comprise a security architecture.

Clearly, even if you intend to farm out your malware management function to a third party, you will need to understand what that function is before you can evaluate the fitness of that party to exercise it properly. By a remarkable coincidence, that is the subject of the next chapter.

Malware Management

IN THIS CHAPTER:

Defining Malware Management

Cost of Ownership Versus Administration Costs

We'd like to think that our previous chapters have added substantially to the malware-related information available to the systems professional. However, that additional information, although needed by anti-virus professionals and more accurate and/or up-to-date than the information to be found in most books on the subject, is similar in kind to that offered in other works.

This chapter, however, deals with management of viruses and other malware as a formal function, within a formally defined organizational infrastructure, and that perspective is rather more novel. Some client organizations have long been aware of the need to define such a function, but have not necessarily done so successfully, for lack of reliable information.

Various writers have considered parts of that function in some detail—ready-made security policies often include an anti-virus policy, though nonspecialists in the field, even security practitioners in other fields, may mislead by giving advice based on misconceptions. In any case, it is the task of the individual or unit responsible for virus management to apply policies and strategies in a technically sound manner.

Defining Malware Management

Virus management is often seen as (primarily) a desktop issue. Historically, this makes some sense. Most viruses target the desktop in some way, though this is less true in the age of the worm. Furthermore, desktop software was, for a long time, the primary focus of most anti-virus product ranges, and maintenance was often seen as a conceptually simple matter. A secretary's time would be allocated to checking incoming media and to distributing update diskettes to individuals, who would apply the updates themselves.

In fact, the virus/malware problem ranges across several areas: desktop management, LAN management, and Internet/intranet/extranet management, as well as less obvious areas such as human resources management. Thinking of anti-virus protection as a desktop issue because that's where the software is visible to everyday users is as inappropriate as treating UNIX support as a desktop issue because the desktop is where the telnet client is located. However, organizations that don't run to a full-time security team, let alone a dedicated virus management team, increasingly consider malware management a network/systems issue. This is a more practical approach in a modern environment, where most viruses and worms are email-borne rather than diskette-borne, and distribution of anti-virus updates over networks is taken for granted. Clearly, individuals cannot be relied upon to respond appropriately and in a timely fashion to threats spreading in minutes and hours rather than months. Furthermore, the convergence we have already noted between classic virus technology and other forms of malicious code traditionally addressed by security teams and network administrators argues for a corresponding functional consolidation.

However, grafting the anti-malware function onto the normal network and systems management functions (even when seriously focused on other aspects of security) is insufficient. Instead, by regarding and defining the malware problem globally, we can work towards holistic solutions that cross boundaries within the organization. This approach is much more reliable than concentrating on the piecemeal relief of individual symptoms. We can best achieve a global definition by considering the anti-virus management function independently of assumptions about who is responsible and where those responsible are situated in the infrastructure. Only then is it practical for the individual manager to consider how to apply that functionality within the security architecture of an individual organization.

Security literature has insufficiently analysed what constitutes a comprehensive malware-management function. General security books rarely consider it at all: they assume anti-virus management to be a matter of (somehow) distributing the software and running it (sometime) to check incoming media or to remove an infected file.

NOTE

Security books almost invariably assume that virus outbreaks are associated with parasitic file viruses, even though historically the most widespread viruses have tended to be boot-sector viruses, macro viruses, and worms, which are not necessarily parasitic.

Specialist anti-virus books (even the competent and fairly current ones) tend to focus on technology rather than strategy, and are often vendor-oriented. We would prefer you to think of malware management as a vendor-independent, enterprise-wide element of the organizational infrastructure. Anti-virus vendors usually fail to address certain significant aspects of malware management, while others require more than an out-of-the-box solution. An individual or team with appropriate expertise and experience must tailor any solution to the needs and attributes of the client organization, irrespective of whether the individual or team works for the client organization, an anti-virus vendor, or a third-party consultant.

Management of viruses and other malicious software can be divided into two main areas: proactive measures and reactive incident management.

Proactive Management

Proactive management includes three main areas: strategy, systems and network administration, and development.

Strategy

The strategic subfunction can be further subdivided into a number of areas:

- ▶ Information gathering
- ▶ Risk analysis
- ▶ Formulation and implementation of standards, policies, and guidelines
- ▶ Education and training
- ▶ Integration of malware management into the IT infrastructure

Information Gathering and Risk Analysis   The broad principles of the analysis-audit feedback cycle are well known and well documented in terms of general security, and we don't intend to consider them at length. The basic principle is to consider the current security status of the organization (*security audit*). This match ignites a fiery cascade of documentation: business impact analysis, security policy, security plan, disaster recovery plan, another security audit, and back round the loop (perhaps we should say Catherine Wheel).

Risk analysis in the malware management field tends, historically, to be threat-oriented. You compile a list of possible attacks, and then assess the system's degree of exposure and vulnerability to each. The main drawback to this approach in the virus context is that it's better at assessing vulnerability to known risks than to unknown risks. As we've seen with macro viruses, DDoS attacks, and email-borne worms, a hitherto unnoticed or insufficiently anticipated loophole may take months or even years to block completely.

Mission-oriented risk analysis is more generic: instead of compiling a list of specific attacks, the analyst examines systems for potential loopholes (*security fault analysis*). Threat analysis examines the capability of a potential attacker to succeed with an attack. Risk reduction aims to ameliorate the exposure to weaknesses identified by the preceding analyses, while security evaluation provides a metric for testing the effectiveness of implemented measures.

Risk analysis in this context is concerned with assessing the likelihood of security breaches and their possible impact on the business if and when they do happen.

Information gathering is a more general, less formal term, and may include risk analysis. It includes such exercises as keeping up with trends in malware and anti-malware technology, strategic and tactical thinking, market trends, legal requirements and other external standards, and product certification status. Tracking such product data actually constitutes the preliminary stage of product evaluation. However, keeping up with anti-malware technology is by no means the same as keeping up with the market. Sometimes a vendor's marketing department makes claims that outstrip the capabilities of the product, or even its readiness for shipping. Information resources for tracking these data are considered in Chapter 8.

Most organizations keep particular watch on products for which they have a current licence. The scope and functionality of a given utility may (in fact certainly will) change, for reasons including the following:

▶ Features are added or removed. For instance, over the last few years, some products based primarily on a known-virus scanner have moved away from providing additional generic tools such as change detectors, behaviour blockers, behaviour monitors, and goat files. On the other hand, they have added other features such as on-access scanning, recursive scanning of compressed files, macro heuristics, disinfection of infected files, and other features we'll consider in more detail when we discuss product evaluation in depth.

▶ Older platforms or configurations are no longer supported. Examples of such platforms include Windows 286, PC/XTs, and Novell 3.*x* and earlier.

▶ Products are removed from or added to a product range. Linux scanners are increasing in popularity, while DOS scanners and Mac scanners that support 68*xxx* processors and Mac OS 6.*x* are hard to find.

▶ Anti-virus professionals who regularly evaluate anti-malware programs probably do so at intervals roughly coincident with the expiry of current licence arrangements. Some reevaluate a program only when extreme circumstances, such as the withdrawal of a core product or inability to meet service levels, force them to do so. Lazy evaluators obtain a number of pseudo-benefits, such as: the avoidance of financial and opportunity costs of regular or rolling (continuous) evaluation, deinstallation of obsolete software, and installation of new products.

▶ A more stable environment (as long as the virus software does work) that doesn't require rejigging of system policies, configuration, and user training.

▶ Larger discounts to encourage brand loyalty.

However, reevaluating only when inertia is no longer enough entails trusting the good faith of the vendor and its competence in fields such as development and maintenance. Development competence is reflected by the vendor's proficiency at meeting new types of threats. Maintenance competence is reflected by such features as regular definitions updates that meet all current threats, and support of older configurations and platforms.

Vendors often emphasize their timely response to new viruses. Where once they offered quarterly or (at extra cost) monthly updates, they may now offer weekly, daily, or even hourly definitions updates, or simply provide updates as often as they are needed. Responding in a timely manner matters when a new virus or variant, especially a destructive one, suddenly becomes widespread through distribution via newsgroups and mailing lists, for instance. While someone has to be the first to be hit by a new "In The Wild" virus, a good and up-to-date anti-virus product, safe computing practices, and a closely monitored global early-warning system can combine to restrict the impact of incoming viruses. Indeed, many administrators are now becoming as reliant on generic blocking of suggestive filenames such as badfile.jpg.vbs or "badfile.txt   .exe", and on formal or informal information exchange networks such as AVIEN (http://www.avien.org/), as they are on vendor information distribution and timely updates.

However, the appearance of a new type of threat can expose computer users to malicious code known to be already In the Wild while vendor labs put together safe and effective approaches to deal with the code. Informed system administrators were aware of the macro virus problem almost as soon as WM/Concept appeared. Some people inside and outside the security industry were aware of the potential for such an attack long before that first successful "data" virus. However, it took some time (and reverse engineering) before vendors were able to implement effective scanning of the complex and sparsely documented Microsoft Office file formats.

The appearance of seriously polymorphic viruses seems to have been a significant factor in the disappearance of some anti-virus products from the market, while the AutoStart worm had a similar effect on Macintosh packages. System administrators (or, in our terminology, malware managers) were for a while reliant upon home-brewed WordBasic and Visual Basic for Applications (VBA) solutions, such as disabling auto macros and filtering generically for the presence of all macros.

The problem is not only with the varying reaction times of vendors, though, but with the perceptions of consumers. The "Viruses & the Mac" FAQ in Appendix B was written to raise awareness of the cross-platform potential of the macro virus problem. It has been six years since the appearance of the first In the Wild Word macro virus and the warnings that such viruses operated across operating systems, yet we still find Mac users who don't realize that their chosen platform is not invulnerable. Now, however, they are also confused by the differences between Visual Basic scripts (to which they are not generally vulnerable) and VBA macros (to which they may be). Vendors must bear some responsibility for these phenomena: marketing departments are much better at talking about strengths than weaknesses, and products are inconsistent in the range of threats they detect (especially across platforms). However, customers are (despite the frequently voiced suspicion that anti-virus vendors write most viruses) often inclined to believe that the vendor knows best. Furthermore, there's often a wide divergence between the ethically and technically informed observations of anti-virus researchers and the pronouncements of the marketing department.

NOTE

Curiously, some computer users go to the opposite extreme, and trust the virus writer before the vendor. Some virus writers and distributors have noted this tendency with glee, pointing out that it is not they who benefit financially from their creations, but the vendors. This view seems to go hand in hand with the self-image of virus writers as performing a public service by educating their victims. But that's enough surrealism for one note.

Policies, Standards, and Guidelines   There is considerable disagreement on how useful policy documents are, depending on the environment. Even when ignored by staff and management alike, these documents define and, in a sense, underpin the whole anti-malware strategy. How effectively and enthusiastically they are accepted and implemented determines how successful they are in practice. However, the formulation process, by defining the aims of the organization, is an important milestone on the road to implementing a security architecture.

Policies define what is to be protected (and why), and define the responsibilities of concerned parties. While the fine detail of malware-related policies is considered in Chapter 11, areas of concern might include the following:

▶ General security policy (anti-virus/anti-malware policies should not be confused with general security policies, but shouldn't be held in isolation, either)

▶ Anti-virus/anti-malware policy

▶ Acceptable use of computing resources

▶ Acceptable use of networking resources

▶ Acceptable use of the Internet

Standards define platform-independent codes of practice and provide a means of measuring performance. They may evolve in response to the need for conformance with internal policies, external standards, and certification processes (ISO 9000 and ISO 7799, for instance). They also respond to the requirements of legislation, such as data protection legislation and laws relating to computer system and network abuse.

Guidelines define how standards are implemented in specific environments.

> **NOTE**
>
> *Policies, standards, and guidelines (however their content is defined) should be sensibly integrated into a properly maintained document tree (a structured body of documents classified by function and appropriately cross-referenced—in some organizations the term* document library *is preferred). At the same time, it has to be emphasized that documentation is a foundation, not a complete building.*

Education, Training, and Information Provision   Education generally takes two main directions:

- ▶ It provides necessary information (urgent alerts, policies, information on procedures and protocols, etc.).

- ▶ It offers training, which may range from general user education in "practising safe hex" (through broad training in remote diagnosis for front-line support staff, and strict hygienic practices for engineers) to specialized training for individuals, or, in larger organizations, for response teams involved with incident management.

Part of the malware management function is not only to keep abreast of malware and anti-malware technology (self-education), but also to arrange internal and external training and information flow. This function may include authoring and delivering in-house courses, arranging third-party training, outsourcing educational services, and so on. Particular targets may include IT support staff, Help Desk staff, dedicated response teams, and management (inside and outside the IT department).

> **NOTE**
>
> *If you can get the message over to the Board of Directors, educating users is a cinch. In fact, you might want to consider exploiting your gifts in other fields, such as herding cats and nailing jelly to walls.*

Other channels for disseminating information may include online services such as mailing lists and the intranet, hardcopy documentation, and in-house periodicals. An established and coherent document tree, available across the whole organization, is an instrument not only of disseminating information, but of enforcing policies such as:

- ▶ Desktop anti-malware policies and configuration
- ▶ Network anti-malware policies and configuration
- ▶ Acceptable use of Internet resources such as the Web, email, and chat

Systems and Network Administration

Responsibility for virus management is often a subfunction of system security in general. This subfunction is inevitably part of a system manager's job description. There is no absolute boundary between systems administration and system security. Tying together desktop administration, network administration, and systems administration is correct in principle, but often breaks down in practice in the security area, especially in the rather specialized area of virus management.

A UNIX administrator, for instance, may and should be well acquainted with issues relating to maintaining system and file integrity on servers. However, working within a comparatively virus-free environment may blind an administrator to the perils of latent viruses. As we've already pointed out, a UNIX box used as an ftp or HTTP server may be a channel for secondary infection through files including code that can't execute at all under UNIX. NT administrators are also at risk of underestimating the direct and indirect vulnerabilities associated with their chosen platform.

Anti-virus/anti-malware tasks tend to be divorced from the mainstream of security, and the same terminology can be applied quite differently according to context. The worms detected by some PC or Mac desktop software are by no means the same threat as was posed by the Internet Worm. An enthusiastic advocate of intrusion detection and a virus management specialist may be talking about two very different phenomena when they talk about signatures. The term *Trojan horse* in the context of multi-user systems has largely been associated with password stealing. In the context of desktop machines, the emphasis has tended to be on programs that trash disks or file systems. This is not to deny that threats against both confidentiality and availability may be encountered in both contexts.

The administrator should be aware of a number of considerations relative to virus management:

▶ The need to protect server-side systems and applications from direct infection.

▶ The need to protect shared files/directories from direct infection.

▶ The need to protect against latent viruses—that is, preventing inadvertent distribution by protecting ftp servers, intranet servers, shared network volumes, and other services against malicious software that cannot activate on the server platform. These considerations must take into account both inbound and outbound situations.

These listed factors may point to a need to establish communication between disparate units. For instance, where virus management is seen as a desktop issue, the latent virus issue may be missed altogether, because no one has the authority, responsibility, or even the technical overview to come to the right conclusions and act accordingly.

Virus management comes within the domain of conventional systems administration (or overlaps with it) because of the need to address such issues as:

▶ Limiting sharing of files (and therefore of file-infecting viruses—in this instance, we can regard macro viruses as a special case of file infection) through access control.

▶ Limiting transitivity through access control—that is, reducing spread by reducing the possible routes by which a virus can fan out.

Clearly, the principle of least privilege applies, by which the administrator assigns the lowest possible level of privileged access to all account holders. By "the lowest possible level", we mean the lowest level compatible with the requirements of each user's job. For example, an account holder who needs to read shared data files may not need to be able to modify or delete those files, and will be given read-only permissions. In general, only systems administrators and operators need write access to shared applications, and even then, good practice is to use a privileged account only when specifically logging on to do systems work. This principle has a direct consequence in the anti-virus context: if an infected account holder doesn't have write access, neither does the virus. Thus, the administration of user and group policies and user authentication through passwords has a direct influence on the system's susceptibility to virus infection.

NOTE

Restriction of privilege can have an adverse impact on automation and transparency. For example, making objects in Microsoft Office read/execute only will increase the need for education on how to answer prompts that result, since MS Office modifies various program files that traditionally shouldn't require write permission. We should therefore stress the necessity to determine and review appropriate levels of access control—being aware that they may have residual effects in some applications.

The anti-virus administrator's sphere of responsibility within the organization extends far beyond the desktop and workgroup to the LAN file server, internal ftp server, intranet web server, and internal mail services. Looking beyond the perimeter, probably no anti-virus professional in the 21st century can afford to ignore Internet mail services, inbound or outbound. An outbound virus may harm the organization's reputation more than an inbound virus harms the organization's data. The problem is not only with outbound infected messages, but also outbound traffic resulting from the infection—such as LoveLetter's attempt to connect to an outside resource and send information to remote locations. While rebroadcasting a virus is not inherently embarrassing, it does expose and publicize the company's vulnerability to outsiders. It may also provide a method to come back into the enterprise network through a backdoor (as allegedly occurred with a recent server at Microsoft). Only administrators with absolute confidence in their desktop product and in the adherence of their customers to safe computing guidelines can afford not to protect the mail gateway.

Other Internet and extranet services also pose risks. Most organizations are both consumers and providers of SMTP (mail), ftp (file transfer), and HTTP (Web) services, and possibly others such as chat and NNTP (USENET), so malicious code can go out as readily as it can come in. The malware manager may not have control over content on web servers and the like, but needs to be in close contact with those who do. Even if the manager has no control, he or she may be able to force some comparisons between known correct web content versus the current state of web content, to detect unauthorized or inappropriate modifications.

Defence in depth entails the use of mix-and-match anti-malware measures, integration of different technologies such as intrusion detection, on-access and on-demand virus scanning, and content analysis, and use of similar software at different locations. It may also entail the use of more than one product line performing the same essential function. We address the issues of best practice and multilayered protection in Chapter 11.

Nor is this the only area in which malware management overlaps with other aspects of security. The association of virus infection with pirated software has been overstated, but exists nonetheless. Regulation through policy and by technical means of software auditing and metering lessens the associated risks.

Business continuity plans (BCPs) or disaster recovery plans (DRPs) may have to take into account the specialized risks associated with the action of malicious software. A BCP starts off from the list of possible scenarios brought to light by risk/business impact analysis, and allocates operational and administrative responsibility for dealing with those scenarios if they arise. Operational issues include, for instance, working through predefined protocols such as traversing a telephone tree, with each node being a person or unit with a need to know. Administration issues include such factors as relocation, insurance, replacement kits, and data restoration or re-creation. The latter may be of particular importance where malware has resulted in the loss (or, worse, gradual corruption) of data. Clearly, simple restoration from the most recent backup will not suffice if a slow-burning data diddler is known to have left its footprints.

> *NOTE*
>
> Data diddling *is a term commonly applied to the unauthorized alteration of data. We regard this as being of particular concern when the diddling consists of long-term, inconspicuous, and often random modifications, because of the difficulty of returning the data to a pre-diddled state.*

Most viruses (but not all malware) target the desktop. Historically, the priority has been to protect the desktop, despite the difficulties of updating, distribution, and maintenance. Gateway protection has long been regarded as a highly effective supplementary defence for an organization that can afford the extra software and the performance overheads. (The better the network and hardware specifications, the less that cost and overhead are issues.) However, this supplementary defence can't be a complete substitute for desktop protection. After all, a high proportion of malware still gains access via removable media. Other danger areas include:

▶ Sharks in the modem pool (any modem connection, even a corporate dial-in or dial-back connection, is likely to constitute a hole in the firewall)

▶ Home machines with concurrent connections to other providers whose security is an unknown quantity

▶ Web-hosted email, such as Hotmail

▶ File/disk transfer between office and home, where home may also involve files/media traded with school, friends, or other businesses

▶ Special risks associated with road warriors, whose systems may rely on intermittent direct connection to the corporate network for anti-virus updates, and may be connected to all sorts of unsafe systems when away from the office

Server protection is an extension of desktop protection as well as a server-side issue. If installed and configured appropriately, it can offer early warning of desktop problems on specific systems, and a tool for distribution of updates (for example, through login scripts). You can still install, distribute, and update anti-virus and anti-malware software by performing one-to-one installations to individual desktops. However, most modern organizations can perform these tasks more efficiently by using the network as a channel for distribution from a central resource, using pull, push, or hybrid distribution models, such as the following:

▶ Email

▶ Snailmail (remote units, home workers)

▶ Pull from a central repository (ftp, HTTP, and automated mail list)

▶ Push from a central repository using remote administration software (provided by the vendor specifically for anti-virus administration, or by a third party for a variety of remote administration tasks)

▶ Update from login scripts

▶ Remote management systems

▶ Pull from an external source, such as a vendor's web site or bulletin board

▶ Push from an external source, such as a vendor's update mailing list

Development

Many organizations do not do a hands-on evaluation of anti-malware software. Instead, they rely on third-party reports from consultants and comparative reviews in magazines to feed their initial short list. Such organizations then filter the final candidates by selecting a product based on criteria such as market share and cost. Clearly, this isn't what we mean by development.

Hands-on evaluation can range from skimming the manuals to conducting configuration testing with limited detection testing, perhaps using the EICAR test file or a virus collection. We will discuss detection testing in Chapter 9, and will note here that large-scale detection testing is not necessarily the best practice. As Bruce Burrell remarked in a 1997 Virus Bulletin conference paper, "...testing is not for general users: it should be done by trained anti-virus professionals". To this statement we would add that there is also a need for a fully resourced test environment, resembling but insulated from live production systems.

All but the largest corporate institutions tend to regard malware management as a fairly low-grade occupation and resent engineers spending time on such issues that they could instead spend changing printer cartridges. Comparison of installation and update rollouts, as practiced by anti-virus vendors with an outsourcing service and as practiced by corporations in-house, indicates quite a different sense of priorities. Vendors are sensitive to the constraints of an accelerated development cycle, since they may have to produce stable definitions files, patches, or recompiled executables with a frequency and regularity inconceivable in other areas of software development. Long beta programs are strictly reserved for new products and major upgrades. Minor updates and patches might be released monthly, weekly, or even more frequently, and vendors are often painfully aware of the fragility of their current product. Perhaps for this reason, they tend to favour a protracted testing phase when they actually roll out an upgrade or update on a customer's site. Customers who do their own rollouts, on the other hand, usually have more faith in the stability of their chosen product, and are happier to take shortcuts. It's surprising that more disasters don't occur, considering how often a product is supposed to "just work". In fact, in a sane environment, development should be an ongoing process. The following list summarizes the elements of the development function:

- ▶ Product evaluation
- ▶ Configuration testing (ease of installation, configuration, and removal)
- ▶ Function testing
- ▶ Performance testing (detection rates, transparency)
- ▶ Installation/rollout/update testing
- ▶ Pilot schemes
- ▶ Compatibility testing
- ▶ Incident management testing
- ▶ Investigating and meeting threats that the market doesn't yet address

Reactive Management

Reactive management of malicious software is essentially incident management—firefighting, in a word, from the logging of a problem with the Help Desk, through identification of the nature of the problem as malware-related, to taking appropriate remedial action and post-traumatic documentation. Thus, reactive management of a problem may include implementing proactive measures (technical, administrative, and educational) to prepare for the next problem, building on experience.

Incident Management

The precise meaning of "appropriate" might vary widely, according to the nature of the incident. An incident might be a hoax alert, a known threat identified at the point of entry and before the malicious code can be executed, a known threat identified post-traumatically, or a completely new threat. The last case presents particular problems in identifying the nature of the threat and taking the necessary countermeasures. A threat that uses a previously unexploited loophole and doesn't broadcast its presence too soon with a conspicuous symptom may evade discovery for many weeks.

The incident management function can be split into many steps:

- ▶ Reporting and logging an incident, and allocating it to the appropriate team or individual.
- ▶ Confirming the existence of a virus, Trojan horse, or other threat, if necessary by submitting samples to a vendor or other research facility.

► Disinfecting a virus, where practical, or removing an infective or otherwise malicious object.

► Dealing with direct damage where malicious code has been executed before diagnosis.

► Recovering damaged files or file systems.

► Backing up or restoring data when recovery by repair is unfeasible.

► Handling forensic issues—finding the breach that allowed the incident, and taking appropriate action to plug it. This may include punitive action against individuals, though we don't recommend punishing the victim as a morale-building exercise.

► Dealing with the direct actions (damaging or otherwise) of the virus payload or infection mechanism; for example, installing scripts that will collect possibly confidential data, or information about vulnerabilites and potential entry points, and send it to remote locations. Understandably, users really want to perform a single point of detection/repair. Sadly, this is no longer enough. Incident management and response require more than using an anti-virus product and backup media. They might entail putting in outbound blocks at the firewall/router, monitoring for access to specific sites as indications of infections, and looking for, altering, or removing ancillary files and system/registry entries that the malware's own installation process may install or modify.

► Advising sources of infection that they have a virus problem, and alerting those to whom the infection may have fanned out subsequently that they, too, may have a virus problem.

► Alleviating secondary damage (limiting damage).

► Discouraging panic responses and inappropriate measures.

► Discouraging damage to morale, such as scapegoating of victims.

► Addressing external fan-out of infection risks that might harm corporate goodwill and damage the organization's reputation, or even inspire litigation. The malware manager must either try to reverse the effects, or put the matter into the hands of those who are better able to limit the damage, whether the effort requires simple public relations, legal, or technical measures.

After recovery, the next stage is assessment. What lessons has the organization learned, and can it avert a similar situation in the future by blocking an entry point or reconfiguring malware-management software? Finally, the incident documentation is completed. This may simply be a matter of signing off a trouble ticket from the Help

Desk. Sometimes it may entail a one-off report to a line manager or someone further up the management hierarchy. Often it will involve adding an entry to a database, for use in the compilation of subsequent routine reports. Metrics are important here when you are asked to provide expanded incident logging information. How can you tell if your AV product or your other efforts are working if you don't record some basic metrics about the situation, such as point of detection, file loss, time expended, and financial impacts?

Incident management isn't always so dramatic, of course. Characteristically, it often involves dealing with false alarms and hoaxes, but the basic steps will be much the same. Indeed, the damage from an uncontrolled hoax may be far greater than that from an initially undetected but comparatively mild virus attack.

> **NOTE**
>
> *Incident management, of course, has a proactive dimension, in that the better you design your incident management initiative, the more effective it's likely to be—although that effectiveness is likely to derive in part from (often painful) experience.*

You need to ask a number of questions when designing incident management protocols:

- ▶ How are problems reported?
- ▶ Who deals with them?
- ▶ How do first- and second-line support staff interact?
- ▶ Who signs off a completed job?
- ▶ How are statistics maintained?

Cost of Ownership Versus Administration Costs

The functions and subfunctions described in the preceding section do not have to be the sole province of one individual. In a large organization, some sharing of routine tasks among teams is inevitable, and indeed desirable. Nevertheless, effective incident management demands expertise, authority, and resources (a sufficiency of finance and manpower) in proportion to the size of the organization and the vulnerability of its systems.

Administering anti-malware technology can be seen as a series of attempts to strike a balance between conflicting factors, such as the following:

- ▶ Cost of potential damage versus cost of ownership of the software
- ▶ Functionality versus transparency
- ▶ Bandwidth versus ease of administration

Cost of ownership is rather conspicuous—it's hard to pass off anti-malware precautions as anything but a cost centre. The accounts ledger shows money going out to the vendors, but no incoming revenue.

Metrics can be crucial for showing trends, potential improvements or reductions in exposure versus infections, and the like—but only if you have metrics before, during, and after implementations of new processes and products. Metrics can then help quantify prevention of damage when compared to incidents that occurred prior to a certain set of implemented processes or products.

Potential damage defies quantification: the more successful an anti-malware strategy is, the less there is to show for it. Indeed, anti-virus vendors currently seem to find that total transparency is a particularly saleable concept. As we've seen, though, transparency is illusory unless you have complete confidence in the ability of your chosen software to handle all eventualities appropriately. Sadly, we have never quite managed that leap of faith. The alternative is to accept one of a number of compromises:

▶ Trust the software and live with its deficiencies, repairing them as best you can after the event.

▶ Be sceptical. Test at the evaluation stage, test before the rollout, and keep testing throughout the life cycle of the software. Live with the cost of scepticism, and hope you can justify the cost by pointing to occasions where caution has forestalled a crisis.

▶ Trust but verify. Test at evaluation and rollout, and test regularly but not obsessively afterwards (unless you really have no other calls on your time).

▶ Hope that something doesn't go drastically wrong at a time when you're looking the other way.

Testing is crucial; experience shows that while a deployment scheme may work in the lab and in pilot tests, it may not work on all systems at all times—typically failing during an important update. It's not unusual—or unreasonable—to undertake random checks of the desktops and other systems to see if the protection status and configurations are in place as they are intended to be. It is not uncommon for automated deployment schemes to be thwarted by users who have their computers powered off during a crucial update. Sometimes the users may not log off, causing login script–based updates to be left in a hibernation state of sorts. Recently we came across an instance where a LAN server scanner could not be updated: an unprivileged user's zombie process had a lock on the on-access component, so attempting to replace it resulted in a sharing violation. Assuming that all systems will be in the state to which they are automatically updated leads to a false sense of security.

Hopefully, one of these compromise positions will result in a comparatively transparent experience for the everyday user, but will tend to be at the expense of the administrator's enhanced need for therapy. Maintaining transparency is often an administrative nightmare. Bulletin boards, newsgroups, and mailing lists dealing with these issues often feature posts from computer users who assert that their chosen product is the best because they've used it since the fall of Troy and have never had a virus. Realistically, these users' *belief* that they have never had a virus doesn't necessarily mean that they actually have not had a virus. It simply means that the user's product has not detected any virus. This could be because there's never been a virus, but it could also be because the product is:

▶ Obsolete or otherwise useless, and can't detect any of the viruses that *have* come a-calling

▶ Misconfigured and can't actually detect *anything*

▶ Configured to disinfect any visiting virus automatically, without making any attempt to notify the user except to write to a log file that no one ever inspects because no one knows that it exists

The last possibility may be the most preferable, but it's far from ideal, and begs a number of questions. Does the product dependably identify malware? Does it disinfect properly? How does it deal with overwriting viruses, Trojan horses, or jokes? Is it generating false alarms and removing or corrupting innocent files? How well does it cope with standard types of file encryption? Answering these questions is the responsibility of the hapless individual who fulfils the malware management function. However, you can gather such information only if you are actively monitoring the situation and collecting metrics by checking log files, Help Desk trouble tickets, and so on. These measures are time-consuming to evaluate, implement, and maintain, and resource costs may be prohibitive in smaller organizations.

Absolute transparency is fine for products in which the malware manager has absolute trust. A more useful aim is moderate transparency for the user, but not necessarily for the malware manager. At the very least, the malware manager may need a record of what has been dealt with so as to have statistics on hand to help justify the budget impact next time the licence is due for renewal. The manager may well be prepared to trade off some transparency for the user against enhanced ability to track incidents, or to intervene where an automated response may not be appropriate: a viral infection that can't be repaired by a given scanner, for instance, or by any scanner, or that could be misrepaired through misidentification. There are also issues that the anti-malware product may not be able to address, such as residual changes to system configuration (for example, disabling of macro protection), additional scripts or files that may be installed, and so on.

Nonreplicative malware and borderline cases such as test files and joke programs can cause particular difficulties in terms of identification. The same program may be defined as a utility or as malware according to context. A disk format is, in a sense, destructive only if it's not what the user intended, and even then it may be the result of accident or misunderstanding rather than malice. Implementing a heuristic to detect possibly destructive behaviour, such as attempting a track format or zeroing a FAT entry, is trivial compared to recognizing whether a program that implements such behaviour is intentionally malicious. Setting appropriate default actions on detection is not necessarily straightforward, either, especially if some form of heuristic analysis is in use:

▶ The Ignore setting is obviously unsafe.

▶ The Alert Only setting is neither transparent nor safe.

▶ Alert and block execution is obtrusive.

▶ The Delete setting is obtrusive and may be seriously inappropriate, depending on the prevailing corporate culture.

While this chapter focuses primarily on malware management and especially virus management, malware and viruses are only part of the problem. Many other applications of content analysis and filtering resist complete automation: these include intrusion detection, spam control, monitoring for illegal or unethical content such as pornography or copyrighted material, and hoax management.

As the virus total rises ceaselessly, the issue of detection impacting on performance continues to preoccupy both users and vendors. Over time, user dissatisfaction with processing overhead has prompted vendors to devote development resources to the reduction of scanning speed and footprint in memory. This is a significant challenge, given the need to detect an ever-increasing range of threats, accessing a widening range of vulnerabilities.

The trend away from routine (scheduled) use of on-demand scanners and towards checking files as they're accessed indicates the need to distribute the processing load and reduce the visible impact on system performance as a whole. Anti-virus suites have, in the past, incorporated a wide range of measures. These may include not only a mixture of known virus scanners (nowadays normally including heuristic analysis for detection of unknown viruses), but also some form of integrity checking. They might also include supplementary tools such as disk editors, bait files, drivers to counterfeit write protection for fixed disks, diskette authentication, and so on. Many of these tools are no longer supplied. In some cases, such tools may be omitted because they're no longer seen as universally safe and effective. Others may be unavailable because there appears to be no particular demand for them in a market that favours more automation or third-party intervention rather than users applying a primarily hands-on approach to virus management.

Are we swimming against the flow by advocating a hands-on approach? While management, vendors, and the media are trying to turn anti-virus into a consumer product, administrators are gritting their teeth and accepting the need to learn the malware management job, since no one else is going to do it properly.

There is a serious shortage of quality data in the anti-virus/anti-malware area. Anti-malware professionals spend a lot of time dealing with "what everyone knows". How well do we measure what we are dealing with? There is a considerable emphasis on quantitative data, which is notoriously hard to gather in the security field. Anti-virus administrators outside large organizations are still likely to have low status unless they're general security people (in which case they may be less virus-literate than their job status might indicate). They don't necessarily have access to sufficient information and resources to offer accurate quantitative data, even if they have the expertise (in malware management and statistics).

What does the everyday customer really want from his or her anti-malware software, and how can the customer (or the periodicals he or she reads) usefully evaluate packages individually or comparatively? Are the methodologies used currently in anti-virus testing applicable to other types of malware?

There's an accepted need for certification of anti-virus and other security software such as firewalls and intrusion detection systems. It's possible for the individual who uses that software to get professional security certification or a higher degree in security, but anti-virus training is somewhat restricted. A few vendors run fairly short workshops—unsurprisingly, they are focused on the products of the vendor running the workshop. Security organizations such as SANS have started to introduce "independent" certification standards for virus management, but still focus on the one or two products with the highest profile and market share. In any case, an organization whose orientation is towards general security may not be best qualified to understand and teach anti-virus management, and we look forward to seeing more real, independent experts give the instant experts a run for their money.

Summary

Concerns with malicious software have increased in scope from classic boot-sector viruses, file viruses, and simple Trojan horses. Recent preoccupations include provider-specific password stealers (especially AOL Trojans), IRC worms, macro viruses and Trojans, scripting viruses, and email-borne worms. Computing platforms requiring protection have changed, too—not just workstation desktops and servers, but mail gateways and firewalls as well—to take into account a proliferation of Internet-related protocols and transmission media.

Administrators are required to provide protection not only from a few hundred viruses known to be formally In the Wild, or the many thousand others that might get lucky, but also from a whole range of other threats. Vendors don't necessarily see these threats as their problem, since they involve technologies presenting quite different technical challenges: spam, intrusion detection, and content analysis for blocking incoming undesirable material or outgoing sensitive data. Consequently, it becomes the malware manager's responsibility to develop strategy and policy, evaluate product, plan and implement rollout, integrate disparate technologies, and plug the gaps that technology can't reach. If this is your role, you need reliable information. In the next chapter, we consider the question of where to find it, and how to assess its value.

Information Gathering

IN THIS CHAPTER:

How Can I Check Whether
Advice Is Genuine or Useful?

Books

Articles and Papers

Online Resources

We have dedicated quite enough space in this book to presenting ourselves as the founts of all viral wisdom. What makes us so smart? As usual, listening to other people.

The listings in this chapter collect sources that we have gathered over the years, and still use today. These are the books, articles, and online sources that you can use to go beyond what we've told you here, and to keep up with the field as it moves beyond the current state.

Organization of this chapter has been a bit of a problem, since the different types of resources don't seem to fit into any of the same categories. Therefore, we present books, then articles and papers, then online resources, arranged as seems suitable within those groups.

We've already indicated that information gathering is an important part of risk assessment and of the malware management function generally. Good information comes from dependable sources. What are good and bad sources? As with most of life, if you can tell good advice from bad advice, you probably don't need any advice. Good judgment, of resources in this case, comes from experience.

Experience, unfortunately, often comes from bad judgment.

How Can I Check Whether Advice Is Genuine or Useful?

Check with an expert. Unfortunately, this isn't as easy as it sounds: everyone is a virus expert. Rob Rosenberger's writing on "False Authority Syndrome" should be required reading for all computer professionals (among others):

> http://www.vmyths.com/fas/fas1.cfm

We have already railed against "instant experts" in this book, and probably often enough that you are beginning to be sick of reading the term. We should, however, address some of the other authorities that people tend to rely on for advice about virus problems and protection. Most of these specialists aren't.

Managers have to pay attention to everything, and can't afford to spend a lot of time on a particularly arcane topic within a specialty in a technical subject that may be only dimly related to the business objective they are supposed to be trying to accomplish. The staff on the Help Desk are run off their feet trying to keep everyone working, and have very little time to educate themselves on side issues. Computer journalists must produce a given number of words on a variety of issues every day, week, or month, and can't devote hours to investigating every issue. Consultants, in our hard-driving, fast-paced, high-energy world, have to sell all the time, and, in all too many cases, sales are more important than knowledge. Computer vendors, even of antiviral products, must similarly concentrate on market share even at the expense of accuracy, or they don't remain vendors for long. Fame is seldom based on erudition, and many a distinguished name in the technical field has made foolish statements in regard to viruses. Retail and repair shops are busy places run on thin margins—a number have become virus vectors without realizing it. And just because someone was once hit by one virus does not mean that he or she has any real knowledge of the rest of the genre.

There is one final population that we should mention, and that is the one consisting of legitimate security experts. Leaving aside the great many consultants who are little more than salespeople, there are those hard-working and knowledgeable souls who spend years educating themselves in the security specialty. They need to know about security management, access control, law and investigation, physical security, business continuity and disaster recovery, security architecture, cryptography, telecommunications and networking, application and systems development, and operations security. Those who are in the field will recognize this list as the ten domains that the (ISC)² (International Information Systems Security Certification Consortium, Inc.) describes in preparing the CISSP (Certified Information Systems Security Professional) examinations. Each one of these fields is a specialty in and of itself. You will notice that viruses don't appear on the list as such. (There is a brief mention of them in one domain—and it probably isn't the one you're thinking it is.)

Most real security experts come from backgrounds in corporate management, mainframe computing environments, network management, physical security, or accounting. (Yes, accounting. For some reason, businesspeople think that someone with the skills to audit financial statements can also audit computer systems.) Security workers obviously try to broaden their horizons and keep up with everything they can, but the task of following any single one of these fields is enormous, and companies generally see security as some kind of cost, with little or no benefit to the enterprise. Therefore, experts have very limited time to study, and actually can pursue only the most important areas in the field. To date, most people have not considered viruses to be a vital area of concern. Security experts will not knowingly mislead you about viruses, but they simply may not know much about them. Later in this chapter, we will point out that many general, and otherwise very useful, security texts contain some serious errors in regard to viruses.

Having said all that, we realize that we are not the final word in all things viral, and you will need to get updated information about new viruses, and virus types, as they appear. Sources of information are available that you definitely can trust.

Advisories from independent security organizations such as CERT (the Carnegie Mellon University Software Engineering Institute's Computer Emergency Response Team) are usually much more formally structured than vendor advisories, with a serial number of some sort, a series of standard fields (problem, platform, risks, damage, solution), a document history, a copyright notice, a disclaimer, a digital signature, and so forth. However, such organizations tend to handle virus alerts less competently than other types of advisories. Nor is a formal structure a guarantee that such a document can't be forged. A digital signature is no test of anything if it isn't checked.

If your organization or ISP has a security specialist you can contact directly, that's a place to start. However, unless you're prepared to try out the source's knowledge of some of the resources listed at the end of this document, you're probably in a poor position to assess that source's expertise.

There is a vacant market niche for an organization with relevant experience on tap to offer a verification service. In the meantime, volunteers offer most of the expertise, which is something of a mixed blessing.

If you feel paranoid, untrusting, and obliged to check these things for yourself, welcome to our world.

Books

As a source of background information, books are often considered your first stop. They cannot, of course, keep you abreast of the latest developments in the field. As authors, we have a vested interest in promoting the medium of "dead trees", but the fact does remain that books are your best bet for an overview of the field. We have included as many titles as we could find, both good and bad. We have also indicated which ones we think are most worthwhile, but, again, we encourage you to form your own opinion—or test ours.

Generally, books on viruses have not dealt specifically with one topic or another, so we have simply grouped all of them by our assessment of quality. We have also included lists of general security texts that touch on virus problems, works on legal issues, examinations of ethics, and fiction involving viruses.

To date, most titles in the field are 180 to 500 pages in large paperback format (with the exception of one video). The lowest-priced title we could find was $10.95, and we believe that it is no longer available. (All the prices here are given in US dollar currency unless noted otherwise; C$ refers to Canadian dollars and UK£ to British pounds).

In addition, only a few books have been published in the field between 1994 and 2000. Scant recent books realistically address the topic of Microsoft Word macro viruses, and, of course, the earlier works don't mention them at all.

Entries in the list include the author, book name, publisher, date of publication, ISBN (International Standard Book Number), and price (if known or available), as well as a short annotation. Entries within sections are sorted by publication date, with the latest first.

Complete reviews of these and other books can be found at the following sites: http://sun.soci.niu.edu/~rslade/mnbkscvr.htm and http://victoria.tc.ca/techrev/mnbkscvr.htm. (These sites should be identical mirrors.)

The Good

Robert M. Slade, *Robert Slade's Guide to Computer Viruses,* 2nd Edition, Springer-Verlag, 1996, 0-387-94663-2, $39.95. In our *completely* unbiased opinion, this is the *best* computer virus book ever written! (And the title was *not* Rob's idea!) However, our opinion is somewhat reinforced by the fact that the book did make the VIRUS-L FAQ, and is, as of mid-2001, the only virus book in the $(ISC)^2$ resource list. This volume contains a number of appendices, lists, and reviews that are definitely dated but still surprisingly (even to the reviewer) applicable, as regards general tone and approach, if not details.

Alan Solomon, *Dr. Solomon's Virus Encyclopedia,* S&S International PLC, 1995, 1-897661-00-2, UK£19.99. A good listing of MS-DOS viral programs but little general information. The book was primarily an adjunct to a software product and may no longer be sold separately.

Fred Cohen, *A Short Course on Computer Viruses,* John Wiley & Sons, 1994, 0-471-00768-4, $44.95. An excellent analysis providing thorough guidance for antiviral policy and procedures. Cohen is considered to be the grandfather of all virus research and very reliable, and his book has some humour as well.

Pamela Kane, *PC Security and Virus Protection Handbook,* M&T Books, 1994, 1-55851-390-6, $39.95. A good overview for the MS-DOS arena, with additional material on general desktop security. It contains Yisreal Radai's exemplary review of the Microsoft Anti-Virus program.

David Ferbrache, *A Pathology of Computer Viruses,* Springer-Verlag, 1992, 0-387-19610-2, $49.00. A good technical overview, considered the classic text for the serious academic researcher.

Harold Joseph Highland, *Computer Virus Handbook,* Elsevier, 1990, 0-946395-46-2, $100.00. This book is a very good overview, unfortunately dated and with little practical material. Despite its age, this book is remarkably prescient and a classic in the field.

Lance Hoffman (ed.), *Rogue Programs: Viruses, Worms, and Trojans,* Van Nostrand Reinhold, 1990, 0-442-00454-0. A good collection of essays for academic study, although not necessarily for the user.

Peter Denning (ed.), *Computers Under Attack,* Addison-Wesley, 1990, 0-201-53067-8, $34.95. A collection of essays roughly related to security and also to the 'Net. The book does not provide all that much material on viruses, but the essays included are classic papers.

The Bad (or Mediocre, at Least)

Roger A. Grimes, *Malicious Mobile Code*, O'Reilly & Associates, 2001, 1-56592-682-X, $39.95. This is not a good book on viruses or malware. The breadth of coverage and detailed content on macro and email virus technology does save it from being really awful: up to the summer of 2001, no other book has dealt with those topics in sufficient depth. And the MS-centrism does have one very positive advantage. If you absolutely must use Microsoft software and applications, the prevention sections of the various chapters do contain a lot of detail that will be useful in reducing the risk that you face.

Robert S. Vibert, *The Enterprise Anti-Virus Book,* Segura Solutions, 2000, 0-9687464-0-3, C$99.95. We are not in complete agreement as to the utility of this book. For the expert, it can provide a useful, though expensive, checklist for reviewing antiviral software. The nonexpert reader, though, may find the material daunting, and not a little confusing. We will be discussing this book in more detail in Chapter 9.

Virus Bulletin, *Survivor's Guide to Computer Viruses,* Virus Bulletin, 1993, 0-9522114-0-8, UK£19.95. A relatively accurate book, but disappointing coming from the *Virus Bulletin,* and now somewhat dated.

Philip Fites, Peter Johnston, and Martin Kratz, *Computer Virus Crisis,* Van Nostrand Reinhold, 1992, 0-442-00649-7. This is a somewhat sloppy book with a number of errors, and little practical user material.

Chris Feudo, *The Computer Virus Desk Reference,* Business One Irwin, 1992, 1-55623-755-3. A collection of basic virus reference sources for readers without online access, but it is now out of date.

Jan Hruska, *Computer Viruses and Anti-Virus Warfare,* Ellis Horwood, 1992, 0-13-036377-4. MS-DOS-specific, this book is technically reasonable but provides suspect commentary. The details and specifics are now out of date.

Alan Solomon, *PC Viruses: Detection, Analysis and Cure,* 1991, Springer-Verlag, 0-387-19691-9. A very accurate book, but somewhat demanding technically. It is now out of date in some areas.

Robert V. Jacobson, *The PC Virus Control Handbook,* Miller Freeman, 1990, 0-87930-194-5, $24.95. Although this book is dated and uneven, it features a good chapter on how to deal with infections.

Allan Lundell, *Virus!,* Contemporary Books, 1989, 0-8092-4437-3, $10.95. This book presents a lot of research, but a lot of errors as well. It will not be much help to the practical user. It is now out of date, and possibly out of print.

The Really and Truly Ugly

For reasonably obvious reasons, it is difficult to get complete information for some of the following titles.

Brian Bagnall, Chris O. Broomes, and Ryan Russell, *E-mail Virus Protection Handbook,* Syngress Media, Inc., 2000, 1-928994-23-7, $39.95. This book doesn't provide enough information about email, and almost nothing about viruses.

Phil Schmauder, *Virus Proof,* Prima Publishing, 2000, 0-7615-2747-8, $34.99. This book does not actually deal much with viruses. It provides undependable information, and is inflated to several times its useful length by repetition and redundant screen dumps.

Ken Dunham, *Bigelow's Virus Troubleshooting Pocket Reference,* McGraw-Hill, 2000, 0-07-212627-2, $19.99. A well-meaning but incomplete and unreliable effort. Two of us saw a few drafts of this text, and one of us requested to be taken off the reviewers list when the disappointing quality of the work became apparent. When the book was finally published, it contained many errors and misleading analyses even though they had been pointed out in the review stage. The author seems to have little understanding of the underlying technologies.

Rune Skardhamar, *Virus Detection and Elimination,* Academic Press, 1996, 0-12-647690-X. Untrustworthy, badly written, and likely from one of the virus exchange crowd.

Janet Endrijonas, *Rx PC: The Anti-Virus Handbook,* McGraw-Hill, 1993, 0-8306-4202-1, C$59.95. This book is ultimately dated and unreliable.

Webster, Gwartney, and Heuckendorf, *PC Virus: Understanding and Prevention,* 1992, 0-922264-01-5. This selection is actually a video and possibly useful, but there are many gaps in the information it provides the viewer.

Peter Norton and Paul Nielsen, *Inside the Norton Antivirus,* Prentice Hall, 1992, 0-13-473463-7. Not much good as a general guide, and provides outdated documentation for the program.

Robert V. Jacobsen, *Using McAfee Associates Software for Safe Computing,* Miller Freeman, 1992, 0-9627374-1-0, $16.95. Printed documentation for the McAfee software of that era. It's out of date and fairly useless.

Bruce Hodge, *Rid Me of This Virus!,* Pickaxe Media, 1992, 0-646-07713-9, $10.95. This book is too short and uneven, and is out of print.

Ralf Burger, *Computer Viruses and Data Protection,* Abacus, 1991, 1-55755-123-5, $19.95. A poorly written book with little solid information, and some viral programs in source code.

Richard B. Levin, *Computer Virus Handbook,* McGraw-Hill, 1990, 0-07-881647-5, $24.95. This vague and undisciplined book presents specifics that are out of date.

John McAfee and Colin Haynes, *Computer Viruses, Worms, Data Diddlers, Killer Programs and Other Threats to Your System,* St. Martin's Press, 1989, 0-312-02889-X, $16.95. Contains some interesting speculations buried in a mass of undisciplined garbage.

Ralph Roberts, *Compute!'s Computer Viruses,* 1988, 0-87455-178-1, $14.95. This book is old and out of print.

Related Topics

Fred Cohen, *It's Alive!,* John Wiley & Sons, 1994, 0-471-00860-5, $39.95. This book provides an intriguing, provoking, and practical exploration of computer programs as "artificial life", but is somewhat narrow.

Mark Clarkson, *Windows Hothouse,* Addison-Wesley, 1994, 0-201-62669-1, $34.95. This book explores lots of artificial life fun with Visual C++.

Ellen Thro, *Artificial Life Explorer's Kit,* SAMS Publishing, 1993, 0-672-30301-9, $24.95. This book is good fun, but offers little analysis.

Steven Levy, *Artificial Life: A Report from the Frontier Where Computers Meet Biology,* Random House/Vintage, 1992, 0-679-73489-8, $13.00. This book takes an interesting wander through fields studying artificial life but has no strong points.

Mark Ludwig, *Little Black Book of Computer Viruses,* American Eagle Publications, 1990, 0-929408-02-0, $14.95. This MS-DOS-specific book is not very accurate, presenting viral source code rather than protection information. The book is also available in French as *Naissance d'un virus,* translated by Jean Bernard Condat.

General Security

Reviews can be found through http://sun.soci.niu.edu/~rslade/mnbksc.htm or http://victoria.tc.ca/techrev/mnbksc.htm.

Anonymous, *Maximum Security,* 3rd Edition, SAMS Publishing, 2001, 0-672-31871-7, $49.99. The first edition was really bad and the second improved to merely mediocre on security overall, but neither edition deals with viruses well at all. The third edition (out since May 2001) does better than the first two on viruses and Trojans, since David Harley overhauled the relevant chapters.

Bruce Schneier, *Secrets and Lies: Digital Security in a Networked World,* John Wiley & Sons, 2000, 0-471-25311-1, $29.99. This book serves as an excellent introduction to security and more. Unfortunately, the chapter that concentrates on viruses is one of the weakest in the book.

Elizabeth D. Zwicky, Simon Cooper, and D. Brent Chapman, *Building Internet Firewalls,* O'Reilly & Associates, 2000, 1-56592-871-7, $44.95. The other classic firewalls text. This book provides realistic consideration of the difficulties and limitations of defending against viruses at the firewall.

Jeff Crume, *Inside Internet Security,* Addison-Wesley, 2000, 0-201-67516-1, $29.95. After starting badly, the book provides a good overview of security in general. It includes a short but reasonable piece on viruses.

Harold F. Tipton and Micki Krause (eds.), *Information Security Management Handbook,* Auerbach, 2000, 0-8493-9829-0/0-8493-0800-3, $155.00. For the most respected work in the general security field, this has a lot of very good material, but a lot of fluff, too. In two volumes, however, only one piece directly addresses viruses (in a very academic tone), and the only other article that does devote some space to the issue has a massive number of mistakes.

Winn Schwartau, *CyberShock,* Thunder's Mouth/Inter.Pact Press, 2000, 1-56025-246-4, $24.95. Aimed at managers, this is a good nontechnical guide to security attacks and dangers on the 'Net, although it is somewhat sensational. The discussion of viruses is not bad, but not very practical.

William C. Boni and Gerald L. Kovacich, *I-Way Robbery,* Butterworth- Heinemann, 1999, 0-7506-7029-0, $34.95. An unfocused and undisciplined "look" at security, this book deals with viruses as poorly as it does with everything else.

Wallace Wang, *Steal This Computer Book,* No Starch Press, 1998, 1-886411-21-2, $19.95. This loose amalgam of roughly security-related topics definitely is not worth buying, including the section on viruses.

Dorothy E. Denning and Peter J. Denning, *Internet Besieged: Countering Cyberspace Scofflaws,* Addison-Wesley, 1998, 0-201-30820-7, $39.95. This is a good collection of essays, although an academic and big iron bias shows. It seems to be the update of *Computers Under Attack,* although almost all the virus material is gone.

Donald L. Pipkin, *Halting the Hacker,* Prentice Hall, 1997, 0-13-243718-X, $44.95. This book offers banal security advice, but includes a good collection of information on the CD-ROM. Unfortunately the coverage of viruses is poor.

Tim Meyers, Tom Sheldon, and Joel Snyder, *Internet Security,* Macmillan Computer Publishing, 1997, 1-56205-760-X, $65.00. This book's coverage is random and incomplete.

Laura E. Quarantiello, *Cyber Crime,* Limelight Books/Tiare Publications, 1997, 0-936653-74-4, $16.95. A pedestrian and frantic warning about security issues; the author misunderstands viruses, as is typical for books on security.

Daniel J. Barrett, *Bandits on the Information Superhighway,* O'Reilly and Associates, 1996, 1-56592-156-9, $17.95. This book provides no useful information on real viruses. However, it does include a short but pertinent section on the Good Times hoax.

Peter T. Davis and Barry D. Lewis, *Computer Security for Dummies,* IDG, 1996, 1-56884-635-5, $19.99. This book has a chapter on viruses, worms, and other such stuff. It gets some general principles right, but is technically weak. There is rehashed material from various widely available FAQs, not always portrayed accurately. Some advice is very poor, such as the suggestion to do a low-level reformat of infected hard disks as a general recommendation for dealing with infected PCs.

Marc Farley, Tom Stearns, and Jeffrey Hsu, *LAN Times Guide to Security and Data Integrity,* Osborne/McGraw-Hill, 1996, 0-07-882166-5, $29.95. This pedestrian guide to security is big on backups, and almost dismissive of viruses.

Michael Alexander, *The Underground Guide to Computer Security,* Addison-Wesley, 1996, 0-201-48918-X, $19.95. This is an OK introduction for desktops, but includes little on viruses.

Simson Garfinkel and Gene Spafford, *Practical UNIX and Internet Security,* 2nd Edition, O'Reilly & Associates, 1996, 1-56592-148-8, $39.95. This is very much a UNIX book, although the authors outline the principles well enough to be useful for readers protecting other systems. It has a brief but pretty accurate page or two on virus implications in a UNIX environment.

David J. Icove, Karl A. Seger, and VonStorch, *Computer Crime: A Crimefighter's Handbook,* O'Reilly & Associates, 1995, 1-56592-086-4, $19.95. This book makes several passing references to virus issues, but is technically very patchy.

Arthur E. Hutt, Seymour Bosworth, and Douglas B. Hoyt, *Computer Security Handbook,* John Wiley & Sons, 1995, 0-471-11854-0, $90.00. Concentrating on big iron and accounting and lacking in depth, this collection of essays has breadth, but also repetition. There is one article on viruses, but it is terrible.

Karanjit Siyan and Chris Hare, *Internet Firewalls and Network Security,* New Riders, 1995, 1-56205-437-6, $35.00. This book makes only one reference to viruses, and that's a pointer to the now defunct VIRUS-L mailing list.

Aaron Weiss, *The Complete Idiot's Guide to Protecting Yourself on the Internet,* Que, 1995, 1-56761-593-7, $16.99. This book devotes a whole chapter to viruses, which doesn't mention boot-sector infectors, multipartite or macro viruses—it assumes that all viruses are file infectors. The book provides brief notes on F-Prot's scanner, Vshield, and Disinfectant, but offers poorly informed material on virus and anti-virus technology and virus control.

Charles Cresson Wood, *Information Security Policies Made Easy,* Baseline Software, 1994, 1-881585-01-8, $495.00. This book is expensive, but if it makes the difference between having a security policy and not having one, it's worth it. Unfortunately, the virus policies were unworkable, but the book changes editions frequently and may have improved.

William R. Cheswick and Steven M. Bellovin, *Firewalls and Internet Security: Repelling the Wily Hacker,* Addison-Wesley, 1994, 0-201-63357-4, $36.95. This is the classic firewalls text. It doesn't consider virus issues beyond vaguely suggesting that PC-heavy sites might want to filter for viruses at the firewall (a somewhat contentious suggestion, especially in 1994).

David Stang, *Network Security Secrets,* International Data Group, 1993, 1-56884-021-7. This book serves as a practical and thorough security guide at the right level for most LAN managers. Although Stang taught virus seminars at one time, this book does not feature much coverage of viruses.

N. Derek Arnold, *UNIX Security: A Practical Tutorial,* McGraw-Hill, 1993, 0-07-002560-6, $26.95. This pedestrian and dated textbook includes source code for a UNIX virus.

Deborah Russell and G. T. Gangemi, Sr., *Computer Security Basics,* O'Reilly and Associates, 1991, 0-937175-71-4, $29.95. This book features several pages on viruses and other programmed threats, but they are not particularly accurate nor helpful. It does include some useful nonvirus material.

Legal

We won't be getting to legal aspects until Chapter 17, but in the meantime, here's a list. Few of these works touch directly on virus issues, and the law surrounding the writing and spreading of viruses is far from clear.

Brian Kahin and Charles Nesson, *Borders in Cyberspace,* MIT Press, 1997, 0-262-61126-0, $25.00. This is an excellent collection of essays on law as it relates to the 'Net.

Jonathan Rosenoer, *CyberLaw: The Law of the Internet,* Springer-Verlag, 1997, 0-387-94832-5, $34.95. This book surveys US case law in regard to the 'Net.

Paul Jacobsen, *Net Law: How Lawyers Use the Internet,* O'Reilly and Associates, 1997, 1-56592-258-1, $29.95. This selection is very useful for lawyers.

Michael Gross, *Law on the Internet,* SYBEX Computer Books, 1996, 0-7821-1792-9, $12.99. This book is a good, well-written guide.

Lance Rose, *NetLaw: Your Rights in the Online World,* Osborne/McGraw-Hill, 1995, 0-07-882077-4, $19.95. This is a good overview of legal matters in relation to the online world, but is still US-centric.

Edward A. Cavazos and Gavino Morin, *Cyberspace and the Law,* MIT Press, 1994, 0-262-53123-2, $19.95. This book explains Internet law for the common person.

Gene K. Landy, *The Software Developer's and Marketer's Legal Companion,* Addison-Wesley, 1993, 0-201-62276-9, $34.95. This book offers good, solid, general guidance.

Lance Rose/Jonathan Wallace, *Syslaw,* PC Information Group Inc., 1992. This book explores legal aspects of BBSs and online systems.

Ethics

The topic of ethics is a major one in all areas of security, but the debate is most heated in the virus arena. Again, we will discuss ethics at more length in Chapter 18, but here is a reading list.

    Reviews can be found at http://sun.soci.niu.edu/~rslade/mnbkscet.htm or http://victoria.tc.ca/techrev/mnbkscet.htm.

Winn Schwartau, *Internet and Computer Ethics for Kids,* Inter.Pact Press, 2001, 0-9628700-5-6, $15.95. To be effective, this book must be used *with* your children, and not simply handed to them. But it is an important and unique work in the field.

Nancy E. Willard, *The Cyberethics Reader,* McGraw-Hill, 1997, 0-07-070318-3, C$17.95. This text is not good on ethics, but is great on netiquette.

Sara Baase, *A Gift of Fire: Social, Legal, and Ethical Issues in Computing,* Prentice Hall, 1997, 0-13-458779-0, $48.00. This book takes a not-very-good look at the social issues and ethics of computing.

M. David Ermann, Mary B. Williams, and Michele S. Shauf, *Computers, Ethics and Society,* Oxford University Press, 1997, 0-19-510756-X, $29.95. This textbook for computer ethics courses is not great.

Peter Ludlow, *High Noon on the Electronic Frontier,* MIT Press, 1996, 0-262-62103-7, $32.50. This book compiles a good collection of essays on philosophical issues related to the 'Net.

Deborah G. Johnson and Helen Nissenbaum (eds.), *Computers, Ethics and Social Values,* Prentice Hall, 1995, 0-13-103110-4, $70.00. This collection of papers doesn't extend Johnson's earlier work, *Computer Ethics* (listed later in this section).

Duncan Langford, *Practical Computer Ethics,* McGraw-Hill, 1995, 0-07-709012-8, $46.45. This book offers a reasonable, fairly lightweight discussion of practical ethics in a computing context.

Deborah G. Johnson, *Computer Ethics,* Prentice Hall, 1994, 0-13-290339-3, $30.67. The basic work in the field, this book provides thorough coverage and is a good discussion starter.

Tom Forester and Perry Morrison, *Computer Ethics,* MIT Press, 1994, 0-262-56073-9, $24.95. This book has lots of great stories, but is short on analytical depth.

Fiction

Why would we include fictional works in a section on resources? Well, primarily because it provides a perspective on the common errors and misconceptions that you will have to correct before you can educate users. And also because, occasionally, fiction does provide neat and accurate examples to use in teaching.

Reviews can be found at http://sun.soci.niu.edu/~rslade/mnbkfc.htm or http://victoria.tc.ca/techrev/mnbkfc.htm.

Bill Buchanan, *Virus,* Ace/Berkley/Charter/Diamond/Jove Books, 1997, 0-515-12011-1, $6.50. It isn't. A virus, that is. Very poor technology in all areas.

Arthur C. Clarke, *3001: The Final Odyssey,* Ballantine/Fawcett/Columbine Books/Del Rey, 1997, 0-345-42349-6, $6.25. The story features generally acceptable science, but a bad idea of what a computer virus is.

Joseph Finder, *The Zero Hour,* Avon Books/The Hearst Corporation, 1996, 0-380-72665-3, $16.95. This story includes some good stuff but is bad on communications and viruses.

Philip Kerr, *The Grid,* McClelland and Stewart, Inc., 1995, 0-770-42740-5, C$8.99. The author employs lousy technology all around and includes some facile ponderings about artificial life.

James P. Hogan, *The Immortality Option,* Ballantine/Fawcett/Columbine Books/Del Rey, 1995, 0-345-39787-8, $5.99. This story expresses some provoking ideas about computer genetics, but the computer virus described is a poor example.

Allen Steele, *The Jericho Iteration,* Ace/Berkley/Boulevard/Charter/Diamond/Jove Books, 1994, 0-441-00271-4, $5.50. Covers the p1 virus, but not as well as the Ryan entry at the end of this section.

John Barnes, *Mother of Storms,* St. Martin's Press, 1994, 0-812-53345-3, $5.99. This story features some interesting explorations of self-replicating programs.

Rudy Rucker, *Live Robots,* Avon Books/The Hearst Corporation, 1994, 0-380-77543-3, $5.99. The author makes interesting points on genetic programming and the "malicious utility" of a virus.

Neal Stephenson, *Snow Crash,* Bantam Books, 1992, 0-553-56261-4, $10.36. This book features sound technical background for nets and programming, an interesting plot line about an "information virus", and is funny.

Dick Francis, *Driving Force,* Macmillan of Canada, 1992, 0449221393, $6.29. This story draws on details (some false) about the Michelangelo computer virus.

Winn Schwartau, *Terminal Compromise,* Inter.Pact Press, 1991, 0-962087000-5, $19.95. The story includes some virus stuff, but the most amusing aspect of the book is playing "spot the error".

John D. Randall, *The Tojo Virus,* Zebra Books/Kensington Publishing, 1991, 0-8217-3436-9, $4.95. Involves corporate insider information from IBM, but no really accurate technical stuff. This book was possibly the inspiration for *Terminal Compromise.*

David Gerrold, *When H.A.R.L.I.E. Was One,* Bantam/Spectra, 1972/1988, 0-345-02885-6/0-553-26465-6. Often cited as the first fictional reference to a computer virus, although it seems to refer to an earlier short story by Gerrold. Interestingly, the two editions describe very different approaches to virus technology.

Thomas J. Ryan, *The Adolescence of P-1,* Ace, 1977, 0-441-00360-5, $5.99. Rob Slade's personal favourite of the classic "computer virus" stories, although p1 is more akin to a worm.

John Brunner, *The Shockwave Rider,* Ballantine Books, 1976, 0-345-32431-5, $6.99. Security literature often refers to this book as including the earliest fictional reference to a virus. Unfortunately, the "tapeworm" in the book has no relation to any real virus or worm. But the book is a good read.

Articles and Papers

No bibliography can be complete without a slew of references to articles, although we sometimes question how useful the practice is for those who don't have a massive periodical archive on hand. The idea, of course, is to be able to cite new data that hasn't yet made it into a book. In the very fast-paced world of computer virus research, even journals are considered to be out of date before they are printed. Online sources are far faster, and are covered in the next section.

We should make mention of the only real periodical dealing with computer viruses, *Virus Bulletin.* Information about it can be found at www.virusbtn.com. *Virus Bulletin* used to have competition in *Virus New International,* but *VNI* is now *Secure Computing,* and no longer specific to viruses. You can find out more at http://www.scmagazine.com/.

Robert Slade, "Computer Viruses", *Academic Press Encyclopedia of Information Systems* (in press).

Max Smetannikov, "Hackers May Profit From Spam", *Interactive Week* (2 July 2001), p. 18.

Chris Conrath, "Computer virus raises new ethical concerns", *ComputerWorld Canada* (29 June 2001), p. 10.

David Thompson, "The Social Engineering of Security", *eWeek* (11 June 2001), p. 25.

Robert Slade, "Computer Security Weekly", *Suite101* (1999–2000) (available at http://www.suite101.com/welcome.cfm/computer_security).

Lynn Grenier, "Seeking the Cause and Prevention of the Common Virus", *Computing Canada* (4 August 2000), p. 13.

David Harley, "Bookworms—and viruses", *Virus Bulletin* (July 2000).

David Harley, "Living with Viruses", *Security Management*, Vol. 44:8 (2000).

David Harley, "Childhood's End—Demythologising Anti-Virus", *Virus Bulletin* (April 2000).

David Harley, "The E-mail of the Species: Worms, Chain-Letters, Spam and other Abuses", *Virus Bulletin* Conference Proceedings (2000) (also at http://www.sherpasoft.org.uk/hoaxfaq/email.pdf).

Sarah Gordon, "Rx for AV", *Information Security* (November 1999), p. 38.

David Harley, "Nine Tenths of the Iceberg", *Virus Bulletin* (October 1999).

U. E. Gattiker and L. Kelley, "Morality and computers: Attitudes and differences in moral judgments across populations", *Information Systems Research*, 10 (1999), pp. 233–254.

David Harley, "Policy, Education, Security and Computer Viruses", *Security Magazine* (1999).

Philip Carden, "Reviews: Antivirus Software", *Network Computing* (8 March 1999), pp. 68–81.

David Harley, "Managing Malware: mapping technology to function", EICAR 1999 Conference Best Paper Proceedings (1999).

David Harley, "Malice aforethought", *BackOffice Magazine,* Vol. 3:11 (1999).

David Harley, "Refloating the Titanic—Dealing with Social Engineering Attacks", EICAR Conference Proceedings (1998).

Andrew Brooks, "Attachments hasten virus epidemic", *Computing Canada* (9 February 1998), p. 23.

Computing, "Hacker turns to vendors as IT PI", *Computing* (4 December 1997), p. 32.

Sarah Gordon, Richard Ford, and Joe Wells, "Hoaxes and Hypes", *Virus Bulletin* Conference Proceedings (October 1997).

David Harley, "Macs and Macros: the State of the Macintosh Nation", *Virus Bulletin* Conference Proceedings (1997).

Virus Bulletin, "Comparative Review", *Virus Bulletin* (May 1997), p. 11.

David Harley, "Useful Techniques for Combating Social Engineers", SANS Network Security Technical Conference Proceedings (1997).

Network Computing, "Vaccinate Your NT File Services ...", *Network Computing* (1 April 1997), p. 94.

David Harley, "Dealing with Internet Hoaxes/Alerts", *EICAR News*, Vol. 3:2 (1997), pp. 10–11 (also at http://webworlds.co.uk/dharley/).

Virus Bulletin, "LAN Antivirals", *Virus Bulletin* (March 1997).

Computer Underground Digest, "Notes from the Underground: 2 interviews with Se7en", *Computer Underground Digest,* Vol. 9:49 (1997).

IBM, "Virus prevalence study", *IBM* (February 1997).

Virus Bulletin, "Comparative Review", *Virus Bulletin* (January 1997).

Frederick B. Cohen, "Information System Attacks: A Preliminary Classification Scheme", *Computers and Security,* Vol. 16:1 (1997), pp. 29–46.

Robert Slade, "Information Security for the Business Manager", *National Seminars* (1996).

Virus Bulletin, "Comparison test", *Virus Bulletin* (October 1996).

Robert Slade, "Evaluating Antiviral Software (series)", *VIRUS-L Digest* (1991–1996).

Bob Violino, "Word Macro Viruses ...", *Information Week* (1 April 1996), p. 22.

Virus Bulletin, "Comparison test", *Virus Bulletin* (April 1996).

Robert Slade, "The Virus File", *DECUS Symposium* (1991–1996).

Bundesamt für Sicherheit in der Informationstechnik, "IT Baseline Protection Manual", *Bundesamt für Sicherheit in der Informationstechnik* (1996).

Robert Slade, "The nightmare has arrived", *Toronto Computes* (December 1995), p. 56.

Patricia Hoffman, "VSUM Certifications", self-published (various dates).

Paul Wallich, "Meta-virus", *Scientific American* (November 1995), p. 34.

U. E. Gattiker and B. Barrett, "Computer viruses in the wild: What is the threat for Canada?" Proceedings of the 95 European Institute for Computer Anti-Virus Research (EICAR) Annual Conference (1995), pp. 173–181.

Al Berg, "Cracking a social engineer", *LAN Times* (6 November 1995), pp. 140–142.

Vesselin Bontchev, "Methodology of Computer Anti-Virus Research", Ph.D. thesis (1995).

U. E. Gattiker and H. Kelley, "Morality and technology, or is it wrong to create and let loose a computer virus", Proceedings of the 28th Annual Hawaii International Conference on System Sciences (1995), pp. 563–572.

British Standard Institution, "BS7799 British Standard Code of Practice for Information Security Management" (1995).

Network World, "Comparison test", *Network World* (9 October 1995).

Jay Milne, "Taking the Measure ...", *Network Computing* (15 September 1995), p. 126.

Symantec, "Understanding Virus Behaviour in 32-bit Operating Environments", *Symantec* (1995).

Joel Conover, "Security Vendors Put Virus ...", *Network Computing* (15 May 1995), p. 106.

Robert Slade, "Computer Viral Programs" (weekly series), *VIRUS-L Digest* (1991–1994).

William F. Katz, "Chips chomp life ...", *PC Week* (24 October 1994), p. N/1.

Gary Stix, "Binary Disinfectants", *Scientific American* (September 1994), pp. 97–98.

Eugene H. Spafford, "The Internet Worm Incident", *Purdue Technical Report* CSD-TR-933 (19 September 1994).

Laura Didio, "Trend ... Enhances ...", *Communications Week* (4 July 1994), p. 35.

Vesselin Bontchev, "Are 'Good' Viruses Still a Bad Idea?", Proceedings of the EICAR '94 Conference (1994), pp. 25–47 (also available at ftp://ftp.informatik.uni-hamburg.de/pub/virus/texts/viruses/goodvir.zip).

The HAQ, "The Hack FAQ Edition 2.07" (11 June 1994).

Data Fellows, "Creating a Virus Prevention Strategy...", *F-PROT Professional 2.13 Update Bulletin* (1994), p. 6.

U. E. Gattiker and H. Kelley, "Techno-crime and terror against tomorrow's organization: What about cyberpunks", Proceedings of the 13th World Computer Congress—IFIP Congress '94 Hamburg (1994), pp. 233–240.

Hilgraeve, Inc., Newsletter (Spring 1994).

Data Fellows, "Polymorphic Generators", *F-PROT Professional 2.12 Update Bulletin* (1994).

Henri Delger, "Comparison review", self-published (1994).

Mitch Wagner, "Possibilities Are Endless and Frightening", *Open Systems Today* (8 November 1993), p. 16.

Alan Solomon (attributed to Sarah Tanner), "A Reader's Guide to Reviews", *Virus News International* (November 1993), p. 40 (reprinted at http://www.softpanorama.org/Antivirus/Reprints/virus_reviews.html).

Eugene Spafford, "Computer Viruses", *ADAPSO* (1989–1993).

Evan Schuman, "Robert Morris in 1993", *Open Systems Today* (8 November 1993), p. 17.

Robert V. Jacobson, "Virus Facts, Not Frenzy", *Information Week* (23 August 1993), p. 6.

Robert Gezelter, "Effective Hardware Protection ...", JAS Technology presentation, Infoexpo '93 (1993).

Information Week, "Viruses: How Big? How Bad?", *Information Week* (19 July 1993), p. 25.

Patrick Flanagan, "Keeping a Watchful Eye on Viruses", *Telecommunications* (July 1993), p. 14.

Communications Week, "Lock Retooled", *Communications Week* (28 June 1993), p. 27.

Scott Spanbauer, "Search and Destroy", *PC World* (May 1993), p. 194.

Charles Haggerty, "An Rx for Viruses", *EBN* (12 April 1993), p. 31.

David Stang, "Fighting the Virus ... with Hardware ...", *Infosecurity News* (March/April 1993), p. 24.

PC Magazine, "Antiviral Software Evaluations", *PC Magazine* (16 March 1993).

Robin Raskin, "Keeping Up Your Guard", *PC Magazine* (16 March 1993), p. 209.

Paolo Del Nibletto, "Viruses face new foe ...", *InfoCanada* (February 1993), p. 13.

PC Week, "First Looks", *PC Week* (8 February 1993), p. 73.

Michael Kei Stewart, "Attack of the Windows Viruses", *Windows User* (February 1993), p. 49.

Tom Williams, "Hardware gives shot ...", *Computer Design* (January 1993), p. 48.

PC Professional, "Comparison Test", *PC Professional* (January 1993).

Paolo Del Nibletto, "Virus management for NetWare", *InfoCanada* (December 1992), p. 15.

InformationWeek, "Cleaning Up the Biosphere", *InformationWeek* (30 November 1992), p. 78.

PC Week, "Buyer's Guide", *PC Week* (9 November 1992), p. 146.

David Stang, "ISCA Antivirus Software Evaluation", *ISCA* (1992).

Vesselin Bontchev, "MtE tests" (October 1992).

Datapro, "Virus Prevalence Report", *Datapro Reports* (1992).

Vesselin Bontchev, "Possible Virus Attacks Against Integrity Programs And How To Prevent Them", Proceedings of the Second International *Virus Bulletin* Conference (September 1992), pp. 131–141.

David Chaum, "Achieving Electronic Privacy", *Scientific American* (August 1992), pp. 96–101.

Kathy Chin Leong, "Networked PCs can suffer ...", *Information Week* (13 July 1992), p. 20.

EICAR, "ChipAway Virus Enabled", *EICAR News,* Vol. 1:1 (1992), p. 4.

Patrick Marshall, "Antivirus Software", *PC World* (July 1992), p. 199.

David Stang, "In Defense of a Virus Description Language", *Virus News and Reviews,* (June 1992), pp. 249–252.

David Harley, "The PC Virus: Protect Your Computer", *IP Networking,* Vol. 3:1 (1992).

Association for Computing Machinery, "Code of Ethics and Professional Conduct", *Association for Computing Machinery* (1992).

IEEE, "The Top 10 PC Viruses of 1992", *IEEE Spectrum* (1992).

Datapro, "Computer Viruses", *Datapro Reports* (May 1992).

Matt Kramer and David Berlind, "LANs Get Cure ...", *PC Week* (2 March 1992), p. 16.

British Computer Society, "Code of Conduct", *British Computer Society* (1992).

Fred Cohen, "A Formal Definition of Computer Worms and Some Related Results", *Computers & Security,* Vol. 11 (1992), pp. 641–652.

Wendy Taylor, "Virus Attacks", *PC/Computing* (February 1992).

Ray Kaplan, "Heterogeneous Network Security", *Demax Software* (February 1992).

Bob Violino, "Networks: No Immunity", *Information Week* (6 January 1992), p. 18.

Carol Ellison, "On Guard", *PC Magazine* (29 October 1991), p. 199.

Mark Schlack, "How To Keep Viruses Off Your LAN", *Datamation* (15 October 1991).

Certus, "Virus Prevalence Survey", *Certus International* (1991).

Fred Cohen, "Trends In Computer Virus Research", *ASP* (1991).

Computer Ethics Institute, "10 Commandments of Computer Ethics", Computer Ethics Institute, Conference on Computer Ethics (1991).

Dataquest, "Virus Prevalence Survey", *Dataquest* (1991).

Corporate Software, "Anticipation may be the Best ...", *Corporate Software,* (January 1991), p. 1.

Peter Tippett, "The Kinetics of Computer Virus Replication", *Certus International* (1991).

PC Magazine, "New & Improved", *PC Magazine* (30 October 1990), p. 56.

Robert Slade, "Computer Virus", *Fisheries & Oceans Canada ITSD* (1990).

Auditor General of Canada, "Report of the Auditor General of Canada Fiscal Year Ended 31 March, 1990" (1990).

Robert Slade, "Data Security" (series), *CAMsoc Update* (1989).

Vinton Cerf, "Thou Shalt Not Create Worms", *Data Communications* (July 1989), p. 69.

Touche Ross, "Computer Viruses", *The Owner Manager* (Spring 1989), p. 1.

Fred Cohen, "Computational Aspects of Computer Viruses", *Computers & Security,* Vol. 8 (1989), pp. 325–344.

Mark W. Eichlin and Jon A. Rocklis, "With Microscope and Tweezers", IEEE Symposium on Research in Security and Privacy (1989).

Network Working Group, "RFC 1087: Ethics and the Internet", *Internet Activities Board* (January 1989).

Eugene H. Spafford, "The Internet Worm Program", *Purdue Technical Report* CSD-TR-823 (28 November 1988).

Peter Rossi, "The Iron Law of Evaluation and Other Metallic Rules", *Research in Social Problems & Public Policy,* Vol. 4 (1987), pp. 3–20.

Fred Cohen, "Computer Viruses—Theory and Experiments", 7th Security Conference DOD/NBS (September 1984), pp. 143–158 (available at http://www.all.net/books/virus/).

John F. Shoch and Jon A. Hupp, "The 'Worm' Programs—Early Experience with a Distributed Computation", *CACM,* Vol. 25 (3 March 1982).

Online Resources

The Internet is the ultimate candy store for data junkies. As Ido Dubrawsky has said, you cannot possibly outgrow the 'Net. However, there are a couple of caveats.

First, while the latest, and often the best, information is available online, the worst, most erroneous, and most opinionated is also there in the same cyberspace. Unless you are very careful, you risk being sadly misinformed. But we've already talked about that.

The second point to make is that the Internet, and particularly the Web, is ephemeral. Links get broken, servers go out of service, pages get old, and companies vanish, taking valuable resources with them. Recently two of the most highly regarded and useful antiviral sites on the 'Net, Dr. Solomon's Virus Encyclopedia and many resources of the IBM anti-virus site, disappeared or changed radically in form, so size and stature are not enough to guarantee continued existence. In the six months between the first and final drafts of this book, fully half of a certain list of URLs (Uniform Resource Locators) went 404—the code indicating that a page has disappeared from a server.

We have provided a web page to address updates and changes at http://www.viruses-revealed.org.uk/, and some tidbits can be found at http://victoria.tc.ca/techrev/vrupdate.htm or http://sun.soci.niu.edu/~rslade/vrupdate.htm. As well, an errata page can be found at http://www.osborne.com/errata/errata.shtml.

There are, of course, some standard actions to take when you find a page has disappeared. You can move from the specific to the general by dropping filenames or subdirectories off the end of the URL until you find a page that works. Or, you might connect to the root index of that particular server, and see if a search engine is available. When all else fails, you can always use the general search engines on the 'Net to try to track down key words in a title or topic.

One other point should be made: the Internet, sad to say, is not perfect, and service is not always reliable. If you don't get through to a specific site, it may be that the particular computer is temporarily overloaded, disconnected, unplugged, or down for service. Try again in a few minutes, hours, or days, and you may get through.

We have arranged some of these references into topics that we hope will be useful. The vast majority of these listings, as usual, will defy categorization. We have also annotated some of the URLs when we think it appropriate, but not all of them by any means. Some URLs are too long to fit on one line in this book; you should type them in your browser as one continuous string, however, with no spaces. Again, some of these are good, some are bad, and most fall in the middle; we'll try to note the extremes.

Mailing Lists and Newsgroups

The most useful entry we could give you would be a reliable mailing list for virus information. Sadly, we can't. VIRUS-L has been quiet for many years, and Henri Delger, who ran different versions of the very valuable VirusHelp newsletter, seems to have retired.

The only active virus mailing list we know of is Virus News. Unfortunately, despite the name, the list has little to do with viruses. The list is a compilation of references to security stories in other online sources, mostly general-media-connected web sites such as CNN.com. SANS and comparable groups run other similar lists. Virus News, and the related Spam News, can be found at www.petemoss.com. For other media-related security mailing lists, you can email sans@sans.org with a subject line of "Subscribe NewsBites", or send any message to security-subscribe@News.WebUrb.dk.

What is left is the alt.comp.virus (or acv, in USENET news parlance, which tends to refer to groups by initials only) newsgroup. This group does discuss virus issues, but beware: the noise-to-signal ratio is extremely high. In addition, acv, as an unmoderated group, tends to be something of a hangout for the VX crowd. Their influence waxes and wanes, depending upon how interested AV types are in reclaiming their turf. There are some related groups, such as alt.comp.antivirus, alt.comp.virus.pro-virus, and alt.comp.virus.source.code.

However, there are a few good general security mailing lists:

> RISKS-LIST: RISKS-FORUM Digest, http://catless.ncl.ac.uk/Risks, is a great source of general security discussion, and one of the best moderated lists on the 'Net as well.

> Crypto-Gram Newsletter, http://www.counterpane.com/crypto-gram.html#sub, provides great general commentary, and specializes in cryptography.

> Cipher, the newsletter of the IEEE Computer Science Technical Committee on Security and Privacy, is at http://www.ieee-security.org/cipher.html.

> PRIVACY Forum: http://www.vortex.com/privacy.html

> Security Mailing Lists: http://xforce.iss.net/maillists/otherlists.php

Free Scanners

So, the first thing you want to know in terms of the Internet is, where can you get good software, right? Preferably, free. Well, the good part we will address at length in Chapter 9. But to answer your question quickly, we recommend the following for home use, emergency use, and even for regular use in many cases:

F-Prot, F-Macro: http://www.complex.is http://www.f-secure.com

F-Prot is tried, tested, and true. In many cases we actually prefer the MS-DOS version, since it can be run on a "cold-booted" machine in order to test for Windows viruses that may interfere with scanning operations when Windows is running. The MS-DOS version is also, as far as we know, still free for home use.

MacroList by A. Padgett Peterson:
http://www2.gdi.net/~padgett/getmacro.htm
http://www.freivald.org/~padgett/getmacro.htm

MacroList is a specific tool for checking Microsoft Word documents for the presence of possible macro viruses. While it is not an automated scanner, it is a utility that is available for both Wintel and Macintosh machines.

garbo: ftp://garbo.uwasa.fi/pc/virus

The garbo archive, at the University of Vaasa, in Finland, is a long-established and highly regarded resource. In terms of antiviral software, it is also an excellent source of older programs and utilities.

Other companies may produce free or demonstration version products from time to time.

Online Scanners

Online scanners present a number of problems, and even dangers. As both Tony Buckland and Bruce Schneier have pointed out in different situations, the client interface is the boundary of trustworthiness. In other words, the online scanner, having submitted a program to run on your machine, really cannot foresee all the possible configurations under which it might be running. It is, unfortunately, quite possible that the online scanner, in attempting to open all files for examination, is really doing identification work for a resident virus. If you already have a virus active in your machine, you may end up infecting all of your files.

In addition, many online scanners require the use of ActiveX or Microsoft Internet Explorer, and these technologies carry their own risks.

Still, this section provides a list of such scanners, for which we thank Axel Pettinger, who posted it recently on alt.comp.virus.

McAfee—AVERT WebImmune: http://www.webimmune.net/

Command on Demand:
http://www.commandondemand.com/cod/index-ns.cfm

Symantec Security Check: http://security1.norton.com/us/home.asp

Trend Micro HouseCall: http://housecall.antivirus.com/

Central Command's Free Online Virus Scanner:
http://www.centralcommand.com/scan.html

Panda ActiveScan: http://www.pandasoftware.com/

DrWeb on-line: http://www.DialogNauka.ru/english/www_av/home.htm

AV-Test made a short test with the preceding scanners (except DrWeb). You can find the results at http://www.av-test.org/sites/tests.php3?lang=en#short.

Encyclopaedias

Lists of specific viruses and their characteristics tend to be called encyclopaedias, after the first, foremost, late, and much lamented Dr. Solomon's Virus Encyclopedia.

F-Secure's Security Information Center: http://www.f-secure.com/v-descs/. Since the passing of Dr. Solomon's Virus Encyclopedia, this is probably the most reliable and accurate source available.

Symantec Security Updates: http://www.symantec.com/avcenter/vinfodb.html

McAfee.com's Virus Information Library: http://vil.mcafee.com/

Trend Micro virus encyclopaedia:
http://www.antivirus.com/vinfo/virusencyclo/

Virus Encyclopedia: http://www.cai.com/virusinfo/encyclopedia/

Mac Virus II: http://www.sherpasoft.org.uk/MacVirus/ or
http://www.macvirus.com

AVP Virus Encyclopedia: http://www.avp.ch/avpve/findex.stm

About.com Antivirus Encyclopedia (this source does not have many entries):
http://antivirus.about.com/compute/antivirus/library/blency.htm

Panda Software: http://www.pandasoftware.com/library/

Sophos virus analyses: http://www.sophos.com/virusinfo/analyses/

Virus Hoaxes and False Alerts

This topic will be dealt with in depth in Chapter 16.

Computer Virus Myths home page (considered the standard virus hoax site):
http://www.Vmyths.com/

Virus Hoaxes: http://www.yale.edu/its/security/virus-hoaxes.html

CIAC Internet Hoaxes: http://HoaxBusters.ciac.org/

F-Secure/Data Fellows HOAX warnings page:
http://www.fsecure.com/news/hoax.htm
http://www.fsecure.com/virus-info/hoax/

SARC—Virus Hoaxes: http://www.symantec.com/avcenter/hoax.html

The Hoaxkill service (let's get rid of hoaxes now!):
http://www.hoaxkill.com/

Computer Virus Hoaxes: http://sassman.net/virus/

Don't Spread that Hoax!: http://www.nonprofit.net/hoax/default.htm

Internet Hoaxes Email Rumors and Urban Legends—Current Netlore:
urbanlegends.about.com/science/urbanlegends/library/blhoax.htm?once=true&

Computer Virus Hoaxes:
urbanlegends.about.com/science/urbanlegends/cs/virushoaxes/index.htm

TruSecure: http://www.icsalabs.com/html/communities/antivirus/hoaxes.shtml

EFF "Hoaxes" Archive: http://www.eff.org/pub/Net_culture/Folklore/Hoaxes/

McAfee.com's Virus Information Library—Virus Hoaxes:
http://vil.mcafee.com/hoax.asp

Symantec Security Updates' Hoax Page:
http://www.symantec.com/avcenter/hoax.html

How to spot a hoax:
http://www.research.ibm.com/ antivirus/SciPapers/Wells/HOWTOSPOT/
howtospot.html

Les Jones' Good Times FAQ:
http://www.public.usit.net/lesjones/goodtimes.html

Hoax verification: http://www.security-sceptic.org.uk

Also:

http://www.sherpasoft.org.uk/hoaxfaq/Mis-IT.html

http://www.sherpasoft.org.uk/anti-virus/hoaxes.txt

http://www.sherpasoft.org.uk/hoaxfaq/email.pdf

http://www.chekware.com/hoax/index.htm

http://www.korova.com/

http://urbanlegends.miningco.com/

Evaluation and Reviews

Oddly, very few sites on the Internet provide reviews of antiviral software. Then
again, perhaps it's not so odd. One of the authors of this book has extensive
experience in the task, and it is a difficult one indeed.

Antiviral Software Evaluation FAQ:
http://www.freenet.victoria.bc.ca/techrev/avrevfaq.html

Alan Solomon (attributed to Sarah Tanner), "A Reader's Guide to Reviews", *Virus News International* (November 1993), p. 40, http://www.softpanorama.org/Antivirus/Reprints/virus_reviews.html

Virus Test Center—University of Hamburg: http://agn-www.informatik.uni-hamburg.de/vtc/eng.htm

Checkmark: http://www.check-mark.com/checkmark/index.htm

C|Net: http://2.digital.cnet.com/cgi-bin2/flo?x=dAEuAugumAwKhAKuu

Response to C|Net: http://www.warlabs.org/portal/advisories.html

Anti-Virus Vendors

Some of these companies provide information and help, whereas others provide only sales pitches.

Virus Bulletin Home Page (*Virus Bulletin* is unique in this list; it is a vendor, but of a magazine rather than of software): http://www.virusbtn.com

F-Secure/Data Fellows World-Wide Web Server Main Index: http://www.DataFellows.com/ (the datafellows.fi, datafellows.com, f-secure.com, and fsecure.com domain names are all equivalent)

Frisk Software home page: http://www.complex.is/

Alwil Software: http://www.anet.cz/alwil/alwil.htm

Sophos home page: http://www.sophos.com/

Stiller Research: Integrity Master Virus Protection/Data Integrity: http://www.stiller.com/

Security Solutions: Virus Clinic: http://www.cai.com/virusinfo/

SBABR home page: http://www.nikosystems.com/index2.htm

Dr. Solomon's On-Line: http://www.drsolomon.com/

ThunderBYTE home page: http://www.norman.com/tbav.shtml

Norman: http://www.norman.com/

Symantec AntiVirus Research Center:
http://www.symantec.com/avcenter/index.html

Trend AntiVirus Center, Antivirus Solutions, Antivirus News:
http://www.antivirus.com/

Panda Software: http://www.pandasoftware.com/

Welcome to Leprechaun Software: http://www.leprechaun.com.au/

Command Software Virus Information:
http://www.commandcom.com/html/virus/virus.html

Sensible Security Solutions, Inc.: http://www.canada-av.com

General Resources

University of Tampere Virus Research Unit (highly regarded):
http://www.uta.fi/laitokset/virus/

Henri Delger's VirusHelp home page:
http://pages.prodigy.net/henri_delger/index.htm

University of Michigan Virus Busters:
http://www.umich.edu/~wwwitd/virus-busters/

IBM Antivirus Research (the collection of papers at this site is particularly
valuable): http://www.research.ibm.com/antivirus/

Thomas Jefferson University Computer Virus Information:
http://www.tju.edu/tju/dis/virus/

Penn State Anti-Virus Page: http://cac.psu.edu/~santoro/cac/virus.html

UK Open University Antivirus home page: http://antivirus.open.ac.uk/

PC Virus Page: http://mft.ucs.ed.ac.uk/pcvirus/pcvirus.htm

Anti-Virus Information Exchange Network: http://www.avien.org

Computer Knowledge Virus Tutorial: http://www.cknow.com/vtutor/

Guillermito et les virus informatiques (French and English information, but probably outdated): http://www.pipo.com/guillermito/darkweb/virus.html

Various Articles

Chat rooms hit by Internet flu:
http://www5.zdnet.com/zdnn/content/zdnn/1216/263771.html

What's NOT a Virus: http://www.bocklabs.wisc.edu/~janda/notvirus.html

alt.comp.virus.pictures: http://members.aol.com/altcompvir/

mIRC SCRIPT.INI Infosheet: http://www.irchelp.org/irchelp/mirc/si.html

Mac Virus/Trojan Horse Alert:
http://www.frostyplace.com/NewsHTML/1998/May/VirusAlert/VirusAlert.html

Doug Muth's Anti-Virus help page: http://www.ezweb.net/dmuth/virus/

Mountain Ridge Dataworks Macintosh Consultants:
http://www.mrdataworks.com/

Descriptions of Common Viruses: http://www.stiller.com/common.htm

Padgett's AntiVirus Page: http://www2.gdi.net/~padgett/av.htm

Computer Viruses—Theory and Experiments: http://www.all.net/books/virus/

McAfee.com World Virus Map:
http://www.mcafee.com/anti-virus/virusmap.asp

Distributed Attack Detection:
http://www.incidents.org
http://www.dshield.org
http://www.mynetwatchman.com

Getting rid of WSH: http://www.F-Secure.com/virus-info/u-vbs/

Sendmail filter for Love Bug: http://biocserver.cwru.edu/~jose/iloveyouhack.txt

Are "Good" Viruses Still a Bad Idea?:
ftp://ftp.informatik.uni-hamburg.de/pub/virus/texts/viruses/ goodvir.zip

VBA Upconversion:
http://www.virusbtn.com/vb2000/Programme/papers/bontchev.pdf

One version of a naming standard:
http://www.symantec.com/avcenter/venc/vnameinfo.html

Macro Protection Techniques:
http://download.nai.com/products/media/vil/pdf/free_AV_tips_techniques.pdf

General Advice

http://ntbugtraq.ntadvice.com/safemail.asp

http://ntbugtraq.ntadvice.com/outlookviews.asp

http://2.digital.cnet.com/cgi-bin2/flo?x=dAEuAugumAwYomouA

http://2.digital.cnet.com/cgi-bin2/flo?x=dAEuAugumAwKhAhuP

Specific Viruses and Vulnerabilities

The articles listed in this section detail specific viruses or events.

Melissa

http://sun.soci.niu.edu/~rslade/melissa.txt

http://victoria.tc.ca/techrev/melissa.txt

http://www.cert.org/advisories/CA-1999-04.html

http://www.ciac.org/ciac/bulletins/j-037.shtml

http://www.antivirus.com/vinfo/security/sa032699.htm

http://www.melissavirus.com

Love Bug

http://www.ca.com/virusinfo/virusalert.htm

cbc.ca/cgi-bin/templates/view.cgi?/news/2000/05/05/lovebug000505

http://www.pcweek.com/a/pcwt0005041/2561671/

http://CNN.com/2000/TECH/computing/05/05/iloveyou.01/index.html

MTX

http://193.247.150.10/avpve/worms/email/mtx.stm

http://161.69.2.149/villib/dispvirus.asp?virus_k=98797

http://www.norman.no/de/virus_info/w32_mtx.shtml

http://www.antivirus.com/vinfo/virusencyclo/default5.asp?VName=PE_MTX.A

AutoStart 9805

http://www.opuscc.com/support/autostart9805.shtml

http://www.virusbtn.com/VirusInformation/autostart9805.html

http://www.sherpasoft.org.uk/MacVirus.archive/reference/autostart.html

http://lowendmac.com/virus/worm.shtml

http://www.unisa.edu.au/itsudesktop/sw/mac/virus/autostart.htm

http://www.internet-security.com/security/lists/security/ciac/0010.html

Shoch and Hupp's Worm

http://ftp.unina.it/pub/docs/rfc/ien/ien159.txt

A German account is available at
http://www.cert.dfn.de/tutorial/wuermer/kap211.html

Linux Worms

Since worms tend to exploit specific loopholes in the operating system, most of these discussions concentrate on the system vulnerabilities rather than the worms themselves.

http://www.sans.org/current.htm

http://www.cert.org/advisories/CA-2001-02.html

http://www.cert.org/incident_notes/IN-2001-03.html

http://www.cert.org/incident_notes/IN-2001-05.html

http://www.kb.cert.org/vuls/id/196945

http://www.sans.org/y2k/t0rn.htm

http://www.redhat.com/support/errata/RHSA-2001-007.html

http://www.debian.org/security/2001/dsa-026

http://www.suse.com/de/support/security/2001_003_bind8_txt.txt

http://www.caldera.com/support/security/advisories/CSSA-2001-008.0.txt

http://www.caldera.com/support/security/advisories/CSSA-2001-008.1.txt

http://www.whitehats.com/library/worms/lion/index.html

DDoS

http://staff.washington.edu/dittrich/talks/cert/

http://staff.washington.edu/dittrich/misc/stacheldraht.analysis

http://staff.washington.edu/dittrich/misc/tfn.analysis

http://staff.washington.edu/dittrich/misc/trinoo.analysis

http://staff.washington.edu/dittrich/misc/ddos_scan.tar

http://staff.washington.edu/dittrich/misc/sickenscan.tar

http://www.cert.org/advisories/CA-2000-01.html

http://www.cert.org/reports/dsit_workshop.pdf

http://www.cisco.com/warp/public/707/newsflash.html

Core Wars and Redstone Code

http://www.koth.org/info/sciam/

http://www.koth.org/info.html

http://www.sci.fi/~iltzu/corewar/guide.html

http://www.cs.ucla.edu/~jperry/corewars.html

http://kuoi.asui.uidaho.edu/~kamikaze/documents/corewar-faq.html

Pranks

hamptonroads.about.com/citiestowns/southeastus/hamptonroads/libr

http://www.supershareware.com/Apps/4072.asp

http://www.btsunlimited.com/shareware_nopass/shareware_prank.htm

http://members.tripod.com/~wiseguysinc/joke.htm

http://www.geocities.com/netsur24/gags.html

http://www.sidor.ru/sick/index1.html

http://looneytunes.acmecity.com/tune/213/

Other

ftp://ftp.microsoft.com/peropsys/IE/IE-Public/Fixes/usa/Eyedog-fix/x86/
q240308.exe

ftp://ftp.microsoft.com/peropsys/IE/IE-Public/Fixes/usa/Eyedog-fix/

http://www.microsoft.com/technet/security/bulletin/fq99-032.asp

http://support.microsoft.com/support/kb/articles/q240/3/08.asp

http://support.microsoft.com/support/kb/articles/q240/7/97.asp

http://www.microsoft.com/technet/security/default.asp

http://www.symantec.com/avcenter/venc/data/bat.chode.worm.html

http://vil.mcafee.com/dispVirus.asp?virus_k=98557

http://www.sans.org/giac.htm

http://www.cnn.com/2001/TECH/internet/03/07/virus.brazil.02/index.html

http://www.virusbtn.com/VirusInformation/michelangelo.html

http://sexyfun.net/
The Hybris virus uses the sexyfun domain in its return address. At the time
that the virus was released, the domain did not exist. Some enterprising souls
have registered it and use it as a platform for providing information about
Hybris and also about spam.

General Security References

TECS (The Encyclopaedia of Computer Security):
http://www.itsecurity.com/

Crypt newsletter: http://www.soci.niu.edu/~crypt/

@stake Research Labs—Advisories:
http://www.atstake.com/research/advisories/index.html

2600: The Hacker Quarterly: http://www.2600.com/

Sarah Gordon's Papers: http://www.badguys.org/papers.htm

Spam, Unsolicited Commercial Email, Etc.

Coalition Against Unsolicited Commercial Email: http://www.cauce.org/

SPAM and the Internet: http://www.spam.com/ci/ci_in.htm

alt.spam FAQ or "Figuring out Fake E-Mail & Posts":
http://digital.net/~gandalf/spamfaq.html

SPAM-L: http://peach.ease.lsoft.com/archives/SPAM-L.html
mailto:listserv@peach.ease.lsoft.com (include the following text line:
SUBSCRIBE SPAM-L *firstname lastname*)

http://www.sendmail.org/antispam.html

http://spam.abuse.net/spam/faq.html

http://www.petemoss.com/

http://www.cybernothing.org/faqs/net-abuse-faq.html

http://members.aol.com/emailfaq/emailfaq.html

http://ddi.digital.net/~gandalf/trollfaq.html

Encryption

Steganography & Digital Watermarking:
http://www.jjtc.com/Steganography/

Tiny IDEA Encryption Program:
http://www.dcs.rhbnc.ac.uk/~fauzan/tinyidea.html

The International PGP home page: http://www.pgpi.com/

Canadian Strategy: http://e-com.ic.gc.ca/english/crypto/631d1.html

Distributed Authentication in Kerberos Using Public Key Cryptography:
http://www.ini.cmu.edu/netbill/pubs/pkda.html

Security Agencies

The United States Navy INFOSEC home page:
http://infosec.navy.mil/content.html

The US Intelligence Community: http://www.cia.gov/ic/index.html

Center for the Study of Intelligence: http://www.cia.gov/csi/index.html

Central Intelligence Agency—Electronic Document Release Center: http://www.foia.ucia.gov/

US Defense Intelligence Agency (DIA) home page: http://140.47.5.4/

National Security Agency: http://www.nsa.gov:8080/

Federal Bureau of Investigation Home Page: http://www.fbi.gov/

Canadian Security Intelligence Service: http://www.csis-scrs.gc.ca/

Canadian Security Establishment: ITS (Information Technology Security): http://www.cse.dnd.ca/cse/english/home_1.html

RCMP Technical Security Branch: http://www.rcmp-grc.gc.ca/tsb/index.htm

Web Information Grabbers and Port Scanners

The Limit Software, Inc.: http://www.thelimitsoft.com/

The Consumer Information Organization's Consumer.Net: http://www.consumer.net/

Privacy Analysis of Your Internet Connection: http://privacy.net/analyze/

Fat-Free Software News: http://www.ffsoftware.com/

Shields UP!—Internet Connection Security Analysis: http://grc.com/x/ne.dll?bh0bkyd2

E-Soft, Inc.: http://www.e-softinc.com/static/audit.html

Security Space: http://www.security space.com/sprobe/probe.html

Eye Digital Security: http://www.eeye.com/html/Databases/Software/nmapnt.html

MC2 Security Wire Computer and Network/Security Solution: http://www.mc2.nu/scan.php3

COTSE-IP Tools: http://www.cotse.com/iptools.html

network tool v2.41: http://nettool.false.net/

DSL—DSLreports.com: http://www.dslreports.com/scan

HACKER WHACKER Remote Computer Network Security Scan: http://www.hackerwhacker.com/

Online Security Check: http://www.it-sec.de/vulchke.html

Security Space: http://www.securityspace.com/smysecure/

Miscellaneous

Smurfing: The Latest DoS Attack: http://www.quadrunner.com/~c-huegen/smurf.cgi

Technical Incursion Countermeasures: http://www.ticm.com/about/knowledge.html

Strategis: http://strategis.ic.gc.ca/sc_mrksv/privacy/engdoc/homepage.html

COAST: http://www.cs.purdue.edu/coast/

Fred Cohen & Associates: http://all.net/

Scott Schnoll's Unofficial Microsoft Internet Explorer Security FAQ: http://www.nwnetworks.com/iesf.html

The WWW Security FAQ: http://www.w3.org/Security/Faq/www-security-faq.html

SekOrg Security Library: http://www.sekurity.org/library/books.comp.infosec.html

DigiCrime, Inc.: http://www.digicrime.com/dc.html

CRACKS: http://www.focus-asia.com/home/mad96/cracks.htm

Gibson Research Corporation Home Page: http://grc.com/default.htm

The Attacks on GRC.COM: http://grc.com/dos/grcdos.htm

Professor Noboru Hidano, "Social Engineering":
http://www.soc.titech.ac.jp/hidano/socialengineering.html

Ontrack Data International, Inc.: http://www.ontrack.com/

The Center for Democracy and Technology: http://www.cdt.org/

Books on the Social Aspects of Computing:
http://dlis.gseis.ucsd.edu/people/pagre/recent-books.html

Cult of the Dead Cow Back Orifice Backdoor:
http://www.iss.net/xforce/alerts/advise5.html

GNUPG—the GNU Privacy Guard:
http://www.d.shuttle.de/isil/crypt/gnupg.html

BugNet home page: http://www.bugnet.com/

National Cryptologic Museum: http://www.nsa.gov:8080/museum/

Media Awarness Network—the Three Little Cyber Pigs:
http://www.media-awareness.ca/eng/cpigs/cpigs.htm

SRI/CSL's Intrusion Detection Page:
http://www2.csl.sri.com/intrusion/index.html

L0pht Heavy Industries Security Advisories:
http://www.l0pht.com/advisories.html

Counterpane home page: http://www.counterpane.com/

Deborah Quilter's RSI Web Site: http://www.rsihelp.com/

PhD Thesis by Suzana Stojakovic-Celustka:
http://www.mystik-tours.hr/teza/teza.htm

Security Search—the Security Search Engine: http://www.securitysearch.net/

Ethics and Information Technology: http://www.wkap.nl/journals/ethics_it

Hack Canada—anything can be cracked when it's forty below:
http://www.hackcanada.com/

SecurityFocus: http://www.securityfocus.com/

Common Vulnerabilities and Exposures: http://cve.mitre.org/

Generally Accepted System Security Principles (GASSP):
http://web.mit.edu/security/www/gassp1.html

Pueblo High Tech Crimes Unit—Slide Shows:
http://www2.co.pueblo.co.us/sheriff/htcu/slides.html

attrition.org: http://www.attrition.org/

Smithsonian Computer History—"The Bug":
http://americanhistory.si.edu/csr/comphist/objects/bug.htm

ICSA Information Security Magazine: http://www.infosecuritymag.com/

ACM: ACM Transactions on Information and System Security:
http://info.acm.org/tissec/

JCS home page: http://www2.csl.sri.com/jcs/

SECURITY Magazine: http://www.securitymagazine.com/

CIPS Vancouver Security Special Interest Group: http://www.infosecbc.org/

(ISC)^2 CISSP Study Guide: https://www.isc2.org/cissp_studyguide

The CISSP Open Study Guide (OSG): http://www.cccure.org/

IT Crime—IT Security and Crime Prevention Methods:
http://www.interpol.int/Public/TechnologyCrime/CrimePrev/ITSecurity.asp

Security News:
http://members.home.net/torelad/SysAdmin/SecurityNews.htm

Handbook of Information Security Management (1998 edition online):
http://secinf.net/info/misc/handbook/

Common Criteria Project home page: http://csrc.nist.gov/cc/

Security Publications: http://csrc.nist.gov/secpubs/

Rainbow Series (US security standards books):
http://csrc.nist.gov/secpubs/rainbow/

Computer Security Resource Center (CSRC):
http://csrc.nist.gov/welcome.html

Information Security Resources: http://security.isu.edu/

Frequently Asked Questions (FAQ):
http://www.alw.nih.gov/Security/security-faqs.html

Auerbach Publications, Information Systems Security:
http://www.auerbach-publications.com/iss/

Illegal Prime Number:
http://www.utm.edu/research/primes/curios/485...443.html

HoneyNet Project: http://project.honeynet.org/

The Security Writers Guild: http://www.securitywriters.org/about.php

SANS Institute Online home page: http://www.sans.org/newlook/home.htm

CERT Coordination Center: http://www.cert.org/

ICAT CVE Metabase: http://icat.nist.gov/icat.cfm

Linux Security—the Community's Center for Security:
http://www.linuxsecurity.com/

Microsoft TechNet:
http://www.microsoft.com/technet/treeview/default.asp?url=/technet/
itsolutions/security/default.asp

rain forest puppy—exploits: http://www.wiretrip.net/rfp/

CyberCitizen partnership: http://www.cybercitizenship.org

Cyber Ethics for Kids: http://www.nicekids.net/indexf.htm

NT Security

Windows NT Frequently Asked Questions (FAQ): http://www.ntfaq.com/

NT Security—Frequently Asked Questions:
http://www.it.kth.se/~rom/ntsec.html

NTBugTraq—NTBugTraq home page: http://www.ntbugtraq.com/

NT Exploit(ed) Page: http://w3.aces.uiuc.edu/DLM/Ntexploits.html

NT Configuration Guide for the Paranoid:
http://www2.sysnet.net/~patton/securing_nt.html

NSA/Windows NT Security Guidelines:
http://www.trustedsystems.com/NSAGuide.htm

Nomad Mobile Research Centre—NT Files: http://www.nmrc.org/files/nt/

Russ Cooper's NT Fixes Status Page: http://www.ntbugtraq.com/ntfixes.asp

Secure Windows NT Installation and Configuration Guide:
http://infosec.navy.mil/TEXT/COMPUSEC/ntsecure.html

Utilities for Windows NT: http://www.sysinternals.com/ntutil.htm

NT Security—Frequently Asked Questions:
http://hackerwhacker.com/faqs/ntsec.html

Product Evaluation and Testing

IN THIS CHAPTER:

Core Issues

Test Match

Further Information

I t may seem strange that, unlike almost every other recent book on anti-virus technology, this one has stayed resolutely vendor-independent. There are three main reasons for this:

▶ We don't have the time or space for furnishing the details of every package you might be using. We know that NAI and Symantec have most of the market share, but many other fine products are strongly represented in both the corporate and the home-user markets, and while the core technology might not be dissimilar, the interfaces can be very different.

▶ Technology changes quickly in anti-virus security, at least on a superficial level. If we provided you with a few pages of illustrative screenshots, the version we used would be obsolete and the product merged with something else by the time this book hit the bookstores.

▶ In general, core functionality doesn't change that much between products. They all detect approximately the same range of viruses found in the wild. As long as detection and provision of definitions updates are up to the mark, it's the details of implementation that matter. However, we cannot tell you which implementation will work best for you (at least, not unless you are prepared to pay substantial rates for individual consultancy). Instead, we feel that this chapter will be more useful if we detail some of the issues that you need to consider when you evaluate anti-virus software that suits your environment.

Before we get into the details of testing antiviral software, whether as part of the corporate evaluation cycle or for purposes of reviewing, we need to consider:

▶ What features and issues are of most interest to you

▶ Which issues are susceptible to quantitative comparative testing

▶ Which features require a more qualitative and subjective evaluation

▶ Whether these latter features can be addressed usefully in comparative testing

Core Issues

The issues that concern most people can be classified quite simply:

▶ Cost

▶ Performance

- ▶ Functional range
- ▶ Ease of use
- ▶ Configurability
- ▶ Support functions

There is some overlap here, of course: functional range and performance are interrelated, as are ease of use and configurability, and the effectiveness of the vendor's support has a major bearing on all these issues. Nevertheless, it is convenient to define each issue in comparative isolation in the sections that follow.

Cost

You won't be surprised to learn that we consider cost to be a somewhat more complex issue than comparing unit costs over a range of products. Not that we consider unit cost to be unimportant. However, many organizations seem to base their evaluations almost entirely on this single factor. Even worse, they may focus on the issue of unit cost at the expense of the operating costs that constitute the hidden 90 percent that comprise the bulk of this particular iceberg. Smaller organizations may find it feasible to procure a package, distribute it, and perhaps remind everyone when and if it needs to be updatated.

> ### NOTE
> *Although the latter solution might be feasible, it may not necessarily be enough. Certainly if your strategy is based entirely on trusting your vendor of choice to make updates available to you as soon as a new threat appears, sooner or later you probably will be hit with the latest fast-burning mass-mailer while it is still making its initial impact, and before updates are available. Of course, we don't advocate such a narrow strategy, and we stress the need to take into account collateral expenses such as education and distribution.*

However, in larger organizations, even the most minimal strategy needs a little more support than this, and realistic cost estimates will reflect that need, rather than a procurement process along the lines of:

- ▶ Which products have I heard of?
- ▶ Which is the cheapest?
- ▶ I'll take it.

Unit Cost

Sadly, even the initial consideration of unit cost can entail hidden costs in terms of licence comprehension, let alone management (not to mention stress and headache management). Like other modern software, anti-virus packages can be licensed in a number of ways—per workstation, per user, per server, or a combination of these. Furthermore, since few vendors nowadays deal exclusively with anti-virus software, the cost may be calculated on the basis of a larger licensing deal including other software such as desktop firewalls, cryptographic software, remote management software, and so on. We are, in general, enthusiastic advocates of multilayering—that is, virus management at a number of key entry points apart from the desktop (the mail server, file servers, web servers, and so on).

Unsurprisingly, vendors who provide scanning services at all these levels are also enthusiastic, and will usually offer highly advantageous licensing terms for all-in-one deals. This reliance on a lone vendor can entail the vulnerabilities associated with any potential single point of failure. You may have a problem with a scanning engine used across a broad product range, or with a particular update, or you may fall foul of a given feature or weakness in the general design specifically exploited by a new threat. Multivendor solutions are less susceptible to such problems, and one brand of scanner in use at the desktop, for instance, may pick up a problem with the gateway scanner, or vice versa. However, this disadvantage may be considered acceptable when weighed against the advantages of a substantial reduction in initial outlay costs, a sole point of contact for all malware-related support needs, and a reduced risk of conflicts between programs. There may be other opportunities for negotiating a reduction in the cost, too: you may be able to act as a reference site, and committing to a two- or three-year licence may carry a considerable discount. However, for every loyalty discount, there's a disloyalty discount. A dealer or vendor who is keen to get your business will often offer the use of the software free until your old licence expires. (Many vendors will not deal directly with customers, but you will often find yourself dealing with sales and technical staff from the vendor as well as from the dealer to whom they hope you will eventually pay the cheque.) This offer is often described, optimistically, as a competitive upgrade. Having the use of a second product when you're already paying for another may not seem much of an advantage, but if you get your timing right, it offers the opportunity for an extended testing and rollout phase.

One consideration that you certainly should bear in mind here is whether the cost of using the software on home or portable machines is a hidden extra. What other hidden costs might you encounter?

Thank You for Your Support

It would be a bold vendor indeed that offered a product without any help-line support at all. However, some vendors have learned over the years to offer less and charge more. A common model is to offer options ranging from a nine-to-five service desk accessed via a premium telephone rate, to 24/7/52 support options with paged and emailed alerts, engineer onsite callout, and so on. The importance of such features is, however, a matter of personal or organizational taste, depending on what other third-party and in-house resources are available.

Via Media

We have been in the game long enough to remember receiving large cartons with disk sets or CDs for each licenced user. Those days are gone—at least, this is no longer a standard service. After all, everyone is connected nowadays, and it often makes sense to distribute upgrades, updates, and interim definitions electronically, with one CD sent to the primary site contact. Such distribution makes sense for small update files and patches transmitted across fast network links. In fact, once a vendor goes this route, updates supplied on conventional media may lag further and further behind the version available on the web site. If, however, you are blessed with large numbers of remote employees working over slow modem links, and a product that is regularly updated as a complete set of programs, some of them recompiled monthly, your mileage may vary considerably. If you find it necessary to burn CDs or even create diskette sets, you will find that the media and opportunity costs (time spent on duplication by staff who could be occupied elsewhere) quickly escalate. Even in a small organization, these costs can grow to the point where purchasing professional duplicating equipment, outsourcing to a third party, or paying an extravagant premium to the vendor become surprisingly attractive options.

RTFM

The days of large boxes of documentation are also long gone. Additional documentation sets are almost invariably an expensive extra. Vendors love electronic manuals, and hate to pay postage. If you can't get away with making .PDFs available on the intranet or a similar resource, look forward to copious laser printing and photocopying. Check the vendor's position on duplicating such materials. In our experience, vendors are often relaxed about this copyright violation—after all, they don't really *want* to produce any more hardcopy documentation than they need to, for obvious reasons. Even the biggest vendors can expect less benefit from economies of scale than you might think, being in a field of publishing where documentation changes and is updated almost as quickly as the software. But don't take our word for it: check with the copyright holder.

Of course, you may be able to condense vendor documentation to something less verbose, paper-intensive, and time-consuming, with some judicious cutting and pasting. However, this solution still imposes (at the very least) an opportunity cost.

Training

Some of the bigger vendors offer product training, on their site or yours. Some also offer less (overtly) product-specific training in virus management, either directly or through dealers. *Caveat emptor*: many (perhaps most) dealers are not anti-virus specialists, and are not always as well versed in the products they sell as you might expect. There are, of course, knowledgeable consultants and vendors. There are also a good number of instant experts. Fortunately, having read this book, you will be in a better position to tell one from the other. Training is usually an optional extra, and in some cases a very expensive one. However, we cannot overstress the importance of having at least one competently trained individual in all but the smallest organizations. Having first-line support staff trained to similar standards may be preferable to having the staff partly trained by an in-house specialist whose expertise might be in demand elsewhere.

Definitions Updates

Let's face it: the days when you could update every three months, perhaps applying interim definitions if a particularly threatening virus appeared between quarterlies, are long gone. Although not every virus that catches the public eye requires urgent attention, sometimes a fast burner not only spreads within hours of its launch, but generates enough copycats and variants to create a serious nuisance. Some vendors still maintain a policy of free updates, but some have moved towards a subscription model, which they usually enforce by requiring authentication before allowing the customer access to updates on web sites. (Vendors that issue a complete, partly recompiled program suite every month usually require authentication, too, not unreasonably.) Clearly, you will need to be sure that the initial licence outlay includes updates (and upgrades).

Customizations

As anti-virus software has endeavoured to become more versatile, in the hope of retaining market share in a high-pressure market, the range of threats (and non-threats) detected has increased. Consequently, customers (especially large customers) want more input into what the software actually detects. For example, some vendors have moved away from detecting by default more or less harmless joke programs such as CokeGift, but have made alternative definitions available on request that *do* detect them. Some customers have gone further and have requested detection of other programs that they consider unacceptable, such as games. Vendors with a gateway scanning product are also asked to address issues such as spam and pornography. These can often be handled more effectively with generic filtering techniques under the control of the systems administrator, but some vendors attempt to comply with customer requests for a more program-specific approach.

NOTE

To take an extreme example, subscribers to and maintainers of some specialist mailing lists are all too aware of the number of unnecessary bounces that can be caused by a mail server that is somehow configured to reject mail that contains a particular virus name in the subject line or message text. The server will bounce the mail even if there is no other realistic indication that a message is any likelier to be at risk than any other message. Indeed, the nonrecipient of such a bounced message may actually be put at greater risk, in that he or she may not be able to receive useful or essential information pertaining to that particular threat.

Older products may allow a degree of customization using a mechanism for entering customer-defined patterns, but vendors have moved away from this model, and are likelier to generate custom definitions themselves, where asked. If this works for you, go for it, but expect additional costs . Where customization is still found, it's likely that it is intended to relax the iron grip of the default configuration rather than to tighten it, as in the context of exclusion lists, whereby a customer can configure a scanner to refrain from scanning certain objects in certain contexts. This customization can reduce security, as when anything in the Recycle Bin is ignored for scanning purposes. On the other hand, reduction of processing overheads entailed by scanning objects that can never be executed may be considered a reasonable trade-off against such a reduction in security.

Administration

We don't intend at this point to go over the details of evaluation and implementation costs again. We must, however, point out again that unit cost is only a fraction of the total cost of ownership. One viable formula goes like this:

Total Cost of Ownership = Licence Cost + Extras + Cost of Evaluation + Cost of Administration

Clearly, even an informal evaluation is at least an opportunity cost. A formal evaluation with extensive testing can involve a number of people, including technical staff, the procurement officer, financial staff, and so on. Watch that counter climb....

Evaluation may be as uncomplicated as comparing reviews from general computing magazines (you may have gathered that we don't think much of these as a resource, in general), specialist magazines such as *Virus Bulletin* and *Secure Computing,* mailing lists, and universities with virus testing facilities and specialist staff, such as Hamburg, Tampere, and Magdeburg. On the other hand, evaluation may be as resource-intensive as a full test environment, involving testing on standard configuration workstations and servers. This may be restricted to installation and configuration testing, a trial rollout, compatibility testing, network performance testing, testing of update and upgrade distribution mechanisms, and so on. On the other hand, it may also involve serious detection testing with live viruses, depending on many factors such as the size of the organization, available expertise, and budget.

Testing the administrative and maintenance issues cannot be considered in detail here: these issues are dependent on the organizational structure and philosophy, resources available, and approach to security architecture. Nonetheless, they constitute a major TCO (Total Cost of Ownership) component, and you will need to factor something in to meet those future costs (not to mention the costs of incident and problem management). Alternatively, you might plan to outsource this testing.

The costs associated with evaluation and testing are only the tip of an administration iceberg. Once a product is selected, deploying and maintaining that product may also include costs such as:

▶ Deploying definitions updates and product upgrades or crossgrades. Who is responsible for regular updates—the vendor, the end user, the systems administrator, or even the user support team? How feasible is an automated solution?

▶ Responding to incidents.

▶ Dealing with false positives.

▶ Accessing and reviewing logs.

▶ Reviewing the contents of a quarantine area (if the product offers such a feature).

▶ Responding to internal user issues. ("How do I turn this thing off?!?")

▶ Selecting disinfection options and assessing the impact of that selection. (For example, selecting deletion instead of disinfection requires the availability of backups and restore options.)

Alas, these are questions that the vendor is unlikely to be able to answer very easily. They are largely specific to the organization, and may take time and much trial and error to establish.

Performance

Performance may be considered in a number of contexts, but detection is the one that matters most. After all, it is the only issue that even the most slippery of vendors cannot weasel out of; the one function that all virus scanners have in common is virus detection. However, just "detecting viruses" is too vague to be very useful, and well-founded testing methodologies target a number of classes of virus:

► In the Wild (usually as defined by inclusion on the WildList). A test set may include all the following classes of malware, though it is increasingly common to advocate the separate testing of pre-Windows file infectors and all boot-sector and partition-sector infectors.

► Boot-sector and partition-sector infectors, usually including file and boot multipartite viruses.

► Macro viruses. These mostly consist of VBA (Visual Basic for Applications) and other Microsoft Office-specific malware, including WordBasic macros and Excel formula viruses.

► Collection viruses (zoo viruses).

► Polymorphic viruses.

With the possible exception of some generic products, it is not usually considered realistic to expect scores of 100 percent in all these categories if a professionally managed, up-to-date virus collection is used—at least, not always, even when testing is intended to be confined to known viruses.

Testing a scanner's heuristic ability by using unknown viruses is a very different ballgame, and we consider some of the pitfalls in the final section of this chapter ("Test Match"). How much store you put by a scanner's heuristic abilities is a somewhat subjective judgment, and may vary according to the kind of heuristics offered and the location of the scanner. On the desktop, "high heuristics" may entail a heavy processing overhead for little gain. On the mail server, even broad-brush heuristics such as filtering by filename wildcards (*.*.vbs, for instance) may pay dividends in discarding or quarantining unknown malware without adding noticeable overhead (noticeable to the desktop user, that is). However, you may also want to know how prone the product is to false alarms (always an increased risk with a heuristic scanner, as with any generic technique).

Home In on the Range

The range of viral threats detected is also a matter for concern. Obviously, it matters if your scanner is not able to detect all the classes of malware that could affect or infect the protected system, and the average PC user would consider it a matter for concern if one of the following major classes of malware were not detected. We include the Trojan category because most anti-virus software detects some Trojans (despite the cries of "This is not anti-Trojan software!"), and the boundaries between certain kinds of virus, worm, and Trojan are somewhat fuzzy. The range of malware you are most likely to be interested in includes:

▶ System viruses that are hardware/firmware-specific. The most obvious examples are PC boot-sector viruses, which may cause damage on Intel-driven machines irrespective of operating system (although the choice of operating system has a bearing on whether the virus can actually replicate).

▶ System viruses that are operating system (OS)-specific. These include file infectors that may target (usually individual) system files under certain operating systems. They also include viruses that work by modifying OS-specific system components such as the Windows Registry.

▶ Parasitics (file infectors), which may also infect system files, but are distinguished from the previous class by the fact that they target executable files in general, irrespective of their actual function. In other words, a file might be infected because it is an .EXE file, irrespective of whether it's a component of the operating system or an application such as a text processing program.

▶ Multipartite viruses. This term is most often applied to bipartite file and boot-sector infectors. However, it can be extended in this context to include, for instance, malware that includes two or more elements of virus infection, worm infestation, and Trojanlike social engineering, or where one type of virus includes a dropper for a different class of virus.

▶ Macro viruses, which can be described as application-specific. This description doesn't mean, of course, that you shouldn't be concerned about receiving infected documents if you don't have the vulnerable application, but then it becomes a matter of responsibility to others. You probably want to let people know that they're showering you with bugs, and you don't want to pass them on yourself passively, as can happen with latent viruses.

▶ Other script malware (such as VBS worms). These may be of specific interest in particular environments—for instance, where the Windows Script Host is routinely used for legitimate purposes.

▶ Worms and email-aware viruses. They are not, of course, always written in VBS, and are not always PC- or Windows-specific.

▶ Trojans, in particular straightforward destructive Trojans. Other nonreplicative malware may also be a concern. Increasingly, though, other classes of malware detection software address Trojan horse programs, in some cases more effectively than anti-virus software does.

From an evaluation standpoint, you should also take an interest in a scanner's capabilities as regards two closely related phenomena that are often not considered:

▶ Latent viruses

▶ Heterogeneous virus transmission

Latent viruses are viruses that have not been executed in the environment under examination. Viruses and worms detected and blocked on arrival as mail attachments are examples of this class of threat. We can also consider viruses that *cannot* be executed in that particular host environment as latent (for example, Windows viruses on a Mac and vice versa, or 32-bit Windows infectors in a 16-bit Windows environment— Windows 3.1, for example). This latter case is an instance of something we have described before as heterogeneous virus transmission. Some readers will certainly want to take into account a scanner's capabilities in a mixed environment. By *mixed environment*, we mean not only offices with Mac and PC desktop machines, but also environments where a mixture of platforms, such as Windows and UNIX, is in use. To take an extreme example, a scanner that detects only UNIX malware if run on a host that includes a mail server is a waste of space unless all the workstations are also UNIX-based. Even then, the question of transmission remains unaddressed, since non-UNIX malware can still be forwarded "passively" without the malicious code being executed as part of the transmission process.

Evaluators should also take into account other targets, such as the following:

▶ Virus kits/generators (we refer here to the recognition of actual kits, not the heuristic detection of kit viruses)

▶ Intendeds, corruptions, and other nonviable threats

▶ Distributed Denial of Service (DDoS) agents

▶ Nondestructive Trojans such as password stealers

▶ Jokes

▶ Games

> ### NOTE
>
> *We are not saying that your software of choice should (or should not) detect all these things. We are, however, saying that if detection of these things is important to you, you need to verify that the software has such capabilities. Some products fail to detect whole classes of real viruses, let alone more equivocal examples of malware and objects that are not universally accepted as malware (jokes, for example).*

Accuracy

We mention in the context of accuracy two factors related to detection that are difficult to test, but are very important to most customers:

▶ Susceptibility to false positives is difficult to test; unless you already know the sort of thing a given scanner misreports as viral (or otherwise malicious), the only testing methodology that is likely to work is to subject it to a huge test suite of applications known to be clean. You can perhaps reduce the load slightly if you have particular classes of false positive in mind.

▶ Gateway scanners can be tested to see if heuristics are set too coarsely grained, by sending mail including known trouble areas, such as plain text mail containing the name of a known virus, or some string known to be associated with a known worm, but out of the context of the particular virus. For example, mail that includes the phrase "Iloveyou" (or even worse, "Good Times") in the body of the message should not, in our opinion, automatically flag that message as infected with LoveLetter. In fact, some might regard it as a false alert if a message with no attachment, but with the subject "Iloveyou", is flagged as definitely infected, even though that subject text normally indicates worm-cast.

While we were writing this chapter, W32/Sircam was making its rounds and demonstrating another oddity we see increasingly often: messages sent by the worm and created by the worm, but with the attachment corrupted or lost altogether. (It is not unusual for gateway scanners or content filters to strip malicious or potentially malicious attachments, but that's not what we are talking about here.) Should anti-virus software flag these accidents and misfires? Yes, because they give the good citizen of the Internet the opportunity to point out to the sender—whether a friend, a colleague, or a complete stranger—that he or she has an infection or infestation of malicious software.

Exact identification is difficult to test; not only do you need a test suite of virus samples, but you also need to know exactly how the antiviral should report those samples. This sort of information is very difficult to verify without specialized resources that are not available to most systems administrators, journalists, and so on. Yet this is an important issue. If a virus isn't identified correctly, it cannot be disinfected with 100 percent reliability. There is further scope for confusion, in that scanners don't always report what they find with a canonical name. For example, sometimes you will see a virus reported as "xyz.gen", suggesting that the virus has been detected and removed using a generic driver that detects a family of viruses, rather than identifying a specific variant.

Appearances may be deceptive, though. How a scanner reports a virus does not necessarily indicate how well it discriminates between variants. After all, most vendors assume that their customers don't care whether the virus in question is W97M/EvilVirus.GP or W97M/EvilVirus.GQ, though this assumption is increasingly unsafe.

In many cases (including CIH, AutoStart, and W97M/Marker), different variants of the same virus have different payloads or levels of destruction or data leakage. The difference between variants may have a serious impact on further containment or source/scope issues, such as where the virus came from and how far it may have penetrated into the organization. For example, a number of recent email-aware viruses and worms write log files or contain internal information about previous addresses "visited". In general, scanners tend to ignore or simply delete such log files, or bury the table along with the worm. However, a systems administrator might well want to know about the log file, perhaps for forensic purposes, or about a residual effect that could be needlessly exposing the presence of a previous infection well after the infection itself has been eradicated.

Furthermore, while a misidentified virus cannot be removed reliably, it isn't always necessary to know the exact variant in order to disinfect a system effectively. If disinfection involves removing all macros in an infected document, or deleting a malicious Visual Basic script, slight variations aren't particularly important. The environment or infected object may not be restored to the state the customer might have expected, even where malware has been exactly and correctly identified, if the virus has made Registry changes or trashed legitimate macros. Registry changes are also an area where variants may differ, and to make manual repairs, the administrator needs to know specifics.

Most readers will not be able to get around these difficulties at first without recourse to the vendor's help line.

Speed of Execution

Scan speed is usually most noticeable when evaluating or testing an on-demand scanner. Fortunately, this is not quite the big issue it was a few years ago, when the on-demand scan was the mainstay of anti-virus strategy. Nowadays, it is common for the on-demand scanner to be used only for removal of a virus already known to be or suspected of being on the system, or in some instances for a weekly or daily scheduled scan. In the latter case, modern multitasking operating environments allow the scan to take place in the background, in which case the speed of operation may matter less, and is certainly dependent on the type and resource intensity of the operations taking place in the foreground. This dependence doesn't make it impossible to test scanning speed comparatively, as long as the testing takes place against the same set of automated foreground processes. However, real-life performance in this respect will vary widely according to the individual workstation, and the tasks being performed at the time. A number of components contribute to overall scanning speed:

▶ How long it takes to load the program initially, before the actual scan starts.

▶ Whether the scanner is set to maximize speed rather than thoroughness, or vice versa. A "deep scan" is likely to incur considerable overhead by examining the whole file, rather than just the part where a given virus footprint is expected to be found. (We are not, by the way, falling into the common trap of thinking of viruses and file viruses as being synonymous, in this case. However, it would be very uncommon to find a system on which the number of files to be examined was less than the number of boot sectors and other system areas, so file scanning is the area in which we would expect to find most of the overhead.)

▶ Whether the scanner is set to examine all files, or only those defined as "executable". Nowadays, "executable" files include infectable documents, such as those created by Microsoft Office applications, as well as system and application files.

▶ Whether the scanner is set for heuristic analysis, whether heuristics are set for all types of infectable object (some scanners have separate settings for file heuristics and macro heuristics, for example), and whether different levels of heuristic intensity can be applied. For example, some scanners differentiate between heuristics and high heuristics, the latter being more resource-intensive.

▶ Whether the scanner allows a form of hybrid detection combining known-virus scanning and checksumming. Specific objects are scanned only for specific viruses if a checksum mismatch suggests that the object has been modified since the last time it was checked. This can give the scanner a significant advantage on a second run against a test suite, but puts it at a disadvantage on a first run, since its speed on the first run will be less impressive than its performance on subsequent runs. How this affects the scanner's performance in a real-world situation will vary widely according to local conditions and patterns of usage.

Similar considerations apply in the testing of on-access scanners. However, unless the scanner is abnormally slow, differences in performance are less obvious on a file-by-file basis, and can only be realistically tested using standardized test procedures and taking into account possible variations introduced by operating system–specific speed reduction strategies such as caching. Use of on-access scanners, which are memory-resident and therefore running all the time, introduces the issue of compatibility and possible contention with other processes running at the same time. It is not uncommon for an on-access scanner to conflict with another memory-resident program (often something not noticeably related functionally, such as a video driver). It is also possible that such a conflict will arise with a given nonresident application, if it happens to be running. On-demand scanners are less often associated with such difficulties, although their use in conjunction with scheduling software has sometimes been observed to cause problems.

It's Not My Default

Modern anti-virus software has a wide range of capabilities and strengths, and some products are better in specific areas than others. Default settings generally put scanning speed before absolute caution, but some vendors' products may vary drastically in regard to a particular default setting. Many a review has castigated a product for poor detection performance when the responsibility actually lay with a tester who had made unsafe assumptions about default behaviour. Here are some issues that you might need to check.

Zipped Files

Most on-access scanners don't check archived (compressed) files such as .ZIP files by default, if at all. (The assumption here is that an infected file within an archive will be detected when the file is actually extracted from the archive, which is when detection is actually needed.) On-demand scanners often do scan inside some types of compressed file, although not invariably. However, they rarely do so by default. Furthermore, while most scanners can scan inside .ZIP files if the appropriate switch is used, they don't necessarily scan nested .ZIP files (that is, .ZIPs within .ZIPs). If they do, they may not scan to an infinite depth of nesting. Most modern products scan in memory (which may cause problems if there are multiple nesting levels or large files), but some may have to extract the contents of an archive to disk before they can scan. Even if other compression formats are supported, it is unlikely that any one product will scan all variations of all likely compression formats, and oddball combinations, such as one type of archive nested inside another, may also lead to difficulties. Even worse, a scanner encountering such problems won't always flag them.

Compressed Executables

Scanning of compressed (packed) executables also leads to complications, though the situation here is somewhat different. This form of compression aims to reduce the amount of space an executable takes up on disk, by allowing it to self-decompress in memory on execution. Clearly, it is desirable for a product to support a variety of packing formats, and anti-virus software has addressed this issue for some years already. However, malicious programs have been known to reappear in a compressed version; in these circumstances, scanners may fail to detect the compressed form. Scanning of packed executables is worth a tick on the features table, but don't expect this process to perform miracles.

Compressed Disks

Disk compression isn't as popular as it was around the middle of the 1990s. Disk capacity is, after all, astonishingly cheap nowadays. Even in environments where disk compression may still be in use, anti-virus software has moved away from routine clean-boot on-demand scanning, which is where problems traditionally arose. In simple terms, disk compression works by funnelling a whole physical disk into a virtual disk, which is in reality a huge file. The virtual disk can be chock full of viruses, but these can be detected only if the software driver is loaded that allows the operating system to see the virtual disk as a disk rather than as a file.

Encryption

Encryption, in terms of password-protected files, causes some confusion, and not only in terms of testing and evaluation. Some decryption, such as the native (invariable) encryption that can be applied to VB scripts, has no impact on detection of malware; if there is a high proportion of content that doesn't change between infections, it doesn't matter whether the content is encrypted or not. Where the contents of a file cannot be scanned effectively unless the file is decrypted, things get a little more complicated. Note that decrypting a file does not always require pre-knowledge of a password, as long as the algorithm is known. However, anti-virus vendors do not normally address decryption issues except where the encryption is part of the virus, as is the case with polymorphic viruses using variable encryption, for instance. The assumption here is that the virus will be spotted when and if the object is decrypted in the normal way.

Obviously, it would not be practical for vendors to include autodecryption routines for every known encryption package, and real-time autodecryption of files enciphered with secure algorithms is not practical, Hollywood fantasies of universal decryption tools notwithstanding. A common exception to this rule is the old-time Word or Excel document. Some older versions of these applications were protected with a simple-enough algorithm that it was feasible to decrypt and scan the files on the fly. And, some vendors did so routinely, although at least one vendor declined to offer this option, on the grounds that the vendor could not guarantee that its product would perform the process correctly every time, and preferred not to risk a false negative. More recently, Microsoft has enhanced the encryption in Office applications later than Office 95, making it no longer feasible to decrypt in real time, so the importance of this feature has declined.

Another commonly found encryption format is the one used by PKZip and other products (notably WinZip) that use the same file format. This encryption, though no longer considered highly secure (a number of "cracks" are available), is nevertheless solid enough to render real-time decryption impractical. Industrial-strength algorithms such as those employed by PGP, for example, should not be susceptible to real-time automatic decryption without a pass phrase.

In general, if a scanner recognizes a file as being inaccessible because it is encrypted (for example, password-protected MS Office files) it is preferable that the scanner report this fact, because there are possibilities for confusion when, for instance, a self-decrypting executable is scanned. The problem here is not dissimilar to that found with self-extracting archive files. The scanner checks the file, finds that it is a legitimate .EXE file, and doesn't find a virus. However, there is no guarantee that when the archived or encrypted component of the file is uncompressed or decrypted that it will be similarly hygienic. However, this is not much of an issue if a reliable on-access scanner is active in memory at the time the file is restored to its original form.

Corporate administrators are generally enthusiastic about gateway scanning; it's far easier to maintain, end users cannot switch it off, and it catches most current malware. However, as more people use encryption routinely, we observe a shift of interest back to desktop scanning. On-access scanning at the desktop, and at the moment of decryption, is currently the best technological means of addressing the problem of transmission of encrypted and possibly infected files. Anti-virus software may be integrated into the Public Key Infrastructure (PKI) so that autodecryption can be effected while the file is in transit between two end users. This latter scenario introduces some interesting questions about technical implementation that does not compromise confidentiality. Unfortunately, these questions are somewhat beyond the scope of this book.

Disinfection and Repair

A moment's thought tells us that disinfection and repair are not altogether the same thing, although the two terms are often used interchangeably. Rather as adding disinfectant to drinking water renders it unfit for its primary purpose, so removing a virus may render a system unusable. It's not only in surgery that a successful operation can leave the patient inert. Low-level formats and ill-advised MBR replacement are drastic surgery indeed. However, dedicated anti-virus software can also kill the patient.

Anti-virus software sometimes replaces an infected boot sector with a generic boot sector that may leave the system unbootable, but this is far less likely to happen with dedicated anti-virus software than with FDISK, the use of which with an undocumented switch is still advocated in some quarters. In fact, we have seen it advocated in anti-virus documentation (and protested accordingly).

Sometimes it isn't possible to repair a true executable file so that it still functions. The effects of the virus may not be altogether predictable, so that the host can't be restored exactly to its pre-infected form. This may not matter, but it may result in side effects. Oddly enough, anti-virus scanners, which usually incorporate a test of their own integrity when they start up, can be particularly vulnerable to this problem: a disinfected scanner program may refuse to run because it can detect that it has been modified.

A macro virus is usually child's play to neutralize. However, it may leave traces that are detected by other scanners, and removal of the macro may not restore the environment. WM/Cap is a classic example, in that it leaves customizations in the global template that render some menu options unavailable. Anti-virus software does not usually address this sort of problem, nor can it restore legitimate macros trashed or corrupted by the virus itself.

A similar problem is found where a virus or worm modifies the Windows Registry. Vendors have avoided making automatic repairs to the Registry, for a number of reasons. The Registry is not a static object. Behind the scenes, changes may be going on all through a computing session, and distinguishing between legitimate and viral modifications is not always straightforward. Restoring a Registry key to a default that usually works may, on occasion, result in destabilizing something else. Furthermore, the Registry changes between versions, and not only between NT-based and $9x$ versions, but between revisions.

Sadly, accurate information on how well a product addresses these issues is rarely available from vendor marketing departments. A well-maintained vendor service desk will have ready access to this information, and will add it to the database as calls on individual incidents come in and are signed off, but this doesn't help much at the evaluation stage. More usually, you can only consider the issue pragmatically, by testing with live samples (oh, dear…) or by talking to people with firsthand experience.

We will not deal at length with the question of product certification here. Not that we regard independent testing and certification as irrelevant or unhelpful, but testing for certification purposes usually focuses on detection. This is understandable: detection is far easier (and cheaper) to test than issues such as disinfection and repair, let alone elusive but expensive issues such as false positives. However, testing and certification processes are changing quite rapidly, and such crucial issues as repair are addressed more often by independent testers and certification specialists such as *Virus Bulletin* (www.virusbtn.com) and ICSA Labs (www.icsalabs.com).

We agree that certification is a much better guide to a product's capabilities if it provides a trustworthy indication of how well the product handles disinfection and repair. To quote Christine Orshesky:

> I cannot tell you how many times I have gone through [situations where] the "cure" was more destructive than the disease scenarios and would have liked to know how a vendor handles disinfection and repair and how it compares to other products before I chose the "auto-detect and repair" option. Lack of confidence or assurance in a given product's disinfection capabilities combined with the need to handle residual effects and the need to determine source, scope, and containment issues, sometimes leads me to disable any disinfection options and simply quarantine or delete.

However, the fact that a product is certified in any respect does not spare you the necessity of understanding what the testing process is intended to evaluate, how appropriate the methodology is to that aim, and how well the certification maps to the needs and requirements of your organization.

Compatibility Issues

Let's consider the problem of virus damage for a moment. We know that some viruses cause dramatic deliberate or accidental damage. However, the most permanent, expensive consequence of virus action doesn't even require the presence of a specific virus, only the possibility that a virus *may* be present at some point in the future. We are, of course, referring to the necessity of taking anti-virus precautions, which usually means scanning software. We are not talking about the cost issues already discussed, but rather the fact that this software has to coexist with other software: the system software and operating system, other utilities (especially those that run memory-resident), and those all-important applications. When PCs were largely DOS-based and single-tasking, and scanning was primarily on-demand, the main issue was "down time" while a system was being scanned, although from time to time a particular combination of software might lead to unexpected side effects. On-access TSR (memory-resident) scanning focused more attention on compatibility issues:

▶ Due to the restricted available memory in a DOS environment, the TSR's footprint had to be as small as possible in order to load at all, and was influenced by such uncertainties as the order in which TSRs were loaded and the state of the network.

▶ TSR programming was always something of a black art, fraught with uncertainties and reliant on mystic incantations.

Inevitably, there were problems, if only the inevitable slowing down of processes where CPU time was shared between resource-intensive or computation-intensive programs.

Windows, as a multitasking environment with a more relaxed memory model and a formally documented programming interface, alleviated some of these problems. However, the increasing complexity of the environment introduced whole new classes of potential instability.

These problems are unpredictable; they can be fully tested only in the target environment, over time. Known problems with particular software, exchange of information in special interest groups such as AVIEN, and customers who are prepared to act as reference sites may be helpful, but someone else's experiences are not a complete substitute for onsite evaluation and compatibility testing.

Functional Range

In a mixed environment (and most large organizations can be described as such), you will need to know what platforms are protected and what virus entry points are covered by antiviral protection:

▶ The desktop

▶ LAN servers

▶ Mail gateways, such as SMTP, Domino, and Exchange servers

▶ Gateways for other data transmission protocols, such as ftp, HTTP, and NNTP

Large organizations will be particularly interested in firewall plug-in scanning, specialized viruswalls, and other content-filtering software and hardware, and the question of how well these functions can be integrated within the same product range.

On-Demand Scanning

The anti-virus industry has moved away from routine on-demand scanning, at least as a prophylactic measure. However, even where a product includes on-the-fly on-access disinfection, on-demand scanners are still needed to deal with incidents where replicative malware has already taken hold. In such cases, the hope is that on-demand scanners will fix the problem, or at least clarify the extent of the problem. In any case, many systems administrators prefer to run scheduled on-demand scans as a supplement to on-access scanning, and sometimes as a substitute, for example, on a low-end system where the processing overhead of on-access scanning is considered too onerous in a low-risk situation, such as a machine that isn't networked. Unless you are very certain that you'll never need it, the effectiveness of the scheduling may be of some interest.

Another likely scenario calling for a scheduled scan is after a new definitions update or version upgrade. In this case, an on-demand scan may be the default or even mandated as part of the installation/update process. If not, it may be desirable to use a wrapper script that calls the installation/update and also runs a scan right after the update. Alternatively, a rescan may be flagged as required at the next restart, and end users may prefer this, since reinstalls and rescans always seem to happen at the worst possible time. However, some machines are never normally powered down, so some means of ensuring that a scan is run before the next weekly scan event (for instance) may be a good idea, to ensure that any infected files that may have slipped through before the update will be detected and handled in a more timely manner. This, in turn, increases the system administrator's ability to respond to a potential latent infection and to contain the infection, but it may also be useful in the comparatively rare case of a virus that isn't properly detected by an on-access scanner when the virus itself is already in memory.

Targeting is also an issue. Sometimes you'll need to run an all-files, all-volumes scan. Sometimes, though, you know exactly what for and where it is you're hunting, in which case it's seriously annoying to have to scan the whole of drive C, knowing that your target is Happy99.exe, and that it's sitting in the attachments directory. Fortunately, few scanners nowadays are this inflexible, but selecting the right module or menu is not always straightforward. Some of the targeting issues that might concern you are these:

▶ Can you select scanning of the whole system, a single selected volume, a number of selected volumes, one or more selected folders, or one or more selected files?

▶ Can you use filename wildcards? Is there a browse button to allow you to navigate to a given file, or do you have to type in a canonical or relative filename? Can you select files or folders on a remote drive using UNCs? (UNC stands for Universal Naming Convention, which is a way of pointing to a server share point using the notation *servername\share\subdirectory\filename* or *servername\volume\ subdirectory\filename* rather than mapping to a virtual drive name. For instance, the "public directory" on the server "rambo" might be mapped to drive Z, but could also be accessed as \\rambo\sys\public. In this case, you would expect the commands DIR Z and DIR \\RAMBO\SYS\PUBLIC to return the same directory listing. As this Novell-flavoured example indicates, the convention doesn't assume an NT server.)

▶   Can you choose to scan or not scan subfolders within the target folder?

▶   Does the scanner support inclusion lists and exclusion lists? For instance, do you want to make sure the Recycle Bin is scanned every time, or exclude the directory tree that contains your virus samples?

▶   Does the scanner look for the tens of thousands of all known viruses, or can it be configured not to look for some classes of malware (such as Macintosh viruses, old-time DOS viruses, joke files, or even viruses unlikely to be found in the wild)?

▶   Assuming that the scanner has a heuristic mode (not all scanners do), is the mode graduated? (Some scanners support "high heuristics" that scan more aggressively for viruslike code than "standard heuristics".) Gateway scanners may offer a particularly wide range of heuristic options, including content scanning within mail messages as well as attachment scanning, scanning for suspicious filename extensions, and so on. If you have particular requirements, you'll want to know that the product supports them.

On-Access Scanning

On-access scanning may offer a similar range of options. Again, if you have particular requirements, you'll need to check issues such as these:

▶   Is the range of malware detected what you expected? For example, DOS TSR scanners don't usually detect complex polymorphic viruses or macro viruses.

▶   Does the scanner have a heuristic mode? Is it configurable?

▶   What does "on-access" actually mean? Does it scan when a file is opened for reading, for writing to, or only for execution? Is a file scanned when it's closed? (More is safer, but less is faster.)

▶   Can the scanner disinfect?

▶   Can it autodisinfect? That is, can it disinfect without prompting? If it can, does it still write a log? If the scanner deals with viruses transparently and creates no record that is available to you, this prevents you from letting the source of an infection know it has a problem. It also means that the cost of the software can't be justified statistically. In this latter case, can alerts or prompts still be sent so that the scanner prevents the administrator from having to review the logs manually looking for infections? Many applications do generate logs, but rarely are the resources available to review or even to act on them.

> ▶ Where alerts are generated, how are they sent? Email or paging might be preferred, in case a server broadcast is not seen for a while (or even at all) because the administrator doesn't happen to be logged on to a particular server, or because a remote console package may not be running at that point.

> ▶ How does the scanner deal with infected files? The most common options are to rename the files with non-executable filenames in order to neutralize them, to place the files in a protected quarantine directory, to disinfect them, and to delete them. Not many scanners nowadays delete all infected objects, but they may delete all examples of a given class, such as file infectors, for example. Of course, some of these issues are applicable to on-demand scanners, too. Most on-access scanners deny access to the infected file and flag it accordingly. On-demand scanners do something similar when they change the filename (for example, from MYFILE.EXE to MYFILE.VXE). However, not all operating systems rely on file extensions to tell them whether a file is executable or not. In Linux and other flavours of UNIX, as well as Mac OS, a filename extension has no special meaning for the operating system, although it may for some applications. Even in MS-DOS or Windows, it isn't necessarily impossible to execute a file with a nonstandard filename extension, or even no extension, but doing so usually requires that you modify the environment by patching a system file or by creating a secondary shell process.

Integrity Checking

This book has largely concentrated on known-virus and heuristic scanning, since this is what the industry usually prefers. However, the day of the change detector (integrity checker) is not yet over. Indeed, as part of a general strategy of integrity management, this class of software is enjoying something of a resurgence of interest in some quarters, and certainly it has its advantages in a multilayered defence strategy. However, a change detector needs a wide range of options offering flexibility in configuration, if it is not to be more trouble than it's worth. In most environments, it needs to be carefully targeted. There is rarely an advantage to detecting modifications to documents; in general, documents are intended to be modified, as are executable files generated by development software used by the owner of the protected system. On the other hand, knowing that a system file or a "frozen" archive has been modified is often an excellent indicator of a virus or some other intrusive program or behaviour.

If you plan to make use of such software, you'll need to be aware of a number of issues. Vendors don't usually advertise the details of the checksum algorithms used to detect modification of a protected object, but they should be able to tell you enough to reassure you that the algorithms aren't simple and relatively easy to spoof.

CRC (cyclic redundancy checking), for example, is perfectly adequate for communications handshaking where security is not an issue, but is unsuitable for secure integrity checking. Secure message digest algorithms such as MD5 are normally considered a minimum requirement. Note, however, that the use of such an algorithm is not an absolute guarantee of the security of an integrity checker, any more than a massive key length is a guarantee of the security of an encryption algorithm.

Integrity checkers are a common target of *retroviruses*, viruses that take advantage of the known characteristics of anti-virus software. A classic attack takes advantage of the fact that integrity checkers are useful only if they check for divergence from a baseline image of a file (or other object) taken at a time when it was known to be uninfected. If the checksum algorithm is feeble enough, a virus may be able to falsify the checksum to conceal the change. If this isn't possible, simply trashing the file containing the checksum might be enough. In a number of notorious instances, if the file was not found, the software simply ran the checksum calculations again to re-create it (or them). If a virus had trashed the file(s), it was now impossible for change detection to detect the presence of the virus, since it had been "absorbed" into the baseline image. Countermeasures include avoiding simple-minded measures, such as writing individual image files for each directory within the imaged directory, in favour of using a single file with a random or user-defined filename and location.

Exclusion and inclusion lists are useful features for integrity checkers, too. Exclusion lists allowing particular directories or files to be excluded can cut down on time wasted checking objects that don't matter or that are expected to change from time to time. Inclusion lists can also be helpful in keeping down the processing overhead by checking only essential objects.

On-access integrity checkers are rarer than the on-demand variety, but have particular advantages where hybrid checksumming and known-virus scanning are used. In these scenarios, a file or other infectable object is scanned for known viruses only if it fails the checksum test, indicating that the file or object has been modified since it was last scanned. Such modification is not necessarily the result of viral action, of course. Also, the one product we know of that makes heavy use of this strategy automatically refreshes the checksums if its known-virus definitions database is updated.

We have not spent much time on old-time behaviour-blocking or monitoring software. Most people get fed up with its false alarms and restrictive behaviour very quickly, and such software isn't very useful if people keep turning it off. If this approach attracts you, you will want to be sure that the software is:

▶ Reasonably configurable (especially in terms of taking it down a notch if it is too aggressive)

▶ Capable of "learning" so that it doesn't set off false alarms monotonously on the same harmless behaviour, day after day

▶ Not so obtrusive as to make your computing life impossible

▶ Economical in the memory and processing time it consumes

▶ Compatible with your standard desktop applications

Other Tools

Not everyone favours the minimal approach. While we don't particularly advocate the Swiss Army knife "blade for every possible job", you may find some use for extra tools, if they're available, such as the following:

▶ Goat or bait files

▶ Tools that take various approaches to scanning for possible companion infectors

▶ Tools for rewriting system areas

▶ Tools for storing and restoring files that shouldn't change

Other tools that may one day fall into the "wish I had one here" class include:

▶ Disk editing and viewing tools (we remember with some fondness a particular tool that was a read-only disk viewer unless you knew the switch that converted it to an editor)

▶ A binary file editor

▶ A small but stable text editor

▶ Last but not least, realistic tools for the deployment and management of the software on remote machines

Ease of Use

If you could choose one attribute above all others for your anti-virus software, what would it be? Detection of every known virus? Availability on every known platform? We suspect that for most people, at least the nonexperts, their first choice would be ease of use. The best virus detection abilities are of little value if it takes a rocket scientist to employ the package.

Ease of use has two closely related aspects: user transparency and ease of configuration and administration. End users want their anti-virus software to toil invisibly, so that they never have to think about their own protection, which equates to expecting a technological solution to solve a psychological problem. Still, wearing our system administrator hats, we share the urge to let our customers get on with their work.

However, there are really only two ways to achieve this enviable state. The first is to use AV security software so easygoing and relaxed that it's useless at providing security. The second is to transfer the burden from the end user to the administrator. This works best if the administrator can effectively generate, maintain, and distribute preconfigured packages to end users. Most modern anti-virus packages with a corporate customer base offer server-based tools for remote installation and maintenance, and some systems also provide remote incident management. The more sophisticated tools of this ilk almost invariably assume the presence of a Microsoft network, rather than less common (nowadays) alternatives such as NetWare or UNIX-based networks. If your network is not of the Microsoft variety, you can attain some of the functionality of such tools by the judicious use of batch files and login scripts. However, our experience is that most vendors don't support such measures as well as they might. The administrator in other environments can generally look forward to hand-coding lots of scripts and macros, and long conversations with staff from the vendor's second-line support office.

Alternatively, you can grit your teeth and accept that end users have to take some responsibility for their own anti-virus arrangements. Implementation in this case can range from complete abdication of central control to the provision of vendor and, if necessary, in-house documentation, training courses, and detailed guidelines. Such measures do not avoid the need for you to provide comprehensive training of first-line and second-line support teams, who will have to be prepared to plug the gaps, whether through detailed telephone talk-downs or through the dispatch of engineers to infected sites.

NOTE

The term talk-down in the context of telephone support seems to derive from those novels and movies where an ex-pilot or other unlikely person finds himself or herself in improbable circumstances, alone at the controls of an airliner, being talked down onto the runway by the control tower.

Configurability

You may be lucky. You may be using an anti-virus solution that comes out of the box with default settings that are ideal for your purposes and environment. But we doubt it, and we would at least urge you to check what the defaults actually are, even if you're administering a single machine. If you are running one or more networks, you may be able to use a standard configuration on all machines, although it's unlikely that it will be the out-of-the-box configuration. (In such cases, you should probably give serious thought to a product that allows you to distribute install-and-run preconfigured packages, preferably over the network.)

Clearly, you will want to set sensible defaults. However, since anti-virus configuration involves a trade-off between speed and transparency on one hand and extreme security on the other, we cannot tell you what is "sensible" for you. Since your own views on what is appropriate in your environment may change according to experience, you will probably want to be able to adjust those defaults easily, when necessary. However, you may also want to be able to lock down the configuration with a password, so that end users don't have the same freedom to change a configuration that you do. Furthermore, you'll probably want to implement such changes remotely, either by use of administration software or by replacing configuration files when the end user logs in to the network.

Other issues that may need to be checked in a mixed environment include the degree of integration between versions for different operating systems:

▶ Is the package available for all the servers and workstations that you run?

▶ If you update the workstations from servers (as is usually the case in a large organization), how effective is the mechanism for automatically invoking the update mechanism when necessary?

Our experience is that most products perform automatic updates quite effectively as long as you run a very conventional network (which usually means Windows everywhere). If you aren't running such a network (and even if you are), we recommend that you test these aspects of the software very thoroughly when evaluating a package:

▶ How does the server or console software check the currency of an attached workstation's protection?

▶ How does the software run the update?

▶ How easy is it to check that the update has "taken"?

▶ If the auto-updating mechanism fails, how easy is it to substitute a hand-crafted replacement using login scripts and batch files?

▶ Can you easily fall back on a previous update/upgrade if the new one causes dramatic problems? How does the console handle regression to previous versions or updates—especially since many products ship small programming changes along with their updated signatures?

▶ How scalable is the console—that is, how many systems can be updated from one console or one task at a console?

Testability

As the previous section may suggest, blind faith has no place in anti-virus implementation. We will explore some of the specifics of detection testing later in this chapter, but you also need to be able to test your implementation. Specifically (but not all-inclusively), you will need to test installation, configuration, updates, logging, and compatibility with other software. Many administrators test every update before releasing it to the organization as a whole (this is particularly important with products that are recompiled every month), and cherish products that allow fast and easy rollback to a previous "safe" version if a problem arises.

Testing your implementation could include spot checks of systems to ensure that what the console (or script) was supposed to make happen really did. In our experience, sometimes scripts report that things have worked as expected, but when you visit a particular system at random, you do not find what you intended. It is worth the effort to check systems periodically and randomly, to ensure that your implementation is working. Checking and assurance avoids difficult confrontations with management, explaining why a system became infected with a virus for which detection capability has been available for weeks or even months.

Support Functions

When we are harassed by marketroids thirsting for a large, exclusive order of anti-virus software, we frequently confound them by remarking that high scores in magazine detection tests are not really the issue. Apart from our hard-earned scepticism in the face of far too many tests that weren't worth the paper on which they were printed, we actually expect major anti-virus packages to score 100 percent on In the Wild tests, but we don't fly into a panic if a product occasionally misses. We are less concerned about zoo tests, though we expect a high score there, and we don't expect much variation between vendors—not, at any rate, in the fairly leisurely world of the magazine detection test. We are very interested in whether a vendor can produce a timely and readily available update to meet the threat posed by a new fast-burning mass mailer, but that isn't the sort of thing that formal tests can easily measure.

The longer we spend in this field, the more concerned we are about the general quality of support. While the primary task of an anti-virus package is to detect viruses, brilliant detection capability is of limited use without an adequate support package.

The Service Desk

Reviews do not address support issues particularly well, so it is worth finding out during the evaluation phase what that gold/platinum/dilithium support package actually entails. You want to know not only when the service desk is available, but how effectively the service desk staff deal with actual problems:

▶ Are the first-line support staff anti-virus professionals? The days when you picked up the phone and found yourself speaking to an internationally recognized guru are pretty much gone. Still, it's worth establishing whether your call will be answered by someone who can deal with common queries competently, or someone who can only refer you (appropriately or otherwise) to someone in second-line support.

▶ Do they have immediate access to good technical information? Do they have good knowledge of their own product range? (This isn't at all the same as being an expert on viruses, by the way. Some support staff have immense facility at telling you exactly how to get to every possible submenu without having the faintest idea of whether those menu options are at all relevant to the problem at hand.)

▶ Are the support/service desk staff professionals? Issues such as Service Level Agreements (SLAs), the promptness with which calls are answered, escalation protocols, and guaranteed call closure times are beyond this chapter's scope, but they are likely to be as important to you in this context as they are in other areas.

▶ Are they equipped for what we might call glitch management, by which we mean the ability to deal competently with known problems? "Yes, that version does that under some conditions. We'll mail you a patch that fixes the problem".

It is also useful to know if the vendor support personnel are available when you have a problem—which is not always between 9 A.M. and 5 P.M., Monday through Friday— particularly if you have signed up for one of the more comprehensive packages, such as the gold or platinum editions. Another issue to look at is how many people can call, and how the support team manages the call-handling process (with access numbers, direct support by a specific individual or team, and so on).

Upgrades and Updates

The routine provision of program updates and patches and definitions updates is a major issue:

▶ Are known bugs dealt with in a timely fashion and adequately documented?

▶ Are patches mailed out (on CD or by email), or are you referred to a URL on an overloaded server?

▶ Is the distribution of definitions updates reliable?

NOTE

For some years, David Harley received monthly updates for a certain product. It invariably arrived (on CD) a few days after the update for the following month became available on the vendor's web site. Clearly, these late updates were a waste of everybody's time. Such ineffective distribution practices are not at all unusual. Distribution targets are exactly the sort of issue you might want to check out before you buy the product, rather than after.

▶ Can you trust the vendor's quality assurance procedures?

▶ Can (and does) the vendor make interim drivers readily available (even in a beta version, if necessary) between scheduled updates, where the appearance of a new threat necessitates them?

Customizations

Some vendors accommodate special, individual requirements (especially from larger companies, of course). Examples include customer-definable definitions for the detection of nonstandard software, games, joke-programs, and so on. If your company intends to go this route, you cannot be too careful about establishing the level of support available before signing any contracts.

The Beta Business Bureau

Products change very fast in this sector, and the effectiveness of a vendor's change management procedures can sometimes be measured in the sudden disappearance of a product's functionality. It is worth checking the vendor's commitment to sound change management by asking a number of questions:

▶ Is there a guaranteed changeover time during which the vendor will continue to support obsolescent versions?

▶ Do existing customers have early access to beta software and documentation?

▶ Are changes flagged well in advance by product circulars, email newsletters, and seminars and briefings?

Information Flow

The quality of seminars and briefings is of major importance in many respects other than changes in the existing product range. You may also want to know well in advance about new additions to the product range (again, access to beta programs is a good thing). Briefings on general virus management and other security issues, and on current malware/anti-malware technology, are a good indication of a vendor's commitment to providing a comprehensive service. If you are able to attend such briefings, you might find it interesting to note whether they attract good independent speakers, and whether the researcher-to-marketroid ratio suits your needs and prejudices.

More specialized training may also be a strong selling point. If it is offered, you may want to consider whether the vendor offers different levels of training for end users, engineers, administrators, and security specialists (for example), and whether onsite training for these groups is an affordable option. If you are considering a vendor that offers a broad range of security solutions, you may be interested in a correspondingly broad range of training options.

We advocate that you gather information on new malware from a variety of sources, including a range of vendor and independent web sites and mailing lists. Nonetheless, whether your specific vendor of choice offers such information will be of particular interest, especially if it's richer in technical information than PR and hype. The information made available from independent sources will be of even more interest to you if early warning systems from the vendor are an expensive optional extra.

From time to time, organizations of any size will inevitably find themselves faced with what may be a new virus or worm. Is your prospective vendor prepared to receive and process suspicious files or media, and in what form will the vendor accept them? Do you have some feel for how fast and accurate the vendor's response is likely to be? It is when you need to answer questions like this that participating in special interest groups (SIGs), such as AVIEN, and checking out reference sites become necessities. In this respect, SIGs and vendors with a global membership or presence have a distinct edge. Not only do you get variety in the level of detail and descriptions, but you get to see what is causing a problem or what has percolated to the top in one area of the country—which can in its own way be an early warning system. One example is the LoveLetter incident, where Europe identified the problem well in advance of when it reached the United States, but US alerts didn't come out until after disaster had already begun. Compare this to the containment of the Kournikova virus, where the presence and the characteristics of the malicious mail spread quickly by a variety of resources (including vendor and researcher mailing lists as well as AVIEN). The containment measures were so timely that some customer organizations were protected very soon after Messagelabs first flagged the problem, irrespective of how quickly their favoured vendors made alerts and updates available, where necessary. Clearly, there are arguments for not making your defences too vendor-specific.

Documentation

What do we really want to know about a virus? Traditionally, all we are expected to care about is whether our chosen product can detect and, if necessary and possible, disinfect it. This position, however, takes a lot for granted. If a product has never raised false alarms, misdiagnosed one virus as another, fluffed disinfection by making a file unusable while cleaning it, or could ever be misconfigured or presented with unexpected bugs, this position might be tenable. However, systems administrators are aware that anti-virus software is an imperfect solution to a growing and mutating problem, and that absolute trust in the vendor's competence is no longer appropriate (and probably never was). Enquiring minds want to know a number of things from an online virus information database, whether it exists on a web site or is supplied as part of the package:

▶   Is the information accurate? How are you supposed to know? We're afraid that you have to be on the way to being an expert in your own right in order to be able to assess quality of virus information. But you know that, and that's why you bought this book.

▶   Is the database up to date? The day of the printed virus encyclopaedia is over; new viruses and variants appear too often for such documentation to be very useful.

▶   Does the database list all the individual threats and classes of threat that concern you, even if the package itself may not deal with all those classes?

▶   How useful is the information? Some technical information is of academic interest only, whereas other detail may be essential. For instance, if disinfection of the virus leaves the Registry in a state of disrepair, it helps to know what changes need to be made. Unfortunately, vendors are sometimes reluctant to give detailed information of this sort, for fear of publishing information useful to other virus writers.

However, the quality of other documentation, whether electronic or printed, is also important:

▶   Is the documentation comprehensive? Does it cover all the platforms applicable within your organization?

▶   Is it clearly written, and does it use reasonably standard terminology? Does it do a good job of explaining basic concepts?

▶   Is the documentation effectively indexed? Does it include contact information and other resources, or does it assume that your 40-page manual contains everything you'll ever need to know?

▶   Does it include advice on generic solutions for unknown viruses?

▶ Does the documentation offer help with policy formulation, sample login/update scripts, batch files, .INI files, and other help with automated implementation in a real-life business environment?

Outsourced Services

If you have outsourced your anti-virus operation, many of the concerns we raise in this chapter regarding testing are of less direct relevance to you. However, from the point of view of contract negotiation and setting SLAs, you will still need to define your requirements, based on the same type of evaluation. You still must track some issues, including nearly all the issues we have described as support functions, and especially the following:

▶ The compilation and distribution of up-to-date documentation, as necessary

▶ The effectiveness of the incident management operations

▶ How well incidents are reported and statistics are compiled

▶ The effectiveness of the outsourcing party's help line or service desk

▶ How well and quickly the service provider reacts to new threats and passes on information accordingly

▶ The quality of that information

> **NOTE**
>
> *The length of this section is itself some indication of how seriously we take the question of anti-virus software evaluation. Anti-virus software is too expensive to buy, implement, and administer to take lightly. If you feel the need of an even more comprehensive and structured resource to help you with evaluation, you might like to take a look at Robert Vibert's* The Enterprise Anti-Virus Book, *which is intended as the basis for an evaluation checklist. Find out more at http://www.segurasolutions.com.*

Test Match

How successful can you expect to be at detection testing on your own account? The short answer is, not very—at least, not if this book is your main resource. This book provides a starting point, but we are not going to pretend to give you all the knowledge and tools you need for professional-quality detection testing. There are a number of organizations that are better equipped and more experienced than most systems administrators, and we recommend that you make as much use of their reports as possible. Such organizations include the magazines *Virus Bulletin* (www.virusbtn.com) and *Secure Computing* (www.westcoast.com), TruSecure (www.trusecure.com, www.icsalabs.com), the University of Magdeburg (www.uni-magdeburg. de), and the University of Hamburg Virus Test Centre (www.agn-www. informatik.uni-hamburg.de). What we *can* do in this section is explore some of the issues and pitfalls of detection testing.

Detection Versus Usability

Before going into detail on the testing of specific types of programs, we must address certain issues that apply to reviewing any antiviral software. Aside from the specific efficacy against large numbers and certain types of viral programs, there are considerations of user aspects of the system in question. These considerations do not relate solely to the chimera of user-friendliness, but to the fact that a given system is intended not only to be somehow effective against viral programs, but must also be run by a "user population" in a given work, social, and technical environment. The user interface of an anti-virus program is an entirely legitimate subject for discussion— indeed, it is the only aspect of its functionality that many reviewers are realistically qualified to consider. However, the value placed on a particular scanner's interface is largely a subjective judgment, whereas the metrics to gauge the effectiveness of its detection are relatively simple—conceptually, at any rate. In the real world, very few non-specialists get the balance between usability and accuracy right. By non-specialists, we mean people without in-depth knowledge of the virus world; it is very possible for someone who is highly experienced at the evaluation and testing of other software to make a complete pig's ear of an anti-virus comparative test.

Other Ranks

It is very easy to "rank" antiviral software on the basis of how many viral programs or strains that it will identify. However, it is only easy to rank known-virus scanning software in this regard. Activity monitors, change detectors, and other generic software have to be tested in completely different ways. Even heuristic analysis, a technique employed (to some extent) by all known-virus scanners, presents special problems in terms of testing—not only technically, but ethically. You can test heuristics by including some rare, or even unknown, viral programs in the test suite. But where do you get them?

Unless you have unusual contacts, the chances are that the vendors' own test suites are much larger and more up to date than yours. Scouring VX web sites and unmoderated newsgroups looking for additions to your collection is unlikely to give you an edge in terms of new viruses, and poses a possible ethical problem, in that to do so expresses tacit approval of such sites. (It also poses a number of problems in terms of maintaining a collection up to "professional" standards.)

Does this mean that vendors do not do this, but simply wait for samples to come to them, either from authors or victims? Different companies deal with this ethical dilemma in different ways. Many take the view that their first priority is to offer the best possible defence to their customers, and if that involves getting their hands a little dirty, the end justifies the means. Others have chosen to take the more spiritually elevated route. This doesn't mean that their products are necessarily less effective against real, in-the-field viruses. Since anti-virus companies share samples, all major companies will, sooner or later, be able to detect viruses in the field (by which we mean not only viruses formally or informally in the wild, but also viruses available from VX resources). It might be suggested that reliance on this sharing of samples means that companies who don't themselves use "darkside" resources are nevertheless implicated in using and encouraging the use of those resources. Personally, we can only record our relief that our everyday work does not normally require us to face this particular quandary. We are not suggesting that companies taking the ethically more "correct" route are in some unscrupulous way taking advantage of the work of other companies. Vendors (or at least researchers) cooperate at many levels, and such companies and individuals make equally substantial contributions in ethically constrained contexts.

Upconversion

A somewhat similar problem is associated with the thorny question of macro *upconversion*, which involves importing a macro virus into a later version of the application (usually Microsoft Word) so as to incorporate proactive detection of the upconverted virus. This enables the product to deal with such a virus, should it later turn up in the field. However, it also involves the creation of a virus that may never otherwise exist, and some researchers have gone to enormous efforts to circumnavigate the horns of this particular dilemma. If an upconverted virus does appear in the field, researchers can incorporate detection in the usual way, and may even benefit from the work of other companies in this area. A number of papers by Vesselin Bontchev have dealt with these issues, and offer good technical background as well as a means of detecting possible upconverted viruses without generating new viruses.

Notwithstanding the difficulties with finding suitably unknown malware, it doesn't seem right to leave unchallenged the assertion by some software producers that they can catch all "known and unknown" viruses. One way to get completely unknown viral programs is to make them up. This is beyond the capabilities of most users, of course, and so it is not a realistic suggestion in most cases. Still, it presents an ethical problem. We know that some bona fide researchers write functional virus code on occasion for testing purposes, under strictly controlled conditions. (*All* testing should be under strictly controlled conditions!) If it's OK for researchers, why is it not OK for you?

In the end, this is a personal decision. If you have the technical skills to write and test viral code in a safe, controlled environment with no risk or intention of making that code available to a wider audience, perhaps we have no right to ask you to desist. But then, if you're that well acquainted with the area, you probably weren't planning to ask for our approval anyway. Be that as it may, if you actually publish test results (as people do, far too often) based on this type of testing, you lay yourself open to accusations of unethical behaviour and incompetent testing. Even the vendor whose product is the "Editor's Choice" is unlikely to come to your defence in this scenario: it may be his turn to cry foul next time.

NOTE

Anti-virus researchers do not conventionally share test code, even within a very restricted "web of trust". That is, you don't share experimental code even with people with whom you are prepared to swap other in-the-wild or zoo viruses.

Another possibility is to test earlier versions of a scanner against viruses that weren't known at the time when that version or definitions set was current. Clearly, such testing is unsatisfactory. If we need to convey just one message in this section, it is "Compare like with like". It's problematical enough to set up comparative testing of current releases so that one scanner doesn't have an unfair advantage over another by virtue of using a later definitions set. To do so with outdated versions is harder still, but if it isn't done, a scanner may benefit by recognizing code non-heuristically that it would be unable to recognize otherwise.

However, writing original code is not usually the problem. More common is to modify existing code to see if the scanner still recognizes it. This is particularly easy to do with script viruses, which are essentially text-based. However, this practice is not a good idea. For one thing, you are creating a new variant. Not only do our previous ethical misgivings about the creation of new virus code still apply, but the results of testing with such variants can be misleading:

▶ Competent scanners don't rely on simple text matching, so changing a comment line, for example, doesn't necessarily tell you anything about the scanner's heuristic capabilities. In the case of script viruses or worms, identification doesn't necessarily *need* to be particularly exact, since the file can often only be deleted, not disinfected.

▶ Other alterations may effectively corrupt the virus, so that it can no longer replicate. In this scenario, whatever your intention, you are no longer testing virus detection, but detection of nonviruses. There may be some justification for testing for detection of corruptions and intendeds, but only if that was what you set out to do. Moreover, in this case you are not even testing detection of known garbage files. There is something intrinsically unsatisfactory about testing heuristic detection of viral code that doesn't work.

▶ It's not always safe to assume that your original sample is either a virus, or the virus you thought you had. Once more, you run the risk of being branded incompetent. We have observed that testers who create new variants do not necessarily test the viruses by replication, as opposed to simply testing for detection, by passing them under the nose of a scanner and seeing if its nose wrinkles. Nor is it particularly helpful to "validate" a sample intended to test detection by declaring it valid if a scanner identifies it as a virus. Yet most amateur testers are totally reliant on this "circular" process.

It is not quite as easy to assess many other, more important, features. More important? Isn't it a scanner's primary job to detect viruses? Certainly. But the best scanner in the world (as regards detection rates) is a waste of disk space if the interface is so hostile that the user cannot or will not use it, or configures it improperly, or if the interface cannot coexist with standard software. It is entirely reasonable and desirable to consider and evaluate these aspects; we only ask that you don't confuse effectiveness at detection with a pleasant interface, as so many poor reviews have done.

Although there may be (depending on how you measure) more than 50,000 different strains of viral programs in the PC world (fewer in the other environments), it is likely that only 1 percent of that number is responsible for 99 percent of infections. Thus it is of far greater importance that, for example, one particular antiviral program does not prevent infection by Magistr or MTX than that it protects against literally thousands of others.

It's All Happening in the Zoo

Thus the choice of a test suite, sometimes called a *zoo,* is made more difficult than it might be otherwise. Certain programs are very significant in terms of danger of attack, and therefore must hold a higher ranking than others. It is not possible to say that any collection of 80 viral programs is better than any collection of 10. If the 80 happen to be all "basement variants" of Jerusalem or Concept, that test suite is virtually useless. First, a decent antiviral program should deal with variants. Second, basement variants have a generally low survival rate in the wild, and are not likely to be a threat. Third, basement variants tend to mutate nonfunctional aspects of viral programs through the insertion of no-operation (NOP) codes and the changing of text.

The test suite should, however, contain a range of viral programs that are functionally distinct. A good test suite should contain programs from different categories of viruses, such as BSIs versus file infectors, and MBR infectors versus BSIs. Self-encrypting, polymorphic, stealth, tunnelling, multipartite, and companion viral programs should all be represented. Some of these programs are very rare in the wild, and so the value of their inclusion may be questionable. (Indeed, there is some evidence that the more sophisticated a virus is, the less likely it is to succeed.) However, it is advisable to test antiviral programs against the known possible viral technologies.

The analysis of virus type and function may even be beyond the capabilities of some reviewers. Many of the problems of numeric reviews are much more basic than that.

The test suites for numeric reviews should now generally contain in excess of 50,000 items. Each of those items *should* have gone through a screening process. At a minimum, one should know certain things about the item, such as, is it actually a virus? Does it reproduce? Under what conditions does it reproduce? Is it the same for each type of object it infects? Is it the same for each succeeding copy? When invoked, does it infect memory?

It is unlikely that each of these items has been tested against all these criteria. Reviewers are much more likely to take shortcuts. One of the shortcuts is to obtain a test suite from someone who has already done the work. The most obvious candidate here is a developer of an antiviral scanner. Scanner developers have to do all of this anyway.

Unfortunately, there are two inherent problems in this approach. One is that if you get a test suite from only one developer, the test suite will exactly match the capabilities of the one product. Viral programs that this one scanner does not catch, but that others do, will not be factored into the review. The other problem is that it is quite possible that the developer has been careless. The zoo may contain nonviral items. The one scanner will detect them, whereas no other scanner will (correctly, since they are not viral). Thus, both factors will tend to boost the rating of the one product.

NOTE

One of the most forceful arguments against the use of real viruses by nonprofessionals is the amount of work involved in correctly maintaining an adequate virus collection. Vesselin Bontchev's paper on "Analysis and Maintenance of a Clean Virus Library" (Virus Bulletin Conference Proceedings, 1993) is required reading on this subject.

An untested zoo may also contain duplicate files. Particularly if one scanner catches them while others don't, duplicates may skew the results. Of course, in some cases you should have duplicate files. If this virus infects more than one type of object, you should have infected copies of the different types.

All of this may give the impression that numeric rankings against a test suite are of no use. This is not the case. Ranking tests have a strong place in the evaluation of scanners.

In passing, we recommend to everyone the "Reader's Guide to Antiviral Reviews", an article (supposedly by one Sarah Tanner but actually by Alan Solomon) in the November 1993 issue of *Virus News International.* It has been reprinted electronically at the following site:

> http://www.softpanorama.org/Antivirus/Reprints/virus_reviews.html

Each of the 26 points that the article discusses is a way to skew the results to favour one product or denigrate another. Some of them strain credulity, but each is known to have been used in major published antiviral reviews.

This begins to point out some of the difficulties in choosing antiviral software. There are, of course, matters of the type of viral program, the test suite against which the system is effective, the user interface, and the style of the program. Still, surely there must be *some* standard by which to measure antiviral software.

In the computer world, the nice thing about standards is that there are so many from which to choose.

However you divide the different types of software, it is extremely difficult to apply the same standards to various categories. Besides the problems of the "numbers game" in testing a given program against a given suite of viral programs, the significance of the test results varies in the context of a scanner, a change detector, and a behaviour blocker. For operation-restricting software, it may be of no consequence whatsoever that the program does not "catch" infections; so long as the restricting software is 100 percent effective in preventing the spread of infection, it does not matter whether it ever identifies any viral programs. Change-detection software may catch all infections, and yet be less effective than a scanner that catches only 90 percent, but effectively identifies them as well. (Unfortunately, we must also factor in the reality that change detectors will generate a *lot* of false positives, particularly because software vendors continue to insist on writing programs that modify themselves.) Therefore, a single numeric standard, based upon the use of a test suite, would be of little utility in assessing the overall effectiveness of antiviral software.

In addition, the environment is constantly changing. The number, specific strains, and types of viral programs are increasing all the time. The companion, spawning, or "precedence" virus does not change the files on disk at all, but rather takes advantage of the order in which programs are "called for". Thus those operation-restricting programs that prevent changes to program files become useless, as do change detectors that peruse only those files in the database at the previous run. Standards, therefore, that are based upon the currently existing viral environment, will be very quickly outdated, and mostly useless.

A single, or even multiple, numeric measure simply does not have sufficient flexibility to gauge antiviral software. It may be possible to construct one that could, after considerable work. However, even if a criterion reference could be made broad enough to cover the various types of antiviral software, the gauge would have to be dynamic. Thus, antiviral software tested at one point would have to be retested each time the standard was renewed; at a minimum, that retest would likely need to be done annually.

As viral programs are constantly developing new methods of attacking files and avoiding detection, so too is antiviral software constantly developing new detection methods, or at least new twists on old methods.

The problem here is the application of a single standard to diverse, and changing, types of antiviral software. It is, however, complicated by the fact that we do not know what the new features of antiviral software may be until they appear. Thus, while it might be possible to gather a series of criteria broadly applicable to the wide variety of antiviral software, and to balance and weight the various gauges in order to come up with a "fair" assessment, it is impossible to use such criteria to judge a feature that you have never considered.

Product suites can include many (not necessarily integrated) products (often for all supported platforms and network environments, and on the same CD set):

- ▶ One or more on-demand scanners (multiple scanning engines, separate Windows and command-line scanners)
- ▶ DOS and Windows on-access scanners
- ▶ Scheduling software (for on-demand scans, retrieval of updates from the vendor's web site, and so on)
- ▶ Behaviour monitors or behaviour blockers, or both
- ▶ On-demand integrity checkers
- ▶ On-access integrity checkers
- ▶ Goat files
- ▶ System console software for remote administration
- ▶ A virus encyclopaedia
- ▶ A rescue disk generator
- ▶ An EICAR test file or product-specific test file, or test file generator

Suites offering this range of functionality are not, perhaps, as popular as they were—at least, a suite may contain many of the preceding components, but they remain unused by most organizations. However, the Swiss Army knife approach lives on in the consumer market in the form of the anti-virus/intrusion detection/ desktop firewall suite. Corporate bodies are also drawn to multilayered security products, but may be likelier to consider a multivendor approach. Also, many brand-new PCs arrive with an all-purpose program suite incorporating anti-virus, personal cryptographic software, a personal firewall, diagnostics and recovery utilities, spam-killing software, and filters for unsuitable web content. Even in the pure anti-virus market, few vendors offer only a single type of utility. This offers the unscrupulous or sloppy tester unlimited scope for marking down apples for not being oranges. A particularly common and frustrating example is the kind of review that includes a generic tool along with a handful of known-virus scanners, then makes the tool the editor's choice because it detects unknown viruses. Yes, such tools are worth considering because they may do better than a known-virus scanner at detecting some kinds of unknown threats. However, these tools are a different kind of software, doing a different job, and they have their own disadvantages that do not always show up in this sort of testing.

Testing for false positives as well as false negatives is even more important with generic products than with known-malware detection products, and we do not know at present of a testing body that has considered in depth the problems associated with testing for false positives.

We Like EICAR

We have previously referred to the EICAR test file as a means of installation testing. (How useful is it as a tool for other kinds of testing?)

The EICAR string is not a virus, and exhibits no viral behaviour. It simply displays a message. (It can be said, very approximately, to simulate an overwriting virus, or else a worm or Trojan that hasn't made any changes in the environment.) A scanner that doesn't recognize EICAR is not failing in its primary function, which is, after all, virus detection. It is, however, ignoring a *de facto* standard for installation testing, which might be taken to imply a staggering insensitivity to consumer demand, an unusual concern for avoiding what could be considered a false alarm, or a disquieting ignorance of its existence.

If a scanner is *supposed* to recognize EICAR but doesn't, that's a minor indication of unreliability. At the time when EICAR was being taken up, some scanners had trouble recognizing it appropriately. At least one scanner recognized it only if it had exactly the right number of characters. The string itself is 68 characters long. However, some people pressed the RETURN key at the end of the line. In MS-DOS, end-of-line is usually flagged by inserting a CR/LF pair (Carriage Return/Line Feed) —that is, two extra characters. Just to make things even more uncertain, some DOS editors add the CTRL-Z character to any text file, as an EOF (End-Of-File) marker. Thus, the actual length of the file could vary by several bytes, resulting in a potential false negative.

At the other extreme, some scanners not only disregarded the length of the file, but alerted on the test string irrespective of where in the file it was found. According to the specification, the EICAR string must make up the first 68 characters, as described at http://www.eicar.org/anti_virus_test_file.htm.

In one highly publicized instance, a scanner alerted on a text file included with another product. The file described the use of the EICAR test, and was reported as "infected" even though the actual string was nowhere near the beginning of the file. Clearly, this alert can be taken as a minor indicator of unreliability or carelessness in the alerting scanner. Of course, it might have been the only bug in the whole program.

EICAR (the file, not the organization) is not universally admired; indeed, one respected researcher has described it as a "very stupid idea". To be strictly accurate, he was describing not the EICAR test, but the principle of a counterfeit virus used for installation and configuration, an idea that did not actually originate with EICAR (the organization, not the file). The idea seems to have originated with Doren Rosenthal, whose virus simulations and (real but short-life) test virus are, from time to time, used (completely inappropriately) as a substitute for real-world viruses in comparative tests. A number of vendors have provided product-specific test files, but most have standardized on EICAR itself.

Rosenthal has claimed for many years that his software is superior to EICAR (mainly because the registered version includes an actual virus), and that the EICAR test was intended as a "spoiler" for Rosenthal's product. In fact, many scanners do detect the Rosenthal product, though they don't necessarily advertise the fact. Rosenthal's product is disliked in the trade, however, for a number of reasons:

▶ Simulations of real viruses are based on the false premise that a product that detects the real virus should also detect the simulation. This premise seems to derive from the popular misconception that a virus "signature" is some sort of constant. This misconception misses two points. First of all, scanners do not detect many viruses by looking for a fixed string (byte sequence), but by using an algorithm. Complex polymorphic viruses cannot usually be detected by scanning for a fixed string; a more complex search algorithm must be used. Second, if a fixed "signature" can be used, that doesn't mean that only one static scan string can be used. In theory, every scanner in the world might use a different scan string than every other scanner, yet they could all detect the same virus. Obviously, a simulation is not the real virus, and may be missed by a scanner that would always detect the real thing. (This objection does not apply only to the Rosenthal simulations, of course.)

▶ If a simulation is not a virus or an official "test" program, it may not be considered appropriate to detect it; technically, it's arguably a false alarm if it *is* detected. Some vendors have actually declined to detect the simulation on those grounds.

▶ The registered product includes a real virus. It isn't destructive, and will remove itself in due course even if anti-virus software doesn't detect it. However, it *is* a virus, and it is usually held to be a bad thing to give real viruses to all and sundry. They may use it inappropriately, or carelessly, or even use it as a template for a new variant. Furthermore, the fact that the product contains what is technically a virus (that is, code which can replicate) gives the product little real testing advantage over a nonreplicative test file such as EICAR.COM. The fact that the virus is or is not detected tells you nothing about the scanner's ability to detect any other virus.

Is EICAR.COM any better, you may wonder? Well, it's free. It definitely isn't a virus. Its functionality is so limited that it's hard to envisage any circumstances under which it could do any damage whatsoever, although virus infected copies have been reported from time to time. As an executable file, EICAR.COM is open to infection by a .COM infector.

However, EICAR.COM isn't universally acclaimed and appreciated as The Answer. One of the reasons for such lack of enthusiasm is the fact that it is sometimes mistakenly considered to tell the user more than is possible. It doesn't even determine whether the product recognizes *any* viruses, because EICAR isn't a virus. A report of the presence of EICAR.COM doesn't give you any information about how many real viruses a scanner detects, but then neither does trying the scanner on 10 or 20 or 200 real viruses. The file can tell you that a product is installed, but not if it's installed (or at least configured) properly. For instance, the fact that a scanner reports correctly that a file called EICAR.COM contains the EICAR string doesn't tell you whether the scanner will detect macro viruses, for example. In fact, the report doesn't actually tell you anything except that the scanner detects the EICAR string.

EICAR *can* tell you a little about what the product does with viruses and worms that it can't disinfect:

▶ If the scanner flags EICAR.COM as the EICAR test file, that's fine.

▶ If an on-access scanner refuses to let you run EICAR.COM as if it were virus-infected, that's a good sign.

▶ If the scanner deletes EICAR.COM and that isn't how you want it to respond, that's a good sign because you can change the configuration.

▶ If the scanner deletes EICAR.COM and isn't configured to do so, that's not such a good sign.

In short, EICAR is useful for convincing management that you're earning your crust by installing working software, or demonstrating to users what happens if a virus does hit the system. You can use it in a limited fashion for testing other aspects of a scanner's functionality (whether it scans compressed files properly, for example). To do this usefully, you need a pretty good idea of how AV software works, in which case it's debatable whether EICAR can tell you anything you didn't know already or couldn't tell by other means. Furthermore, you need to understand the limitations of this method of testing.

Randy Abraham's paper "Giving the EICAR Test File Some Teeth" (Virus Bulletin Conference Proceedings, 1999) describes in considerable detail some techniques for extending the test file's capabilities by wrapping it in nested zip files, or as an embedded OLE-2 object in Office documents. If you wish to test these issues, there is usually no reason to use a specific (real) virus to do so, and EICAR will do fine. EICAR will also give you a limited means of checking on how your software is deployed (and to a lesser extent, configured), or of checking or demonstrating corporate incident-handling procedures.

To make use of the EICAR test string, type the following text into a file called EICAR.COM, TEST.COM, or a similar filename, or else download the file from www.eicar.org:

```
X5O!P%@AP[4\PZX54(P^)7CC)7}$EICAR-STANDARD-ANTIVIRUS-TEST-FILE!$H+H*
```

(The third character is an uppercase *o*, not a zero.) Running the file displays the text "EICAR-STANDARD-ANTIVIRUS-TEST-FILE!"

> **NOTE**
>
> Sarah Gordon's 1995 article "Are Good Virus Simulators Still a Bad Idea" provides an interesting and by no means dated view of the pros and cons of the use of simulators as educational and testing tools. You can find the article at www.commandcom.com/virus/simulator.html.

Further Information

Professional detection testing is beyond the scope of this book. It takes access to substantial resources and a degree of expertise that you cannot expect to get from a single book. If you wish to explore further and increase your understanding of the field, here are some references worth checking:

► Sarah Gordon and Fraser Howard, "Antivirus Software Testing for the New Millennium", the 23rd National Information Systems Security Conference, 2000. You can find this paper at http://csrc.nist.gov/nissc/2000/proceedings/papers/038.pdf.

► Ian Whalley, "Testing Times for Trojans", www.research.ibm.com/antivirus/SciPapers/Whalley/inwVB99.html.

► Ian Whalley and Richard Ford, "Testing the Untestable: the Hidden Roadblocks to Anti-Virus Testing", Virus Bulletin Conference Proceedings, 1998.

► Sarah Gordon and Richard Ford, "Reviews and Evaluation of Antivirus Software: The Current State of Affairs", www.badguys.org.

► The WildList is commonly used as a basis for detection testing, and a number of papers and articles at www.wildlist.org deal with related issues.

Summary

This has been an exceedingly long chapter. This is because our intention in writing this book is not to give you all the answers, but to give you the baseline information to enable you to ask the right questions and come to the conclusions that are right for you. In the next chapter, we look at what might be thought of as the other end of the process: incident management.

CHAPTER 1

Risk and Incident Management

IN THIS CHAPTER:

Risk Management

The Best Form of Defence Is Preparation

Reported Virus Incidents

Assume that at some point you are going to fail.

Or rather, not to be too fatalistic about it, don't assume you are going to succeed. Any program that claims that it will be able to deal with all future viral and other malicious programs is flat-out lying, and the software byways are littered with the corpses of software developers who figured they knew it all. Make redundant provisions for checking, and don't trust any one antiviral program or system. Keep testing your protection, and keep up to date. And remember our earlier advice: two antivirals are better than one (although probably not if they're both running on-access at the same time, on the same machine). And as we keep saying, we're talking about a social problem here. There is no technology so secure that your users can't break it: they may bypass it, or they may literally break it so that they are unable to use anything any more.

The essence of effective incident management is preparation. Risk management is about knowing what the potential problems are (which is why you need the sources of information in Chapter 8) and being prepared to manage them if and when they arise. Incident management is dealing reactively with security breaches as they occur, whereas problem management is concerned as much with taking proactive measures as it is with managing crises.

Which brings us to a crucial point: inform yourself and inform others. Not every computer user needs to read alt.comp.virus all the time. But every computer user should know of someone who does read a decent virus or security publication on a regular basis. You can't trust CNN for the latest virus bulletin; the media still think the US National Security Agency (NSA) shut down Iraq's air defence with a printer.

NOTE

In fact, alt.comp.virus and its spin-off groups should carry a data health warning. The site posts some excellent information from time to time, but the signal-to-noise ratio is excruciating, and the quality of misinformation that is sometimes found there is impressive. It's a fine place to study the instant expert in his natural habitat, but caveat lector. Do not believe everything that you read in the group.

By the same token, let the word out a bit more if you find you have been attacked by a virus. If you get hit, make sure you send a copy of the infection to a researcher. (It's terribly frustrating to try to deal with the aftermath of a bad disinfection when you don't have a copy of the virus to work with. "Oh, we just reformatted the drive".) If you get hit, admit it. Don't imagine that you can ignore the problem and it will go away. (We are continually asked how bad the virus situation is … by the same people who will not answer surveys so that we can find out how bad the problem is.) This last word of advice is a bit of a touchy issue with those who feel that anti-virus experts should not say anything for fear of giving virus writers ideas. Never fear: virus writers don't need any help. Clifford Stoll's book *The Cuckoo's Egg* (Pocket Books, 2000) proves that the only result of keeping information to yourself is that the people who really need the data won't have it. What we do counsel against is making available copies of viruses or virus code to everyone who asks for them, or even to everyone on a particular mailing list or newsgroup. There's no good reason to give such goodies to people who may not want or need them, and who may be tempted to experiment.

Risk Management

Risk management and analysis are standard parts of information security management practice. The general security texts cover this topic very well, and we will not try to duplicate that material. Instead we will provide a very brief outline in case you have not studied the topic, and quickly examine the virus topic in risk management terms.

A *threat* is the broadest concept in risk analysis. A threat may be something like the possibility that the earth may fall into the sun, thus destroying our computing capability (among other things). The threat discussed in this book is the existence of malicious software, and the predilection of certain people to write new forms of it.

The next level down the risk chain is a *vulnerability*. This is, in a sense, the reason that the threat is a potential problem for you. For example, the earth falling into the sun could be bad since computer hardware is generally not sufficiently hardened to withstand temperatures in excess of 6,000 degrees Celsius. Computer installations are vulnerable to viruses since viral programs use only normal computer functions and, therefore, can affect any computer system, can consume system resources, may carry dangerous payloads, and take time to eradicate.

Having identified vulnerabilities, risk management next looks at *exposures, attacks,* and *exploits.* These terms detail the specifics of a weakness in the system under consideration. An exposure for the earth is that the sun exerts a gravitational force, and the only thing keeping the earth away from the sun is orbital dynamics. In viral terms, the fact that you are using a given operating system means that you are potentially exposed to viruses able to infect that platform. Exploits may be the parts of that system particularly susceptible to viral operations, and attacks would be the specific viruses themselves.

In assessing the threats, vulnerabilities, and specific risks, the management planner will also want to factor in probabilities. How likely is it that a problem will occur?

Good news: the earth probably will not fall into the sun any time soon. Viral risk, however, is increasing steadily. The best estimates are that large companies now encounter viruses several times each week, and that infections probably take hold more than once per month.

The impact of an exposure or attack must be considered. If the earth did happen to fall into the sun, that event very likely would cause the long-predicted "Death of the 'Net". The impact of a virus infection varies greatly, but the computer support department will likely have to devote many hours to checking computers, disks, mail queues, and file servers—and that would be the impact for the smallest potential problem. An impact that is seldom fully considered is that of publicity: if your company does become infected by an email worm, and the fact that employees or systems send out infections to others becomes public, how would that affect the corporate standing, customer goodwill, and perhaps even the stock price?

On the other side of the risk management page are safeguards. What actions can you take to reduce the vulnerability for your company or systems? We could, for example, equip the earth with rockets to keep it away from the sun. We can write policies about practices that increase or reduce the risk of virus infections, educate users, install scanners, and make backups of important data and programs.

Safeguards will range in effectiveness, and the security planner must gauge how much a particular safeguard will mitigate a specific exploit, and then must calculate the residual risk. The net danger, multiplied by the expected impact, multiplied again by the number of times you expect it to happen over the year gives you a rough idea of the problem.

Such a calculation also gives you some ammunition in support of budgeting for antiviral protection, since senior management wants to know what the company is getting for what it spends. Unfortunately, potential losses are seldom convincing to management until they happen.

Chapter 11 will provide more specific details regarding risk analysis and virus management policies.

The Best Form of Defence Is Preparation

Your best defence against malicious software is not some specialized program, but something you should already have: data. Documentation is vital to programming, network management, and desktop support. One of the horrible ironies of the information age is that computer system records are possibly more neglected than any others.

The Computer

Each computer should have basic details close at hand. "Close at hand" does not, in these days of networks and faxes, have to mean physically close to the computer. Having such details handy can help enormously in other areas, such as technical support quite aside from virus detection. With this in mind, an archive in the support office makes a lot of sense, along with the documentation and software libraries. The support department is also a likely site for remote-administration software. No large site can ignore the potential of remote-access software for virus-specific and general administration. Most industrial-strength anti-virus software includes some tool for distributing upgrades and definitions updates, and in some cases for dealing with disinfection, capturing quarantined viruses, and performing other incident-management functions.

There should be a list of the programs run at start-up time. With the number of background and resident programs running on computers today, it's a wonder anything can operate at all. If you don't know what your computer is supposed to be running, how can you know when something unusual has crept in? In the MS-DOS world, you could obtain this list simply by printing a copy of the CONFIG.SYS and AUTOEXEC.BAT files. The more recent versions of Windows, however, have a bewildering variety of places to check. Some of these may not even be on the local computer itself, since most networking systems provide for programs to be run at login. Larger organizations will make heavy use of standardization, which is, after all, a very efficient means of reducing support costs. Such an organization will build workstations (and even servers) from a library of standard images, using tools such as Ghost, rather than adding applications and configuration tweaks to an operating system installed according to the manufacturer's defaults. In tandem with an effective backup strategy, this use of pre-configured software will usually mean that even in the worst case, an infected machine can be rebuilt from scratch and data restored as of the most recent safe backup. Use of mirrored servers, RAID technology, and the other trappings of third-millennium risk management can actually make "recent" very recent indeed.

Even where a rebuild or heavy use of imaging software and backups is considered overkill, there can also be a description of the boot-sector and partition boot record. This description can be as simple as a copy on a separate diskette or a "hex dump" listing. But even this description is a formidable object for a novice user to understand, let alone produce. The technical difficulty is not, however, an insurmountable problem. The user does not have to understand what the listing means. The qualified people who installed the system can generate the listing. Again, this data can help support people with problems other than viruses.

From the esoteric, we move back into the mundane, and some uncontroversial measures.

Once again, backup "originals" of software could be kept in the support, or main IT, office. The copies should be made after installation, should there be any customization involved. These copies serve two purposes. First, they allow for quick access to known clean software for reinstallation, if necessary. (These copies of the software "originals" may reduce or eliminate the need for full backups of the system, as the software is often the larger portion of material on the user's disk, and generally the most stable.) The copies also provide a baseline for a quick check for any changes to the software.

The Office

"Each computer" is pretty easy to define. An office is less so.

For the purposes of this discussion, an office is defined as a group of people who interact on a regular basis. "Regular", for this purpose, need be no more than once per week.

An office, therefore, is defined less in terms of locale and walls than in terms of communication. For this definition, an office may consist more of those working on a common project in far-flung cities than of those in the next cubicle to whom we never speak. However, a group need not follow "official" reporting lines either. An office could be defined more in terms of how fast you can find information when you need it. The items in this section are those that may not be referenced for long periods of time as long as things are going well, but that may need to be found quickly once an anomaly has been identified.

Each office should have a description of current common viral programs and hoaxes, or access to a common source of information, such as an intranet page. Whatever list is used must be kept up to date, and it is essential that each organization of any size assign someone to support the prepared lists with additional information.

The office should keep a minimal list of local virus information contacts.

One of the items that should be a part of any office computer "kit", simply on the basis of good management, is a list of all hardware and software purchased, including the suppliers and serial numbers. The reason for including such a list in your virus-fighting arsenal is partly to track the source of a virus. More and more companies are becoming aware of the need to audit software, and the audit practice may also become very helpful in fighting viruses. The hardware list is also valuable, because certain pieces of hardware will affect the operation of the computer. Corporate support staff will immediately nod and say in unison, "Modems!" Locking down

Virus-Busters?

However, we do recognize the immediate problem. After all, we've raised it ourselves: Who are you going to call? It is very difficult to advise anyone on this problem. For our part, we can probably cite, with confidence, perhaps 100 people in the world who are competent in the field. There may in fact be more, but it is an esoteric field, with few standards by which to judge practitioners. The information is hard to find, for one thing. The popular and even the technology trade media have very little appreciation for the difficulties and traps of virus hunting.

Virus experts, in common with most system-level hackers, tend to be charter members of "Egos-R-Us". This is bad enough. However, what is worse is that everyone with an outdated copy of McAfee or Norton thinks he or she is a virus expert and assumes the arrogance without necessarily having the expertise to back it up. (Given that the general population, even of advanced computer users, has very little background in the subject, the problem of proving credentials is often moot.) We are not, by the way, slamming NAI or Symantec here (though we have been known to do so elsewhere). Both products are, in the right hands, extremely capable. In the wrong hands, any product can be a disaster.

In fact, in writing this book, Rob Slade went back to some earlier suggestions he had made, and found that almost all the indications of a "good" antiviral expert had become useless in the intervening six years.

So, if you can't find a good local expert, the following indications will at least help avoid the bad ones. Run from anyone who tells you that "one antiviral fits all". Anyone who boasts of the size of his or her virus collection is more interested in collecting scalps than in keeping you safe, and very likely has contacts in the virus exchange community. Anyone who warns against shareware and online services doesn't know the realities. Anyone who tells you that X is the best scanner and Y is a waste of space should be required to defend his or her position statistically, and be humanely disposed of if he or she fails to do so convincingly. ("CNN said so" counts as a failure.)

systems so that unauthorized software cannot be installed or maintained will be too draconian for many organizations. However, where such measures can be implemented, they may help control the influx of new threats, such as just-launched fast-burners received through an unauthorized Hotmail account, or remote-access Trojans picked up from warez servers.

The recommendation to have a designated machine for receiving and testing new disks or software is bound to stir up a storm. Why spend good money on a machine that is going to be used for nothing except testing software?

This argument appears to be based in the deeply rooted prejudice that says that the only important part of a computer system is the part that you can see, feel, and throw through windows at times of stress. Let's look at the picture in real financial terms. If you buy two copies of a commercial antiviral program (for an office of, for example, 20 computers), plus the upgrade fees for a year, you've spent about $400. Three hundred dollars will easily get you a bare-bones used machine for testing. Besides, you probably already have a computer that no one in the office will use because of its age and obsolescence. In addition to performing antiviral testing, you can use the check-in machine to detect Trojans, which relatively few anti-virus programs do. A designated machine also allows you proactive rather than reactive protection.

We should stress that you may need to make sure that the hard disk you use for testing is not empty. (Some prima donna viral programs refuse to operate unless it is worth their while in terms of the amount of file space used.) Keep the drive about 80 percent full.

Along with the catalog of hardware and software, there should also be a log of disks and/or programs received. Many large companies think they already have such a log. Many small companies see this measure as far too draconian. As usual, the truth lies somewhere in between.

Corporations, both large and small, and government departments often have policies controlling the use of software. Usually these schemes make some statement regarding bringing disks and software into the office. These policies are, of course, universally disregarded, even by those who drafted them. Such procedures are unnecessarily restrictive and unworkable, and they fail to address the issues that prompted them in the first place.

The intent of such policies is good: the institution wishes to protect the copyrights of authors and other companies (or at least wishes to avoid being sued for failing to do so). The policies are also supposed to prevent the intrusion of viral and Trojan software into the company and, in some cases, the extraction of sensitive data from company files.

Preventive Maintenance

Some actions should be performed regularly. What is "regularly"? The definition will depend on your situation, but, in general, it will mean more often than you do now. The items under this section of our list of good practices are particularly those that should be conducted for good maintenance and support in any case.

Here Be Draconians

Unfortunately, we have yet to see such a policy actually achieve its intended objectives. In most cases, the procedures are both insufficient for the intended outcome and are damaging to normal business practice. We will use some examples from the federal government in Canada. (Anyone gloating over the foolishness of this particular institution does not know the policies in his or her own company.)

The Treasury Board is the governing body in financial matters, and therefore publishes directives covering pretty much all aspects of Canadian federal government practice. Several years ago, the board published a circular stating that all computer-related software or hardware had to have an associated purchase order (PO) before it entered government premises. At first glance, this policy would appear to be sound, and even an advantage for software companies. Not so. If you are reviewing software, a local government office cannot afford to purchase the necessary variety of software and still keep within its budget. Of course, it is possible to cut a PO for the software for no money. However, this takes about as long as the review process itself, and can also potentially put the software company at risk (if the company has other policies regarding minimum and maximum pricing). Even if you intend to purchase the software during next fiscal year, you cannot review it in this fiscal year if you have no funding left for that line item or cannot afford to "lose" that funding this year.

This policy was, of course, intended to keep pirated software out of the organization and to ensure that software publishers were paid for their efforts. In fact, however, the policy was ignored, and evaluation software was obtained under the table. In the end, all this policy did was prevent publishers who had standardized policies for review software from competing in reviews by local offices.

Canadian federal government policy also provides for tracking all inventory through accession numbers. The system works well for desks and cars, but not so well for computers and software. (Rob Slade had a hard time convincing the "materiel management" people in one office that it made no sense to issue one accession number to 12 video cards, but that it did make sense to issue one number to one card, three disks of set-up software, and one manual—for the same card.) Because of the difficulty involved in putting items into inventory (personnel had to obtain the inventory coding for the item, obtain an accession number, affix a label—have you ever had to try to find space for a 2×6cm label

Here Be Draconians *(continued)*

on a video card?—and enter up to 46 fields of data into the inventory database by paper form, since only two people in the local office had access to the database itself), very few software-related items were ever entered into inventory. Data disks were never labelled—after all, what do you do with a carton of 100 blank disks that are probably headed for 30 different offices?

To track infections effectively, however, users need to be able to identify even data diskettes and customer data diskettes. The system for doing so must be easy, must not interfere with normal work, and must be rigorously enforced—by the *users*.

The trouble with most policies of this type is that these considerations are not planned for from the beginning. Trying to make transitory computer materials fit an inventory system designed for permanent fixtures, or forbidding the entry of disks into the company, simply leads people to ignore the policies in order to achieve greater productivity. The specifics of recording and tracking will have to vary with the corporate climate and culture. If an intent and some relevant background (rather than a mandated procedure) are presented to employees, the users will come up with a solution—and one that is far more effective than that imposed by the head office.

Back Up Data

Our good old friend, the backup. Why stress data? For three reasons. First, programs and structure should be backed up at installation and at every change in configuration. They need not be backed up between these times, however. Second, backing up only data reduces backup time and increases the frequency with which people are willing to do a backup. Third, you can buy another copy of Perfect Writer tomorrow, but can you buy another copy of your last month's receivables?

In dealing with backups, of course, you must decide on the type. Full, differential, and incremental backups all have their particular advantages and disadvantages. Full backups are the simplest, comprising the whole of your data, but require the greatest amount of time and number of tapes. Differential backups, storing only the data that have changed since the last full backup, are quicker to perform but more complex to set up. Backing up only the data that have changed since the last backup operation of any type, and saving the incremental changes, makes for the fastest save operation, but requires that you have access to the last full backup and every backup done since.

Back Up Software Changes

Actions that you perform when installing or changing software should not require any further explanation. We should, however, mention one thing in regard to the term "change". Unfortunately, a number of programs still modify their own code when a change is made in the configuration. We are not including these minor amendments in our definition of "change". When changes have been made that affect the size or composition of a program file, the program should be backed up (either by itself or as part of a full system backup), and the printout list of program file sizes should be redone.

Protecting original software is not as important as it used to be, now that most packages come on CD-ROM. Make sure it is ROM, though; CD rewriteable disks are just as vulnerable as floppies, and maybe more so.

First, Do No Harm

Once again, a trial run on an isolated system should be a part of general practice, regardless of the existence of viral programs. A trial run allows you to find any bugs in the program and to review the program's usefulness. We recall that a Trojan version of SCAN was uploaded to bulletin boards. It created all kinds of havoc because the boards "approved" the version—on the basis, of course, of its having passed a virus scan. A single run on an isolated system would have detected the problem.

If you do find an infection, perform a minimal disinfection. Please let us stress *minimal*. Do the least that you can do and still ensure security. Although there is some doubt as to the wisdom of disinfecting program files, it is surely better to delete one file than to restore the whole directory. It is better to delete and restore one directory than to restore the whole disk.

AND. No one. Ever. (Yet.) Has found a virus that requires a low-level format. No LLFs. Got that?

However, do perform a thorough disinfection. Many people, while going too far in gouging an infection out of their workstation, will fail to check out their floppy diskettes, backups, and Word documents. One of the most frequently asked questions on every virus mailing list used to be, "I cleaned off Stoned, but now it's back. How come?" Easy answer: "You didn't check your disks".

Also, with few exceptions, power down cold when you are disinfecting and start fresh. If you have a virus in memory, none of your disinfection methods can be guaranteed, and some may even cause harm.

Overkill

Once upon a time, Rob Slade's little brother started an organization for computer users who also happened to belong to the same religious group of which they were members. The brother, of course, hit Rob up for some articles for his newsletter, and got a series on computer virus protection. In trying to get a certain bible college to join the association, the brother happened to mention the benefits of virus education. The college declined.

Shortly thereafter, a rather simple boot-sector infector virus infected the college computer system, a local area network serving the administration and library. The college packed up the entire network and shipped the whole thing back to the computer reseller. The computer geniuses at this particular shop reformatted every single hard disk and shipped it back to the college. The college had to hire additional staff and spend weeks retyping all the student records, and the entire library catalogue, back into the system.

An hour or so with one of the many freeware or shareware antiviral programs would have fixed the whole thing.

Yes, We Mean *All* Disks

Rob Slade was once asked to help clean up the laptop computer belonging to the legal counsel for a government department. The lawyer was clearly annoyed that the virus had hit him again: he had previously had the machine disinfected by the technical support office. Rob explained that, since the virus had come back again, all diskettes would have to be checked in addition to the computer itself. The lawyer complied, although his attitude quite plainly betrayed that he didn't believe a word of this nonsense, and was only going along with it in order to have grounds for really throwing the book at the next person who failed to correct the problem.

Rob cleaned not one but two viruses off the laptop. He then tested the diskettes, and found that a third of them were too badly corrupted to recover, while a similar number were infected with various combinations of no less than five different viruses.

The lawyer got back his clean laptop, clean disks, and the explanation. After he picked his jaw up off the floor, he scrambled around the office and found another 40 diskettes that had been missed on the first, rather cursory, pass. Thirteen of those were infected as well.

Reported Virus Incidents

In general, the first point of contact when a virus incident takes place is the Help Desk. However, the quality of computer-virus awareness in IT support units is variable. If you haven't already done so, pick the best wannabe guru you have available, find him or her some third-party training (product-specific, if necessary), and point this individual to the sources of information included in Chapter 8. Then refer all action on suspected virus incidents to your newly appointed guru in the first instance, while you get everyone else up to speed. Start with the Help Desk staff.

Dealing with a virus outbreak is not just a question of cleaning the infected disk with the current flavour-of-the-month scanner. At the very least, your reaction should involve, as far as is practicable, stopping the loophole by which the malicious software entered the enterprise, and limiting damage caused by any secondary infection that might possibly have spread before the virus was detected. Cleaning only the infection found is purely a matter of treating the symptom rather than the illness. If technical training in general comes under the purveyance of the Help Desk or a specialist documentation officer or unit, users and first-line technical support staff faced with evidence of an infection must check with the designated person.

Certainly, the Help Desk staff should not mark virus reports as "closed" unless all relevant staff are suitably qualified to do so. Any virus report should, in the first instance, be treated as urgent.

Help Desk Investigations

What constitutes a virus incident? Any case where a program reports a potential virus or Trojan symptom, such as the following:

▶ Microsoft Diagnostics (MSD) or a similar utility reports less than 640KB base memory.

▶ Windows 3.x or Windows 95 reports problems with 32-bit disk access.

▶ Norton Utilities reports a possibly virus-related problem with, for example, the Master Boot Record.

▶ Any anti-virus program, however weak, reports a possible virus.

▶ Classic visual or audio/visual virus symptoms are evident.

▶ A Microsoft Office application puts up a "macros and customizations" message or displays a VBA error message.

Anything along the lines of "There's a problem here that I don't understand" qualifies as a possible virus incident. In such a case, it's perfectly legitimate to run an up-to-date and reputable anti-virus package under controlled conditions. By this, we mean taking precautions, such as using a certified clean and write-protected boot disk, disconnecting the machine from the network while scanning, scanning all files, including archived files, and taking whatever other measures may seem appropriate. In fact, it's legitimate to scan for viruses even where there are no perceived virus indicators whatsoever. It should be second nature for support staff to check that anti-virus software is present, active, and up to date on any system they are working on, irrespective of how relevant that software may seem to the job in hand. After all, any end-user system on which it's necessary for support staff to work should be regarded as potentially hostile. (In real life, of course, we often find support staff disabling anti-virus programs to stop them from getting in the way, in the hope of dealing with a job as quickly as possible.)

Oh, Yes It Is!

A certain security system for laptop computers involves the installation of a nonstandard Master Boot Record. While the product was in development, the sales team called on many computer stores in the local area, in order to demonstrate the system and, just incidentally, test it on as many different types of computers as they could.

One particular store carried a new brand of laptop, and the security system would not install properly on any computer of this new model. The development team was sure that the problem must be due to the presence of a virus, but the sales team members swore up and down that they had faithfully scanned all the computers they tested.

After much trial and effort, it was found that the problem was a virus; almost every machine in that computer store was infected. The sales team was using a virus scanner that the security company had recently dismissed as inadequate. They preferred the old scanner to the new one, because the old scanner didn't cause them as much trouble. The trouble to which the sales staff were referring, of course, was the message telling them that a virus was present.

Dealing with Virus Incidents

If possible, calls suggesting a virus incident should be referred initially to the person in the support hierarchy with virus knowledge (or training, at least). Often, we hope, this will be the support person taking the Help Desk call. If front-line staff don't have any particular expertise, they can still follow a well-constructed protocol, even a checklist along the lines suggested in the section "Virus Incident Checklist" later in this chapter. The appropriate system manager should be informed immediately of any problem relating to file servers and other central systems, but any problems with a possible virus content should be referred or copied to the Help Desk in the first instance, or to the local virus guru directly.

In general, the ideal short-term solution is to do as little as possible until you have access to a competent source of advice, and you should strongly advise the user to do likewise.

Help Desk Advice to Users

The following are pieces of advice for the Help Desk personnel to proffer to users:

- ► Do not attempt to continue to work with an infected system.

- ► Generally, it's probably better not to switch off an infected machine until it's been inspected by a competent person, but make sure no one else tries to use it in the meantime. (The obvious exception is where some malicious act seems to be in the process of execution on the affected system.)

- ► If you have the means of checking other machines in the office for infection, you should do so, and then take appropriate steps if you find an infection.

- ► If you are unable to check other machines, you must assume that all machines are infected, and take all possible steps to avoid spreading infection any further.

- ► Infected and potentially infected systems should be quarantined—don't use them, and don't let anyone else use them.

- ► Users of infected machines should not trade disks or email with other users until the computer is declared clean by a competent authority.

- ► If the infected system is connected to any local area network, it should be logged off all remote machines. If necessary, physically disconnect the machine, but first advise the network's administrator.

- ► No files should be exchanged between machines by any other means until you've established that this can be done safely.

▶   Ensure that all people in your unit and any other units at risk are aware of the situation.

▶   Get all floppy disks in the unit together and ready for checking.

Virus Incident Checklist

You can use the following rough list as a starting point for gathering information:

▶   Why does the client think a virus is present?

▶   What sort of virus does the client think it is?

▶   What virus name did the anti-virus package report?

▶   If the virus was reported by an anti-virus package, which product was used?

We have seen instances where the operating system or a general diagnostic package has suggested the presence of a virus—in a few cases, correctly. It's unlikely that the package will be considerate enough to name the virus, but it may still be helpful to know the name of the package. While we were wearing our Help Desk hats, users would contact us and report that "SCANDISK says we have a virus". Since SCANDISK is pretty limited as a disk diagnostic utility, it's unlikely to do a better job as a virus utility. Further questioning may elicit the following information:

▶   The person at the next desk thought the utility signified a virus.

▶   A real anti-virus program with a similar name made the suggestion.

▶   A completely different program running at about the same time displayed the alert box that raised the alarm.

Knowing that one of these scenarios is applicable can make the difference between solving the case over the phone and having to send in the anti-virus SWAT team, possibly quite unnecessarily. (Trust us: we have been that SWAT team.)

To continue with the original checklist, you will need to know the following information:

▶   What type of system is it? What type of hardware, operating system, and network environment?

▶   What specification of hardware is involved, what version of the operating system, network, and scanner is being used, and how recent are the virus definitions?

▶ Is there an apparent infection, or was the virus blocked at entry? (You may have quite a problem eliciting the answer to this question. Most naive users, and quite a few support professionals, don't see a distinction. Does the hard disk appear to be infected, or only a floppy? Or is just a single file flagged as infected and located in the mail attachments directory?

Virus Identification

The principal reason for needing to identify a PC virus is to estimate the likelihood of its spreading if work continues until the system has been cleared. A virus that is identified as a boot-block infector (boot-sector virus [BSI or BSC], partition-sector virus, DBR [DOS Boot Record] infector, or MBR [Master Boot Record] infector) normally spreads when a PC is booted with an infected floppy in drive A, and therefore doesn't usually present a direct threat to a network. However, systems infected with a virus that has a destructive payload or known destructive side effects must be kept quarantined. In any event, you should disallow the use of diskettes unless absolutely necessary. Diskettes should in all cases be write-protected wherever possible.

General Protective Policies

Since the central characteristic of a virus is that it spreads, any means of data communication is a potential vector. Such vectors include internal network links, external network links, email, new software, disk exchange, and any other means of getting ones and zeros between machines. The more rigorously you control the channels of transmission, the safer you will be.

Disks brought in by engineers, sales representatives, and others are particularly suspect, as are disks that have been used by friends, college students, computer bureaux, or your children. Preformatted disks (including hard disks and CDs) are also questionable, as are newly repaired systems.

Email file attachments should be, by default, untrusted. Firewall or gateway-based virus or content scanners may help to reduce the risk of an email virus or worm, but they definitely can't eliminate the danger. Verify any attachments, and be quite specific in describing anything you send by email. When in doubt, don't double-click.

Seriously consider security when evaluating software, particularly when planning company standards. Ensure that software is up to date with regard to security patches or recommended configurations. (Don't be the first one on your block to buy the latest new program; 1.0 releases are notoriously buggy.)

Configuring for Safety

As we write this book, the most problematic type of virus is the email script worm. Most of these programs use the Windows Script Host (WSH), which is installed, by default, on every Windows 98 and Windows 2000 system. It is also active on other Windows systems if Microsoft Internet Explorer 5.5 has been introduced, or if WSH itself was downloaded from Microsoft. You can get rid of the script capability by following the instructions for the appropriate system:

▶ **Windows 95**   On the desktop or in Windows Explorer, right-click on My Computer. Select Open from the menu. In the My Computer window, open the View menu and select Options. Click on the File Types tab. If VBScript Script File is in the list of file types, select it and click the Remove button.

▶ **Windows 98**   From the Windows taskbar, select Start | Settings | Control Panel. In the Control Panel screen, double-click the Add/Remove Programs icon. In the Add/Remove Programs window, open the Windows Setup tabbed page. Select Accessories and double-click. In the Accessories list, find Windows Script Host. Uncheck the Windows Script Host checkbox. Click OK to return to the Add/Remove Programs window. Then click OK.

▶ **Windows NT 4.0** or **Windows 2000**   Log on as Administrator. On the desktop or in Windows Explorer, right-click on My Computer. Select Open from the menu. In the My Computer window, open the View menu and select Options. Click the File Types tab. If VBScript Script File is in the list of file types, select it and click on the Remove button. If the program prompts you to do so, confirm that you want to remove the file type.

Summary

Having taken a brief look at some general guidelines for handling the virus situation, in the next chapter we look in more detail at the entities responsible for initiating most data transfers: the users.

User Management

IN THIS CHAPTER:

Richard's Laws of Data Security apart, how possible is a 100 percent secure environment? The single computer user might get pretty close to that degree of security as long as he or she avoids:

► Local networking

► Electronic access to remote systems (including, of course, the Internet)

► Receiving data except as hard copy (that is, no incoming data via serial links, removable or external media from any source but the owner of the system, and so on)

We might stretch a point and allow such a reclusive user to give data to someone else on write-protected media. However, he or she might not be able to use the media again subsequently, in case someone had inadvertently or deliberately write-enabled the media or introduced malicious code. There are, for instance, a number of ways in which a write-protected diskette can be written to, even with the protect tab physically removed.

Until someone comes up with a *real* virus that spreads via powerlines, they don't provide too many entry points for a virus. We could have fun putting together some far-fetched ideas, such as malicious code embedded in printed material that takes advantage of a buffer overflow vulnerability in OCR (optical character recognition) software to install itself onto a system with a scanner attached. Apart from that, such a system would be about 99 percent secure—we have to allow for unusual (but not unheard of) vectors such as compromised hardware (a trojanized keyboard, for example) or software (a virus-infected shrink-wrapped application, for example).

Does the system we're describing sound like yours, or that of a significant number of the computer users you support? Nevertheless, your aim is probably to keep the systems in your domain risk free. Unless you are in the unusual position of having absolute control over your users' systems, you will need to assume that you are going to fail.

Panicking your users by drawing their attention to the fragility of what they may perceive as secure technologies isn't always productive. Users are subject to attacks of vertigo when they find that their assumptions about the privacy of their email or the efficacy of the firewall at countering all sorts of threats are unfounded. However, a little user paranoia is a healthy corrective to corporate complacency.

Managing the Managers

Managers frequently display a degree of paralysis when they are urged to ponder security issues. Consider initiating a pilot project: task an individual or a working group with information-gathering and making recommendations. It can be expensive to engage outsiders for long enough to do a realistic assessment of the needs of your organization, and there are too many anti-virus consultants whose expertise derives from the back of a box of software. However, if you opt for in-house research, you're probably trading off knowledge of the organization against lack of experience in an area where even security professionals are often not well-versed—and in many organizations, security administration is not allocated to security professionals. If you go this route, you must ensure that the individuals tasked with the mission have the motivation, time, and resources to learn as they go along. And, of course, they need to have a copy of this book.

Policies Count

Security policies are often regarded as a time- and paper-consuming waste of space, or, alternatively, as a substitute for action. In the real world, the truth lies somewhere in between. But, as a first principle, and as a means of prompting management to take some kind of action, two facts are noteworthy. First, any reputable security auditors will give you a terse report if you have no security policy: no policy, no security. Second, you must have some kind of security policy in order to have any chance of dealing with even the most egregious and blatant failures of employees. You can't necessarily (or reasonably) discipline a user for not conforming to an unpublished policy, but you can begin to exert some leverage. This may be particularly so where individuals in the higher echelons are responsible for poor practice and could resent being brought to account for it.

Nor is it enough for management to pursue a policy of nonintervention while the resident expert slogs away at the problem. If someone higher up the organizational tree decides to stamp on the expert's fingers, management must offer positive support.

Covering your back shouldn't be the main concern in a healthy corporate environment, but there's no need to paint a bull's-eye on the aforementioned posterior. If management is concerned enough about the sorts of threats examined here to task someone with establishing countermeasures, that person should not be expected to handle the task wearing manacles. In this context, we like to quote Eugene Spafford:

> Spaf's First Principle of Security Administration: if you have responsibility for security, but have no authority to set rules or punish violators, your own role in the organization is to take the blame when something big goes wrong. (Simson Garfinkel and Eugene Spafford, *Practical UNIX and Internet Security*, O'Reilly and Associates, 1996)

Without management support, the best you can hope for is the probably part-time and strictly reactive application of band-aid solutions.

Security and Insurance

Security in general and anti-virus security in particular constitute a cost centre and rarely offer opportunities for profit (except for security vendors). Like fire insurance, security represents a large expense set against the risk of an attack that may never come, and may not seem to have been worth the cost of proactive protection. Security policies are not generally popular. They take time to put together properly and are of no practical use without a realistic educational program to back them up.

However, policies represent the organization's recognition of the problems to be faced, the assessment of vulnerabilities, the degree of commitment to managing security problems, and the fundamentals of practice. Without laying the foundations of an informed implementation, you cannot fully understand the causes of such breaches, so as to lessen the impact of similar future incidents. Policy issues, including specimen policies, are examined in detail in Chapter 17.

Viruses and Insurance

It is possible to purchase virus incident insurance. Such insurance may require a considerable initial outlay: many insurance companies display little enthusiasm for including computing-related risks in a policy at all, let alone viruses. This reluctance suggests the need to observe "due diligence" in the implementation of protective measures, before purchasing or making claims under malware-specific clauses in insurance policies. There is also a clear need to articulate losses accurately (or at least convincingly), supporting our contention of a serious need for policies and reporting.

It seems likely that insurance companies will shortly start taking the issue of information security more seriously. Obtaining insurance against business interruptions may soon become difficult unless you can demonstrate that realistic security policies and business continuity plans are in place.

Risk/Impact Analysis

Start off with a little risk analysis. If you cannot demonstrate the problems, management will be understandably reluctant to allocate resources and alarm the users. A well-written preliminary conceptual report may be sufficient to encourage the freeing of funds for a serious risk analysis project. At the very least, it should be possible at this stage to task a suitable person or persons to carry the project forward. Take time to consider their qualifications. Do they have the expertise, or are resources available to enable them to acquire expertise? Do or will they also have authority, resources, and time to implement defences? This isn't a job for the office boy, but neither is it a particularly technical job, although technical knowledge is rarely a drawback.

Most people today are aware that viruses are a significant threat. The big security organizations and consultancies who used to consider virus management a minor distraction now offer information, advice, and even training in the field, though not always of particularly high quality. By definition, the risks are to some extent specific to the organization, but this section lists some of the factors we find recurring time after time.

Viruses generally stop or hinder the use of computing resources, create hidden damage in a system, generate visible changes to computer operations, and engender fear, uncertainty, and doubt among the users affected. We can break these impacts down into more detailed effects.

Loss of Productivity—Denial of Service Costs

▶ Degraded performance of infected systems

▶ Unreliability of damaged applications

▶ Unavailability of damaged systems

▶ Unavailability of damaged or inaccessible data

Unobserved Effects

▶   Performance degradation

▶   Undetected data damage

▶   Application damage

▶   Disk I/O impairment

▶   Illicit resource utilization

▶   Undetected propagation and secondary infection

Observed Effects

▶   Serious performance degradation

▶   Unintentional side-effects

▶   Undiagnosed system faults

▶   Long-term damage to disks or data

▶   Cost of service time spent on undiagnosed faults

▶   Unreliable applications

▶   Loss of competitive advantage due to loss of productivity

Post-Traumatic Psychological Damage

▶   Post-traumatic vertigo—being overwhelmed by the task ahead

▶   Post-traumatic shock—being overwhelmed by the amount of damage done

▶   Scapegoating and witch hunts—which are no substitute for real incident and problem management

Management Costs

Against these costs, you should also consider the costs of virus management. After all, higher management will have to justify the benefits of amelioration against the attendant costs.

The benefits aren't easily quantifiable, although attempts have been made to use data such as that uncovered by the TruSecure surveys. You cannot usefully assemble a spreadsheet that shows exactly how much you'd save if you implemented virus protection for the first time, because you don't know how much damage is being done now. If you already have virus protection (and some large organizations still do not), you are unlikely to be able to input realistic figures to indicate how much it saves you. Even the presumptive savings to be made by increasing or decreasing the level or type of protection are hard to measure, not least because of the unavailability of a standardized reporting methodology.

In fact, even the post-traumatic losses inflicted by a virus attack seem to present difficulties in assessment. The highly publicized cases of Christopher Pile (a.k.a. the Black Baron) and David Smith (a.k.a. VicodinEs) are instructive. Estimates of the damage suffered by a single company as a result of infection by Pile's Pathogen virus ranged from £40,000 to £500,000 (or about $58,000 to more than $700,000 in US dollars). The damage caused by Melissa seems to have been estimated on the basis of "think of a (big) number and double it". If this is the best we can do by way of estimating consequent damage in the rigorous context of the criminal justice system, what chance do we have of usefully quantifying hypothetical attacks?

This doesn't mean, however, that keeping good metrics about incidents, exposures, and such is less than crucial. Damage costs are important and need to be measured accordingly in an organization of any size. While such costs cannot directly articulate savings from having virus protection, they can provide insight into trends, changes in exposures, effectiveness of products, and time spent chasing windmills. Collecting virus incident metrics continues to be a difficult and arduous task. However, it is also necessary when and if insurance policies are in place and claims are to be made. It won't take insurance companies long to determine that not all claims are actual virus infections, or that the damage estimates may be inflated. After all, they are in the business of making money, not paying claims.

Some costs to consider include those discussed in the following sections.

Pre-Implementation Costs

- ▶ Gathering information
- ▶ Establishing criteria and terms of reference
- ▶ Benchmarking against peer organizations
- ▶ Formulating a policy
- ▶ Evaluating options such as:
  - ▶ Outsourcing versus in-house
  - ▶ Outsourcing *and* in-house

Cost Analysis

- ▶ Cost of procurement (unit cost)
- ▶ Cost of installation
- ▶ Cost of testing
- ▶ Cost of upgrading
- ▶ Cost in performance (overhead from memory-resident scanners)
- ▶ Cost in time (on-demand scanners, checksummers)
- ▶ Cost of failure (spread of undetected viruses despite the implementation of virus management software)
- ▶ Incident management (this may seem an odd thing to list, but sometimes dealing with a breach is more expensive than leaving it alone)
- ▶ Reaction to false negatives
- ▶ Accelerated spread of undetected file viruses
- ▶ Cost of monitoring effectiveness and other revaluation
- ▶ Cost of revaluation
- ▶ Cost of switching (reimplementation)
- ▶ Personnel opportunity costs (time that could have been spent on more glamourous activities)

The Management Feedback Loop

- ▶ Arriving at decisions
- ▶ Reporting to higher management
- ▶ Fine-tuning
- ▶ Seeking endorsement from higher management
- ▶ Communicating strategy and policy to IT staff and their user constituency, and incorporating feedback:
  - ▶ Meetings
  - ▶ Documentation

Training and Education

- In-house or third-party training:
  - Training a response team
  - Training Help Desk personnel
  - Training users
  - Training trainers
- Monitoring of training, including its short-term and ongoing effectiveness
- Ongoing revaluation of the malware management function, which should consider:
  - Changing needs
  - Changing trends
  - Changing policies or strategies
  - Cost-effectiveness

Policy Issues

Draft as many policies as you need, not to mention guidelines and procedures. A policy is not necessarily an acceptable substitute for action (it's often a delaying tactic, coming somewhere between the working party, steering committee, and management approval), but it may be a very useful first step. At this point, it needn't (and probably can't) be comprehensive. Having a policy at least demonstrates that a problem has been identified and that the will exists to address it. Securing higher management approval is the vital first step in securing an organization. Once you have an acceptable draft policy, you have some authority, even before detailed planning and implementation.

Some organizations still have no clear policy regarding the use of the Internet (including electronic mail, the World Wide Web, newsgroups, etc.) or the desktop. It is a mistake to leave the novice cybernaut without direction. It isn't necessary to teach everyone the fundamentals of TCP/IP or the history of ARPANET, but it might be good practice to make sure that your system's users know the following:

- Email is not necessarily private, but may be read by authorized or unauthorized persons, and is increasingly likely to be scanned automatically at the gateway, not only for malware but for other unacceptable content. A policy might contain a notification to all employees that the company regards *any* email sent to or from a company account to be open to company authorities, and that a message may be read for diagnostic, quality control, investigative, disciplinary, or other purposes. In fact, a good idea might be to have email sigblocks carry this warning, to avoid later hassles over privacy.

▶ Email doesn't always come from the source whence it appears to originate. The fact that it comes from a trusted person's account does not mean it was sent with his or her knowledge or consent.

▶ Quoting or forwarding mail and other material without permission may not only be a breach of netiquette, but may also have copyright implications. Legislation applicable to the printed word may also apply to email or postings to newsgroups, and material available for viewing on the Web is not necessarily in the public domain. In some cases, however, textual content is not all that is being forwarded. Attachments can, of course, contain or constitute malware, but message text and HTML can also contain malicious embedded scripts.

▶ In most organizations, a degree of recreational browsing or Internet social interaction is acceptable, but if that degree is quantified (and it probably should be), users should be made aware of what is considered acceptable and what is not. If it's acceptable to use work resources *at all* for extracurricular (especially commercial) activities, an organization may need to draw the boundaries very clearly. Encouraging non-work-related use of the 'Net has some advantages. As one example, getting people to use company email for contacting net-connected relatives is a good way to get them used to using email and the various options available. It might be considered preferable to state that company resources are provided for company purposes, but that not all breaches may be subject to discipline, according to company judgment. Such a policy statement allows some leeway for turning a blind eye to personal email, while leaving available the option of prosecuting blatant and flagrant misuses such as distributing pornography, harassing fellow employees, or using Microsoft Outlook. However, it also allows a degree of interpretation and uncertainty that won't find favour in every organization.

The user of a desktop machine should understand clearly (when applicable) that the desktop belongs to the organization, not the user, and be aware of the organizational expectations that the user must meet regarding the following types of policies and concerns:

▶ The system's users should understand the proper use of authorized and legitimate software and peripherals, especially modems, that may breach security in a number of respects.

▶ Users must conform to company guidelines on such security issues as virus management (of course).

▶ Mail-agent software on the desktop should be secured as much as possible. Such systems rarely have the same rigorous safety provisions that are available on a multi-user system, and often are very insecure, indeed, in default mode.

▶ It will probably also be necessary to address issues specific to the use of laptop computers and other portable equipment, either in the policy at hand or in a separate AUP (Acceptable Usage Policy). Such matters might deal with additional levels of access-restricting software, encryption of data, and remote-access concerns.

Good policies are an essential weapon in the fight against security breaches. Effective implementation of policy entails not only raising the overall awareness level among general users, but also paying special attention to a number of critical support issues. We suggest that the company's legal counsel should be involved, at some point, in the wording of security-management policies—although, in the interests of comprehensibility, the legal team probably shouldn't write them.

Help Desk Support

Users frequently make a point of emphasizing the importance of their roles or those of their superiors in order to gain preferential treatment. They may exaggerate the length of time a trouble ticket has been outstanding or the gravity and/or urgency of the problem. They may bypass normal channels, in order to get quicker, more senior, or more expert service. In the context of social engineering, we have noted in other publications some of the ways in which users can try to subvert normal processes for their own gain, at the expense of others:

▶ Subtle intimidation

▶ Bluster

▶ Pulling rank

▶ Exploiting guilt

- ▶ Pleading for special treatment
- ▶ Exploiting a natural desire to be helpful
- ▶ Appealing to an underling's subversive streak

Help Desk staff need a proper framework within which to work. First and foremost, they need a superior who is willing, authorized, and knowledgeable enough to make sensible decisions about when, if ever, to bend the rules, and who won't throw a thorny problem back at them. The staff needs a good understanding of what the rules actually are, what their responsibilities are, and what recourse they have in the event of a grievance. They also need to know that when they have a run-in with a difficult user, they will have the backing of management, as long as they conform to policy.

Malware management makes particular demands. First-line support staff must be equipped to deal with false, real, and real-but-useless alerts, and know enough to distinguish between them, or where to refer them if in doubt. Hoax management is dealt with in some detail later in this chapter, as well as in Part IV.

Who Owns the Problem?

Rob Slade once did some management consulting for a technical company attempting to implement a middle management layer for the first time, in order to grow and meet competition. He found that the owners, used to running everything, were still making direct contact with support and development staff even after the appointment of managers for those sections. It took a lot of time and careful preparation to prove to the owners that this was the case, but finally they admitted that he was right. After thinking it over, however, they acknowledged that while he was right, they still preferred to keep things as they were.

The company continued on as before, struggling against competitors that grew ever larger, and was finally bought out by one of the larger outfits. Sadly, and because they were unwilling to change their management style, the owners essentially lost their company. However, they did it with full knowledge of what was happening, and it is important for security professionals to understand that they are *not* the ones responsible for the ultimate protection of the company: senior or executive management holds the reins of power. But security workers *are* answerable for educating the top dogs—or at least trying.

First-line support staff should have enough knowledge and experience to diagnose a possible virus-related incident, even when it's reported as something else. On the other hand, they should also know enough to avoid the "Something's not working: it must be a virus!" trap. It rarely hurts to check that anti-virus software is working and up to date, or to scan the system, and such checks might be included as part of the standard diagnostic procedure for indeterminate incidents. However, any IT professionals finding themselves using an unidentified virus as an explanation for an indeterminate system problem should immediately volunteer for urgent reeducation. It never hurts to refer a "Could this be a viral problem?" call to second- or third-line support (a process often referred to, disconcertingly, as *escalation*) or to a third party (a consultant or vendor helpline).

The support staff should also have the confidence in themselves and line management not to allow the customer to dictate priorities.

They should have enough informed scepticism to know when point-and-click use of anti-virus software is or is not appropriate. Elimination of an incoming threat that hasn't infected is usually safe, barring such (hopefully unusual) circumstances as known false positives. However, once malicious code has been executed, even known threats may require manual intervention as a supplement or even as a substitute for anti-virus software. The possible circumstances where such complications may arise are too numerous to list, but we have in mind such instances as:

▶ Anti-virus software that deletes what it cannot clean

▶ Malware that modifies the Registry so that anti-virus software cannot execute properly and thus may hinder more than it helps

▶ Disinfection or disinfestation that causes damage through misidentification of the malicious program

Help Desk staff and technicians (and their management) also need training and support to get past the "single point of detection and repair" syndrome. A staff suffering from this syndrome will report to a user who suspects a virus, clean the affected system, never ask about source and scope of what was detected, then close that trouble ticket—only to have another user (or recipient) call in with the same virus infection on his or her system. While this syndrome increases the Help Desk's turnaround statistics on individual trouble tickets, and reduces the staff's response time, in fact, it actually elevates the total incident time as the staff members run around putting out individual fires. This syndrome also distorts the reporting process, as these trouble tickets now appear to be individual and distinct infections/incidents but may in fact be symptoms of the same incident.

Other IT Support Staff

IT staff in general both pose and are vulnerable to special risks. They're often assumed to have a wider range of knowledge than is really appropriate. We have already referred to the dangers of "instant experts", who overestimate their own abilities. After all, IT professionals are often highly knowledgeable in their own areas. They may have undergone training in other support areas that has actively reinforced common misconceptions about security and malware. Courses leading to Microsoft professional qualifications, for instance, tend to adhere to a very narrow and Microsoft-centred view of security issues; this focus gets engineers through examinations, but discourages them from questioning the built-in assumptions. You may have gathered that we do not always regard Microsoft as the ultimate authority on all things security-related, especially virus issues. We should not give the impression that Microsoft owns this problem exclusively; we are aware of general security courses, for instance, that are appallingly ill-informed on viral issues.

Support staff are under pressure to reinforce the view of themselves as experts, not only to bolster their own self-image but to reflect well on the unit to which they belong. They may have privileged access to particular systems (but not necessarily expert knowledge of those systems). They are often encouraged to experiment, and are usually expected to teach themselves as much as possible, and sometimes more than is possible. This applies especially in the anti-virus arena. The people in the virus management industry who know most about virus internals are, more often than not, committed to strictly limited disclosure, while the people who are committed to full disclosure are rarely in a position to display the same breadth of knowledge.

IT staff constitute a classic virus vector. In the absence of proper controls, they are apt to flit from user to user without taking elementary precautions. Many organizations virtually ignore training in security issues for staff in general—not altogether surprisingly, given the cost and administrative overheads of enforcing training in areas that are not often seen as relevant to the average user. However, organizations that withhold training in these areas for IT support teams take serious risks: IT team members make tempting targets for all manner of security attacks.

IT Security and Other Units

Physical and IT security personnel often have an uneasy and distant relationship, even in institutions where they share a common node of the management tree:

▶ IT personnel should at least understand the need for physical controls and may need some involvement in the physical securing of IT equipment, for instance, when sophisticated technical controls such as hand-held authentication devices are employed.

▶ Non-IT security people need at least a basic understanding of how IT hardware hangs together in order to appreciate where the weaknesses are—not only in terms of virus damage, sabotage, theft, and espionage, but even in terms of accidental damage.

It's not only people formally employed in security who need to be involved with security and malware management. Staff who have access to critical systems or data should be subject to special contractual and other controls and policies, and temporary/contract staff should not be overlooked. Staff leaving or changing jobs within an organization may entail changes to access controls in a number of contexts, and it's essential that access privileges reflect the current status of the individual. Status should, in turn, be partly determined by exposure to relevant training and experience.

Staff who work in personnel departments are tempting targets for social engineering attacks, since they have privileged access to all kinds of interesting and saleable information. But they are also prime targets for incoming macro virus infections, since these employees receive curricula vitae (resumés) from individuals outside the organization's defensive perimeter.

Training and Education

General users should not be expected to become security experts. Indeed, it's unrealistic to assume them to be IT-literate beyond the requirements of their work. This makes the quality of the educational and other resources available to them particularly important, not only in terms of accuracy and pertinence, but also accessibility. Training and first-line documentation should be as brief and clear as possible, but more detailed resources should be available and *known* to be available. In particular, such documentation should make as few assumptions as possible about the technical knowledge of the reader; unfortunately, this objective is not always consistent with the equally pressing requirement that the documentation be as *short* as possible.

Make it clear what is forbidden (disabling anti-virus software, substituting an unapproved package, and so on) and what the penalties are. Leave as few "I didn't think it mattered just doing such-and-such" loopholes as possible. Management should be co-opted into setting a good example. Why should lower grades take security more seriously than management? Furthermore, managers who are "too important" or "too busy" to be inconvenienced by security precautions are excellent targets for the social engineer, cracker, or virus writer.

It is commonly held to be secretaries and other low-status workers who are most likely to be responsible for breaches of security. However, our experience out in the field suggests that in a reasonably well-protected organization, management is likelier to be responsible for the widespread dissemination of virus hoaxes, real viruses, and worms. This may well reflect comparatively low levels of computer literacy among older managers, though these levels are changing as business adjusts to ubiquitous information technology. It can reflect impatience with anything perceived as taking up valuable time; the proper response to this complaint is to point out the loss of time and other damage that the company may sustain by post-infective incident management.

Heads of departments require particular cultivation. They need to have a sufficient understanding of the technological and other risks to which their staff may be vulnerable, so that they take whatever measures are appropriate, including encouraging subordinates to take advantage of educational opportunities and conform to guidelines. Furthermore, many war stories are told at conferences of how a CEO propagated a hoax or chose to favour functionality over security in the company's choice and implementation of email services, or how employees received a message from the CEO, and assuming that the message was important, opened worm- or virus-ridden attachments. We heard recently that this same CEO had been quoted in a security publication on the topic of viruses, stating that eliminating vulnerabilities can be one of the most positive steps an organization can take.

If management doesn't take malware-related threats seriously, staff cannot be expected to, either. Resources must be allocated to assessing the risks, defining policies, and making sure that users know what management expects of them by way of a realistic user-awareness programme. We repeat: you don't have to turn everyone into a security expert, but you do have to ensure that everyone has a minimum of training to raise awareness of the issues and, most importantly, to ensure that employees know where to go for information and guidance if they need it. Managers and system administrators must also set a good example by personally conforming to good practice.

Different job functions require different levels of training. IT staff usually need a deeper knowledge of security than most users, and a realistic appreciation of what is required of them. Non-IT security staff need a passing acquaintance with technology, even if they never use a computer themselves, if they're to handle physical security effectively. Units that are particularly vulnerable, such as personnel/human resources departments, may need special consideration, too.

Nevertheless, technical inexpertise presents its own distinctive problems, and the hoax management problem provides a telling example. A reactive response to a user's report of an email virus is relatively simple. You could simply say, "No, there is no Good Times virus—it's a hoax.", which may be enough if your user is considerate enough to ring the Help Desk and say, "I've just received a message about a virus called Good Times".

A more attractive approach might be to enhance your users' technical grasp by demonstrating the absurdity of the alert they've received. "You can't burn out a CPU by making it perform the operations it was built to perform, and anyway there's no such thing as an nth complexity binary loop". Adding value by educating a customer is, in principle, a good thing.

But what if the customer rings back and says "I know Good Times is a hoax, but apparently there's a Trojan horse virus that..." You can, of course, continue to raise your user's technical awareness: "Trojan horses and viruses aren't the same thing". Should you then expound on the differences and disputed areas?

- ▶ Isn't a virus a special case of Trojan horse?
- ▶ Isn't a virus dropper a Trojan horse?
- ▶ Could a virus overdrive an antique monitor?
- ▶ Could it reprogram a modem or a flash BIOS?

It seems that the more you explain, the more questions you have to answer. The logical end to this road is the point at which your user has become a security expert. This is all to the good if your business is creating security experts, but *that* is a market which is easily saturated.

Alternatively, you could focus on technical issues that relate specifically to hoaxes rather than to computing and computers in general. "Here are some of the features of the email you've received that imply that it's a hoax. It's all in capitals. It has far too many exclamation marks. It asks you to forward it to everyone you know". This response is much better. It equips a receptive user with a heuristic to trap any chain letter and most hoaxes (most of which are special cases of chain letters). Such heuristics are actually as far as most of the current literature on the hoax virus phenomenon goes, and we consider them at length in Chapter 16.

But let's consider a warning that says, "There's a new virus that [insert the usual improbable characteristics here]. Don't panic, I've enclosed a program as an attachment that cures it". This is a very rough approximation of what the Red Team virus does. The virus it describes doesn't exist, but the attachment *is* virus-infected. The virus description in this case would be trapped by the previous heuristic ("P.S. Make sure you warn all your friends of this new threat!"), but that's no guarantee that the real virus won't get its place in the sun. The world is full of people who haven't caught up with this heuristic. Those who have are not safe. "It does sound like a hoax, but just to be on the safe side...."

How should you react to a virus alert that acknowledges all the heuristics that might be deployed against all known hoax viruses, but claims to be a special case? What if the alert misrepresents a standard instance of social engineering as an exception? How about, "Please warn everyone you know not to pass on alerts to everyone they know"? What about an alert that avoids such crass hoax symptoms as capitalization and multiple exclamation marks?

You could, of course, continue to attempt to raise the level of technical awareness of your system's users. Or you could go back to first principles: "If it doesn't say quack, doesn't waddle, says it hates water, but has an orange beak, maybe it's a duck after all". Red Team still says "quack". Your hypothetical alert might not. It might not say anything at all, and leave the victim to deduce that it would be a good idea to pass the warning on. The alert might bypass all your anti-hoax heuristics: however, it would still have to persuade its intended victim to execute it. In a well-protected environment, such an alert would still fall foul of the Prime Directive: "Thou shalt not run unauthenticated programs". In this case, "a well-protected environment" clearly implies educated users.

You can't make realistic rules to cover every potential future threat. If you did, no one would read all the way through the manual. The trick is to keep the rules few, simple, and general, but concentrate on helping your system's users to extrapolate from a broad principle to a specific instance. That's where education can counter social engineering.

We often suggest that quite basic IT training, even where security is not normally considered an issue, should include an introduction to computer ethics. Such an introduction would raise awareness of what the Evil Hacker or Vile Virus Author may be up to, but also highlight the responsibilities of users in terms of awareness of the problem and the techniques involved. It also would give users a reinforced appreciation of what is acceptable in their own computing activities. It is received wisdom that most targeted attacks are still directed from inside rather than outside. The majority of staff won't have the knowledge or desire to write viruses or hack into prohibited, secured areas, but may be seriously careless about using other people's systems, software, or data files without authorization. Indeed, some staff members may be tempted to commit a small act of rebellion such as installing a joke program or semi-Trojan, not realizing that an apparently small indiscretion may create enormous breaches. If you train staff members to think about the grey areas, they will be less likely to be pulled across the line that separates more-or-less legitimate corner-cutting from breaches of policy or even illegal acts.

NOTE

The not particularly standard term semi-Trojan *refers to software that occupies the hazy hinterland between jokes and Trojans, which might, according to context, be regarded as trivial or threatening. An example is a program that claims to overwrite the hard disk.*

Positive Reinforcement

Employees are more likely to take pride in doing their jobs properly if they see that management:

- ▶ Values the job function. Nothing is more dispiriting than feeling that no one cares whether your job gets done or not.

- ▶ Values the contribution of the individual performing that function.

- ▶ Considers it important that the job is done *well*.

- ▶ Doesn't shoot the messenger. A virus report is an indication that anti-virus software and the people who use it are functioning as they should. There never was a time when the mere presence of a virus constituted reasonable grounds for dismissal of the person who received it, the engineer who set up the PC, the systems administrators responsible for the local file server or mail server, or the head of IT.

People with security responsibilities often respond well to being given a more impressive job title or increased formal responsibility, enhancements that may cost little or nothing. Of course, bigger paychecks help, too. On the other hand, inappropriate use of such incentives can be seriously nonconstructive. There is such a thing as an overenhanced sense of one's own worth.

Proactive Malware Management

In the age of the fast-burning mass mailer, there are two ways to go: either we can take the decisions out of the customers' hands by applying extensive blocking or quarantining of suspicious inbound (and preferably outbound) mail and other network traffic, or we can eschew transparency and conscript customers by encouraging them to follow good practice.

Safe Hex Guidelines

This section provides some guidelines to what is sometimes called Safe Hex, but might be called (less amusingly but more accurately) safer computing. You will find some tips on avoiding a few of the most common risks actually faced by computer users today, and can form the basis of an informational resource. Some of the suggestions here will be implemented by IT departments rather than individual users, in organizations of any size. However, these suggestions are included because anyone who works (or plays) at home, and does not have access to an IT department, is advised to think about whether he or she needs to take similar precautions.

Check All Alerts and Warnings with Your IT Department

Warnings from any individual within the organization who is not authorized to forward them should not be assumed to be accurate, but should still be checked with the Help Desk facility or the security administration team. At the end of this chapter, we include a Help Desk response form and quick guide to hoaxes that you can use as the basis for dealing with the problem of users who forward inappropriate material. Home users and the like might want to consider checking with their anti-virus vendor of choice or an independent resource. David Harley maintains an advisory verification service at http://www.security-sceptic.org.uk, while Rob Rosenberger's site at http://www.vmyths.com, an essential resource for checking hype and hoaxes, also offers a mail-out service addressing major hoax-related issues.

Don't Trust Attachments

In general, up-to-date anti-virus software and sensible precautions are still the best bet for most people. Don't open mail attachments from people you don't know; check with the sender if you get an attachment from someone you do know but from whom you weren't expecting an attachment, especially if there is no accompanying message, or if the accompanying message doesn't seem to make sense. (Worms usually mail themselves without the knowledge of the person from whose mail account they're sent.)

A common entreaty is to trash anything you can't trust. This solution may be safest for the individual, but at the expense of others. If everyone trashed everything unsafe, perhaps it wouldn't matter whether we identified new threats, but that won't happen in the foreseeable future. Until it does, it's better to avoid executing untrusted code, and, instead, send it to a competent authority for examination or other appropriate action. Individuals might want to forward such code to the vendor of their choice; larger organizations should have an in-house designated individual or team competent to make such decisions.

What, in any case, *is* trust? It's reasonable to distrust anything from anyone you don't know, but more often than not, you will receive worms and viruses from people you know and trust (for their goodwill, if not for their security awareness). Should you mistrust an attachment from your boss, your spouse, or your mother? Probably, but perhaps wholesale discarding of anything these users might send you is not worth the embarrassment and ill feeling it is likely to entail. Better to verify that they know they sent it (to lessen the risk from self-mailing viruses and worms) and that what they sent is what you see before you. The problem with exhortations to beware of attachments from unknown or untrusted sources is that they will be read as equating "known" and "trusted". Most viruses are received from known and trusted sources. Trusting the source (i.e., the goodwill of the sender) doesn't mean it's a good idea to trust the object.

We are sometimes told not to open anything from a trusted source unless it has been verified, but this advice alone is not enough. A file intentionally sent is unlikely to be a mail worm, but it can be virus-infected, without the knowledge of the sender, and opportunities for infection are not restricted to attachments. This principle addresses in some measure threats like Melissa and ExploreZip, but applies just as much to floppy disks as it does to attachments or ftp downloads. The trick is not to focus on the particular and miss out on the general. Better still, state the general principle *and* the particular instances, probably in some detail. If you're avoiding MIME attachments, you need to avoid embedded uuencodes as well.

Take Care in Newsgroups and on the Web

Distrust executable files from unmoderated newsgroups, or any newsgroup that doesn't normally approve binary files. In fact, take the same care as you would with email, but more so. After all, the chances are that more of the people in your web of trust contact you through regular email than do through USENET. You should also regard data files with suspicion, especially if they are Office documents. Pure text and graphics files are fine, but only if you can verify them before you open them.

You should probably be particularly careful in groups specializing in erotica (or worse), pirated software, hacking/cracking/virus-related material, and ethically murky areas such as MP3 exchange. We say this not because these items are inherently more likely to be infected, or even because of personal issues with the ethics of these types of activity. The real problem is that such groups have a large pool of unregulated materials that are highly desirable to many people. A virus or Trojan stirred into the mix has a much higher chance of being downloaded and run. For this reason, virus and Trojan writers are more likely to use these venues to launch their beasts into the wild while feeling good about themselves for being "morally superior" to their immediate victims.

You should be similarly cautious on web sites, ftp sites, and even chatrooms and email lists dealing with similar material. Infected subscribers to mailing lists may result in inadvertent forwarding of mass mailers. Accepting executable content from someone you meet in a chatroom is asking for trouble.

Don't Install Unauthorized Programs

Trusting the sender doesn't mean you have to trust the message or attachment: most virus victims receive the infected object from a trusted source (who normally isn't aware he or she has a virus problem). If someone does send you a program file such as a joke program, screensaver, or game, even if the sender claims that the file is something less frivolous such as a disk or file utility, you should regard the file as potentially dangerous and forward it to an appropriate resource for analysis. We would discourage you from using any unauthorized programs of any sort, whether received by email, on floppy, as a download from the Web, or from any other source.

Joke program files, in particular, often generate a virus alert from anti-virus software, and dealing with such alerts can be more of a problem than straightforward detection and removal of a real virus.

Be Cautious with Microsoft Office Documents

Microsoft Word documents and Excel spreadsheets are frequent targets for macro viruses. Other documents may also carry viruses, but far less frequently. If people you don't know send you unsolicited documents (or any other type of file), regard the files as potentially dangerous and send them for analysis. If people you do know send such documents unexpectedly, this may mean that a virus or email worm has infected their system and is mailing itself out from their account without their knowledge. Ask them to confirm that they sent the file.

Use and Ask for Safer File Formats

To lower the risk of receiving and forwarding macro-infected documents, use Rich Text Format (.RTF) word processed documents (which do not directly support Microsoft's macro languages) and .CSV documents for spreadsheets, and ask other people to send you documents in these formats where possible. Note, however, that following this advice doesn't provide complete safeguards.

A document that has the .RTF extension is not necessarily a Rich Text Format document. Some viruses can intercept the attempt to save a document as RTF and save it as a normal document, but with an .RTF extension, so that macros are preserved and will be run as usual when the document is opened in Word.

It's also possible to insert a Word document, Excel spreadsheet, or other potentially infected or infective objects into an .RTF document created or edited with Word, complete with macros, which may be executed when the embedded document is opened even if Word's own macro virus protection is active. A patch is available from Microsoft to counter this latter type of attack. Many anti-virus products now include .RTF as a default scanning option, rather than checking for .RTF files only during an "all files" scan.

Where formatting is not crucial, plain text remains the safest option, and may be less resource-intensive.

Continue to Use Anti-Virus Software

Always using these file formats does not, therefore, relieve you of the need to run anti-virus software that scans files as or before they are opened. Additionally, while you should not place your entire trust in the macro virus protection included in recent versions of some Microsoft Office applications, it's highly recommended that you make full use of them. While this software will not identify specific viruses, it will normally indicate the presence of "macros and customizations". Any document that gives rise to such a message should be forwarded to a responsible individual or agency, such as an anti-virus vendor, for analysis.

Keep Your Anti-Virus Software Updated

Make sure that someone in your organization is ensuring that your anti-virus software is up to date. If your scanner can be auto-updated from the vendor's web site (or some similar source), make sure that you or an administrator has configured it that way. If you can't or choose not to use some sort of automated scheduling, make sure that updating manually is part of your regular routine.

Up to Date Doesn't Mean Invulnerable

Scanning for known viruses is always second best. By the time you see an update, other viruses have been found, and new viruses can go from unknown to a global threat in hours, even minutes. At the moment, viruses don't often spread that rapidly, but that can change, and even an occasional Melissa or Love Bug can be very costly. The fact that you're running up-to-date software doesn't mean you can't possibly have a virus.

Super-users Aren't Super-human

Don't assume that because someone else is responsible for keeping your anti-virus software updated, it must be happening. An administrator may not have all the necessary information about your system. The software or the updating mechanism may have a problem. If you get messages from the software itself that it isn't up to date, or that there may be some sort of problem (including a possible virus), report it; don't assume that someone else will notice sooner or later. Someone may, but perhaps too late.

Disable Floppy Booting

By default, most PCs will attempt to start up from a floppy disk, if there is one in drive A. (Note that some systems can be made to boot from another floppy drive, though such a configuration is unusual.) Changing CMOS settings so that booting from a floppy disk doesn't happen by default lowers the risk of infection from boot-sector viruses such as Form, Stoned, Michelangelo, and Monkey.

Some systems allow you to disable floppy booting altogether, while others allow you to change the boot sequence from A, C, to C, A, so that the system will boot from drive A only if there is a problem with the hard drive or if the boot sequence is changed back. It isn't always obvious how to implement this sort of protection, but that's what Help Desks are for.

Write-Protect Diskettes

If you have to take a floppy disk to another system, write-protect the disk first. Write-protecting the disk will not protect the other system from any viruses on the diskette, but may protect the diskette from any infection present on the other system.

Office Avoidance

Avoiding using Microsoft Office applications is an obvious means of avoiding trouble, but isn't very practical for many corporate users and others who are required to use a particular application, or even a particular version of an application. Use the built-in configuration options for warning of the presence of macros, and other protective measures, such as those described in Jimmy Kuo's "Free Macro Protection" white paper at the NAI site (http://download.nai.com/products/media/vil/pdf/free_AV_tips_techniques.pdf).

Reconsider Your Email and News Software

Certain email software is particularly vulnerable to abuse, notably Outlook and Outlook Express. If you don't need the particular functions they offer, you might consider using another (arguably more secure) mail client such as Eudora, or even accessing mail from a less vulnerable platform (such as Macintosh or UNIX). If you do use Outlook, consider upgrading to the more secure but less user-friendly versions. These can be found at the Microsoft Office Outlook download page:

    http://office.microsoft.com/downloads/
    default.aspx?Product=Outlook&Version=95|
    97|98|2000|2002&Type=Update|Converter|Add-In|Assistant|Stationery|
    Document|Viewer|Template|Anti-Virus|Updates

(This URL is long enough that it must be wrapped in the book. It should all go on one line with no spaces when you plug it into your web browser.) You will probably want to download the "Outlook 97 Email Attachment Security Update" (published 6th September, 2000), the "Outlook 2000 SR-1 Update: E-mail Security" (published 7th June, 2000), or the related Macintosh versions. There are also updates that deal with some security problems related to inappropriate use of Java. Be advised, though, that these versions make the program much less functional, and you can't restore the functionality of the less secure versions without considerable hassle and extensive reinstallation.

Whatever your email client, it makes sense not to let it do any of the following automatically:

▶ Execute attached programs

▶ Open Office documents with any application (Word, Excel, PowerPoint, Access) that will let macros run automatically

- ▶ Open your web browser and open embedded links
- ▶ Run any HTML scripts such as JavaScript, VBScript, and so on (an even better idea is to decline HTML support altogether)

Show All File Extensions in Windows Explorer

You should configure Windows Explorer and, indeed, any other environment that displays filenames to show all file extensions. Note that such a configuration doesn't guarantee defence against deceptive icons or double extensions intended to persuade you that a file is of a trustworthy file type (myfile   .txt.vbs, for instance). In Windows, the icon is determined by the (last) file extension, but in some environments, the icon can be edited into something deceptive.

Disable the Windows Script Host

Internet Explorer and Outlook are both subject to a particular vulnerability associated with the Windows Script Host (WSH). If you don't need this feature, disabling WSH protects you against a whole class of email viruses and worms. File types associated with this vulnerability include (among others) VBScript (.VBS) files and scrap (.SHS) files.

   Detailed information on disabling the Windows Script Host is given in Chapter 10.

Introduce Generic Mail Screening

Discarding or quarantining messages containing scripts or attached executable files at the mail server or at the desktop rather than relying on detection of known scripting viruses significantly increases security. Certainly any file that includes a double extension, such as myfile.txt.vbs (so that it appears to be a simple text file), or that contains a large block of spaces before the extension (so that the extension itself may not be visible to the recipient), should be treated as suspicious.

Utilize Microsoft Security Resources

Microsoft maintains a number of security resources, including mailing lists for the circulation of security bulletins. For the IT professional or the concerned home user without an IT unit on which to rely, these are good sources of information on security issues relating to Microsoft products (Windows in general, Microsoft Office, Internet

Explorer, Outlook, and so on) that are, unfortunately, often implicated in security problems. They can be found at:

http://www.microsoft.com/security/default.asp
http://www.microsoft.com/technet/security/current.asp

Of course, Microsoft is far from being the only source of such information. Other vendors offer discussion lists and advisory mail-outs for users of their software and/or hardware, while third-party consultants offer similar services.

Subscribe to Anti-Virus Vendor Lists

Some anti-virus vendors maintain mailing lists relating to specific virus outbreaks and alerts as well as to version upgrades, definitions updates, and so on. Although it may expose you to a higher proportion of marketing hype and scare-mongering, subscribing to several of these lists may also give you a more balanced view.

Scan Everything

Before opening any new or modified object, you should scan it with current anti-virus software. At this point, it's probably too much to hope that customers will run on-demand scanners unprompted at *any* time, let alone every time you would like them to. Fortunately, on-access scanning has removed most of the need to run scheduled or on-demand scans for most people, though many competent administrators prefer to run scheduled scans as a backup. After all, rigorous testing suggests that even today, on-access scanners do not always dependably detect the same range of threats as the corresponding on-demand scanners.

Don't Rely on Anti-Virus Software

An organization that relies entirely on its anti-virus software, however reputable, is dicing with disaster. Nowadays, a reasonably secure corporation protects itself with multilayered anti-virus systems, intrusion detection systems, and firewalls. DSL (Digital Subscriber Line) and cable modems introduce to the home user the joys of continuous (fast) connection to the Internet, but also the increased risks of a connection that is, potentially, always there and always identified by a consistent IP address. Major hardware/software defensive measures such as a corporate firewall are not an option for most people with one or two home machines, but "personal firewalls", anti-Trojan software, and other scaled-down weaponry are options (and are sometimes very cheap or even free).

Back Up, Back Up, Back Up

Backing up is not the complete answer to viruses and other threats that it's sometimes claimed to be, but a well-planned backup strategy goes a long way towards aiding recovery from the most destructive viruses. Lengthy consideration of backup issues is worth a book in itself, but you should consider the following points.

Prioritize Data Backup

It's usually more practical in cases of severe damage to restore a complex operating environment from scratch by reinstalling from a standard image or from a "day zero" backup, adding nonstandard applications, then restoring data. This strategy has the advantage of minimizing the need for a full backup, requiring less expenditure of time and resources, and placing the emphasis where it should be—that is, on the data.

Beware of Data Diddling

Remember that not all virus damage involves sudden catastrophic effects. Slow corruption (viral or otherwise) of data that goes back over several generations of backup makes it unsafe to rely on recycling media too frequently. Backing up data to a diskette and leaving it there instead of (or, better, as well as) recycling media may pay dividends one day. Don't be afraid of redundancy (but manage it carefully).

Write-Protect Your Backups

If you do need to restore data, irrespective of whether you suspect virus action, do it where possible from read-only media (write-protected diskettes, for instance). We know of cases where attempting to repair damage from write-enabled media has resulted in the progressive loss of backups as well as the original data.

Back Up Your Backups

If you back up your data to a server, it's wise to ensure that the server is backed up too.

Test Backup Procedures

It's also a good idea to test your backup procedures from time to time. Nothing is sadder than to breathe a sigh of relief, and then discover that your diskettes are corrupted, that your tapes haven't been recording everything you thought they were, or that the operator wasn't aware that the tapes don't rewind automatically.

Backups Are Dumb

Backup systems are not typically intelligent systems; they simply make a copy of whatever is found on the item to be preserved onto the backup media. This means that data, programs and infected files are backed up just as well—and so are empty files or files of zero length, as in the case of ExploreZip-affected systems. The backup system neither knows nor cares about the content of the files, their size (unless they won't fit), or whether or not they are infected. It is therefore important to ensure that your backup strategy fits your needs, is not overused or recycled too quickly, and is checked periodically for accuracy.

Hoax Management

It is usually considered good practice to request that users not distribute virus warnings without checking with an individual qualified to assess the accuracy and urgency of such warnings. Even better practice is to bar any dissemination of warnings at all, except by one or more individuals authorized to do so.

Form Response

We sometimes find it useful to produce a form response for use by Help Desk staff. A copy should be sent to the administrator or team responsible for anti-virus and related security issues, along with a copy of the original alert, especially if it was received as email, in which case it should be sent with all the original headers if possible. An appropriate response form would contain the following suggested wording:

> Thank you for the message concerning the <alert/advisory identifier>. We appreciate notification of such things, and even more we appreciate it if people check with us rather than send them on. Indeed, we ask that all virus warnings be forwarded to the Help Desk and copied to <the anti-virus administrator>, whose job it is to forward them if appropriate.

> <The anti-virus administrator> is always pleased to advise on whether the warning is authentic or accurate, whether it's advisable or appropriate to forward it to anyone, and whether any further response to the apparent source of the warning is indicated.

> This alert <delete as applicable>:

> ▶ Is a known hoax <insert source of further information>.

- ▶ Is probably or possibly a hoax—research continues <insert grounds for mistrust>.

- ▶ Contains some element of truth but is not very/completely accurate <enumerate inaccuracies as appropriate>.

- ▶ Is correct, but we wouldn't regard it as particularly useful to forward it indiscriminately.

- ▶ Raises an important issue and we take it seriously. A statement will be/has been issued accordingly.

<Insert expanded material pertaining to this particular advisory/alert/ warning/hoax here.>

We would be grateful if you could point out to anyone in doubt that warnings from any individual within the organization who is not authorized to forward them should not be assumed to be accurate, and should still be checked with the Help Desk. This applies irrespective of:

- ▶ The status of the sender. It is our experience that managerial status and knowledge of security issues do not necessarily go together.

- ▶ Apparent endorsement of the warning by authoritative individuals or organizations, including anti-virus and other security companies or agencies.

- ▶ Your belief in the good intentions and technical competence of the source of the warning.

A Quick Guide to Hoaxes

We have spent some years researching hoaxes, hoax management, and related issues, and that body of work cannot be condensed to a few paragraphs. Hoaxes and other manifestations of email abuse are considered at much greater length in Chapter 16. However, this section offers a minimal guide to the field that you can use as a basis for an informational supplement to the preceding form response.

Most of the hoaxes we see derive from the Good Times virus hoax that wasted so much bandwidth in the mid-1990s. Usually the message says something like "Don't open mail with a particular subject". "GOOD TIMES", "DEEYENDA", "IT TAKES GUTS TO SAY JESUS", "HOW TO DEEP FRY A CAT", and "WIN A HOLIDAY" are a few examples of subject lines that are alleged to be associated with "lethal" email viruses. It is usually claimed that if you read the message it will eat your hard drive (or at least reformat it) and send all your credit card details to the "Legion of Doom". (Hoaxes can be and occasionally are a lot subtler than these examples. However, we have no intention of giving away a guide to writing a hoax that might fool us.)

We used to say that viruses simply aren't distributed this way, and that it's not possible to be infected by a virus simply by reading email. This is still true if you define your terms rather carefully. Unfortunately, however, virus writers have muddied the waters since the mid-1990s, when hoaxes really started to become a nuisance. Current generation email viruses often do arrive in your mailbox with a characteristic subject line. However, it's very easy to change the subject line and the name of the infected or otherwise dangerous file attachment each time it's passed on, which makes it more difficult to detect possibly infected attachments. (Virus and worm authors are increasingly making use of this technique.) Any mail that asks you to forward its contents to other people is, arguably, a chain letter, whomever or wherever it comes from, and should be regarded with scepticism.

You should also be sceptical of a virus warning that states that "There is no cure for this virus". Anti-virus vendors have usually managed to address the high-profile, high-impact, fast-spreading viruses and worms that excite the most profound media attention in a matter of hours (or less), and it is most unlikely that there will ever be an undetectable virus from which there is no protection. There *are* viruses whose effects are so drastic that recovery of data (or, in rare instances, of systems) is impractical; however, such viruses are no more difficult to detect and protect against than any other virus.

Many virus alerts are pure fantasy, and are intended only to frighten you into forwarding the message. Even if a message isn't virus-related or a hoax, it doesn't necessarily serve any useful purpose to forward such a warning indiscriminately. New viruses appear at a rate of several hundred per month, and unless the circumstances are very unusual, it isn't productive to point out the existence of a specific virus. You might just as well say, "Keep your anti-virus software up to date", which is good advice but doesn't bear undue repetition.

Except in this book.

Summary

This chapter reflects our conviction that malware is essentially a people problem, and cannot be resolved by purely technological means. Indeed, the root problem can be eradicated only by social means (teaching responsible behaviour and controlling those users who cannot or will not be responsible), and we explore those issues further in Part IV.

Case Studies: What Went Wrong, What Went Right, What Can We Learn?

CHAPTER 2

Case Studies: The First Wave

IN THIS CHAPTER:

I t would be nice if we could give you a detailed analysis of every virus you might need to know about. Unfortunately, to do so would make this book much too long, even if we included *only* the few hundred viruses definable as In the Wild by their inclusion in the WildList. Even then, detailed analyses of many viruses and variants wouldn't necessarily be particularly useful to you.

The case studies in this section aren't always typical of all viruses, or even all viruses of a particular class. They all have some intrinsic interest, and they tell us something about virus technology, anti-virus technology, society and viruses, or all three. At the very least, they will give you some insight into the strange, twilit worlds in which virus writers and anti-virus researchers move. In the first chapter of this section, we consider in more detail some of the oldest known viruses.

Brainwashing

Although old and seldom seen nowadays, the Brain family (Pakistani, Pakistani Brain, Lahore, and Ashar), raises a number of interesting technical points.

Brain itself was the first known PC virus, aside from those written by Fred Cohen for his thesis. Unlike Cohen's viruses, however, Brain is a boot-sector infector. The two earliest viral programs (for the Apple II family) were "system" viral programs, and it has been suggested that these earlier, similar programs influenced the writer of Brain.

Brain has been described as the first stealth virus. A request to view the boot sector of an infected disk on an infected system will result in a display of the original (pre-infection) boot sector. Early editions of Dr. Solomon's Anti-Virus Toolkit included an account of how Alan Solomon, in his first encounter with the virus, infected a number of diskettes before realizing that the virus was hiding the boot sector from his disk editor. (Solomon, at that time a data recovery specialist, went on to become one of the world's best-known experts on viruses and anti-virus technology.) The volume label of an infected diskette is set to "(C) Brain", "(C) Ashar", or "Y.C.1.E.R.P", depending on the variant. When the virus was written, there was no widely used graphical alternative to the DOS prompt. If you wanted to see what files were on a disk, the chances were that you used the DIR command to display a list of filenames and file information. At the very beginning of such a listing (depending on the version of DOS and any command-line switches in use), comes something like this:

```
Volume in drive A is (C) Brain
Volume Serial Number is 3AF1-41A7
Directory of A:\
```

Brain was not, it seems, intended to blush forever unseen.

Who Wrote the Brain Virus?

In one of the most common Brain versions, you will find text, unencrypted, giving the name, address, and telephone numbers of Brain Computer Services in Pakistan. The virus is copyright by "Ashar and Ashars" or "Brain & Amjads", so we have two brothers running a computer store who have written a virus. Simple, right?

David Shenk's Eleventh Law of Data Smog applies: beware stories that dissolve all complexity (David Shenk, *Data Smog: Surviving the Information Glut,* Abacus, 1997).

Solomon's analysis (which we are no longer able to trace in any public form) indicates that Ashar is older than Brain. In fact, the address text isn't present in the most common version of Brain, and it would have been a very simple matter to have overlaid the text in the Ashar or Brain programs with the address text.

Why would the owners of Brain Computer Services have written a virus? It is frequently stated that they were selling pirated software, a practice that is legal in Pakistan but not in the United States. According to this theory, the infected disks were sold to Americans as punishment for their use of pirated software. One has to wonder why Brain would have been intended to "punish" the United States (its major source of software). In any case, the Brain infection was never limited to the Western world—viruses are better at scattergun effects than at precision marksmanship. This story has nevertheless been cited as a curious example of Islamic logic. Cultural biases aside, this justification for Brain rests on the same kind of argument that you will find in any virus exchange, 'zine, or web site—that viruses are cool because they affect only people who deal in pirated software and pornographic material, who are careless about backing up, and who open mail attachments. As usual, blame attaches to the victims, not the perpetrators.

> ### NOTE
>
> *It is true that viruses have been injected into the wild by way of sources of illegally copied software, erotica, and so on, such as warez servers and alt.sex hierarchy newsgroups, with the perpetrators blaming the downloaders for their vile appetites. It doesn't seem to us, though, that the same logic necessarily applies to a more or less legitimate commercial venture.*

It has also been suggested that Brain Computer Services may have written some software of its own, and was incensed when it became a victim, itself, of other software pirates. This theory doesn't seem particularly convincing, either. If infected disks were sold by Brain Computer Services, a clean copy would more likely have been pirated than a legitimate copy. It has been suggested that Brain is some kind of copyright device. This theory also defies logic, since the virus would then "legitimize" bootleg copies whenever it infected one.

Brain is not intentionally or routinely destructive, and it is possible that the virus was written to publicize the company. It was the earliest known PC virus, at a time when computer viruses did not inspire the same revulsion that they tend to do now. Even some time after the later, more destructive viruses, Lehigh and Jerusalem, viruses were still seen as possibly neutral or even in some way beneficial. It may be that the author saw a self-reproducing program that "lost", at most, 3KB of disk space as simply a novelty. In a way, such a virus would not be dissimilar to those ludicrous Easter Egg applets that programmers working for major application publishers use to express their individuality.

It has recently been noted that Brain Computer Services appears to be alive, well, and represented on the World Wide Web. Given the fact that poachers often aspire to becoming gamekeepers in the wacky world of security, it seems surprising that they aren't offering anti-malware consultancy services.

Banks of the Ohio

Fridrik Skulason, whose F-Prot has provided the engine for a number of anti-virus products over the years, analysed exhaustively the apparently later Ohio and Den Zuk versions of the Brain virus.

The Ohio (Den Zuk 1) and Den Zuk (Venezuelan, Search) variants contain some of the same code as Brain, so the virus will not infect or overlay them. Brain issues an "Are you there?" call to ensure that a targeted disk is not already infected. However, Ohio and Den Zuk identify Brain infections and overwrite them with themselves. They can be described as single-shot anti-virus utilities targeting the Brain virus (at the expense, however, of causing the Ohio and Den Zuk infections).

NOTE

Substitution of one virus for another has not seemed to us to be a useful basis for an anti-virus program, in general, but viruses that seek out and overwrite older viruses have been surprisingly common. We know of instances where virus writers have pleaded, on discovery, that they were drawing attention to a security loophole ("Hey, look, you can write viruses in VBA!"). However, we cannot think of an occasion where a serious attempt was made to justify the spreading of a virus by passing it off as an anti-virus utility. Marketing remote-access Trojans as network administration utilities might almost qualify. We also recall the author of a notorious "test virus" utility describing his product as an anti-virus utility, apparently on the grounds that it removed the test virus after the test. This leading contender for the 1990s Golden Chutzpah Award has also complained about the fact that his test virus has never been featured on the WildList. Apparently, no publicity is bad publicity...

Skulason also found that the Den Zuk version would overwrite an Ohio infection. (This "seeking" activity gives rise to one of Den Zuk's aliases: "Search".)

It was also suspected that "denzuko" might have referred to "the search" for Brain infections. Extensive searches for the meaning of the words "den zuk" and "denzuko" in a number of languages, as an attempt to find clues to the identity of the virus author, turned up closely related words meaning "sugar" and "knife" as well as "search". However, these turned out to be quite beside the point.

Both Den Zuk and Ohio contain text that suggests that they were written by the same author. Ohio contains an address in Indonesia (and none in Ohio—the name derives from Ohio State University, where it was first identified). Both contain a ham-radio licence number issued in Indonesia. Both contain the same programming bug. The FAT (File Allocation Table) and data areas are overwritten if a floppy disk with a higher capacity than 360KB is infected. Den Zuk is a more sophisticated exercise in programming. Skulason concluded, therefore, that Ohio was, in fact, an earlier version of Den Zuk.

The virus's author, apparently a college student in Indonesia, confirmed Skulason's hypotheses. In fact, Den Zuko turned out to be the author's nickname, derived from John Travolta's character in the movie *Grease*.

Full details of Skulason's analysis and his contact with the author were published in an early edition of *Virus Bulletin*, but we do not know of a currently available source.

The MacMag Virus

On 7th February, 1988, users of Compuserve's HyperCard Forum received a warning message to the effect that the NEWAPP.STK HyperCard stack file had been removed from the system. The message advised anyone who had downloaded the file not to use it. A Mac user had earlier downloaded the same HyperCard stack from the GEnie system. When he ran it, an INIT resource was copied into his system folder, suggesting a program that was intended to be executed at start-up. INIT programs include control panels and system extensions. These have similar background functionality to DOS TSR (Terminate and Stay Resident) programs, Windows VxDs, NT services, and other utilities that run in the background throughout a computing session.

The Forum suggested that there was no danger of any such activity, since HyperCard "stacks" are data files rather than programs. In fact, we recall almost the same objection on the now defunct ICARO mailing list when WM/Concept, the first In the Wild Word macro virus, was reported. The moderator checked and confirmed the warning and found that everything happened as the user had said. Furthermore, the INIT resource was "viral": it spread to other systems with which it came in contact. (At that time, "system" disks were as common among Mac users as "bootable" disks were among MS-DOS users.)

Give Peace a Chance

The MacMag virus did no apparent significant damage. It simply attempted to reproduce until 2nd March, 1988. If an infected computer was started up on that date, the virus displayed the following message:

> RICHARD BRANDOW, publisher of *MacMag,* and its entire staff would like to take this opportunity to convey their UNIVERSAL MESSAGE OF PEACE to all Macintosh users around the world.

Fortunately, on 3rd March the message appeared only once, and then the virus erased itself. As a result, the virus is hardly ever found outside collections.

NOTE

MacMag was programmed to trigger on the first anniversary (2nd March, 1988) of the introduction of the Macintosh II line. Oddly (but probably coincidentally), a bug in the virus caused system crashes on the Mac II, but no other model of Macintosh.

Brandow was the publisher and editor of the Montreal-based *MacMag* computer magazine, which had a circulation of about 40,000 and its own electronic bulletin board. He claimed to have been thinking about the "message" for two years before creating the virus. Brandow claimed "authorship" of the virus, according to an article in the *Chicago Tribune* on 14th February, 1988. However, it appears that he actually commissioned the programming of the virus, and the internal structure contains the name of Drew Davidson, apparently a professor at an American university.

Brandow, like many subsequent virus writers and distributors, gave various inconsistent reasons at different times for writing the virus. He claimed he wanted to make a statement about software piracy, though neither the statement nor the logical connection between piracy and viruses is particularly obvious. More often he fell back on the somewhat irrational "message" that would somehow promote world peace. In this regard, he made reference to the impressive number of handgun owners in the United States. The logic behind any of these connections is tortured at best. It seems, however, that Brandow did at least have disciples in Europe, among the free spirits of the Chaos Computer Club and the Belgian virus factory, and they sometimes applauded his actions.

The MacMag virus seems likeliest to have been intended as a publicity stunt, and Brandow milked it for all it was worth, and more.

Viruses and Warez

Are viruses and software piracy connected? The assumption that such a connection exists is often used as an argument against piracy. We do not in the least advocate piracy, of course; we are aware of the compelling moral and legal arguments against theft. We know of occasions when infected software or Trojans (and even virus-infected Trojans) have been found on warez servers (networked sources of pirated software) and dubious newsgroups. It is likely that infected software has, from time to time, been deliberately made available as a means of punishing those who use such resources, and some virus writers have sought moral justification by claiming that "if people don't use pirated software, they won't catch viruses".

When David Harley first compiled the alt.comp.virus FAQ, he asked a number of expert contributors, "Is the connection between viruses and piracy a myth?" Most agreed that it was, and one said (more or less), "It's a myth, but I don't object to you using it as an antipiracy argument". There is an obvious ethical problem here: surely the "good guys" should try to be more "honest" than the "bad guys". It seems to us, though, that there is another problem: if we push this argument, are we not giving the impression that pirated software is the major vector of virus transmission? It is doubtful whether this was ever true.

In 1995, boot-sector viruses were still the main virus problem. There is no reason to suppose that diskettes carrying illegally copied software are, in general, more likely to be virus-infected than are other diskettes. As the decade wore on, macro viruses became the main problem, and there is no obvious connection between macro viruses and pirated software; even a black market copy of Word is not intrinsically more vulnerable to this class of virus. Modern worm authors use a variety of hooks to trick their victims into executing their malicious code, and programs that masquerade as ripped-off software are not common if used for this purpose. We must conclude, therefore, that the connection between piracy and viruses is at best overstated. Of course, you should respect the rights of software authors and publishers, but you should be cautious about executing *any* code. Malicious code is not restricted to program files, and often arrives from innocent and legal sources.

The Wanton Seed

MacMag is one of the few viruses whose entry point into the field is documented, albeit by a somewhat unreliable source. Brandow claimed that he infected two computers in *MacMag*'s offices in December 1987 in order to "seed" the infection. It has been suggested that some deliberately infected diskettes were circulated in order to help it along.

Mac OS can be configured and customized by "dropping" resources into the system folder. In this case, a resource (named DREW in the HyperCard stack and DR in its viral form) was copied into the system folder on Mac systems.

Bootable Mac disks contain a system folder, in the same way that bootable MS-DOS disks contain the hidden system files and COMMAND.COM. In those days (1988, remember), system diskettes were commonly used as the means of starting up a Mac or PC, although floppy-drive-only personal computers are rarely seen outside museums now. In addition, Mac users would often create system disks with specialized configurations. A number of Macintosh programs worked only with one specific version of the Finder, so the user would have to "downgrade" the computer each time one of these programs was to be run. The Mac OS "opens" each disk inserted into the machine. On an infected machine, the MacMag virus found its way in the form of an INIT into the system folder of any diskette that was inserted into the drive. Thus the virus became one of the "initial" programs automatically run on system start-up; it would remain resident throughout the computing session. While memory-resident programs are often regarded as a test of a programmer's abilities, MacMag, according to analysis, was not a sophisticated piece of programming.

Early reports of the MacMag virus related to its appearance on the Compuserve system, however Compuserve actually had nothing to do with the production of the file. It was uploaded and distributed through other systems (notably GEnie) as well, but the MacMag virus was distributed, among other routes, via a HyperCard stack (that was for a time posted on Compuserve).

HyperCard, though often described as a solution in search of a problem, was the first widely available implementation of the hypertext or hypermedia concept. Related items of information are linked so that associated data can be seen concurrently, or at least accessed quickly and in the nonlinear fashion exemplified by the World Wide Web.

HyperCard was also seen as a development tool, and still has its adherents, even though Apple has all but stopped offering any support whatsoever. In fact, for several years HyperCard infectors were the only new viruses seen on the Macintosh platform at all, apart from Word and Excel viruses. HyperCard stacks are essentially databases with internal link information. As such, the initial report of the fact that NEWAPP.STK, supposedly a file of information on new Apple products, actually altered system data met with scepticism. Even then, it was assumed that a viral program could not spread via data files. It was erroneously reported that MacMag was an example of a virus that could. In fact, the NEWAPP.STK might better be described as a "dropper", and HyperCard viruses are better described in general as precursors to later macro viruses.

Macros Mess with Your Mind

Increasingly, programs are being invested with the ability to interpret macros and scripts, blurring the distinction between data and program code. HyperCard stacks can contain a substantial command set as well as data. Originally, these commands governed the ability to navigate between cards. The XCMD extended command set allowed for additional functions used to effect the system changes.

Other systems, such as Lotus 1-2-3, had macro capabilities associated with data files. In theory, it was always possible for a virus to be able to switch forms from object to macro in the same way that multipartite viral programs switch from file to boot-sector format. Macro and script viruses have become seriously widespread problems in recent years, and some examples are discussed in the next chapter.

MacMag seems to have been the first virus to infect shrink-wrapped commercial software. The president of MacroMind, a company producing educational material for computer training, was given an infected copy of the Mr. Potatohead program. MacroMind apparently delivered some infected training software to Aldus Corporation. The virus eventually spread to the production copy of the new Freehand drawing program. Seven to ten thousand copies of the program had been infected over three days of production, and many of them were distributed by the time the infection was discovered.

The characteristic media warning to avoid shareware and use only commercial software seems to have been first observed with regard to this virus (http://www.ciac.org/ciac/virdb/VIRS0068.TXT). The warning seems somewhat at odds with the reported dissemination of the virus through commercial software. On the other hand, MacroMind's customers included Microsoft, Lotus, Apple, and Ashton-Tate, but no infected copy was ever reported to have been shipped from those companies.

Scores

You may be surprised that we include two major analyses of Macintosh viruses in this chapter, given the overwhelming preponderance today of PC and Office (Word and Excel) viruses. At the time, however, there were no Office viruses, and the disparity between the number of viruses for each platform was very much smaller.

The Scores Mac virus is of particular interest, as it was probably the first virus to target a specific company and application.

Scores was probably detected in 1988, if not in late 1987. It did not appear to carry any payload, but, when the actual code was studied and disassembled, it was found to include a search for Mac "resources" identified as VULT or ERIC. At the time, no applications containing such resources were known. In May 1988, EDS, of Dallas, disclosed that these identifiers turned out to be used by resources internal to the company. The company never did say whether these resources were associated with a strictly internal utility or if they had been part of a project that was never released in that form. Either way, it is clear that the Scores virus was "aimed" at EDS since the resources are not part of any other program. It may be that the virus was supposed to spread throughout the company and then interfere with vital internal applications. Alternatively, the virus may have been intended to lie in wait until a certain application was released for general use, so that infected Macs would misbehave, leading to complaints, bug reports, or a bad name for the company in general.

NOTE

The Scores virus was first described by John Norstad, who also gave detailed instructions for disinfection. He decided not to write a specific disinfection program for the virus, since two others had already been produced. However, his reviews of the disinfection programs available at the time noted their serious shortcomings. Norstad went on to create the widely acclaimed (and free!) program Disinfectant. Until macro viruses became a major problem, Disinfectant provided the Mac-using community with effective and unobtrusive protection from viruses at no cost; however, it has not been supported or maintained for some years.

One of the early copies of Scores examined by researchers was recovered from the NASA headquarters in Washington. This led to reports of the NASA virus, and long afterwards major IS trade papers and security texts reported how the Scores virus had swept through NASA, trashing hard disks. In real life, Scores was never known to have done any actual intended damage.

In July 1988, a Texas man was charged with computer-related sabotage and burglary, and it was reported, in error, that he was the author of Scores. In December 1988, Apple sources were saying that they knew the author's identity, and that the matter was in the hands of their lawyers. In December 1990, it was reported that the Dallas prosecutor's office would be proceeding with charges and that reports of damage were being solicited. We are not aware of any subsequent reports or proceedings.

Scores uses complex mechanisms, but starts simply enough. When an infected application is run on a new system, the system folder is infected. The virus creates two invisible folders, one named Desktop and the other Scores (hence the name). Thus the Scores infection was launched early in the start-up process and went resident. The virus then proceeded to accomplish the following:

▶ It created INITs of 6, 10, and 17. This led to later problems with other INITs using the same numbering, since these INITs were sometimes assumed, incorrectly, to be infected.

▶ The virus created the Notepad and Scrapbook files, if they were not already present.

▶ It changed the file types, as well as the normal icons, for these files.

▶ The virus waited two days before beginning to infect applications.

▶ Four days after the infection of the system folder, the second part of the virus would start up, scanning for applications that, when run, identified themselves as ERIC or VULT. If such an application were ever executed, it would be terminated after 25 minutes of operation.

▶ Seven days after the system folder infection, the final part of the payload would come into play, affecting applications with the VULT resource. If such applications were found, the virus would force them to display a series of errors and eventually to crash, making use of a complicated sequence of timings and operations.

NOTE

Scores might almost be seen as an early form of the multipartite virus, since it toggles between system and application files. However, the other activities take place only after the infection has entered the system folder. Thus, Scores is actually analogous to some PC multipartite viruses that spread more effectively through boot-sector infection than through file infection. However, terms such as bipolar and tripolar are sometimes used to describe threats that include more than one type of malicious program, but may have only one replication vector.

The timing sequences and arrangements for triggering errors and program termination suggest that the author intended the virus to interfere with an application in a normal environment and generate "normal" problems. An intermittent bug would be difficult to trace and less likely to be effectively handled as a virus. This supposition would tend to support the idea that the author meant to cause trouble for ERIC and VULT as a released application. It does not, however, rule out the possibility that the author of Scores intended to create trouble for an in-house utility.

Lehigh

For all the damage that the Lehigh virus caused, we should at least be grateful that it generated sufficient interest for Ken van Wyk to start the VIRUS-L mailing list. For a while this mailing list was also mirrored on USENET news as comp.virus. Unfortunately, VIRUS-L seems to have disappeared, but it was, for a number of years, the primary source of accurate virus information, and was largely responsible for ensuring that the anti-virus research community did, in fact, become a community.

Not all students are even minimally computer literate. Student consultants at universities and colleges are presented with a steady stream of disks from which files have "mysteriously" disappeared. In November 1987, however, it appeared that certain failed disks were due to something other than user carelessness.

File-infecting viruses generally (though not exclusively) attach to a file in one of three ways. Some file viruses prepend, or bind themselves, to the beginning of the file, so that they run first. Other files append, or connect themselves to the end of the file, but modify the beginning of the file so that the virus runs first. Others overwrite some part of the existing file. In the case of an overwriting virus, often a redirection is also made at the beginning of the file so that the virus runs first. Sometimes the virus overwrites code that is important to the original program, and sometimes a virus looks for some section that it can overwrite without creating damage.

The Lehigh virus overwrote the slack space at the end of the COMMAND.COM file. This meant that the virus did not increase the size of infected files. A later report of a 555-byte increase in file size was due to confusion over the size of the overwriting code. When an infected COMMAND.COM was run (usually upon booting from an infected disk), the virus stayed resident in memory. When any access was made to another disk—via the TYPE, COPY, DIR, or other normal DOS commands—the virus would infect any uninfected COMMAND.COM files. The virus kept a counter of infections; after four infections, the virus would overwrite the boot and FAT areas of disks with bytes copied from BIOS.

Lehigh (the virus, not the campus) is remarkably stealthfree. The primary defence of the virus, at the time, was that no one would have been looking for it. The virus altered the date stamp of infected COMMAND.COM files. If attempting an infection on a write-protected disk, the virus would not trap the "WRITE PROTECT ERROR" message. This message was a serious giveaway if seen as a result of typing DIR: generating the directory listing should not require writing to the diskette (unless output is being redirected).

The virus was limited to targeting those disks that had a COMMAND.COM file, and, more particularly, those that contained a full operating system. Admittedly, in those heady bygone days, more users kept copies of the operating system on their disks. However, the virus was also self-limiting in that it would destroy itself once activated, and would activate after only four reproductions. To the best of our knowledge, the Lehigh virus never did spread beyond the campus in that initial attack. Although it is found in a number of private virus collections and may be released into the wild from time to time, the virus has no real chance of spreading given the change in computing environments.

CHRISTMA EXEC

CHRISTMA EXEC, the Christmas Tree Worm, sometimes referred to as the BITNET chain letter, was probably the first major malware attack across networks. It was launched on 9th December, 1987, and spread widely on BITNET, EARN, and IBM's internal network (VNet). It has a number of claims to a small place in history:

- ► It was written, unusually, in REXX.
- ► It was hosted on mainframes (on VM/CMS systems) rather than on minicomputers, quaint though that distinction sounds nowadays when the humblest PC can run UNIX.
- ► It was not self-launching; it presented itself as a chain letter inviting the recipient to execute its code. When it was executed, the worm drew a Christmas tree on-screen and mailed a copy of itself to everyone in the account holder's equivalent to an address book, the user files NAMES and NETLOG. Conceptually, there is a direct line of succession from this worm to the social engineering worm/Trojan hybrids of today.

In 1990, the spirit (though none of the code) of the worm was invoked by a message displayed between 24th and 31st December, along with a Christmas tree graphic, on systems infected with the XA1 (Tannenbaum) virus. "Und er lebt doch noch: Der Tannenbaum!"—that is, "And it still lives: the Christmas tree!"

The Morris Worm (Internet Worm)

In autumn 1988, most people were blissfully ignorant of both viruses and the Internet. Robert Slade, however, recalls that VIRUS-L had been established and was very active. "At that time it was still an 'exploder' mailer, rather than a digest, but postings were coming out pretty much on a daily basis, so I was quite surprised when I didn't receive any on November 3rd. I didn't get one on November 4th, either. It wasn't until November 5th, actually, that I found out why".

The Morris Worm didn't actually bring the Internet in general, nor email in particular, to the proverbial grinding halt. It was able to run and propagate only on machines running specific versions of the UNIX operating system on certain hardware platforms. However, given that the machines that are connected to the Internet also comprise the transport mechanism for the Internet, a minority group of server-class machines, thus affected, degraded the performance of the 'Net as a whole. Indeed, it can be argued that despite the greater volumes of mail generated by Melissa and LoveLetter, and the tendency of some types of mail servers to achieve meltdown when faced with the consequent traffic, the Internet as a whole has proven to be somewhat more resilient in recent years.

During the 1988 mailstorm, a sufficient number of machines had been affected by the Morris Worm to impair email and distribution-list mailings. Some mail was lost, either by mailers that could not handle the large volumes that backed up, or by mail queues being dumped in an effort to disinfect systems. Most mail was substantially delayed. In some cases, mail would have been rerouted by way of a possibly less efficient path after a certain time. In other cases, backbone machines, affected by the problem, simply processed mail much more slowly. In still others, mail routing software would crash or be taken out of service, with a consequent delay in mail delivery. Ironically, electronic mail was the primary means by which the various parties attempting to deal with the problem were trying to contact each other. Some things haven't changed.

By Sunday 6th November, mail was flowing, distribution lists and electronic periodicals were running, and the news was getting around. However, an enormous volume of traffic was given over to one topic—the Internet Worm.

The Internet Worm still inspires fascination. Even today, no virus story in the popular media is complete without some reference to it. In many ways, the Internet Worm is the story of data security in miniature. The Worm used trusted links, password cracking, security holes in standard programs, standard and default operations, and, of course, the power of viral replication.

"Big Iron" mainframes and other multi-user server systems are generally designed to run constantly—to be ready for action at all times, and to execute various types of programs and procedures in the absence of operator intervention. Many hundreds of functions and processes may be running at all times; some cooperate with each other, while others run independently. In the UNIX world, such small utility programs are referred to as *daemons,* after the supposedly subordinate entities that take over mundane tasks and extend the "power" of the "wizard", or skilled operator. Many of these

Mail Management

A typical pattern for dealing with a worm-related mailstorm in the 21st century runs something like this:

1. An administrator receives alerts from vendors, security organizations, or peer networks (the Anti-Virus Information Exchange Network, or AVIEN, is the most public of these discussion lists, at present; you can find out more about AVIEN and the Early Warning System, or EWS, at http://www.avien.org), or notes attacks on his or her own network.

2. The administrator gathers information (by talking to vendors and other sysadmins or by trawling web sites).

3. The administrator takes any available generic blocking measures (such as discarding mail with a characteristic subject).

4. He or she applies and distributes anti-virus updates to desktop machines.

5. The administrator manages any subsequent incidents.

Characteristically, these peripheral measures take up much of the first hour or two of an outbreak. The administrator is more likely to spend the next two or three days handling public relations: forestalling or fielding enquiries from customers, management, Help Desk staff, mailing lists, newsgroups, and, for high-profile administrators or organizations, the media.

utility programs deal with the communications between systems. "Mail", in the network sense, covers much more than the delivery of text messages between users. Network mail between systems may deal with file transfers, routing information for reaching remote systems, or even upgrades and patches to system software.

When the Internet Worm was well established on a machine, it would try to infect another. On many systems, this attempt was all too easy, since computers on the Internet are meant to generate activity on each other, and some had no protection in terms of the type of access and activity allowed.

The finger program is one that allows a user to obtain information about another user. (Please: we've heard all the jokes.) The server program, fingerd, is the daemon that listens for calls from the finger client. The version of fingerd common at the time of the Internet Worm had a minor problem: it didn't check how much information it was given. It would take as much as it could hold and leave the rest. "The rest", unfortunately, could be used to start a process on the computer running fingerd, and this process was used as part of the attack. This kind of buffer overflow attack continues to be very common, taking advantage of similar weaknesses in a wide range of applications and utilities.

The sendmail program is the engine of most mail-oriented processes on UNIX systems connected to the Internet. In principle, it should allow only data received from another system to be passed to a user address. However, a debug mode allows commands to be passed to the system. Some versions of UNIX were shipped with the debug mode enabled by default. Even worse, the debug mode was often enabled for testing during installation of sendmail and then never turned off.

When the Worm accessed a system, the main program from the previously infected site was fed to the new machine. Two programs were used, one for each infected platform. If neither program could work, the Worm would erase itself. If the new host was suitable, the Worm looked for further hosts and connections derived from the new host.

The program also tried to break into user accounts on the infected machine. It used standard password-cracking techniques such as simple variations on the name of the account and the user. It carried a dictionary of words likely to be used as passwords, and would also look for a dictionary on the new machine and attempt to use that as well. If an account was successfully accessed, the Worm would then look for accounts that this same user had on other computers, using standard UNIX tools.

The Worm did include an "Are you there?" call, a means of checking for copies already running on a target computer. However, it took some time to terminate the program, and through a bug, the Worm regularly produced copies of itself that would not respond to the request for termination at all. The normal copies of the Worm did destroy themselves—having first made new copies. In this way, the process ID number would continually change.

The Worm was not intentionally destructive. However, the mere presence of the program had implications for the infected systems and for those users associated with them. Because the multiple copies of the program ran simultaneously on the host machines, there was a serious impact on the performance of other processes. Also, communications links and processes were being used to propagate the Worm rather than to support the legitimate work for which they were intended.

Although the media usually misrepresent even the simplest virus attacks, it managed to report the Morris Worm with astonishing accuracy. Highly accurate newspaper reports were appearing even in regional newspapers as early as 5th November. Even the inaccurate stories were better than we have come to expect. A story from the *New York Times* on Sunday 6th November stated that Robert Morris was able to track the progress of the Worm because "[e]ach second each virus broadcast its location to a computer named Ernie at the University of California". While this was not altogether correct, it *was* true that the Worm was intended to send packets to ernie.berkeley.edu, but the code that should have accomplished this was faulty. Nevertheless, had the Berkeley system been configured as intended, it would have been possible to track the Worm's progress, albeit roughly.

One of the factors that contributed to this unprecedented (and unequalled until Melissa) media accuracy has to be the number of researchers involved. Across North America, dozens and perhaps hundreds of people were involved in a detailed examination of the Worm, since very little other work was being (or could be) done until the problem was resolved. Even nonresearchers were following the developments closely so as to be able to repair their own systems. Also, there was less time for misinformation to spread by way of "friends of friends" who had once seen a copy.

Robert Tappan Morris, son of Robert Morris of the National Security Agency (NSA), was a student of data security at Cornell University when he wrote the Worm. The release of the Worm seems to have been accidental, whatever the motive for actually writing it may have been. This view is supported by the unfinished nature of some of the code, and the fact that the author seems to have attempted to generate (moderately) early alerts. The first recorded warning was sent anonymously by a friend, about 10 hours after the initial release.

In general, expert opinion seems to favour the view that Worm exhibits a considerable knowledge of security holes and demonstrates (mostly) competent but unspectacular programming. The Worm contains a number of concepts that reoccurred in subsequent self-launching worms and other malware.

Morris was convicted on 16th May, 1990, of violating the Computer Fraud and Abuse Act, and was sentenced to three years' probation, a $10,000 fine, and 400 hours of community service. His appeal failed, and the appeal court's decision is instructive, depending as it does on questions of intent and whether right of access to a computer confers the same right of access to the network to which it is attached.

Debate over the sentence began even before the last copy of the Worm had been shut down. It ranged from "Hanging's too good for him", to "He's done us all a great favor". A range of opinion still exists today.

Estimates of the damage done by the Worm ranged from $100,000 to $97 million. This "think of a number" approach to quantification is also typical of high-profile virus reports or estimates used in actual trials of virus writers. The approach isn't confined to the virus arena, though. In *The Hacker Crackdown*, Bruce Sterling describes how Craig Neidorf, a.k.a. Knight Lightning, was tried for the fraudulent theft of a document called "Control Office Administration of Enhanced 911 Services for Special Services and Major Account Centers", which he published in the electronic phreaking/hacking magazine *Phrack*. In the course of the proceedings, Southern Bell variously estimated the value of the stolen document at $74,449 and $24,639.04. The trial foundered in part because similar documentation was available from a Bellcore catalogue priced at a whopping $13.

The WANK Worm

In October 1989, another network worm was found slithering around the Internet. This time, rather than affecting UNIX machines, the worm targeted VMS machines connected through DECnet. While it is open to debate as to what Morris originally intended to do with the Internet Worm, the WANK (Worms Against Nuclear Killers) worm was clearly intended as propaganda.

WANK could not use the same exploits as the Morris Worm (not least because it ran on a different platform), but it had a number of comparable characteristics. It was spread from system to system using mail functions, and exploited default "system" and "field service" accounts and passwords to gain access. In fact, the author seems to have borrowed ideas from the Morris Worm and from a previous DECnet worm (HI.COM).

In addition to guessing system passwords, the WANK worm also attempted to change them. As the program would have no further use for passwords, once running, the purpose of changing passwords would appear to have been to inconvenience the system operator, although it also mailed the new (random) DECNet account password to a user on a SPAN node.

The worm carried a message (which was displayed if the worm breached an account with system privileges) that announced that the infected system had been "WANKed" and that contained the quotation, "You talk of times of peace for all, and then prepare for war". Apparently the author had encountered and believed reports of the Internet Worm that had spoken of massive numbers of military computers being affected. Ironically, few, if any, of the people who saw the WANK worm's message would have had anything to do with the military.

Some aspects of the worm were just plain obnoxious, such as:

▶ Appearing to delete all of a user's files at login (it didn't actually delete user files)

▶ Paging users with the PHONE program

▶ Attempting to find accounts where the account name and the password were the same ("joe" accounts) or the password was null

▶ Disabling mail to the system account

Jerusalem

In terms of the number of infections (copies or reproductions) that a virus produces, boot-sector viral programs long held an advantage with microcomputers. Among file-infecting viral programs, however, the Jerusalem virus was the clear winner. It has another claim to fame as well: it almost certainly has the largest number of variants of any virus program known to date, at least in its class (parasitic file infectors).

Initially known to some as the Israeli virus, the version reported by Y. Radai in early 1988 (also sometimes referred to as "1813" or Jerusalem-B) was the most commonly encountered version. Although it was the first to be very widely disseminated and was the first to be discovered and publicized, analysis suggests that Jerusalem was the outcome of previous viral experiments.

A few things are common to pretty much all of the Jerusalem family. They usually infect both .COM and .EXE files. When an infected file is executed, the virus installs itself into memory, thus remaining active even after the originally infected program has been terminated. The virus code appended to the file infects .EXE programs executed after the program goes resident. Prepending code infects .COM files. Most variants carry some kind of date logic-bomb payload, often triggered on Friday the 13th. Sometimes the logic bomb is simply a message; often it deletes programs as they are accessed.

Although Jerusalem tends to work well with .COM files, the differing structure of .EXE files has presented the virus with a number of problems. As David Chess, a well known researcher working for IBM, has noted, it is a minor wonder that such a buggy program has spread so widely. Early versions of Jerusalem, not content with one infection, will reinfect .EXE files again and again so that they continually increase in size. This growth renders pointless the attempt at stealth that the programmer built in when he ensured that the file creation date was conserved and unchanged in an infected file. Also, .EXE programs that use internal loaders or overlay files tend to be infected in the wrong place and have portions of the original program overwritten.

Although the virus was reported to slow down systems that were infected, it seems to have been the continual growth of .EXE files that led to the detection of the virus. Jerusalem variants often don't check the infection status of a file, so that a single executable can be reinfected time and time again, until the delay on startup becomes noticeable. An early infection was found in an office belonging to the Israeli defence forces, giving rise to the occasional alias IDF. This pseudonym was actually problematic, since it was more often used as a reference for the unrelated Frodo virus.

The great number of Jerusalem variants has contributed towards severe naming and identification problems. Because a number of the variants are very closely based on the same code, the signatures for one variant will often match another, thus generating even more confusion. This situation is not unique to the Jerusalem family, of course, and is an ongoing concern in the anti-virus research community, as systems administrators grow increasingly vociferous in their demands for a unified nomenclature.

The common Jerusalem payload (file deletion on Friday the 13th) begged the question as to why the logic bomb had not activated on Friday 13th November, 1987. Subsequent analysis has shown that the virus will activate the payload only if the year is not 1987. The next Friday the 13th was 13th May, 1988. Since the last day that Palestine existed as a nation was 13th May, 1948, it was felt that the virus might have been an act of political terrorism. This supposition led to another alias, the PLO virus. However, Israel celebrates its holidays according to the Jewish calendar (no surprises there), and the independence celebrations were slated for three weeks prior, on 13th May, 1988. These facts, and the links between Jerusalem and the sURIV family, suggest that there is no intentional political link. It is almost certain that the Jerusalem virus is, in fact, two viral programs combined:

▶ sURIV 1.01 is a .COM-file infector, .COM being the easier file structure and therefore the easier program to infect.

▶ Virus sURIV 2 is an .EXE-only infector and has longer and more complex code.

▶ Virus sURIV 3 infects both types of program files and contains considerable duplication of code; it is, in fact, simply the first two versions concatenated together.

Although the code in the sURIV programs and the 1813 version of Jerusalem is not absolutely identical, the program duplicates all the same features. The payload date for sURIV is 1st April, and the year has to be later than 1988. Although this seems to suggest that sURIV is a descendant of Jerusalem, in fact the reverse is probably the case. Certainly the code is less sophisticated in the sURIV variants.

The Jerusalem virus was immensely successful as a template for variants. The code is reasonably straightforward and, for those somewhat familiar with assembly language programming, an excellent primer for the writing of viral programs affecting both .COM and .EXE files. It has a number of annoying bugs, though. It can misinfect some .EXE files (this applies, to an extent, to *any* file virus that predates changes in the .EXE format introduced by recent versions of Windows, for instance). It can conflict with Novell NetWare, which requires the use of Interrupt 21h subfunctions that are also used by the virus. One of the "Sunday" variants is supposed to delete files on the seventh day of the week. The author didn't realize that computers start counting from zero and that Sunday is actually the "zero*th*" day of the week. Since there is no seventh day, the file deletions never actually happen.

The "AIDS" Trojan

We have included the AIDS Information Diskette Trojan in this section for a number of reasons:

▶ It deserves a place in the history of malware as one of the more successful Trojans.

▶ For sentimental reasons. David Harley traces his assimilation into the security industry from the day he was asked for help with this Trojan.

▶ It was so widely—and incorrectly—reported as a virus. As it happens, a number of unrelated computer viruses, on a variety of platforms, are sometimes known as AIDS. The one that everyone remembers, though, was not a virus at all.

In the fall of 1989, approximately 10,000 copies of an "AIDS Information" package were sent out from a company calling itself PC Cyborg. Some were received at European medical establishments, and a number were received at other types of businesses. The packages appeared to have been professionally produced. Accompanying letters usually referred to them as sample or review copies. However, the packages also contained a very interesting "licence agreement":

In case of breach of license, PC Cyborg Corporation reserves the right to use program mechanisms to ensure termination of the use of these programs. These program mechanisms will adversely affect other program applications on microcomputers. You are hereby advised of the most serious consequences of your failure to abide by the terms of this license agreement.

Warning: Do not use these programs unless you are prepared to pay for them.

The disks contained an installation program and a simple AIDS information and risk assessment package. The installation program appeared only to copy the AIDS program onto the target hard disk. However, a hidden directory was created with a nonprinting character name, and a hidden program file with a nonprinting character in the name was installed. The AUTOEXEC.BAT file was renamed and replaced with one that called the hidden program and then the original AUTOEXEC. The hidden program kept track of the number of times the computer was rebooted, and, after a certain number, encrypted the hard disk. The program then presented the user with an invoice and a demand to pay the licence fee in return for the encryption key. One version, which waited for 90 reboots, was thought to be the "real" attempt; an earlier version, which encrypted after one reboot, alerted authorities and was probably released erroneously.

The Panamanian address for PC Cyborg turned out to be real. Four principals were identified, as well as an American accomplice who seems to have had plans to send 200,000 copies to American firms if the European "test" worked. The British trial of the American was suspended, as his bizarre behaviour in court was seen as an indication that he was unfit to plead. An Italian court, however, found him guilty and sentenced him in absentia.

Everybody Must Get Stoned

The Stoned virus seems to have been written by a high school student in New Zealand— hence its other name, New Zealand. All evidence suggests that he wrote it only for study and that he took precautions to prevent its spread. These precautions proved to be insufficient, as it turned out. It is reported that his brother stole a copy and decided that it would be fun to infect the machines of friends.

NOTE

Tequila seems to have escaped into the wild under somewhat similar circumstances. On that occasion, a friend of the author stole a copy and infected other disks. Sometimes virus authors seem to be as careless about their choice of confidant as the rest of us.

The original version of Stoned is said to have been restricted to infecting floppy disks. The current most common version of Stoned, however, infects *all* disks. It is an example of a second class of boot-sector-infecting (BSI) viral programs, in that it places itself in the Master Boot Record (MBR), or partition boot record, of a hard disk instead of in the boot sector itself. As with most BSIs, Stoned moves the original sector to a new location on the disk. On hard disks and double-density floppies, this movement is not usually a problem. On high-density floppies, however, it can overwrite system information, resulting in loss of data. One version of Stoned is reported not to infect 3.5-inch diskettes; this version may well have been the template for Michelangelo, which doesn't infect 720KB disks either.

Stoned has spawned a large number of mutations ranging from minor variations in the spelling of the payload message to the functionally different Empire, Monkey, and No-Int variations.

Michelangelo, Monkey, and Other Stoned Variants

Michelangelo is generally believed by researchers to have been built on, or "mutated" from, the Stoned virus. The similarity of the replication mechanism, down to the inclusion of the same bugs, puts this theory beyond all reasonable doubt. Any successful virus is likely to be copied, to some degree. Michelangelo is unusual only in the extent to which the payload has been modified.

Michelangelo has been widely reported to have been discovered in Europe in the spring or summer of 1991. However, Roger Riordan in Australia had reported and named the virus in February 1991. He suspected that Michelangelo had entered the victim company on disks of software received from Taiwan, but this hypothesis remains unproven.

His report indicates that the virus existed prior to 6th March, 1991 (the trigger date), which means that the virus can survive even though it destroys itself along with the system tracks of disks overwritten on that date. This resiliency is not really surprising: few computer users understand that boot viruses can, in principle, infect any disk from any other disk, whether or not the disk is bootable, contains program files, or contains any files at all.

Riordan determined that 6th March was the trigger date. It is often assumed from the name of the virus that it was intended to trigger on 6th March because that is the birthday of Michelangelo Buonarotti, Renaissance artist, sculptor, and engineer. In fact, this misunderstanding was revived yet again in 2000 by Phil Schmauder's book on viruses. However, the body of the virus has no text, no reference to Michelangelo, and no evidence of any sort that the author of the virus was aware of the significance of that particular date. The name is simply the one that Riordan chose to give it (and it has nothing to do with Ninja turtles, either).

By the beginning of 1992, production software was being shipped on Michelangelo-infected floppies, and at least one company was shipping infected PC systems. It has been suggested that by the end of that February, when the general public was becoming aware of the problem, the number of infected floppies out in the field may have been in the millions. Fortunately, most infected machines were checked and diagnosed before 6th March of that year.

The replication mechanism of Michelangelo is basically that of Stoned. It replaces the original boot sector on a floppy disk with a copy of itself. The virus moves the original boot sector to sector 3 (for 360KB diskettes) or 14 (for 1.2MB or 1.44MB diskettes), and the virus contains a "loader" that points to this location. After the virus loads itself into memory, the original boot sector is run, and to the user, the boot process appears to proceed normally. On hard disks, the original partition sector is moved to (0,0,7).

> ### NOTE
>
> *This (x,x,x) notation is frequently used to identify a particular sector. It denotes (head, cylinder, sector), so in this case the partition sector is moved to head 0, cylinder 0, sector 7. Fridrik Skulason's detailed analysis of the virus can be found on the Virus Bulletin web site at http://www.virusbtn.com/VirusInformation/michelangelo.html.*

Michelangelo is no stealth virus. Examination of the boot blocks shows a clear difference between a "valid" sector and the infected one. (The absence of the normal system messages should also be a tip-off: Michelangelo contains no text whatsoever.) In addition, Michelangelo reserves itself 2KB at the "top" of memory; a simple run of DOS's CHKDSK utility will show total conventional memory on the system, and if a 640KB machine shows 655,360 bytes, then the machine does *not* have Michelangelo. (If the number is less, there may be reasons other than a virus, and if the number is 655,360, that does not, of course, prove that a virus is not present or active.)

CHKDSK is still found on modern PC systems, but the information obtained from the command MEM /C is a better tool for checking memory in recent versions of Windows. Its output is similar to the following:

```
Modules using memory below 1 MB:

Name            Total             Conventional        Upper Memory
--------    ----------------    ----------------    ----------------
MSDOS          33,008   (32K)       33,008   (32K)          0   (0K)
HIMEM           1,168    (1K)        1,168    (1K)          0   (0K)
CDROM           4,224    (4K)        4,224    (4K)          0   (0K)
IFSHLP          2,864    (3K)        2,864    (3K)          0   (0K)
SETVER            832    (1K)          832    (1K)          0   (0K)
WIN             3,728    (4K)        3,728    (4K)          0   (0K)
vmm32           7,488    (7K)        7,488    (7K)          0   (0K)
COMMAND         7,472    (7K)        7,472    (7K)          0   (0K)
Free          594,336  (580K)      594,336  (580K)          0   (0K)
```

```
Memory Summary:
Type of Memory         Total          Used           Free
-----------------   -----------    -----------    -----------
Conventional           655,360         61,024         594,336
Upper                        0              0               0
Reserved               393,216        393,216               0
Extended (XMS)      15,728,640        176,128      15,552,512
-----------------   -----------    -----------    -----------
Total memory        16,777,216        630,368      16,146,848

Total under 1 MB       655,360         61,024         594,336

Largest executable program size       594,320     (580K)
Largest free upper memory block             0     (0K)
MS-DOS is resident in the high memory area.
```

Disinfection is a simple matter of placing the original sector back where it belongs, thus wiping out the infection. This can be accomplished with sector-editing utilities, or even with DEBUG, though of course it is normally easier and safer just to use an anti-virus utility (especially for viruses that have been around this long).

NOTE

There have been "cocktail" cases where a computer has become infected with both Stoned and Michelangelo. In this situation, the boot sector cannot be recovered, since both Stoned and Michelangelo use the same "landing zone" for the original sector, and the infection by the second virus overwrites the original boot sector with the contents of the first virus.

When an infected computer boots up, Michelangelo checks the date via Interrupt 1Ah. If the date is 6th March, the virus then overwrites the first several cylinders of the disk with the contents of memory (which doesn't amount to much at this stage in the start-up process). Interrupt 1Ah was not usually available on the earliest PCs and XTs, with some exceptions. However, the disk that is overwritten is the disk from which the system is booting; you can save a hard disk simply by booting from a floppy. Also, the damage is triggered only at boot time, although this is not altogether a positive. The fact that the damage occurs during the boot process means that the payload, like the infection mechanism, is no respecter of operating systems, it can and does trash non-DOS operating systems such as UNIX.

A number of suggestions were made in early 1992 as to how to deal with Michelangelo without using anti-virus software. Since so many antiviral programs—commercial, shareware, and freeware—identified the virus, it seems odd that people were so desperate to avoid this obvious step of using a scanning program to find the virus. Robert Slade observes:

> The "computer expert" in one of our local papers wrote an article on Michelangelo for his weekly column. It was packed with errors, and he was roundly chastised by many people. A large contingent of his detractors were local BBS sysops who urged him simply to get one of the shareware scanners and make certain. His response, the next week, was to publish a column stating that no self-respecting business would be caught dead with a modem.

Other people recommended backing up data, which is *always* a good idea. And, given that Michelangelo is a boot-sector infector, the virus will not be stored on a tape backup. However, diskettes are a natural target for BSIs. Nowadays, diskettes are much less favoured for major backup purposes; zipdisks, tapes, and other high-capacity writeable media are cheap and highly available. At that time, however, many popular backup programs used proprietary non-DOS disk formats for reasons of speed and additional storage. These, if infected by Michelangelo, would become unusable.

Changing the computer clock was also a popular suggestion. Since Michelangelo was set to go off on 6th March, theoretically users could just set the computer clock to make sure that it never reached 6th March. However, many people did not understand the difference between the MS-DOS clock and the system clock read by Interrupt 1Ah. The MS-DOS DATE command did not always alter the system clock. Network-connected machines often have "time server" functions so that the date is reset to conform to the network. The year 1992 was a leap year, and many clocks did not deal with it properly. Thus, for many computers, 6th March came on Thursday, not Friday.

NOTE

An even sillier suggestion was to test for Michelangelo by setting the date to 6th March and then rebooting the computer. This strategy became known as "Michelangelo roulette". One vendor actually reported an incident where a customer switched on a machine on the fatal morning, and when the machine promptly died, switched on the other machines in the office to see if the same thing happened. It did.

Many people suggested a modem avoidance strategy. Such a strategy is, of course, no defence worth mentioning against any pure boot-sector virus. Neither the master/ partition boot record nor the boot sector is an identifiable, transferable file, and neither can be transmitted as a file over a modem or Ethernet connection, although an infected disk can be transferred over a network connection as a binary image. While dropper programs are theoretically possible, they are rarely used as a means of disseminating a virus through unsuspecting users. The danger of getting a Michelangelo infection from a BBS was therefore so small that, for all practical purposes, it did not exist. Warnings against the use of bulletin boards or, more recently, web sites merely proscribe a major source of advice and utility software.

Unlike the Columbus Day/Datacrime hypefest of 1989, the epidemic of Michelangelo in the spring of 1992 had its basis in fact. Vendors were making unsubstantiated claims for the numbers of infections, which, in retrospect, turned out to have been surprisingly accurate. More importantly, the research community as a whole was seeing large numbers of infections. The public was seeing them as well. No fewer than 15 companies shipped commercial products that turned out to be infected with the Michelangelo virus.

Instant experts arose to fill the need for press releases, confusing Michelangelo with every other virus that had ever put a message on a screen. (One such "consultant" called a researcher of our acquaintance for a "professional courtesy consultation"— to ask what a "boot sector" was.)

Two producers of commercial antiviral programs released crippled freeware versions of their scanners. The programs *did* briefly mention that they checked only for Michelangelo, but certainly gave users the impression that they were checking the whole system. Happily, the trend over recent years has been for vendors to produce small, single-shot freebie programs, rather than crippled versions of free packages, for dealing urgently with high-profile viruses. Even this approach has its drawbacks: we recently came upon an instance where a Hybris infection was almost overlooked because the freebie program used could detect only a single variant. Oddly, it was a later variant than the one actually found on the machine in question: it seems that the vendor assumed that anyone using it would already have updates of its product for the previous versions. Since the vendor in question was also responsible for one of the freebie Michelangelo scanners, perhaps the average vendor's level of ethical responsibility has not been raised as far as we would have hoped.

Because of the media attention, a number of checks were made that would not have been done otherwise. Hundreds, even thousands, of copies of Michelangelo were found within single institutions. Because many copies had been found and removed, the number of "hits" on 6th March was not spectacular. Hundreds, perhaps thousands, of machines were struck, but the damage was not nearly as great as it might have been. Predictably, perhaps, media reports on 6th March started to dismiss the Michelangelo scare as another overhyped rumour, completely missing the reality of what had transpired.

In spite of its self-destruction on the trigger date, Michelangelo infections continued to be discovered after March 1991, and even after the widely publicized trigger date of 6th March, 1992. We no longer receive yearly media enquiries around the trigger date (nowadays people ask us about CIH's trigger date in April), but the virus continues to be found in the field, and is still featured on the WildList.

Don't Monkey with the MBR

Another Stoned variant, unrelated to Michelangelo, is Monkey (often classified as Empire.Monkey). It was even more widespread than most realized because Central Point Anti-Virus (and Microsoft Anti-virus, essentially the same program) misidentified it as Stoned 3. Monkey added a further twist: the common "generic" forms of boot-sector/MBR eradication did not work well against it. The classic method for cleaning the Master Boot Record is to use the DOS utility FDISK with the /MBR switch. However, using this method to clean Monkey will actually result in loss of data, though the data loss is not irrevocable as long as no further inappropriate action is taken.

If your computer is infected with Monkey and you boot from a clean system floppy disk, you will find that you cannot access the hard drive. In addition to repositioning the MBR, Monkey also encrypts it. The encryption is not a serious problem, as it uses a simple XOR function with the 2Eh byte. However, the encryption does ensure that you do not have valid partition-table data anywhere on your hard disk, and that you will have to go through an extra step to get rid of the virus. Many single-virus detectors and disinfectors have been developed, and few are considered to be important. In the case of Monkey, though, Tim Martin's KILLMONK has performed sterling service.

Monkey is still reported as being In the Wild, even though all competent known-virus scanners have detected it for many years. It is one of the primary reasons that virus experts discourage the use of FDISK /MBR. Indeed, for years, some of us have referred in public to the command as FDISK /MUMBLE, to make it a little harder for the unwary to fall prey. Since we've let the genie out of the bottle in this chapter, we feel obliged to go into a little more detail about why you should, in Bruce Burrell's words, "Just say no to FDISK /MUMBLE". The following points are loosely based on material contributed by Bruce (anti-virus guru in residence at the University of Michigan), Graham Cluley (who has many years of AV experience at Dr. Solomon's and Sophos), and David Harley (whoever he may be) for the alt.comp.virus FAQ:

Use of FDISK /MUMBLE is contraindicated under the following circumstances:

▶ If you have reason to believe that the victim PC may be infected by a virus (such as Monkey) that doesn't preserve the partition table.

▶ If the PC may be infected by a virus (such as One_Half) that encrypts (parts of) the hard drive and keeps the decryption key in the Master Boot Record. One_Half gradually encrypts the infected hard drive, starting from the last sector and working back towards the beginning, and the MBR stores the information about how much of the disk has been encrypted. If the MBR is replaced, that information is irrevocably lost, and part of the disk will remain encrypted.

▶ When security software that encrypts (parts of) the hard drive is in use.

▶ If your system is an older one that uses software such as Disk Manager, EZDrive, or DriveRocket to overcome the restrictions in older operating systems as to how large a hard drive can be used and how large a partition can be.

▶ When the system uses a controller card that stores data in the sector occupied by the bootstrap program and partition table.

▶ If you have reason to believe that more than one boot-sector infector is active (a condition sometimes known as a *cocktail*). This condition is particularly a problem when both viruses move the original MBR to the same location, so that the second infection overwrites the original MBR with the first infection.

▶ If you have reason to believe that a data diddler such as Ripper is active. In anti-virus circles, a data diddler is a virus that gradually corrupts the contents of the hard disk. If this corruption consists of random disk writes, a conventional scanner will not be able to repair the damage; however, it can take some steps to compensate for the possibility of specific problems.

▶ If you're unsure of your ground. "When in doubt, don't".

Most people will have "reason to believe" only if they have already identified the presence of a specific virus, which usually means that they have used a virus scanner. If you have a scanner, you don't usually need to use FDISK /MUMBLE. However, we recognize that, on occasion, the method might be useful to someone with a better-than-average grasp of the potential problems—preferably someone basking in a life-long lucky streak. You can reduce the risks considerably by taking the following steps:

1. Boot from a clean system floppy (this is mandatory). You must generate the floppy from a recent and appropriate version of DOS/Windows, and the floppy must contain guaranteed clean utilities.

2. Check that memory appears to be as you would expect (MEM or CHKDSK can be helpful here).

3. Check that partitioning is as it should be with FDISK or UNFORMAT, as appropriate.

4. Check that DOS can see your hard disks with DIR. If you can't see all the drives/partitions, you should abandon both hope and FDISK /MUMBLE.

5. Then start looking for a scanner that can name that virus.

Nonetheless, we would hate for you to think that we actually recommend the use of FDISK as an anti-virus utility. If you are in doubt, don't use FDISK. If you are not in doubt, worry about whether you should be.

Form

Form is a boot-sector virus with an innocuous payload. If the current date is the 18th of the month, the virus hooks Int 09h, so that every time a key is pressed, there is an audible beep. (This payload is dependent on the keyboard driver loaded.) Infected disks are marked as having 1KB in bad sectors, but the "bad" clusters actually contain the original boot sector and part of the virus's own code, which contains a string, "The FORM-Virus sends greetings to everyone who's reading this text. FORM doesn't destroy data! Don't panic! Fuckings go to Corinne". However, contrary to common reports, the message is never actually displayed.

The fact that Form infects the DOS Boot Record (DBR) rather than the Master Boot Record (MBR) on a hard disk has some interesting implications. One is that you cannot disinfect an infected disk simply by cleaning the MBR using FDISK (or an alternative tool), since the virus code is not contained in the MBR. Another is that while the virus's payload is innocuous, it can prevent a Windows NT system from booting up simply by infecting a bootable NTFS partition, thus corrupting the bootstrap loader program. This is generally true of viruses that infect the DBR rather than the MBR on hard disks (diskettes do not have an MBR). However, a DBR infector that uses stealth techniques (Form does not) may stay active long enough to allow the system to boot.

This discussion offers an opportunity to summarize the implications of using Windows NT or 2000 rather than Windows 95, 98, or ME, in the context of boot-sector viruses:

▶ "Pure" boot-sector viruses are hardware-specific rather than operating system–specific. They can infect NT, NetWare, and UNIX machines just as easily as they can a Windows desktop machine, if the machine is started or restarted (intentionally or otherwise) with an infected floppy (bootable or otherwise) in drive A (assuming CMOS defaults).

▶ Dropper programs and multipartite viruses that use BIOS and DOS services to install into the Master Boot Record cannot do so in an NT/Windows 2000 environment. However, NT machines that multiboot into DOS or a non-NT version of Windows can be infected while the less secure operating system is running.

▶   A boot-sector virus that succeeds in installing itself in the MBR can go memory-resident and execute boot-time code in much the same way as it does on other versions of Windows. However, once NT has loaded, direct disk services provided by the BIOS are no longer available, since NT uses protected mode drivers. This lack of available disk services blocks secondary infection of diskettes.

▶   Boot-sector viruses that don't preserve the original boot record can prevent the system from booting.

▶   Boot-sector viruses that infect the DBR rather than the MBR will probably stop a machine booting from an NTFS partition unless they use stealth.

The Modem Virus Hoax

The Modem virus was first reported in *VIRUS-L 1*, No. 42 (December 1988), and came from JPL (the Jet Propulsion Laboratory, a NASA research institute). Although the reporting of this virus doesn't constitute the very first virus hoax, it is worth close examination, since many subsequent hoaxes have borrowed circumstantial detail from it. The original report, which was supposed to have come from a telecommunications firm in Seattle, claimed that the virus was transmitted via the "subcarrier" on 2,400bps modems, so you should use only 300 or 1,200bps.

NOTE

Some versions of the later PKZip Trojan semihoax claimed that the virus affected transmissions "at 14,400 or greater". Hoaxes are, it seems, a renewable resource.

The subcarrier was alleged to be some secret frequency that the modem manufacturers used for debugging. The frequency turned out to be so secret that no modem manufacturer had ever heard of it; of course, all the bandwidth available is used for modem transmissions, and unused pins in a serial (RS-232) cable are still assigned, and are therefore not available for covert transmissions. The reports claimed that the virus modified the internal registers of the modem (but registers are data, not programs). They did not explain how the virus commuted between the modem and the PC. The initial source of the hoax seems to have been a posting on Fidonet (apparently on 6th October, 1988) by someone who gave his name as Mike

RoChenle. Ken van Wyk later suggested this pseudonym might be read as "microchannel", the then-new bus for IBM's PS/2 machines.

The virus was frequently reported for most of 1989. Why, apart from the average computer user's ignorance of the technology and tendency to accept incomprehensible pseudojargon without question, did the rumour persist for such a long time? The rumour itself may have prompted a lot of interest in computer viral programs among computer and modem users. Even though these people joined virus discussion groups and saw that these groups were not discussing the modem virus, they continued to post reports of it. One of the most likely reasons, however, is that people were primed to believe the rumour. Bulletin boards and, by extension, modems have had consistently (and unfairly) bad press over the years. BBSs were seen, despite all the evidence to the contrary, as the ultimate source of all "evil" programs—viruses and Trojans—and people seemed to accept without question anything bad said about them.

The Iraqi Printer Virus

In early 1992, reports surfaced of a virus that shut down Iraq's air defence system during Operation Desert Shield/Storm. This story seems to have started with *Triumph without Victory: The Unreported History of the Persian Gulf War* by *U.S .News and World Report* staff, and the serialization of the book in the periodical. The articles were rerun in many papers and recycled by CNN, ABC, and other networks. The story claimed that a French printer had been smuggled into Iraq through Jordan. Allegedly, US agents intercepted the printer and replaced a microchip in the printer with one reprogrammed by the NSA. The reprogrammed chip is supposed to have carried a virus that invaded the air defence network to which the printer was connected and then erased information on display screens when "windows" were opened for additional information on aircraft.

Could a chip in a printer send a virus? Doesn't a printer just *accept* data?

Both parallel/Centronics and serial RS-232 ports are bidirectional. Serial ports are probably used more often for bidirectional exchanges of byte streams between networked computers than for printer control. Centronics ports, though primarily used to link PCs to printers, are also used for exchanging information between PCs. Installation and execution of popular programs such as LapLink can literally be initiated from a controlling PC, using appropriate cabling—either a null modem cable or a suitable Centronics-to-Centronics cable.

NOTE

Cabling is not always bidirectional. Robert Slade recalls that in the early days of PCs, he had to deal with serial ports that had been used as printer ports and could no longer be used as modem ports because the "return" pin had been sheared off, a common practice used then to "fix" balky printers.

Even where a Centronics cable is used for printer control, the information flow has to be two-way. Otherwise, the printer driver on the PC is unable to determine whether printing is taking place successfully and thus will usually display an error message.

A group of ROM BIOS functions is concerned with printer traffic. Int 17h function 02h is specifically intended to ascertain the status of the printer, and the function returns a bit in the AH register accordingly. Other functions initialize the port or send a character to it, but return the same values, so that the program calling the function knows whether the operation was successful. Table 12-1 lists the status values.

However, the information that comes back over the line is concerned strictly with whether or not the printer is ready to accept more data. The host never accepts this information as a program.

The case of network printers is somewhat more complex. There are two possible cases—network print servers and network printers (such as the Mac LaserWriters)—and they are quite distinct. The print server may be a networked computer or a small, dedicated computer appliance, accepting files from other network sources and spooling them to a printer. This computer/printer combo is unable to submit programs to other hosts on the 'Net. The program on the client workstation is controlled by the server only in the sense that the program acts on information supplied from the server. The Mac case is substantially different, since the Mac laser printers are attached as peers

Value	Meaning
7	Printer not busy
6	Printer acknowledge
5	Out of paper
4	Printer selected
3	I/O (input/output) error
2	Unused
1	Unused
0	Printer timed-out

Table 12-1   *Printer Status Report Bits*

and have the ability to submit programs to other computers on the network. One Mac virus was at one time reported to use the LaserWriter as a vector. However, it is unlikely that the Iraqi air defence system was Mac-based, and few other systems see printers as peers.

> ### NOTE
>
> *Windows NT terminology is instructive here. NT administrators distinguish between the print server (a computer administering requests to print), the printer (a software interface between the application and the print device), and the print device (the actual printer hardware). Printer hardware that includes print server functionality (either built-in or as an add-on card) is widely used in corporations nowadays, but the server is still under the control of the client PC and the user or administrator using it. The client machine receives information from the server, rather than instructions.*

If it *were* possible to send some kind of program from the printer to the computer system/network, could it have been a virus?

Given the scenario of a new printer coming into an existing system, any damaging program would probably have to be a virus. A Trojan horse could have the same payload and would be far easier to implement, but would be reliant upon the printer being attached to the network. In general, the first thing an engineer does when the system malfunctions after a new piece of equipment has been added is to take out the new part. Unless the chip could send out a program that could have survived by itself in the network or system, or install itself elsewhere in the system, removing the printer would also remove the problem. Furthermore, the program, irrespective of how it entered the system, would need to be capable of self-installing and running on that system (well, duh...), so the programmer would have to have very specific knowledge of the target system. The program would need to know exactly what the air defence software was and how it was set up in order to display the information. It would also have to be sophisticated enough to masquerade as a bug in the software, and persistent enough to avoid elimination by the reloading of software that would immediately take place in such a situation.

There is, however, telling (if circumstantial) evidence that the Desert Storm virus never existed. *Infoworld* (April 1991) carried an article reporting a computer virus that the US authorities had used to shut down Iraqi computer systems. The *Infoworld* article was an obvious April Fool's joke (supported by the name of the virus: AF/91). The article ended with the warning that the virus was out of control and was now spreading through systems in the Western world. This hoax seems to have been intended to satirize the rise of the then-new (and startlingly popular) Windows 3 operating environment.

The *Triumph without Victory* story was confirmed by sources in the Pentagon. A book by James Adams called *The Next World War* (Random House, 1998) relates in some detail how unspecified virus-bearing hardware had been inserted into supplies intended for Saddam Hussein's command and control network, but that American bombs had destroyed the building before the virus could actually begin its work. We know that US agencies have researched the use of malware in electronic warfare (who hasn't?). Yet the similarities to the *Infoworld* AF/91 prank article are simply too great to ignore. Is this a case of official "sources" taking their own information from gossip that had mutated from reports of the joke, or did the joke have its basis in a real incident?

An earlier article in a French military aerospace magazine could have prompted the *Infoworld* joke. This article stated that a virus had been developed that would prevent Exocet missiles, which the French had sold to Iraq, from hitting French ships in the area. The author used a mix of technobabble and unrelated facts, somehow inferring from the downloading of weather data at the last minute before launch, the programmability of target information on certain types of missiles, and the radio destruct sequences used in testing, that such a "virus" was possible.

It *is* true that, at the time, the US military was calling for proposals regarding the use of computer viral programs as computer weapons. The military subsequently issued three contracts giving $50,000 to develop further proposals. At least one of those contracts subsequently entered the second phase, which allowed a half-million dollars for further refinement. It should be noted that the proposals were to have covered defence against viral programs as well. We have received information from normally reliable sources, far closer to the US government than any of the authors are ever likely to be, suggesting that the story was closer to the mark than we would have expected.

We remain sceptical: after all, a sophisticated grasp of computer security in general and malware in particular has not generally been characteristic of government agencies anywhere. Nevertheless, we are unable to back up our prejudices with irrefutable evidence. What, then, do we learn from this case study, and why have we paid it so much attention in this section? Obviously, we find it intrinsically interesting, and its lack of a complete resolution adds to its piquancy, perhaps because computer science teaches us to expect binary precision in our dealings with technology. Most of all, though, it reminds us that the virus phenomenon is more psychological than technological, and that the walls between fact and fiction are at least as thin in the security arena as they are in society at large. We will return to this theme in Chapter 16, when we discuss hoaxes and urban legends in exquisite detail.

Summary

We have now considered a number of virus-related events, from the earliest PC viruses and first-generation worms, through the early 1990s. The next chapter continues this series of case studies with a closer look at the Good Times hoax (the model for most of the hoaxes that followed), the rise of the macro virus, and the first intimations of the mailstorms that accompanied us across the divide between millennia.

CHAPTER 13

Case Studies: The Second Wave

Nearly all classic computer virus books were written during the period covered by the preceding chapter and don't address the topics we will cover here. The obvious exception is *Robert Slade's Guide to Computer Viruses* (second edition, copyright 1996, Springer-Verlag, New York, Inc.), of which included a little material on the (then) brand new Word macro virus threat. More recent virus books have addressed what we think of as "second wave" viruses—mostly macro viruses, 32-bit Windows infectors, and the earliest email-aware viruses—but not, we feel, particularly successfully or accurately, in general.

Of course, the previous generation of viruses did not all vanish as the second-wave viruses that we discuss in this chapter began to appear. Some imposed their own expiry date by self-destructing after the execution of a hard-coded, date-related trigger. Others assumed technologies such as low-capacity 5.25-inch media, floppy-only systems, obsolete processors like the Intel 8088 and other pre-80386 chips, and obsolete operating environments such as MS-DOS and Windows 3.*xx*. These were shed as hardware and operating systems progressed. No doubt some of these viruses still linger on forgotten floppies somewhere, but are otherwise seen only in collections, and it has been suggested that some of these museum pieces (Old- Fashioned File Viruses) should be withdrawn from standard virus test suites. This is not a debate we choose to enter here, however.

Still, a glance at any recent WildList indicates that some oldies but goodies continue to maintain a foothold in the virus charts. Boot-sector infectors such as Form or Jumper do not make number one with a bullet any more, but their continuing presence in the WildList is a constant reminder that someone, somewhere, still sees no reason to use anti-virus software.

Nevertheless, the case studies in this chapter bring us much closer to the present day. We will focus less on particular examples (with the exceptions of Good Times and WM/Concept) and more on classes and trends. For instance, a number of the macro viruses cited in this chapter are worth mentioning because they add a piece or two to the macro composite profile, but don't require the same in-depth analysis as many of the others that we have discussed.

By 1995 or thereabouts, a number of paradigm shifts had altered the viral landscape:

▶ Windows 95 was widening the range of virus vulnerabilities. Windows 98 and ME, along with ancillary applications such as Internet Explorer and the various flavours of Outlook, continue this trend into the present day. Windows 95 also demanded serious work on the part of anti-virus vendors to port their on-access scanners to a radically different environment.

▶ Good Times became (arguably) the most successful hoax virus to date.

▶ Interpreted viruses brought do-it-yourself (D-I-Y) virus creation to a level at which the comparatively inexperienced programmer could join the game. Writing a macro virus required more programming skill than generating a kit virus, but the result was much more satisfying to the virus author and was harder to catch generically. Kit viruses usually have a family resemblance that makes detecting new ones surprisingly simple. However, sometimes the only resemblance between a macro virus and its derivatives is that both are macros, making automated detection conceptually more difficult.

▶ Viruses had become enough a part of everyday computing that only the occasional instant expert, black hat, or conspiracy theorist continued to assert that viruses were the invention of anti-virus vendors' marketing departments. The Web was well on the way to making electronic communications accessible to people who would have had a panic attack at the thought of learning to use Archie or command-line ftp.

▶ More people had access to email at work or at school and, increasingly often, at home. At the same time, the shift from boot-sector viruses to data-borne (macro) viruses increased the susceptibility of email users to mail-borne viruses, real and imagined.

▶ These and other factors were increasing the rate at which viruses could spread, so that the vendors' quarterly update cycle was starting to lose ground to the monthly update cycle, pointing to the weekly, daily, and even hourly updates boasted by some today.

The Black Baron

In terms of its technology and strict chronology, the Black Baron's SMEG (Simulated Metamorphic Encryption enGine) and the Pathogen and Queeg viruses derived from it could be said to belong to the previous generation. However, the legal and social consequences, which are arguably of more interest than the actual malware, continued to reverberate into 1996. SMEG.Pathogen and SMEG.Queeg were highly polymorphic DOS file infectors, using variable encryption. The viruses infected .COM and .EXE files when they were executed or opened. Both viruses incremented an internal counter when a file was infected, and triggered when the counter reached 32. Depending on the time and day, either virus would display a message and overwrite the first 256 cylinders of the hard disk, effectively trashing the system.

In May 1995, the Black Baron was charged (under his real name, Christopher Pile) with 11 offences under the UK's Computer Misuse Act 1990. These included five charges of unauthorized access, five of unauthorized modification, and one of incitement. In an article in *Virus Bulletin* ("*Regina v Christoper Pile:* The Inside Story," February 1996), Jim Bates describes how police searched Pile's home in Plymouth and found only a Sinclair Spectrum computer. This is not an IBM-compatible computer, and appeared to have been used for games-related programming. However, a search of other premises uncovered a Tandon PC, a modem, and a number of diskettes. Though the contents of the disk had been defragmented and wiped, Bates found two documents that proved to be job applications in Pile's name, clearly linking him to the PC. Eventually, Pile admitted his connection, and later supplied the password to an encrypted file on one of the diskettes containing virus source code and documentation.

Bates disassembled and analysed a number of specimens supplied to the police by complainants, and confirmed that they were instances of Pile's virus. Nine of the charges related to infection from a file shown to have been uploaded by Pile to a bulletin board, from whence the victim downloaded the virus. The tenth charge related to Pathogen infection sustained by software publishers, Microprose Limited. This charge was particularly interesting, in that the infection did not appear to derive directly from any BBS used by Pile. As Bates commented, "This shows that, if someone writes a virus and someone else becomes infected by [the virus], it is not essential that the link between the writer and the victim should be proven: presence and identification of the virus is enough".

The 11th charge (incitement) related to the distribution of the SMEG engine and its documentation. According to other reports, the file SMEG03.ZIP contained instructions on writing viruses with SMEG "as easily as possible". Pile also expressed the hope that SMEG users would "have fun with SMEG" and pass the software on to their friends. While Pile seems to have suggested that the code had positive uses, the judge disagreed. Pile was sentenced to six months, imprisonment for each of the charges of unauthorized access and modification, to run concurrently; however, on the incitement charge he was sentenced to 12 months' imprisonment to run consecutively.

Good Times Just Around the Corner

Good Times is probably the most famous of all false alerts, and was certainly the earliest that received wide distribution. Some controversy persists over the identity of the originators of the message, but it is possible that it was a sincere, if misguided, attempt to warn others. The hoax probably started in early December 1994. In 1995, the variant of the hoax including mention of the FFC began circulating.

It seems most likely that the Good Times alert was started by a group or an individual who had seen a computer failure without understanding the cause, and associated it with an email message that had "Good Times" in the subject line. (In fact, there are indications that the message started out on the AOL system, and it is known that there are bugs in AOL's mail software that can cause the program to hang.) The announcement states that there was a message, identified by the title of "Good Times", which, when read, would crash your computer. The message was said to be a virus, even though there is nothing viral about that sort of activity (even if it *were* possible).

Text Appeal

At the time of the original Good Times message, email was almost universally text-based. Elsewhere, we discuss the possibility of ANSI bombs and other text-based malicious software. Suffice it to say here that the possibility of a straightforward text message carrying a virus in an infective form is remote. The fact that the warning contained almost no details at all should have been an indication that the message wasn't quite right. It provided no information on how to detect, avoid, or get rid of the "virus", except for its warning not to read messages with "Good Times" in the subject line. (The irony of the fact that many of the warnings contained these words seems to have escaped most people.)

Blowing in the Wind

Pathetically (and, sadly, characteristically), a member of the VX community actually did produce a Good Times virus. Like the virus named after the older Proto-T hoax, the "real" Good Times was an uninteresting specimen, having nothing in common with the original alert. It is generally known as GT-Spoof by the anti-virus community, and was hardly ever found in the field. The source code, credited to virus author Qark, also known as Rhincewind, appeared in issue 4 of *VLAD (Virus Labs And Dist)*, an underground e-zine. The code included the comment, "Remember to email all your friends, warning them about Good Times!" but displayed no similarity to the virus described in the hoax alerts.

Loop de Loop

The Good Times virus and its primary variants were predominant in 1994–95, though close variants continue to appear. However, an extract from a report by the Y2K Risk Assessment Task Force, chaired by Sam Nunn, illustrates that the mythical "nth complexity binary loop", characteristic of a common version of the Good Times hoax, is not dead, although it has mutated somewhat.

Three other malicious viruses will actually lock a processor in a divide-by-zero loop, which, if left running for a sufficient amount of time, will overheat the Central Processing Unit, causing it to melt down and effectively reducing the computer to scrap metal.

Big Bang

Les Jones' FAQ describes the wide impact that Good Times had across the globe. (The following extract omits some minor personal data, mostly email addresses.)

The virus hoax infects mailing lists, bulletin boards, and USENET newsgroups. Worried system administrators needlessly worry their employees by posting dire warnings. The hoax is not limited to the United States. It has appeared in several English-speaking and non-English-speaking countries. One reader sent me an English transcription of a radio broadcast in Malta.

Adam J Kightley [...] said, "The cases of 'infection' I came across all tended to result from the message getting into the hands of senior non-computing personnel. Those with the ability and authority to spread it widely, without the knowledge to spot its nonsensical content."

Some of the companies that have reportedly fallen for the hoax include AT&T, CitiBank, NBC, Hughes Aircraft, Microsoft, Texas Instruments, and dozens or hundreds of others. There have been outbreaks at numerous colleges.

The U.S. government has not been immune. Some of the government agencies that have reportedly fallen victim to the hoax include the Department of Defense, the FCC, NASA, the USDA, U.S. Census Bureau, and various national labs. I've confirmed outbreaks at the Department of Health and Human Services, though they had the good sense to question the hoax, and ask for more information on Usenet, before passing the hoax along to their employees.

The virus hoax has occasionally escaped into the popular media. [A correspondent] reports that on April 4, 1995, during the Tom Sullivan show on KFBK 1530 AM radio in Sacramento, California, a police officer warned listeners not to read email labelled "Good Times", and to report the sender to the police. Other radio stations, including Australia's ABC radio, have also spread the hoax.

The Good Times FAQ also gives an interesting example of how a real virus, a hoax, and a misapprehension can converge and spread confusion further:

> There has been one confirmation of a person who received a message with "xxx-1" in the header, but an empty message body. Then (in a panic, because he had heard the alert), he checked his PC for viruses (the first time he checked his machine in months) and found a pre-existing virus on his machine. He incorrectly came to the conclusion that the E-mail message gave him the virus (this particular virus could NOT POSSIBLY have spread via an E-mail message). This person then spread his alert.

While the Good Times FAQ has not been updated for several years, it remains an excellent source of information, not only on the hoax itself, but on the hoax phenomenon, and it has had as profound an influence on later writers and researchers as the hoax itself did on the content of later hoaxes. (We are pleased to acknowledge Les Jones's kindness in allowing us to quote the FAQ at some length here. You can read the full document at http://www.public.usit.net/lesjones/goodtimes.html.)

Proof of Concept

WM/Concept was by no means the first macro virus. HyperCard viruses were already commonplace in the Macintosh arena when WM/Concept appeared, and a number of anti-virus researchers had explored WordBasic and other malware-friendly macro environments (notably Lotus 1-2-3) long before the virus appeared in 1995.

NOTE

The term malware-friendly may require some expansion here. Much has been made of the fact that at least one proof-of-concept virus was created (and very strictly controlled) long before the first Microsoft Office virus was written. However, 1-2-3 viruses were never much of a threat, even when the package was at the height of its popularity. This was not just because only the "good guys" had thought of the possibility or had thought it worth trying, but also because of the comparative simplicity of the macro language and the fact that file access had to be via the menu system, rendering a stealth infector almost impossible.

However, WM/Concept was the first macro virus to be publicly described as such, and certainly the most successful in terms of spreading. For a while, it was easily the most widely found virus in the world. Oddly enough, though, some quarters greeted its appearance with disbelief. After all, a Word file is usually considered to be data rather than a program file. However, there is no absolute distinction between program and data.

Those of us concerned with the control of damage from viruses and other programmed threats have held to a number of working assumptions, while aware of theoretical possibilities that these assumptions may not be correct in every case. One of these is that viruses can spread only by attaching themselves to executable code, and cannot, therefore, be spread by data files. While the first part of this proposition holds true, the second doesn't, unless we reexamine our definition of what constitutes a data file.

Programs Versus Data

We cling to the belief that because executable files run programs, and data files contain data, there is a clear-cut distinction between the two types of file. In fact, this has never been true. An executable file may contain a great deal of data: it may, for instance, contain a whole database, as well as the instruction set for accessing, entering, and deleting records. An extreme example might be a program that consists of a series of instructions to write text to the screen, such as the following pseudo-code:

```
begin
      string1="Hello World"
      string2="Goodbye, Cruel World"
      write string1
      write string2
end
```

In this case, the two text strings that comprise the data are an intrinsic part of the program.

What may be perceived as a data file may be, in reality, a program. A PostScript file is, in fact, a program read and acted upon by a PostScript interpreter program. A printer normally executes this program, but a program such as GhostScript can also interpret a PostScript file and print it to the screen on the host computer. While the syntax may be very different, the basic concept of a PostScript program is pretty much the same as in the preceding pseudo-code.

After summer 1995, a number of viruses appeared that spread through data files, specifically data files produced by applications using complex macro languages. Data files written by or for such applications may include macros, which are no more or less than small (and sometimes not-so-small) programs interpreted by the application for which they were produced.

The first in-the-wild examples specifically targeted Microsoft Word version 6, but code for viruses infecting Excel and Ami Pro also appeared very quickly. All versions of Word for Windows and Word 6, and later for the Macintosh, include a sophisticated macro language (WordBasic in older versions, and Visual Basic for Applications, or VBA). The simplest form of macro language is based on the ability to store and replay a sequence of keystrokes. Such applications are capable of all the functions normally associated with a high-level programming language such as BASIC. In fact, macro languages used by Windows applications are often versions of BASIC based on Microsoft's Visual Basic, and are capable of much of the functionality (if not the efficiency) of a full-scale programming environment such as Visual C++. More recently, other applications in the Office suite have included VBA, and non-Microsoft applications sometimes also include the macro language, under licence.

The Name of the Game

Since Concept was the first (officially) of its kind, the usual problem of what to call a newly discovered virus was intensified. Microsoft, anxious to avoid the "V" word, referred to it as Prank Macro. Some of the names you may still encounter include WW6Macro and WinWord.Concept. In Mac circles, it was known for a while as Word Macro 9508.

Concept spread far and (for its time) fast. It got something of a boost when two companies accidentally shipped it in infected documents on CD-ROM. The first instance was a Microsoft CD called *MicroSoft Windows '95 Software Compatibility Test.* The CD was shipped to a number of large original equipment manufacturing (OEM) companies in the summer of 1995, as a means of checking compatibility with Windows 95, which was due for imminent release. However, the CD contained a document called OEMLTR.DOC, which was infected with Concept. It is possible, but unproven, that a staff member at Microsoft wrote the virus. A few months later, Microsoft UK distributed the virus on another CD, *The Microsoft Office 95 and Windows 95 Business Guide*, in a document called HELPDESK.DOC. (It wasn't exactly Microsoft's year: only a little earlier, the corporation had distributed Form-infected demo floppies.)

Meanwhile, another company called ServerWare distributed 5,500 copies of a CD called *Snap-On Tools for Windows NT*, which contained a number of infected documents. To its credit, ServerWare immediately withdrew the CD, warned recipients, and sent out a clean copy. This is in some contrast to Microsoft's reaction: it was autumn before Microsoft admitted to the first infected CD. They did, however, make available a macro-based fix for the virus, a somewhat tortuous piece of code that tended to fall over on a system with multiple infections. Eventually, Microsoft also beefed up its quality assurance considerably by employing a virus specialist to engineer a process for intensive checking of outgoing media. (Nowadays, Randy Abrams is a respected speaker in his own right at security conferences.)

Concept was fairly obvious, and could be forestalled and even fixed (with patience) without the aid of anti-virus software. When a Concept-infected file was opened, a message box appeared containing the number 1 and an OK button. Clearly, we are not talking extreme stealth here. You could also detect the virus's presence by checking the Tools | Macro submenu for the presence of macros. A WM/Concept.A infection, specifically, is characterized by the presence of the following macros:

- ▶ AAAZFS
- ▶ AAAZAO
- ▶ AutoOpen
- ▶ PayLoad
- ▶ FileSaveAs

Any document might legitimately use AutoOpen or FileSaveAs. However, macros with the names Payload, AAAZFS, and AAAZAO are something of a giveaway. The macros are not encrypted, and so it's easy to spot the virus. On the other hand, this lack of encryption also makes it easy to modify the code. Virus writers learned almost straight away to conceal the internals of their macros by implementing them as execute-only macros, which cannot be edited or easily viewed. With the onset of Word 97, Microsoft managed to turn this technique against virus writers, by disallowing the "upconversion" of execute-only Word 6/95 macros to Word 97 format. Thus, there are upconverted versions of Concept, but not of Cap. You can identify upconverted Concept variants by using a scanner that distinguishes between (for instance) WM/Concept.A and W97M/Concept.A.

When Is a Payload Not a Payload?

Even though Concept.A has a Payload macro, it has no actual payload. Famously, it contains the following string:

```
That's enough to prove my point
```

This string no doubt explains the name *Concept* (as in "proof of concept").

To the Next Level

We are not sure whether Microsoft's blocking of execute-only upconversion was intended as an anti-virus measure. Technically, this blocking derives from the fact that VBA applies protection to projects, not individual macros. Upconversion of viral macros is something of a problem in more respects than one, and there has long been discussion as to how far anti-virus companies should go in anticipating future upconverted viruses, especially if providing detection means creating a variant that does not currently exist. Some companies have taken the stance that they are entitled to give their customers maximum protection. However, the the fact that some products already protect against the upconversions is evidence that virus authors have been inspired to play with upconversions of specific Word 6.*xx* viruses. A problem also arises if the customer expects to be protected against upconverted viruses that may not exist. In this case, the customer may not know whether his or her vendor of choice offers detection. Conference papers by Vesselin Bontchev have examined many of these issues in some depth, for example, the *Virus Bulletin* conference paper at http://www.virusbtn.com/vb2000/Programme/papers/bontchev.pdf.

Concept.A was fairly harmless, as viruses go: it tampered with Word 6's global template (usually NORMAL.DOT, or Normal on a Macintosh) so that files were saved as templates and ran the infective AutoOpen macro. This gave Mac users an additional advantage, in that template files on the Mac have a different icon to document files. As long as the virus infected only template files, this icon was a frequently found heads-up to Mac users that they might have a virus problem. However, in later versions of Word, the distinction between documents and templates is less absolute, so this particular heuristic has become less viable.

In a sense, the main importance of Concept was that the code could be altered very quickly to incorporate a destructive payload, alternative infection techniques, and evasion of the first attempts at detecting it. This virus has been described as the first cross-platform virus in that it works on any platform. However, this description isn't altogether accurate: it infected only systems running Word 6 or Word 95, though versions are known that can infect Word 97 and later. Platforms capable of running Word 6 included the following:

▶ PCs running Windows 3.*x* and Windows 95

▶ PCs and DEC AXP workstations running Windows NT

▶ Macintoshes and Power Macs

Infection took place when infected files were read in Word 6, but not by the Word 6 document viewer, which can't run Word macros. Later versions of the Word viewer had some limited ability to run macros, but did not constitute an effective vector for viral macros. Even in Word, Concept could not infect if auto macros (AutoOpen, AutoClose, AutoNew, and AutoExit) were disabled. Indeed, it took the anti-virus companies some time to fully appreciate the extent of the macro virus problem, and one of the first suggestions was to run an AutoExec macro that would disable auto macros. This simple technique was defeated very early on in the game as a comprehensive protective measure, but we include a snippet of the sort of code that was published at the time, just for completeness.

From the Tools menu in Word 6, select Macro. If you don't already have an AutoExec macro, use the Create option to create an AutoExec macro similar to the following:

```
sub Main

MsgBox "Killing off Automacros", 48

DisableAutoMacros 1

end sub
```

A number of other measures were also suggested at the time that weren't altogether reliable, such as the following examples:

- ▶ Starting up Word with the /m switch, or starting up Word while holding down the SHIFT key. These methods bypass only AutoExec, not the other auto macros, and there are quite a few reports that they don't work.

- ▶ Making NORMAL.DOT read-only with ATTRIB.

- ▶ Enabling the "Prompt to save NORMAL.DOT" option available from the Tools menu. Word.Nuclear disables this option.

- ▶ Holding down the SHIFT key while opening a document. This technique allegedly disables auto macros, but there were many reports of its not working reliably, either.

Auto Macros

Many modern versions of these applications include autoloading macros that, by default, run when a file is opened or closed, without requiring the intervention of the person running the application and reading the file. The following examples are taken from Word, but many applications have similar facilities:

Macro Name	When It Runs
AutoExec	When Word starts
AutoNew	Each time a new document is created
AutoOpen	Each time an existing document is opened
AutoClose	Each time a document is closed
AutoExit	When the application closes

Auto macros can be defined either globally or for a particular template, except for the AutoExec macro, which will not run automatically unless it is stored in the Normal template or a global template stored in the directory specified as the Startup directory. Disabling auto macros worked fine for viruses like Concept and Nuclear, which relied on the presence of auto macros. Unfortunately, it wasn't long before virus writers learned alternative infection techniques. Also, remember that AutoExec macros continued to run when Word 6 or Word 7 was started up, even with auto macros disabled.

The Empire Strikes Back—Slowly

Anti-virus vendors faced a number of problems in adding macro virus detection and disinfection to their products. The Word document format was difficult to parse. Microsoft met with anti-virus researchers to discuss the problem early on, and offered documentation on the relevant file formats to researchers who signed a Non-Disclosure Agreement (NDA). However, this documentation turned out to be sparse and inaccurate, and some researchers found it easier to reverse engineer, with or without the help of the documentation. Unfortunately, this problem has recurred to some degree with any version of Office that uses a change of file format and one that, in theory, doesn't. Office 2001 (for Macintosh) was essentially file-compatible with earlier versions, but it turned out that recompiling the application had altered the way macros were stored just enough to stop some scanners from recognizing some macro viruses in documents that had been saved in 2001.

A more basic problem was that adding routine scanning of files with a .DOC or .DOT extension added significant overhead to on-demand scans. In fact, there is no absolute requirement for a vulnerable Word file to use these filename extensions, or any extension at all—on Macs, there is no requirement for *any* file to have a filename extension. This problem matters less for a memory-resident scanner that scans every file on access. However, at that time, some vendors had not yet successfully ported their Windows 3.*x* VxD scanners to Windows 95, and most DOS TSR scanners never did incorporate scanning for macro viruses (which were, after all, never operational during a DOS session).

These problems may have influenced the spate of anti-virus scanners that appeared over the next year or two, and that were themselves Word-hosted. In other words, the scanners were macro-based, though often they made use of Word's ability to incorporate functions in .WLL (Word Link Libraries) library files compiled in other languages. Some were at least in part virus-specific, and a few used a more generic macro-blocking approach.

Microsoft's Macro Virus Protection (SCAN831.DOC) was a Word 6 document that included an AutoOpen macro to scan for infection by Concept and innoculate NORMAL.DOT. The tool provided minimal protection, and was available on CompuServe, AOL, and MSN, as well as from http://www.microsoft.com/. In addition to detecting Concept.A (and adding detection for one or two of the other early contenders later), this tool installed some protective macros. A Mac version of SCAN.DOC was also available. The early releases of SCAN.DOC were notable for the fact that they contained a notorious typographical error:

```
Dlg.Pat$ = "*.doc; *.dot"
```

This line set up the .Name argument for FileFind. However, the superfluous space between the semicolon and the second asterisk effectively stopped the macro from looking for .DOT files.

WM/Nuclear

The Nuclear virus was also known as Winword.Nuclear, Wordmacro-Nuclear, and Wordmacro-Alert. It could be described as either multipartite or hybrid, since as well as infecting Word documents, it attempted to drop a DOS file infector. (It is also notable as the virus that nearly got David Harley into a great deal of trouble, as described in "How to 'Nuke' Your Job", just ahead.)

Nuclear is a two-stage missile. Stage one attempts to drop (install) a DOS/Windows file virus called Ph33r.

NOTE

Malware authors, vandals, crackers, and so on often favour a somewhat idiosyncratic approach to spelling involving the substitution of numerals for alphabetical characters, as well as eccentric capitalization. Clearly, the name of the virus is supposed to strike Ph33r (fear) in the hearts of those of us who are not 3l33t (elite).

The code is so buggy that the virus is never dropped. In stage two, Nuclear attempts to erase system files if it happens to be 5th April. This routine is also buggy, but *can* sometimes do minor damage.

How to "Nuke" Your Job

I was at a "seminar" (that is, a marketing session) at the headquarters of an anti-virus company in London. After one presentation, the subject of macro viruses came up during a table discussion. He recalls: It turned out I already had a sample of Nuclear, and the anti-virus company didn't. Since I actually had a copy on a diskette that I had with me at the time, I offered the company's representatives a copy of the infected file, and they ran it on a test PC in my presence. A few days later, a friend rang me and, knowing my interest in viruses, asked whether I had seen that morning's *Observer* (a UK Sunday newspaper). Imagine how pleased I was to read, among other hysterical claptrap, that the company to whom I had given that sample was credited with having "helped" an "unnamed medical charity" (at the time I worked for a cancer research organization). According to the *Observer*, a member of staff had "unknowingly" infected PCs in the workplace by running a file found on the Internet and had to be rescued from his or her own stupidity. Fortunately, my employers either didn't notice the article or didn't make the connection, and I was never asked to account for my alleged incompetence. (The infected file was identified as soon as it was downloaded, and was examined and executed only on one of my own test machines at home.) This was just as well, since I never did receive the promised written apology, and the newspaper never retracted nor corrected any of its errors. On the other hand, the company in question lost any chance of ever doing business with me, and I learned a great deal in the process about trust and business ethics.

The virus is characterized by the existence of the following macros:

- ▶ AutoExec
- ▶ AutoOpen
- ▶ FileSaveAs
- ▶ FilePrint
- ▶ FilePrintDefault
- ▶ InsertPayload
- ▶ Payload
- ▶ DropSuriv
- ▶ FileExit

Nuclear could be detected by running the Macros command under the Tools menu. If the macros InsertPayload, Payload, and DropSuriv were listed, then it was reasonably likely that the system was infected. As well as using execute-only macros, Nuclear camouflaged its presence by disabling the "Prompt for changes to NORMAL.DOT" option. Despite the name DropSuriv, the DOS virus concerned was not a member of the Jerusalem/sURIV family described in the previous chapter.

NOTE

At the time Nuclear was discovered, the Tools | Macro command was frequently recommended as a means of detecting macro viruses (both of them!). However, using this command can be misleading. Some viruses modify the command as a primitive stealth measure, so that no macro names are observed. Reportedly, Colors (described in the next section) actually executes its harmless but irritating payload if Tools | Macro is executed.

The InsertPayload macro could add the following text to the end of printouts when printing documents (but only if the system clock's seconds counter is reading between 55 and 59 seconds):

```
"And finally I would like to say:

STOP ALL FRENCH NUCLEAR TESTING IN THE PACIFIC!"
```

According to Richard Martin's Macro Virus FAQ, this macro could also affect faxes sent via a FAX Print Driver.

Reportedly, the macro Payload attempts to delete IO.SYS, MSDOS.SYS, and COMMAND.COM on 5th April. In general, this attempt fails, as WordBasic cannot reset the attributes of a file that has the system attribute set; however, the sample examined by David Harley did successfully delete COMMAND.COM.

The DropSuriv macro routine didn't appear to work on any system, due to a syntax error. Its author apparently intended the routine to use the standard DOS utility DEBUG to generate an executable from the dropped debug script.

Nuclear found its way into the field by a particularly unpleasant route. While anti-virus companies were working on assimilating macro virus detection into their scanners, a number of fixes consisting of Word documents running protective macros were made available, including WVFIX.DOC (from Command Software) and a document by Eugene Kaspersky, developer of the AVP anti-virus utility. Unfortunately, Kaspersky made some of the macros in this document execute-only, meaning that the macros could not be edited or inspected. This seems to have given some bright soul the idea of producing a document looking remarkably like Kaspersky's, but infected with a *different* virus.

Colors

Unfortunately, using the Tools | Macro option to see what macros were currently in memory turned out to be potentially misleading, since a virus can subvert this function. Indeed, one of the problems with having the macro programming language so tightly bound into an application infrastructure is that it makes it depressingly easy to subvert almost any function. Tools | Macro isn't a safe check for macro viruses. Colors, the next macro virus down the pike, not only intercepted the Tools | Macro call and hid the macros, thus adding a measure of stealth to the macro virus repertoire, but (reportedly) triggered if that call was made. It was, however, still possible to detect the presence of unexpected macros using the File | Templates | Organizer | Macros submenu.

Colors derived its name (and the occasionally found alias Rainbow) from its payload. The virus maintained a counter in the [windows] section of WIN.INI. When the counter reached 299, and then every 300th time thereafter, the virus changed Windows colour settings to random values. This payload failed on Macs, of course, except if they used some Windows emulation. However, like so many macro viruses, Colors replicated quite nicely.

The virus is thought to have originated in Portugal, and its perpetrators launched it by posting to USENET newsgroups in October 1995.

The following macro names may signify infection by the Colors virus:

- ▶ AutoClose
- ▶ AutoExec
- ▶ AutoOpen
- ▶ FileExit
- ▶ FileNew
- ▶ FileSave
- ▶ FileSaveAs
- ▶ ToolsMacro

These macros are all named after perfectly legitimate WordBasic functions, and therein lies the danger. If you open a document (or, strictly, a template—WordBasic macros spread by passing templates off as documents) to which these macros are attached, the infected file becomes the default template, so that closing the file, for instance, calls the infective FileSave routine rather than the internal routine. This scheme enables the virus to hide the presence of infective macros.

All macros included in Colors were execute-only. Legitimate macros with the same names were overwritten at infection. The AutoExec macro was actually empty, and may well have been intended to overwrite AutoExec macros such as the one listed earlier that disables auto macros. Auto macros were reenabled, and the prompt to save changes to the global template was disabled.

DMV

In the late 1980s, Professor Harold Highland wrote what may have been the first (PC, or DOS, as opposed to Windows) macro virus. At the 1995 Virus Bulletin Conference in Boston (Massachusetts, not Lincolnshire!), he described how he had used Lotus 1-2-3 to test the concept. He subsequently destroyed all copies of the virus. Then, as reported in December 1994, American security specialist Joel McNamara wrote two demonstration macro viruses (one for Excel, one for Word). Both viruses were called DMV (Document Macro Virus), and were also written as a test as well as forming the basis for a paper. However, after Concept appeared, McNamara chose to make some code available via the World Wide Web.

Reportedly, the Excel virus did not actually work. The code as published was, in any case, not a direct threat, since McNamara made no attempt to incorporate stealth.

The DMV viruses are mostly noteworthy because they were published supposedly as "educational aids". Publication raised the question as to whether the full disclosure of virus code (macro or otherwise) is more useful as an educational aid to virus writers, to anti-virus researchers, or to virus victims, a debate that rumbles on into the 21st century. It also served to remind anyone who hadn't been paying attention that Excel was also a vulnerable platform. Curiously, the later WM/Imposter was largely noted for the fact that it masqueraded as DMV: when it infected, a dialog box appeared containing the single word, "DMV".

Wiederoffnen and FormatC

Wiederoffnen is notable for two reasons. It was not a virus, but one of the first macro Trojans. Furthermore, the document was actually a Word for Windows version 2 document; however, it worked perfectly well under Word 6. Wiederoffnen worked by intercepting AutoClose and manipulating AUTOEXEC.BAT. As its name implies, this Trojan appears to have originated in Germany.

FormatC, which found its way into the field by way of a newsgroup posting, attempted to format drive C when the document was opened. The Trojan contained only one AutoOpen macro. The macro was execute-only, but could be seen in the macro list. When it triggered, the macro ran an unconditional format of drive C in a minimized DOS box.

On the whole, Word macro Trojans haven't had much impact in the general computer world. Some macro programming environments (notably Lotus 1-2-3) saw more Trojans than viruses, but these Trojans were rarely encountered in the field, and we mention them only for completeness.

Diddling: Green Stripe and Wazzu

Concept was not, of course, the only proof-of-concept virus. There were others that failed to capture the VX community's imagination (if the word isn't too inappropriate) in the same way. Green Stripe, named from its main macro procedure, was not an Office virus, but targeted Ami Pro. Like pre-VBA versions of WordPerfect, Ami Pro stores macros in a separate file, instead of embedding them in data files or template files. Since most people don't knowingly share macro files, Green Stripe was never likely to be a major contender, and is notable mainly because it indicates that no activity is too banal or pointless to escape a virus author's attention.

Green Stripe was first published in the final edition of Mark Ludwig's virus writing newsletter *Underground Technology Review*. Its presence was less than stealthy, since the infection process was quite slow, due to the number of files it attempted to infect. Removing the infected macros was simply a matter of deleting the macro files, which had the .SMM filename extension. In the unlikely event that the virus actually spread, Green Stripe reportedly changed all occurrences in a document of the word *its* to *it's*.

The logistic difficulties of tricking a potential victim into accepting the .SMM file along with the .SAM main document probably would have sufficed to ensure that Green Stripe's place in virus history stayed unique, but Ami Pro's spiral into comparative oblivion sealed the virus's fate. Much the same applies to such curiosities as Galadriel (which is CorelScript-specific), AutoCad and Visio viruses, and the handful of Access and Powerpoint infectors.

The primitive data diddling, however, may have appealed to the author of WM/Wazzu, an otherwise unexceptional virus that takes this principle one step further. Wazzu, which got an extra push into the wild when a victim, asking for help in identifying it, posted a copy to alt.comp.virus, changed the location of words within the infected document. Since the change was random, its effects could not be repaired automatically. The virus also inserted the word *wazzu* into random locations in the document.

WM/Atom

Atom appeared in February 1996 and did not spread significantly. It could infect only via auto macros, and did not stop the prompt to save changes to the global template. When active, Atom infected all files that were saved with FileSaveAs or opened with FileOpen.

Atom had two destructive payloads. On 13th December, it attempted to delete all files in the current directory. Also, if the system clock's seconds count was 13 at the time that a file was being saved, the virus would password-protect the file, using the password ATOM#1. There followed something of a fad among virus writers for password payloads, and one anti-virus vendor began offering a decryption utility to address the problem. This decryption was easy enough: the document encryption in older versions of Word is trivial. In fact, some anti-virus products routinely decrypt Word 6 documents on the fly to enable scanning. However, Word 97 and later versions use an algorithm that is more difficult to crack.

WM/Cap

The Cap virus, to some extent, supplanted Concept as the world's number one virus. It had no payload, but did cause some collateral damage because of the way in which it infected, deleting any macros that it could not identify as its own. Utilizing a primitive stealth mechanism, Cap used empty macros to remove ToolsMacro and associated menu items, so that active macro inclusions couldn't be checked. As stealth goes, this mechanism was less than effective. David Harley got used to checking menus on problem machines even where no suspected virus action had been reported, and was often able to identify a Cap infection over the telephone.

By default, Cap.A installed ten macros:

- ► AutoClose
- ► AutoExec
- ► AutoOpen
- ► FileClose
- ► CAP
- ► FileOpen
- ► FileSave
- ► FileSaveAs
- ► FileTemplates
- ► ToolsMacro

Of these, only the CAP macro contains substantial code; the others are empty or call subroutines within the CAP macro. The virus also installs local language versions of the equivalent macros, and flourishes under foreign versions by virtue of its sophisticated (if ponderous) handling of infection of the global template: it installs localized extra copies of FileClose, FileOpen, FileSave, and FileSaveAs. Subsequent infections under English versions retain the extra macros.

WM/Cap does not rely on auto macros as an infection mechanism. Macros such as FileOpen correspond to internal Word functions. In Word 6 and 7, such macros attached to an open document are executed in preference to the internal function, even when called through the menu system, so that infection is independent of auto macros. The writer of Cap did not invent this technique, but certainly made the most of its potential for spreading: the virus continues to feature strongly in virus report statistics.

> **NOTE**
>
> *Cap also had an impact on recommended procedures for dealing with file attachments and documents. Until the more recent discovery of additional functions and tags added by Microsoft, virus researchers had recommended the use of RTF (Rich Text Format) files instead of Word's standard DOC format. RTF is a text-only format, and cannot contain Word macros. However, the fact that Cap contained a FileSaveAs macro allowed it to intercept the function called when the user tried to "SaveAs" a different file type. All documents are saved in the Word DOC format, regardless of the format you choose. So, for example, if a user tries to save a document as an RTF file, the extension of the document will become .RTF, but internally the file is still a DOC and still contains the virus.*

Excel Viruses

XM/Laroux was the first bona fide Excel virus, appearing in 1996, and continues to be widely reported. It is actually a fairly simple virus (no one said that successful viruses have to be sophisticated), consisting of two macros. AutoOpen runs when an infected document is opened; it calls the check_files macro, then opens a file, containing the viral macros, in the XLSTART directory. Since this file is opened every time Excel is started (that's why it is put into XLSTART), it infects all subsequent workbooks. The original has no destructive payload, and doesn't infect on Macintoshes. A number of variants exist and are found in the wild, including upconverted Excel 97-specific variants.

XM/Sofa uses a slightly different infection mechanism, putting the BOOK.XLT file into the alternate startup directory. When an infected file is opened, the virus changes the caption at the top of the screen to "Microsofa Excel" instead of the normal "Microsoft Excel". XF/Paix, however, excited a surprising amount of short-term interest when it appeared early in 1998, considering that it didn't spread far outside France. Paix was mildly interesting in that it used an Excel 4.0 formula rather than a VBA macro—hence the use of the *XF* prefix rather than *XM*.

X97M.Papa.A was intended as a macro worm, although it is not viable because of a bug in the macro code. X97M.Papa.B, however, *is* a viable worm, mass-mailing itself to addresses in Outlook's address books. The mail arrives with the following subject line:

L 13-6   `Fwd: Workbook from all.net and Fred Cohen`

The body of the email text was intended to circumvent Excel's built-in macro virus protection (such as it is), and reads as follows:

```
Urgent info inside. Disregard macro warning.
```

The payload, which is triggered randomly, involves using the ping utility to repeatedly check two different IP addresses, thus creating the possibility of a mild denial of service (DoS) attack through its potential impact on the network.

On every 24th April at 14:00 (2 P.M.), X97M/Barisada.A prompts the infected user to answer a question or it threatens to clear the cells in the current spreadsheet. However, the payload does not work as intended.

There are far fewer Excel viruses than there are Word viruses, and fairly common viruses such as Barisada tend to inspire less interest than their Word equivalents, perhaps because fewer people routinely use spreadsheets.

Variations on a Theme

There is, essentially, only one intentionally programmed WM/Cap, although WM/CopyCap is very closely based on Cap. However, there are many variants. How can this be? A variant can be generated "accidentally" in a number of ways without deliberate human intervention. These scenarios are not restricted to Office viruses or to macro viruses in general, or even to PC platforms, but the activities are particularly noticeable and prevalent in WordBasic, though VBA macros may also mate with each other. The following are some of the possible scenarios:

▶ Where more than one virus infection exists on a single system, it is sometimes possible for them to mate. Mating between macro viruses is particularly likely to happen if the two viruses incorporate one or more macros with the same name, so that one virus copies the corresponding macro from the second virus. The composite virus (if it remains viable) then infects other systems.

▶ A single virus may also acquire legitimate macros from the global template (usually NORMAL.DOT) and copy them along with the viral macros during subsequent infections.

▶ There are many ways of "disinfecting" a macro virus, one of the simplest and least effective of which is simply to toggle the template bit so that macros are left intact, but are unable to execute. This method is viable (if unforgivably sloppy) in versions of Word up to and including Word 95 (Word 7), since one of the distinctions between a document and a template is the ability to run (but not contain) internal macros. More recent versions do not preserve this distinction. A "better" product that checks more than just the template bit will report the presence of the virus, even though the virus is inactive unless the template bit is flipped (turned back on). There are, however, other ways that you might neutralize a document without completely removing the macro code. Businesses that change their primary anti-virus product fairly regularly find that a document thought to have been disinfected suddenly triggers an alert in a new product (or, less often, a new upgrade to an old product). Characteristically, this alert will not result in identification of the original virus. The alert is likely to report that a document contains "traces of WM/xyz", is "like WM/xyz", or is even an "unknown variant of WM/xyz".

▶ An incompletely disinfected macro virus may not only leave traces, but leave whole macros intact. Such a circumstance can arise when the disinfecting scanner misidentifies a virus. Indeed, it has been suggested that problems with disinfection associated with certain scanners partially accelerated the initial explosive growth of the Word virus phenomenon. In this scenario, anti-virus software that takes a generic approach and discards *any* detected macro has an advantage. Publishers of virus-specific scanners, however, generally prefer to keep the baby, even if it means keeping some of the bath water, and assume that the virus victim might have legitimate macros and other customizations that he or she might want to keep.

▶ We all know, of course, that viruses are the creations of "misunderstood genius". However, it appears that even a genius can occasionally write imperfect replication code, so that under certain circumstances some component macros are not copied to the next generation. This can result in a "devolved" variant. If the loss of macros stops the virus from functioning, the resulting "nonviable devolved virus" is normally still detected, and the scanner may still refer to it as a "virus", even though it no longer replicates. Sometimes, not all the blame attaches to the virus author. In Word 6 and 7, I/O (input/output) errors during macro copying are likely to result in corrupted macro copies. In fact, in a highly recommended series of articles on macro viruses published in *Virus Bulletin* in late 1999, Igor Muttik suggested that the 200 or so WM/NPad variants were all the result of such corruption by copy errors. NPad was seen extensively around the same time as Cap.

▶ VBA versions 5 and 6 are not susceptible to the same copy errors; they are not immune to the "mating" mechanism, however, where two viruses use the same class module. Again, the resulting cocktails may have a variety of effects. VBA errors resulting from conflicting calls to the same functions may result in a nonviable virus. On the other hand, a viable hybrid may be produced and continue to replicate.

Word 97

Office 97 brought a slight respite in the virus war, though virus writers were experimenting with the new requirements of Visual Basic for Applications before the application left beta testing. Any hope that the renovated VBA technology, and the improved native measures for detecting the presence of macros and customizations, would prove a major obstacle to the generation and spread of viruses proved ill founded.

   WM97/Class was first identified in summer 1998, and was found in the wild shortly thereafter. While some WordBasic viruses had achieved a measure of polymorphism, Class managed to refine the technique. W97M/Ethan proved once more that simplicity is no barrier to viral success. W97M/Marker added data leakage to the mix: it mailed summary information to the Codebreakers site. W97M/Caligula developed this theme a little further, by leaking PGP-related information. While this leakage didn't constitute a major security breach, it was close enough to make people nervous. W97M/ColdApe was remarkable only in that it targeted Nick FitzGerald, former editor of *Virus Bulletin* and an outspoken critic of VX immorality and incompetence. ColdApe infected through the AddFromString operator, but also dropped the VBScript virus Happy, and used Outlook to mail a somewhat saucy message to FitzGerald.

Thank You for Sharing

In some ways, though, the most significant macro virus of this period was another WordBasic virus. Technically, WM/ShareFun was mediocre; however, its importance does not lie in its internal complexity, or lack thereof, but in its use of social engineering and email as aids to dissemination. With the benefit of hindsight, the virus appears to be a sort of precursor to Melissa, which itself is a bridge between the macro viruses of yesteryear and the worms of today.

   ShareFun passed from document to document within Word in an unremarkable manner. However, its payload was rather more interesting. On a machine running Microsoft Mail, ShareFun would attempt to mail itself to three randomly selected mail addresses from the victim's list of correspondents. If it succeeded, the next potential victim would receive a message headed "You have GOT to read this!", with an infected file enclosed as an attachment. (Nowadays, even comparative newcomers to computing are becoming aware that trusting the sender doesn't mean you have to trust the attachment, but that message was, at that time, still hard to convey.) ShareFun did not, of itself, make huge waves. However, other virus writers had taken note.

Macro Virus Nomenclature

Virus nomenclature has always been a sensitive issue, because of the lack of standards. Where a "standard" naming system (most often that implemented by the Computer Antivirus Research Organization, or CARO) is imposed retrospectively, it is rarely universally adopted by vendors, let alone anyone else. VBS/LoveLetter.A continues to be known as the Lovebug (or Love bug, or Love Bug), and who remembers the real name of the Kournikova worm? (The answer is VBS/VBSWG.J@mm, should you find yourself asked this question on a quiz show.)

However, there is a logic behind the standard(ish) naming system applied to macro viruses. Names have three main parts: the platform identifier (followed by a slash, /), the family name (e.g., Cap), followed by a period and the variant suffix. The platform identifier indicates the vulnerable application. The variant suffix is a guide to the exact variant in question. The first known version of the virus usually has the suffix .A, and subsequent variants proceed alphabetically to .Z, then start again at .AA. A number is appended to a devolved variant, as in WM/Rapi.A1, for example. Macro viruses that are also considered to be worms may also have an "-mm" (mass mailer) suffix appended, as in the case of W97M/Melissa.U-mm. Where a variant replicates only under a specific language version of Word, a country code preceded by a colon may be appended, as in WM/Boom.A:de, which replicates only under the German version of Word 6.

Table 13-1 is by no means all-inclusive (or universally used), and includes only Office macro viruses. It doesn't include other common prefixes, such as VBS (for VBScript), JS (for JavaScript), or other suffixes such as .HLL (high-level language),

Platform Identifier	What It Denotes	Example
WM	WordBasic macro	WM/Cap.A
XM	Excel macro (VBA 3)	XM/Laroux.A
A97M	Access 97 macro	A97M/AccessiV
W97M	Word 97 macro	W97M/Marker.AD
X97M	Excel 97 macro	X97M/Laroux.NU
O97M	Office 97 macro (infects all applications running VBA)	O97M/Tristate.A

Table 13-1   *Common Platform Identifiers*

.HLLC (C language), @M (mailborne virus), or @MM (Mass Mailer). A web page giving a number of conventions used by Symantec can be found at

http://www.symantec.com/avcenter/venc/vnameinfo.html

But it must be stressed that the conventions used by this vendor are not exactly the same as those used by others, and there is no true universal standard.

Anti-Macro Techniques

Macro viruses presented unique virus management problems in the mid-1990s. Basic detection techniques did not work quite so well in this area as they had done in previous contexts:

▶   One approach that immediately became obsolete was checksumming. Documents are not necessarily designed to be static. Obviously, they change while they're under development. Furthermore, the development lifetime of some types of documents might extend over many years, while an archived document that could be considered static in itself might be hauled out of cold storage to serve as a pattern for a different document. In some environments, attempts were made to check Word .DOT (template) files regularly for changes. However, Word makes changes in NORMAL.DOT, the default template file, every time the user changes a setting, allowing lots of scope for false alarms. In fact, many checksummers (change detector programs) do not have an option for checking files of a type not usually considered to be an executable file—such as any Word document or template. Other generic techniques such as behaviour monitoring and blocking have similar problems, though heuristic analysis has proved comparatively successful in detecting unknown macro viruses.

▶   On-demand scanners are now routinely upgraded to scan .DOC and .DOT files and recognize known macro viruses and Trojans. However, Office has never relied on filename extensions. Even in MS-DOS (there was a series of versions of Word for DOS), data files are not *required* to have an approved extension, or any extension at all. On some operating systems (Mac OS and UNIX, for instance), filename extensions have no special meaning to the operating system at all. Macro viruses rendered the "executables-only" on-demand scan conceptually obsolete, though scanners still offer a choice and rarely use "scan all files" as a default. Scanning data files introduced substantial overhead to any on-demand scanning (scanning that you specifically call up from the command line or by double-clicking on a program icon). This overhead became less of an issue as memory-resident scanning under Windows became more common. DOS TSR (memory-resident) scanners were never very effective in this context. In general, they detect a subset of possible viruses—otherwise, just about any disk I/O would slow the whole system while opened files were checked for all known viruses, a problem aggravated by the limited memory available to a DOS application. One of the more obvious advantages of a Windows environment is that it acts as a "DOS extender", allowing an application access to extended memory.

▶ Polymorphic viruses, which cannot be detected with a simple scan string, present a particular memory and processing overhead problem for TSR scanners. Again, this issue has become less significant as more people use Windows VxDs to do on-access or concurrent scanning.

In fact, there are very simple expedients that would eliminate most of this new subclass of virus. (These are *general* principles and apply as much to WordPerfect for DOS, for example, as to Word 6 or Visual Basic for Applications.)

▶ Don't allow code to run automatically if you cannot trust it. (So would there ever be a time when you could trust auto macros?)

▶ Don't run *any* macro unless you know what it does.

Unfortunately, both of these expedients have problems:

▶ Many corporate applications rely on running macros of one sort or another. If even one of these is an auto macro, disabling automatic macros becomes a major problem.

▶ There is no simple command for turning off auto macros, let alone macros in general, which are a fundamental part of the Word infrastructure. However, later versions of Word make it possible to display a dialog box warning if a document contains macros and offering a choice of opening with or without macro execution (or not opening at all). In fact, this dialog box is an installation default, though it is far too easy to disable permanently. There are, of course, ways of hardening Word with third-party applications that detect and/or block macros. Padgett Peterson's MacroList, for example, is a free utility; a macro-based generic tool available at http://www.freivald.org/~padgett/. (Padgett is also the author of the highly regarded DiskSecure, available at the same site.)

▶ We are not much in favour of running untrusted macros (especially unreadable macros), or, in fact, reading *any* untrusted documents without some sort of checking. However, it's not always practical to enforce a policy of the following sort:

1. Where practical, disable auto macros on all machines.
2. Establish guidelines as to what constitutes trusted and untrusted documents and sources.
3. Check all untrusted documents on a sheepdip PC (just as you would check an unvalidated program file). (Sheepdip machines have declined drastically in popularity in recent years. They represent a major processing bottleneck, an intrusive and obstructive anti-virus tool at its worst. The rise of the on-access scanner has made this unpopular measure less necessary.)
4. Strictly control any exchange of documents. (Even before VBScript worms became hot news, it was becoming unsafe to assume that anything *received* from a given individual was knowingly *sent* by that individual.)
5. Enforce access control where considered necessary by using appropriate software, so that only authorized diskettes can be used on critical machines. (Keep in mind, however, that such access control is an extension of the sheepdip principle, and subject to similar problems.)
6. Conduct training in virus control and general security issues.

Jimmy Kuo of Network Associates has published an excellent collection of free macro anti-virus techniques, both in *Virus Bulletin* and elsewhere:

http://download.nai.com/products/media/vil/pdf/free_AV_tips_techniques.pdf

Hare

The rise of the macro virus did not result in the disappearance of older virus classes. Hare was a multipartite, stealth, memory-resident, polymorphic virus. This sounds pretty scary, but in fact, it was, comparatively, a damp squib. Its social impact was out of proportion to its actual spread.

On 26th and 29th June, 1996, several forged posts with Hare-infected attachments were posted to USENET. Since the target newsgroups included groups where erotic material was commonly posted, victims were often assumed to be pornographers, perverts, and pirates. Of course, this assumption ignored the fact that, irrespective of how a virus is launched originally, its subsequent spread cannot be controlled or predicted.

On 22nd August and 22nd September, when the system was booted for the first time, diskettes in drives A and B were to be erased, as were the contents of drive C. However, despite the astonishing media attention it received, the principle interest in Hare lies in the comparative thinness of its spread.

Chernobyl (CIH.Spacefiller)

There is still no known virus that causes incontrovertible damage to hardware, though we are not about to say that such damage could never happen under any circumstances. However, the PC virus CIH can cause comparable damage to firmware.

NOTE

If the virus's name is CIH, why is this section titled "Chernobyl"? Because we figured that anyone looking for information on this specific virus might, thanks to the media, look for it under that specific name. The virus actually acquired this name retrospectively. It was first identified in summer 1998, and was most commonly referred to as CIH. Later, a particular vendor's marketing department noticed that one of its variants would trigger on 26th April, 1999, the 13th anniversary of the infamous meltdown at a Russian nuclear power plant, and started to use the name as a hook to catch public and media interest. In fact, there are several versions of CIH, and others trigger on 26th June or the 26th of any month. Nonetheless, the name has stuck, and a recent book has perpetuated the small but irritating myth that the virus author specifically chose the date to commemorate the meltdown. The name of the virus actually derives from the initials of its author, Chen Ing-Hau.

CIH is a Portable Executable (PE) infector. (PE is the format used by 32-bit Windows programs under Windows 9x, Me, NT, and 2000.) Apart from the matter of its trigger date, it has a particularly interesting feature. The Chernobyl variant includes a highly destructive two-fold payload. Part of Chernobyl's payload that makes recovery difficult is quite commonplace: it overwrites the first 2,048 sectors of each hard disk with random data. However, the virus also takes advantage of a vulnerability in PCs that use flash ROM BIOS technology (as most do nowadays).

Flash ROM technology allows a computer user to implement BIOS upgrades and bug fixes without specialist skills or hardware. However, CIH takes advantage of this capability to rewrite part of the system's internal bootstrapping routine—actually, the virus rewrites only a single byte, but this is enough to invalidate the boot block and prevent a vulnerable machine from booting at all. This problem is independent of damage to the hard disk, and booting from a system diskette doesn't help. The machine cannot boot at all until the BIOS is replaced. In some systems, the cost of replacing a soldered chip is probably higher than replacing the motherboard. However, this part of the payload can only trigger under very specific circumstances, including an appropriate combination of chipset and ROM, and the availability of a programming voltage. A jumper setting often enables the voltage on the motherboard. The setting can be used for protection, but the default is often to enable the voltage. After all, PC users may be happy to reflash ROM from diskette, but not to dive under the hood and change jumper settings. Systems (such as many Compaq machines) that restrict the initial boot code to a read-only stub have an advantage here, in that the machine can still get far enough into the boot process to be reflashed. This arrangement is also safer in the event of a mishap, such as a power outage, while flashing is in progress.

Esperanto

The Esperanto virus is less interesting for what it does than for what it has been claimed to do. This virus can infect a wide range of file types, depending on the environment, including the following:

▶ DOS .COM files

▶ DOS .EXE files

▶ Windows 3.*x* NewEXE files

▶ Windows 95 PE .EXE files

▶ Windows NT PE .EXE files

However, it was by no means the first Portable Executable infector: that dubious honour goes to Boza.

In the unlikely event of its infecting without corrupting the host file, Esperanto is intended to trigger on 26th July, when it displays the following poem:

[Esperanto, by Mister Sandman/29A]
Never mind your culture / Ne gravas via kulturo,
Esperanto will go beyond it / Esperanto preterpasos gxin;
Never mind the differences / ne gravas la diferencoj,

> *Esperanto will overcome them / Esperanto superos ilin.*
> *Never mind your processor / Ne gravas via procesoro,*
> *Esperanto will work in it / Esperanto funkcios sub gxi;*
> *Never mind your platform / Ne gravas via platformo,*
> *Esperanto will infect it / Esperanto infektos gxin.*
> *Now not only a human language, but also a virus...*
> *Turning impossible into possible, Esperanto.*

Esperanto has also been credited with being the first and only virus (macro viruses excepted) that infects Macintoshes as well as PCs. It appears that the author embedded a mangled version of the Mac virus MDEF into the body of the PC virus. The chances of it actually infecting a Macintosh system are slightly less than our chance of turning this book into a Hollywood screenplay.

Esperanto has also been described as multipartite. This description is probably more defensible: it is both a file infector and a hoax.

Summary

Some of the viruses reviewed in this chapter are seen comparatively rarely today. Nevertheless, macro viruses continue to be a major problem, even if they are no longer the *main* problem. The techniques developed by virus writers reviewed in this chapter helped to shape the malware that dominates the present-day virus scene.

The next and final chapter on case studies takes us up to the present day and to the dominance of the fast-burning mass mailer.

Case Studies: Turning the Worm (the Third Wave)

403

I n Chapters 2 and 13, we gave a great deal of attention to macro viruses. Clearly, the existence of macro virus technology is not a threat that conveniently went away as soon as the Age of the Worm began. It is true that as worms and email viruses have become more common, macro viruses have declined in "market share". A similar phenomenon was observed as macro viruses became more prevalent and boot-sector viruses declined. However, the cases are not quite the same. Boot-sector viruses were always a minority interest, being harder to write than file viruses. They were more successful in the wild, so more recorded virus incidents involved boot-sector infectors (BSIs), but fewer were written. New macro viruses and variants, however, continue to be commonplace.

Macro viruses were an order of magnitude easier to write, and did not lose that advantage when mail viruses kicked in. Indeed, as we've already indicated, there is a close relationship between Visual Basic for Applications, the language of choice for recent macro viruses, and VBScript, the Visual Basic scripting language in which many worms are written. Later in this chapter we will examine this relationship a little further. We will also examine Melissa, the macro virus/worm hybrid whose appearance marked a watershed in email virus development, and perhaps was the first "fast burner". Before that, however, we examine a worm whose origins lie in a field outside the mainstream of virus development, being neither a macro virus nor PC-based. It was one of the first indications that worms were no longer restricted to big corporate server systems.

The AutoStart Worm

AutoStart 9805 is usually considered to be a worm, rather than a virus—that is, it replicates by copying itself, but doesn't attach itself parasitically to a host program. It affects only Power Macs; earlier models running a 68KB series Motorola CPU cannot run the replicative code. The original took hold rapidly in Hong Kong and Taiwan in April 1998, and, along with five later variants, subsequently spread worldwide.

AutoStart does not require a particular version of Mac OS, the Macintosh operating system, but it does require that QuickTime 2.0 or later be installed, and that CD-ROM AutoPlay be enabled in the QuickTime Settings control panel. Disabling AutoPlay on a clean system removes the vulnerability, though it doesn't help significantly on a system that is already infected, and the Disable option exists only in version 2.5 or later. Also, infection can still take place if the system is booted from a volume with an infected Extensions folder.

The AutoPlay setting enables a program contained on a CD to be launched when the CD is inserted. CDs are not the only possible transmission media; any HFS (Hierarchical File System) or HFS+ volume (hard disk, diskette, zipdisk, or even disk images) can carry the infective program. However, audio CDs cannot carry the infection, and it is not necessary to disable Audio CD AutoPlay in the QT (QuickTime) control panel.

Infected media contain an invisible application file named DB, BD, or DELDB in the root directory. Macintosh files include a file type identifier, in this case APPL, and a creator field, in this case ????.

This is an AutoStart file; it will run automatically if CD-ROM AutoPlay is enabled. If the host Mac isn't already infected, the worm copies itself to the Extensions folder. The new copy is renamed Desktop Print Spooler, Desktop Printer Spooler, or DELDesktop Print Spooler, respectively (changing the file type to APPE). Unlike files with the legitimate Desktop Printer Spooler extension, the worm file has the invisible attribute set, and isn't listed as a running process by the system software, although the file can be seen with Process Watcher or Macsbug.

Initially, the most noticeable symptom of an infected system is that it will lock up and churn with unexplained disk activity every 6, 10, or 30 minutes. This happens because the system is rebooted after infection, and the worm launches every subsequent time the system restarts. The disk activity matches the intervals at which the worm examines mounted volumes to see if they're infected; if they aren't, the worm writes itself to the root directory and sets up.

Most versions of AutoStart attack data. Files with names ending *data, cod,* or *csa* are targeted if the data fork is larger than 100 bytes. The worm also attacks 2MB files with names ending *dat.* AutoStart damages files by overwriting the data fork (up to the first megabyte) with garbage.

AutoStart 9805-B can cause irreparable damage to files of type JPEG, TIFF, and EPSF. AutoStart 9805-C and AutoStart 9805-D do not intentionally damage data.

The July 1998 edition of *Virus Bulletin* included a comprehensive analysis of AutoStart and some of its variants. CIAC Bulletin I-067 was based on Eugene Spafford's information release on the original AutoStart worm, and can still be found at http://www.ciac.org/, though the information contained in quick-response virus advisories can become outdated quite rapidly.

AutoStart is notable for being the only Macintosh malware to be featured on the otherwise PC-centric WildList. However, David Harley is working with the WildList Organization on a MacWildList to track Mac-specific and crossplatform malware.

W97M/Melissa (Mailissa)

She came from alt.sex.

Now, as the old joke goes, that we have your attention ...

In this instance, though, the lure of sex was certainly employed to launch the virus into the wild, and the statement is literally true. The source of the infestation of the Melissa Word macro virus (more formally identified as some variation on W97M/Melissa) was a posting on the Usenet newsgroup alt.sex. The message had an attachment, a Word document, and the posting suggested that this document contained account names and passwords for web sites carrying salacious material. As one might expect in such a newsgroup, a number of people read the document, which actually carried a macro that used the functions of Microsoft Word and the Microsoft Outlook mailer program to reproduce and spread itself—rather successfully, as it turns out. Melissa is not the fastest burning email-aware malware to date, but it certainly held the record for a while.

Many mail programs, in the name of convenience, were by this time becoming more and more automated. Much of this automation focused on running attached files, or scripting functions included in HTML-formatted messages, without requiring the intervention of the victim. (HTML, *HyperText Markup Language*, is the data structure for web pages.) Padgett Peterson, author of MacroList, one of the best available macro virus protection tools, has stated, "For years we have been saying you could not get a virus just by opening E-Mail. That bug is being fixed".

Consider Her Ways

To be susceptible to the effects of Melissa, a victim needed to be running Microsoft Word 97 or later and Microsoft Outlook 98 or later. It was also necessary to receive an infected file and read it into Word without disabling the macro capability. However, all of these conditions are normal for many users. Microsoft, like any software publisher (and yes, that does include anti-virus vendors), is in the business of locking customers into an upgrade cycle. Receiving infected documents has never been a problem, from WM/Concept onwards. Melissa increased the likelihood that any given user would eventually receive an infected document by the sheer volume of reproduction of copies. However, by judicious social engineering, the virus also increased the chances of persuading a victim to open an infected document. Many mail programs will now detect the type of a file from its extension and start the appropriate program automatically. If you need to simply look at MS Word documents, a document viewer is available (free, as it happens) from Microsoft, which will not execute most macros, thereby protecting your system from infection. But you need to download and install the program, and make it your default "reader" for .DOC files. Microsoft's stranglehold on the corporate market seriously reduces the possibility of computer users taking the trouble to implement this solution.

On execution, the virus first checks to see whether an infectable version of Word is running. If so, Melissa reduces the level of the security on Word so that it will not display any future warnings regarding macro content. Under Word 2000, the virus blocks access to the menu item that allows you to raise your security level and sets your macro virus detection to the lowest level—that is, none. Restoring the security level requires the deletion of the NORMAL.DOT file and the consequent loss of legitimate macros and customizations.

The virus checks for the Registry key HKEY_CURRENT_USER\Software\Microsoft\Office\Melissa?\ with a value of "... by Kwyjibo". (The "Kwyjibo" entry seems to be a reference to the "Bart the Genius" episode of *The Simpsons* television cartoon program where Bart Simpson used this word to win a Scrabble match.) If Melissa does not find that key, the macro starts up Outlook and sends itself as an attachment to the "top" 50 names in *each* of your address lists. Most people have only one (the default is "Contacts"), but if you have more than one, then Outlook will send more than 50 copies of the message. Outlook also sorts address lists so that other mailing lists are at the top of the list. In addition, if you have a Microsoft Exchange Server, the macro can send copies to the "global" address lists on the server. Therefore, a single infected machine may distribute far more than 50 copies of the message/virus in the next "hop".

Infection Versus Dispersal

Like most macro viruses, Melissa works by infecting the global template, then infecting all documents thereafter. Each document created or reviewed is infected when closed. Each infected document activates the macro when the file is opened. Avoiding Outlook does *not* offer protection from the virus; it only means that the 50 copies will not be sent out automatically. If you use Word but not Outlook, you can still be infected, and can still send out infected documents on your own.

The virus cannot invoke the mass-mailer-dispersal mechanism on Macintosh systems, but it can be stored and re-sent from Macs. There was a great deal of confusion when it was reported in early 2001 that Melissa had now "become" a Mac problem. David Harley posted the following information to a number of Macintosh resources:

> A number of people on Mac-related lists have been misled by a news report at ZDnet suggesting that a new variant of Melissa has been found that targets

Macs. This is a travesty. The virus concerned is a common variant of Melissa. Since Melissa is a macro virus (or virus/worm hybrid, if you prefer) any variant may be infective (to a degree) on a Mac, but the mass mailing component only works in Windows. This variant is no more or less a danger to Mac users than the others, in principle.

However, there is an issue. It turns out that an accidental (minor) change in the Office 2001 document format means that many scanners have not consistently been able to detect macro viruses in documents saved in 2001 format. This affects PC scanners as much as it does Mac products.

Sans Souci

As with any Word macro virus, the source code travels with the infection, and so it was very easy to create modifications to Melissa. Many Melissa variants with different subjects and messages began showing up shortly after the original virus appeared. The first similar Excel macro virus was called Papa, though this and its progeny have never had the same global impact as Melissa. In fact, the source code was more than usually widely published, in newsgroups, on the Web, and elsewhere.

In one distressing instance, a major security organization issued a "flash advisory" including a range of information of varying quality and relevance. Unfortunately, it also included the entire source code, trivially modified so that it would not run without some tweaking. We understand that some security people view the question of whether or not to publish substantial virus code differently than most people in the anti-virus community, who are usually opposed to the practice. Indeed, we will return to the full disclosure/nondisclosure debate in Part IV of this book.

Nevertheless, we consider the inclusion of the source code irresponsible and inept, not only because it made the virus source code available to individuals who might not otherwise have seen it, but because of those very modifications. While the changes might have defeated the most terminally clueless of aspirant virus writers, it would require only minimal understanding of VBA programming to restore the code to functionality. It gets worse, however: the changes which were made effectively turned the virus into an intended or nonviable virus. Restoring its functionality would probably not restore the original virus, except possibly by accident. Instead, it would create a variant. We doubt that the organization in question intended to encourage systems administrators, the primary audience of the advisory, to create new viruses, but it did unfortunately provide them with the means to do so.

Furthermore, it was already known that the "Dark Side" kept track of the mailing list; indeed, someone had already distributed a spoofed version of the organization's newsletter not long before, using the organization's own mailing list.

The Commercial Virus

At the height of Melissa mania, one rather appalling discussion took place on an Internet marketing newsletter, in which the editor was exalting this new marketing tool, seeing it as a kind of automatic spam. This idea, or something very similar, was taken up in due course in the UK press. We are not aware that anyone has actually gone so far as using an actual virus as a marketing tool, though chain letters and spam certainly invite comparison with "memetic viruses". Sooner or later, though, we fear that someone will try. Such use of viruses is being referred to as "viral marketing", though nowadays the term also refers to such variations as services that are free as long as the user accepts advertising material along with the service. We hope that any organization that would go so far as to use a real virus as a marketing tool would gain only some short-term notoriety at the expense of losing all its credibility. However, the worst consequence of these discussions is that gradually they extend the borders of acceptability. Such issues as implementing program code that covertly modifies the Registry to include an advertisement or that passes information back to a remote site are increasingly regarded with indifference.

A classic example is the automatic insertion of an advertising type signature block that encourages the recipient to visit a specific web site to sign up for the free email, as is prevalent with services such as Hotmail and Yahoo! mail. *Entrepreneur Magazine* printed an enlightening article by Mark Henricks on viral marketing, titled "Viral Marketing: You Want to Catch This 'Bug'" (May 2000, pages 96–103). Henricks cites an example of a company that (very profitably) used "viral marketing" to force recipients of its client's encrypted messages to visit the company's web site— presumably to decrypt the message. No wonder that an article at the time asserted that "Melissa is a marketing tool".

I Used to Love Her (But It's All Over Now?)

As with many more recent mail-borne nuisances, a number of fixes, such as sendmail and procmail recipes for mail servers and mail filtering systems, were devised very quickly. However, these fixes were often not fully tested or debugged. One version would trap most of the warning messages about Melissa. Mail filters can, of course, become problems themselves. In the initial mailing of Robert Slade's contemporary report on the virus, the message was bounced from one system because of an automated filter that interpreted it as a "hoax" virus warning.

Melissa was something of a nine-day wonder. The massive infection hit over a single weekend and, almost immediately everyone learned how to protect against the virus and the clones that quickly followed. (Of course, everyone knows how to protect against Form, but it still turns up in the field, after more than ten years.)

Mail-based viral programs have always had a serious impact. In 1987 there was CHRISTMA EXEC, in 1988 the Internet Worm, and in 1989 H.COM and WANK. These viruses were all spread on and between mainframe and minicomputer systems, but had rather startling similarities to Melissa, including short lifetimes. A problem so obvious tends to be identified and dealt with in short order. However, the explosive growth of simple data communications technology presents new opportunities for viral infection and spread. A slow infector could be started on a web page and then sent around via email, carrying a logic bomb set to go off on a specific future date. A simple mail virus could itself do serious damage in the short term. Melissa shut down email contact for many companies using the Microsoft Exchange Server for mail. Properly timed, the release of just such a program could be part of a sabotage campaign against either a corporate or a military target. The association with salacious sites could be used as black propaganda against a victim. Furthermore, viruses like Melissa may send sensitive internal information out on a quick trip around the world when a confidential document is first opened after infection.

W32/Happy99 (Ska), the Value-Added Virus

Happy99 is another good example of the success of the mail-borne approach to viral dissemination: it has spread very widely by sending itself out as an email attachment whenever it infects a system. In this case, however, the virus is actually a full-blown Windows application, not a macro or script virus. When run, it shows a "fireworks display" claimed to commemorate New Year's Day 1999. Spanska, the virus's author, has observed in alt.comp.virus that he likes to give his victims something interesting to look at while he infects their systems. Indeed, he was a frequent poster to the newsgroup at one time, and even contributed to some useful debates on ethics and morality that attracted input from both sides of the Black Hat/White Hat divide.

When Happy99 infects, it modifies WSOCK32.DLL. After the modified .DLL runs, then each time an email is sent, a second message—including a copy of the worm as an attachment—is sent to the same recipient at the same time. The worm's presence is easy to detect (apart from the graphics). The original WSOCK32.DLL is copied to a file called WSOCK32.SKA, and a file called LISTE.SKA is created, containing a list of the addresses to which the infective mail has been sent. This list is meant to ensure that the worm is mailed to each correspondent only once. Files called SKA.EXE and SKA.DLL are also dropped when the system is infected.

Happy99 is kind of interesting. For a virus, it's almost cuddly: it isn't intentionally destructive, it's fairly easy to recover from (even without anti-virus software), and it has some visual interest, which may explain why it continued to spread long after New Year's Day 1999. And it doesn't even use sex as a hook.

PrettyPark

PrettyPark is versatile: not only is it a worm, it also steals passwords and has backdoor functionality. PrettyPark had become widespread by the summer of 1999, and variants also continue to be widely seen. Something of a resurgence of panic arose the following year when a version appeared that some anti-virus products could not detect. Although this version was not essentially a new variant, the executable had been packed somewhere along the line. Packing is a form of compression; however, unlike archive formats such as zip files created by compression utilities such as WinZip, packed files are ready-to-run executables that take up less space than their unpacked version. They do not have to be extracted, and differ from self-extracting files. A self-extracting file's function is to extract itself, not to run the application. In the case of a packed file, part of the file is decompressed into memory in the execution of the application; decompression is not a separate function.

PrettyPark arrives as an email attachment called the Pretty Park.Exe file. The file icon represents a character from the *South Park* cartoon series. PrettyPark's staying power is impressive, given that it contains no significant social engineering. The nearest it gets is to offer the unexplained attachment filename C:\CoolProgs\Pretty Park.exe.

On execution and self-installation as \Windows\System\FILES32.VXD, PrettyPark mails itself out to addresses in the Windows Address Book. It also mails certain Internet Relay Chat (IRC) servers with system settings and password information, and modifies the Registry setting as follows:

```
HKEY_CLASSES_ROOT
exefile\shell\open\command
```

This modification ensures that FILES32.VXD runs whenever any .EXE file is executed. This has ugly side-effects when anti-virus software is updated on an infected system. Memory-resident anti-virus software normally blocks access to applications that it recognizes as virus-infected or malicious. If the memory-resident software is unable to disinfect or remove the program itself, the victim may be unable to use an on-demand scanner to disinfect if the scanner itself is an .EXE file, since the memory resident software is probably unable to get past FILES32.VXD to execute the scanner. Even if this were not the case, scanners do not reliably reverse Registry settings. If a victim removes FILES32.VXD without amending the Registry, it still is not possible to run .EXE files. As with many more recent worms and viruses, removing PrettyPark from an infected system may require manual intervention by a knowledgeable individual, rather than just point-and-click disinfection. Increasingly, vendors are having to make available one-shot disinfection utilities with step-by-step instructions for removal, and often with the sort of detail they would prefer to keep from their customers and the prying eyes of virus authors. These utilities range from simple .REG files to reverse Registry changes, to complex applications run from the MS-DOS command line. Indeed, we often find it easier to clean worm-infested systems with an assortment of command-line utilities than with the installed Windows anti-virus applications.

The PrettyPark backdoor allows a remote machine to create and remove directories, and to send, receive, delete, and execute files. However, this functionality is rarely reported to have been exploited. Later in its history, the worm was sometimes found to be infected with unrelated file viruses.

Keeping to the Script

Script viruses started in a small way. VBS/First is an unsophisticated overwriting virus that appeared towards the end of 1998, and is not particularly interesting, from a technical standpoint. VBS/First.B added a little camouflage, to conceal the fact that it shelled to DOS. VBS/First.C was minimally bipartite: it infected VBS and JavaScript files. VBS/First has one other interesting feature: on the 15th day of any given month, it tries to connect to a VX site.

VBS/Seven.A was not an overwriter. However, it added a type of payload that became almost a VBS virus standard within two years: it included a time bomb that overwrote all .DOC and .TXT files with a graphic.

VBS/Internal infects HTML files using an infective Visual Basic script. For the script to execute, the victim must be running a VBScript-aware browser. VBS/Luser.A added self-encryption to the mix. JS/Charlene and VBS/Charlene try to infect over the Internet, as well as locally, using vulnerabilities in Internet Explorer. VBS/Hopper infected VBScript, Word, and HTML files.

These were small beginnings, but the genie was finding his way out of the bottle. For more information on early VBS viruses, a useful resource is Katrin Tocheva's article "From VBS to VBA" (*Virus Bulletin,* March 1999). Marius van Oers considered some of the technical issues associated with VBS in "Automating MS Outlook VBScript" (Virus Bulletin Conference Proceedings, 1999).

VBS/Freelink

VBS/Freelink is an email worm, found in Europe in July 1999, which used encryption similar to that of VBS/Luser (VBS/Zulu). The worm arrived as email with the subject line "Check this" and an attachment called Links.VBS. The body of the message contains the following text:

```
Have fun with these links.

Bye.
```

If the victim accepts the invitation and the worm is executed, an encrypted script called RUNDLL.VBS is dropped into C:\Windows\System. The script modifies the Registry to execute RUNDLL.VBS each time the system is started. A dialog box now displays the following text:

```
This will add a shortcut to free XXX links on your desktop. Do you want
to continue?
```

Clicking on Yes creates a shortcut called FREE XXX LINKS on the desktop, pointing to http://www.sublimedirectory.com. If there are any mapped network shares, the worm is copied to the root of each share.

The worm uses Outlook to mass-mail itself to every address in all address books. In an attempt at camouflage, the infective messages sent out by the worm are removed from the victim's Sent Mail folder.

After restart, Links.vbs is dropped to the Windows directory. If mIRC or Pirch98 (IRC chat clients) are found, the script modifies their .INI files so that the worm is spread when the victim accesses an IRC channel.

I Wrote a Letter to My Love—VBS/LoveLetter

The Love Bug, as it will probably always be known, first hit the nets on 3rd May, 2000. It spread rapidly, arguably faster than Melissa had done the previous year. However, the Love Bug was not particularly sophisticated.

NOTE

Harley first became aware of the Love Bug early one morning when a customer reported receiving an attachment containing gibberish. (One of the advantages of working in an environment where Outlook was not commonly used as a mail client is that the client that was used, could not interpret the program.) The Help Desk analyst who received the call, realizing that "gibberish" might indicate program code, referred the call to Harley. Sure enough, cursory inspection of the code indicated that the attachment was clearly meant to be infective. Harley forwarded a sample to an AV vendor and prepared for an interesting day.

The original Love Bug came in an email with a subject line of "I LOVE YOU". The message consisted of a short note urging you to read the attached love letter. The attachment filename, LOVE-LETTER-FOR-YOU.TXT.vbs, was a fairly obvious piece of social engineering. The .TXT bit was supposed to make people think that the attachment was a text file and, thus, safe to read. At that point, many people had no idea that a .VBS extension indicates a Visual Basic script, and, in any case might not have been aware that if a filename has a double extension, only the last extension has any special significance to Windows. Putting *vbs* in lowercase was also likely meant to play down the extension's significance. However Windows, like DOS before it, is not case sensitive.

If you clicked on the attachment, nothing much happened—unless you happened to have Windows 98, Windows 2000, Internet Explorer 5, or Outlook 5. Since most users have a combination of these applications, clicking the attachment had an effect for most recipients. If any of those applications (or a few others) are present, then Windows Script Host (WSH) will also be on your machine, and you will have a file association binding the .VBS extension to wscript.exe. In that case, WSH would read and interpret the contents of the "love letter".

The infection mechanism included the installation of some files in the Windows and System directories. These files were just copies of the original .VBS file, in one case keeping the name of LOVE-LETTER-FOR-YOU.TXT.vbs, but in other cases renaming files (to MSKERNEL32.vbs and WIN32DLL.vbs) to fool people into thinking that they were system files.

The virus made changes to the Registry so that these files would run when the computer started up. Notice that the .VBS extensions kind of give the game away.

We Love Macs

Macintosh users were more or less immune to the Love Bug, since Mac OS has no Windows Script Host. A number of infectees first realized they had a problem when Mac users mailed their "admirers", asking how to open the file. However, the Mac community should not be too complacent. There have also been instances where Mac users whose systems remained uninfected passed on infected attachments. (We have referred to this previously as *heterogeneous virus transmission*.) In some instances, a Mac user has forwarded the attachment to a PC user, asking that PC user to open and print the attachment for them. David Harley sometimes refers to this as "Wormhausen-by-Proxy Syndrome". However, passive forwarding of attachments is not the only way in which a Macintosh user can be implicated in the spread of PC-specific script viruses. As discussed shortly, when we consider KAK and BubbleBoy, the use of HTML- aware browsers allows scripts to be invisibly embedded in the body of a message. In this scenario, simply forwarding the unedited text spreads the worm quite effectively, perhaps not quite as efficiently as Good Times, but at a rate too great for comfort.

Nowadays, many organizations routinely quarantine or bounce files with a .VBS extension (especially a double extension) at the mail gateway.

LoveLetter infects files with the extensions .VBS, .VBE, .JS, .JSE, .CSS, .WSH, .SCT, .HTA, .JPG, .JPEG, .MP2, and .MP3. The infection routines search local drives, but also all mounted networks, so shared directories can be an additional source of infection. The routines overwrite most of these files with a copy of the script (that is, the original file is not preserved anywhere, even though the new file has a different name), and change the filenames from (for example) picture.jpg to picture.jpg.vbs. In some cases, the virus simply deletes the original file. MPEGs, however, are not overwritten. The original file, say song.mp3, is marked as hidden, and a new file, song.mp3.vbs, is created with a copy of the virus. The .VBS extension must, of course, be added for the virus to be effective.

Once the virus has copied itself all over a host machine, it starts to spread to other machines. If Outlook is present, the virus will use any addresses found in any address book associated with the mail program to send copies of itself to each of those addresses (but only once). As with Melissa, this means that when you get a copy of the Love Bug, it will appear to come from someone you know. In addition, the program tries to make a connection to IRC, using the mIRC chat program, and spread that way. The Love Bug creates another copy of the file, LOVE-LETTER-FOR-YOU.HTM, in the Windows System directory, and then sends that copy to any user who joins the IRC channel while the session is active.

When a system is infected, the worm attempts to download a Trojan application from a web site in the Philippines by changing the startup URL in Internet Explorer. The file, named WIN-BUGSFIX.exe, will try to collect your various password files and email them to an address in the Philippines. If the file is executed, the Trojan also creates a hidden window called BAROK and remains resident and active in memory. However, this site was probably overloaded in the early hours of the Love Bug infection, and was quickly taken down.

A very large number of Love Bug "cleaners" were made available (the same was true for the AutoStart Mac worm, incidentally). Interestingly, most of them were Visual Basic scripts themselves. Unfortunately, at least two variants of the virus pretended to be disinfecting tools and did more damage than the original virus.

Since the virus is an unencrypted script file, it carries its own source code with it, which meant that variants started appearing within hours. Over a dozen were reported during the weekend after the virus first struck, and many more have been observed since. One of the more successful of these variants thanked the recipient for the order of a Mother's Day gift, and claimed that the recipient's credit card had been charged $326.92 as per an attached invoice. Obviously, this ruse relied on people being too angry to think about how anybody could charge their credit card when they had not given the number to a vendor. The invoice, of course, was no such thing, merely a modified version of the original script. The variants showed a certain amount of innovation in the field of social engineering, if not in the actual code. One derivative targets UNIX systems using shell scripts, but uses a very similar mechanism.

There are estimates of damage stemming from Love Bug in the billions of dollars, but justifying such figures would be very difficult. Certainly, a number of email systems were clogged, including those of some very large organizations. Many administrators shut down mail entirely, rather than resort to the work of filtering. In addition, the resetting of Registry entries is likely to be somewhat time-consuming. Text in the virus includes the string "Manila, Philippines".

The code also contains the two Philippine email addresses and the web site's URL. It doesn't take too much brain power to figure out that somebody in the Philippines might have some information about the origins of the bug. However, the Manila Department of Justice eventually dropped all charges against the long-suspected culprit.

VBS/NewLove-A

NewLove is an ugly little VB Script worm that has a number of aliases, including VBS/Loveletter.Gen, SPAMMER, and Herbie. NewLove is a polymorphic Visual Basic Script worm that changes its appearance in an attempt to avoid detection. Not only does the body of the script change, but the worm randomly chooses a filename in your Windows\Recent folder and attempts to forward itself to all addresses in the Microsoft Outlook address book. The name of the file it forwards remains the same as that of the randomly chosen file, but the worm appends a .VBS filename extension. (Thus, MYFILE.DOC becomes MYFILE.DOC.VBS.) The filename attached will have one of the following extensions, which makes filtering by extension comparatively simple: indeed, any organization with extensive mail-filtering would probably cover most of these combinations (and might well discard or quarantine *all* .VBS files in any case). And, of course, disabling the Windows Scripting Host pretty much removes the problem in any case.

► BMP.VBS

► DOC.VBS

► GIF.VBS

► HTM.VBS

► JPG.VBS

► MDB.VBS

► MOV.VBS

► MP3.VBS

► TXT.VBS

► URL.VBS

► XLS.VBS

The message has the subject line: "FW: *filename*", where *filename* is the name of the file it is forwarding, less the .VBS extension. The message itself contains no text. The worm attempts to truncate all files on local and remote drives to a zero-byte file.

The worm increases in size each time it infects, so it could, in principle, have a heavy impact on mail servers. However, the effect of the virus on the real world proved far less than its reputation would suggest. Many email systems had been configured to deal with such a close relative of the Love Bug, but the press were glad of another chance to show off their newly acquired virus knowledge.

Call 911!

The first announcement concerning the BAT/W95/911/Chode/Firkin worm was made on 1st April: the coincidence of its date and the inept manner of its announcement led many to assume it to be an April Fool's joke. A slightly hysterical FBI advisory on this virus was widely distributed by other organizations. Because of its apocalyptic tone and relentless use of uppercase "shouting" throughout the message, and the fact that the message exhorted its recipients in classic chain-letter fashion to pass it on, many people took it for a hoax.

This virus can also be spread via the Microsoft Windows networking "share" function, when a resource connected to a local area network, a drive, folder, file, or printer is set so that it is "readable" by anyone who accesses it. The 911 worm looks for resources such that remote users have write permissions as well as read permissions.

When the virus finds a likely host, it tries to copy a number of files to it, including some that will ensure that the virus executes at next boot time. After completing the infection routine, the virus may display a message on the local machine, or it may format a range of hard drives. Interestingly, the current version seems to avoid deleting itself in the damage process. The worm may delete other files at specific times. It may also attempt to place a call to 911 through the modem. Since the infection and spread tend to be localized to one network, a major infestation in a given area could have had some serious consequences for emergency services.

The best protection against a threat like this is to turn down the level of access to your shares, or to turn off the share function altogether. On both Windows NT and 9*x*, bring up the control panel, either through the My Computer icon or under the Settings entry on the Start menu. On Windows 9*x*, select the Network icon. Under the Configuration tab, the File and Print Sharing button allows you to disable access to files and printers. Under the Access Control tab, you can do a bit more tuning, but it takes some work. On Windows NT, you can check what shares have been created under the control panel, by clicking Server, then Shares, but restricting access is somewhat more complicated.

The virus creates hidden directories on the local hard disk, with directory names of chode, foreskin, or dickhair. Secondary infections were logged in C:\PROGRAM FILES\chode\chode.txt or c:\PROGRAM FILES\foreskin\cool.txt. Infected computers contained the files ASHIELD.EXE and ASHIELD.PIF somewhere.

On an infected system, on the 19th of each month, a .VBS script deletes files from C:\Windows, C:\Windows\System, C:\Windows\Command, and the root directory. It then displays two message boxes:

▶   You Have Been Infected By Chode

▶   You may now turn this piece of sh*t off!

Manual disinfection is usually possible by removing these directories and files, where they exist:

▶   C:\Program Files\Chode

▶   C:\Program Files\Foreskin

▶   C:\Windows\Start menu\Programs\Startup\Ashield.pif

▶   C:\Windows\Start menu\Programs\Startup\Netstat.pif

▶   C:\Windows\Start menu\Programs\Startup\Winsock.vbs

VBS/Stages

VBS/Stages, also known as I-Worm.Scrapworm and IRC/Stages.ini, among other names, spread via Pirch, mIRC (both Internet chat clients), email, and mapped network drives. If it arrived by email, it displayed the following characteristics:

▶   The subject line is a combination of three variable terms. The first term is always "FW:" or blank. The second term is always one of the following: "Life stages", "Funny", or "Jokes". The third term is either "text" or blank.

▶   The message always contains the text "The mail and female stages of life".

▶   The attachment is always called LIFE_STAGES.TXT.SHS.

The .SHS extension denotes a Windows scrap object, a file that can, in principle, be any kind of file. Windows Explorer does not show the .SHS file extension, irrespective of whether file extensions are set to be displayed. If you check the file under Properties, its type is shown as Scrap Object, but the Properties box and the General tab show its name as LIFE_STAGES.TXT. However, the MS-DOS name is shown in 8.3 format (LIFE_S~1.SHS), and the DOS DIR command shows the full filename, complete with the .SHS extension. It is possible to change this behaviour by editing the Registry entry HKEY_CLASSES_ROOT\ShellScrap from "NeverShowExt"= to "AlwaysShowExt". Remember, however, that a subsequent virus could quite possibly change the entry back. (We gave details about testing the visibility of the ShellScrap extensions in Chapter 6.)

The "Stages of Life" name derives from the text file displayed while the virus installs itself. This text consists of an extended joke. The following extract gives some of the flavour:

```
Age. Seduction Lines.
17 My parents are away for the weekend.
25 My girlfriend is away for the weekend.
35 My fiancee is away for the weekend.
48 My wife is away for the weekend.
66 My second wife is dead.
```

The virus moves REGEDIT.EXE to the recycle bin and renames it REGEDIT.VXD, and modifies the Registry to use the relocated file. It also creates a handful of files with fixed names, such as C:\Windows\System\Scanreg.vbs, and spreads over all available drives a number of others with randomly generated names. Random filenames are built. First, the name begins with one of the following words:

- ▶ IMPORTANT
- ▶ INFO
- ▶ REPORT
- ▶ SECRET
- ▶ UNKNOWN

This is followed by a hyphen or an underscore character, then a random number between 0 and 999, then .TXT.SHS. A typical filename would therefore be something like INFO_97.TXT.SHS.

BubbleBoy and KAKworm

In reports about Melissa, many references were made to the mythical and nonexistent Good Times virus. Simply reading the text of a message still cannot infect a system, with a rather important exception. BubbleBoy and JS/KAK take advantage of a security hole in older, unpatched versions of Internet Explorer and

Outlook that allows two ActiveX controls (scriptlet.typelib and Eyedog) to run at an inappropriate level of trust. This vulnerability allows a script virus embedded within the body of a mail message to infect a system without attaching a separate file.

Infective email arrives with the subject line "BubbleBoy is back!" The message contains the following text:

```
The BubbleBoy incident, pictures and sounds

http://www.towns.com/dorms/tom/bblboy.htm
```

It also contains an embedded HTML file containing the viral VBScript. The message has no attachment. If the recipient is using MS Outlook, the script is executed when he or she opens the email. In Outlook Express, the script can be run from the preview pane as well.

BubbleBoy drops a file called UPDATE.HTA into the Windows start-up directory. When the system next starts up, this file runs and edits the system Registry. The virus then mails a copy of itself, using Outlook, to every address in the Outlook address books.

BubbleBoy was a proof-of-concept virus rather than a serious threat in the field. While JS/KAK employed used the same concept, it had a much greater impact. The worm is embedded in an email message as an HTML signature. The recipient of the message doesn't see any evidence of the script running, because it contains no displayable text, but the script is run if he or she opens or previews the message. The file KAK.HTA is dropped into the Windows\Start Menu\Programs\Startup folder. The next time the system starts, KAK.HTA creates C:\WINDOWS\ KAK.HTM and modifies Outlook Express Registry settings so that KAK.HTM is included as a signature in all outgoing messages. On the first day of any month, after 5 P.M., the worm displays the message "Kagou-Anti-Kro$oft says not today" and shuts Windows down.

Microsoft Security Bulletin (MS99-032), originally posted on 31st August, 1999, has information on patching the scriptlet.typelib/Eyedog vulnerabilities in Internet Explorer 4.0 and 5.0.

MTX (Matrix, Apology)

MTX is a particularly unpleasant piece of malware. It consists of three main components: a worm, a parasitic virus, and a backdoor Trojan. The virus decompresses and installs both the worm and the backdoor onto the system, then infects. The backdoor downloads and spawns plug-in components, then infects 32-bit Windows executables, which can usually be disinfected. It is common to find 60–70 or more infected files when the virus has taken hold. Oddly, the worm cannot infect the system on its own: it spreads because it is itself infected by the virus, which installs the worm when executed. The virus code contains the following strings:

```
Software provide by [MATRiX] VX TeAm: Ultras, Mort, Nbk, LOrd DArk,
Del_Armg0, Anaktos

Greetz: All VX guy in #virus and Vecna for help us

Visit us at:

http://www.coderz.net/matrix
```

The worm and backdoor components contain similar (but not identical) text.

So as to make detection and disinfection more difficult, the virus component uses EPO (Entry Point Obscuring) technology. The entry point for the virus code is not at the infected program's entry point, as would be expected from a prepending virus, but further inside the code block. When the virus code executes, it decrypts itself, then checks the Win32 kernel for the Win32 API functions needed in order to proceed. It also checks for the presence of a number of anti-virus programs and exits if any of them are found. Otherwise, it installs three decompressed files to the Windows directory:

- ▶ IE_PACK.EXE is the worm itself.
- ▶ WIN32.DLL is also the worm, but is infected by the virus component.
- ▶ MTX_.EXE is the backdoor.

The virus then infects Portable Executables in a number of directories, characteristically Windows and Windows\System, before exiting. In our experience, 60 or more executables may be infected.

The worm uses a replication mechanism similar to that used by Happy99. It modifies C:\Windows\System\WSOCK32.DLL so that a copy of the worm is sent in a second message (unknown to the sender) that follows each legitimate mail message sent. Since the WSOCK32 file controls the connection to the Internet, the victim is also prevented from visiting a number of Internet sites and from sending email to the same domains, mostly anti-virus and other informational sites. The virus detects them by using four-character combinations such as the following:

afee	mapl	pand	yman
avp.	nai.	soph	
f-se	ndmi	tbav	
lywa	nii.	yenn	

The worm also blocks any attempt to send email messages to the following domains, which include a number of anti-virus vendor sites or other informational sites.

bca.com.nz*	f-secure.c*	maple.com.*	perfectsup*
beyond.com*	HiServ.com*	mcafee.com*	singnet.co*
bmcd.com.a*	hiserv.com*	meditrade.*	sophos.com*
cellco.com*	il.esafe.c*	metro.ch*	successful*
comkom.co.*	inexar.com*	netsales.n*	symantec.c*
complex.is*	inforamp.n*	newell.com*	trendmicro*
earthlink.*	mabex.com *	pandasoftw*	wildlist.o*

These measures make it difficult for the victim to obtain help or anti-virus updates, so as to deal with the infection. Even with up-to-date anti-virus software, disinfection can be awkward and time-consuming. It is often best done with a command-line scanner, booting from DOS, so that the virus is not active in memory. Infected files cannot always be safely disinfected, and must be replaced from .CAB (cabinet) files (usually compressed system files) or other sources. Files dropped or modified by the worm, as opposed to those infected by the virus, usually have to be deleted and, in the case of modified files such as WSOCK32.DLL, replaced.

NOTE

One of the originators of the worm may have felt some subsequent remorse, or a need for some PR-related damage limitation. At any rate, a page was put up suggesting ways of getting around the blocking of some vendor web sites, notably by using IP addresses in URLs rather than domain names. However, when we checked recently, the page had disappeared.

When the worm mails itself out, the target address receives two messages: the original message, written by the sender, followed by a message with no subject or message text. The second includes an attached file that contains one of the names that is selected by the worm, based on the current date:

```
ALANIS_Screen_Saver.SCR
ANTI_CIH.EXE
AVP_Updates.EXE
BILL_GATES_PIECE.JPG.pif
BLINK_182.MP3.pif
FEITICEIRA_NUA.JPG.pif
FREE_xxx_sites.TXT.pif
FUCKING_WITH_DOGS.SCR
Geocities_Free_sites.TXT.pif
HANSON.SCR
I_am_sorry.DOC.pif
I_wanna_see_YOU.TXT.pif
INTERNET_SECURITY_FORUM.DOC.pif
IS_LINUX_GOOD_ENOUGH!.TXT.pif
JIMI_HMNDRIX.MP3.pif
LOVE_LETTER_FOR_YOU.TXT.pif
MATRiX_2_is_OUT.SCR
MATRiX_Screen_Saver.SCR
Me_nude.AVI.pif
METALLICA_SONG.MP3.pif
NEW_NAPSTER_site.TXT.pif
NEW_playboy_Screen_saver.SCR
Protect_your_credit.HTML.pif
QI_TEST.EXE
READER_DIGEST_LETTER.TXT.pif
README.TXT.pif
SEICHO-NO-IE.EXE
Sorry_about_yesterday.DOC.pif
TIAZINHA.JPG.pif
WIN_$100_NOW.DOC.pif
YOU_are_FAT!.TXT.pif
zipped_files.EXE
```

Naked Wife

W32/Naked (W32.HLLW.JibJab@MM) is a worm written in Visual Basic (actual VB, not VBScript or Visual Basic for Applications). It cannot execute unless the Visual Basic 6.0 or later run-time files are present.

The worm arrives as an email attachment called NakedWife.exe, and uses social engineering techniques to persuade the victim to run it. If executed, the worm copies itself to a temporary directory and displays a fake Flash movie window with a message that reads "JibJab Loading". However, no movie ever loads, and the worm proceeds to mail itself to all the addresses in the Windows Address Book. It also tries to delete all .COM, .DLL, .EXE, .BMP, and .INI files found under C:\Windows and C:\Windows\ System. Choosing the HELP|ABOUT menu in the Flash window displays a message box that reads "You're are now FUCKED! (C) 20001 by BGK (Bill Gates Killer)". The counterfeit Flash movie displays a logo like the one which belongs to JibJab Media, Inc., based in New York. According to CNN, a JibJab executive was quoted as saying that, "The virus did not come from the company and that the worm creator likely used its logo to gain the trust of e-mailer readers".

The message arrives with the subject "Fw: Naked Wife". The body of the message says, "My wife never look like that! ;-)", and is signed with the sender's name (though without his or her knowledge, of course). The attached file, NakedWife.exe, is 70KB.

The worm itself is less interesting than the confusion concerning its origins, as discussed in Chapter 15 and in the story found at the following URL:

http://www.cnn.com/2001/TECH/internet/03/07/virus.brazil.02/index.html

W32/Navidad

W32/Navidad is a mass-mailing worm that appeared around the beginning of November 2000. When it infects, the worm sends a copy of itself, via Outlook or any other MAPI (Messaging Application Programming Interface) aware client, in reply to all incoming messages that include a single attachment. The outgoing message has the same subject line as the mail to which it poses as a response, and the worm is attached as a file called NAVIDAD.EXE.

Responding only to mail that arrives with an attachment, thus indicating that the user of the host system is already on attachment-exchanging terms with the sender of the incoming mail, increases the likelihood that the recipient of the attachment will open it. Bugs in the virus code, resulting in an inability to restart the infected system properly, do not affect the worm's ability to mail itself out, since the problem doesn't arise until after the system is rebooted.

When the worm infects, it displays an Error dialog box containing the letters *UI*. Under a Windows 95 or Windows 98 system, the worm adds the following Registry key:

```
HKLM\SOFTWARE
\Microsoft\Windows\CurrentVersion\Run
\Win32BaseServiceMOD=\Windows\System\Winsvrc.exe
```

Under Windows NT or Windows 2000, the worm adds this key:

```
HKLM\SOFTWARE\
Microsoft\Windows\CurrentVersion\Run
Win32BaseServiceMOD=\Winnt\System32\Winsvrc.exe
```

However, when the worm is copied into \Windows\System (Windows 9*x*) or \Winnt\System32 (NT or W2K), the new file is called WINSVRC.VXD, not WINSVRC.EXE.

Under Windows 95 or Windows 98, the worm changes

```
HKEY_LOCAL_MACHINE\SOFTWARE\CLASSES
exefile\shell\open\command
```

and

```
HKEY_CLASSES_ROOT
\exefile\shell\open\command
```

to

```
\Windows\System\winsvrc.exe "%1" %*"
```

Under Windows NT or Windows 2000, the worm changes

```
HKEY_LOCAL_MACHINE\SOFTWARE\CLASSES
\exefile\shell\open\command
```

and

```
HKEY_CLASSES_ROOT
\exefile\shell\open\command
```

to

```
\Winnt\System32\winsvrc.exe "%1" %*"
```

The intention is to run the worm every time any other .EXE is launched. However, the filename error effectively renders the PC unusable, since there is no WINSVRC.EXE.

Anti-virus software isn't actually very good at removing the worm, once it infects; in fact, it may be easier to copy regedit.exe to regedit.com so as to be able to edit the Registry, reverse the changes, and delete the worm's files, including WINSVRC.EXE, WINSVRC.VXD, WINTASK.EXE, WINTASK.VXD, NAVIDAD.EXE, or EMANUEL.EXE. The exact filenames vary according to whether the virus is the original Navidad or the Emanuel variant, which corrects the filename error that makes Navidad so obvious.

W32/Hybris

The Hybris worm started to make its mark in late September 2000. It's disseminated by an email message that is often but by no means always sent with a From: field of hahaha@sexyfun.net. This address is actually forged to make it harder to trace the infected source. However, the sexyfun.net domain was later set up and used as an Hybris information resource. The worm may sometimes check the language settings of the host computer and select a "story" relating to Snow White and the Seven Dwarfs in English, French, Spanish, or Portuguese, used as message text to accompany the copy of the worm when it is mailed out.

The attachment may have one of several different names, including, but not limited to, the following:

- ▶ anpo porn(.scr
- ▶ atchim.exe
- ▶ branca de neve.scr
- ▶ dunga.scr
- ▶ dwarf4you.exe

- ▶ enano porno.exe
- ▶ joke.exe
- ▶ midgets.scr
- ▶ sexy virgin.scr

It may also come with a filename comprising a semirandom set of eight letters, of which the first two and the last two always seem to be the same, in the same order, such as abxxxxab.

When the worm attachment is executed, the WSOCK32.DLL file is modified or replaced, so that it can track email and other Internet traffic. When the worm detects an email address, it waits, then sends infected email to that address. It also connects to alt.comp.virus and uploads encrypted plug-in modules to the group. If it finds newer plug-ins, the worm downloads them for its own use. For several months, alt.comp.virus was almost unusable because of the sheer number of plug-ins clogging the group.

VBS/VBSWG.J@mm (Anna Kournikova)

This worm, also known as SST, Anna, Lee-O, or OnTheFly, appeared out of nowhere on 12th February, 2001. The first indication of the problem came from MessageLabs, which specializes in scanning email traffic on behalf of ISPs and other major corporate customers, using multiple virus-specific scanners as well as generic tools. Shortly afterwards, systems administrators in AVIEN (the Anti-Virus Information Exchange Network) started to track the worm, and had blocked many thousands of infective emails by the time most vendors had developed detection for it.

Anna is a VBS email worm generated using a virus creation kit. It was reported subsequently that the worm's author had been offered work and encouragement by the mayor of his hometown, apparently on account of the author's programming skills. In fact, he didn't write a line of code. He simply chose some menu options.

Infective mail arrives with an attachment called AnnaKournikova.jpg.vbs. The message contains the following text:

```
Hi:
Check This!
```

The message has the following subject header:

```
Here you have, ;o)
```

This header made blocking infective mail a snap, even for systems administrators who weren't able to block by filename or filename extension.

On execution, the worm emails itself to everyone in the victim's Microsoft Outlook address book. On 26th January, the worm directs your web browser to a Dutch web site, apparently chosen more or less at random, simply because it was a menu option. The worm also creates the following Registry key:

```
HKEY_CURRENT_USER\Software\OnTheFly
```

It avoids sending infective mail more than once by setting the following key to 1:

```
HKEY_CURRENT_USER\Software\OnTheFly\mailed
```

VBS/Staple.a@mm

VBS/Staple is also known as Injustice or Justice. It is a Visual Basic script that spreads by way of Outlook. Staple arrives attached to email with the subject "RE: Injustice". The message text reads:

```
Dear (name),

Did you send the attached message, I was not expecting this from you !
```

The attachment is called injustice.TXT.vbs; if executed, it copies itself to the Windows\System directory and mails itself out to the first 50 names in the Outlook Address Book, and to several other (mostly Israeli) email addresses, including:

- ▶ amuta@ehudbarak.co.il
- ▶ arie@kba.org
- ▶ doar@mof.gov.il
- ▶ doar@shaam.gov.il
- ▶ foundation@habonimdror.org

The virus updates a value in the Registry to ensure that a particular recipient receives the email with the virus only once.

```
HKEY_CURRENT_USER\Software\Microsoft\WAB\"&malead,1,"REG_DWORD
```

A political message is displayed, followed by some URLs. The version shown next has been snipped so as to give you the flavour without undue propaganda content:

```
PLEASE ACCEPT MY APOLOGIES FOR DISTURBING YOU.

Remember that one day YOU may be in this situation.

We need every possible help.

Israeli soldiers killed in cold blood 12 year old Palestinian child
Mohammad Al-Durra, as his father tried to protect him in vain with
his own body …... Similarly, approximately 40 children were slain,
without the media taking notice or covering these tragedies. THESE
CRIMINAL ACTS CANNOT BE FORGIVEN OR FORGOTTEN!!!!"

        HELP US TO STOP THE BLOOD SHED!!
```

The code contains the following comment:

```
'Do not worry. This is a harmless virus. It will not do any thing to
your system.
'The intension is to help Palestinian people to live in PEASE in
their own land.
'S/N : 881844577469
```

Linux Worms

By spring 2001, a number of examples of Linux malware were indicating that anti-virus researchers had not been joking when they argued that Linux users could not count indefinitely on avoiding the attentions of virus authors. Interestingly, while the Windows worms generally followed the CHRISTMA EXEC style of having users run the scripts and programs, the new Linux worms are similar to the Internet/Morris/UNIX worm in that they rely primarily on bugs in automatic networking software.

Ramen

The Ramen worm makes use of security vulnerabilities in default installations of Red Hat Linux 6.2 and 7.0 (first edition) using specific versions of wu-ftp, rpc.statd, and LPRng. The worm defaces web servers by replacing index.html, and scans for other vulnerable systems. It does this initially by opening an ftp connection and checking the remote system's ftp banner message. If the system is vulnerable, the worm uses one of the exploitable services to create a working directory, then downloads a copy of itself from the local (attacking) system.

Compromised systems send out email messages to two Hotmail and Yahoo! accounts, and ftp services are disabled. Ramen's SYN scanning may disrupt network services if the network supports multicasting.

Ramen is pretty much a proof-of-concept attack, since it makes no attempt to conceal itself. However, similar attacks quickly followed Ramen.

Linux/Lion

Lion uses a buffer overflow vulnerability in the bind program to spread. When it infects, Lion sends a copy of output from the ifconfig command, /etc/passwd and /etc/shadow, to an email address in the china.com domain. Next the worm adds an entry to etc/inetd.conf and restarts inetd. This entry allows Lion to download components from a (now closed) web server located in China. Subsequently, Lion scans random class B subnets in much the same way as Ramen, looking for vulnerable hosts. The worm may install a rootkit onto infected systems. This backdoor disables the syslogd daemon and adds a trojanized ssh (secure shell) daemon.

The worm replaces several system executables with modified versions:

- ▶ /bin/ls
- ▶ /bin/netstat
- ▶ /bin/ps
- ▶ /sbin/ifconfig
- ▶ /usr/bin/du
- ▶ /usr/bin/find
- ▶ /usr/bin/top
- ▶ /usr/sbin/in.fingerd

The files /bin/in.telnetd and /bin/mjy provide additional backdoor functionality and attempt to conceal the rootkit's presence by hiding files and processes.

Linux/Adore (Linux/Red)

Adore is a Linux worm, similar to Linux/Ramen and Linux/Lion. It uses vulnerabilities in wu-ftpd, bind, lpd, and RPC.statd that enable an intruder to gain root access and run unauthorized code. The worm attempts to send IP configuration data, information about running processes, and copies of /etc/hosts and /etc/shadow to email addresses in China. It also scans for class B IP addresses.

Adore drops a script called 0anacron into the /etc/cron.daily directory so that the script runs as a daily cron job (the cron utility executes scheduled tasks at predetermined times). This script removes the worm from the infected host. A trojanized version that conceals the presence of the worm's processes replaces the system program /bin/ps, because the real ps program would show the processes.

Lindose (Winux)

Lindose is a proof-of-concept, cross-platform virus that can infect both Windows PE and Linux ELF executables. At the time of writing, this virus has not been seen in the field. While it does not look particularly likely that it will be, Lindose is, perhaps, an indicator of things to come. If executed from Windows or Linux, Lindose searches for and infects both PE and ELF executables. It is less unusual than you might think to find both types of executables on the same system. Some Linux versions can live on a DOS/Windows partition, and Windows emulators for Linux are available.

Lindose infects ELF files by prepending the viral code. The virus infects PE files by overwriting relocation data. If there is no relocation data section in the program, or it is too small to accommodate the code, infection does not take place.

W32/Magistr@mm

Magistr is a memory-resident Win32 email worm/virus hybrid that was found in the field in March 2001. It has a notably vicious payload: it may overwrite the contents of hard disks with a vulgar message, and may corrupt flash BIOS in much the same way as W95/CIH does. The virus is, unusually for one of its size, written in pure assembly language. Its size derives from its unusual complexity: a similar program in a high-level language would be quite a lot larger. Apart from the expected infection and dissemination routines, a double polymorphic engine, and its payload mechanism, Magistr incorporates a number of routines that make it harder to detect and remove.

The virus infects a file in the Windows directory and modifies the Registry and WIN.INI so that the code is activated every time Windows starts up. It makes no attempt to hand back control to the infected application. Magistr scans and infects PE files, including both .EXE and .SCR files. Although the .SCR extension is normally associated with Windows screensavers, .SCR files are essentially standard executables and are run as such by Windows—hence the frequent use of .SCR as an extension (sometimes following a harmless fake extension such as .JPG) for worms distributed as email attachments. The virus spreads both to local directories and to shared volumes. If it is able to find and write to the Windows directory on the remote machine, it infects the remote system by modifying WIN.INI so that an infective file will be executed at the next start-up.

The virus is not restricted to using Outlook to mail itself; it can also use Netscape Messenger. Infected messages may have no subject or message text, but may have a randomly constructed subject and message using text from .DOC and .TXT files found on the system. Magistr may also use an internal dictionary of words and phrases in several languages. The attachment is a file found and infected on the victim system, so the virus is difficult to block by gateway filtering unless standard filtering practice is to discard or quarantine attachments with an .EXE or .SCR filename extension. The virus avoids mailing recently infected victims from a newly infected system by maintaining an internal list of the last ten victims. The destructive payload triggers one month after infection. Before that, the virus may prevent the victim from accessing desktop icons by moving them away as the mouse cursor approaches. This less destructive payload may have been suggested by joke and Trojan programs with similar warheads, and may even be intended to suggest to the victim the presence of a joke rather than destructive malware.

After the destructive payload triggers, the virus displays another vulgar message. The virus code contains the following text:

```
ARF! ARF! I GOT YOU! v1rus: Judges Disemboweler. by: The Judges
Disemboweler. written in Malmo (Sweden)
```

Because the message attachment is a real file that has been infected, the filename is that of a legitimate program. This became important in a false alarm, or hoax, message that was prevalent while this book was in preparation. Many people were warning each other about the file SULFNBK.EXE. Since it was a real file, found in later versions of Windows, a number of people gave credence to the hoax, and thought that they had been infected when they found the file. Most of the files thus found, of course, were simply the original, uninfected, versions.

BadTrans

BadTrans is a Win32 email worm with backdoor functionality. It was found in the wild in April 2001.

The worm uses MAPI functions to access and respond to unread messages (as does ExploreZip). The Trojan component is a version of Hooker, a password-stealing Trojan, and mails system information to ld8dl1@mailandnews.com.

On infection, the worm copies itself to \Windows as INETD.EXE and drops the HKK32.EXE Trojan also to the Windows folder. The password stealer is executed, then moved to the system directory as KERN32.EXE, dropping a keystroke-logging DLL (Dynamic Link Library) at the same time. The worm modifies WIN.INI (Windows 9x) or the Registry (Windows NT/2000) so that it is run on start-up.

When infective mail is sent, the worm randomly selects the attachment filename from the following variants, some of them obviously influenced by previous worms:

- ▶ Card.pif
- ▶ docs.scr
- ▶ fun.pif
- ▶ hamster.ZIP.scr
- ▶ Humor.TXT.pif
- ▶ images.pif
- ▶ Me_nude.AVI.pif
- ▶ New_Napster_Site.DOC.scr
- ▶ news_doc.scr
- ▶ Pics.ZIP.scr
- ▶ README.TXT.pif
- ▶ s3msong.MP3.pif
- ▶ searchURL.scr
- ▶ SETUP.pif
- ▶ Sorry_about_yesterday.DOC.pif
- ▶ YOU_are_FAT!.TXT.pif

The subject field in worm messages is the same as in the original message, preceded by "Re:" so that it appears to be a response to that message. The message body also looks like a "reply" to the original, which the body quotes in full. At the end of the quote, there is a single line:

```
> Take a look to the attachment.
```

The worm attempts to avoid answering the same mail twice, or answering its own messages from other victim systems, by adding two spaces to the end of the subject field and not responding to any mail with such a subject line. This mechanism is unreliable, however, since mail servers are likely to discard trailing spaces. In this event, an infective message received on a machine already infected will generate a response from the local instance of the worm, thus initiating a potential loop. A loop can also be initiated if the worm is unable to mark answered messages, as can happen with certain mail clients. Such a loop can result in a mail server meltdown.

Summary

This chapter could have considered many other examples of malware. However, our purpose in Chapters 12 to 14 was not to provide a complete encyclopaedia of malware, interesting and instructive though such a project might be, but to look at innovative features and trends. This chapter, we hope, has better equipped you to understand the underlying technological and psychosocial mechanisms.

In accordance with our assertion that malicious software is as much a social problem as a technical issue, the next section will focus on social issues rather than technology.

Social Aspects

Virus Origin
and Distribution

On 8th March, 2001, CNN announced that "Tech firms disagree on source of Naked Wife". You can read the article at the following URL:

http://www.cnn.com/2001/TECH/internet/03/07/virus.brazil.02/index.html

Briefly, CNN reported from Sao Paulo that Brazilian and US anti-virus specialists disagreed about the origin of the Naked Wife virus. Like the MTX virus in the preceding autumn, this virus happened to spread across North America and Europe while a major security conference was winding down (in this case, EICAR). Symantec (in the US) reported that the virus appeared to have been written on Monday 5th March on a personal computer owned by a company called AGF Brasil Seguros, the Brazilian arm of a French insurance company, and registered to a user named M. H. Santos. However, a Brazilian representative of McAfee said it was certain the virus did not originate in Brazil, but from the United States. A representative of Symantec in Brazil reported that the virus "could have possibly originated in Brazil" but couldn't confirm the involvement of a specific company. AGF Brasil Seguros said in a press release that "The company found out about the incident through press reports and is investigating them now".

It would be nice to tell you where the virus really originated, but it seems to have come and gone, leaving the anti-virus establishment and the public equally confused. If you've read the case studies in the preceding chapters, you won't be surprised that anti-virus companies contradict each other, that victim companies are cagey about their susceptibility to virus infection and distribution, or even that national pride alters the onlooker's viewpoint. What will probably be most obvious, though, is that when it comes to virus dissemination, computer forensics seems to have regressed since Alan Solomon and Fridrik Skulason analysed Brain and its siblings. Such a regression is probably inevitable. Since then, more than 60,000 PC viruses have been added to the VX arsenal. Even at the time Whale was discovered, researchers still had time to play with its code. Nowadays, with multiple viruses appearing on a daily basis, no one has the time, and only anti-virus marketing departments really care about naming those possibly responsible.

A few years ago in alt.comp.virus, anti-virus people used to point to Christopher Pile as an example of the terrible things that can happen to an unmasked virus writer. Pile was convicted under the UK's Computer Misuse Act and sentenced to 18 months' imprisonment. After a while, pro-virus people started to jeer, "Isn't there anybody else?" They had a point. Virus writing is a comparatively low-risk occupation, in terms of risk of discovery. No other high-profile virus-related trial took place until the author of Melissa, David Smith, managed to attract the attention of law enforcement agencies with the seriously disruptive and damaging impact of his creation, and was obliging enough to leave the electronic equivalent of a footprint. In fact, the importance of the GUID match in the infective document may have been overrated: Smith seems to have been under police surveillance even before Richard M. Smith (one of the founders of Phar Lap Software, and no relation to David) suggested using GUID matches as a forensic tool. Somewhat inconsistently, Richard M. Smith has subsequently cultivated a reputation as a crusader against privacy abuse. Indeed, he had posted information about Microsoft's hard-coding of hardware information into Word documents some time previously as an illustration of privacy abuse. Moreover, we have found in testing that the presence of the GUID information in Word documents was somewhat inconsistent. Thus, the GUID match seems to have afforded some confirmatory evidence, but might not have stood up so well if it had been the *only* evidence.

Who Writes This Stuff?

There are certain widely known stereotypes. Every so often, it occurs to someone (often very publicly) that those with the most to gain from an ever-increasing virus glut are the vendors of anti-virus software.

> ### NOTE
> *We are not necessarily among the biggest fans of the anti-virus industry. However, we have to point out that if the industry, some representatives of whom are almost compulsively ethical, turned its attention to virus creation and dissemination, the quality of code in the average virus would improve drastically. Furthermore, who needs professionals when there are so many devoted amateurs in the game?*

In the anti-virus industry, quite a different stereotype reigns. The typical virus writer, we are told, is young, almost invariably male, and tends to "grow out" of the virus writing game as soon as he gets a real life. Anti-virus researchers tend to be dismissive of the technical abilities of virus writers, a viewpoint with which we have considerable sympathy. There exist virus writers who can write competent code; there are many more who do not.

The industry's lack of respect for the abilities of virus writers is well counterbalanced by the media, who continue to be fascinated by the mythical boy genius running rings around the incompetent anti-virus geeks and suits. Virus writers seem to like this cliché too, and many go to some lengths to encourage the stereotype, whether or not they believe in it. We suspect that a vociferous majority of wannabe virus writers subscribe to the stereotype uncritically. The more competent virus authors tend to monitor anti-virus technology as closely as anti-virus researchers watch malware, and are generally less vocal about their views.

In fact, the undirected nature of virus epidemiological patterns means that tracing an infection back to its original source is a little like tracing your ancestry back through the aeons. Unless you have a little help from the Book of Genesis, you're unlikely to get back as far as Adam and Eve.

Unsurprisingly, there is little quantitative research available. Sarah Gordon, who has written extensively in this area, has done some very capable qualitative and ethnographic research, and her papers on "The Generic Virus Writer" are required reading for anyone needing to understand this topic. Indeed, our heading for this subsection is blatantly stolen from the title of one of her papers. "The Generic Virus Writer" papers make heavy use of interviews with a handful of virus writers, and challenge all the stereotypes described in this subsection. Many of Gordon's papers are available at http://www.badguys.org/papers.htm, and we recommend them.

Social Engineering

Naive and uninformed curiosity has been causing problems since Alice swallowed the contents of a bottle labelled "Drink Me". Nowadays, we have hostile applets with a nice big button labelled "Click Me", and Trojan horse programs that promise interesting cultural experiences. There's an element of social engineering in every Trojan horse. Pornographic images are frequent carriers of viruses and Trojans in some newsgroups. It's often said (often by us) that viruses identifiable by subject headers such as "Good Times" or "Join The Crew" are sheer fantasy, but the ShareFun macro virus almost fit this description—it sent mail with the header "You MUST read this!" and an infected Word document as an attachment. Such a header is, of course, a nice piece of psychological manipulation later emulated by the Red Team virus. In this latter case, an infected program is sent as an attachment to a classic virus hoax alert. However, the attachment was claimed to be a cure for the hoax virus. Many times in the past we have seen hoaxers subvert actual anti-virus software by using it as a carrier for real viruses. Recent worms, except for the rarer self-launching species, have used increasingly sophisticated social engineering techniques to trick the victim into running malicious code.

We are not generally impressed by books that purport to be about viruses, but consist largely of some thin chapters on viruses padded with some chapters on topics that are included because the author thought he could write about them, not because of their relevance to virus management. However, the term *social engineering* is widely used in the context of worms and email viruses, yet poorly documented, and we make no apology for exploring the subject in more detail.

Social engineering attracts such a range of definitions, covering such a variety of activities (from password stealing, to scavenging through waste for useful information, to spreading malicious misinformation) as to be confusing at best. The question is, do accepted definitions of social engineering meet the needs of those tasked with addressing this class of threat? The term originally derives from the social sciences, but even there, it seems to have several shades of meaning.

While most managers and general users (and not a few security practitioners) are still at the "Social engineering? What's that?" stage, the bad guys are cheerfully making use of psychological manipulation to subvert systems, and the poachers turned gamekeepers are giving considerable attention to this type of threat in conferences, training courses, and articles. They are not restricting themselves to the password-stealing issue, and neither should we. We do not advocate uncritical acceptance of bad guys past and present as the ultimate authorities on what social engineering is and what we should do about it. Rather, we believe that people should recognize there *is* a problem needing to be addressed, with useful resource available.

In order to advance our understanding of the problem, it's necessary to examine some classic social engineering techniques and countermeasures. Formalizing the problem makes it easier to work towards effective solutions, making use of realistic, pragmatic policies. Effective implementation of such policies, however good they are in themselves, is not possible without a thoughtful user education programme and cooperation from management, and considerable attention should be paid to the need to apply constructive social engineering to both management and users.

When David Harley first started talking about spam, hoaxes (especially hoax virus alerts), and distribution of some real viruses and Trojan horses in the context of social engineering, his approach was seen as somewhat controversial. However, the method derived from the increasing recognition among some security practitioners of a growth in the range and frequency of threats based on psychological manipulation. Whether such threats qualify as social engineering might be an interesting topic for debate, but is not a major issue as far as this book is concerned. What *is* important here is that educational solutions to social engineering issues also equip computer users to make better and more appropriate use of their systems in terms of general security and safety.

The Tokyo Institute of Technology devotes considerable resources to social engineering as an area of academic study. A 1996 paper by Noboru Hidano defines the purpose of social engineering as resolving social problems, specifically by "social recognition and measurement method, integrated theory of Psychology,

Sociology and Economics, spatial and social design theory, and people's participation and decision forum".

A paper by J. J. Jacobs uses the definition "the discipline and quantitative constraints of engineering ... applied to social legislation". This describes rather well the basis of laws that criminalize racial discrimination, for instance. However, legislation has proved in practice a poor environment for the application of engineering principles. As Jacobs pointed out, "The one engineering principle most often violated is the obligation to recognize and acknowledge that the proposed process does not work, and to learn from that experience".

A paper by Ross Parish on the application of social engineering to the marketplace echoes this theme. "The problem of evaluating programmes is compounded by the tendency of governments and their agencies to attack any problem on a broad front using several policies so it is difficult to disentangle the effects of any one of them from those of the others".

In malware management, we are already moving from too little recognition that the social engineering problem exists, to a flurry of piecemeal attempts at resolution. Clearly, we need to learn from past mistakes in the wide world of social legislation, and attempt to deal with related problems in a holistic manner, rather than chipping away at one problem at a time. Otherwise, we will inevitably fall foul of Peter Rossi's brass law of evaluation: "the more social programmes that are designed to change individuals, the more likely net impact of the programme will be zero". (Peter Rossi, "The Iron Law of Evaluation and Other Metallic Rules". *Research in Social Problems & Public Policy,* Vol. 4 [1987], 3–20.)

Social Engineering Definitions

Here are a number of definitions of social engineering from a more vandal-oriented perspective:

► "The skillfull (sic) manipulation of a governed population by misinformation to produce a desired change". —Keytel

► "Deceptive practices that attempt to obtain information from people using social, business or technical discourse". —SRI International

► "A method of 'sounding' information which is not generally accessible. Often, perpetrators will pose as insiders by using pertinent keywords during conversations and thus receive information useful for other purposes". —Bundesamt für Sicherheit in der Informationstechnik IT Baseline Protection Manual

► **"social engineering** n. Term used among crackers and samurai (hackers for hire) for techniques that rely on weaknesses in wetware (people) rather than hardware or software". —*Jargon File*

► "The use of non-technical methods to obtain information". —Ira Winkler

► "Plain old con games". —Robert Slade

► "Psychological manipulation of an individual or set of individuals to produce a desired effect on their behaviour". —David Harley

Harley's formal writings on this subject have made much use of the last definition, since it allows consideration of a wider range of attacks: not just breaches of privacy (attempts to steal passwords through primarily nontechnical means), but attacks on the other cornerstones of IT security. It also has the advantage of allowing us to reclaim the term and the methodology for user management. Let us consider the classic tripod model of information security:

► **Confidentiality/Privacy**   Information should be available only to those who are entitled to it.

► **Integrity**   Information should be protected against accidental or deliberate but inappropriate modification.

► **Availability**   Information should be available to those who are entitled to it when they need it.

Social engineering is most often thought of as an attack on confidentiality (password stealing). However, psychological manipulation can also be used as an attack on integrity. Indirectly, password stealing can be a means of gaining unauthorized access so as to effect unauthorized modification. We are using terminology here borrowed from the UK Computer Misuse Act, but comparable terminology is used in legislation worldwide. Social engineering can also be used directly as a means of persuading/conning a mark (a victim or target) into introducing an inappropriate modification. Most of today's worm programmers gain access to a victim system by tricking the victim into executing malicious code. The program then modifies the host environment to facilitate the worm's dissemination.

However, social engineering can also be seen as an attack on availability: for instance, dissuading the victim from using a legitimate resource can be as effective a denial of service (DoS) attack as flooding the target organization's Internet gateway with bad packets. Social engineering as described in the previous paragraph is also a part of the process of flooding a mail server with worm-infested mail.

NOTE

We acknowledge here that we are making use of Simon Widlake's distinction between worms and viruses: "Viruses infect: worms infest". This admittedly simplistic distinction between infection and infestation is rather important. It's the difference between the transparency of viral infection and the worm writer's characteristic need to trick the victim into actively running malicious code. Like the Trojan victim, the worm victim must take the first step towards his or her own downfall. While we dislike any image that encourages the quasidiabolical fantasies of self-aggrandizing vandals with satanic nicknames, the worm really is rather like a vampire: it cannot enter uninvited.

Some virus writers attempt to maximize their creations' chances of survival by programming their viruses to replicate in a restrained manner (sparce infectors). Other viruses are far more overt, and attempt to spread as far and fast as possible. However, the fast infectors are not necessarily strongly reliant on social engineering to reproduce, except as they might need it to kick-start themselves into the field in the first place. We have lots of information on the file-to-file or system-to-system infection mechanisms used by all common viruses. We know quite a bit about the way in which certain individual viruses have been catapulted into the field, but these are a minority, though a significant one:

▶ Tequila's author probably did not intend the virus to spread. However, a friend acquired a copy and infected his father's master disks. Unfortunately, father was a shareware vendor. The Swiss police arrested two people in connection with the event.

▶ The AIDS Trojan diskette carried a Panamanian address that turned out to be the real thing. Well, an extortionist has to have a drop box for his ill-gotten gains. A man was arrested in the UK, but didn't stand trial because he was considered unfit to plead. (He was, however, tried and sentenced in absentia in Italy. The incident is discussed in much more detail in Part III.)

▶ WM/Concept was probably written at Microsoft. It found its way onto at least two official Microsoft CDs, among others. Harley recalls with some amusement finding it infecting on-disk documentation for a trial version of a content-scanning utility well known in anti-virus circles.

▶ Eugene Kaspersky wrote a fix for the original version of Concept in the form of a Word template. The author of WM/Nuclear uploaded a version of the same document infected with the new virus. The infected file was quickly removed, as we remember, but collectors had already taken copies that were soon freely available on VX sites, though Nuclear's spread was far more restricted than Concept's.

▶ Hare-infected files were posted to USENET on 26th and 29th June, 1996, and spread from there. The posts were forged, and the files posted were an assortment of alleged utilities. Warez web sites and bulletin boards (where pirate software is to be found) and newsgroups that allow the posting of binary files (pirated and legitimate, pornographic or otherwise) have often been the injection site for malicious software.

▶ The Black Baron (Christopher Pile) is reported to have uploaded infected files (including an anti-virus utility) to public resources.

▶ According to Phil Schmauder's less-than-competent book *Virus Proof: The Ultimate Guide to Protecting Your PC* (Prima Publishing, 2000), macro viruses are spread when "...the hacker would e-mail the document to multiple recipients to spread the virus". This is not, of course, normally the case. Most macro viruses are received from innocent victims, not evil hackers with long lists of potential victims. However, the author of Red Team did claim to be disseminating the virus using spamming techniques—that is, mass mailing to a precompiled list.

▶ More recently, the techniques used by the writer of Hybris include harvesting email addresses from sources other than the victim's address book (web cache files and postings to alt.comp.virus, for example) and modifying headers to make it harder to trace the sender's real address. We should emphasize that in the case of Hybris and other email worms, the sender is a victim of the virus, not the perpetrator. The main issue here is not that it makes it harder to trace the original source (though it does not help), but rather that it makes it harder to let the sender know that he or she has an infection, since they may not be readily identifiable.

We can trace other viruses back to their apparent source (the writer or distributor), but not usually by tracking them back along a trail of infections. In most cases, we don't know exactly where the virus made the jump from the author's PC to the wild, and very few virus writers have even pretended to consider the question. However, outside the realm of hoaxes, no one has yet figured out how to create malware that can self-replicate or trigger without someone, somewhere, executing a program. Of course, that person will often be the author, in the first instance, but not invariably; surprisingly often, virus writers are too nervous to test their creations on their own systems. If they do, and the replication or self-replication that takes place is confined to that system, it's of little interest to the rest of us. If the virus escapes accidentally, or through the malicious action of another, that's a different matter. In the case of a very small subset of malware that seems at present to consist almost entirely of self-launching worms, it may be enough for the author to run the program, whereupon the worm goes its own way, freed of its originator's control.

In most cases, some minimal social engineering is required to initially get the program into circulation. This might consist of sending to an individual, newsgroup, or mailing list a message which contains an infected attachment (or not, in the case of KAK or BubbleBoy, for instance, where the viral code is embedded into the message itself) and a deceptive subject line and/or message. In the case of a fast-burning mass mailer, someone deliberately injecting the infective program into the global bloodstream can easily fade into oblivion, one pseudo-victim among many real victims. Even where the malware is comparatively lightly distributed, it's not that difficult to stay invisible. Many victims still have a problem with the idea that viruses are received from people they know. It's difficult to prove that victims are not victims if no one has a search warrant and the will to suspect them. Short of a major shift in the general consciousness away from unthinking trust towards moderate paranoia, we see little likelihood of this changing. Potential victims may have learned not to trust love letters from unlikely sources, but they haven't always learned to extrapolate from the particular to the general. The Kournikova virus had less impact than LoveLetter. However, we are not sure that this was because the level of general awareness had risen in the interim, or even because anti-virus programs are performing better than they used to. We suspect that better networking between systems administrators and increased use of perimeter scanners and generic attachment blocking in corporate institutions also play a large (perhaps larger) part.

Password Stealers

Social engineering in virology is not limited to the initial promotion of worms. In fact, a whole subculture of password-stealing malware is disseminated by email. Mail apparently sent from a systems administrator, yet asking for a password, should triggera red light. We cannot think of one multi-user system worth having where the systems administrator *needs* your password, and many sites and providers tell you specifically that "You will *never* be asked for your password".

On AOL, password stealers are a way of life; there are hundreds, maybe thousands of them, although they have a pretty strong family resemblance. If your anti-virus software alerts on an object that begins APS.something, you're probably looking at a password stealer. Some are fairly specific; one quoted by Gordon obviously targets children, where the sender claims to be one of the child's father's colleagues: "Daddy needs to know the password...".

This Time It's Personal

Increasingly, you'll find social engineering via email tailored to you personally. Some spammers send email that includes your name in strategic places (such as the subject line) in the same way that mail-merging has allowed terrestrial junk mailers to lend a spurious personalization to their messages. Harley notes:

> I had a couple of instances where one genius mailed me with the subject line, "Hey, Harley, wazzup?" Nice piece of targeting, apart from the fact that it assumed:
>
> ► That I'm in the States
>
> ► That Harley is my first name
>
> ► That I'm about 14 years old
>
> ► That even a 14-year-old wouldn't be suspicious of someone claiming to be in my class but with an unfamiliar mail address
>
> ► That I'm the sort of k00l d00d who uses slang with digits substituted for letters
>
> ► That I'm sad enough to take my credit card to porn web sites. Or presumably my father's credit card...

This pseudo-personalization is not restricted to spammers, however. We note with disquiet that some virus/worm writers have proved quite inventive at creating a generic message that looks more personal than it is. For instance, they might foster the impression that the message is a continuation of correspondence that has already been exchanged between the owner of the infected system and the recipient of the infected mail. Using the same subject line as such correspondence is a simple and effective means of achieving this impression, and has been used successfully several times.

Trojan horses (programs that masquerade as one type of program while covertly doing something you wouldn't want them to do) can certainly be described as incorporating an element of social engineering. "Click here and see somebody naked, or download a cool screensaver, or run a cure for a mega-destructive virus or the Y2K bug".

You can say the same of viruses, though the view that a virus is a special case of Trojan has lost favour in recent years. However, it has become fashionable to refer to email viruses (or worms—that's a can of viruses we won't reopen for this chapter), such as ExploreZip, as using social engineering techniques to con the recipient into executing them. The writers of such viruses—or worms—are becoming more creative, using spamlike techniques to capture attention. ExploreZip, for instance, mails itself out in reply to email from the next potential target. Suppose that you mail me a message with the subject "Let me buy you lunch". (Please do!) If I happen to be infected with ExploreZip, you'll get a message back from my account (though it will be from the virus, not from me!) with the subject "re: Let me buy you lunch". The body of the message will say, "Hi [whatever your name is]! I received your email. I shall send you a reply ASAP. Until then, take a look at the attached zipped docs. Bye". So you look at the attachment, see a file called zipped_files.exe, and think, "OK, a self-extracting zip file". It isn't, though; it's just a plain old worm file. If you run it, your system becomes infected.

The social engineering element comes from the fact that the worm has been sent to you by someone you know—unless you regularly offer lunch to complete strangers—and is apparently a coherent response to mail you just sent to me. However, this misses an important point: you're far likelier to receive a virus from someone you know than from a complete stranger—unless you're in Human Resources and get lots of resumes. (Careless job-hunters seem to have become one of the major infection vectors in recent years.) Virus writers have been engaging in social engineering all along, but it took the worm epidemic to make social engineering a compulsory component of the infection process.

Why Do They Write This Stuff?

Most research into the motivation of computer vandals tends to focus on hackers and crackers rather than virus writers. So, although this section is somewhat speculative, we are including it because virus writers, hoax writers, and other mail abusers probably share some motivation. Indeed, much of the literature in the security field suggests a hierarchy in which the old-style hacker, the virtuoso tuner of systems, sits atop the tree. A branch or two down sits the cracker or computer vandal, who has successfully usurped the title of hacker in the media. Further down sits the social engineer, whose virtuosity is psychological rather than technical. Much further down comes the virus writer, whose skills are restricted to one specialized field. Lower still sits the writer of simple Trojan horses. Below him is the hoaxer, unable to construct a "real" threat. This model is seriously oversimplified, but offers one convincing aspect in its emphasis on the aspirations of each group member to be accepted as or at least mistaken for a member of the next higher group.

The following suggestions are drawn from observation and from personal exchanges of views with virus writers as well as with anti-virus researchers, rather than from any formal research. The first batch of observations is drawn from years spent on the alt.comp.virus newsgroup, and is based on an entry in the FAQ for that newsgroup. We must urge caution: you should not assume that people who claim to be ace virus writers in a public forum are real virus writers at all, as knowledgeable as they claim to be, or even "typical" of all or any particular group of virus writers. These suggestions are built on impressions, not on research data, indicating that virus writers:

▶ Don't understand, or prefer not to think about, the consequences for other people, or they simply don't care.

▶ Draw a false distinction between creating/publishing viruses and actually distributing them. Apparently, they consider it perfectly reasonable to make a virus available to anyone who cares to distribute it.

▶ Consider it to be the responsibility of someone else to protect other systems from their creations. They think it is the responsibility of the victim to defend himself or herself from encroaching malware, not the responsibility of the creators to keep their handiwork away from systems other than their own.

▶ Get a buzz, acknowledged or otherwise, from vandalism.

▶ Believe that they're fighting authority.

▶ Like "matching wits" with anti-virus vendors.

▶ Feel (or claim to feel) that they are keeping the anti-virus vendors in a job.

▶ Believe they are performing a service to the community by drawing attention to security weaknesses.

NOTE

This "ethical hacking" approach doesn't seem very convincing to us, in general. We already know that it is possible to write viruses in VBA or worms that can take advantage of the Windows Scripting Hoax. Where an innovative technique is used, is there an advantage to the victim in implementing it as a real virus and making it freely available or launching it directly into the wild?

Here are some suggestions about the motives of virus writers based on a wider range of information exchanges, speculations, and discussions. Again, this information is not based on research data.

▶ **Aggression** Sometimes this aggression arises out of resentment against being characterized as "nerdish". "I can't kick butt on the football field, so I'll trash some lamer's 'puter". Some virus writers seem to like the power to induce fear and panic, hence the satanic nicks (nicknames) and the naming of unexceptional viruses after terrifying filoviruses and other pathogens such as AIDS, cholera, Marburg, and Ebola.

▶ **Distant and anonymous damage**   Virus writers may like the thought of being capable of violating distant systems, even though they can't usually observe the process and potential damage it may cause.

▶ **Displacement**   Virus writers substitute a low-risk activity (where it is easy to be anonymous) for a high-risk physical activity.

▶ **Rebellion**   Getting up the noses of the suits and wrinklies may be a significant plus.

▶ **Deindividuation**   Their personal sense of identity is overwhelmed by the sense of belonging to an "alternative group". They thereby attenuate personal, individual guilt. Deindividuation may give the virus writer a real or perceived sense of anonymity, and diffuse his or her sense of responsibility.

▶ **Disinhibition**   The lifestyle of virus writers reduces socializing factors. They believe that their anonymity leads to reduced risk of detection. They also fail to recognize that transgression of *local* legislation is not the only risk.

▶ **Dehumanization**   They blame the victim. Melissa was the fault of "lazy administrators" and users who didn't check that Office's "macro-protection" wasn't disabled, rather than the fault of the virus author. Virus victims are at fault because they don't know enough to protect their systems/data. Characteristic terminology is suggestive: users, lamers, AV parasites, clueless newbies.

▶ **Hostile attributional bias against the potential victim**   For instance, virus authors express aggression against the victim because of perceived aggression from other interested parties, especially those identified as being formally anti-virus, such as vendors, researchers, and consultants. "My next virus has a destructive payload because Nick FitzGerald called me an onanist".

> ### NOTE
> *Nick FitzGerald is moderator of the VIRUS-L mailing list and comp.virus newsgroup, a former editor of Virus Bulletin, an independent consultant, and a researcher of considerable experience. He also has a reputation for outspokenness. The "Nick FitzGerald was mean to me" example is drawn from a real-life exchange on alt.comp.virus.*

▶ **Projection**   The virus writer attributes "unacceptable" traits to the victim or to other parties. "It's OK for me to trash other people's systems because

Microsoft does it all the time". "It isn't my responsibility if people spread my code maliciously".

▶ **Fascination with the mechanics of self-replicating and/or self-modifying code**

▶ **The "15 minutes of fame" syndrome**   Some virus writers get a kick out of seeing their virus on the WildList, or listed in a vendor's virus information database.

▶ **Ignorance**   Virus authors often fail to realize the potential seriousness of disseminating viral material, even as source code. This myopia is not restricted to virus writers: compare the wit and wisdom of Microsoft (re: VBS/BubbleBoy). "This is not a malicious virus, but will send itself to every address in every address book in Outlook". Real viruses such as Melissa and imaginary viruses such as Join the Crew have caused infinitely more damage simply by replicating than most viruses that intentionally trash files or data. After all, as the existence of hoaxes points out, a virus doesn't even have to exist to cause damage.

We have also suggested several times in this book that there is a convergence between virus writers and other mail abusers. Here we speculate on some associated phenomena.

Ascribing motivation for the distribution of hoaxes and chain letters has to be based, again, more on speculation than on formal research. We know generally why people pass them on, as discussed in the next chapter, but we don't usually know the originator of a full-blown hoax, and so are unable to examine his or her motivation. Nevertheless, people always ask the question, and we'll attempt a tentative answer. Possible motives for starting a chain letter may include the following, but there are many other possibilities, as well.

▶ **To see how far a letter will go**   One group of cancer victim hoaxes claims that the chain was started by a cancer victim wishing to "live forever" through the chain letter. A wish to break some sort of record may be the starting point of a hoax; indeed, at least one email chain letter includes a reference to *The Guinness Book of Records.*

▶ **To promote fraudulent or (less often) legitimate moneymaking schemes**   For example, pyramid, Ponzi, and multilevel marketing schemes.

▶ **To advertise and promote**   Sometimes this motivation gets confused with viral marketing, whereby mail or news posts include an explicit advertisement also called *banner advertising* in the industry. Often the advertiser is the provider of the service by which the mail/post is sent. However, the chain letter itself includes what might be regarded as an explicit or implicit advertising message.

▶ **Harassment of an individual or group (cf. revenge spam) by attempting to implicate them in the spreading of a chain letter**   For instance, several chain letters claim (untruthfully) that the American Cancer Society (ACS) will contribute a fixed sum to cancer research for each forwarded letter. Each recipient of the hoax may also be instructed to mail a copy of each forwarded message to the ACS.

▶ **To counter other chain letters**   Several instances of hoax virus alerts may have originated as an attempt to counter the spread of an existing chain letter by claiming that mail with a given subject field (title) contains a virus and shouldn't be opened. Good Times, one of the best-known virus hoaxes, may have started this way.

▶ **To maximize hoax distribution**   A hoaxer may seize upon the chain letter mechanism as a way of getting more mileage out of the hoax.

Motivations for hoax virus alerts likely have something in common with those that drive the writers of real viruses, probably more so than those motivations associated with other types of chain letters. Some of these motivations are listed here:

▶ **Sheer malice and mischief**

▶ **Perhaps sometimes the same motivations that lead people to create real viruses**   However, it's easier to write a hoax, because no programming skill and experience are required. Frequently, the only contribution of the creator is to change the title (subject header) of a previous hoax, to merge two or more hoaxes into the same chain letter, or to add circumstantial detail in the hope of increasing the hoax's credibility.

▶ **Anonymity**   This is one of the attractions to a vandal of real virus writing. However, it's even easier for the writer of a virus hoax to remain anonymous/pseudonymous, since there is no need to persuade someone to run viral code. The hoaxer can just play on the recipient's ignorance about real virus/anti-virus technology. If traced, the initiator can simply claim to have been forwarding someone else's warning, out of goodwill and ignorance.

▶ **Ignorance and misunderstanding**   A number of hoaxes are passed on out of ignorance and misunderstanding, but some actually owe their creation to such accidents. Many misleading stories originate from a misunderstanding of a problem and mistaken attribution of its cause to some form of malicious code.

▶ **Genuine efforts to address real problems or security breaches**   Some such attempts acquire layers of embellishment (deliberate or otherwise) that make it hard to pick out the underlying fragments of truth.

▶ **Humour**   Some of the hoaxes listed on hoax information web sites are actually spoofs, intended humourously rather than maliciously. Their descriptions are so incredible that the authors probably never expected anyone to take them seriously. Unfortunately, hoax writers seem to have had the last laugh. It appears to be impossible to write a spoof so far-fetched that no one will believe it, and ideas from hoax spoofs often turn up subsequently in malicious hoaxes.

Secondary Distribution

Why do people pass on real malware? The short answer is that they don't know it's malware. "Classic" viruses are generally as inconspicuous as their biological counterparts: you cannot usually tell that an object is infected without using (up-to-date) anti-virus software or some other means of close inspection. Even then, you can't be sure that you don't have something too novel or too stealthy to be detected yet. Binding the malicious code to a legitimate object (a Word document, for instance) gives the malicious code a free ride.

It's probably reasonable to assume that most people wouldn't pass on objects they knew to be infected except to people they assumed were competent to deal with them (such as anti-virus researchers, systems administrators, and so on).

Why do people pass on hoaxes and chain letters? Again, usually because they don't recognize hoaxes. They may also be fooled by unexpected content into failing to notice that a chain letter has the primary characteristic of all chain letters: a request to forward. Forwarding email is so easy that most people will do it even if they are not certain of the facts.

Some of the reasons that people pass on virus hoaxes include the following:

▶ **Altruism/social responsibility**   Like other forms of social engineering, virus hoaxes are objectionable precisely because they exploit their victim's desire to be helpful and responsible. It's easy to look back to a golden age when the Internet was less noisy and founded on cooperation and mutual support. While the Internet was once a more civil place, there have always been those who've exploited not only the ignorance and gullibility of newbies but their eagerness to learn and help others.

▶ **Caution**   "It sounds a bit odd, but I'd better pass it on anyway". Many, if not most, computer users are aware that they can't possibly know everything about technology, and are deferential to people who they believe must know something they don't.

▶ **Self-interest/reciprocity**   People pass on information in the hope of gaining brownie points or competitive advantage, or to bolster their image. Vendors are particularly prone to passing on virus alerts, genuine or otherwise, essentially as a public relations exercise. This is certainly likely to rebound if the alert is a hoax: why would you trust a vendor that doesn't check its sources? However, if a vendor passes on a warning that concerns a real threat but isn't particularly helpful, you will probably be equally concerned about the vendor's competence. Unfortunately, most customers are not knowledgeable enough to evaluate such information, so useless or hoax alerts continue to consume bandwidth.

▶ **Modelling behaviour**   Several pages of prior recipients increase the likelihood that the victim will pass the warning on. After all, 350 previous suckers can't be wrong. This is much less likely to happen in an environment where the accepted protocol is to clear alerts with someone qualified and authorized to pass them on.

Does Education Work?

There are two disparate schools of thought in corporate virus management as regards education. One is that user education is a key component of anti-virus strategy. The other is that education doesn't work, so the security manager is advised to assume that system users are incompetent and to tailor AV strategy accordingly.

In fact, both viewpoints contain an element of truth. In most organizations, education in security issues *doesn't* work—not because it's impossible for education ever to work, but because it isn't implemented properly. An overwhelming temptation is to treat training as an unpleasant but temporary malaise: grit your teeth, sign the cheque, and move on. Unfortunately, real life isn't like this. Education is an ongoing process, not a one-off event. Individuals come and go, and their replacements have to be trained. Strategy evolves as threats and countermeasures evolve, and policy and training requirements change accordingly. A few years ago, anti-virus measures were all about detecting known viruses. Now such measures are about transparency, real-time scanning, and heuristic analysis; meanwhile, other types of threats have become more prominent.

However, transparency doesn't fix everything, except in the most Draconian environments. Users are, perhaps, more sensible than we sometimes give them credit for. The real enemy is misinformation, and there's plenty of that on offer, from crackers, hoaxers, virus writers/distributors, poorly informed colleagues, managers, spouses, and even vendors and consultants. With so much low-grade information around, no wonder users get confused. Isn't there something to be said for increasing the amount of quality information available and giving the users a fair chance?

Perhaps the best approach to education is hybrid. Give (or at least offer) users the best training your resources allow. However, don't assume that all your users are fully trained, or that your training is so comprehensive and yet memorable that, once trained, your users will always act completely appropriately in all possible circumstances, and will never need any further training.

Virus management isn't rocket science. However, it is poorly understood, even by security professionals who may have considerable expertise in other areas, such as firewalls or cryptography. So what constitutes the best training?

It's not usually helpful to try to turn everyday users into virus experts, or indeed any kind of security experts. Most of them aren't interested (indeed, why should they be?) and don't have technical backgrounds in the areas that the field demands. Giving a clerk or a technophobic manager a detailed map of the physical and logical characteristics of a PC hard disk is likely to instill deep panic rather than a keen appreciation of the inner workings of boot-sector viruses. In any case, such a map isn't what they need. Broad guidelines as to what constitutes safe computing practice are more useful.

It is usually far more appropriate to implement a "minimum that you need to know" approach: how to avoid booting from a virus-infected diskette; how to ensure that an anti-virus package is properly installed, configured, and updated; and what to do if the existence of a virus-related problem is suspected. It is not a good idea to swamp customers with technical detail. It's helpful to make sure they know where to get further help and information if and when they need it. If software can be configured to remove viruses and update itself without the user's intervention, the user has less to remember and is less likely to make inappropriate modifications.

Of course, this minimalist approach doesn't work at all levels:

▶ Few small organizations can afford the services of a full-time virus expert, but there has to be someone, somewhere, who has sufficient expertise, authority, and resources to make executive decisions on anti-virus strategy. This does not necessarily have to be an individual within the organization. Like any other anti-virus functions, these decisions could be outsourced.

▶ Help Desk staff are often the first point of contact for a user with a problem. Staff need to know at least enough to give competent advice concerning the problems they are able to diagnose. In the case of a problem flagged by anti-virus software, initial identification is not an issue, though clarifying the real nature of the problem in the face of a misleading error message may be a major undertaking. Sometimes (and especially where it concerns a previously unknown virus), ascertaining that a problem *is* virus-related may not be trivial. Most importantly, first-line support staff need to know when to defer to someone with more expertise.

▶   Top management are not only users (and not necessarily computer-proficient), they also control the resources available for virus management, and therefore need a realistic appreciation of the risk and cost implications, as well as the same appreciation of good practice as everyone else.

Global Education

In the security community, it is an accepted axiom that security risks in general and viruses in particular are a social issue, rather than a technical problem, even if we tend to throw technical solutions at them. Perhaps corporate institutions in the third millennium will be more likely to consider social factors such as policy and education when attempting to reduce security risks. However, even if an organization takes education seriously, training addresses only part of the problem.

For many years, we have been irritated by reports that have confidently stated that 80 percent of security breaches are internal, and we note with amusement that the same agencies now state with equal confidence that the proportion is 50/50. Either way, addressing problems of individual and corporate responsibility within business environments clearly is not enough, even in an age when the workforces of most developed countries consist largely of people who are in some sense computer professionals. In other words, increasingly fewer jobs will not require some use of a computer at some point in the process. However, there is a huge gap between being computer-proficient enough for specific tasks, such as basic data entry and word processing, and being trained in general good practice that should be characteristic of a well-founded training or induction course, but often isn't. In fact, many computer science courses are no better thought out, judging from the number of requests we get from students who are required to work with and even write real viruses as an academic assignment.

Such measures as education at the workplace in the practice of safe hex, ethical guidelines, and codes of conduct, if implemented widely enough, may eventually trickle down to the general population, but that doesn't help us right now. Wannabe virus writers are not always of working age, or even old enough to be in further education. Even if they are exposed to suitable practical and ethical education, immaturity sometimes militates against their deriving as much benefit as might be hoped. The problem can be alleviated over time, but not necessarily resolved. The US Department of Justice and the Information Technology Association of America Foundation (ITAA) announced in September 2000 an interesting "CyberCitizen" partnership, intended to teach basic rules of appropriate online behaviour to teachers, parents, and children. You can find more details at http://www.usdoj.gov and www.cybercitizenship.org.

Summary

Many people in the security business prefer to think in terms of technical solutions to technical problems. Who cares why vandals vandalize, or why customers are so resistant to good security practice? We hope that we've convinced you that some understanding of psychosocial factors is necessary if we are to deal with problems that we regard as being essentially social rather than technical, vital though an understanding of the technical issues continues to be.

In Chapter 16, we will discuss the issues of hoaxes and other email abuses in considerably more detail, before moving on to discuss the practicalities of education and policy in Chapter 17.

CHAPTER 6

Metaviruses, Hoaxes, and Related Nuisances

T he phenomenon of virus warning hoaxes was first discussed in the earliest days of virus research. In February 1988, Jeffrey Mogul proposed the "metavirus", a fake virus warning that told people that their systems would become so badly infected that they should essentially destroy all their data and software, then start again from scratch. This concept has been variously called *metavirus, false alert, false alarm,* or *warning prank,* but is now generally referred to as a *virus hoax.*

The basic idea is that the originator describes a virus with horrible consequences, and one that is incredibly infective. *Incredible* is the operative word: most hoaxes describe viruses that not only don't exist, but couldn't exist. The message tries to whip up terror to the extent that people will pass along the message without thinking through the consequences. Of course, if people do forward warning messages to everyone they know, mail queues get clogged and an enormous amount of time is wasted as people try to run down details of the nonexistent virus.

These messages were extremely prevalent in the late 1990s, and were very difficult to correct. The Good Times hoax, three years after it was known to be false, was still being faxed between government offices and taken as a serious threat. While we see the original Good Times virus comparatively rarely this side of the millennium divide, the newbies (newcomers to the Internet) currently leaping into cyberspace keep finding the virus's derivatives and mailing hoax warnings to all their new-found friends on the Net. Hoax alerts are usually transmitted as a special case of chain letter, and other forms of nuisance are often considered in the context of exponentially exploding email.

Chain letters, hoaxes, and spam tie up network resources that may scarcely be able at the best of times to cope with the traffic they have to carry. Systems administrators, Help Desk staff, anti-virus vendors and experts, support engineers, and security managers have to deal not only with the manifestations of an overloaded system, but also with the work load resulting from anxious customers needing support and information. Everyday computer users must live with unnecessary and undeserved fear, anxiety, anger, and the feelings of helplessness, foolishness, and inadequacy when they discover that they've been victimized. In this chapter, we'll concentrate mostly on virus and other security alerts, and also consider phenomena such as spoofs and hype alerts. We will also, somewhat briefly, consider the relationship between these nuisances, real worms, and other forms of network abuse, especially spam (loosely definable as electronic junk mail). First, we need to consider some basic definitions.

Spam, Spam, Spam (Part 1)

Yes, the term "spam", used in reference to masses of unwanted email or newsgroup postings, does derive from SPAM the canned meat. There is an opinion that says the term was used because spam pretends to be information in the same way that SPAM pretends to be ... well, Hormel is a good sport about the neologistic appropriation of its tradename, so we won't belabour the point, beyond noting that the same speculation also makes an analogy between nonsense-content and fat-content.

The more commonly accepted derivation is that the term derives from a Monty Python sketch involving a restaurant where the menu items contain increasing amounts of SPAM, and the Viking clientele eventually drown out all conversation by singing about "SPAM, SPAM, SPAM, SPAM, SPAM, SPAM, SPAM, SPAM". Hormel even notes this in a page at http://www.spam.com/ci/ci_in.htm.

(And where did Monty Python get the idea for the sketch? Well, Hormel also claims the honour of the world's first commercial radio jingle. You can hear it, as a UNIX .au format audio file, by going to their "SPAM in Time" page for the 1930s at http://www.spam.com/it/it_30frame.htm. You'll have to enable JavaScript to click on the link for the jingle, but the danger is almost worth it. Listen for yourself and see if you think there is a similarity between the jingle and the Viking's song.)

Chain Letters

A simple definition of the chain letter can be found in *The Oxford Reference Dictionary*: "a letter of which the recipient is asked to make copies and send these to others, who will do the same". *Webster's* offers a slightly more complex definition: "a letter directing the recipient to send out multiple copies so that its circulation increases in a geometric progression as long as the instructions are carried out". These definitions offer a starting point for considering the *mechanism* that the chain letter author seeks to exploit. We tangentially consider motivational aspects in Chapter 18.

CIAC (Computer Incident Advisory Center), among others, describes the chain letter as having a tripartite structure: hook, threat, and request (see the CIAC web page at http://www.ciac.org/ciac). While it's not always straightforward to separate these elements, they do seem to be common to most chain letters, electronic or otherwise.

The hook is there to catch your interest. Some of the ways in which it might attempt to do this include:

▶ Appealing to greed (e.g., make money fast, win some reward).

▶ Exploiting fear of technology (e.g., virus hoaxes) and the consequences of its perversion or breakdown.

▶ Invoking sympathy (e.g., cancer victim hoaxes). In fact, it's striking how often chain mail and cancer coincide.

The threat is there to persuade you to keep the chain going. Traditional chain letters threaten bad luck, even death. Virus hoaxes threaten the destruction of systems—physical damage, file-trashing, leakage of confidential data. One chain letter threatens unlimited spam if you don't forward it. Others are more subtle: if you don't pass it on, you will miss out on the opportunity to make money or to earn the undying gratitude of your friends. Sometimes the threat is to others: if you don't forward the letter, a little boy's dying wish won't be honoured, or cancer will continue to flourish. The threat may be implicit or explicit.

Sometimes it pays to look for form, not content. Most chain letters share some common characteristics. The request expresses the core function of the chain letter, which is to have you replicate the letter by forwarding it to your friends and acquaintances. The term *replicate* is not used lightly. Chain letters, especially virus hoaxes, are often considered to be "meme viruses", or "viruses of the mind". Instead of using the infective code used by computer viruses, chain letters rely on suggesting to recipients that they pass the message on to others.

Virus hoaxes ask you to "help" others by disseminating "information". Cancer victim hoaxes, for example, ask you to generate money for medical research by forwarding identical messages. However, the common aim in each case is not to inform, to improve society, or even to sell a product: it is (purely or primarily) self-replicative.

Mailing list sales pyramid schemes, however, ask you to send money, add yourself to the list, and "sell on" the list, or sell another token product. A "successful" scheme might make large sums of money for the originator. It seems likely that the popularity of this type of scam is related to the perceived possibilities for high response when the scam is implemented as a chain letter.

Hoaxes

The Oxford Reference Dictionary defines hoax as "to deceive, especially by way of a joke…a humorous or mischievous deception". Other definitions incorporate the concepts of "mockery or mischief" and "deliberate trickery intended to gain an advantage…fraud, fraudulence, dupery, put-on".

There are certainly stories circulated for commercial advantage, the content of which is barely distinguishable from that of chain letter hoaxes. For instance, some Y2K and security consultants (including anti-virus vendors) occasionally have been noted for their use of scare-mongering and black propaganda to advance their own interests. The distinction between hype and hoax can be too fine to measure: some vendor advisories inflate minor threats to such a degree that the only definable difference between hype alerts and hoax alerts is the fact that the source (unlike the content) is verifiable. Such misinformation makes its own dishonourable contribution to the hoax problem, in that a few of the heuristics applicable to hoax detection also apply to advertising material, making it harder for the nontechnical reader to distinguish fact from fiction.

Urban Legends

Urban legends (ULs) are a little different from hoaxes, but sometimes listed in the same web sites. The alt.folklore.urban FAQ defines an urban legend as follows:

▶ It appears mysteriously and spreads spontaneously in varying forms.

▶ It contains elements of humour or horror (the horror often "punishes" someone who flouts society's conventions).

▶ It makes good storytelling.

▶ It does *not* have to be false, although most are; accordingly, ULs often have a basis in fact, but it's their life after-the-fact (particularly in reference to the second and third points) that gives them particular interest.

Clearly ULs resemble hoax chain letters in several respects, according to this definition. Both hoaxes and urban legends often derive from unknown originators and diverge into variant forms. Both have a hook (they make a good story). Both may contain threats; in the case of the urban legend, the threat is often implicit in the reinforcement of conventional behaviour. Both may have a basis in fact, an aspect that is often overlooked in discussions of hoax alerts. The biggest difference is that the urban legend doesn't carry an overt replicative function: the further dissemination of the story depends largely on its storytelling appeal rather than an explicit request.

Curiously, the urban legend also resembles the extreme hype alert. The projected horror is promoted as punishment for those who don't take due precautions and buy into the vendor's solution. It "makes good storytelling".

As Indra Sinha remarked in *The Cybergypsies: A True Tale of Lust, War, and Betrayal on the Electronic Frontier* (Viking, 1999), "The stories don't have to be plausible. These people will swallow any scare you throw at them. Wilder the better. They *want* these fucking nightmares to be true".

Chain Letters and Hoaxes

Not all chain letters are hoaxes, of course. Some are, in a sense, socially responsible, such as the many that are associated with an appeal (genuine or otherwise) for aid to charity. One well-known group of hoaxes claims that the reader will get money or goods from such companies as Disney, Microsoft, and Nike, if the individual forwards the mail. Another group of hoaxes claims that the reader will make money for cancer research by forwarding the mail he or she just received. Clearly, the precise nature of the hoax is generally secondary to the opportunities for mockery or simply spreading chain email.

However, it is arguable that forwarding any chain letter, regardless of its content, opens up enough opportunities for abuse to outweigh any possible advantages to this method of distribution. The only profit we can see for the use of a chain letter for a legitimate message is that the message might achieve a wider distribution than it would by any other means, except maybe spamming, which involves the use of potentially massive distribution lists. Even that benefit is questionable: what do you gain by creating a completely undirected bulk of email, as opposed to a semi-directed mass?

Hoaxes and Virus Alerts

Not all hoaxes are virus alerts. In fact, the programs described in most "virus" hoaxes would be better classified as Trojan horses, if they really existed at all, but our reservation here is less technical. Some hoaxes are concerned with computer security threats; some are concerned with other types of threats. For instance, cellular telephone networks seem to be a popular target for hoaxers. David Harley recalls one hoax that warned that new legislation would result in floods of London taxis becoming illegal for the purpose of carrying fare-paying passengers. The hoax message claimed that such cabs would be sold off to private individuals, who would buy them with the intention of duping potential robbery, rape, and murder victims. Apart from the fact that no such legislation existed, the idea of cities clogged with fake taxis piloted by psychopaths argues a grimmer view of humanity than even a Y2K consultant would feel able to get away with.

Obviously, not all virus alerts are hoaxes. However, anti-virus vendors and security organizations do not normally distribute security alerts as chain letters.

Even if you're on the mailing list of a reputable organization that sends out virus and other security alerts, it's not uncommon for spammers or hoaxers to subvert such lists. If you receive forwarded mail that appears to derive from an advisory or press release, there's always the possibility that even if the source is genuine and the original content accurate, the version passed on may have lost (or gained) something in translation.

One difference between a hoax alert and a "sincere" alert is not the accuracy of the content, but rather the distributive mechanism. Misleading alerts may arise from trusted sources, either because of a genuine error or as a marketing ploy. Hype alerts may diverge from the truth enough to be seriously misleading, such as the press releases by certain vendors that misuse the term "In the Wild" or that describe boot-sector viruses as "network viruses". However, it should be emphasized that while it is unusual for a security vendor to release information as a chain letter, this convention could be subverted at any time. Experience indicates that vendors may protest when other vendors go against accepted practice, but may eventually follow suit when they seem to be at a serious competitive disadvantage by not doing so. Furthermore, suppliers of third-party services (consultants, including those not directly in the security business) frequently pass on information (or misinformation) to clients and potential clients hoping to earn brownie points and competitive advantage.

NOTE

We are aware of an alert, the collaboration of a commercial security organization and a law enforcement agency, that included an appeal to forward, like a chain letter. Indeed, the alert incorporated so many of the stylistic features associated with chain letters and hoaxes that it was widely assumed to be an April Fool's joke. In fact, it dealt with a real if somewhat overstated threat. We include some heuristics for hoax-spotting later in this chapter, but there is clearly a danger in equating form with content. Just as a real threat can be presented in such a way that the alert's recipients mistake the message for a hoax, an advisory apparently sent from a reputable organization could perfectly represent the style of that organization but still be a hoax or spoof.

Nor are hoax alerts met only as chain letters. Misinformation, black propaganda, and hoax alerts may be spammed to newsgroups and mailing lists, or found on web sites. Furthermore, hoax victims often redistribute hoaxes initially received as email via other communication channels, such as newsgroups, static web sites, postal mail, and fax machines.

Misinformation under the Microscope

We have already mentioned Good Times, and will consider it in more detail in Part III. This section introduces one or two other examples of hoaxes and legends.

The terms *virus* and *damage* are so closely connected in the minds of most computer users that *virus* is now being used to describe any situation in which a computer is damaged, unavailable, or simply not doing what the user wants. The truth is that relatively few viral programs perform any overt damage to a system—as we've pointed out previously, a damaging payload increases the likelihood that the virus will be spotted. Viruses that destroy their target files or disks are, by definition, self-revealing and self-limiting.

All viral programs make some kind of change to the system, of course. Even those not designed to cause damage may do so, simply because the author did not anticipate a particular set of circumstances. Most "header" or "integrity" checks in self-checking programs were intended only to trap bad copies or disk sectors, but they will stop programs from operating if a viral infection occurs. In these days of increasingly complex and multitasking operating systems, a resident virus is almost certainly going to result in unforeseen interactions.

BIOS, CMOS, and Battery

We in the virus research community frequently get questions about the BIOS virus, CMOS virus, or Battery virus. These three are all variations on a similar theme and are regularly reported.

First of all, BIOS is ROM BIOS. The *RO* in ROM stands for *read only*. A virus, therefore, cannot infect the BIOS—at least, not yet. Flash EEPROMs are now almost universally used as "upgradeable" ROMs for the BIOS. These are vulnerable to virus damage, as is indicated by the comparative success of CIH in the field, but vulnerability is a different issue than infectability. A virus that flashed the BIOS with an infective upgrade would probably be ridiculously host-specific. It *is* possible to get "bad" ROMs, and it is even possible that a run of BIOS ROMs would be programmed so as to release a virus. It hasn't yet happened, though, and it is extremely unlikely since it would be easy to trace. On the other hand, we have already seen the occasional BIOS trojanized in the factory.

The CMOS can certainly be changed. Some viruses, for example, change the boot settings to make it more difficult for the victim to boot clean from a floppy known to be virus free. The CMOS table, however, is stored in a very small piece of memory. It is highly unlikely that a virus could fit into the leftover space, even though the theoretical limit of the "minimal" family is about 31 bytes. More importantly, in normal operation the contents of the CMOS are never actually "run", but are simply referenced as data by the operating system, so any such virus would remain forever latent.

There have been "joke" reports of electrical "metavirals" (e.g., "They cluster around the negative terminal, so if you cut off the negative post you should be safe ..."; "They transmit over the 'third prong', but occasionally leak over onto the others"). However, there are also a number of reports that changing the battery in a computer damages the CMOS. People probably report such damage because no matter how fast you change the battery, there is a loss of power during that time, and, therefore all the data is lost. Some computers, but by no means all, have a backup system that gives you about ten minutes in which to change the battery without loss of data.

The JPEG Hoax

The JPEG virus hoax is a straightforward prank, released on 1st April of both 1994 and 1995. The announcement was rather carefully crafted of technobabble that recalled, for example, the data overrun bug in sendmail that was used by the Internet Worm. The warning was said to be the result of research by Dr. Charles Forbin who is the main character in the science-fiction book *Colossus* and the movie *The Forbin Project*. (That story is along the usual line of computer-takes-over-the-world.)

> **NOTE**
>
> *Many hoax viruses are described in terms of confusing technobabble, such as the Good Times "nth-complexity infinite binary loop", or with the use of inappropriate terminology such as "a Trojan virus". Unfortunately, most users of computers and the Internet do not have the technical expertise to distinguish between geekspeak (writing in jargon, rather than English) and technobabble (technical-sounding gibberish).*

While the announcement of the JPEG virus was an obvious hoax for those who understood the references, the concept of a virus hidden in a graphics file is a complex one. In general, the data in a graphics file would never be executed as a program and therefore would be of no use as a viral vector. During 1994, however, a .GIF (Graphics Interchange Format) file caused much alarm when posted to a USENET newsgroup. The file header contained a very odd section of data, with suspicious text references. Those who examined it ultimately decided that the file was harmless, and that the file was possibly a hoax aimed at a select and suspicious few on the 'Net. You should not, however, interpret this example as meaning that JPEGs are always safe. Apart from the well-known double extension trick (virusfile.jpg.exe, for instance) to which we've alluded several times already, a file with a filename whose extension really is .JPG, or an icon suggesting an association with a graphics program, is not necessarily what it appears to be. A true JPEG is not an executable file, and cannot be run; it can only be displayed by a suitable graphics application. Such an application will not execute an .EXE masquerading as a .JPG, but a command shell may interpret the file as an executable irrespective of its extension.

The Budget Virus

Few outside of Canada will have heard of the Budget Virus of 1995. When the federal budget is introduced, the Canadian government sends copies to all major financial institutions, along with explanatory and background material. In February 1995, the government was to distribute this material on diskette rather than in printed form. The Finance Department apparently checked the master disk for viral infection with two different scanners (which were never publicly identified). The Department then sent the floppy to a duplication house, for a run of more than 5,000 copies. The duplicators, seemingly *after* the copies had been made, themselves checked the disk with ThunderByte Scan—and were warned of a "suspect virus" on the disk.

Neither the duplication house nor the Canadian agent for ThunderByte were reticent in talking to the press. Senior management in accounting firms pontificated on the disaster that could have overtaken the economic structure of the nation, with this virus paralysing all of its financial institutions.

The specific damage that the virus could have done was left unstated. In fact, the virus was only identified as being "unknown", the clear implication being that it was new and that only the advanced technology of one particular scanner was able to find it. Further, the virus never *has* been identified. Given that any moderately competent virus researcher can tell you a number of things about a virus within hours, and that ThunderByte was known for its aggressive heuristic scanning techniques (not, in itself a bad thing), it is hard to believe that there ever was any virus at all. The old saw, "It ain't that folks is so ignorant, it's that they know so much that ain't so", is true in the computer virus field as in no other. For a variety of reasons, hard facts about computer viral programs are extremely difficult to come by, while rumours, innuendo, and outright lies abound.

Rude Awakening

Could such a SNAFU arise again? Apparently so. As we were writing this chapter, a trade periodical focussing on computing networks featured an item concerning a spoofing attack on an IT company's weekly newsletter to its customers, into which the "rudest word in the English language" (that would probably be "consultant") had been inserted 47 times. The report mentions that the company was "...also concerned that the newsletter contained a virus, but this fear turned out to be unfounded". However, further on, the CEO is quoted as saying that "...he was annoyed the server was crashed, covering what the virus was or how it got in. It was probably a Trojan backdoor virus, but we are not sure how it got in".

In fact, the item in question took four columns to say "Our newsletter was defaced, and we don't know how, so it must have been a virus". Of such stuff are the myths of undetectable viruses wrought.

NOTE

The acronym SNAFU is normally rendered in polite society as Situation Normal: All Fouled Up.

Wheat and Chaff

You want to be informed of new viral programs. You also want to inform your friends and community. But you do *not* want to spread false alerts, which make people waste time and resources protecting against dangers that don't exist. Yet, false alerts can often, to the nonexpert, look like the real thing. How can you tell?

The quickest way to check a report is to know its source. However, as the saying goes, if you can tell good advice from bad advice, you don't need any. You won't be able to identify trustworthy people unless you also know how to spot a hoax. There are some items you should always find in a real alert. Detail is one: what objects are affected, how much the program files increase in size, what text or search strings are in the infectious portion, and how much memory is taken by resident programs. All valid alerts should state how an infected program or disk can be identified *before* it is run, not just the effects of the virus on the computer. The report should also state which scanners (and which specific versions) have been tested against the new virus and what they report. (Most of the time, the better scanners will report *something,* even with a new virus.) Finally, a valid alert will identify virus researchers and antiviral developers who have received samples. Often alerts, while not actually inaccurate, don't provide all of this information; opinion may vary on whether a useless alert is invalid.

One approach, of course, is to check reliable sources of information on current hoaxes and chain letters (the dictionary or encyclopaedia approach). Useful resources for "exact identification" of known hoaxes are considered in the "resources" section of this book, Chapter 8.

Hoax Identification Heuristics

There are many heuristics (rules of thumb) that can be used with some success to identify common types of hoaxes, even where the researcher is unfamiliar with the specific hoax, and some of these heuristics are listed here. Bear in mind, though, that a hoax could evade all these heuristics and still cause major damage. An alert might also have one or more of these characteristics and yet be genuine.

In some instances, we include samples from a few of the more common hoaxes.

Warn Everyone!

The "Warn Everyone" type of hoax is the one that led Jeffrey Mogul to coin the term *metavirus*. Hoaxers want to create a "virus of the mind" and have you, your friends, and their friends act as the infective agents. You are to pass the message along to everyone. As an act of charity, of course, you need to warn all your friends, relatives, coworkers, distant acquaintances, e-pen-pals, and random additions to your address book to make sure that they know about this horrid threat. Generally these hoaxes pass through multiple generations, and you have to page down past dozens of screens full of the email addresses of those who have received the warning. And passed it on. And on. And on. And on ... Table 16-1 describes some examples of "Warn Everyone" hoaxes.

Appeal to False Authority

Some hoaxes claim to quote highly convincing information sources such as real anti-virus vendors and their representatives, the Computer Emergency Response Team (CERT), and so on. These attributions are intended to add "credibility by association". In fact, organizations, publications, and individuals with lesser claims to relevant expertise have certainly issued or forwarded such warnings, sometimes to comic effect, all of which adds to the problem. Claiming to quote a known anti-virus vendor is another common indicator. It is not unknown for anti-virus companies to hype a virus in press releases or on their web sites, but they don't broadcast alerts to every mailing list on the Internet—at least, not yet.

Almost all warnings cite some kind of authority. Oddly, most cite an authority that has nothing to do with viruses. AOL doesn't know anything about viruses. IBM

Source	Example
California, aka Wobbler	"Please pass this message on to all your contacts and anyone who uses your e-mail facility....Forward this letter to as many people as you can".
Bug's Life	"Please pass it on to anyone you know who has access to the Internet...Please copy this information and e-mail it to everyone in your address book. We need to do all we can to block this virus...pass this information on to your friends, acquaintances and work colleagues".
Budweiser Frogs	"Please distribute this message...Please share it with everyone that might access the Internet. Once again, pass this along to EVERYONE in your address book so that this may be stopped".
It takes guts to say Jesus	"Pass this warning along to EVERYONE in your address book and please share it with all your online friends ASAP so that this threat may be stopped".
"It takes guts to say Jesus" variant	"Please practice cautionary measures and tell anyone that may have access to your computer. Forward this warning to everyone that might access the Internet".

Table 16-1   *Warn Everyone!*

releases its advisories through CERT. Microsoft may release an advisory from time to time, but generally to a limited group, and well after the fact. (Microsoft advisories are certainly worth tracking, but their primary importance lies in their links to patches for repairing security loopholes in Microsoft products.) The FCC (US Federal Communications Commission) has nothing to do with viruses, and announced at the time of the Good Times scare that it would never release virus-related information, but some prevalent hoaxes still claim to quote the commission. Recent virus hoaxes refer to Symantec or McAfee, but real warnings from these companies should come with references to details on the relevant web sites. Even then, you might want to check the actual URL before even thinking about passing on such a warning. Table 16-2 describes a few of these appeals to authority.

It Works on Everything

Some hoaxes do not specify the affected hardware, application, mail client, and so on. Again, this lack of specificity is not conclusive by itself. Anti-virus vendor advisories often assume that the entire computing world uses PCs, and frequently that a particular version of Windows is universally employed. On the other hand,

Source	Example
California, aka Wobbler	"IBM and AOL have announced that it is very powerful, more so than Melissa [The same hoax contained an internal contradiction]...information was announced yesterday morning from Microsoft".
Bug's Life	"This information came from Microsoft yesterday...AOL has confirmed how dangerous it [the virus] is".
Budweiser Frogs	"This information was announced yesterday morning from Microsoft".
It takes guts to say Jesus	"…was announced yesterday morning from IBM; AOL states that this is…".

Table 16-2   *Appeal to False Authority*

claims that a virus plays tricks with mail software or address books, without specifying the type of mail client affected, are a good indicator that such information is unreliable, hoax or not. Similarly, if a claim states that a virus will leak information such as passwords or credit card details, but fails to specify which passwords are targeted or where the virus looks for credit card details, these are all strong indications of an intent to frighten rather than to inform.

It Works Immediately

Some claims warn of immediate and devastating damage when the "infected" email is opened. Hoax viruses rarely seem content with popping a rude message up onto the screen, preferring instead to render targeted systems unusable. In fact, if the viruses described in many hoaxes really existed, they wouldn't be viruses at all: they'd be Trojan horses with no reliable means of replication, since they'd burn themselves out on every system they landed on and trashed. Such a virus wouldn't discriminate between opening the email and opening an attachment. However, it has never been entirely accurate to say that just reading mail is safe from any kind of malware (malicious software); as we've described elsewhere, some current viruses can take advantage of a loophole in unpatched versions of Outlook.

No Fix, No Fee

The claim states that no means of detection or recovery are known. This is a fairly dependable heuristic. In general, it's possible for an anti-virus vendor to supply detection for a newly discovered threat within hours, or less. There are exceptions, though. It took anti-virus vendors many months to properly implement detection and disinfection of macro viruses, and for a while, the best help a vendor could offer was guidance on disabling auto macros. It's not impossible that a completely new threat could arise that would require similarly extensive reengineering, but it happens rather rarely.

Recovery is a more complex matter, and depends on the tools available to the victim, the backup strategy that has been employed, and so forth. A virus warning that doesn't take these factors into account is automatically suspect. One that claims that no disinfectant is available yet, and that the virus is impossible to remove, is an instant candidate for the trashcan. Such a claim is flatly impossible. There is always a way to get rid of any virus: after all, it is only software, and, in the famous USENET phrase, "It's all just ones and zeros". Table 16-3 lists some typical claims.

Is It a Bird? Is It a Plane?

Claims that superhackers have somehow managed to write a program to do something that was previously thought to be impossible invite deep suspicion.

Anti-virus experts spend much time out of the public eye exchanging ideas about potential nightmare scenarios, and responsible individuals tend to keep such discussions away from the marketing department and journalists. Nonetheless, if a scenario is possible, someone has probably hypothesized it.

Furthermore, belief in the supernatural powers and intellects of hackerz and crackerz, virus writerz, and other 3l33t kewl d00dz (elite cool dudes) is not common among anti-virus experts, who will, if anything, go out of their way to belittle a vandal's abilities. Alerts that indicate such beliefs are more likely to originate from a member of one of those groups, a journalist, or a security expert talking about a field outside his or her own competence.

Source	Example
California, aka Wobbler	"...there is no remedy".
Death Ray	"'So how do you protect yourself? I wish I knew,' said Heriden. 'You either stop using the Internet or you take your chances until we can get a handle on this thing and get rid of it for good'".
Budweiser Frogs	"...a very dangerous virus and that there is NO remedy for it".

Table 16-3   *No Fix, No Fee*

Warnings about Phrases in Subject Lines

For some reason, almost all successful hoaxes refer to email viruses. And all of them warn you about reading messages with some specific phrase in the title. Now, of course, many email viruses and worms, such as Melissa, can be and have been identified by a specific phrase in the subject line. However, when virus hoaxes such as Good Times began to appear, this was not the case.

NOTE

This classic hoax characteristic has created a user-support problem all of its own. At first, we could simply point out that viruses are not normally associated with particular filenames, although a Trojan horse or virus dropper might be. Then we had to admit that certain filenames (and even Subject: fields) could be associated with particular malware, while continuing to make the point that anyone can change a Subject: field or filename. Then, if the customer was curious and persistent enough, we found ourselves having to explain that worms, viruses, and Trojans are not exactly the same thing, but that particular examples are sometimes assigned to different categories by different observers. Now we have to explain once more that even worms are not always identifiable by a characteristic mail subject or filename. Perhaps this explains why anti-virus researchers are such grumps.

Worm writers quickly figured out that the subject line was a giveaway, and thus learned to program changing subject lines. However, most hoaxes still warn you about the subject. Some hoaxes have suggested extreme polymorphism in the subject line, but these do not seem to have caught on very well. Perhaps even the most credulous victim needs to have *something* apparently useful to pass on by way of identification. If a virus is ever created that works on any platform, cannot be identified by any anti-virus software, and doesn't have standard subject, source, or message content, there will be no obvious way to identify it. What use, then, is the warning? Perhaps even some of those who can't distinguish a vaguely possible payload or infection mechanism from sheer fantasy balk at passing on a warning that observes that a threat exists without offering any way of dealing with that threat. Table 16-4 lists some characteristically subject-specific hoax warnings.

Utter Destruction

All hoaxes seem to threaten massive destruction, often including damage to hardware. Some viruses can, and will, erase data on your computer, sometimes to the extent of overwriting everything on the hard disk. But no known virus actually damages hardware, and most researchers believe it would be pointless to try and create such a beast, since any possible damage to hardware that can be accomplished with

Source	Example
California, aka Wobbler	"Very Urgent VIRUS(s) Warning with titles: 'Win a Holiday' OR 'California'".
PenPal Greetings	"If anyone receives mail entitled: PENPAL GREETINGS! please delete it WITHOUT reading it".
Budweiser Frogs	"Also do not open or even look at any mail that says 'RETURNED OR UNABLE TO DELIVER'".
It takes guts to say Jesus	"If you receive an E-mail titled, 'It Takes Guts to Say "Jesus"....'"

Table 16-4 *Warnings about Phrases in Subject Lines*

software would be very hardware-specific. In any case, most email viruses have been relatively tame in the damage department. Table 16-5 lists a few of these.

Don't Contact the Experts

In an apparent attempt to stop you from contacting somebody who just might be able to tell you that the claim is a load of rubbish, most hoaxes make the point that not many people know about the alleged problem yet. Look at the message time-stamp.

Source	Example
Death Ray	"But suffice it to say that the virus affects the computer's hardware, creating conditions that lead to dangerous short circuits and power surges. The end result? Explosions—powerful explosions. And millions of Internet users are at risk".
California, aka Wobbler	"It will eat all your information on the hard drive and also destroys Netscape Navigator and Microsoft Internet Explorer".
Bug's Life	"Once opened, you will lose EVERYTHING on your PC. Your hard disk will be completely destroyed".
Budweiser Frogs	"This virus will attach itself to your computer components and render them useless".
It takes guts to say Jesus	"It will erase everything on your hard drive [...] Some very sick individual has succeeded in using the reformat function from Norton Utilities causing it to completely erase all documents on the hard drive....It destroys Macintosh and IBM compatible computers".

Table 16-5 *Utter Destruction*

Source	Example
A.I.D.S. Hoax	"IT WILL ATTACH ITSELF INSIDE YOUR COMPUTER AND EAT AWAY AT YOUR MEMORY THIS MEMORY IS IRREPLACEABLE. THEN WHEN IT'S FINISHED WITH MEMORY IT INFECTS YOUR MOUSE OR POINTING DEVICE. THEN IT GOES TO YOUR KEY BOARD AND THE LETTERS YOU TYPE WILLNOT REGISTER ON SCREEN. BEFORE IT SELF TERMINATES IT EATS 5MB OF HARD DRIVE SPACE AND WILL DELETE ALL PROGRAMS ON IT AND IT CAN SHUT DOWN ANY 8 BIT TO 16 BIT SOUND CARDS RENDERING YOUR SPEAKERS USELESS.'"
The Bad Times spoof hoax alert	"It will rewrite your hard drive. Not only that, but it will scramble any disks that are even close to your computer. It will recalibrate your refrigerator's coolness setting so that all your ice cream melts and milk curdles. It will demagnetize the strips on all your credit cards, reprogram your ATM access code, screw up the tracking on your VCR, and use subspace field harmonics to scratch any CDs you try to play".

Table 16-5   *Utter Destruction* (continued)

If it is more than an hour or so old, then we guarantee that the experts do know about it. Those in the anti-virus industry, particularly, have mechanisms in place to deal with the rapid spread of email viruses, and they don't rely on "catch as catch can" email forwarding. Increasingly, virus-literate systems administrators are using formal or informal webs of communication to share information at a rate comparable to communications within the industry.

NOTE

What's the difference between a hoax telling you to ignore experts, and us telling you to ignore instant experts? We're trying to get you to study and think for yourself. A virus hoax is trying to stop you from thinking until you click the Send button.

Table 16-6 lists some examples of such claims.

SHOUTING!! AND EXCLAMATION MARKS!!!!

In an attempt to get you to see how VITALLY IMPORTANT! their message is, virus hoax writers often use a lot of words typed all in uppercase letters (known in

Source	Example
California, aka Wobbler	"Not many people seem to know about this yet so propagate it as fast as possible....This is a new, very malicious virus and again, not many people know about it".
Bug's Life	"As far as we know, the virus was circulated yesterday morning. It's a new virus, and extremely dangerous".
Budweiser Frogs	"IT JUST WENT INTO circulation yesterday, as far as we know....This is a new, very malicious virus and not many people know about it".
Win a Holiday	"This is a new, very malicious virus and not many people know about it".

Table 16-6   *Don't Contact the Experts*

email circles as "shouting"), and tend to use a lot of exclamation marks. Real virus warnings tend to be rather dull reading, and advisories are less likely to overstate the urgency of a virus problem than hoax alerts. Consistently poor spelling, grammar, syntax, and presentation are also suggestive of a hoax. Anti-virus companies often exaggerate threats for competitive advantage, but they generally employ literate professionals to write their press releases or advisories. Table 16-7 shows some examples of REALLY IMPORTANT hoaxes.

Don't Confuse Me with Facts

A major characteristic of virus hoax messages is their lack of technical detail. They include, instead, lots of details about false authorities, the (literally) incredible damage the virus can cause, "infinite binary loops" (technobabble: they don't exist), and the newness of the virus.

Source	Example
E-mail or Get a Virus	"IM SORRY GUYS>>I REALLY DONT BELIEVE IT BUT SENDING IT TO YALL JUST IN CASE!!!!!!!!!!!!"
California," aka "Wobbler	"Remember, DO NOT DOUBLE CLICK THE FILE!!!"
Win a Holiday	"If you receive an email titled 'WIN A HOLIDAY' DO NOT open it".
Bug's Life	"DO NOT OPEN IT UNDER ANY CIRCUMSTANCES"

Table 16-7   *SHOUTING!! AND EXCLAMATION MARKS!!!!*

As well as providing much more hard data, real virus warnings worth receiving will tell you:

- ▶ What the virus infects
- ▶ How it activates
- ▶ What actions to take to avoid activating it
- ▶ How to get rid of it
- ▶ Which antiviral programs will detect it
- ▶ Where on the Web to find more information or updates
- ▶ Which company or person is responsible for the report

These facts simply aren't present in virus hoaxes. For instance, a hoax that reads like a news item or press release may give no indication of its origin (or may give a false origin, of course).

Hoax alerts tend to be concerned with self-replication, not with pointers to additional help or information. They rarely include:

- ▶ Verifiable sources of further information. Fake URLs are common, as are URLs pointing to inappropriate/suspicious sites. It's easy to set up a web page without having to supply any sort of verification/authentication (free of charge: credit card details aren't necessary), so a genuine web page can contain very unreliable information. An alert that claims to originate with Symantec, but includes a pointer to a site on geocities.com, suggests foul play. Such a link doesn't prove that an alert is phony, though: plenty of well-meaning amateurs and guru wannabes offer security information, some of it genuinely useful.

- ▶ Full details of the source of the information or a contact within the originating organization for further clarification. There is unlikely to be a digital signature or any sort for authentication. However, the presence of a digital signature is not, in itself, proof of a bona fide alert. Many people don't bother or don't know how to check these.

General Chain Letter/Hoax Characteristics

Virus hoaxes are simply a special case of normal chain letters. Very few hoaxers, irrespective of the nature of their hoax, can resist asking you to pass on their creation and including a threat or inducement to reinforce the request: "Pass this on to everyone you know, otherwise something undesirable and virus-related will happen". However, hoax alerts prey on the altruistic and nonaltruistic impulses of their victims, and an explicit request to forward is not always necessary.

Some general characteristics of a hoax include the following:

▶ The mail is undated, or shows no realistic or verifiable date. "Yesterday" or "just issued by…" isn't good enough. However, a convincing date doesn't prove that the message is not a hoax.

▶ There is no "best by" or expiry date on warning. Nonetheless, the presence of such a date doesn't verify the alert, either.

▶ No identifiable organization (or individual within the organization) is quoted as the source of the information. (If an individual is cited, it is still worth checking whether he or she actually exists.)

Spam, Spam, Spam (Part 2)

What does spam have to do with hoaxes and viruses? At first sight, not very much. The fact is, though, that spammers, purveyors of scams and snake oil, hoaxers, and writers of real viruses are increasingly finding common ground, and the latter-day fascination with "viral marketing" is suggestive.

Spam is a term applied to a number of abuses involving the indiscriminate use of email or newsgroup postings to broadcast "information". Some purists still apply the term exclusively to newsgroup abuse, and classification of USENET spam includes the following:

▶ **EMP (excessive multiposting)**   Messages posted individually to each of many groups (classic spam)

▶ **ECP (excessive crossposting)**   One message crossposted to many groups (velveeta) (one message with many groups in Newsgroups header)

▶ **Commercial postings**

However, most people today probably think primarily of spam email, which includes the following classifications:

▶   **UCE (unsolicited commercial email)**   Junk mail

▶   **UBE (unsolicited bulk email)**   Sent in bulk to many addresses. Such mail may include a commercial message, but by no means necessarily.

Motivations

Sometimes people say, "If it's something you want to receive, the mail isn't spam". A more appropriate definition might be that if the message contains information the recipient has neither asked for nor has any interest in, the message can be considered spam. Spammers intend to advertise a product or a web site (especially sites where each hit earns money from a sponsor), but other motivations may also apply, including:

▶   **Advertising**

　　▶   Sex/porn sites

　　▶   Legitimate entertainment

　　▶   Consumer items

　　▶   Services

▶   **Aggression**   Violation of remote systems/system users

　　▶   Revenge

　　▶   Flooding systems with unwanted mail (denial of service, mailbombing)

　　▶   Implication of a disliked person (especially an antispammer) in spamming activities by using the mail server of the targeted person's web site as a relay, fraudulently inserting the person's details into the mail headers, using the person's details in the body of the message, and so on. With the increasing sophistication of worms such as Hybris, virus writers are using similar camouflage techniques to eliminate true information about the sender. The victim of revenge spam may subsequently become the victim of various sanctions applied by groups and individuals who oppose spamming and who believe the victim to be guilty of the practice.

▶   **Sheer mischief**   Some junk mail is clearly not expected to achieve anything other than to annoy or in some way distress the recipient.

▶ **Hoaxing**   Some junk mail is clearly deceptive.

▶ **Virus/Trojan distribution**   Virus/worm writers are increasingly making use of spamming techniques to inject real viruses into the wild.

▶ **Soapboxing**   Using spam as a means of disseminating a non-commercial message, rather than commercial advertising. From time to time, a virus will also carry a propaganda message.

▶ **Scamming**   A scam is an attempt to con the victim out of money, services, or information.

Scams always involve an element of deception and social engineering, and may be distributed as a chain letter, among other means (including spam). Here are some detection heuristics:

▶ Giveaway phrases such as "Make Money Surfing the Web". (Anything that offers you money is suspicious.) Material like this may be received as spam or as a chain letter.

▶ The absence of any real product. The scam sells on the franchise, so that there are no real customers either. Everyone is a brochure salesperson, for instance, selling to other brochure salespeople.

▶ Claims that "This isn't a pyramid scheme", or "This is genuine MLM", or "This is not illegal". Such claims are characteristic, and usually plainly untrue. We see this Big Lie technique elsewhere, too: spammers frequently claim "This is not spam!" A current favourite claim is "This is not a SPAM. You are receiving this because you are on a list of email addresses that I have purchased for marketing", begging the question of how this particular spammer defines "real" spam. Virus/worm writers employ similar measures to persuade the victim to open a dubious attachment, flying in the face of accepted definitions and common sense. We have seen instances where the writer has gone to considerable lengths to persuade the prospective victim to read a Word document with macros enabled.

▶ Testimonials from well-known people, major TV shows, and so on, intending to prove that the alleged opportunity is genuine, except that the quotes can't be verified.

▶ Anonymous, forged, or otherwise untraceable senders.

▶ The overuse of CAPITALS, $$$$$, and !!!!!. Like spammers and hoaxers, scammers often use shouting to try to reinforce their point.

▶ Limited subscriptions. It frequently amazes us that we are so well known that benefactors from far-flung corners of the globe favour us with the opportunity to join highly selective lists of investors. We seem to be particularly well known in Nigeria, which appears to be awash with government officials wanting to pay us millions for the use of our bank accounts. Curiously, they usually seem to like using Hotmail accounts.

▶ Of course, the lack of any real, substantial information about what you have to do to earn all that money.

Common Themes

For what it's worth, while we were writing this chapter, we compared notes on what type of spam we were seeing.

▶ Pyramid/MLM/work scams

▶ Chinese political messages (seemingly related to Falun Gong)

▶ "Find out anything about anyone" software or services

▶ Viagra (or herbal substitutes) sales

▶ Sex sites

▶ Begging letters

▶ Sales of spamming services

▶ Gambling-related advertisements (for lotteries, online casinos, and so on)

▶ Sales of web services

Spamology and Virology

Subject fields including characteristic phrases designed to suggest easy money, pirated software, marketing opportunities, or sex-related content/information are no longer restricted to spammers.

Some spammers long ago realized that many people discard mail with obvious headers, and some have progressed beyond headers to subject content intended to fool the recipient into thinking the mail contains a personal message. Others include the recipient's email address in the same way that mail-merged junk mail sometimes includes a name and address in the body of a form letter. Virus writers have learned from this: several recent viruses/worms use similar techniques to stop recipients from discarding the mail unseen and persuade them to open attachments or click on links to web sites. Examples of such Subject fields include "Urgent mail from *X*" (where *X* is a previous victim) and "The information you wanted".

If you get as far as reading the message, that's usually enough to identify a sales pitch. On occasion, though, it's not a commercial product or a pet idea you're being sold, but a scam. Nevertheless, the problem from a content-filtering perspective is automatic detection, rather than identification by reading.

From time to time, the attachment is malicious. Red Team demonstrates a convergence of three types of abuse. It consisted of a nuisance chain letter that spread information about a nonexistent virus. However, Red Team also included an attachment that claimed to be a fix for the virus. The attachment was in fact intended to install a real (not particularly interesting) virus. The author tried or threatened to disseminate the virus by using spamming techniques to launch the chain letter. The expressed intention was to increase the load on anti-virus support teams by blurring distinctions and making it harder to define a virus hoax "generically". In other words, the author attempted to define the general characteristics of the hoax so that AV support teams could detect a previously unseen hoax by matching it to those criteria. Red Team was something of a damp squib, but more recent threats have also served to blur the distinctions. It's now widely known, for instance, that VBScript viruses can, in certain environments, infect the target system as soon as the mail is opened—it isn't necessary to execute an attachment.

Thinking of each type of abuse totally in isolation from the others is not practical. As you can see from the following rough detection heuristics, detecting spam has some similarities with detecting email worms. Spam is generally easier to identify just by scanning the content by eye, and often just from the Subject: line. However, the heuristics that the recipient normally uses to identify junk mail on sight are not always easy to transcribe algorithmically. This makes automatic detection of spam a tougher nut to crack than some content-filtering vendors would like you to think.

Some detection heuristics for detecting spam include the following:

▶ An unreadable subject and/or sender. Strange characters here and in the body of the mail imply an exotic language that your mail program can't interpret properly. Some spam from exotic locations has readable headers, but the body is unreadable.

▶ Certain headers are characteristic. For example, friend@public.com in the From: field is an old favourite, just as hahaha@sexynet.fun is characteristic of some instances of the Hybris worm. Sender IDs composed of random strings of characters such as 65eK8y872@edssng.edssing.com.sg also suggest spam, as do obviously forged headers like your own account name being used in the Sender: field.

▶ Mail from web-based free-email services such as iname.com, Hotmail, Yahoo!, etc. may denote a "disposable account" used to send mass mail until the account is closed as a result of complaints. Service providers who offer short-term evaluation of their services may also be used for disposable accounts.

▶ Mail that isn't addressed to your actual address suggests a mailing list. If you're unfamiliar with a list name or sender, that may suggest spam, or even a subscription bomb. Sometimes a vandal will subscribe someone else to multiple high-volume mailing lists, so that unwanted mail swamps the victim's mailbox. Again, viruses and worms commonly piggyback mailing lists and address books to somewhat similar effect.

▶ Certain anomalies in the headers, such as impossible IP addresses and domain names, or time zone mismatches, indicates forged messages. Anti-spamming software sometimes uses such anomalies as a detection heuristic.

Metaviruses and User Management

If you're concerned about defending a whole department or organization, it's probably a good idea to incorporate measures against hoaxes, spam, and chain letters into an acceptable use policy for email and USENET.

First, you need to appoint a competent person to verify potential hoaxes by checking PGP (Pretty Good Privacy) signatures, personally contacting trusted individuals, and checking reliable sources and URLs. It makes sense for this person to have in-depth knowledge of computer software and hardware and, even better, real virus and anti-virus technology, so that he or she can evaluate a wide range of reported threats from experience. Alternatively, you could outsource this function to your anti-virus vendor or some other suitably qualified third party. At present, David Harley maintains an email hoax verification service at www.security-sceptic.org.uk.

In addition, you should have policies in place that discourage people from passing on virus alerts (even real ones), chain letters, and so on, and absolutely forbid them to do so without having them verified. Be as general as possible in your definitions: you don't want people who would recognize a Good Times clone easily to fall victim to a chain letter hoax, so discourage unverified mass mail-outs rather than just discouraging the passing on of virus alerts.

Consider passing a standard response form to individuals who've passed on a hoax, and asking them to pass the form on to anyone they've alerted. Reading the headers of their mail and copying the response to everyone who seems to have received it may have worked a few years ago when the phenomenon wasn't so widespread. But doing so now is probably not worth the bandwidth problems, redundancy, and general annoyance it's likely to create. We have included in Chapter 11 a specimen response form for general use by the support desk.

These policies could be integrated with other, more general recommendations for good practice:

- ▶ Considering the privacy of others
- ▶ Respecting intellectual property rights
- ▶ Discouraging transmission of unacceptable material (threats, pornography, defamation, etc.)
- ▶ Discouraging the waste of network resources
- ▶ Discouraging unacceptable commercial usage
- ▶ Encouraging good disk and file hygiene and protection

What Should I Tell My Customers?

Primarily, you should tell your customers to follow policy. We include some specimen policies later in this section that should be of help. You might want to consider a simple guidelines document suggesting that they don't forward any form of email flooding, which just wastes bandwidth and annoys recipients who've heard it all before. Examples of email flooding include the following:

- ▶ Chain letters
- ▶ Good luck letters
- ▶ "Words of wisdom"
- ▶ "Love chains"
- ▶ Stories about kids wanting to get in the record books
- ▶ Stories about Neimann Marcus cookies or other urban legends
- ▶ Messages that will somehow result in a donation to some charity if you forward them (although nobody can trace whether you've forwarded a message)

> **NOTE**
>
> The last comment may seem to contradict what you have heard about web bugs. Web bugs are links to web sites that can be embedded in HTML email. Fully web-enabled email clients will contact the web site, and hostile sites can obtain information about the people who read "bugged" email. However, this bugging applies only to people who are using such web-enabled email clients, and generally there is no way to determine whether email has been forwarded or to whom.

Ask yourself, is this information *useful* to anyone? If, by passing it on, you're simply shouting "fire" without offering any indication as to where the fire is, or where the fire extinguishers are, think again. At the very least, you should include a source of reliable further information. If you don't know whether your source is reliable, think again. As an example, how useful would it be to anyone if you forwarded a warning such as the following:

> There's a new strain of meningitis going around. There is no known cure, and everyone who comes into contact with a carrier catches the strain and dies. Please pass this warning to everyone you know.

Handling Spam, Chain Letters, and Hoax Alerts

What should you do if you get one of the following? Count your blessings. If we had only ever received one hoax alert, chain letter, or spam mail (or even just one copy of each example that comes our way), we'd be happy. You may or may not get as much as we do, but the nature of the phenomenon means that getting a little spam is as likely as being a bit pregnant. Here are some suggestions to pass on to your customer base.

Spam

If you get copious spam, don't take it personally. Most spammers don't know anything about you. In general, they're rather sad and stupid, more than sinister. Your mail address is harvested from a variety of sources (newsgroup postings, mailing lists, web sites, and so on) and added to lists that are sold to others—just like terrestrial junk mail. Spam that attempts to implicate you by name and/or mail address in its dissemination is sometimes called revenge spam, and that form of spam usually *is* personal: anti-spammers (those who try to isolate people and sites involved in sending spam) are frequent targets for this sort of unpleasantness.

Be sceptical. If the message says you're receiving the mail because you logged on to the sender's web site, or were subscribed to a mailing list, the sender is probably lying. If it includes an apology in case you were mailed "in error", that's in the hope of dissuading you from tracing the sender and lodging a complaint with his or her provider. If the sender says that you can opt out of the mailing list by following instructions, take it with a pinch of salt. You may well find that your reply bounces because the sender has given you a forged address or one that goes to an innocent third party. If instructions do work, or you're able to submit a removal request to a web site, you're likely to find that far from receiving less spam, you'll receive more—after all, you've just proved that you have a working email address. Spamming isn't like conventional marketing through junk mail: it's much cheaper (for the spammer, anyway), so the spammer has no incentive to target victims accurately. In fact, the recipient is not the only victim here; the other victim is the sad little person who thinks he or she is maximizing his or her sales potential by using a purchased mailing list.

NOTE

Does all this mean that you, as an administrator, have to put up with spammers? Of course not, but we don't recommend that you take any action that involves trying to attack people who seem to be spamming your customers, unless you intend to spend substantial time on research. There are people who spend most of their time dealing with this particular threat, keeping their filters tuned and hounding the perpetrators. There's a lot to learn if you want to hit the right targets, and spammers have a vested interest in misdirecting your anger. If you are not absolutely sure of the identity of the sender, limit your response to sending a copy of the message (with full headers) to the abuse account at the various sites the message has passed through.

Chain Letters

Whatever the content, if a letter contains a request to forward it, *don't* forward the letter without verifying. Better still, don't forward the message even if you have verified it with the originator and checked the facts. If the message is important enough to send on, it is important enough to write a new one to send to people that you know.

Hoaxes

Of course, if you know that an alert is a hoax, you won't forward it. If you have any doubt about an alert's veracity, don't forward the message unless you are sure of the facts. Better still, don't forward the message even if you have verified the alert except under very exceptional circumstances. Is there an echo in here? Well, we *did* say that a hoax is a special case of chain letter.

Summary

This has been a long chapter, considering how much of it focuses on viruses that don't actually exist. It has also dealt with a subject that the anti-virus vendor community has tended to neglect, some seeming to feel that they did their bit around 1997. Conference papers and articles were written, known hoaxes were listed on vendor web sites, and enquirers were referred to Rob Rosenberger's site at www.kumite.com/myths, more recently www.vmyths.com, as the last word on all things hoax-related. However, this is not enough. The encyclopaedias are not all- inclusive, the simple heuristics of yesteryear don't catch all the variations of hoax, semi-hoax and hype alert, and no web site has a monopoly on Truth. While Good Times derivatives continue to appear, more subtle blends of hoaxes and real viruses make the job of evaluation more difficult, and the convergence of types of mail abuse increases the complexity of the administrator's job. So, too, does the increased sophistication of tools, both at the perimeter and at the desktop, some of them spanning more than one type of network threat. While this sophistication increases the range of weapons in the administrator's arsenal, it also increases his or her learning curve. Next, we look at legal and quasi-legal issues, and consider how we can manage real and imagined viruses through policy.

CHAPTER 17

Legal and Quasilegal Imperatives

nformation protection is the protection of information assets, based on risk analysis and reduction of threats to data integrity, data confidentiality, and modification. We have already examined technological solutions to the virus problem (or partial solutions, more accurately) in detail, especially in Part II. Such solutions can display considerable sophistication and are, within limits, surprisingly successful. Yet the virus problem continues to grow, largely because technological solutions miss the social dimension.

As anti-virus professionals, systems administrators, security managers, and the like, we are not in a position to change human nature. We can, however, effect a significant degree of behaviour modification within the organizations for which we are responsible. Indeed, the virus/worm problem could be reduced to near-trivial proportions within corporate enterprises simply by enforcing appropriate caution through education and policy. However, policy does not exist in a vacuum; it reflects social mechanisms and constraints originating beyond the enterprise perimeter: social convention, criminal law, civil law, contractual obligations, and compliance with external codes, standards, and guidelines.

In this chapter, we concentrate largely on the expression of malware management through internal policies, but we also consider some of the external elements that inform them.

Malware and the Law

It isn't possible in this chapter to deal even briefly with all the legislation that *may* be relevant in one country, let alone all of them. In the United States, local statutes may be much more rigorous than federal legislation, which is generally more concerned with computers in which the government has an interest than it is with those belonging to individuals.

Legislation is usually more concerned with the spread of viruses than with their creation. In most countries, it is not an offence to write a virus. In a minority of countries, this is not the case. Legislation in many countries can be used against individuals implicated in the spread of viruses by infection of systems where the owner or user of the system is unaware that malicious software is present. Exchange of malware between individuals who are both aware of what it is they are transferring is less likely to attract proceedings under criminal law. In countries where the creation of a virus is an offence, distribution is almost invariably also an offence; characteristically, even the sharing of virus code between anti-virus researchers is, at least technically, also an offence in such states. Switzerland is a frequently cited example.

Once a virus is released into the wild, it is likely to cross national boundaries, making the writer and/or distributor potentially answerable for his or her actions under a foreign legal system, in a country that he or she may never have visited. You might think this particularly true of fast-burning email worms and viruses, and potentially, it is. However, none of the infrequent recent cases where someone has been identified has resulted to date in prosecution outside the individual's own country. In fact, the only instance we can bring to mind at present is the case of Dr. Popp and the AIDS Trojan, which we considered in a case study in Part III. (An Italian court tried and sentenced Popp in absentia.) However, the principle of trying a foreign national in a country where an offence was committed is firmly established in international law, and has been tested a number of times in areas of computer crime unconnected with virus distribution, as well as cases other than computer crime.

Where criminal action against virus writing and distribution is local in a particular case, the perpetrator may nevertheless be subject to civil action. In other words, even where no offence is thought to have been committed, the individual may still be sued for damage, if he or she is thought to be implicated in the distribution of a virus, for instance. Clearly, such offences can include the unwitting distribution of infected material such as macro-infected documents. A possible example would be proceedings launched for recovery of the costs of damage to data, systems, or reputation due to negligence and lack of "due diligence". This scenario has resulted in an upsurge of contracts that specify whether an individual or organization is responsible for management of virus-related risks. It is also possible that an alleged perpetrator could be acquitted of any criminal offence, but still face civil litigation.

Grounds for Criminal Proceedings

Some of the grounds on which virus writing or distribution may qualify for criminal proceedings include:

- ▶ **Unauthorized access**   You may be held to have obtained unauthorized access, even to a computer you've never seen, if you are responsible for distribution of a virus that infects that system. In some cases, users who may have been unknowing virus victims have been subjected to legal proceedings because of presumed involvement with the distribution. (This is quite different than a virus victim facing civil proceedings because of presumed neglect in letting the virus take hold on his or her system and thus spread to other victims.)

- ▶ **Unauthorized modification**   Modified objects might include an infected file, boot sector, or partition sector, as well as data.

▶ **Loss of data** This might include liability for accidental damage, as well as intentional disk or file trashing. In real life, modification of data might well be considered more serious than complete loss of data, especially where sound backup and recovery practices are in place. However, outright trashing of data is the consequence of viral action that people fear most, even though intentionally destructive viruses are in the minority. It is likely that this preoccupation would be reflected in judicial proceedings.

▶ **Incitement** This is the act of encouraging others to commit an illegal act. Acts that might be considered incitement where virus writing or distribution is considered illegal might include making virus-related material available, such as actual viruses, virus code, information on writing viruses, and virus engines.

▶ **Denial of service** This is usually considered an attack in its own right or a consequence of nonviral malware such as distributed denial of service (DDoS) agents. However, it has been argued that all viruses also entail a degree of denial of service. Some viruses might include a payload that results (intentionally or otherwise) in reduced or denied service of some sort (including, of course, access to data). Sometimes a virus or worm that doesn't have such a payload can nevertheless be the indirect cause of denial of service when anti-virus software notices an infection. Denial of service may also result when a virus conflicts with legitimate software when both are in memory at the same time. Viruses are not normally associated with these phenomena. However, *any* unauthorized virus steals memory, disk space, or clock cycles (processor time), and sometimes all three.

▶ **Endangerment of public safety** A Canadian statute, for example, indicates that anyone who willfully commits an act likely to constitute "mischief causing actual danger to life or to constitute mischief in relation to property or data", or who fails to do something that it is his or her duty to do, resulting in danger or mischief, is guilty of an offence.

▶ Application of any of the preceding with reference to computer systems or data in which the relevant government has an interest.

Of course, these grounds cannot all apply at all times in all countries. Some countries do not recognize the right of foreign states to influence or institute legal proceedings locally, for instance. It is, however, possible to break the law of another country, state, province, or other locality without ever leaving your own, and to face subsequent extradition.

Some pro-virus residents of the United States (at least as represented in USENET) seem to hold the unshakeable belief that US law is universal law, and have, in any case, limited knowledge of their own legal systems (as do most people who aren't in the legal profession). None of the authors of this book are lawyers (in fact, we aren't even US residents), so we don't offer the following observations from a position of uncontestable authority. If we were qualified to do so, this chapter would not be the place to tackle a subject of such complexity. However, the Internet crosses national and legal boundaries. An action you take (legally) in your state that affects me may be illegal where I live, in which case you may expose yourself to legal sanctions.

Local interpretation of the statutes may hold that it is legal to distribute viruses, for example, on a VX web site, as long as the people who are downloading the virus know what they are getting. Certainly virus writers and distributors tend to assume that this is the case, and lean heavily on this defence, except where they *intend* to slip a virus into circulation covertly. In most countries, exchanging viral material is legal if the recipient knows what he or she is getting (more or less), and if there's no suggestion of incitement to commit a crime. Specifically, sending a clearly labelled sample to a bona fide researcher or vendor is usually legal. Someone who intentionally infects a file and makes it available for downloading without any sort of warning is far likelier to face legal action. In the United Kingdom, for instance, the Computer Misuse Act specifically criminalizes unauthorized access and unauthorized modification. If a virus covertly accesses a major system, especially if it damages or otherwise modifies the system or its contents, the chance of prosecution rises dramatically, if the perpetrator can be traced. Note that any virus modifies the host environment in some way, and usually does so without the knowledge or permission of the owner of the computer.

The Computer Misuse Act

Section 1 of the UK's Computer Misuse Act is aimed at outlawing unauthorized access to programs or data if the offender knows at the time of access that he or she doesn't have the right to do so.

Section 2 expands this concept into the area of "ulterior intent": that is, it identifies instances where unauthorized access is gained with intent to commit or facilitate further offences (blackmail or extortion, for instance).

Section 3 deals with the offence of intentionally causing "an unauthorized modification of the contents of any computer".

Many countries have equivalent legislation dealing with the key concepts of unauthorized access and unauthorized modification. Legislation addressing criminal damage, incitement, and interference with telecommunications equipment may also be relevant. The Copyright, Designs & Patents Act deals with software piracy, and is often cited in anti-virus and information protection documentation in the UK, presumably because of the slightly dubious but time-honoured association of piracy with virus infection.

In general, unwitting dissemination of a virus by someone whose system is infected is not a crime, as there is no question of intent. The individual may, of course, have to carry the "burden of proof" that he or she was unaware of spreading a virus, and may be liable to civil proceedings for negligence.

Under certain circumstances, laws in other countries may be applicable in cyberspace, where there are no formal territorial boundaries. For instance, the Canadian Criminal Code stipulates that everyone, "while in a place outside Canada", who conspires to commit an offence in Canada "shall be deemed to have conspired in Canada to do that thing".

Some Broad Concepts

Writing a virus is not usually illegal, though it may contravene acceptable use policies, conditions of employment, and so on. Legal sanctions are likely to be directed towards those who may be guilty of more generalized misdemeanours, such as criminal mischief, which might include:

▶ Damaging or destroying property

▶ Rendering property dangerous or impairing its ability to function

▶ Obstructing the lawful use of property

The concept of criminal mischief is unlikely to be invoked where an individual is simply eliciting or exchanging information, as long as he or she has the right of access to that information.

The concept of incitement arises where one person suggests to others that an offence be committed. Legal proceedings may ensue even if the offence is not or could not actually be committed, if the offence is committed in a different way than that suggested, or if the individual who actually committed the offence is not charged. Ignorance of the fact that a suggested act would be illegal is not necessarily a defence, although intent to act criminally is certainly a significant factor.

No wonder legal advice is so expensive.

Data Protection Legislation

Data protection legislation such as the UK's Data Protection Act does not necessarily deal exclusively with electronic data (although protection of electronic data was added with the 1998 revision). Clearly, your mileage may vary if you don't happen to be in the UK. However, the UK legislation is based on the same European Directive to which other European Community members are obliged to conform, so there is a distinct family resemblance between laws enacted in member states. Meanwhile, most non-European states address similar problems, if not in exactly the same way. We will therefore concentrate on the Data Protection Act in particular and the European Directive in general as examples, rather than as being universally applicable. Nevertheless, well-founded data protection legislation will tend to address the same range of issues.

If data processing in general is to be defined as lawful, at least one of a number of conditions must be met:

▶ The subject must have consented to the processing.

▶ Processing must be necessary in order to enter into or execute a contract to which the party is subject.

▶ The data controller is under a legal obligation (other than contractual) entailing a need for the processing.

▶ The processing is necessary to protect the vital interests of the data subject— that is, necessary to save life.

▶ The processing is necessary for the administration of justice, for the exercise of tasks necessary for administrative functions within the public sector or by government, or for other functions necessary to the public interest.

▶ The processing is necessary for the data controller's legitimate interests without being detrimental to the legitimate interests of the data subject.

Lawful processing in terms of sensitive data is subject to additional conditions. The Act defines sensitive data as that relating to the following:

▶ The subject's racial or ethnic origin

▶ The subject's political opinions

▶ The subject's religious beliefs

▶ The subject's trade union membership or non-membership

- ▶ The subject's physical or mental health
- ▶ The subject's sexual life
- ▶ The subject's criminal record or being subject to criminal proceedings

One or more of the following conditions (which include some of the conditions already defined) must be met if processing of sensitive data is to take place:

- ▶ The subject has given explicit and informed consent to processing.
- ▶ The controller is legally bound to undertake processing.
- ▶ Processing is in the vital interests of the subject or of another (in an emergency situation).
- ▶ Processing is in pursuit of legitimate nonprofit activities.
- ▶ The data subject has deliberately made the data public.
- ▶ Processing is necessary in relation to legal rights. These might include obtaining legal advice; establishing, exercising, or defending legal rights; or conducting ongoing or prospective legal proceedings.
- ▶ Processing is necessary for the administration of justice, public sector interests, or the public interest.
- ▶ Processing is necessary for medical purposes, including (but not confined to) preventive medicine, medical diagnosis, medical research, provision of care and treatment, or the management of healthcare services. The inclusion of "medical research" is specific to the UK's Data Protection legislation; it does not appear in the European Directive.
- ▶ Processing is necessary to trace equality of opportunity between peoples of different racial or ethnic backgrounds.
- ▶ Other conditions apply, specifically listed by the secretary of state. The European Directive requires such conditions to be in the public interest and suitably safeguarded, but the UK Act does not include this requirement.

Data Protection Principles

Data protection legislation in the European Union (like the UK's Data Protection Act) is based on the European Data Protection Directive 95/46/EC. Member states may make additional conditions in the public interest, as long as they incorporate suitable safeguards. In general, there is far more harmonization of data-protection legislation between member states than is the case in other areas of security-related legislation. Other countries have similar concerns and legislation, although the expression of such legislation may be very different.

Data processing requires the consent of the data subject, except when:

▶ Processing is necessary to execute a contract to which the subject is party.

▶ Processing is necessary to fulfil a legal obligation.

▶ Processing is necessary in the vital interests of the data.

▶ Processing is necessary in the public interest or in the exercise of official authority.

▶ Processing is necessary if the data controller is to pursue legitimate interests (but only if those interests are compatible with the interests, rights, and freedoms of the subject).

Categories of data are defined which correspond to the categories earlier defined as sensitive and which can be processed only under strict conditions, including the explicit consent of the data subject.

The data subject has the right to know the identity of the data controller, and the purpose for which the data are collected (from the subject or from a third party). The data subject also has the right of reasonable access to the data and the right to have inaccurate data corrected or deleted. The subject has the right to object to and even block the processing of data, the right to object to their use for direct marketing, and the right not to be subject to a legally binding decision based solely on the automatic processing of data.

Personal data must be protected against accidental or unlawful destruction or loss, or unauthorized alteration, disclosure, or access. The level of security must be appropriate to the risk, the nature of the data, and the cost and availability of remedial technology.

The eight Principles that underpin the UK legislation are listed here, not because they carry any universal force of law, but because they encapsulate most of the issues that data protection legislation is intended to address. They do, however, reflect the content of the European Directive, which has implications for American companies with an interest in the transfer or processing of protected data by European partners or subsidiaries. For more information, try:

> http://www.privacy.org/ pi/intl_orgs/ec/eudp.html
> http://www.privacy.org/pi/intl_orgs/ec/ final_EU_Data_Protection.html

▶ **First Principle**   "Personal data shall be processed fairly & lawfully". (This principle can be roughly defined as satisfying Schedule 2 of the Act, and, in the case of sensitive data, Schedule 3.)

- ▶ **Second Principle**   "Personal data shall be obtained only for one or more specified and lawful purposes, and shall not be further processed in any manner incompatible with that purpose or those purposes".

- ▶ **Third Principle**   "[Data] shall be adequate, relevant, and not excessive in relation to their purpose".

- ▶ **Fourth Principle**   "[Data] shall be accurate and, where necessary, kept up to date".

- ▶ **Fifth Principle**   "[Data] shall not be kept for longer than is necessary..."

- ▶ **Sixth Principle**   "[Data] shall be processed with the rights of the data subject under this act".

- ▶ **Seventh Principle**   "Appropriate technical and organizational measures shall be taken against unauthorized or unlawful processing of personal data and against accidental loss or destruction of, or damage to, personal data".

- ▶ **Eighth Principle**   "[Protected data] shall not be transferred...outside the European Economic Area unless an adequate level of protection [is] assured by the target country or territory".

What do these principles have to do with malicious software? While they do not explicitly mention specific malware, the need to protect against malicious programming is woven into the very fabric of the Act. The third and fourth principles require by implication that the integrity of protected data should be preserved, and all malicious software is, potentially, a threat to integrity. The seventh principle is more specific, and could be held to cover not only threats to integrity, confidentiality, and availability, but also the very presence of malicious software on a system used for data processing within the terms of the Act. Unauthorized processing is characteristic of malicious software, if not altogether a defining characteristic, and often entails a risk to data (including personal data) on the affected system. It is difficult to see how a data processing system unprotected against malicious software could escape breaching this principle unless it could be proved that the system had *never* held "personal" data and never would.

BS7799 and Virus Controls

The British Standard Code of Practice for Information Security Management (BS7799) is commonly used as a basis for organizational security standards, and is now the foundation for the international standard. It was originally the result of a collaboration between the Department of Trade and Industry, the British Standards Institution, and a number of large corporate bodies in the United Kingdom, put together in an attempt to codify "best practice". However, many security professionals regarded the Code of Practice in general as an inadequate basis for a standard, and the section on virus control was particularly weak, displaying little evidence of input from anyone with significant expertise in virus management. The size of the sampled institutions apparently does not guarantee their understanding of the security field in general, nor virus management in particular. We have to wonder whether other documents based on "best practice" within industry are similarly founded on the unverified assumption that size is related to competence.

Protection from hostile software is a requirement for conformance with BS7799, so as to maintain the integrity of data and programs. While the 1995 version mentioned other forms of malware (malicious software), such as worms and Trojans, as requiring special measures "as appropriate", it singled out virus detection and prevention as a "key control", although the guidelines were somewhat vague. The standards emphasized the following points:

▶ The need to educate users in virus control, and in particular the need for a proactive virus strategy.

▶ The need to encourage general security awareness.

▶ The need to implement appropriate system access controls. The reader was directed to the section later in the Code of Practice dealing with system access control, but that section did not specifically cover virus management. This omission may have been unfortunate, since there is indeed a place for access control in virus management. For instance, access control can ensure that network users have, by default, no write access to executable files on servers or other workstations. Another example might be the use of access-control software to ensure that a workstation cannot access media until the media are scanned and authorized by a "sheepdip" or "gateway" machine using a known-virus scanner.

The Code of Practice required the establishment of a formal policy insisting that users comply with software licences, and that unauthorized software not be used. This linking of software piracy with virus infection is common in security writing, although some evidence suggests that the implication of software piracy in virus dissemination is generally overestimated. The later section to which the Code refers the reader is actually concerned with copyright issues. Certainly a security policy should address these issues, but we remain sceptical as to how relevant they are to a virus-management policy.

The use of reputable anti-virus software was required as follows:

▶ Known-virus detection must be performed with a regularly updated scanner. The Code of Practice specifies that this scanning be required either as a "precautionary measure" or routinely. Since experience indicates that users are not always very good at remembering to take precautionary scans, most institutions might prefer to emphasize the use of regular routine scans, using a scheduler or a call to an on-demand scanner from AUTOEXEC.BAT, for instance. Such a pattern of usage might reasonably be modified, however, where an on-access scanner is permanently active in a multitasking environment, or where unobtrusive background scanning can realistically be scheduled to run automatically.

▶ Change-detection or integrity-checking software is recommended "where appropriate". Over the years, the issue of scanners versus generic anti-virus software, of which change-detection software is one type, has generated some controversy. The press and other sources have often represented some products as making known-virus scanners redundant. Unfortunately, the issue is rather more complex than this. Under the present state of the technology, considering generic anti-virus software (which may be defined roughly as software that doesn't recognize known viruses as such, but which detects and in some cases repairs changes to executable code) as a replacement for known-virus scanning remains unsafe, though such software increasingly is being regarded as a useful supplement. However, the emphasis has shifted away from change detection on the desktop (although it certainly continues to play its part on servers) towards generic blocking of suspicious email and email attachments at the gateway.

▶ The Code suggests that the use of anti-virus software to repair damage to infected files be undertaken only with caution. Repairing infected files or boot sectors is probably safer with a utility that actually recognizes the virus concerned than by other means, but it's reasonable to recommend that caution be exercised. In some circumstances, an infection cannot safely be removed, or unusual factors may make repair particularly complicated. Even vendors that make a big marketing point of their ability to repair infected files will usually admit that, where possible, it is safer to replace an infected file. Fortunately, serious disinfection difficulties arise much more rarely with macro viruses, and some components of worm infestation can simply be removed, although repair to the Windows Registry is usually required.

▶ The Code recommends that critical systems be regularly examined for unauthorized changes to software, the presence of unexpected files, and the quality and integrity of data.

▶ Checking of diskettes of dubious provenance is mandatory. This recommendation seems a little quaint nowadays, given the decline in use of diskettes (and indeed zipdisks and other high-capacity removable media). We would still recommend, though, that this caution be extended to all removable media, including those that arrive shrinkwrapped containing new software, and that recycled media be subjected to particularly stringent precautions before reuse.

▶ The Code specifies that procedures and responsibilities be defined for reporting and recovery. Elsewhere the Code of Practice states general guidelines for the establishment of such procedures, but the Code implies that there should be a clear channel so that the best person or team to deal with an incident hears about it at the earliest possible moment. The establishment of virus-specific business continuity plans is required, with particular emphasis on backup and recovery. Given the existence of viruses such as Dark Avenger, Ripper, and some macro viruses that are intended to cause random damage over a period of time, this issue deserves more virus-specific attention. However, business continuity planning is another of the key controls emphasized in the Code of Practice.

The standard suggests that these issues are particularly important as regards network file servers. This is certainly so where a server is used as the primary backup storage medium for workstations; however, a properly configured server usually should not allow unprivileged users to modify shared applications.

The revised version of BS7799 places far less reliance on detailed specification of controls, and instead advocates the use of third-party consultancies to certify compliance with the standard. It consists primarily of a Code of Practice (Part 1) and Specification (Part 2). The "Specification for information security management systems" essentially defines an objective (to protect the integrity of software and information), the required controls (detection and prevention controls), and the need for implementation of "appropriate user awareness procedures". (Simple and straightforward: the difficulties of this virus-management business are really overrated, don't you think?)

The Code of Practice is only a little more detailed. The objective is, again, to protect integrity, so the Code does not formally address the implications of malware action that results in threats to availability, service provision, accountability, or confidentiality. This may tell us something about mindset, and certainly gives ample opportunity for an incompetent certification authority to miss some important points. While we can hardly say that no virus has ever damaged data or software, such damage constitutes a comparatively small percentage of the total cost of virus impact. Curiously, the 1999 revision emphasizes protecting PCs, implying workstations, rather than protecting servers.

The Code defines protection in terms of "security awareness, appropriate system access, and change management controls". Specific areas singled out include:

▶ Compliance with software licences and prohibition of unauthorized software.

▶ A formal policy addressing the risks associated with obtaining files and software from external networks.

▶ The installation and maintenance of anti-virus software. (Detection and repair are both mentioned.)

▶ Regular reviews of software and data content. (This appears to refer to the presence of unauthorized files or modifications to authorized files.)

▶ Scanning of material from untrusted sources before use.

▶ Scanning of mail attachments and downloaded files before use.

▶ Management procedures and responsibilities, including systems management, product training, incident reporting, and recovery.

▶ Business continuity issues (backup and recovery).

▶ Verification of information. Particular attention is paid to distinguishing between hoaxes and real viruses. The revision suggests that staff be made aware of the hoax problem and of what to do if one is received. (The problem of how to recognize a hoax in the first place doesn't seem to merit much attention.)

The 1999 revision is intended to supersede the 1995 original. However, we have considered the original in some detail, as it tends to influence the thinking of organizations implementing conformance, either directly or through the recommendations of consultants.

In fact, institutions using BS7799 as a basis for their security architecture may be obliged to trust the recommendations of third-party consultants, if they do not have in-house expertise. This is a particular disadvantage where virus issues are concerned, since many security consultants are not particularly well acquainted with the low-level operations of microcomputers. When it comes to viruses, which are mostly confined to PC-compatibles and (to a lesser extent) Macintoshes in the business and academic worlds, consultants may lack the technical knowledge to grasp some crucial elements of the virus problem. They may be reluctant to admit to imperfect understanding of virus issues, and even be genuinely unaware of any problem with their understanding.

ISO 9000

ISO 9000, also known as BS5750, is not concerned directly with viruses, or with security in general, but with quality management. However, quality assurance (QA) in an IT context can be a useful adjunct to (but not a substitute for) sound security management. The principles of quality management are much the same in anti-virus security as they are in widget manufacture:

► People have defined roles so that they know the jobs for which they are responsible. QA analysts love organization charts.

► Procedures are documented.

► Documentation is subject to a formal change-management procedure, which in turn is documented. We are reminded of the old programmer's dictionary joke: "Loop: see *Loop*".

► Sound procedures are supplemented by good record-keeping, to assist in troubleshooting and to demonstrate whether procedures are followed.

► Regular checks and audits are carried out.

► Problems are identified and corrected.

► Good communication is maintained.

You may wonder whether it's worth the price of this book to learn this, let alone the cost of consultancy and certification. And yes, this is essentially formal methodology applied to commonsense measures. Good management often is. Bad management tends to substitute formality for common sense, but this book is not the arena in which to ride that particular hobbyhorse.

Security Architecture

A security architecture based on policy presupposes an educational strategy: policies that no one knows about are useful only for scapegoating purposes. Underpinning the educational strategy, there should be a firm foundation of documentation. There is a classic model for a security architecture that works as well for anti-virus protection as for other areas of security, embracing policy, standards, and guidelines.

Security policy broadly defines:

► What is to be protected

► Why protection is necessary, and from what threats

► What the responsibilities of all concerned parties are

Standards are more detailed, but still independent of specific platforms and applications. They define platform-independent codes of practice, and the way that performance is measured.

Guidelines (or system policies) define how standards are implemented in specific environments. The corporate anti-virus policy could be contained within an overall security policy. This, in turn, could be quite specific about systems, and sample policies along these lines have been published. However, a modular approach makes maintenance easier, especially if the main source of policy information is Web-hosted.

A security policy should, in any case, make specific reference to anti-virus practice and policy. It's too easy to regard anti-virus security as an isolated desktop issue, rather than as a systems issue ranging across the whole enterprise and impinging upon other security issues. An anti-virus policy might consist of:

► A mission statement to define the objectives of the policy, and of the organization's anti-virus strategy. Essentially, the statement defines what you're protecting.

► An explanatory section in non-technical, non-legalistic terms, essentially to define what it is you're defending against. This section might include a historical summary of the virus problem, but should certainly include some sort of description of the problem. It is, of course, possible to address policy issues in terms of "Do this, don't do that, and the rest is up to you". However, if users or customers can see the logic behind the instructions they are given, they are likelier to remember those instructions. It therefore makes sense to make sure they have some idea of what viruses are, what they do, and what cost and damage implications they entail. These costs and damages may include corrupted data, leakage of information, and system damage, but may also include psychological factors such as damage to morale, reputation, and goodwill, as well as legal considerations such as breach of contract and breach of data-protection legislation.

► Cross-reference to other security policies is essential. An anti-virus policy should certainly refer to and be referenced by the overall corporate security policy. Other policy issues that may overlap include:

   ► Use of the Internet and the World Wide Web, email, IRC and other protocols and information channels

   ► Authorized and unsanctioned software

   ► Piracy and software licensing

   ► The use and reuse of electronic storage media

▶ Backup of servers and workstations

▶ Formulation of standard contracts with suppliers of software and hardware

Some organizations also have a separate information protection policy, dealing with ownership of data and systems. This policy leads naturally into the definition of responsibilities of individuals and groups, including top management, unit managers, contractors, visiting firefighters, and just about anyone else who ever goes near a computer.

The local anti-virus guru may be a security specialist, a systems administrator, an engineer, or even a power user with special skills, training, and interests. To whom is this guru responsible? What authority and resources does the guru have, and what responsibilities does he or she own? (These may include software evaluation, implementation, maintenance, testing, distribution, policy, and education.)

Systems management personnel have special privileges, and therefore should be required to meet high standards of caution and ethical behaviour. Systems managers often don't see virus management as being any of their concern. However, viruses should never be regarded as solely a desktop issue. A file server with no direct anti-virus protection is potentially a major source of infection, irrespective of whether it runs under a vulnerable operating system.

Unless top management accepts the ultimate responsibility for ensuring that suitable software and expertise are available and adequately resourced, implementation of anti-virus and other security measures is likely to be shelved every time that something more urgent or glamourous needs attention. Everyone likes a "quick win"; security, however, if it's done properly, needs constant care and feeding, and those who implement it get more complaints about its nuisance value than compliments on how well-protected everyone feels.

In large organizations, implementation will be much harder without the cooperation of middle management and department heads and their willingness to accept change and monitoring.

IT staff in general have to conform to good practice as regards electronic hygiene. Clue-challenged IT staff can be a significant source of infection. They may also, if suitably trained, be in a position to spot a virus-related problem onsite before the user has identified it or reported it to the Help Desk, and may thus play an important role in the early containment of a virus outbreak.

Help Desk staff need to be able to spot a possible virus problem as early as possible in the diagnostic process; otherwise, they may advise inappropriate action instead of referring the problem to someone with more expertise.

What is expected of those to whom Help Desk staff are responsible? General users and customers need to know what their own responsibilities are. (Remember that security responsibilities run in several directions: up towards the top of the management tree, down to every other member of the unit, across to other parts of the organization, and outward to peer organizations.)

▶ On many sites, up-to-date anti-virus software is available, but distribution isn't automated, so the users need to know when and where updates and upgrades are available. Remote users present particular difficulties regarding automated distribution, although these difficulties are by no means insurmountable.

▶ They need to know what anti-virus software to use on home machines and laptops.

▶ They may also need to know how to install and configure such software in the absence of an automated system. In general, people who use laptops or home machines for work purposes should be encouraged or even required to maintain a standard of protection on those machines as good as, or even better than, that maintained onsite.

▶ If it is decided to take a stern position against removing anti-virus software (to improve system performance, for instance), general users and customers have a particular need to know of this strict policy, since their systems are likely to be less open to central control.

▶ They need to know whom to contact in an emergency.

▶ They need to know about particular issues such as machines that are used by more than one person, loan pool machines, and "gateway" machines that are used to check incoming or outgoing storage media. General users and customers need some idea of legislative obligations, contractual obligations, codes of connection, and national and international standards with which they are required to conform.

▶ They will be required to conform to stated policies and conditions of employment.

▶ They may be required to take advantage of educational opportunities where they are offered.

▶ They will usually be required to use recommended software and update it as updates become necessary and available.

Policy documents should cross-reference to standards and guidelines, if applicable. Particularly vulnerable systems may require platform-specific measures. Remember, though, that a policy is worthless unless:

- ▶ It is supported by management.

- ▶ It is flexibly and knowledgeably implemented.

- ▶ It is supported by realistic protocols.

- ▶ People know where to look for advice if they need it, and they don't have to be virus experts or lawyers to understand it.

- ▶ It is cross-referenced to other security policies, such as:

  - ▶ The overall security policy

  - ▶ An information protection policy, dealing with data and system ownership issues, or, more brutally, the ownership of problems associated with data and systems

  - ▶ Restrictions on what software may be used, and from whence it may be sourced

  - ▶ An email usage policy

  - ▶ An Internet and Web usage policy

  - ▶ A media usage policy

  - ▶ Standard contracts with suppliers

  - ▶ Backup policy and issues (affecting both servers and workstations)

Guidelines entail specific implementation requirements. They attempt to answer a number of questions.

Who Is Responsible for Security in a Given Context?

How and when can Help Desk staff be contacted? And what are their responsibilities? This is standard policy fodder, but the answers are apt to be fuzzy or skipped altogether in the context of malware management, which is still often seen as a minor branch of systems security requiring no special attention.

What Systems Are Protected?

Workstations and LAN servers are obvious candidates for protection. Gateways for email, HTTP, ftp, IRC, and other vectors for malicious software certainly should not be neglected. Firewalls, viruswalls, and contentwalls may confer protection, but they require protection too. Intranet, extranet, and Internet servers also require protection.

What Are the Details of Implementation and Configuration?

In the context of virus management, these details may include product-specific recommendations, but will certainly address broad strategic issues such as the use of on-access scanning, on-demand scanning, and scheduled on-demand scanning.

Detailed protocols will deal with incident management and virus cleanup and recovery. They may also address other measures such as access control, hardware and software configuration, and change control. Special considerations may be addressed, such as shared access machines (machines that don't have a single "owner"), including machines (especially portable machines) from the loan pool and sheepdip machines for the testing of incoming and outgoing media.

Everyone, especially the person primarily responsible for virus management, needs to know where to go for further information. IT staff do not have diplomatic immunity. They should, in fact, be *exceptionally* scrupulous. Systems administrators do not emerge from the MCSE course fully expert in virus management. Virus management isn't rocket science, but it's a skill that requires some work—mostly research.

An engineer or user who thinks he or she must have a virus because a problem has arisen is grasping at straws. Most reported virus incidents turn out to be something else. Many anti-virus professionals spend more time dealing with hoaxes than with real viruses. A real but known virus is still rarely more than a nuisance, if dealt with properly. (Almost any of the fast-burner epidemics of recent years could have been avoided for the most part by purely generic filtering.) Panicking users cause more damage than most viruses.

One means of lessening the FUD (Fear, Uncertainty, Doubt) factor is to be proactive. If people know that information is generally made available to system and security administrators, and everyday users where appropriate, they will tend to react more calmly and rationally. Sometimes, though, it's difficult to decide when information should be shared, and with whom.

It may be helpful to concentrate on broad issues (types of virus, types of anti-virus technology, hoaxes) rather than individual threats, and to assume that most general users and customers have only minimal understanding of virus and anti-virus technology, and thus will not understand or retain detailed information very well. Much information gathered from mailing lists, newsgroups, and web sites can be seriously misleading, and not fit to present to an untrained audience without modification. Most administrators don't have time to translate jargon or black propaganda into information that most technically ill-equipped users would find particularly useful.

It may be useful to make a distinction between everyday users and IT personnel. Some of the latter may have a little formal training in the use of a particular vendor's AV software and/or some one-to-one or one-to-not-very-many training from the local guru. This is a mixed blessing: the larger the organization, the more necessary it is to spread the load. However, a little knowledge is *still* a dangerous thing.

There's an element of risk assessment here. How much do you share, and when? There are three main reasons for passing on virus or malware information to colleagues or users:

▶ Because there's a real danger of its being seen on your site. Risk assessment of this sort obviously demands serious expertise, or access to a vendor Help Desk you can trust to give you dependable information.

▶ Because there's a likelihood the customers will become aware of it, so you need to forestall a deluge of reports and questions.

▶ To stop customers from taking inappropriate action, perhaps through panic.

This may mean being prepared to field or forestall quite a few threats that don't exist (such as "It takes guts to say 'Jesus'!") as well as those that do.

In real life, you may have to react to an enquiry rather than be proactive, simply because of time pressures. If an enquiry arises, assume that there's a likelihood that someone else will come up with the same question, and alert other IT personnel (especially the Help Desk). This particularly pays off with regard to hoax alerts and chain letters, which seem to cluster as a result of their rapid spread through an organization.

Policy Outlines

The following suggested policy outlines cannot be expected to work for everyone, nor in all respects, but they highlight and to some extent address most of the core issues. It is generally advisable to include a more-or-less standard clause in most or all such policies, specifying that conformance to each policy entails respecting all apposite legal and other obligations. These might include (but won't necessarily be restricted to) the following:

▶ Data protection legislation

▶ Copyright legislation

▶ Legislation concerned with unauthorized access or modification to systems or data, such as the UK's Computer Misuse Act

▶ Trade secrets legislation

▶ Antidiscrimination legislation

▶ Obscenity and pornography legislation

It might be appropriate to state explicitly that conformance is required to all internal policies and other policies, standards, and agreements by which the company is bound.

Acceptable Use of Facilities and Resources

Use of email, as well as access to the World Wide Web and other networks and internetworks, using resources owned by the employer is intended for work purposes only. Use for purposes not strictly work-related may be acceptable in moderation, subject to management approval, depending on the organization, if such use doesn't interfere with work. Many organizations might consider it appropriate to proscribe the use of company resources for administration of private business ventures.

All use of company resources is required to be in accordance with all binding legal and other obligations, as specified at the beginning of the "Data Protection Legislation" section.

Acceptable Use of Email

Who owns email? To some extent, the answer is a matter of local corporate culture and applicable (local) case law. However, it's important to make the position clear to employees (including contractors and volunteer workers). On many sites, any email is considered liable for inspection by duly authorized personnel, and some governments have gone out of their way to push responsibility for email content onto employers and Internet service providers (ISPs). Is personal email allowed? Is that also open to inspection and monitoring? If not, how do authorized personnel differentiate between private and corporate mail? Under what circumstances might mail be examined? Much as we'd love to answer these questions for you, they must be resolved within the organization.

However, email users must be aware that while they're using a company account, what they write may be seen to represent the views and policies of the company. They are therefore required to conform to appropriate standards of accuracy, courtesy, decency, and ethical behaviour, and to refrain from the dissemination of inappropriate mail content.

Inappropriate behaviour may make not only the employee but also the company open to accusations of libel/defamation, harassment/discrimination, copyright infringement, or invasion of privacy. Employees are therefore required to act in accordance with the company's published policies as well as all applicable legislation and other binding agreements.

The company is not able or obliged to maintain constant surveillance of employees' use of its facilities, especially where such use is not specifically authorized. However, users of these facilities have no automatic right to privacy in that mail may be monitored or checked from time to time to maintain network support, enforce security, and so on, as well as to ensure that the mail meets prescribed standards.

Email should not be used as if it were a secure communications channel for the transmission of sensitive information or messages. Use of encryption, though, should be in accordance with the company's policy.

Is legitimate use of email defined anywhere? Are there guidelines as to what uses (if any) of company mail resources for private purposes are legitimate? Are particular activities explicitly proscribed? For instance, using company time and resources to run a private business or subscribing to (or even running) particular types of mailing list might be proscribed.

What about corporate identity? Any mail from a company account is, to some extent, seen by the outside world as in some way representing that company. Are there restrictions on the use of the company name in signatures? Should there be a compulsory disclaimer? Are there restrictions on who can speak for the company in particular contexts? Even if nothing is actually formally specified, you can bet that someone is going to trip an alarm sooner or later. Codification may lessen the chances of undue unpleasantness and, if incidents do occur, at least make managing the situation more practical.

Acceptable standards of conversational intercourse should be maintained. It's easy to write and send email, and sometimes doing so is more convenient than using the phone. Email is potentially less prone to "circular whisper" syndrome than the telephone, and it doesn't rely on the other person's being immediately available. People who are comfortable with email probably favour it over the telephone, but think of it as more like making a phone call than writing a memo. However, this isn't the case. Email isn't necessarily temporary or transient. Once mail is sent, there are likely to be two copies immediately: one in the sender's "sent" mailbox, and one in the recipient's inbox. Within 24 hours, both copies may have started to replicate across backup media.

Here are some of the issues, not necessarily virus-related, that you might want to address in an email policy:

▶ **Flamebait**   Mailing lists, newsgroups, and so on have widely differing codes of conduct. Contravening them may provoke responses, from a few sharp words to mailbombing or worse. Offensive action of the latter variety is not only unpleasant as an expression of direct anger, but may have indirect consequences as a result of the inconvenience, or worse, to the organization. If one of your users does cross someone's anger threshold, response in kind may result in escalation of unpleasantness, and that user may compromise his organization as well as himself. An angry response on the part of a member of your organization might also have unpleasant repercussions.

▶ **Speaking about the company**   Corporations may not have formal guidelines about what users can say to third parties, but such problems will arise in any event, especially if the corporation doesn't encourage its employees to treat email in much the same way as other channels of communication, such as "real" mail. Obviously, security professionals and other professional paranoids learn to be ultra-careful about discussing their sites. And this is all before we even start to consider leakage of *real* confidential data.

▶ **Anonymization**   This is one way to avoid compromising the employer when using a work account, as long as the anonymization isn't circumvented. However, it invites assumptions and curiosity.

▶ **Libel**   Obviously, users aren't likely to flout local libel legislation deliberately. However, they may not realize the implications of an unguarded statement in what they think of as a transient medium, and one in which both they as individuals and the company they are seen to represent are at risk.

▶ **Unauthorized quoting of private email**   Old hands usually consider such quoting to be bad form, but many people don't think twice about it. Some who are aware of the ethical and legal implications may be perfectly prepared to ignore them, of course.

▶ **Quoting other sources of information**   This may include cutting and pasting, or even scanning. Such quoting makes it very easy to be careless about taking material from email, newsgroups, the Web, and so on, and running the risk of infringing copyrights or intellectual property rights, with or without due attribution.

You might also consider it appropriate to include restrictions on the use of Web-hosted mail services such as Yahoo! and Hotmail. Messages sent through these channels bypass mail-server-hosted safeguards, and may entail risks, viral and nonviral, for companies that are not equipped to handle them technologically.

Anti-Chain Mail Policy

Chain email is a drain on network resources, system resources, and support staff. Any mail that includes a request to forward the message widely and inappropriately should be regarded with suspicion. On no account should staff originate chain mail, however good the cause it promotes.

No email that warns of viruses, Trojan horses, or other security threats should be forwarded without checking and authorization from IT or its authorized representatives, however trustworthy you consider the source to be.

Some virus hoaxes may have been intended to discourage the forwarding of previously existing chain letters. This is *not* an acceptable reason for passing on a hoax or chain letter.

Passing on warnings about hoax warnings can be a difficult area. Some individuals and groups have recommended passing information about hoaxes and chain letters back to other recipients of a hoax or chain letter, and in some extreme instances, to everyone in the recipient's address book. The following are suggested guidelines for handling hoaxes:

▶ Passing on an anti-hoax message to everyone you know with instructions to do the same is simply a chain letter, and not acceptable.

▶ Passing back an anti-hoax message to other hoax recipients may be justifiable if there are only a few of them and you're reasonably sure they'll benefit from the information. Even then, you should pass it back only if you're sure that the information is accurate and you have the approval of the IT manager or security manager.

▶ Not all hoaxes are security-related. Do not pass on, for instance, appeals to forward mail to raise money or support for a worthy cause. Even if it isn't a hoax, it may not be considered an appropriate use of company resources.

Anti-Spam Policy

A good policy will state that employees should not use company resources for the dissemination of spam, junk mail, and other forms of inappropriate mass email for private or work-related purposes. Mailing lists specifically set up for dissemination of particular types of work-related information might be excepted from this stricture, as long as the type of information broadcast is appropriate. However, spamming a mailing list is never considered appropriate.

Employees should be expected to react appropriately to spam by reporting and forwarding it to IT, and by following ITs advice on what further action to take, if any. Direct response to spam (including making angry replies or following instructions to unsubscribe) can cause more damage than ignoring or simply deleting the offending messages. (Damage in this context includes lack of cooperation on the part of administrators who might otherwise be helpful; increased volume of spam; the spammer having ascertained that he or she has a "live one"; and mail-bombing, revenge spam, and such from a malevolent spammer.)

Spoofing, or forging mail headers in the headers of email or news postings, should be forbidden—either as a means of disguising the source of mass email (there is no legitimate business reason for doing this) or as a means of making it more difficult for spammers to add your address to their lists of targets. The latter may be a legitimate aim, but spoofing is likely to ease the spoofer's burden of junk mail at the expense of other legitimate users. If you need to take some action along these lines, discuss the means of doing so with the appropriate IT staff or the Help Desk. Measures such as sending virus-infected mail or Trojan horses to suspected spammers are totally unacceptable, and a clear breach of organizational security policies.

Acceptable Use of the World Wide Web and USENET

Access to the World Wide Web, IRC, USENET, and other Internet information resources is allowable as far as is necessary to achieve work-related goals. Access to sites or newsgroups that aren't directly work-related may be permitted, subject to management approval, as long as this doesn't interfere with work. Access to resources that customarily carry pornographic material, pirated software, and other illegitimate information and resources, such as malicious software (binaries or source code), including viruses, Trojan horses, backdoor/Remote Access Tools (RATs), password-cracking tools, and hacking tools, is unwise.

Anti-Virus Policy

It may seem strange that an explicit anti-virus policy should be a relatively small item in a whole sheaf of policies, given that this is a book on malware management, not security in general. However, it isn't practical to look at malware management as if it were totally isolated from the rest of the security management function. There are points specific to an anti-virus policy, and points that belong in other policies that have a bearing on virus management too. For instance, there are restrictions on software download that are also relevant to acceptable use of the World Wide Web. Some of the anti-virus-specific points are the following:

► All possibly virus-related problems should be reported to the call centre (the service desk or Help Desk) and logged to the appropriately qualified person or team.

► Help Desk and second-line support staff attempting to handle such incidents should advise qualified personnel at the earliest possible point in the incident management process, to determine whether expert intervention is necessary.

► Sharing of games, joke programs, screensavers, and other nonessential executable files (programs) is not recommended. Any attachment is potentially hostile, irrespective of what the source claims it to be or the trustworthiness of the source. Viruses and worms are characteristically distributed furthest, unwittingly, by innocent third parties, rather than directly by malware authors. A joke program that generates an anti-virus alert may be as serious a nuisance as most viruses.

► On no account should users disable or reduce the functionality of security software without authorization from the security officer. Nor should a user install software that increases the risk of infection from outside. This clause, in a policy, could be used to deter the use of unauthorized products from warez sites (as an anti-malware measure but also as an anti-piracy measure), the use of communications software, such as instant messaging packages, that might have security implications, and the download of "grey hat" software such as RATs. Of course, such concerns could be addressed specifically here or in other policies, such as the draft policy on Web use that precedes this section.

► Customers should be expected to use the corporate standard anti-virus package. Systems running unsupported packages would be regarded as unprotected, as this practice can have general support implications as well as the obvious security implications.

► Unqualified staff (including IT personnel) should not pass on warnings of viruses, Trojan horses, and other security breaches without authorization. Rather, they should consult qualified IT staff who can distribute the information if it is considered appropriate. You can't expect to teach a non-technical user everything that he or she needs to know to identify any hoax, known or unknown, on sight. Rather than providing a complete analysis and history of the hoax phenomenon, mention common names, core heuristics (if a message asks you to forward it, it may well be a hoax), and basic concepts (keep your anti-virus software up to date, and be careful with programs and documents from unexpected sources).

Summary

There are three main approaches to virus management: technological, political, and educational. The technological solution is to rely on carefully configured and maintained anti-virus (or anti-malware) software. The political solution is to make sensible virus management a matter of policy. To do so demonstrates the management and corporate will to address the problem, and to conform to legal and quasilegal imperatives. It allocates specific responsibilities and duties to management, administrators, and end users. However, the political solution needs to be backed up by both the technological and educational solutions. To do otherwise is the equivalent of removing fire alarms and fire extinguishers and discontinuing fire drills because the building has been declared a no-smoking area.

In Chapter 18, we discuss the issues of responsibility and education. Who is responsible for fire drills, for putting up the non-smoking signs, and for dealing with the problem of those who are unable to give up tobacco? How do we reduce the ability of staff to use lack of guidance as an excuse for "incorrect" behaviour?

18

Responsibility, Morality, and Ethics

IN THIS CHAPTER:

As security professionals, we are not required to conform to a global code of ethics, and that lack of direction mirrors uncertainties throughout the computer-using population as to how to apply ethical standards to computing. To quote the Professional Code of Ethics for Psychologists of the German Association of Professional Psychologists, "A code of ethics is always an expression of a profession's self-comprehension". We are aware, of course, that a number of organizations inside and outside the security domain do attempt to codify standards of professional conduct, of which the codes of conduct of the Association for Computing Machinery (ACM) and British Computing Society (BCS) are probably the most widely quoted, but these cannot be described as universal. Nor, of course, are they specific to the anti-virus field, if we can sidestep the question of whether virus management can be described as a profession.

For decades, computer professionals have attempted to come to terms with the fact that computerization has ethical implications. More recently, though, many more people have become in some sense "computer professionals", and computers have become a recreational commonplace. Thus, as computers have ceased to be restricted to use as a professional tool, ethical issues are no longer confined to the workplace. However, attempts to "regulate" ethical development tends to be restricted to professional or quasiprofessional contexts, including specialist AV lists and organizations such as AVIEN, EICAR, the WildList Organization, and the confidential mailing lists used to facilitate the exchange of information and samples between research professionals.

The Two-Minute Guide to Ethics

Ethics has been defined elsewhere by Urs Gattiker as the "higher order" that belongs to every culture or nationality, representing the goals and ideals of that culture while depicting rules that guide personal behaviour in daily life. Morality provides "an impartial constraint on the pursuit of individual interests". A code of conduct might be described as a series of prescriptive (normative) statements or guidelines about what constitutes appropriate professional behaviour in a particular organizational context.

Morality is interpersonal and involves issues of harm, rights, or justice. Proponents of cognitive development theory suggest that, by studying conventional or consensus-based obligation, we might be better able to determine how morals affect people's behaviour. Whereas ethics focus on overall values and beliefs (such as those based on religion and culture), morals provide the individual with the necessary constraints to function in a society and with other Internet or computer users. Morals can be grouped into three domains, discussed later in this chapter (also see Table 18-1).

	Moral Domain	**Conventional Knowledge Domain**	**Personal Morality Domain**
Means of Learning	Direct observation of harm or injustice caused by a transgression	Exposure to group consensus	Exposure to others (e.g., during childhood) and past behaviours' outcomes
Material Conditions	Objective obligations: justice, harm, rights, welfare, allocation of resources	Actions that are right or wrong by virtue of social consensus: social uniformities and regularities, food, clothes, forms of address, gender roles	Psychological states, personal tastes, and preferences
Formal Conditions	Rational, universal, unalterable, objective, self-constructed, more serious	Arbitrary, relative, alterable, consensus-based, socialized, less serious	Rational and irrational, arbitrary, relative, alterable, self-constructed
Description	Intrinsically harmful acts perceived directly, or inferred from direct perceptions	Acts that are not harmful, have interpersonal consequences, and are meaningful in a specific social context	The domain is outside the realm of societal regulation and moral concern
Infractions	1. Hitting another individual 2. Pirating software	1. Sending junk mail 2. Loading a computer virus program onto an electronic newsletter/list server	1. Committing indecent acts 2. Using encryption devices
Consequences	1. Social group may castigate 2. Legal or institutional (e.g., a school may suspend a student, or an employer might issue a warning)	1. People may be puzzled or upset about behaviour 2. Individual may be encouraged to change or face the consequences (e.g., social outcast)	1. Individual may feel uneasy or good about behaviour 2. Based on input from reference group(s) or close friends/family, person may feel uneasy/good about behaviour

Table 18-1   *A Social and Interactional Approach to the Domain Theory of Moral Development*

The *personal domain of morality* is outside societal regulation and is based on personal preferences and tastes. The use of encryption software for sending and receiving email is sometimes said to fall into this domain, because private email is sent using encryption software only if the person wants to keep information secure while maintaining privacy for all parties involved. However, the personal morality aspect of privacy doesn't seem to prevent governments from attempting to subvert the principle of personal privacy, at least in the context of electronic communications. Indeed, for many years, discussions of privacy in computing have centred on the question of to what extent the rights of the individual to personal privacy override the perceived needs of law enforcement. If a man's home is his castle, as the English say, what about his mailbox?

It might be argued that virus writing comes into this domain when it does not involve making viral programs and source code available to others. Indeed, many anti-virus professionals over the years have adopted a position of "We don't care what you do on your own computer, as long as you keep your creations to yourself". As we saw in the last chapter, legislation tends to reflect this viewpoint. Comparatively few countries have attempted to outlaw virus creation per se, focusing instead on laws forbidding unauthorized access, unauthorized modification, and inciting or enabling others to commit a criminal act.

The *domain of conventional knowledge* includes acts that have interpersonal consequences and are meaningful in a specific social system but are not harmful. For example, designing a virus and distributing it to friends as a prank may be perfectly acceptable in one country, but may be objectionable, if not punishable by law, in another nation. There is a distinction here between the acts of virus creation and that of dissemination. Sharing information about virus creation may also come under this heading. While few cultures would deliberately discourage anti-virus researchers, vendors, and the like from sharing information (although this can be a side effect of attempts at regulation), many cultures would likely consider virus writers exchanging information (including source code and samples) to be crossing moral or legal boundaries. Legally, the question of whether the exchange indicated malicious intent may sometimes resolve the issue. Morally, the issues are more complex. Is a vendor that takes samples from a VX site inciting the maintainers of such sites? If the use of such samples by that vendor as a research tool is beneficial to the community as a whole because it provides protection against the virus, does the end justify the means? Since, as the bad guys never tire of pointing out, the vendors (indeed, all anti-virus professionals, including ourselves) are making a living and sometimes a profit from the existence of viruses, does this compromise vendors (or us) because virus writers are "necessary" to their present livelihoods? We believe not, since the logical extension of this argument is that medical staff should not be paid to treat disease, nor law enforcement agents to fight crime.

Harmful acts, such as violence and theft, pertain to the *moral domain* (see Table 18-1). Intrinsic harm is perceived directly, or is inferred from direct perceptions. Both children and adults reason that the act is universally wrong because the harm is intrinsic to the act. Hence, the act is not tolerated.

Table 18-1 was adapted from Schweder et al. (1987, 24) and adopted by Gattiker, Janz, Greshake, Kelb, Schwenteck, and Holsten (1996). It is generally assumed that if the majority of a society considers something harmful, such behaviour or action will be outlawed, thus resulting in legal sanctions if the person committing the action is caught. In contrast, a substantial minority of people may perceive something as being immoral, but such behaviour may be quite common and in some cases accepted.

Demographics

As Table 18-1 suggests, people have different ways of interpreting situations, based on their culture, values, and norms. Research indicates that demographic variables have been used extensively to assess whether people differ based on such variables as age and gender, and most social phenomena can be better understood by also taking into consideration demographic factors. This section addresses these issues in the context of computer viruses, morality, and ethics.

Age

Demographic variables already result in significant differences between groups, such as younger people compared to their older peers, as far as computer viruses are concerned. For instance, Gattiker and Kelley, in a 1995 study, reported that younger individuals were far more open to sharing various programs and viruses with each other. By comparison, older respondents were far less open to the idea of sharing, and were likelier to view their actions in a moral context.

People seem to find it difficult in general to think of the exchange of copies of copyrighted software as theft or piracy. The same is probably true of books, videos, and music, but these usually present more of a challenge in terms of copying. Yet people are far less likely to commit outright theft where copying is not an option (shoplifting, for instance). This probably relates to the increased likelihood of discovery, of course: it is easier to trace the theft of an original object than it is to detect the fact that a copy has been made. However, it may also be that people have difficulty with the concept that the theft of intellectual property is in principle no less stealing than the theft of a vehicle, money, or items of clothing, especially when they can easily accomplish theft of intellectual property by copying diskettes or burning a CD.

Why do older people find it easier to see the "wrongfulness" in these actions? Perhaps because they were educated in a less morally ambivalent age? Perhaps because they are likelier to be able to look back at a world where copying technology was more expensive and less available? Is their abhorrence of viruses based on an extrapolation of strict moral standards to new technological contexts, or is it an expression of their fear of technologies that hardly existed in their school years, and with which they are, in consequence, uncomfortable? Perhaps younger people are less concerned not because they are less moral than their elders, but because they are less afraid of the consequences of malicious software.

If abhorrence of malicious software is influenced by technophobia and fear of the unknown, does this mean we don't regard these issues as having a moral dimension? Not at all. However, ethical behaviour is most amenable to analysis when it comes from knowledge, rather than a semi-instinctive fear of the unknown.

Considering age differences and attitudes towards computer viruses results in differences as outlined previously in this section. However, what may be important in this context is that younger people's influence on the Internet may be disproportionate considering their population statistics. Just a few years ago, millions of students joined the Internet population every semester by entering university and getting their email account for study purposes. Today, ever more high schools offer their pupils access to the Internet, and some data suggest that more than 60 percent of households with school age children have Internet access compared to just about 30 percent for a country's population overall. Accordingly, younger people tend to make up a larger percentage of Internet users than their percentage of the overall population. Hence, younger people's interpretation of issues and their subculture, including their ethics and morals, are influencing Internet users or the Internet culture much more than they might in other areas of life (for example, playing golf, snowboarding, or eating at restaurants). This influence may be offset to some extent as the proportion of older people joining the user population rises, but this rising proportion will not necessarily exert an equal influence.

This line of reasoning is supported by the fact that younger people are more likely to adopt technologies earlier. For instance, while about 60 percent of Denmark's population have cellular phones, this percentage rises above 80 for teenagers and young adults. Earlier adoption of technology or more extensive use of the Internet becomes of particular relevance if the ethics and morals of younger people differ from their elders. Hence, user statistics and customer preferences with new technologies often reflect the influence of early adopters. Gauging customer preferences primarily by charting the younger generation's tastes could shift the results due to positions of subcultures that do not necessarily reflect the overall population's values and norms.

The Napster phenomenon primarily attracted younger people. To limit the use of bandwidth for person-to-person file sharing, some universities have even restricted the proportion of their network and bandwidth resources that can be used for person-to-person file sharing through Napster (for example, no more than 10 percent of the system's bandwidth capacity at any time), or blocked person-to-person file sharing altogether. The entertainment industry is trying to limit this property right violation or copyright infringement of sharing music files by developing a content scrambling system (CSS). Unfortunately, digital files cannot be made impossible to copy, any more than water can be made dry. Unless younger people accept property and copyrights as being an issue within the moral domain, and one that should not be tolerated (see Table 18-1), they will continue to infringe upon the rights of musicians and affect their revenue stream adversely.

Napster is a phenomenon somewhat beyond the scope of this chapter, but the attitudes held by the young regarding this issue can usefully be compared to their perception of virus writing and virus distribution. If they are indifferent to the subsequent consequences of spreading a virus or making it available for others to distribute, other people may suffer negative consequences due to virus infection. Younger people's hypothetical lack of interest in the consequences of poor information security may also be of importance for technologies that are still under development. For instance, younger people are not only more likely to use cellular or mobile phones than their elders, but, as importantly, are likely to use palm and other wireless devices more than their older counterparts. Unfortunately, malicious software has begun to affect palm top devices, and concerns about the possibility of malware capable of affecting wireless devices still to be released (UMTS phones, for example) have also aroused considerable attention and speculation.

Gender

A substantial body of research indicates that people assess ethical and moral matters differently according to gender. However, how these issues may affect the virus domain is less clear, with some notable exceptions. For instance, using a hypothetical scenario describing a person posting a virus on a bulletin board, a study by Gattiker and Kelley indicated that women were less permissive than men. The study also found that women were more likely to be bothered by the virus scenario than men. Hence, women appeared more cautious regarding the application of moral criteria in the context of computer usage. It has also been observed that women are often less interested than men are in computers and other machinery. Women regard computers primarily as instruments for achieving other goals, even if those goals are recreational, such as gameplay. Men, on the other hand, seem likelier to invest a higher proportion of their time maintaining and tweaking machinery, whether it's fine-tuning a motorcycle or automating the desktop. We will delicately sidestep the issues of whether these gender differences are real or stereotypical, and whether they are, if real, innate or conditioned. It seems possible in either case that this emphasis on the mechanical aspects of hardware and software results in some displacement of computers and computer usage away from the moral domain.

Some research indicates that women in general are far more concerned about how their actions and behaviours affect others. Gattiker and Kelley also reported that males were more likely to have the attitude that computer users are responsible for protecting themselves, and that virus writers or even virus distributors should not be ostracized or otherwise punished. Women felt that such behaviour was not acceptable simply because it could result in harm to others.

These findings confirm gender differences as reported in other research addressing ethical and moral issues. Simply, the research suggests that women tend to differ from men in how they assess situations and feel about other people's behaviour. Some people may be little surprised that research also indicates that as far as computer viruses are concerned, women are far more cautious than men. But as importantly, women worry more about how their computer-related behaviour (for example, information security) or carelessness with a computer virus may affect others. We do not know how closely this research reflects universal gender differences. We do know that reports of female involvement with virus writing, distribution, and other intrusive activities are notably rare. Even the anecdotal accounts and out-and-out bragging in forums such as alt.comp.virus rarely hint at virus-writing activity arising from the distaff side.

Cultural and National Norms

The preceding section suggests that age and gender are two demographic variables that do affect ethical and moral viewpoints about computer viruses. Specifically, men are less cautious with computer viruses than women, and younger people are less likely to feel that it is in some sense wrong to write a computer virus, or to pass on such code to others.

Cultural issues may also have a bearing on how we regard virus creation and distribution. It is a matter for debate whether carelessness about basic computing hygiene is also a matter for ethical concern, or simply a practical issue. In either case, this is an area where social engineering in its more traditional, sociological sense (that is, as a means of reinforcing socially desirable behaviour, rather than as a tool employed by crackers and virus writers) may be of more practical use than ethical debate.

National Issues

When discussing cultural issues, we must make a distinction between cross-national differences or similarities (that is, country A as opposed to country B) and differences among groups of people or subcultures within a nation. Unless the country represents a closely knit society, wherein values and norms are shared and abided by the large majority of the population, diversity will result in differences in values, norms, and the way in which people see virus issues fit the domains of morality.

Various countries have undertaken efforts to reduce dysfunctional cultural differences through legislation and law enforcement as a means of social control. But results have been mixed. For instance, the impact of the United States' "war on drugs" has not always been beneficial. "Mandatory sentencing" laws are, it is sometimes argued, the main reason for the country's huge prison population. Moreover, it is reported that one in four of the country's 2 million prisoners are incarcerated for drug offences, and these prisoners have only a limited chance of becoming productive members of society when they are released. This book is not the forum for an extended debate on retribution versus rehabilitation, and we will not explore the issue. Clearly, however, while a majority of citizens may agree that drugs are harmful and thus part of the moral domain, a substantial minority does not and, therefore, consumes drugs and/or sells them for profit.

People who distribute or write computer viruses pose a somewhat similar problem. Some virus authors seem to gain satisfaction from being able to claim "credit" and garner media attention for a computer virus disaster, even though they normally prefer to do so anonymously. Although many people see computer viruses as harmful, members of a subculture may see it as being an issue of the personal morality domain. If this were to be the case, then the matter is a personal issue and depends upon one's preferences. Sarah Gordon's interviews with computer students show responses typical of many studies in this area. The base attitude appears to be, "If I find it interesting, and I can do it, why do you say I shouldn't?" And indeed, this is a fair question, which we can answer convincingly only if we can demonstrate plausible harmful consequences. The question of what constitutes harm (or damage) is considered further in the section "Do No Harm" later in this chapter.

Some advocates promote virus writing on the grounds of freedom of speech. Americans often cite First Amendment rights, referring to the First Amendment to the *U.S. Constitution,* which some Americans seem to see as some universal law rather than as a local political document, however desirable.

We have made frequent reference to Gordon's writings in the context of VX psychology and ethics. Unfortunately, we cannot do justice to such an extensive body of work in this short chapter, and recommend that you check out her papers covering these topics, many of which are available at her web site (www.badguys.org).

We should, however, take this opportunity to explore Gordon's observations regarding the ethical development of virus writers, which indicate that adolescent virus writers tend to exhibit ethics normal for their age group. Normality, in this analysis, is taken as conforming to Lawrence Kohlberg's "Stages of Moral Development" model. Kohlberg's levels have been the most quantitative of the various tools for assessing moral development and maturity, and are based on the rationales used to explain moral choices. The six stages are divided into three groups: pre-conventional, generally referring to the reasoning of children; conventional, used by most adult members of society; and post-conventional. The two post-conventional stages are somewhat controversial. Kohlberg and his adherents would state that post-conventional reasoning is used by those who are morally superior and have progressed beyond the need for rules, while others would point out that there is no distinction between a stage six who chooses to live by higher values, and a psychopath who does not care about anyone beyond himself. (Kohlberg himself has admitted that he could not point to a specific person who operated at a stage six level.)

The specific stages are defined as follows:

Pre-Conventional Morality

1. Obey the rules to avoid punishment.

2. Obey the rules to get rewards or satisfy needs.

Conventional Morality

3. Judge actions on good intentions and concern for others. Conform in response to peer pressure.

4. Behave morally, based on acceptance of authority. Conform to avoid censure by legitimate authority.

Post-Conventional Morality

5. Become more flexible in judgment. We may question the moral bases of the rules we live by, but conform for the good of the community.

6. Live by "normative ethics". We choose (to some extent) the principles by which we live, based on what we perceive to be universal principles. Clearly, there is still room for considerable cultural bias here: we are not impervious to the influence of the society in which we live. However, the "mature" personality can admit the possibility that the principles of his or her own culture may not be universally applicable.

Although Kohlberg's model of moral development has the most detailed construction, its utility is questionable. His system is not so much one of values education as of values measurement. There is great difficulty, however, in determining the "stage" of a given individual. Most ethical discussions will be judged as having reasoning at all of stages three, four, and five.

Acknowledging that young virus writers are not abnormal in terms of their ethical development is not the same as saying that virus writing is in principle normal or desirable. However, it certainly suggests that virus writing should not be regarded as *de facto* evidence of a psychopathic personality. It also suggests the likelihood that virus writers might "age out" of what society would regard as antisocial behaviour. This does indeed happen, although Gordon has also noted that ambivalence in many groups about how "wrong" virus writing is appears to "push up the age of aging out, if the process occurred at all" ("Virus Writers: The End of the Innocence" [www. research.ibm.com/antivirus/SciPapers/VB2000SG.htm]). Given that the authorship of CIH and the Kournikova virus was seen in some quarters as indicating suitability for jobs in the software industry (although not the anti-virus industry!), such uninformed public perception certainly seems to be less than a deterrent for impressionable youth. At the same time, there is little evidence that the heavy sentencing faced by the author of Melissa has had a significant deterrent impact, either. Nonetheless, virus writing does not yet appear to have become accepted as "cool" except by a (significant) minority, and members of that minority do indeed age out.

In alt.comp.virus (where two of the authors of this book have spent far too much of their extracurricular time in the past), we have seen evidence that virus writers and other pro-VX individuals can engage in rational ethical debate with "the other side". Indeed, representatives from either side may, on occasion, accommodate opposing viewpoints. We have indeed seen representatives of more than one generation of VX move towards the centre. In some instances, a virus writer will publicly retire. Sometimes this act of withdrawal is considered in terms of a shift of interests, change of lifestyle, work or domestic reasons, and so on. In other cases, however, a virus writer has made explicit a change in his or her ethical viewpoint, and may even apologize publicly. Rarely, a former virus writer has retained a public profile of sorts. This public profile may work to the advantage of the virus-hating community, in that a reformed virus writer may be a more influential role model than an anti-virus personality (if that isn't a contradiction in terms) representing the forces of authoritarianism and conformity.

A country with substantial cultural diversity must, therefore, cope with different social approaches to the computer virus challenge exhibited by various groups (such as organizations, private users, hackers, computer geeks, and teenagers). Legislation that is ignored by a small but substantial minority could result in the incarceration of many people, while not really eliminating the root of the problem. To illustrate, because people copy music onto tapes, many countries have tried to deal with this issue by adjusting legislation so that any sales price for blank tapes includes a copyright fee paid to the recording industry. Similar examples are copyright fees included in charges incurred for photocopying materials. Hence, protecting every group's rights or balancing rights and responsibilities makes life easier for all, and can reduce potential conflicts. However, given the invasive nature of malicious software and the generally anonymous nature of the perpetrators, it is hard to see how such a strategy could accommodate the "rights" of virus writers without legitimizing actions that offer no significant advantage to the victim.

Some virus writers (especially those who have faced legal action) have argued that virus writing is a legitimate activity because it draws attention to potential security breaches and vulnerabilities in programs and operating systems, and educates victims. Certainly, coding an exploit may be acceptable under some circumstances, and software vendors cannot be trusted to repair shortcomings if reports of such exploits are not made public. However, we fail to see how releasing yet another kit-generated VBScript or macro virus variant can be justified by its benefit to the user community. Does this mean that the use of a novel technique justifies the release of a virus? Perhaps, if we ever see a technically sound, well-coded virus that does no deliberate damage and is tested to a professional standard against the possibility of accidental damage, that does not conceal its presence and intentions, and is thus in accordance with the spirit and the letter of most of the relevant legislation, we might consider debating the matter. None of us is holding his breath.

Motivational Factors

Why do virus writers create viruses? Damage is far from being the only factor:

- ▶ A somewhat academic interest in replicative software in its own right, under controlled circumstances.
- ▶ An interest shared between members of virus writing groups.
- ▶ Peer acceptance and recognition.
- ▶ Recognition by anti-virus companies (such as being listed in encyclopaedias and README files).
- ▶ A misplaced sense of humour or mischief, associated with a lack of understanding of the consequences for the victims.

▶ WildList fever: the buzz from getting their creation out into the world and, even better, recognized as a big issue by the media. However, it sometimes seems that the media do not consider a virus newsworthy unless it is deliberately or accidentally destructive, or even mistakenly thought to be. A destructive but rare virus is apt to get more publicity than a widespread but innocuous specimen.

▶ A desire for revenge on a person or group, irrespective of how far beyond the original target the ripples spread, or a quasi-arsonist desire to watch the servers melt down.

Cross-National Differences

Cultural differences can result in diverging behaviours that may be perceived as being within acceptable norms in one cultural setting but offensive in another. Some countries (such as Switzerland and Italy) may have legal means of prosecuting anybody whose code could damage data if the other party's computer or information system gets infected. But in some countries, playing with a computer virus or spreading malicious code may be perfectly acceptable behaviour.

More commonly, crucial distinctions are drawn between creating code out of purely personal interest, sharing code between VX enthusiasts, and releasing code into the wild, so that the question of unauthorized access may arise. Different countries have a different understanding of ethical and moral obligations about data security issues, as longstanding differences between the United States and Europe on the export of encryption might indicate. However, one could claim, without prejudice, that neither the European Union nor the United States has a monopoly of truth on this issue; they both simply offer legal or regulatory frameworks that reflect their own cultures. Moreover, the professional codes discussed in this section indicate quite clearly that even associations whose members are computer security experts impose different ethical demands on their members. These are often rooted in diverging values and norms inherent in their respective memberships.

The differences outlined may be major, and sometimes even result in international wrangling and name-calling by politicians and diplomats; nevertheless, these differences also apply to how a particular country deals with computer viruses and hacking. For instance, Gattiker and Kelley's 1995 study reported that US respondents were most relaxed about posting a computer virus on a bulletin board, whereas respondents from Germany, for example, felt that this practice was wrong. Similarly, Gattiker and Kelb, in a 1998 study, reported that while German respondents felt that legal regulation should protect their privacy, Canadians were less trusting and US respondents felt that they had to fight for their privacy themselves.

The preceding differences are echoed in divergent approaches to legislation and computer viruses. Although some countries may see a computer virus in the knowledge domain, others put it into the moral domain, and have therefore introduced legislation accordingly. Even within the European Union, no comprehensive and united legal framework exists that would make it easier for businesses and users alike to address the computer virus issue in ways analogous to the very specific terms of the EC directive on data protection. However, some predirective drafts now under consideration indicate a willingness to deal with more general network security issues on a community-wide basis.

Familiarity and Ethics

The preceding sections suggest that cultural differences (contrasts among groups within a society such as younger people or the underground) as well as cross-national ones (how we deal with unauthorized access and modifications to systems and information) will remain with us for years to come. But besides these differences or similarities that could influence our ethical and moral understanding of malware-related matters, familiarity with computer virus incidents may also moderate people's willingness to abide by moral standards.

One of the difficulties with surveys is that people may answer a question but not be familiar with the subject. Accordingly, asking people what they think about computer viruses or whether they think viruses are harmful may result in respondents adopting a moralizing or draconian stance. Accordingly, a person may say viruses are harmful or virus writers should be punished. However, such statements say little about the responsibilities of the victims, or how they could exacerbate the problem themselves by being careless with file attachments or by deactivating the virus scanners on their desktops.

The virus vignette used by Gattiker and Kelley provided subjects with the context link, thereby attempting to address the familiarity issue. Most computer users have either had a personal experience with a virus, have tried to protect their machines and software from virus contamination, or have known end users who have experienced the hassles and headaches of computer virus contamination (or of anti-virus configuration and maintenance). Furthermore, familiarity and acquaintance of the subject with the behavioural outcomes makes it possible to assess the effect on moral decisions. Therefore, computer users are probably more conscious of the possibility that a virus may do harm to others than they are of the implications of encryption, simply because of their context-specific experiences. That is, far more people have firsthand experience of virus-related problems, whether with anti-virus software or with actual viral infection. At the time of writing, far fewer people use encryption routinely, and may not be fully aware when it does affect them. For instance, a surprising number of people are unaware that when they "password" a local file, encryption of the file is usually an integral part of the process. "We don't want strong encryption, we just want to know that our files can't be read without the password".

End Users and Responsibility

When we ask people about a specific situation, responses become more realistic and reflective of what the individual might do personally. What is especially important is how familiar a person is with a particular scenario. For instance, having previously suffered from a computer virus makes people far more sensitive to anti-virus issues (although not necessarily more knowledgeable—indeed, it's likely that victims of a virus attack will become both more exposed and more receptive to misinformation). It has been suggested that a virus incident such as the Kournikova virus results in a 90-day post-traumatic recovery period during which most users are quite careful to observe good hygienic practices. During this period, it is argued, they tend to follow procedures, such as having all incoming email scanned by the anti-virus software installed on their desktops. They might even regularly back up their data and update their anti-virus software.

> ### NOTE
>
> *We suspect that this view is based on a widespread misunderstanding of how modern anti-virus software works, and the amount of routine manual maintenance it requires of end users. In fact, organizations that depend on end users doing a manual on-demand scan of all incoming files and media—running regular manual backup procedures and manually updating their anti-virus software—are in need of a reality check. Not only is it naive to expect corporate staff to execute routine security procedures, but it should be unnecessary. Modern security software is sophisticated enough to automate such tasks, although we would stress the need to check that automatic mechanisms are working as they should.*

However, the argument runs, the time intervals between new fast-burner virus incidents are becoming ever shorter. The question must be raised whether users simply become desensitized and thus careless. Besides the ever-smaller time window between incidents, security or anti-virus policies in firms may not be enforced with sufficient rigour. Some research suggests that people start forgetting the norms and rules to which they should adhere about 60–90 days after they have read or signed a firm's IT policy. Hence, it is suggested, IT security and anti-virus policies are important but effective only if people get reminded regularly and within 60-day time intervals about their policy content and why and how the policies work. On the other hand, experience in large institutions does not always suggest that viruses are always spread through the same victims, hit time and time again by the latest variation on the LoveLetter theme. Our observations in the field suggest clustering of incidents in vulnerable units (human resources departments and public relations departments are a particularly frequent entry point), but not necessarily involving the same individual.

Some individuals and some classes of end user (higher management and their satellites, for instance) do seem particularly prone to involvement in virus incidents, but we are not convinced that desensitization is the only factor, or even the most important factor. Other factors that seem to play a part include gender (again), curiosity about technical issues, and status. While it is embarrassing and even job-threatening to the lower orders if a VIP is implicated in a virus incident, it is also more difficult culturally for the IT staff responsible for anti-virus administration to regulate the security awareness and practices of higher management. Contrary to the popular stereotype, the same cultural difficulties involved with regulating higher management aren't primarily a problem with clerks and secretaries. Administrative staff are often as obsessive as any systems administrator could wish about reporting suspicious attachments, anomalies with security software, and high-volume messages about the latest microchip-devouring impossible super-virus, especially if they know that a sound mechanism exists for dealing effectively with such reports. In a moderately well-regulated environment, problems are more likely to derive from the spread of malware from the mailboxes of those who are too high powered to be subject to draconian restrictions. To make the problem worse, lower ranks who are generally cautious with email attachments are less likely to take normal precautions when the attachment comes from someone higher up the tree of command.

However, if people play it safe when opening any kind of unannounced attachment from a trusted source, such as a friend or business partner, such caution should reduce their vulnerability to virus attacks drastically (although novel approaches to technology or to social engineering are always likely to claim some victims). Familiarity with computer viruses (for example, having suffered from a computer virus by having lost time, face, and even data) seems likely to make a person more cautious and aware about safety matters. However, it doesn't necessarily make a user better informed.

Someone who has suffered from a computer virus in the past may subscribe to a social consensus that frowns upon virus programming. Moreover, he or she may feel that opening an attachment without adequate precautions is simply careless or even negligent. Such an individual may also take the necessary steps in order to reduce the likelihood of unintentionally passing on a computer virus. Someone who hasn't suffered negative virus experiences and/or does not understand the possible threat may simply find all this concern about viruses irrational and unnecessary. On the other hand, awareness of negative consequences may be of little benefit if accompanied by poor advice. Often, this awareness involves recommending draconian restrictions that make normal work difficult and unpleasant, while failing to address defensive gaps wide enough for the proverbial carriage and pair. In fact, the need to address such issues has prompted us to suggest that organizations should consider making it compulsory for IT users to adhere to a code of practice along the lines discussed later in this chapter.

Is Anti-Virus a Profession?

We suppose that we should ask this question, though we cannot give an authoritative answer. An anti-virus professional may be as skilled in his field as a doctor or lawyer, but he or she is not compelled to achieve a minimum standard of competence, proven by a universally recognized qualification. There are, of course, general security qualifications that carry a great deal of weight, but they are not usually considered a reliable guide to expertise in computer virology. And many quite competent professionals don't have them and have never needed them. On the other hand, we are aware of security professionals whose capacity for giving bad advice about viruses is quite independent of their possession or nonpossession of formal qualifications.

Anti-virus professionals, being (by implication) computing professionals, do have the advantage of being more familiar with and less nervous about information technology in general, and viruses in particular, so they do not have to be "ethical" out of fear of the technological consequences. Like virus writers and distributors, they may (and usually do) feel that end users should take some responsibility for their own safety and practice basic anti-virus hygiene. They may even underestimate the difficulties of comprehension that bedevil others who are less fascinated with viral and antiviral technology. Unlike the virus exchange community, however, they are unlikely to adopt the position that computer illiteracy, naivete, or downright stupidity on the part of the end user justifies the actions of the black hat brigade.

We are not assuming here that all "legitimate" anti-virus researchers are plaster saints. However, the closed-loop, nondisclosure model of security to which this field generally adheres tends to hold anyone who behaves unacceptably subject to sanctions, including expulsion from crucial sources of information. Such sources might include the exchange of samples, without which it's difficult to maintain a competitive position in the commercial anti-virus market. Such sanctions sound like a further instance of the use of fear as an ethical driver, but we believe that a distinction between researcher ethics and vendor ethics is necessary here. In a short web site article, Gordon suggests that a researcher in this field is likely to display a number of characteristics, including:

▶ Having technical proficiency

▶ Working with viruses only in a secured research environment intended to minimize the risks of accidental release of viruses, and open to audit by third parties

▶ Owning an ethical responsibility to practice only within his or her own competence, and accountable to a generally accepted ethical code

Vendors and Ethics

Researchers are, of course, more often than not employed by vendors, but may consider themselves bound by a more restrictive code than generally applies within the organization that employs them. There are instances, for example, of anti-virus software that doesn't detect whole classes of malicious software because of the difficulties of gaining entry to the inner circles where samples are exchanged. We have in mind, for instance, certain Macintosh anti-virus products that don't detect macro viruses. An ethical issue probably arises here, however, only if the marketing of such a product misleads the customer into thinking that he or she has full protection. In fact, many would consider a product that provides substantially incomplete detection of a class of malware (for example, some common Trojans but not others) as being in greater danger of crossing boundaries of acceptability, although this would, again, be at least in part a marketing issue.

There is a related problem outside the commercial anti-virus arena, but not quite the same one. An honourable tradition endures of semi-altruistic programmers making available anti-virus software of limited functionality, including one-shot scanners that detect and (sometimes) disinfect one or two viruses and/or variants, and some generic tools that block a limited range of malware classes.

NOTE

You may wonder at the term semi-altruistic. We intend no disrespect to those who have made such tools available at no cost, but would only point out that not all rewards are financial.

We applaud the community-spirited endeavours of those who make such tools available, but sometimes they may mislead the computer user into a false sense of security. Real-life examples include:

▶   A scanner that detected only a handful of obscure viruses that had never been
seen in the field

▶   A scanner that was claimed to detect a particular worm, but consistently failed
to detect one of the known variants

At the other extreme, we have encountered a scanner that consistently reported a
virus when it was unable to open a file. You might call this a false sense of insecurity.
The problem here is that it seems churlish to chide a volunteer for not meeting
professional standards. You get what you pay for, the argument runs, and half a loaf
is better than none. We have some sympathy with this viewpoint, but it takes us back
to the issue of user responsibility. If the weaknesses of a product are adequately
documented, then perhaps the programmer has done as much as necessary to meet
minimum ethical standards. This is not, however, always the case, even with
commercial software.

We have previously alluded to free "Michelangelo editions" of commercial software
that appeared to scan for all known viruses but detected only one. This may well
have been an honest error in presentation. However, one of us had a lively debate
with a vendor who had a "Lite" evaluation version of his or her product, which was
claimed to detect "all known viruses" generically. About a year after the appearance
of the first Word macro virus, the product was distributed in a magazine in the United
Kingdom. Since the distributed product was an obsolete version, it knew nothing about
Word documents and macro viruses. Generic detection based on change detection
doesn't usually help much in this area: data files are usually dynamic, not static, and
are intended to be changed during their lifetimes. Clearly, changes in viral technology
had overtaken any claims to complete invincibility, yet the defensive arguments
employed by various representatives of the company concerned ranged from threats of
litigation, through "It's just an evaluation copy: the full version detects macro viruses",
to "We're not responsible for the documentation that was distributed with the
software". The problem with such an incident is not that "You get what you pay
for". It's a question of whether you get what you expect, and whether the vendor has
employed "due diligence" to make it clear that the free lunch is missing a couple of
courses: the full menu is available only to those who deploy a credit card.

It's also possible for "ethical" concerns to mask (or at least become confused with)
other motivations, such as commercial advantage, or to preserve the mystique of the
Inner Circle. Most anti-virus vendors take a rather paranoid, and almost obsessive,
position with regard to the sharing and distribution of viral code. At least, researchers
usually do; sometimes the marketing department is less scrupulous. However, most
major companies have arrangements by which virus samples are shared, so that the
customer is not placed at undue risk if he or she chooses not to buy every anti-virus
program on the market.

Commercial Ethics

The preceding section may give the impression that we do not believe it possible for an anti-virus vendor to conform to an ethical standard. This is far from true. While any company (or individual) may sometimes fall short of ethical perfection, it is normal for anti-virus companies to expect their staff to conform to codes of behaviour. In some instances, aware perhaps that anti-virus companies are often suspected of unethical activities such as soliciting or creating viruses, a company may make public its code of ethics. A good example is Symantec's, which you can read at www.symantec.com/avcenter/reference/sarcethics.html.

Why are people so ready to believe the worst of vendors? Perhaps this cynicism arises simply from the assumption of universal self-interest, but perhaps more complex mechanisms are at work. We observe that computer professionals (including ourselves) often find a particular fascination in viruses and other malware, and may solicit examples of malicious code. The anti-virus establishment is often seen as frustratingly uncooperative in its refusal to make such code available for testing, experimentation, and education; indeed, this lack of cooperation runs counter to practice even within other areas of information security.

While in our more cynical moments we are apt to suggest that the term *commercial ethics* is probably an oxymoron, we acknowledge that Adam Smith's famous dismissal of benevolence as a significant factor in economic interaction does not tell the whole story:

> It is not from the benevolence of the butcher, the brewer, or the baker that we expect our dinner, but from their regard to their own interest. We address ourselves, not to their humanity but to their self-love, and never talk to them of our own necessities but of their own advantage. (*The Wealth of Nations,* Ch. 2, 1776.)

Even if vendors in general and security vendors in particular were always and exclusively driven by commercial self-interest, this would neither prove nor disprove the need for codes of conduct.

A code of business practice may be highly moral but platitudinous, and totally at odds with practice within the organization that owns it. On the other hand, it may be an honest recognition of duties and responsibilities, and an expression of intent to meet those obligations. It may be a useful guide to making decisions in difficult circumstances, or it may be a means of avoiding taking personal responsibility for a difficult decision by falling back on a ruling that may never have been intended to meet such a case. The anti-virus industry may be regarded as a special case, in that it must demonstrate its intention to be "whiter than white" as a counterbalance to the popular conception that the industry is reliant on poachers turned gamekeepers.

An article from 1980 by John Ladd ("The Quest for a Code of Professional Ethics: an Intellectual and Moral Confusion", *AAAS Professional Ethics Project: Professional Ethics Activities in the Scientific and Engineering Societies,* eds. Chalk, Frankel, and Chafer) discusses some of the difficulties presented by passing off a code of conduct as a code of ethics. (We have tried to talk about codes of conduct rather than codes of ethics.) Ethical principles are not very susceptible to conversion to a series of flat statements of prescribed conduct: "ethics must, by its very nature, be self-directed rather than other-directed". A code of conduct can be evaluated in ethical terms, but to describe it as a code of ethics to indicate that it isn't a legal code is somewhat misleading. Being a professional "does not automatically make a person an expert in ethics". (Actually, it doesn't even make a person an expert in his or her profession.) Ladd also draws attention to the "mischievous side-effects" that can arise from adoption of a code of ethics:

▶ It encourages complacency. Having a code of ethics may be seen as an acceptable substitute for ethical behaviour.

▶ Since a code of ethics prescribes a minimum standard, it may actually excuse the signatory from having to exceed that minimum.

Do No Harm

We acknowledge the force of these arguments, yet we consider that there is some value in guidelines, even guidelines as general as "Do no harm", if they help the signatory to develop a better understanding of what "harm" actually is. We encourage a shift toward "Do as you would be done by", away from "Do others before they do you". We have previously hinted at the suggestion that different cultures and subcultures may have different views of the damage done by the dissemination of malicious software. It is commonly suggested that viral "harm" is synonymous with damaging payloads. This misses a number of points:

▶ Most viruses are not intentionally damaging in this sense. However, accidental damage, social consequences, and other factors frequently ignored by commentators may be every bit as damaging as a wanton destroyer of files.

▶ On occasion, anti-virus software does more damage when it deals with a threat than is entailed by leaving the virus where it is but attempting to attenuate its impact. (In such cases, separating the vendor's responsibility from that of the virus author can be an interesting exercise.) Friendly fire can still be fatal.

▶ We find ourselves considering the virtual equivalent of a culture in which the common cold is considered to be as "bad" as leprosy or Ebola, or where a "benign" tumour is routinely treated with the same rigour as a malignant growth, resulting in all the physical damage associated with chemotherapy or radiation therapy.

The responsibility for the side effects associated with these measures lies ultimately with the virus writer. But the question must be asked, do vendors bear some responsibility for their reliance on the "easy" solution of known-virus detection technology and their berating of customers for their ignorance of "safe hex" principles?

Developing Codes of Conduct

Developing codes of conduct is considered important in that they can provide members of professional associations with the guidelines and moral constraint to help them manoeuver through today's minefields of regulations and expectations that society and clients may have. However, there's an argument for giving even general computer users a minimum set of guidelines to work from, if only to help them make the connection between expected standards of conduct in everyday life and the application of those same standards to their computing activities.

A Minimum Code of Conduct

The following specimen code might be a suitable jumping off point for an organization wishing to explore this approach. Many of the same issues are examined in more depth when we move on to consider the specialist requirements of professional computing organizations, especially those with a particular awareness of and interest in security.

All staff should be required to meet prescribed ethical standards, but particular attention should be paid to staff (such as technical management and IT personnel) with special skill sets and corresponding privileges. You might specify that they are expected to:

▶ Promote public health and safety

▶ Advance public/customer knowledge

- ▶ Respect the legitimate rights of others—property rights, copyrights, and intellectual property rights

- ▶ Comply with and maintain knowledge of standards, policies, and legislation

- ▶ Conform to and maintain relevant professional standards

- ▶ Exert due care and diligence

- ▶ Avoid conflicts of interest

- ▶ Avoid representing customers financially where inappropriate

- ▶ Refuse inducements

- ▶ Maintain confidentiality

- ▶ Support fellow professionals

- ▶ Work within the limits of their own expertise or authority

- ▶ Upgrade skills where opportunities exist

- ▶ Accept professional responsibility

- ▶ Follow through what they begin, rather than offload awkward jobs onto others, irrespective of whether the job is in their remit, authority, or competence

- ▶ Resist temptation to evade their own responsibilities by assigning blame to others

- ▶ Access systems, data, and resources only when authorized and when appropriate

EICAR

The European Institute of Anti-Virus Research (EICAR) has long required members to acknowledge and conform to a brief statement of ethical intent. This takes the form of:

- ▶ A general statement of intent to take virus issues seriously and responsibly

- ▶ Avoidance of "trading on people's fears"

- ▶ Renunciation of unrealistic claims for advertising purposes in relation to security software

- ▶ An embargo on trading malicious code or information that could be useful to a virus writer, except with legitimate researchers and other individuals fighting the good fight

The organization has been developing a more comprehensive code for its members since late 1999. This code is still under discussion, and it would not be appropriate to distribute it in its present form (or at all, without formal permission). However, one proposed draft is based on a more general document written by David Harley and used in discussions with a number of organizations, and a version of that document is included in this section. The draft attempts to distinguish clearly between legal issues, public matters, employer and client concerns, and those of the profession and keeping one's professional competence and integrity intact and abreast of new developments. The draft is based on two assumptions:

▶ Computing professionals are accountable for their ability or inability to meet their social responsibilities, whether or not they are enshrined in law.

▶ Standards of conduct are not imposed by an organization on its members arbitrarily, but as an expression of the group's common will to view such conduct as an integral part of its members' professional activities.

Article 1: The Public Interest

This section addresses what the Association for Computing Machinery's Code of Ethics and Professional Conduct refers to as "general moral imperatives", but we have preferred, in accordance with the British Computing Society usage in its Code of Conduct, to use the more specific term "the Public Interest".

1.1 Members are required to promote public health, safety, and the welfare of the environment.

1.2 Members are required to recognize the rights of individuals and groups to information privacy and confidentiality. They are not to access or modify systems or data without proper authorization.

1.3 Members are required to abstain from activities or publications that could cause or foster panic (i.e. "trade on people's fears").

1.4 Members are required to refrain from discrimination according to sexual preferences, gender, or religious beliefs.

1.5 Members have a duty to support efforts undertaken to advance information security as well as enhance privacy.

Article 2: Legal Compliance

2.1 Members are required to respect legally binding constraints such as copyrights, patents, and licence agreements.

2.2 Members are required to respect ethically binding constraints that may not always be subject to legal provisions, such as trade secrets and other privileged information.

2.3 Members are required to acknowledge and respect the intellectual property rights of others.

2.4 Members are required to be conversant with the legal provisions applicable to their professional activities, to conform to them, and to contribute to their continuing revision and amendment with a view to enhancing their accordance with the common good.

Article 3: Duty to Employers, Clients, and Colleagues

3.1 Members are required to be honest and trustworthy, in advertising and marketing, and in dealing with customers and clients, with their employers, and with their colleagues and peers, as much as in other aspects of their professional lives.

3.2 Members are required to conform to local policies and working practices.

3.3 Members must treat all parties, including colleagues, with respect, while conducting their business or interaction in a just and fair manner while also acknowledging the rights of others.

Article 4: Duty to the Profession

4.1 Members are required to refrain from unnecessary dissemination of malicious code, in particular the exchange of virus source code other than with bona fide anti-malware researchers.

4.2 Members are required to refrain from the dissemination of computer malware, tools, or applications that encourage or enable the recipient to engage in immoral, illegal, or illegitimate conduct. Distribution of such software to trustworthy individuals and organizations in the pursuance of bona fide research objectives is excepted from this requirement.

4.3 Members are required to be proactive in changing laws that are either incorrect or simply unworkable regarding information security and privacy.

Article 5: Specialist Competence

5.1 Members are required to improve their own specialist competence constantly so as to keep in step with scientific and technological development.

5.2 Members shall seek to conform to recognized good practice, including quality standards that are in their judgment applicable.

5.3 Members shall only offer to do work or provide service that is within their professional competence and shall accept professional responsibility for their work.

Do Codes of Conduct Make a Difference?

While developing a code of conduct is important, experience in EICAR illustrates that a code's ratification and acceptance by members can be a time-consuming process, due to the vastly different cultural backgrounds of members.

Most professionals are members in one or more professional organizations serving their interests and concerns. Nearly all have either a specific code of conduct or a consensual but unwritten set of rules. A specific code, for instance, is currently under development and discussion at AVIEN (www.avien.org). This code covers a somewhat similar range of concerns. In this case, the code of conduct is associated with initiatives concerned with education and certification. However, organizations with a grounding in anti-virus security—with its emphasis on trust (or mistrust), confidentiality, and nondisclosure—often have quite a different point of view on matters relating to virus exchange. For instance, security organizations, whose grounding is in other areas of security, where full disclosure and cooperative development are more valued, may exchange malicious code freely. This can lead to serious cognitive dissonance for anti-virus specialists participating in other areas of security.

Two philosophically opposite camps tend to form around this issue. The first states that security information should be restricted. This restriction will limit the information available to those who would try to break security systems. The second philosophy often refers to this first position as "security by obscurity", and proposes that restriction of information serves only to keep it out of the hands of those who need it. The "crackers", so this second theory goes, already have the information.

The experience of the Internet Worm must be said to favour the latter position more than the former. The fixes, "workarounds", and patches that enabled systems to recover and prevent reinfection were developed by an informal "network" of individual researchers who freely broadcast their results. (This "free broadcast" was somewhat hampered by the fact that the primary means of communication was the same system that was under attack. The important factor is that the information was not being censored as it was discovered, nor was it being provided by a central authority or clearinghouse.) More recently, however, confusion between routine anti-virus activities and initiatives out of the AV mainstream to deal with other malicious software (such as Linux worms, DDoS attacks, and various kinds of Trojans) has led to practical and ethical problems. The practical problems include duplication of effort in some areas (dealing with common Trojans, for example, which are addressed both by anti-virus software and by Trojan-specific security software) and a confusion of aims in others. The Code Red worm, for instance, which was a burning issue as this chapter was being written, generated a great deal of cooperative research outside the AV establishment, but it seemed to be widely assumed that the AV vendors would deal with the actual eradication of the worm itself. These vendors tended to see the worm as a general security threat rather than as an anti-virus issue, and thus tended to concentrate on providing sources of information rather than a technical fix. In consequence, the worm was rather widespread before other parties began to address the problem. Issues of responsibility and ethics arise when organizations on either side of the AV/security fault line take inappropriate action because of technological and philosophical misunderstandings.

We are not necessarily against full disclosure under all circumstances, and we agree that it's possible that anti-virus vendors sometimes favour nondisclosure at least in part because it offers them a means of maintaining competitive advantage over newer entrants to the field. We believe, however, that the free exchange of virus code—especially comparatively "easy" macro and script code, for instance—is more advantageous to wannabe virus writers and script kiddies than it is to everyday users, since it increases the likelihood of knock-off malware and malware variants.

People who need to implement effective anti-virus defences do not generally need the source code, a disassembly, or a sample for do-it-yourself (DIY) analysis. An explanation of what the virus does and the mechanisms that it exploits is usually sufficient, and sometimes surplus to requirements. What people really need to know is how to prevent or contain the virus, not explicit detail about how it works. Sometimes, though, it is impractical to block entry or contain the spread of the virus, or to perform an effective cleanup, without such detail. The industry's traditional adherence to the model of nondisclosure and nonsharing of samples and source can cause major difficulty if a patch or update is not immediately available. The industry in general tends to err on the side of caution, and this caution sometimes leaves the end user with insufficient information to manage the problem until updates, interim detection drivers, or single-shot detection/removal tools become available. This situation makes more understandable the readiness of some security resources outside the industry to make detailed information available. It also makes it easier to understand the increasing demands from pressure groups, such as AVIEN, that the anti-virus industry move away from its paternalistic "Gods and Ants" stance, and tell the systems administrator what he or she needs to know—especially where nondisclosure leaves the industry's own customers more exposed than they should be.

Whether an anti-virus professional (within the industry or otherwise) releases code to people outside the Inner Circle is a matter of individual responsibility. However, the provision of *sufficient* information is most certainly the responsibility of the industry as a whole, and a challenge it has not always met successfully. Nor is it sufficient to say, "If people need this stuff, they can get it elsewhere". That constitutes an evasion of the responsibility to ensure that the available information is the best possible. Information and code made available through open-disclosure resources are likely to be subject to ongoing peer review rather than initial screening.

Publication of virus code is often compared to publishing details of nonviral exploits, which many people consider acceptable. We believe, however, that publication of any code (or indeed exploit details) should be considered against criteria such as the following:

▶ Will publication be limited to people who can be trusted not to make malicious or inappropriate use of the code, or is access available to anyone who asks?

▶ Will publication help actual or potential victims?

▶ Does it enable victims to fix something themselves?

▶ Will it increase the risk of this specific attack being employed by knowledgeable black hats?

▶ Will it increase the risk of copycat attacks?

▶ Will it increase the risk of variant attacks from other sources, requiring different defensive measures in each instance?

▶ Will a vulnerability be eliminated as a result of publication that would not otherwise be eliminated?

▶ Does the likely benefit to potential victims from publication outweigh the likely benefit to vandals, script kiddies, and the like (not to mention those who are inclined to experiment inappropriately)?

Whether or not to publish in the light of such criteria is always a personal decision, perhaps influenced by membership in organizations that require commitment to a specific code of conduct. We believe, however, that the criteria *should* be taken into consideration.

Further complications arise in the areas of testing and product evaluation as practiced by journalists, consultants, and such. We do not propose to revisit these issues in depth (see Chapter 9), but would point out that there is a major ethical problem when individuals carrying out these activities do so without a sufficient understanding of the technology to implement competent methodologies.

Organizations that don't offer security services or products, but are interested in security only as a means of protecting their other interests, will often have yet other viewpoints. We suggest that compiling codes of conduct such as the minimum code described earlier in this chapter could be, if nothing else, a valuable exercise for helping such organizations clarify their own standpoints.

The question with an unwritten code or constitution is whether people do have a clear understanding of its existence, the ramifications for their conduct, and the content of the code. Here research indicates that even if people know a code by heart, following its guidelines is sometimes a big step that people often fail to take. Hence, a code may actually exist in a vacuum or on its own because it is very much ignored by members as they conduct their daily business. Gattiker, Greshake, Schwenteck, Janz, Holger, and Kelb, in a 1997 study, compared adherence to codes of conduct in the United States, Germany, and Canada, and concluded that "The code of conduct does not appear to affect how people assess moral conduct in either scenario (i.e., conventional and moral domains) in any of the three countries". This study may support suggestions that ethical codes in the computing context are of more cosmetic importance than real effectiveness.

Other research indicates that after about three months, people simply forget a code of conduct's content and may inadvertently breach it in some way, unless somehow reminded. We are not altogether in agreement on this: it is not certain that being obliged to acknowledge such a code by signing it at regular intervals (such as quarterly) or by renewing an annual subscription is either effective or appreciated. Nevertheless, you may wish to consider such a strategy.

Summary

In Economics 101, students are taught that market demand will always result in somebody's producing and selling the supply needed to satisfy the demand. Legal efforts are unlikely to stop buyers from securing the product from producers, even if illegally, as is the case with drugs. Moreover, moral constraints develop and may differ across countries and cultural groups within a society.

Outlawing virus writing and exchange does not, of itself, make matters easier or less dangerous for users concerned about their digital data. Codes of conduct can and maybe should be developed, understood, and committed to by all employees and user groups. While these codes may differ widely according to context, at least they can provide guidance to users and impose constraints. However, the problem requires a more educational solution. Rote learning of safe hex guidelines and codes of conduct may be better than a free-for-all approach, but rote learning is not education: it's a strategy for taking responsibility away from the end user. As long as we maintain the fiction that malware management can be totally transparent to the user, we are doomed to generation after generation of VX wannabes repeating the same experiments and mistakes, and writing the same old graffiti.

Anti-virus security is not the solution. There is no absolute technological solution. The advocates of personal firewalls, anti-Trojan software, IDS, Linux, integrity management, code-signing, and other flavour-of-the-month panaceas are not entitled to claim an exclusive licence to the truth, either. These are all different sizes and shapes of Band-Aids. Salves and bandages are very useful in the event of a playground injury, but they are not the answer to bullying.

Viruses are part of a social problem with a social solution—not necessarily a *realizable* social solution, but we could do better at dealing with the problem than we do. Education is not the answer, either, but it plays a major part in addressing the root of the problem rather than the symptom. We are not only talking about simple computer hygiene and the principles of safe hex, but acknowledging that computing has a moral and ethical dimension. Truly safe computing is considerate computing. Spreading this message among corporate users is a start, but it also needs to be considered in the computer science class, in the home, even in the nurseries and junior schools. If more educationalists catch that thought, they may eventually make more of a difference.

At this point, we'd like to quote Simon Widlake, for an extreme statement of a view we often hear from the hugely experienced, one that goes some way towards explaining why so many anti-virus professionals don't routinely run anti-virus software on their home machines. In a discussion on the alt.comp.virus newsgroup, Simon said:

> Block *ALL* unsolicited executable/interpretable files... End Of Story; Game Over; *NO* AV required.

And, of course, he's right, in a sense. There are no fires in an oxygen-free environment. However, most of us (corporately speaking, at least) have to live in an oxygen-rich habitat. Let's look at an analogy:

> Problem: Some parcels contain plastic explosive.

> Solution: Suspend all mail services.

> Result: No more parcel bombs, except where people use illegal mail services, in which case they deserve what they get. No sniffer dogs or emergency services required.

Now *that's* a social solution. Unfortunately, it's not a very good one, unless you favour government by curfew, enforced by military patrols, in a world where communication is discouraged.

Moving from parcel bombs to mail bombs, once it becomes more important to avoid malware than to receive legitimate traffic, the bad guys have won and we might as well go home. While we're at it, we'd better close down the Web because some sites are pornographic. There are lots of intermediate steps between "wide open" and "bolted shut". For most people, "bolted shut" means replacing service with security, and that's the tail wagging the dog. But we can deliver a fully effective service only if we all understand the nature of the problem that prevents us, at present, from achieving that level of service.

Wrap Up

IN THIS CHAPTER:

Predictions

Closing Comments

Stop Press

Last chapters tend to be either prognostication or opinion. Foretelling the future is a bit chancy. As Daniel Delbert McCracken has usefully put it, you shouldn't make predictions about computing that can be checked in your lifetime. At the beginning of 1995, we would have been willing to say that data files presented no viral danger. And then along came Microsoft Word macro viruses. In 1997 we would have said that merely reading an email message could never infect you. And then along came the latest version of Microsoft Outlook, which could fire up an attachment not only when you read the message, but also if you previewed it. Statements about the future of technology have a disturbing tendency to be confounded by new technologies. So we will keep our predictions mercifully brief, and then move on to the editorial.

Finally, we will wrap up with some late-breaking stories that happened as we were completing the book.

Predictions

Viruses are here. Virus numbers are growing. New viruses and variants will continue to grow for the foreseeable future, and will become an increasing problem in all areas of computing.

A number of security specialists have stated that viruses are a passing fad, and that when desktop operating systems become as secure as mainframe systems, viruses will disappear. It is certainly true that desktop operating systems have not, to date, been in any way secure. It is also true that, as desktop operating systems have changed over the years, certain types of viruses that were previously major threats have become almost extinct.

However, take note of Gene Spafford's point in the foreword: operating system vendors have not been very diligent at "hardening" systems. A decade ago, both Microsoft and IBM were offered a proven technology that would have almost completely eliminated the threat of boot-sector viruses, without compromising any system functions. They were offered this technology free of charge, but neither company incorporated it into its products. More recently we have seen evidence of Microsoft's attitude towards making its products more secure: the corporation brought out a version of Outlook that deleted any email that carried any attachment. This example of overkill was an obvious attempt at proving to the market that shielded products have a drastic cost inherent in their use. Therefore, we do not foresee commercial desktop products becoming much safer in the near future.

Taking another look at the original point about desktop operating systems, it is instructive to examine the recent spate of Linux viruses. A version of UNIX, Linux is actually a very secure system. Yet, as the use of Linux grows, our assertion that more use of a given platform means more viruses is proving prescient. Linux does not have anything like the number of viruses that are extant in the DOS and Windows worlds, and the types of virus that plague Linux tend to be different. However, viruses are a problem in all environments. Remember that Fred Cohen did his initial experiments with mainframes. A new operating system is not going to make the virus threat disappear, although a properly designed system could definitely reduce the problem.

We are also seeing a very disturbing trend towards convergence in virus writing. Until now, viruses have been a problem all on their own. The major issue in dealing with viruses was the cost of detecting them and the time spent cleaning them. Occasionally a virus with a destructive payload endangered data, but that was pretty much the most we had to be concerned about.

Viruses are no longer an isolated threat. They are being used to launch attacks from one operating system platform, aimed at another. Invasions of privacy, with attendant social and legal problems, are being carried as payloads in recent viruses. Viral programs are using a variety of technologies to update themselves on the fly, and make their presence known once they have invaded a system. We have not yet seen specific viruses successfully used to install Trojans, trap doors, RATs, and/or DDoS zombies on the machines they infect, but there have already been attempts, and we predict the trials will achieve that end shortly.

When malware starts to use the viruses' power of self-reproduction effectively, we had better be able to deal with the new virus threat.

Closing Comments

If you have actually read the book to this point, and not just skipped ahead to see how it ends, you may be feeling a little nervous right now. Don't despair—at least, not entirely. The virus danger is real—but it isn't absolute. Like most of life, it's a bit of a bad-news/good-news situation.

Bad News: Security Specialists Don't Know Much—About Viruses

We have noted in Chapter 8 that most security experts are not really informed about viruses. Our list of general security texts, in the same chapter, noted that many otherwise excellent works fail when they attempt to address the virus topic. The CISSP CBK (Common Body of Knowledge) course takes a full eight days to complete, and, at the moment, contains roughly 2,000 slides of material. Only four of those slides deal with viruses. Again, we do not fault people who are trying their best to stay on top of a variety of important issues, of which viruses are only one, and the CBK course shows how big a task this is. You have no way of knowing whether an "expert" is giving you valid information about viruses unless you are educated about viruses yourself.

Yes, we are quite well aware that we have been sounding this same alert over and over again throughout the book. However, in our experience, many of the problems we encounter professionally have been caused by people taking bad advice, very often from "experts". You are just as smart as most of them, and, now that you've finished this book, possibly even better informed. And in this case, a little knowledge can help you quite a lot. Which brings us to...

Good News: A Little Education and Basic Policies Can Really Help

In our not-so-humble opinion, you've taken a good first step in buying this book. (You... did buy it, didn't you?) Finding out about the reality of viruses will prepare you to begin addressing the problem.

You can take a bigger step by training your systems' users. We'd love to have you buy copies of this book for all of them, or recommend that they get copies themselves, but, more realistically, we'd be almost as happy if you copied (small) relevant portions of this book for your training materials and gave us credit for what you use. A half-day session would probably do for a simple virus course, covering a few foundational security policies.

What kind of policies? Well, we've gone over a number of them in Chapter 7, a few more in Chapter 10, and another group in Chapter 17. But, as a quick recap, here are a few that can really help in the current environment:

▶ *Don't double-click on attachments.* Don't open attachments until you've checked them out. You can check them by using an up-to-date scanner, or by contacting the person who sent you the attachment, to be sure of what it is.

▶ *When sending attachments, be really specific.* Don't just reply with the same subject line, or a vague "Here's the stuff you wanted". Use a subject line that says, "Here is a WordPerfect document file containing the Anderson contract". In the body of the message, tell your correspondent "Frank, this is Mary. This file is the third version of the contract with Anderson Corporation, as you requested on Thursday. The file is called 'Anderson Contract 3.wpd' and is 34,958 bytes long". This gives the person on the other end some assurance that the message, and file, really is from you, and isn't just some ambiguous, "Hi, I'm fun! Open me!" virus or Trojan come-on.

▶ *Don't blindly use Microsoft products as a company standard.* We know this point will be controversial, but consider it carefully. You can read MS Word documents with StarOffice or other office suite packages, or even with WordViewer, which is available from Microsoft. MS Internet Explorer is more dangerous than Netscape. MS Outlook is more dangerous than Pegasus. MS Windows...well, you get the picture. You do have options.

▶ *Disable Windows Script Host. Disable ActiveX. Disable VBScript. Disable JavaScript. Disable cookies, although that's more for privacy than for viruses.* Run with those dangerous technologies disabled by default. When you come across a web site that requires them, ask yourself whether you really need what that site has to offer. Don't send HTML-formatted email. (It might be as well to eschew Rich Text Format as well.) Be very wary of receiving HTML-formatted email, and use a mailer that informs you when you do receive such email. If you receive email that requires JavaScript, then you should very seriously question why someone wants his or her email to run programs on your computer.

▶ *Use more than one scanner.* Have defence in depth. A content scanner on a firewall is convenient, but probably will take shortcuts. An on-access scanner is handy but must operate within the confines of the operating system. Do a manual scan with a different product every once in a while, just to make sure. Of course, defence in depth is more than using multiple scanners—it is having protection at each layer of your network: at desktops, file servers, email servers, gateways, and each point of entry into your network. It is also reasonable to have more than one vendor's product in this mix—such as one vendor on the desktop and a different vendor on the email servers. This prevents having the "all your eggs in one basket" philosophy that so many organizations fall victim to in an attempt to minimize contracts and maintenance or training efforts.

▶ *Don't think you're safe: everybody is at risk.* The best current estimates are that every large company gets hit at least once a month, and that each infestation affects roughly 100 computers. Even virus experts get caught. You can too.

Bad News: Convergence Is Going to Get Worse

As noted earlier, the different forms of malicious software are starting to converge. Trojans are beginning to install trap doors, RATs are initiating zombies, and viruses are sending spam. As these forms combine, new and more powerful attacks will begin to make computing more dangerous for everyone.

An additional hazard is associated with convergence. We have tried to be clear, in this book, on the various forms of malware, and the dangers of each. When new forms arise, the media aren't likely to be as careful. You will hear about weird and wonderful programs, described in ways that confuse what is really happening. Try to keep in mind the specific types of bad software, and the real operations that might be present.

Good News: Just the Same, but More

Viruses don't really present a new threat; it's just the same old rancid wine in new bottles, and more of them.

In reality, there truly is almost nothing new under the sun. There have always been people trying to damage your data, or your computers, or your operations. Almost as soon as there was software, there was also bad software. All that viruses do is to permit multiple attacks, from multiple sources, faster than used to be the case.

An example of the quantitative, rather than qualitative, change in the problem is the situation with regard to laws addressing computing. Lots of people have called for legislation to make writing viruses a crime. It is extraordinarily difficult to draft such edicts, and, in fact, we don't believe that such specific decrees are absolutely necessary. There are already ordinances prohibiting mischief and vandalism. Companies can bring lawsuits against individuals or groups who have harmed them. So it would be perfectly possible to bring a suit or charges against the author of a virus, assuming you are game to track down the perpetrator. All that is needed is the care and will to do it. If you can't be bothered to collect and prepare the evidence for a prosecution, then a new law declaring virus writing to be illegal will not help, and may add to the thrill for virus writers and wannabes.

Existing laws are suitable for computer crimes, given some work and education. For mischief, prove mischief. For theft, prove value and loss. Unless we learn how to use Common Law against computer crime, we shouldn't try to write new laws against new crimes. Until then we are going to have more cases of new laws making certain prime numbers illegal, or people facing 15-year prison terms for installing screensavers.

NOTE

Don't believe numbers can be illegal? Have a look at the following sites:
http://www.utm.edu/research/primes/curios/485...443.html,
http://www.utm.edu/research/primes/curios/207...957.html, or
http://www.utm.edu/research/primes/curios/945...469.html.
If the pages have changed, go to http://www.utm.edu/research/primes/curios/swish/
and search for the term illegal.

Bad News: Multiple Points of Attack Can Scale the Problem

Still, viruses present a greater risk than many other forms of malicious software. A virus need only be created and released once. If it is successful, it spreads on its own, attacking systems as it goes. Each system compromised becomes another source of infection. If you aren't part of the solution in the viral world, you are most definitely part of the problem.

> **NOTE**
>
> *Rob Slade wanted to call his first book* The Binary Hydra. *In Greek mythology, Hercules had to kill a beast. Every time he cut its head off, it grew two more. The same thing can happen with viruses. Once you have been infested, you must eradicate every trace of the virus, or it will simply start to replicate all over again. This means eliminating every copy in every email message on every disk in every machine.*

We've seen the result in other fields. Denial of service (DoS) attacks have been around for years. They were a nuisance, but major sites on the Internet had so much capacity that the small DoS attacks were just shrugged off. Then came February of 2000, and suddenly major corporate sites on the Internet were no longer available. Distributed denial of service (DDoS) used the same kind of multiplication of power that viruses make possible.

Good News: Existing Tools and Some Diligence Can Work

Fred Cohen has actually proved that a perfect defence against viruses is not possible. And, as we have seen, the protection provided by operating systems and antiviral tools is often very much less than perfect. Even so, the tools that do exist, and the policies that we have suggested, can keep you very safe. With a proper set of guidelines and some knowledge of the field, you can reduce your risk so thoroughly that, for all intents and purposes, your protection is complete. Two of the authors of this book have spent many years working with and testing viruses, and exploring data networks, and have never yet become infected from a virus in the wild.

Reread this book. Check up on the other sources of information that we've pointed out. Consider some good antiviral policies for your workplace. Get some antiviral tools in place, at various points in your enterprise. Keep up with the field. Read news reports and virus warnings with scepticism. Don't panic.

And, hey: be careful out there.

Stop Press

It takes a long time to write a book, and changes can happen pretty fast in the technology business. Therefore, we have intentionally kept this space blank until the book is almost complete. What we want to cover in this section are new viruses and virus-related events and technologies.

We don't expect this material to be vital to your protection. In fact, we fully expect that any late-breaking news will confirm that the recommendations made elsewhere will keep you safe. With that in mind, we anticipate that each entry here will follow a "what's new" and "what's not" structure, telling you about the new virus or technology and then reminding you about established virus security principles that apply.

If you would like to look up details on the specific viruses covered here, go to the virus encyclopaedia web sites listed in Chapter 8, and use the search functions available.

RTF Is Not a Panacea

What's New

When Microsoft Word macro viruses appeared, many people recommended the use of Rich Text Format (RTF) files. RTF has been around for a long time, and is a file structure that can be used to exchange documents between different types of word processing programs. Since RTF is a text-only format (it uses legible tags that people can, with a little work, understand), it cannot contain executable code and, in particular, cannot contain macros and macro viruses.

The WM/Cap Word macro virus (see Chapter 13) presented a bit of a problem. When MS Word users tried to save files as RTF, Cap would intercept the function and generate an infected Word document file, but with a filename that had an .RTF extension. However, looking at the file with a simple text editor such as Notepad would show the difference. True RTF was still safe.

However, that is no longer the case. Microsoft has extended its handling of RTF with its own programs, particularly Word. A tag, created by Microsoft and not part of the basic standard, now allows an .RTF file to link to another file, and this file can be a Microsoft Word document or template. Therefore, when MS Word opens a file that is written in Rich Text Format, it may also open an additional file. If Word's macro detection feature is active, it will check the original .RTF file for macros, but will pronounce the file clean since it doesn't have any macros. The feature will not check the second file, however. Therefore, you now can become infected by opening an .RTF file in Word.

You might note that another file must be involved, and may object that you should become suspicious when asked to copy two files to your computer where one should be enough. However, the link to the second file can take place over the Internet, so the second file would be invisible to the user unless he or she examines the tags in the .RTF file.

So far this function has not been used in a virus, but there is a Trojan horse program called Goga that uses it to steal your account and password information. More information can be found at
http://www.kaspersky.com/news.asp?tnews=0&nview=1&id=191&page=0.

Microsoft's take on the issue can be found at
http://www.microsoft.com/technet/security/bulletin/MS01-028.asp, which contains
a reasonable outline of the situation, plus pointers to patches that can help.

What's Not

Well, we told you not to trust Microsoft, now, didn't we?

Leaving that aside, this is still a situation where you are most likely to encounter an
attack from an email attachment. Don't trust unknown files. Don't double-click on them.

In addition, you can configure your system so that .RTF files are not associated
with Microsoft Word. You can open them with WordViewer, WordPad, Notepad,
or a non-Microsoft word processor, and be safer.

Poly/Noped

What's New

This VBScript worm displays a message about stopping child pornography. The code
does the usual Melissa and LoveLetter trick of sending itself to entries in the Microsoft
Outlook Address Book. After it does that, it scans for JPEG files on the hard disk,
looking for specific strings in the filename that the virus author obviously thought might
relate to pornography. The worm will collect these files and email them to addresses
thought to belong to law enforcement agencies.

What's Not

So, are virus writers trying to prove that viruses really are useful? Well, they've
tried that before. One old program carried a payload that would encrypt your data
for you, while another tried to compress the data on your disks, in order to save space.
Unfortunately, both of those programs stole the utility code from legitimate programs,
and both had serious bugs.

Is the VX crowd showing us how to use viruses as spy tools? That's been thought
of before, and thoroughly discussed more than a decade ago. The problems relating to
such viruses should be fairly obvious. Most countries have laws against illegal searches
and invasion of privacy. In addition, you are going to harvest a great many cute bathtub
pictures before you ever get to serious child pornography. Finally, what is to stop
someone writing a worm that *places* illegal material on your computer?

Mandragore

What's New

Mandragore spreads itself as an executable file. Users must download the file and
run it in order to become infected. However, the virus uses the Gnutella file-sharing

system to advertise itself. A copy of the virus registers itself as an active node within the Gnutella network, and intercepts requests for file searching. Mandragore will return a positive result, and create a copy of itself named appropriately for the request. The virus sends itself only in response to requests, so computers without software such as Gnotella, BearShare, LimeWire, or ToadNode will not obtain copies, unless Gnutella users send the files obtained to others. The virus carries no damaging payload, and you can detect infections by looking for a file called GSPOT.EXE in the Windows startup folder.

What's Not

Didn't we tell you not to put that file in your computer? You don't know where it's been! Actually, this might be the closest thing we've ever seen to a virus that really is associated with pirate software, if it were not for the fact that peer-to-peer file sharing has many other legitimate uses. Other than responding to a request rather than promoting a come-on, this virus is just another example of social engineering trying to get you to run something on your computer.

SULFNBK Hoax

What's New

The SULFNBK hoax warning caught a lot of people. This was because many users, when they followed the instructions, actually did find a file named SULFNBK.EXE on their computers, and believed that they had been infected. Thus, the hoax wasn't just a simple chain letter: each new generation was created by someone who was really convinced that he or she had been hit by the virus.

That many people found the SULFNBK.EXE file was not surprising. It is part of later versions of Windows, and appears on every version of Windows 98, among others. The file is a utility that will restore long filenames if the file system has been damaged somehow—by the use of a DOS disk utility program, for example.

What's Not

Actually, we aren't really sure that the SULFNBK warning started out as a hoax. The Magistr virus infects Windows system files when it mails itself out, and SULFNBK is one of the files that may be so infected. It's quite possible that a user was infected with Magistr, and, not knowing all the details, sent out a warning with one vital mistake.

We tried to make this point in Chapter 16 with regard to virus hoaxes. Verify the validity of what you read, and what you send. Even if a message does not contain all the characteristics of a classic hoax, you may very well be spreading misinformation, and wasting bandwidth, mail queue space, and, most importantly, the time and attention of many people.

Sadmind

What's New

Sadmind is a fairly classic Internet worm. It propagates itself using a buffer overrun exploit on Solaris (a version of UNIX) systems. While it searches for new Solaris machines to infect, it also probes for Microsoft Internet Information Server (IIS) web servers. It will attempt to deface the main page on the IIS server.

What's Not

Buffer overruns aren't new. Patch your software when one is discovered (and teach the next generation of programmers not to be so sloppy).

Web page defacement attacks aren't new. Secure your public data from tampering. (No, this isn't a book on Web security. If you are responsible for a server, go to http://victoria.tc.ca/techrev/mnbkscnt.htm or http://sun.soci.niu.edu/~rslade/ mnbkscnt.htm and choose a book on Web security from those reviewed there.)

Cross-platform attacks aren't new. As long as someone is only mounting an attack, they can send probes from any computer to any other reachable system.

Cheese

What's New

Cheese is a Linux worm that searches for computers that have been infected by a previous Linux worm, based on a trap door that the prior worm left on the infected machine. Cheese fixes the security loophole. The worm contains text that indicates it was written with good intent, to try to help secure systems.

What's Not

It's been done before. The Ohio and Den Zuk viruses were supposed to eradicate copies of the Brain virus, but Ohio and Den Zuk actually created more problems than Brain did. Cohen has suggested that "good" viral programs could undertake network management, and security patching is part of network management. However, "useful" viral programs need to be a lot more sophisticated than Cheese is before they can be considered genuinely safe to release.

Lindose/Winux

What's New

There is a virus that can infect both Linux ELF files and Windows PE-EXE files.

What's Not

Big deal. Jerusalem and sURIV3 could infect both .COM and .EXE files back in 1987.

MacSimpsons

What's New

MacSimpsons is a virus written in AppleScript. It mails itself out to users listed in the Outlook Express or Entourage mailer programs.

What's Not

Script viruses exist. Don't download and run files—even if you are using a Mac.

Outlook View Control

What's New

The Outlook View Control is an ActiveX control, supplied by Microsoft and related to the Digital Dashboard system, that allows users to display and view their Outlook mail or calendar data through a web page. The control is supposed to allow only passive viewing, but it contains a bug that permits manipulation of the data and even lets an attacker run malicious code. This bug can be exploited from a malicious web page or HTML format email, even if the user only previews the message. Outlook or Internet Explorer users do not need to open or click on any attachments to invoke the control.

What's Not

ActiveX is a dangerous technology. Disable it. Disable VBScript and JavaScript while you're at it.

Code Red/Bady

What's New

Microsoft's Internet Information Services (IIS) contains a buffer overrun vulnerability in the index server. A worm called Code Red now exploits this vulnerability in order to deface web pages on the server and search for other IIS servers to infect. Of course, a number of worms use buffer overflow bugs. Code Red, due to the way in which it tries to find other IIS servers to infect, may create bandwidth flooding and denial of service situations for certain IP addresses. It would be difficult to say that this constitutes a DoS attack, since the problem appears to be related to sloppy coding rather than a deliberate assault. There also seems to be a deliberate DoS attack against whitehouse.gov.

An estimated quarter of a million (250,000) servers were infected in the first week, and possibly hours, after the release (or discovery, at least) of the worm. The whitehouse.gov site did not have any problem defending against the DoS attack: since the flood used a hard-coded IP address, that address was simply taken out of service. Some security experts were, however, concerned that Code Red would launch successive waves of attacks, between periods of dormancy. In addition, a number of variants appeared soon after the initial wave.

You can find out more about Code Red from any of the virus encyclopaedias or at http://www.eeye.com/html/Research/Advisories/AD20010618.html, or get details and patches at http://www.microsoft.com/technet/security/bulletin/MS01-033.asp.

What's Not

Buffer overruns aren't new. Keep your systems patched. Defacing web pages isn't new. Keep your servers patched. Bugs in virus code aren't new. And we warned you about convergence—even if it is by accident.

Code Red was definitely a media virus. Some anti-virus vendors promoted it as a means of increasing their own visibility. Some security organizations hyped it for the same reason. However, for some reason it caught public imagination, and even the US FBI held a press conference predicting dire catastrophes resulting from the worm. Since the cure was known, and only a few percent of Internet users could possibly have been affected in any case, it is difficult to see what all the fuss was about. Code Red only served to take attention away from a much more serious problem: Sircam.

Sircam

What's New

As the book goes to the final stages, the big virus news is W32/Sircam@mm. The virus has been hugely successful. It is also huge. The size of the executable itself is around 150,000 bytes. Sircam uses all kinds of virus techniques: like Melissa, it can mail out your private files; like Love Bug, it uses the double filename extension to fool people into opening it; like Stages, it uses variations in the message it sends.

When Sircam is active on your machine, it will search for .GIF, .JPG, .JPEG, .MPEG, .MOV, .MPG, .PDF, .PNG, .PS, and .ZIP files that you have. It will choose one, incorporate the file into the body of the virus, and create a message with itself as a file attachment. Rob Slade received a message with a company's personnel file attached, as well as other files from around the world. Confidential files from the government of the Ukraine ended up being sent to news services.

The filename of the attachment will use the original name of your file, with an added .BAT, .COM, .EXE, .LNK, or .PIF extension, so that Windows will see it as an executable file. For example, your file "Property Values.ps" will become "Property Values.ps.com". The subject of the message created will depend upon the filename, so it will always be different.

Sircam uses information from the Microsoft Outlook mailer program to obtain email addresses for generating mail, the network mail server to use if available, and information to use in regard to the sender, but it contains code for creating and transmitting the mail itself. It will also harvest email addresses from temporary cache files, and contains addresses for SMTP servers to use if no information is found on the infected machine.

The virus hides a copy of its code in the Recycled folder, and creates a Registry key that directs all calls for .EXE programs to run the virus first. In addition, Sircam will infect other machines across local networks, using Microsoft networking shares.

At the time of writing, the virus has not yet been fully analyzed. It may have payloads causing file deletion and filling of disk space with text files.

What's Not

All other considerations aside, somebody has to open the file for it to get a hold. *Don't double-click on email attachments!* At the time of writing, all the technologies known to be used in Sircam were previously used in other viruses.

Summary

That's all we wrote. Except for the appendixes.

Hopefully we've told you what viruses are, where some of them came from, how they work, and how to protect against them. You've got some resources to draw upon, and suggestions about policies for safer computing. Some material has touched upon social and legal aspects of viral programs.

But the book has to end sometime. So, until the next edition, it's over to you, now.

Appendixes

A

Frequently Asked Questions on VIRUS-L/comp.virus

K en van Wyk set up the VIRUS-L/comp.virus mailing list and newsgroup following 1987's LeHigh virus incident. Release 1 of the FAQ (Frequently Asked Questions) document was reprinted in Pamela Kane's *PC Security and Virus Protection Handbook* (M&T Books, 1994). However, the much more comprehensive Release 2.00 has never been reprinted, to the best of our knowledge, and is reproduced here by kind permission of Nick FitzGerald, moderator of the comp.virus newsgroup and FAQ maintainer. It was last updated on 9th October, 1995, and so does not deal with all the issues that concern today's malware manager. However, it remains a very well-written and comprehensive primer with contributions from highly reputable researchers, and answers questions that are still asked today.

The mailing list and newsgroup have not been publicly active for some years, so we have removed administrative detail concerning the newsgroup mailing list, and have added notes where necessary in the light of more recent developments. Author notes retain the same format as within the main chapters of this book. Many of the questions answered are also addressed in detail within this book. This appendix doesn't present such material unless it adds substantially to the information already included or represents a valid alternative view.

The complete 1995 version of the FAQ is periodically posted to USENET. A rough HTML version is available from www.faqs.org/faqs/computer-virus/faq/.

Primary Contributors

The following people, listed in alphabetical order, have provided significant content and/or editorial input to this FAQ sheet:

Mark Aitchison, Vaughan Bell, Claude Bersano-Hayes, Matt Bishop, Vesselin Bontchev, Bruce Burrell, David Chess, John-David Childs, Olivier M. J. Crepin-Leblond, Nick FitzGerald, Richard Ford, Alan Glover, Yaron Y. Goland, Sarah Gordon, Mikko Hypponen, John Kida, Kevin Marcus, Anthony Naggs, Donald G. Peters, A. Padgett Peterson, Y. Radai, Brian Seborg, Fridrik Skulason, Rob Slade, Gene Spafford, Otto Stolz, and Ken van Wyk.

What are the known viruses?

The reader should be aware that there is no universally accepted naming convention for viruses, nor is there any standard means of testing. As a consequence, nearly *all* virus information is highly subjective and open to interpretation and dispute.

There are several major sources of information on specific viruses. Probably the largest one is Patricia Hoffman's hypertext VSUM. While VSUM is quite complete, it covers only PC viruses and is regarded by many in the anti-virus field as inaccurate, so we advise you not to rely solely on it. You can download VSUM from most major archive sites.

NOTE

While the web site http://www.vsum.com/ still exists, neither the web resource nor the VSUM database itself seems to have been updated for some years. None of us has ever rated its accuracy highly. We do not know of a current source for the Computer Virus Catalog or for CAORbase, although the Virus Test Center in Hamburg is still operational. We have removed obsolete URLs and contact information from this appendix.

A more precise source of information is the Computer Virus Catalog (CVC), published by the Virus Test Center in Hamburg. It contains highly technical descriptions of computer viruses for several platforms, including DOS, Mac, Amiga, Atari ST, and UNIX. Unfortunately, the DOS section is quite incomplete.

Another small collection of good technical descriptions of PC viruses, called CAORbase, is also available from the University of Hamburg.

A fourth source of information is the monthly *Virus Bulletin,* published in the UK. Among other things, it gives detailed technical information on viruses; a one-year subscription, however, costs $395.

NOTE

Check the Virus Bulletin web site at http://www.virusbtn.com/.

The book *Virus Encyclopaedia,* which is part of the printed documentation of Dr. Solomon's AntiVirus ToolKit (a commercial DOS anti-virus program) is more complete than the CVC list and just as accurate; however, it lists only DOS viruses. This book may be available separately from the ToolKit.

NOTE

Dr. Solomon's (the organization and the product) have been subsumed by Network Associates. The Virus Encyclopaedia ran to two editions (the second coauthored by Dr. Alan Solomon and Dmitry O. Gryaznov). It remains a good source of information on early PC viruses, but the older version is more likely to be found separate from the product.

Where can I get more information on viruses and related topics?

Five very good books on computer viruses that cover most of the introductory and technical questions you might have are described here.

Computers under Attack: Intruders, Worms and Viruses, edited by Peter J. Denning (ACM Press/Addison-Wesley, 1990). This is a book of collected readings that discuss computer viruses, computer worms, break-ins, social aspects, and many other items related to computer security and malicious software. It is a very solid, readable collection that doesn't require a highly technical background. Price: $20.50.

Rogue Programs: Viruses, Worms and Trojan Horses, edited by Lance J. Hoffman (Van Nostrand Reinhold, 1990). This is a book of collected readings describing in detail how viruses work, where they come from, what they do, and so on. It also has material on worms, Trojan horse programs, and other malicious software programs. This book focuses more on mechanism and relatively less on social aspects than does the Denning book; however, there is an excellent piece by Anne Branscomb that covers legal aspects. Price: $32.95.

A Pathology of Computer Viruses, by David Ferbrache (Springer-Verlag, 1992). This is an in-depth book on the history, operation, and effects of computer viruses. It is one of the most complete books on the subject, with an extensive history section, as well as sections on Macintosh viruses, network worms, and UNIX viruses. Price: $49.00.

A Short Course on Computer Viruses, 2nd Edition, by Dr. Fred B. Cohen (Wiley, 1994). This book is by a well-known pioneer in virus research, who has also written dozens of technical papers on the subject. Price: $35.00 ($45.00 with accompanying diskette).

Robert Slade's Guide to Computer Viruses, by Robert Slade (Springer-Verlag, 1994). This book is a comprehensive introduction to computer viruses, written in a clear and easy style for non-experts. Price: $29.00.

A somewhat dated, but still useful, high-level description of viruses, suitable for a complete novice with little computer background, is *Computer Viruses: Dealing with Electronic Vandalism and Programmed Threats*, by Eugene H. Spafford, Kathleen A. Heaphy, and David J. Ferbrache (ITAA [Arlington, VA], 1989). ITAA (Information Technology Association of America) is a computer industry service organization and not a publisher. While many people have indicated they find this book a very understandable reference, it is now out of print; however, portions of it have been reprinted in many other places, including Denning's and Hoffman's books (described earlier in this section).

It is also worth consulting various publications such as *Computers & Security* and *SECURE Computing* (both of which, while not limited to viruses, contain many relevant papers).

What are computer viruses?

Fred Cohen "wrote the book" on computer viruses, through his Ph.D. research, dissertation, and various related scholarly publications. He developed a theoretical mathematical model of computer virus behaviour, and used this to test various hypotheses about virus spread. Cohen's formal definition (model) of a virus does not easily translate into English, but his own, well-known, informal definition is "a computer virus is a computer program that can infect other computer programs by modifying them in such a way as to include a (possibly evolved) copy of itself". Note that a program does not have to cause outright damage (such as deleting or corrupting files) in order to be classified as a "virus" under this definition.

The problem with Cohen's popular definition is that it doesn't capture many of the subtleties of his mathematical model—as indeed, few informal definitions do—and questions arise that can be answered only by checking his formal model. Using his formal definitions, Cohen classifies some things as viruses that most readers of VIRUS-L/comp.virus (and many experts) would not consider as viruses. For example, given certain circumstances on an IBM PC running DOS, the DISKCOPY program is classified as a virus by Cohen's formalisms.

This has led to some tension between what Cohen considers a "virus" and what is usually discussed on VIRUS-L. Several other definitions of *virus* have been proposed, but it is probably fair to say that most of us are concerned about things that the following definition identifies as viruses:

> A computer virus is a self-replicating program containing code that explicitly copies itself and that can "infect" other programs by modifying them or their environment, such that a call to an infected program implies a call to a possibly evolved copy of the virus.

Probably the major distinction between Cohen's definition and "viruses" as we tend to use the word is that we see them as deliberately designed to replicate (although there is some debate over this too). Cohen's definition does *not* require deliberate replication (and this would be difficult to build into his formal model).

Note that many people use the term *virus* loosely to cover any sort of program that tries to hide its possibly malicious function and/or tries to spread onto as many computers as possible, though some of these programs may more correctly be called "worms" or "Trojan horses". Also be aware that what constitutes a "program" for a virus to infect may include a lot more than is at first obvious—don't assume too much about what a virus can or can't do!

These software "pranks" are very serious; they are spreading faster than they are being stopped, and even the least harmful of viruses could be life-threatening. For example, in the context of a hospital life-support system, a virus that "simply" stops a computer and displays a message until a key is pressed could be fatal. Further, virus writers cannot halt the spread of their creations, even if they wanted to. It requires computer users making a concerted effort to be "virus-aware" rather than continuing the ambivalence that has allowed computer viruses to become such a problem.

Computer viruses are actually a special case of something known as "malicious logic" or "malware", and other forms of malicious logic are also discussed in VIRUS-L/comp.virus. It can be important to understand the distinctions between viruses and these other forms of malware.

What is a worm?

A computer *worm* is a self-contained program (or set of programs) that is able to spread functional copies of itself or its segments to other computer systems (usually via network connections).

Note that unlike viruses, worms do not need to attach themselves to a host program. There are two types of worms: host computer worms and network worms.

Host computer worms are entirely contained in the computers on which they run and use network connections only to copy themselves to other computers. Host computer worms where the original terminates itself after launching a copy on another host (so there is only one copy of the worm running somewhere on the network at any given moment) are sometimes called *rabbits*.

Network worms consist of multiple parts (called *segments*), each running on different machines (possibly performing different actions) and using the network for several communication purposes. Propagating a segment from one machine to another is only one of those purposes. Network worms that have one main segment that coordinates the work of the other segments are sometimes called *octopuses*.

The infamous Internet Worm (perhaps covered best in "The Internet Worm Program: An Analysis", Eugene H. Spafford, Purdue Technical Report CSD-TR-823) was a host computer worm, while the Xerox PARC worms were network worms. (A good starting point for these is "The Worm Programs—Early Experience with a Distributed Computation", Communications of the ACM, 25, No.3, March 1982, pp. 172–80.)

What is a Trojan horse?

A *Trojan horse* is a program that does something undocumented that the programmer intended, but that some users would not approve of if they knew about it. According to some people, a virus is a particular case of a Trojan horse—namely, one that can spread to other programs (i.e., it turns them into Trojans too). According to others, a virus that does not do any deliberate damage (other than merely replicating) is not a Trojan. Finally, despite the definitions, many people use the term *Trojan* to refer only to *nonreplicating* malware, so that the set of Trojans and the set of viruses are disjoint.

What are the indications of a virus infection?

Many people associate destruction—file corruption, reformatted disks, and the like—with viruses. Machines infected with viruses that do this kind of damage often display such damage too. This is unfortunate, as usually viruses can be detected or prevented from infecting long before they can inflict any (serious) damage, although many viruses have no "payload" at all. Note that viruses that simply reformat the hard disk shortly after infecting a machine tend to wipe themselves out faster than they spread, and don't get far.

Thus, the more successful viruses typically try to spread as much as possible before delivering their payload, if any. As these tend to be the viruses you are most likely to encounter, you should be aware that there are usually symptoms of virus infection before any (or much) damage is done.

Some virus authors have written various kinds of symptoms into their programs, such as messages, music, and graphical displays. The main indications, however, are changes in file sizes and contents, changes to interrupt vectors, or the reassignment of other system resources. The unaccounted use of RAM and a reduction in the amount reported to be in the machine are important indicators. Examination of program code is valuable to the trained eye, but even a novice can often spot the gross differences between a valid boot sector and some viral ones. These symptoms, along with longer disk activity and strange behavior from the hardware, may instead be caused by genuine software, by harmless "joke" programs, or by hardware faults.

The only foolproof way to determine that a virus is present is for an expert to analyse the assembly code contained in all programs and system areas, but this is usually impracticable. Virus scanners go some way towards performing this analysis by looking in that code for known viruses; some even use heuristic means to spot "virus like" code, but these are not always reliable. It is wise to arm yourself with the latest anti-virus software and to pay close attention to your system. In particular, look for any unexpected change in the memory map or configuration as soon as you start the computer. For users of DOS 5.0+, the MEM program with the /C switch is very handy for this. If you have DR DOS, use MEM with the /A switch; if you have an earlier DOS version, use CHKDSK or the commonly available MAPMEM utility. You don't have to know what all the numbers mean, only that they have changed *unexpectedly*. Mac users have "info" options, which give some indication of memory use, but may need ResEdit to supply more detailed information.

If you run Windows on your PC and you suddenly start getting messages at Windows start-up that 32-bit disk access cannot be used, this often indicates that a boot-sector virus has infected your PC.

What steps should be taken in diagnosing and identifying viruses?

Most of the time, a virus scanner program will take care of diagnosing and identifying viruses for you. To help identify problems early, run a virus scanner:

▶ On new programs and diskettes. (Write-protect diskettes before scanning them.)

▶ When an integrity checker reports a mismatch.

▶ When a generic monitoring program sounds an alarm.

▶ When you receive an updated version of a scanner (or you have a chance to run a different scanner than the one you have been using).

Because of the time required, it is not generally advisable to set a scanner to check your entire hard disk on every boot.

If you run into an alarm and your scanner doesn't identify anything or doesn't properly clean up for you, first verify that the version you are using is the most recent. Then get in touch with a reputable anti-virus researcher, who may ask you to send in a copy of the infected file.

What is the best way to remove a virus?

To keep downtime short and losses low, do the minimum that you must to restore the system to a normal state, starting with booting the system from a clean diskette. It is *never* necessary to low-level format a hard disk to recover from a virus infection!

If backups of infected or damaged files are available, and if appropriate care has been taken to ensure that the backups do not include infected files, restoring from backup is the safest solution, even though it can be a lot of work if many files are involved.

More commonly, a disinfecting program is used, though disinfection is somewhat controversial and problematic. If the virus is a boot-sector infector, you can continue using the computer with relative safety (if the hard disk's partition table is left intact) by booting from a clean system diskette. However, it is wise to go through all your diskettes removing any infections, because sooner or later you will carelessly leave an infected diskette in the machine when it reboots, or give an infected diskette to someone who doesn't have appropriate defences to avoid infection.

You can cure most PC boot-sector infections by using the following simple process—pay particular care to make the checks in steps 2 and 3.

Note that removing an MBR virus in the way described here may not be desirable, and may even cause valuable information to be lost. For instance, the One_Half virus gradually encrypts the infected hard drive "inward" (starting from the end and moving towards the beginning), encrypting two more tracks at each boot. The information about the size of the encrypted area is *only* stored in the MBR. If the virus is removed using the following method, this information will be irrecoverably lost and part of the disk with unknown size will remain encrypted.

1. Boot the PC from a clean system floppy—this must be MS-DOS 5.0 or version 6.0 or higher of PC-DOS or DR DOS. This diskette should carry copies of the DOS utilities MEM, FDISK, CHKDSK, UNFORMAT, and SYS.

2. Check that your memory configuration is "normal" with MEM. Check that your hard disk partitioning is normal, by running FDISK with the Display partition information option selected. MS-DOS 5.0 (or later) users can use UNFORMAT /L /PARTN.

3. Try doing a DIR of your hard disk(s) (C, D, and so on).

   You should continue with step 4 *only* if all the tests in step 2 and this step pass. Do *not* continue if you were unable to access *all* your hard disks correctly, as you will quite possibly damage critical information, making permanent data damage or loss more likely.

4. Replace the program (code) part of the MBR by using the MS-DOS or PC-DOS FDISK /MBR command. If you use DR DOS 6.0 or later, select the FDISK menu option Re-write Master Boot Record.

5. Replace the DOS boot sector using the command SYS C (or whatever is correct for your first hard disk partition). For this step, the version of DOS on your boot diskette must be *exactly* the same as is installed on your hard disk. (This may mean you first must reboot with a clean boot diskette other than that used in step 1.) If you are using a disk compression system, such as DoubleSpace or DriveSpace, check the documentation on how to locate the physical drive on which the compressed volume is installed, and apply the SYS command to that drive instead. Usually this is drive H or I.

6. Reboot from your hard disk and check that all is well—if not (which is unlikely if you made the recommended checks), seek expert help.

7. As you will get reinfected by forgetting an infected diskette in your A drive at boot time, you have to clean all your floppies as well. This is harder, as there is

no simple way of doing it with standard DOS tools. You can copy the files from each of your floppies, reformat them, and copy the files back, but this is a very tedious process (and prone to destructive errors!). At this point, you probably should consider obtaining some good anti-virus software.

FDISK /MBR will overwrite only the boot loader code in the MBR of the *first* hard drive in a system. However, a few viruses will infect both drives in a two-drive system. Although normal PC configurations never boot from the second hard drive, should the second drive from such a machine ever be used as the first drive in a system, it will still be infected and in need of disinfecting.

What are "false positives" and "false negatives"?

A *false positive* (or Type-I) error is one in which anti-virus software claims that a virus has infected a given object when, in reality, the object is clean. This error is a failure of *detection.* A *false negative* (or Type-II) error is one in which the software fails to indicate that an infected object is infected. Clearly, false negatives are more serious than false positives, although both are undesirable.

Following from some of Cohen's work, it has been proven that every virus detector must have an infinite number of false positives, false negatives, or both. In other words, detection of viruses, either by appearance or behaviour, is *undecidable.* The interpretation and practical significance of this finding depends upon the interpretation of the terms used.

In the case of virus scanners, false positives are rare, but they can arise if the scan string selected for a given virus was not well chosen and is also present in some benign objects. In modern scanners, most false positives probably occur because some virus encryption engines produce very "normal looking" code, and scanners that only try to decide if a piece of code could have been generated by a known virus encryption procedure will occasionally identify "innocent" code as "suspicious". False negatives are more common with virus scanners because scanners will miss completely any new or heavily modified viruses.

One other serious problem could occur: a positive that is misdiagnosed. As an example, imagine a scanner faced with the Empire virus in a boot record that reports it as the Stoned virus. In this case, use of a Stoned-specific "cure" to recover from an Empire infection could result in an unreadable disk or loss of extended partitions. Similarly, sometimes "generic" disinfection can result in unusable files, unless a check is made (e.g. by comparing checksums) to verify that the recovered file is identical to the original file. The better generic disinfection products all store information about the original files to allow verification of recovery processes.

A particular type of false positive, where (part of) an *inactive* virus is detected, is known as a *ghost positive*. Ghost positives usually occur in one of four situations (the first two of which are examples of anti-virus programs "upsetting" each other):

▶ Ghost positives can be caused when the disinfection routine of an anti-virus program "unhooks" a virus from its target (be it a file or boot sector) but it does so in such a way that part of the virus code is left intact (although that code will never be executed). Another anti-virus program might see this code and report it is an infection. In this case, the second anti-virus program is seeing a "ghost"—part of a virus that was there.

▶ A scanner may "see" the unencoded scan strings of another scanner, left in memory after the first program has run, or held in memory by a resident scanner, and report these "ghosts" as active viruses.

▶ As explained elsewhere, a copy of an infected diskette boot sector, sitting in the disk buffers, may be detected and reported as an active virus.

▶ Disinfection procedures can result in virus "remnants" being left in "slack space" (disk space allocated to files but not actually occupied). As in the case of copies of infected diskette boot sectors being held in disk buffers, these remnants can be detected and incorrectly reported as being active. Ghost positives of this nature should disappear after running disk defragmentation or "optimization" programs with the option to "clean" slack space. Occasionally running a defragmenter (like MS-DOS 6's DEFRAG) after a full data backup is a good idea anyway—especially before installing new software. Unfortunately, DOS's DEFRAG does not have a "clean slack space" option, although some third-party defragmenters do. There are also utilities that clean unallocated and slack space, and these should remove ghost positives caused by remnants.

Could an anti-virus program itself be infected?

Yes, so it is important to obtain this software from good sources, and to trust results only after running scanners from a "clean" system. But there are situations where a scanner appears to be infected when it isn't.

Most anti-virus programs try very hard to identify viral infections only, but sometimes they give false alarms. If two different anti-virus programs are both of the "scanner" type, they will contain "scan strings" from which they identify viral infections. If the strings are not "encoded", then they may be identified as a virus by another scanner type program. Also, if the scanner does not remove the strings from memory after it has run, then another scanner may detect a virus string "in memory".

This often causes the second scanner to report that your system is "infected", but *only* after you have run the first scanner (which may be a memory-resident one). The major contributors to this FAQ are so tired of dealing with nonvirus reports of this sort that they *strongly* recommend users to avoid anti-virus software that doesn't keep its scan strings encoded in memory.

Some change-detection anti-virus programs add a snippet of code or data to a program in order to "protect" it. (This process is sometimes called *inoculation,* but this term is also used for other anti-virus techniques.) These file changes will likely be detected by other change-detection programs, and may therefore raise a warning of a suspicious file change. (See a later question for a discussion of the inadvisability of adding self-checking code to *existing* programs.)

It is good practice to use more than one anti-virus program; however, by their nature, multiple anti-virus programs may confuse each other!

NOTE

Anti-virus programs worth the disk space that they take up use change-detection self-checking techniques to see if they might have been infected with an unknown virus. Virus writers have been known to use techniques that specifically address known self-checking mechanisms in anti-virus software.

Where can I get a virus scanner for my UNIX system?

Basically, you shouldn't bother scanning for UNIX viruses at this point in time. Although it is possible to write UNIX-based viruses, we have yet to see any instance of a nonexperimental virus in that environment. Someone with sufficient knowledge and access to write an effective virus would be more likely to conduct other activities than virus writing. Furthermore, the typical form of software sharing in the UNIX environment does not easily support virus spread.

NOTE

The first sentence of this section was accurate enough in 1995, but as we were writing this book, Linux viruses were an increasing problem.

This answer is not meant to imply that UNIX viruses are impossible, or that there aren't security problems in a typical UNIX environment—there are. In fact, Cohen's first experimental virus was implemented and tested on a UNIX system. True viruses in the UNIX environment are, however, unlikely to spread well. For more information on UNIX security, see the book *Practical Unix Security* by Simon Garfinkel and Gene Spafford (O'Reilly and Associates, 1991). Price: $29.95 (it can be ordered via email from nuts@ora.com).

> ### *NOTE*
>
> *This excellent book went to a second edition some years ago: the title was changed to* Practical Unix and Internet Security *(O'Reilly and Associates, 1996).*

There *are* special cases in which scanning UNIX systems for non-UNIX viruses does make sense. For example, a UNIX system acting as a file server (e.g., PC-NFS) for PC systems is quite capable of containing PC-file-infecting viruses that are a danger to PC clients. Note that, in this example, the UNIX system would be scanned for PC viruses, not UNIX viruses. Also, *any* PC is vulnerable to PC MBR infectors, so you should take special care to prevent booting a PC-hosted UNIX OS from a floppy infected with an MBR virus.

In addition, a file integrity checker (to detect unauthorized changes in executable files) on UNIX systems is a very good idea. (One free program that can do this test, as well as other tests, is Tripwire, available by anonymous ftp from its home site of coast.cs.purdue.edu in /pub/COAST/Tripwire and from several other anti-virus sites.) Unauthorized file changes on UNIX systems are very common, although they are not usually due to virus activity.

Why does my scanner report an infection only sometimes?

There are circumstances where part of a virus exists in RAM without being active. If your scanner occasionally reports a virus in memory, it could be due to the operating system buffering diskette reads or harmlessly keeping disk contents that include a virus in memory, or because another scanner left scan strings (again harmlessly) in memory. These are known as *ghost positive* alerts.

I think I have detected a new virus; what do I do?

Whenever you have doubt about a virus, you should obtain the latest versions of several major virus scanners (not just one). Some scanning programs now use heuristic methods (F-PROT and TBSCAN are examples), and activity monitoring programs can report a program as being possibly infected when it is in fact perfectly safe (odd, perhaps, but not infected). If no scanner finds a virus, but a heuristic program raises some alarms (or there are other reasons to suspect a virus—for example, change in size of files, or change in memory allocation), then it is possible that you have found a new virus. However, the chances are probably greater that it is an "odd but OK" disk or file.

CHKDSK reports 639KB (or less) total memory on my DOS system; am I infected?

If CHKDSK displays 639KB (654,336 bytes) for the total memory instead of 640KB (655,360 bytes)—so that you are missing only 1KB—it is possibly due to reasons other than a virus, but there are a few common viruses that take only 1KB from total memory (Monkey and AntiEXE). Non-virus reasons for a deficiency of 1KB include:

▶ A PS/2 computer. IBM PS/2 computers reserve 1KB of conventional RAM for an Extended BIOS Data Area—that is, for additional data storage required by the computer's BIOS.

▶ A computer with a BIOS that is set to use the upper 1KB of memory for its internal variables. (Most BIOS chips with this option can be instructed to use lower memory instead.)

▶ Some SCSI controllers use additional memory.

▶ The DiskSecure anti-virus program uses some memory.

▶ Mouse buffers for older Compaqs use memory in a non-standard way.

If you are missing 2KB or more from the 640KB, 512KB, or whatever amount of memory is conventional for your PC, the chances are greater that you have a boot-record virus (e.g. Stoned, Form, or Michelangelo)—although, even in this case there may be legitimate reasons for the missing memory such as:

▶ Many access control programs prevent booting from a floppy

▶ H/P Vectra computers

▶ Some special BIOS chips that use memory for a built-in calendar and/or calculator

However, these are only rough guides. In order to be more certain whether the missing memory is due to a virus, you should:

▶ Run several virus detectors.

▶ Look for a change in total memory every now and then.

▶ Compare the total memory size with that obtained when cold booting from a "clean" system diskette. The latter should show the normal amount of total memory for your configuration (although several BIOS chips now steal 1KB of conventional memory when booting from a floppy but none when booting from a hard drive).

> **NOTE**
>
> *In all cases, you should run CHKDSK without software such as MS Windows or DesqView loaded, since these operating environments seem to be able to open DOS boxes only on 1KB boundaries (some seem to be even coarser). Thus, CHKDSK running from a DOS box may report unrepresentative values.*

Note also that some machines have only 512KB or 256KB instead of 640KB of conventional memory.

I have an infinite loop of subdirectories on my hard drive; am I infected?

Probably not. This happens now and then, when something sets the "cluster number" field of a subdirectory to the same cluster as an upper-level (usually the root) directory. On PCs, the /F parameter of CHKDSK should be able to fix this problem (as should many other popular disk-repair programs), usually by removing the offending directory. *Don't* erase any of the replicated files in the "odd" directory, since that will erase the copy in the root as well. (This is not really a copy at all, just a second pointer to the same files.)

Can a PC not running DOS be infected with a common DOS virus?

Yes! There are three distinct possibilities here.

One is Novell's NetWare (and possibly other network operating systems), which boots from a DOS disk and loads a "standard" DOS executable that takes complete control of the system from DOS. This executable—SERVER.EXE—could easily be infected by a DOS file infector. For example, you may need to move a server's NetWare boot diskette from the server to a DOS PC to edit some of the configuration and start-up files that have to be on that diskette. If the PC where the editing is done is infected with a file-infecting virus, SERVER.EXE may well be infected when the new start-up files are saved to the diskette. Such infections are virtually guaranteed to render SERVER.EXE inoperative, and the server would fail at its next restart. No viruses are known to target the NetWare kernel specifically.

Another possibility is the case of a 386 (or better) system running NetWare or a self-loading OS, such as UNIX, NeXTStep486, Windows NT, or OS/2. Such a system is still vulnerable to infection by MBR infectors (such as Stoned or Michelangelo), as these are OS-independent. Note that an infection on such a system may result in the disabling of non-DOS disk partitions (possibly beyond easy recovery) because the tricks and system conventions that these viruses employ may not apply to operating systems other than DOS. The issue here is that MBR infectors are not really "DOS viruses" so much as "PC-BIOS viruses"—they can infect any machine with a PC-compatible BIOS.

Third, *any* OS that offers a "DOS box" or "DOS emulator" to run DOS programs can, potentially, run a virus-infected DOS program. Such activation of a virus should allow the virus to spread to any "targets" available to it under that DOS emulator. For example, a DOS program infected with a multipartite virus, when run under OS/2, would probably be able to infect other DOS executables, but not the MBR/DBS, as OS/2 only allows privileged programs to read these critical areas of the hard drive. With the increasing sophistication and power of computing environments, DOS emulators running on non-PC computers are increasingly available and able to run DOS viruses.

My hard disk's file system has been garbled; do I have a virus?

Many things apart from viruses cause corruption of file systems.

With DOS machines, possibly the most common source of problems is Microsoft's SmartDrive disk cache program that came with Microsoft Windows 3.1 and subsequent versions of MS-DOS. Most versions of this software not only cache disk-reads but, by default, also cache disk-writes. This means that recently "written" files (for example, a document that you recently saved in your word processor) may not have all the information about the associated file system updates written to disk by the time you exit the application, close Windows, and turn off your PC. Users who simply save work and then turn their PCs off are even more likely to suffer from the type of problems induced by disk caching.

Regardless of what caused your file system corruption, you should probably seek expert help *before* trying to fix anything yourself. While there are many powerful and interesting-sounding utilities of the "disk fix" kind available, *all* of these have the stunning ability to render your file system all but unfixable (or at least fixable to a much lesser degree) when presented with unusual situations that their authors hadn't considered when designing the programs. Unfortunately, as these programs (by definition) do not recognize these situations, they confidently pronounce that you have such-and-such a problem, then ask your permission to fix it. Even when these utilities have "undo" options, they often cannot restore your file system to its originally "broken" state in order to give human experts their best shot at fixing it. Thus, detecting whether it is safe to let one of these programs loose on your disks is something you should normally seek expert help in deciding.

Is it possible to protect a computer system with only software?

Not perfectly, although software defences can significantly reduce your risk of being affected by viruses *when you apply the software appropriately*. All virus defence systems are tools—each with its own capabilities and shortcomings. Learn how your system works, and be sure to work within its limitations.

Using a layered approach, you can achieve a very high level of protection and detection with software only:

▶ Using the ROM BIOS password to control access to the computer, and to prevent the computer from booting from a floppy diskette. (Some may consider this a hardware approach.)

▶ Boot-sector change detection software can readily detect the existence of boot-sector infectors.

▶ Operating system programs should be checked via integrity management for existing programs, and scanning for unknown programs. Authentication values should be checked for any new or transmitted software.

▶ Software locks can prevent writing to a fixed or floppy disk.

As each layer is added, undetected invasion becomes more difficult. Nevertheless, complete protection against any possible attack cannot be provided without dedicating the computer to preexisting or unique tasks. International standardization on the IBM PC architecture is both its greatest asset and its greatest vulnerability.

Is it possible to write-protect the hard disk with software only?

The answer is no. Several programs claim to do this, but *all* of them can be bypassed with techniques already employed by some viruses. Therefore, you should never rely on such programs *alone,* although they can be useful in combination with other anti-virus measures.

What can be done with hardware protection?

Hardware protection can accomplish various things, including write-protection for hard disk drives, memory protection, monitoring and trapping of unauthorized system calls, and so on. Again, no single tool will be foolproof, and the stronger the hardware-based protection is, the more likely it will interfere with the normal operation of your computer.

While the popular idea of write-protection may stop viruses from *spreading* to the disk that is protected, it doesn't prevent a virus from *running*.

Also, some existing hardware protection schemes can be easily bypassed, fooled, or disconnected, if the virus writer knows them well and designs a virus that is aware of the particular defence.

The big problem with hardware protection is that there are few (if any) operations that a general-purpose computer can perform that are used exclusively by viruses. Therefore, making a hardware protection system for such a computer typically involves deciding on some (small) set of operations that are "valid but not normally performed except by viruses", and designing the system to prevent these operations. Unfortunately, this means either designing limitations into the level of protection that the hardware system provides or adding limitations to the computer's functionality by installing the hardware protection system. Much can be achieved, however, by making the hardware "smarter". This solution is double-edged: while it provides more security, it usually means adding a program in an EPROM to control the protection. The fixed location allows a virus to find the program and to call it directly after the point that allows access. It is still possible to implement this solution correctly, though—if this program is not in the address space of the main CPU, has its own CPU, and is connected directly to the hard disk and the keyboard. An example is a PC-based product called ExVira, which seems fairly secure, but it is an entire computer on a board and is quite expensive.

Does setting a file's attributes to read-only protect it from viruses?

Generally, no. While the read-only attribute will protect your files from a few viruses, most simply override the setting and infect normally. So, while setting executable files to read-only is a good idea (providing protection against accidental deletion), it certainly does not provide thorough protection against viruses!

In some environments, the read-only attribute does provide some additional protection. For instance, under Novell NetWare, a user can be denied the right to modify file attributes in certain directories on the server. This means that a virus that infects such a user's machine will be unable to infect files in those server directories if the files have their read-only attribute set.

Do password/access control systems protect my files from viruses?

All password and other access control systems are designed to protect the user's data from other users and/or their programs. Remember, however, that when you execute an infected program, the virus in it will gain your current rights and privileges. Therefore, if the access control system provides *you* with the right to modify some files, it will provide the same privilege to the virus, too. Note that the extension of rights does not depend on the operating system used—DOS, UNIX, or whatever. Therefore, an access control system will no better protect your files from viruses than it protects your files from you.

DOS offers no memory protection, so a virus could disable the access control system in memory, or even patch the operating system itself. More advanced operating systems (such as UNIX, OS/2, and Windows NT) make it much harder or impossible for a virus to disable such protection measures. Even so, viruses will still be able to spread, for the reasons previously noted. In general, access control systems (if implemented correctly) are only able to slow down virus spread, not to eliminate viruses entirely.

Of course, it's better to have access control than not to have it at all. Just be sure not to develop a false sense of security or come to rely *entirely* on your access control system to protect you.

Do the protection systems in DR DOS work against viruses?

Partially. Neither the password file/directory protection available from DR DOS version 5 onwards nor the secure disk partitions from DR DOS 6 were intended to combat viruses. If you have DR DOS, it is very wise to password-protect your files (to stop accidental damage too), but don't depend on this measure as your only means of defence.

The use of the password command (e.g. PASSWORD/W:MINE *.EXE *.COM) will stop more viruses than the plain DOS attribute facility, but that isn't saying much! The combination of the password system plus a disk-compression system may be more secure, because to bypass the password system a virus must access the disk directly. However, under SuperStor or Stacker, the physical disk will be meaningless to a virus. Some viruses, rather than invisibly infecting files on compressed disks, may very visibly corrupt such disks.

The main use of the "secure disk partitions" system, introduced in DR DOS 6, is to stop people from fiddling with your hard disk while you are away from the PC. The way this system is implemented, however, may also help against a few viruses that look for DOS partitions on a disk.

Furthermore, DR DOS is not fully compatible with MS/PC-DOS, especially when you get down to the low-level tricks that some viruses use. For instance, some internal memory structures are "read-only" in the sense that they are constantly updated (for MS/PC-DOS compatibility) but not really used by DR DOS. So, even if a sophisticated virus modifies these structures, it will not have any effect, or at least not that intended by the virus's author.

In general, using a less compatible system diminishes the number of existing viruses that can infect it. For instance, the introduction of hard disks made the Brain virus almost disappear, the introduction of the 80286 and DOS 4.0+ made the Yale and Ping Pong viruses next to extinct, and so on.

Does a write-protect tab on a floppy disk stop viruses?

In general, yes. The write-protection on IBM PC (and compatible) and Macintosh floppy disk drives is implemented in hardware, not software, so viruses cannot infect a diskette when the write-protection mechanism is functioning properly (although many "friend of a friend" stories abound contesting this).

But remember:

► A computer may have a faulty write-protect system (this happens!). You can test the system by trying to copy a file to a diskette that is apparently write-protected.

► Someone may have removed the tab for a while, allowing a virus to infect the disk.

► The files may have been infected before the disk was protected. Even some diskettes "straight from the factory" have been known to become infected during the production process.

Thus, you should scan even new write-protected disks for viruses. You should also scan new preformatted diskettes, as there have been known cases of infected, shrink-wrapped new diskettes.

Do local area networks (LANs) help to stop viruses, or do they facilitate their spread?

Both. A set of computers connected in a well-managed LAN—with carefully established security settings and minimal privileges for each user, and without a transitive path of information flow between the users (that is, the objects writeable by any of the users are not readable by any of the others)—is more virus-resistant than the same set of computers if they are not interconnected. The reason is that when all computers have read-only access to a common pool of executable programs, there is usually less need for diskette swapping and software exchange between them, and therefore fewer chances for a virus to spread.

However, if the LAN has lax security and is not well managed, it could help a virus to spread like wildfire. It might even be impossible to remove the infection without shutting down the entire LAN. Stories of LAN login programs, shared copies of which are run on every workstation, becoming infected are, unfortunately, not uncommon.

A network that supports login scripting is inherently more resistant to viruses than one that does not *if* the login script is used to validate the client before allowing access to the network.

What is the proper way to make backups?

A good backup regime is at the heart of any comprehensive virus defence scheme. No matter what combination of software and hardware defences you install, nor what "policy" you implement, there is always the possibility that some new virus will be devised that can beat your defences *or* that someone will fail to follow "proper protocol" with "foreign" media or file sources. In corporate settings, you cannot overlook the possibility of the latter as a form of directed attack by disgruntled employees.

Planning to minimize the impact of a virus infection on your computing is much like planning to minimize the effect of an earthquake or fire. You cannot be sure where, when, or even *if* you will ever be "hit"; the potential impact could fall anywhere in a very wide range of possible damage; being "completely safe" can involve enormous expense; and you cannot adequately test your preparations without exposing yourself to serious risk of damage. Therefore, selecting the defence scheme that suits you involves deciding on the level of loss you can afford and probably settling on a system that, while not "perfectly watertight", is "good enough".

Despite the importance of a good backup scheme, it is really beyond the scope of this FAQ sheet to provide a definitive guide to planning your backup procedure—that could easily take another document the size of this one! All this said, however, we provide the following advice as, we hope, a good starting point.

Planning an effective backup scheme really starts with answering some important questions. Consider:

- ▶ Who is dependent upon the files on this system? Is it a home computer mostly used by the kids for games, a stand-alone workstation running a small business, a networked workstation in a medium-sized company or the same in a large corporate environment, or a server with many (hundreds of) users?

- ▶ How long can the most important user be without access to these files? One hour (or two, four, eight) a day, a week? Remember to assume that your problems will arise at the worst possible moment (like 24 hours before a tax audit is due to start!).

- ▶ What proportion (and volume!) of files is "fixed" (in the sense that they seldom change) versus those that change? Do all changes have to be backed up, or is a "once-some-given-time-period" backup acceptable?

- ▶ What type of information is in the regularly changing files?

The answers to these (and other) questions help shape backup and recovery plans and are fairly well understood issues among computer systems professionals. Highly critical systems containing crucial data will be designed from the outset to have high redundancy (disk mirroring, disk arrays, uninterruptable power supplies, maybe even redundant servers), though such system options *alone* provide no real protection from virus attacks. You may opt for a backup system that records every change to any files on your system (server-only or clients and servers) or regular (often nightly) backup of changed data files, and so on.

When it comes to planning backup regimes with an eye to the possibility of recovering from a virus attack, you also have to consider that regularly backing up executables (loosely, "programs") can cause problems. If you back up executables and are infected by a virus, unless you can be *absolutely sure* of the date of first infection (despite sounding simple, this is not something that can commonly be done), you may have quite a few problems finding the best backup set from which to restore, as you will probably have several sets that include infected executables.

For home or small business use, it may be best to maintain two kinds of backups. One would contain only your data files and the other your operating system and program files. (Issues to consider are covered in the next two paragraphs.) You might facilitate such a scheme by maintaining a strict separation of the two kinds of files, perhaps by putting the operating system and programs on one drive or partition and your data files on another. While this scheme is probably not practical for many existing machines, enforcing adherence to the "rule" that data files should only be placed in appropriate subdirectories (folders) within a prescribed data directory may not be a bad thing.

The best way to manage backup of data files depends on the answers to most of the previously listed questions and precludes our giving definitive advice here. While planning your backup regime, bear in mind that some viruses damage some kinds of data files, while others make small, occasional, random modifications as files are written to disk. While viruses with either of these "features" are quite rare, both of these possibilities mean that vital data files should probably be backed up to long-cycle media sets as well as to shorter-cycle sets. You should also take other steps to ensure that you can re-create the sequence of changes. (For example, you should retain all transaction records so they can be reentered.)

You should probably back up executables once after installing them, and only *after* you are sure they are virusfree according to your current anti-virus screening procedures. *Never* make a backup containing executables over media that hold *any* of your current backups. More cautious administrators maintain several cycles of executable backups. These precautions should ensure that you don't face the problem of infected executables outlined several paragraphs ago. Also, if a newly installed program is infected with a virus that your current defences don't detect, you can easily restore your system and installed software to how it was before the infected software was installed, after you become aware of the virus's presence. You will probably have to reinstall manually any programs that you installed subsequent to installing the infected program.

Having referred to this second kind of backup as "executables only", we should point out that a complete system backup is also acceptable for this type of backup. However, note that a sequence of full system backups with interim incremental backups (when only those files that have changed since the last complete backup are saved) is *not* what we are advocating. Such systems tend to be too "broad brush" to be truly useful for recovering from an unknown, future virus attack. Unfortunately, this tends to be the preferred or recommended backup scheme for small to medium-sized systems (including most personal computers), and is typically what most popular backup software for such systems is designed to do. This doesn't mean that popular backup systems and software aren't useful, just that you have to exercise some care in using them (such as excluding executable files from your incremental backups).

Having said all this, there are still a few other problems to consider, especially, which files should you count as "data" files? This question can be problematic, as most people immediately think of their word processor and spreadsheet files, and the like, as data, and that's about it. What about the files in which your programs store their configuration information? In a sense, these are as much "your data" as they are program files, because they reflect your preferred screen colors and layouts, default fonts, personalized button bars, and so on. When you look at the time that people spend finding the (often obscure) options settings in their programs and making them work "just right", and how upset they can become if they lose these settings, it makes sense to treat such configuration files as you treat other "personal data files" in your backup regimes. Similarly, people tend to treat system configuration files (in DOS/Windows PCs, CONFIG.SYS, AUTOEXEC.BAT, WIN.INI, and SYSTEM.INI at a minimum) as part of the system, often ignoring the (sometimes considerable) fine-tuning that these configuration files go through *between* system and executable backups.

One last point: we cannot stress enough that you *must* have, in a safe place, a full, working copy of the software you need to restore your backups. You must be able to guarantee that this software is not virus-infected should you ever have to use it, *and* that it is fully usable should you be facing a machine that has had its entire hard drive "wiped clean".

Can boot-sector viruses infect nonbootable DOS floppy disks?

Any DOS diskette that has been properly formatted contains some executable code in its boot sector. (There is some debate as to whether this code should be called a program or not. The important thing here is that this code is *executed* at system start-up if the diskette is in the system's boot drive.) If a diskette is not "bootable", all that boot sector (normally) does is print a message (on a PC, typically something like "Nonsystem disk or disk error; replace and strike any key when ready").

However, the boot sector is still executable and therefore vulnerable to infection. Should you accidentally boot your machine with a "nonbootable" diskette in the boot drive, and see such a message, it means that any boot virus that may have been on that diskette *has* been run, and has had the chance to infect your hard drive or perform other mischief. So, when talking about viruses, the words "bootable" and "nonbootable" are misleading. All formatted diskettes are capable of carrying boot-sector viruses.

Most current computers will try to boot from their (first) floppy drive before trying to load an operating system off their hard disks. Because of this and the fact that every floppy disk is possibly infected with a boot-sector virus, it is a *very* good idea to set your computer to try to boot from its hard disk. Many newer PCs offer the option to select boot order in their system CMOS set-up routines. If your computer has such an option, set it to try to boot from your hard disk first.

Can a virus hide in a PC's CMOS memory?

No. The CMOS RAM in which PC system information is stored and backed up by batteries is accessible through the I/O ports and not directly addressable. That is, in order to read the contents of the CMOS, you have to use I/O instructions rather than standard memory addressing techniques. Therefore, anything stored in CMOS is not directly "in memory". Nothing in a normal machine loads the data from CMOS and executes it, so a virus that "hides" in CMOS RAM would still have to infect an executable object of some kind in order to load and execute whatever had been written to CMOS. A malicious virus can, of course, *alter* values in the CMOS as part of its payload, but it can't spread through, or hide itself in, the CMOS.

Further, most PCs have only 64 bytes of CMOS RAM, and the IBM AT specification predetermines the use of the first 48 bytes of this memory. Several BIOS chips also use many of the "extra" bytes of CMOS to hold their own machine-specific settings. This means that anything that a virus stores in CMOS can't be very large. A virus could use some of the "surplus" CMOS RAM to hide a small part of its body (such as its payload, counters, and so on). Any executable code stored there, however, must first be extracted to ordinary memory in order to be executed.

This issue should not be confused with whether a virus can *modify* the contents of a PC's CMOS RAM. Of course, viruses can modify these contents, as this memory is not specially protected (on normal PCs), so any program that knows how to change CMOS contents can do so. Some viruses do fiddle with the contents of CMOS RAM (mostly with ill intent), and these have often been incorrectly reported as "infecting CMOS" or "hiding in CMOS". An example is the PC boot-sector virus EXE_Bug, which changes CMOS settings to indicate that no floppy drives are present.

Can a PC virus hide in Extended or in Expanded RAM in a PC?

Yes. If one does though, it has to have a small part resident in conventional RAM; it cannot reside *entirely* in Extended or in Expanded RAM. Currently there are no known XMS viruses, and only a few EMS viruses (Emma is an example).

Can a virus hide in a PC's Upper Memory or in High Memory Area?

Yes, it is possible to construct a virus that will locate itself in Upper Memory Blocks (UMBs—640KB to 1,024KB) or in the High Memory Area (HMA—1,024KB to 1,088KB). Some viruses (e.g., EDV) do hide in UMBs, and at least one, Goldbug, will use the HMA if it is available.

You might think that there is no point in scanning in these areas for any viruses other than those that are specifically known to inhabit them. However, in some cases, even ordinary viruses can be found in Upper Memory. Suppose that a conventional memory-resident virus infects a TSR program that the user has loaded high (for instance, from AUTOEXEC.BAT). Then the virus code will also reside in Upper Memory. Therefore, an effective scanner must be able to scan this part of memory for viruses too.

Can a virus infect data files?

Some viruses, such as Frodo and Cinderella, modify non-executable files. However, in order to spread, the virus code must be executed. Therefore, "infected" non-executable files cannot be sources of further infection. Such "infections" are usually mistakes, due to bugs in the virus.

Even so, note that it is not always possible to make a sharp distinction between executable and non-executable files. One person's data can be another's code, and vice versa. Some files that are not directly executable contain code or data that can, under some conditions, be executed or interpreted.

Some examples from the PC world are .OBJ files, libraries, device drivers, source files for any compiler or interpreter (including DOS .BAT files and OS/2 .CMD files), macro files for some packages like Microsoft Word and Lotus 1-2-3, and many others. Currently there are viruses that infect boot sectors, master boot records, .COM files, .EXE files, .BAT files, .OBJ files, device drivers, Microsoft Word document and template files, and C source code files, although any of these objects theoretically can be used as an infection carrier. PostScript files can also be used to carry a virus, although no currently known virus does this.

Aside from viruses using the preceding vectors, however, there is an increasing possibility that viruses may spread through the sharing of data files. More and more we see the ease with which software producers enable their programs to embed "objects" of many kinds into document files, and into fields in databases and spreadsheets. Perhaps the best known of these systems are Object Linking and Embedding (OLE) in MS Windows and the OpenDoc format. As these embedded objects often have the ability to "display" themselves, many files traditionally considered to be data-only are increasingly serving as containers carrying data and executable code. We are not aware of any virus that specifically targets such executable "objects", but it is now a trivial task to embed an executable file into some kind of document file so it will be run when the icon representing it is clicked in the finished document. There is nothing to prevent infected executables from being embedded in this way, and thus for viruses to be spread through the distribution of "data files".

Can viruses spread from one type of computer to another?

The simple answer is that no currently known viruses can do this. Although some disk formats may be the same (e.g., Atari ST and DOS), the different machines interpret the code differently. For example, the Stoned virus cannot infect an Atari ST, as the ST cannot execute the virus code in the boot sector. The Stoned virus contains instructions for the 80x86 family of CPUs that the 680x0 CPU family (used in the Atari ST) can't understand or execute.

NOTE

This section of the FAQ remains accurate as long as macro viruses, which are usually application-specific rather than hardware-specific, are considered separately.

The more general answer is that such viruses are possible, but unlikely. Such a virus would be quite a bit larger than current viruses and might well be easier to find. Additionally, the low incidence of cross-platform sharing of software means that any such virus would be unlikely to spread—it would be a poor environment for virus growth.

Are mainframe computers susceptible to computer viruses?

Yes. Numerous experiments have shown that computer viruses spread very quickly and effectively on mainframe systems. To our knowledge, however, no non-research computer virus has been seen on mainframe systems. (Despite often being described as such, the widely reported Internet Worm of November 1988 was not a computer virus by most definitions, although it had some viruslike characteristics.)

Many people think that computer virus infections are impossible on mainframe computers, because their operating systems provide means of protection (e.g., memory protection, access control, etc.) that cannot by bypassed by a program, unlike the operating systems of most personal computers. Unfortunately, this belief is false. As demonstrated by Cohen in 1984, access controls are unable to prevent computer viruses—they can only slow down the speed at which viruses spread. If there is a transitive path of information flow from one account to another on a mainframe computer, then a virus can spread from one account to the other, without having to bypass any protections.

Consider the following example. The attacker (A) has an account on a machine and wants to attack it with a virus. To do this, A writes and releases a virus. Due to the protection provided by the operating system, the virus can infect only the files writeable by A. On a typical system, those would be only the files owned by A.

However, A is not alone on the system. A works with B on some joint projects. At some time, B might want to check how far A has progressed in his or her part of the project. This might involve running one of the programs that A has written— programs that are now all infected with A's virus.

On a system with protection based on discretionary access controls (e.g., UNIX, VMS, and most other popular operating systems), the program that is being executed usually runs with the privileges of the user who is executing it—not with those of the program's owner. (The few instances where this is not the case present a different kind of security threat, unrelated to viruses.) That is, when B runs A's infected program, the virus in it will run with B's privileges and will be able to infect all programs writeable by B.

At some later time, A and B's boss, C, might want to check whether they have completed that joint project. Even if the boss has reasons to suspect A (as a disgruntled employee, for example), C is likely to trust B and execute one of B's programs. This results in the virus running with C's privileges (which are likely to be significantly greater than those of A and B) and infecting all programs writeable by C. Quite possibly, these programs will include many owned by other employees, thus creating many more distribution chains that nobody suspects.

The virus may interfere somehow with C's normal work, which causes C (who is probably not very knowledgeable about such things as computer security and viruses) to ask the system administrator, D, for help. If D executes one of C's infected programs (and D is much more likely to trust a respectable person like C, who is quite probably D's boss as well, than any of C's employees), this will cause the virus that A wrote a long time ago to run with system administrator privileges and do whatever it wants with the system—infect other users' files, attack other systems, and so on.

A trivial improvement of the preceding scenario (in terms of speeding up the virus's spread) would be for the attacker to place the virus in some kind of Trojan horse— for example, in an attractive game or utility—placed in a publicly accessible area.

Why, then, are there fewer viruses for mainframe computers than for personal computers? The answer to this question is complex. First, writing a well-made mainframe virus—one that does not cause problems and is likely to remain unnoticed— is not a trivial task. It requires a lot of knowledge about the operating system. This knowledge is not commonly available, and the typical youngster who is likely to hack a quick-and-dirty PC virus is unlikely to possess such knowledge or be in a position to learn it. People who possess this knowledge are likely to use it in more constructive, satisfying, and profitable ways. Second, the culture of software exchange in the mainframe world differs considerably from that of the PC world—we don't see many VMS users running around with a bootable tape of the latest game. Third, very often it is easier to attack a mainframe computer by using some security hole or a Trojan horse instead of by using a virus.

So, computer viruses for mainframe computers are definitely possible and several already exist. Also, some IBM PC viruses can infect any IBM PC-compatible machine, even if it runs a "real" OS such as UNIX.

Forms of malware other than computer viruses—notably Trojan horses—are far quicker, more effective, and harder to detect than computer viruses. Nevertheless, many more viruses than Trojan horses have been written to attack personal computers. There are two reasons for this:

▶ Since a virus is self-propagating, the number of users to whom it can spread (and cause damage) can be much greater than in the case of a Trojan.

▶ It's almost impossible to trace the source of a virus since (generally) viruses are not attached to any particular program.

For further information on malicious programs on multi-user systems, see Matt Bishop's paper, "An Overview of Malicious Logic in a Research Environment", available by anonymous ftp on Dartmouth.edu (IP = 129.170.16.4) as pub/security/mallogic.ps.

Some people say that disinfecting is a bad idea. Is that true?

Disinfection is "safe" only if the disinfecting process completely restores the noninfected state of the object. That is, not only must the virus be removed from the object, but the original length must be restored exactly, as well as any system attributes (such as time and date of last modification, fields in the header, etc.). Sometimes it is necessary to be sure that the object is placed on the same sectors of the disk that it occupied prior to infection. (This is particularly important for some system areas and some files from programs that use certain kinds of self-checking or copy protection.)

None of the currently available disinfecting programs do all of this. For instance, because of the bugs that exist in many viruses, and because some infection processes involve overwriting (part of) the objects of infection, some of the information about the original object may be irrevocably destroyed. Sometimes it is not even possible to detect that this information has been destroyed, nor to warn the user. Furthermore, some viruses (such as Nomenklatura and Ripper) corrupt information very slightly and randomly, so that it is not even possible to tell which objects have been corrupted.

Therefore, it is usually better to replace infected objects with clean backups, provided you are certain that your backups are uninfected or from the original media. You should try to disinfect files only if they contain some valuable data that cannot be restored from backups or recompiled from their original source.

NOTE

If the FAQ had been updated more recently, it would probably have gone into more detail about Registries and the like that are also affected by malware. Anti-malware products do not typically address Registry modifications introduced as part of the malware's installation process. Such modifications may also apply to residual files and scripts that the malware may install as part of the "infection" process and that may continue to perform actions regardless of whether the "infected" files are still present on the system.

Can I avoid viruses by avoiding shareware, free software, or games?

No. There are many documented instances in which even commercial shrink-wrapped software was inadvertently distributed containing viruses. Avoiding shareware, freeware, games, and the like only isolates you from a vast collection of software (some of it very good, some of it very bad, most of it somewhere in between).

The important thing is not to avoid a certain type of software, but to be cautious of *any and all* newly acquired software and diskettes. Merely scanning all new software media for known viruses would be rather effective at preventing virus infections, especially when combined with some other prevention/detection strategy, such as integrity management of programs.

Can I contract a virus on my PC by performing a DIR of an infected floppy disk?

Assuming the PC you are using is virus free before you perform the DIR command, then the answer is no.

When you perform a DIR, the contents of the boot sector of the diskette are loaded into a buffer for use in determining disk layout and so on, and certain anti-virus products will scan these buffers. If a boot-sector virus has infected your diskette, the virus code will be contained in the buffer, which may cause some anti-virus packages to produce a message like "XYZ virus found in memory...". In fact, the virus is not a threat at this point since control of the CPU is never passed to the virus code residing in the buffer. Even though the virus is really not a threat at this point, you should not ignore this message. If you get a message like this, and then reboot from a clean DOS diskette, scan your hard drive, and find no virus, then you know that an infected boot sector loaded into a buffer has caused the false positive. You should thus disinfect the diskette before using it. The use of DIR will not infect a clean system, even if the diskette on which it is being performed does contain a virus. Note, however, that running DIR on a diskette can result in the infection of a clean diskette if the PC is already infected.

Despite our categorical "no" answer, there is a small risk that a virus infection could be transferred from a floppy through a DIR listing. If you use an ANSI console driver that allows key remapping, it is possible that a specially prepared diskette could reprogram your keyboard so that pressing a particular key causes an infected program on the diskette to run the next time the reprogrammed key is pressed. The risk of such an attack is very low and can easily be negated by following the general advice for preventing ANSI bombs.

Mac users with system software prior to version 7.0 should be aware of a greater threat in their environment. Various system resources (which can contain executable code) are loaded from the automatic access to a diskette that is part of the system building its desktop view of the diskette's contents. When such a resource is required, the most recently loaded one will be used. Thus, if a diskette with a virus-infected resource in the Desktop file is in your Mac's drive, and an uninfected copy of that resource has not subsequently loaded from elsewhere, the next time that resource is required, the infected copy will be executed, along with the virus. The possibility of this kind of attack was removed with the introduction of version 7.0 (and later) of the system software, which handles such things quite differently. A common Mac virus, WDEF, uses this infection path, as do a few others.

Early versions of AmigaDOS are susceptible to a threat similar to the Mac WDEF virus—after the user inserts a diskette into the drive, the operating system runs the

Disk Validator from the diskette. At least one Amiga virus, Saddam, attaches itself to Disk Validator to help spread itself. Version 2.0 of AmigaDOS eliminated the threat of this type of attack by removing the need for the Disk Validator.

Is there any risk in copying data files from an infected floppy disk to a clean PC's hard disk?

Assuming that you did not boot or run any executable programs from the infected disk, the answer generally is no. There are two caveats:

▶ You should be somewhat concerned about checking the integrity of these data files as they may have been destroyed or altered by the virus.

▶ If any of the "data" files can be interpreted as executable by some other program (such as a Lotus macro), then you should treat these files as potentially malicious until the symptoms of the infection are known.

The copying process itself is safe (given the preceding scenario), although you should be concerned with what types of files are being copied to avoid introducing other problems.

Can a DOS virus survive and spread on an OS/2 system using the HPFS file system?

Yes, both file-infecting and boot-sector viruses can infect HPFS partitions. File-infecting viruses function normally and can activate and do their dirty deeds, and boot-sector viruses can prevent OS/2 from booting if the primary bootable partition is infected. Viruses that try to address disk sectors directly cannot function under OS/2 because the operating system prevents this activity.

NOTE

HPFS (High Performance File System) was the OS/2 precursor to NTFS, and was also supported by early versions of Windows NT.

Under OS/2 2.0+, could a virus-infected DOS session infect another DOS session?

Each DOS program is run in a separate virtual DOS machine (OS/2 keeps each program's memory space separate from the others). However, any DOS program has almost complete access to the files and disks, so infection can occur if the virus infects files; any other DOS session that executes a program infected by a virus that makes itself memory-resident would itself become infected.

Also, bear in mind that generally all DOS sessions share the same copy of the command interpreter. Hence if *it* becomes infected, the virus will be active in *all* DOS sessions.

Can normal DOS viruses work under MS Windows?

Most of them cannot. A system that runs MS Windows exclusively is, in general, more virus-resistant than a plain DOS system. The reason is that most resident viruses are not compatible with the memory management in Windows. Furthermore, most existing viruses will damage Windows applications if they try to infect them as normal (i.e., DOS) .EXE files. The damaged applications will stop working and this will alert the user that something is wrong.

Virus-resistant, however, is by no means virus-proof. For instance, most of the well-behaved resident viruses that infect only .COM files (Cascade is an excellent example) will work perfectly in a "DOS box". All nonresident .COM infectors will be able to run and infect too. Aside from being subject to DOS viruses, MS Windows users can also contract several currently known Windows-specific viruses, which are able to infect Windows applications properly (i.e., they are compatible with the NewEXE file format).

Any low-level trapping of Interrupt 13, as by resident boot-sector and MBR viruses, can also affect Windows operation, particularly if protected disk access (32BitDiskAccess=ON in SYSTEM.INI) is used.

NOTE

While this answer is accurate as far as it goes, since this FAQ was revised, many Windows-native file infectors have been written (Win32 infectors, PE infectors, and so on, as well as viruses that can distinguish between types of .EXE files and infect accordingly and appropriately). Obviously, these infectors will usually work under an appropriate version of Windows, and have been rather more successful than might have been expected in the mid-1990s.

Can I get a virus from reading email?

In general terms, the answer is no. Email messages and postings on BBSs and newsgroups are text data and will not be executed as programs. Computer viruses are programs, and must be executed to do anything, so the simple act of reading online messages doesn't pose a threat that you will catch a computer virus.

There are a few provisos to be made. If your computer uses ANSI screen and keyboard controls, you may be susceptible to an ANSI bomb. An ANSI bomb may, merely by being placed in text read on the screen, temporarily redefine keys on the keyboard to perform various functions. It is, however, very unlikely that you will ever see an ANSI bomb in email, or that it could do significant damage while you are reading mail.

Another possibility is that mail can be used to send programs. To do this, program files have to be encoded into a special form so that the binary (eight-bit) program files are not corrupted by transfer over the text-only (seven-bit) email transport medium. Probably the most common of these encoding schemes is uuencoding, although there are several others. If you receive an encoded program, you normally have to use a decoding program or special option in your email program to extract and decode it before it can be run. Once you have extracted the program, though, you should then treat it as you would any other program whose source you do not know, and test it before you run it.

A third possibility is with the newer, highly automated online systems. Some of these attempt to make online access much easier for the user by automating such features as file transfer and program updates. At least one commercial online service is known to be capable of sending new programs to the user and to invoke those programs while the user is still online. While there is no reason to assume that any service that does this *will* infect you, any time things are going on that you are not being told about, you are at greater risk.

NOTE

Yes, we know about the hole in some versions of Outlook exploited by some viruses and worms (KAK, for instance). But at the time that this FAQ was written, that hole lay some distance in the future, which makes the prescience (or pessimism) of this section all the more impressive.

Can a virus "hide" in a .GIF or JPEG file?

The simple answer is no. The complete answer is more complex.

.GIF and JPEG (.JPG) files contain compressed graphical information. Every now and then, rumours arise that it is possible to infect those files with a virus in such a way that it will spread when you display one of these images. This is technically impossible—no part of the GIF or JPEG format contains code that is executed by the viewer program.

It *is* possible to use the least significant bit of the colour information for each pixel in .GIF files to store additional information without visibly altering the quality of the picture contained in the file. This is called *steganography* and is sometimes used to transmit secretly encrypted messages. Since a virus is nothing more than information, it is possible to "encode" it into a .GIF file and transmit it this way.

However, the recipients must be aware that the .GIF file contains such hidden information and take some deliberate steps to extract it—the transmission cannot happen against the recipients' will.

> **NOTE**
>
> *Often what appears to be a JPEG or other graphics file may, in fact, be a program. A particularly common example is the double extension trick used by many contemporary worms, whereby a file called "badfile.jpg.vbs" or "badfile.jpg   .scr" may look like a graphic, but is, in fact, something quite different.*

How often should we upgrade our anti-virus tools?

This is a difficult question to answer. Anti-virus software is a kind of insurance, and these types of calculations are difficult.

There are two things to watch out for here: the general "style" of the software, and the scan strings that scanners use to identify viruses. Scanners should be updated more frequently than other software, and it is probably a good idea to update a scanner's set of scan strings at least once every two months. In the six months or so prior to January 1995, most of the popular PC-based virus scanners typically added detection of about 500–600 new viruses or variants—this averages out to between two and three new viruses per day!

Some anti-virus software looks for changes to programs or specific types of viral "activity", and these programs generally claim to be good for "all current and future viral programs". However, even these programs cannot guarantee to protect against all future viruses, as virus writers are continually developing new "attack" and anti-anti-virus methods. Thus, even this type of anti-virus software needs to be upgraded occasionally.

Of course, not every anti-virus product is effective against all viruses, even if upgraded regularly. Thus, do *not* depend on the fact that you have upgraded your product recently as a guarantee that your system is free of viruses!

Is it possible to use a computer virus for something useful?

This question reflects a very hotly debated topic that has flared up dramatically several times in VIRUS-L/comp.virus. The answer to this question is not simple and largely hinges on your definition or interpretation of the term *computer virus*.

By definition, viruses do not have to do something "bad" (although many people argue that the uninvited "resource wasting" that is almost inherent in viral activity is necessarily bad). From this point (and based on his somewhat esoteric definition of the term *computer virus*), Cohen has argued that "good" or "useful" computer viruses are a serious possibility. In fact, Cohen offered a reward of $1,000 for the first clearly "useful" virus; despite several potential claimants, however, he hasn't paid up.

Although these discussions have not resulted in a widely agreed-upon position, many contributors to this forum believe that there are serious problems with the idea of implementing useful computing functionality through self-replicating programs. Vesselin Bontchev's paper originally delivered at the 1994 EICAR conference, titled "Are 'Good' Computer Viruses Still a Bad Idea?", is available by anonymous ftp from ftp.informatik.uni-hamburg.de (IP = 134.100.4.42), as pub/virus/texts/viruses/goodvir.zip. It contains many strong arguments against the idea of "good computer viruses", and some prescriptions of how good viruses would have to be implemented and distributed to deserve the label "good". To date, no strong arguments countering the points in this paper or otherwise arguing in favour of the concept of good viruses have been posted to the group.

Wouldn't adding self-checking code to your programs be a good idea?

Every few months, somebody suggests the idea of adding a small piece of code to existing programs. This code would check for virus infections when the program is executed by comparing a previously computed CRC or cryptographic checksum (hash value) of the file in its known clean state with its current value. The idea is that this code would detect any virus infection immediately, and thus would be effective against unknown viruses.

This idea is simple and intuitively attractive—in fact, some anti-virus programs have included options to implement just such a strategy. This approach, however, has some serious flaws. It cannot prevent the program from infection in the first place. Further, if a program that has been protected this way becomes infected later, whenever it is run, the virus code will be activated first. The virus may then be able to detect or even remove the self-checking code, or it might make it totally ineffective by using stealth techniques, so the self-checking code "sees" only the original, noninfected program.

Some programs—much anti-virus software, for example—contain an internal self-check. Such internal code might also be unable to detect stealth viruses, but unless the external self-check code uses stealth techniques too, the result will be a conflict, where the internal check will notice the newly added code and decide that it has been "infected".

Moreover, this method is ineffective against "companion" viruses that don't modify the applications they infect.

It may not be possible to protect all programs this way. For example, under DOS it is relatively easy to add code of this type to most .COM files (unless the original program is slightly less than 64KB, and the resulting file would break that limit). However, .EXE files are more of a problem—especially those containing internal overlays, where one cannot append the code to the file, as the resulting file might become too big to load. Windows applications are also a problem, as they have two different entry points and you have to take special care to handle that situation correctly.

On the other hand, adding internal self-checking to programs as part of their development is a good idea. Although internal self-checking has the same limitations regarding stealth viruses, it does not cause the conflicts previously described, and can be put in any program at compile time. Such self-checking is also much more difficult for viruses to bypass.

Is my disk infected with the Stoned virus?

Of course, the answer to this, and many similar questions, is to obtain a good virus detector. There are many to choose from, including ones that will scan diskettes automatically as you use them. As Stoned is a boot-sector infector, remember to check all diskettes, even nonsystem or "data" diskettes.

It is possible, if you have an urgent need to check a system when you don't have any anti-virus tools, to run CHKDSK or MEM and note the values reported, boot from a known clean system diskette, then compare the results returned by CHKDSK or MEM. If the total amount of conventional memory reported is different between the two boots, then you may have a viral problem. However, this information alone cannot tell you whether the problem is Stoned. If you cannot see the PC's hard disk (usually the C drive), then it is even more likely that you have a virus problem, though definitely not Stoned. If you have a "disk editor" type program, looking at the boot sector of a suspect floppy or the MBR of the suspect hard drive may be helpful. If you have Stoned, the first byte will indicate the characteristic far jump of the virus (hex: EA) instead of the more common short jump (hex: EB) of the boot loader. Even if that is the first byte, you could be looking at a perfectly good disk that has been "inoculated" against the virus *or* has been infected with some other virus that makes similar changes, or at a diskette that seems safe but contains a totally different type of virus.

I was infected by both Stoned and Michelangelo. Why has my computer become unbootable?

These two viruses store the original Master Boot Record at one and the same place on the hard disk. They do not recognize each other, and therefore a computer can become infected with both of them at the same time.

The first of these viruses that infects the computer will overwrite the Master Boot Record with its body and store the original MBR at a certain place on the disk. So far, this is normal for a boot-record virus. But if the other virus then also infects the computer, it will replace the MBR (which now contains the virus that had come first) with its own body, and store what it believes is the original MBR (but in fact is the body of the first virus) *at the same place* on the hard disk, thus *overwriting* the original MBR. When this happens, the contents of the original MBR are lost. Therefore, the disk becomes nonbootable.

When a virus removal program inspects such a hard disk, it will see the *second* virus in the MBR and will try to remove it by overwriting it with the contents of the sector where this virus normally stores the original MBR. However, now this sector contains the body of the *first* virus. Therefore, the virus removal program will install the first virus in trying to remove the second. In all probability, the program will not wipe out the sector where the (infected) MBR has been stored.

When the program is run again, it will find the *first* virus in the MBR. By trying to remove it, the program will get the contents of the sector where this virus normally stores the original MBR, and will move it over the current (infected) MBR. Unfortunately, this sector still contains the body of the *first* virus. Therefore, the body of this virus will be reinstalled over the MBR ad infinitum.

There is no easy solution to this problem, since the contents of the original MBR are lost. The only solution for the anti-virus program is to detect that there is a problem, and to overwrite the contents of the MBR with a valid MBR program, which the anti-virus program has to provide itself. If your favorite anti-virus program is not that smart, consider replacing it with a better one, or try using the boot-sector disinfection procedure described elsewhere.

In general, infection of the same file or area by multiple viruses is possible, and vital areas of the original may be lost. This can make it difficult or impossible for virus disinfection tools to be effective, and replacement of the lost file/area will be necessary.

I was infected with Flip, and now a large part of my hard disk seems to have disappeared. What has happened?

Flip contains a logic error, probably because its author only had knowledge of hard disk partitioning schemes under DOS 3.*x* (where partitions could not exceed 32MB).

Part of Flip's infection routine decrements by six the "total number of sectors" field in the BIOS Parameter Block (BPB), a table of critical disk geometry data, in the DOS boot sector of the boot partition. For partitions of 32MB and under, this field is meaningful, but in larger partitions, this field is set to zero and a field in the "extended BPB" contains the "big number of sectors" for that partition instead. Not knowing about larger partitions, Flip renders the large partitions it meets a shade under 32MB. The fix for this is to use a disk sector editor to set the word at offset 13h of the affected DOS boot sector to "00 00". (It should be set to "FA FF" if the situation described in this paragraph applies.) If you don't understand these instructions, do *not* attempt to follow them; instead seek the help of a more technically knowledgeable person.

What does the GenB and/or the GenP virus do?

There is no such thing as *the* GenB or GenP virus. They are both part of a heuristic used by a very popular scanner to detect boot-sector viruses. The scanner notes something in the boot sector (GenB) or in the MBR (GenP) that it strongly suspects is a virus, but has no idea which particular virus it might be. If you want to know which particular virus you have, you should run a scanner that has better recognition and identification capabilities. One advantage of the GenB/GenP report is that you can often use the disinfection utility from the same producer to remove the virus, even if no other scanner can remove it. When told to remove the GenB/GenP "virus", the utility scans the disk for something that looks like a saved copy of the original boot sector or MBR and will put it back in place, thus removing the virus. Or, alternatively, if there is an apparently valid partition table in the virus MBR, the utility may write a good generic MBR.

How do I "boot from a clean floppy"?

"Put it in the A drive and turn the power on".

This facetious answer aside, the real question here is usually more one of "How do I ensure that I have a clean boot floppy?"

As with so many issues concerning viruses, the important thing is to be prepared *in advance*. A current, clean boot disk should be a standard part of every personal computer system. This is because there are occasions, other than facing a real or suspected virus infection, when being able to boot your computer to a "known good" state is useful or desirable (for example, when you accidentally delete your disk-compression driver from your hard disk). As with backups, a current, clean boot disk is one of the standard parts of a personal computer system most commonly missing.

The important thing in preparing a clean boot diskette, especially if you have to use it with a (suspected) virus infection, is that it must *not* run a single byte of code from your hard disk. This means your boot floppy must contain all the basic operating system files, device drivers, and configuration commands necessary to make your system minimally usable. This diskette must be prepared on a system that is, itself, guaranteed "clean", and you should write-protect it immediately after it is completed. Aside from holding a basic, minimal operating system, your emergency boot diskette should contain the utilities necessary to install your OS to a hard disk *and* basic diagnostic or "fix it" programs, and your favourite anti-virus tools. Depending upon disk space considerations, you may need additional diskettes to hold all these utilities. For example, if you use DOS, it is a good idea to copy the following utility programs to your emergency boot disk (if your version of DOS includes them): FDISK, CHKDSK and/or SCANDISK, FORMAT, SYS, MEM, UNFORMAT, UNDELETE, and MSD.

When rebooting your computer from a clean system disk, it is most important that you perform a "cold start". On a PC, this means pressing the reset button or turning the power off and then on again, *not* pressing CTRL-ALT-DEL. Regardless of the machine type, if you are unsure, turn the power off and then power on again. To configure your machine correctly, it is even more important to try booting from the floppy first. Most contemporary BIOS chips have an option to select the boot order (A then C, or C then A)—this must be set to A then C for this procedure, though normally we strongly recommend that you set this option to C then A.

As systems change from time to time, you may occasionally need to update this most critical of diskettes so that it will still boot your system to a usable state. Since you may have recently contracted a new virus that bypasses your current anti-virus precautions, this update process can put you at risk of infecting your "clean" emergency boot diskette. Because of this, it is prudent to have two such diskettes. With system changes, you would update these in a "leap frog" manner. This means your previous emergency boot diskette might still bring your machine up to a minimally useful state (such that you may still be able to make repairs) should a previously unknown virus infect your updated emergency boot diskette.

Unfortunately, this isn't the whole story either! A PC virus known as EXE_Bug can fake out the boot process by setting the PC's CMOS to look as if there are no floppy drives in the machine. Most BIOS systems don't even try to boot from a floppy in this case, and go straight to the hard disk, loading the virus from the MBR. When EXE_Bug first loads into memory, it checks to see if there is a diskette in the first floppy drive, and if there is, it loads the boot sector from the diskette and lets the floppy boot as normal. Most people don't notice the subtly different boot time and drive access order involved in this, so they think they have booted clean, when in fact the virus is active in memory! To circumvent this possibility, you have to check the PC's CMOS settings before letting the floppy boot proceed, make sure that your PC "knows" it has a floppy drive, *and,* with some PCs, make sure that the boot order option is set to A then C. This presents a chicken-and-egg situation on some machines, as you may have to boot DOS on the machine to be able to run the utility program that lets you change its CMOS settings.

Remember, if you changed your BIOS boot order option, set it back to C then A after disinfecting your PC.

My PC diagnostic utility lists "Cascade" among the hardware interrupts (IRQs). Does this mean I have the Cascade virus?

No! This is quite normal on AT-style (286 and better) PCs (and on a few 8086 [XT] class machines). The original IBM PC design had one Programmable Interrupt Controller (PIC) to handle hardware interrupts generated when devices such as disk controllers, serial and parallel ports, LAN adaptors, and so on have to be serviced. While developing the AT, IBM decided that the eight Interrupt ReQuest (IRQ) lines that the original PIC supported were probably insufficient for likely future expansion needs, so the AT developers added a second PIC. The two PICs had to cooperate so that both didn't interrupt the CPU concurrently. The developers achieved this by having the second PIC use an IRQ to signal the first PIC when it has an IRQ to service. IRQs 2 and 9 were used for this signal and are commonly called the "cascade" IRQs, as they allow the second PIC to cascade an IRQ down to the first PIC.

When I do a DIR | MORE, I see two files with random names that are not there when I just use DIR. On my friend's system, they cannot be seen. Do I have a virus?

No. DOS's default command-line interpreter (COMMAND.COM) creates two temporary files with unique names for every pipe character (|) used on the command line. Starting with DOS version 5.0, these files are created in the directory pointed to by the TEMP environment variable, not in the current directory as they were in earlier DOS versions. If your TEMP setting is invalid, or if you have an earlier version of DOS, you will see these files in the current directory when you pipe the output of a DIR command through MORE (or any other filter). If you don't see these files in the current directory's listing, performing the command DIR | MORE on the directory specified by the TEMP variable will reveal them.

Generally, using DIR /P instead of DIR | MORE is better, as the latter command avoids the creation of the temporary files. If you use an alternative command-line interpreter, none of the preceding concerns may apply.

Viruses and the Macintosh

IN THIS CHAPTER:

How Many Viruses Affect the Macintosh?

Mac-Specific Viruses

PC Viruses on Emulated PCs

Esperanto.4733

PC Scripting Viruses

The EICAR Installation Test File

Information Resources

Mac Troubleshooting

Questions Received at Mac Virus

The "Viruses and the Macintosh" FAQ was originally written by David Harley around 1996, at a time when the Mac-using community had become complacent about the rarity of Mac viruses. Most were reliant on a brace of freeware anti-virus tools (Disinfectant and Gatekeeper, both of which detected only Mac-specific threats). Few Mac sites had yet come to terms with the fact that Word and Excel macro viruses were a problem on Macintoshes as well as on PCs (albeit not the same problem). Drawing attention to this fact didn't save Mac users from being a major source of macro virus infection for a while, but provided a reference point for victims of WM/Concept, WM/Npad, and WM/Cap, shocked to find themselves in the firing line.

Comments, suggestions, and additional material were received from Ronnie Sutherland, Henri Delger, Mike Groh, Eugene Spafford, Bruce Burrell, Michael Wright, Peter Gersmann, David Miller, Ladd Van Tol, Eric Hildum, Jeremy Goldman, Kevin White, Bill Jackson, Robert Slade, Robin Dover, John Norstad, and Susan Lesch, who for some time was the principal maintainer of the FAQ, and gave it a home at her hugely influential Mac Virus site. When Lesch was forced by pressure of other commitments to give up maintaining Mac Virus and the FAQ, both moved to Harley's site at http://www.sherpasoft.org.uk (http://www.macvirus.com now points to www.sherpasoft.org.uk, where Mac Virus II is hosted). The ICSA and EICAR web sites have also hosted Mac Virus, but neither carries the Mac Virus II or the latest versions of the FAQ.

This appendix is not the FAQ, but a digest of some of its more relevant and up-to-date information.

How Many Viruses Affect the Macintosh?

There are, depending on how you measure, between 40 and 100 Mac-specific viruses and related threats. Most of these are not regularly found in the field. We have to say "in the field", because there is at present no Mac equivalent to the WildList that provides a way of tracking what viruses are in the wild.

However, there is a project under development by David Harley in association with the WildList Organization to track Macintosh-specific viruses.

Mac-Specific Viruses

This section does not list all variants. However, it does include more detailed information on one or two common Mac viruses that are not well documented elsewhere. The main problem affecting Mac users nowadays is the spread of macro viruses. Cataloguing all individual macro viruses individually is beyond the scope of this appendix, so they are only considered as a general class.

Native Mac viruses are rather rarely seen nowadays, and most people don't need to know about them in detail—in fact, what they need most is to know that their favoured anti-virus can deal with them.

Mac-Specific System and File Infectors

The following are some of the Mac-specific system and file infectors:

▶ *AIDS,* an nVIR B strain, infects application and system files, but inflicts no intentional damage.

▶ *Aladin* is a close relative of Frankie.

▶ *Anti (Anti-A/Anti-Ange, Anti-B, Anti Variant)* can't spread under system 7.*x* or system 6 under MultiFinder. The infector can damage applications so that they can't be 100 percent repaired.

▶ *The AutoStart worm* is considered in some detail in Chapter 14 of this book; see that section for more details.

▶ *CDEF* infects desktop files. It does not inflict any intentional damage, and doesn't spread under system 7.*x*.

▶ *CLAP* is an nVIR variant that spoofs Disinfectant to avoid detection (Disinfectant 3.6 recognizes it).

▶ *Code 1* is a file infector that renames the hard drive to "Trent Saburo". Accidental system crashes are possible.

▶ *Code 252* infects application and system files. It triggers when run between 6th June and 31st December. The macro virus runs a "gotcha" message ("You have a virus. Ha Ha Ha Ha Ha Ha Ha Now erasing all disks..."), then self-deletes. Despite the message, the virus does no intentional damage, though Norstad points out that shutting down the Mac instead of clicking to continue could cause damage. Code 252 can crash system 7 or damage files, but doesn't spread beyond the System file. It doesn't spread under system 6 with MultiFinder beyond System and MultiFinder. The virus can cause various forms of accidental damage.

▶ *Code 9811* hides applications, replacing them with garbage files with names similar to FIDVCXWGJKJWLOI. According to Ken Dunham, who reported this virus, "The most obvious symptom of the virus is a desktop that looks like electronic worms and a message that reads 'You have been hacked by the Pretorians'".

▶ *Code 32767* once a month tries to delete documents. This virus is not known to be in circulation.

▶ *Flag* is unrelated to WDEF A and B, but was given the name WDEF-C in some anti-virus software. The virus is not intentionally damaging but, when spreading, it overwrites any existing WDEF resource of ID '0', an action that might damage some files. This virus is not known to be in circulation.

▶ *Frankie* affects only the Aladdin emulator on the Atari or Amiga. It doesn't infect or trigger on real Macs or the Spectre emulator. The virus infects application files and the Finder. Frankie draws a bomb icon and displays "Frankie says: No more piracy!"

▶ *Fuck* (an nVIR B strain) infects application and System files. It inflicts no intentional damage.

▶ *Init 17* infects the System file and applications. It displays the message "From the depths of Cyberspace" the first time it triggers. It can cause accidental damage, especially on pre PowerMac machines.

▶ *Init 29 (Init 29 A, B)* spreads rapidly, infecting system files, applications, and document files (document files can't infect other files, though). It may display a message if a locked floppy is accessed on an infected system: "The disk 'xxxxx' needs minor repairs. Do you want to repair it?". The virus inflicts no intentional damage, but can cause several problems, including multiple infections, memory errors, system crashes, printing problems, MultiFinder problems, and start-up document incompatibilities.

▶ *Init 1984* infects system extensions (INITs). The virus works under systems 6 and 7. It triggers on Friday the 13th and damages files by renaming them, changing file TYPE and file CREATOR, changing the creation and modification dates, and sometimes deleting the files.

▶ *Init-9403 (SysX)* infects applications and Finder under systems 6 and 7. The virus attempts to overwrite the whole start-up volume and disk information on all connected hard drives. This virus is found only on Macs running the Italian version of MacOS.

▶ *Init-M* replicates under system 7 only. It infects INITs and application files. The virus triggers on Friday the 13th. Its damage mechanisms are similar to those of Init 1984. The virus may rename a file or folder to Virus MindCrime. Rarely, Init-M may delete files.

▶ *MacMag (Aldus, Brandow, Drew, Peace)* was first distributed as a HyperCard stack Trojan, but only infected System files. The virus triggered (by displaying a peace message, then self-deleting) on 2nd March, 1988, and thus is very rarely found today.

▶ *MBDF (A,B)* originated from the Tetracycle, Tetricycle, or "tetris-rotating" Trojan. The A strain was also distributed in Obnoxious Tetris and Ten Tile Puzzle. This Trojan infects applications and system files, including System and Finder. MBDF can cause accidental damage to the System file and menu problems. A minor variant of MBDF B appeared in summer 1997.

▶ *MDEF (MDEF A/Garfield, MDEF B/Top Cat, C, D)* infects the System file and application files (D doesn't infect System). It causes no intentional damage, but can cause crashes and damaged files.

▶ *MDEF-E and MDEF-F* are both described as simple and benign. They infect applications and system files with an MDEF resource ID '0', but do not otherwise cause file damage. These viruses are not known to be in circulation.

▶ *nCAM* is an nVIR variant.

▶ *nVIR (nVIR A, B, C⁻AIDS, Fuck, Hpat, Jude, MEV#, nFlu)* infects the System file and any opened applications. Extant versions don't cause intentional damage. The payload is either beeping or (in the case of nVIR A) speaking the phrase "Don't panic" if MacInTalk is installed.

▶ *nVIR-f* is an nVIR variant.

▶ *prod* is an nVIR variant.

▶ *Scores (Eric, Vult, NASA, San Jose Flu)* aims to attack two applications that were never generally released. The virus can cause accidental damage, though, including system crashes and problems printing or using MacDraw and Excel. The virus infects applications, Finder, and DA Handler.

▶ *SevenDust* consists of a family of five viruses that spread through MDEF resources and a System extension created by that resource. Some versions are highly destructive. It is also known as MDEF 9806, although it isn't related to other viruses called MDEF.

▶ *T4 (A, B, C, D)* infects applications and Finder, and tries to modify the System file to alter the start-up code. Under system 6 and 7.0, INITs and system extensions don't load. Under 7.0.1, T4 may render the Mac unbootable. The virus masquerades as Disinfectant, to spoof behaviour blockers such as Gatekeeper. Originally included in versions 2.0/2.1 of the public domain game GoMoku, T4-D spreads from application to application on launch by appending itself to the "CODE" resource. It deletes files other than the System file from the System folder, as well as documents, and is termed dangerous. The D strain is not known to be in circulation.

▶ *WDEF (A,B)* infects desktop files only. The virus doesn't spread under Mac system 7. It inflicts no intentional damage, but causes beeping, crashes, font corruption, and other problems.

▶ *zero* is an nVIR variant.

▶ *Zuc (A, B, C)* infects applications. When an infected application is run, the cursor moves diagonally and uncontrollably across the screen when the user holds down the mouse button. The virus does no other intentional damage.

HyperCard Infectors

HyperCard infectors are a somewhat esoteric breed, but continue to appear, and most of the commercial scanners detect them:

▶ *Antibody* is a virus-hunting virus that propagates between stacks, checking for and removing MerryXmas, then inserting an inoculation script.

▶ *Blink* was reported in August 1998. The infector is nondestructive but spreads; infected stacks blink once per second starting in January 1999.

▶ *Dukakis* infects the Home stack, then other stacks used subsequently. It displays the message "Dukakis for President", then deletes itself, and thus is not often seen.

▶ *HC 9507* infects the Home stack, then other running stacks and randomly chosen stacks on the start-up disk. On triggering, this infector displays visual effects or hangs the system. It overwrites stack resources, so a repaired stack may not run properly.

▶ *HC 9603* infects the Home stack, then other running stacks. The virus has no intended effects, but may damage the Home stack.

▶ *HC "Two Tunes"* (referred to by some sources as *"Three Tunes"*) infects stack scripts. It has several visual/audio effects: it displays a "Hey, what are you doing?" message, plays the tune *Muss I denn*, plays the tune *Behind the Blue Mountains*, displays HyperCard toolbox and pattern menus, and displays "Don't panic!" 15 minutes after activation. Even sources that describe this virus as "Three Tunes" seem to describe the symptoms consistently with the description here. This virus has no known connection with the PC file infector sometimes known as "Three Tunes".

▶ *Independance* [sic] *Day* was reported in July 1997. It attempts to be destructive, but fortunately is not written well enough to be more than a nuisance. You can find more information at http://www.hyperactivesw.com/Virus1.html#Iday.

▶ *MerryXmas* appends to a stack script. On execution, the virus attempts to infect the Home stack, which then infects other stacks on access. There are several strains, most of which cause system crashes and other anomalies. At least one strain replaces the Home stack script and deletes stacks run subsequently. Variants include Merry2Xmas, Lopez, and the rather destructive Crudshot.

▶ *WormCode*, a nondestructive HyperCard infector, was reported in February 2000. You can find more information at http://www.hyperactivesw.com/Virus1.html.

Mac Trojan Horses

Trojan horses are often unsubtle and immediate in their effects. While these effects may be devastating, Trojans are usually very traceable to their point of entry. The few Mac-specific Trojans are rarely seen, but of course the commercial scanners generally detect them. We refer here to destructive Trojans, not worms and remote-access tools, which are virtually unknown in the Macintosh arena, to date.

▶ *ChinaTalk,* was distributed as a system extension. It was supposed to be a sound driver, but actually deleted folders.

▶ *CPro* is supposed to be an update to Compact Pro, but attempts to format currently mounted disks.

▶ *ExtensionConflict* is supposed to identify extensions conflicts, but installs one of the six SevenDust (also known as 666) viruses.

▶ *FontFinder* is supposed to lists fonts used in a document, but actually deletes folders.

▶ *MacMag* is a HyperCard stack (from New Apple Products) that was the origin of the MacMag virus. When run, MacMag infected the System file, which then infected system files on floppies. The Trojan is set to trigger and self-destruct on 2nd March, 1988, and so is rarely found.

▶ *Mosaic* is supposed to display graphics, but actually mangles directory structures.

▶ *NVP* modifies the System file so that users cannot type any vowels. The Trojan was originally found masquerading as New Look, which redesigns the display.

▶ *The PostScriptHack* referred to by some sources was basically a PostScript job that toggled the printer password to some random string a number of times. Some Apple laser printers had a firmware counter that restricted the number of times the password could be changed, so eventually the password would get stuck at some random string that the user would not know.

▶ *Steroid*, a control panel, claimed to improve QuickDraw speed, but actually mangled the directory structure.

▶ *Tetracycle* was implicated in the original spread of MBDF.

▶ *Virus Info* purported to contain virus information but actually trashed disks. This Trojan is not to be confused with the Virus Reference HyperCard stack.

▶ *AppleScript Trojans* have been discovered on a couple of occasions. A demonstration destructive compiled AppleScript was posted to the newsgroups alt.comp.virus, comp.sys.mac.misc, comp.sys.mac.system, it.comp.macintosh, microsoft.public.word.mac, nl.comp.sys.mac, no.mac, and symantec.support.mac.sam.general on 16th August, 1997, apparently in response to a call for help originally posted to alt.comp.virus on 14th August, 1997, and followed up on 15th August, 1997. On 3rd September, 1997, *MacInTouch* published Xavier Bury's finding of a second AppleScript Trojan horse, which, like the call-for-help follow-up, mentioned Hotline servers. The "MacSimpsons" AppleScript worm was reported in the summer of 2001 (see Chapter 19).

Macro Viruses, Trojans, and Variants

At the time of the longstanding second-to-last upgrade of Disinfectant (version 3.6 in early 1995), there were no known macro viruses in the wild, apart from HyperCard infectors. In any case, Disinfectant was always intended to deal with system viruses, not Trojans or macro/script viruses. However, many users are unaware of these distinctions and still assume that Disinfectant is a complete solution, even after its effective demise. (In fact, people were still relying on Gatekeeper long after its author disowned it.)

Unfortunately, the number of known macro viruses now runs into several thousand, though the number in the wild is far fewer. Most macro viruses (if they have a warhead at all) target Intel platforms and assume FAT-based directory structures, so they usually have no discernible effect on Macs when they trigger. Many of them do, however, infect effectively.

Viruses that manipulate text strings within a document may work just as well on a Macintosh as on a PC. In any case, the main costs of virus control are not of recovering from virus payloads, but of establishing detection and protection (or of not establishing them). The costs of not establishing these measures can be considerable, irrespective of damage caused on infected machines, especially in corporate environments. Secondary distribution of infected documents may result in:

▶ **Civil action**   For instance, inadvertent distribution of an infected document to external organizations may be in breach of contractual obligations.

▶ **Legal action**   In terms of breach of data-protection legislation such as the UK Data Protection.

▶ **Damage to reputation**   No organization wants to be seen as being riddled with viruses.

Mac users with Word 6 or later versions of Word or Excel supporting Visual Basic for Applications (Office 98 and Office 2001) are vulnerable to infection by macro viruses that are specific to these applications. Indeed, these viruses can potentially infect other files on any hardware platform supporting these versions of these applications.

Office 98 applications are in principle vulnerable to most of the infective threats to which Office 97 applications are vulnerable, though again, payloads are another matter. In fact, an increasing number of VBA infectors seem not to work as expected in Office 98 and 2001. Word 2001 uses a file format that is (accidentally) slightly different from that used in Office 97, 98, and 2000. This has created some problems for anti-virus software on Macs and on PCs, depending on which parts of the macro the software actually scanned.

Early in 2001, a number of people on Mac-related lists were misled by a news report at ZDNet suggesting that a new variant of Melissa had been found that targeted Macs. This was a travesty. The virus concerned is a common variant of Melissa. Since Melissa is a macro virus (or virus/worm hybrid, if you prefer), any variant may be infective (to a degree) on a Mac, but the mass mailing component works only in Windows. This variant is no more or less a danger to Mac users than the others, in principle. It took a while to remind people that macro viruses have an impact on Macs too, and even then most commentators outside the anti-virus industry completely misunderstood the implications.

However, there was an issue. It turned out that an accidental (minor) change in the Office 2001 document format meant that many scanners were unable to detect macro viruses consistently in documents saved in 2001 format. This change affected PC scanners as much as it did Mac products.

PC Viruses on Emulated PCs

Files infected with a PC-specific file virus (this excludes macro viruses, which are not PC-specific) can execute only on a Macintosh running DOS or DOS/Windows emulation, if then. They can, of course, spread across platforms simply by copying infected files from one system to another.

DOS diskettes infected with a boot-sector virus can be read on a Mac with Apple File Exchange, PC Exchange, DOS Mounter, etc., normally without risk to the Mac. However, leaving such an infected disk in the drive while booting an emulator such as SoftPC can lead to unpredictable results when the virus attempts to infect the logical PC drive. (Informal testing with common boot-sector infectors has indicated that they often work pretty much as they do on real PCs.)

Esperanto.4733

Esperanto is a PC file infector that works with a number of PC executable file formats. When it was first seen, Esperanto was reported to be a multiplatform virus capable of executing under some circumstances on Macintoshes. Subsequent reports indicate that this belief is the result of misinformation on the part of the virus's author. However, at least two reputable PC anti-virus vendors still list Esperanto as capable of activating on a Macintosh. No Mac scanner is known to attempt to detect it in Mac-specific mode, and it has rarely been reported in the field.

PC Scripting Viruses

MacOS doesn't, of course, support the Windows Script Host, on which the current crop of VBS viruses and Trojans rely, as a distribution mechanism. However, PC emulation packages do support it. Not all Mac anti-virus software detects such viruses. It is, of course, possible for Mac users to forward them. In particular, several instances have occurred in which Mac users have forwarded the KAK worm, because it's not an attachment and isn't obvious to Outlook users on either platform.

Welcome Datacomp

From time to time Mac users report that the message "Welcome Datacomp" appears in their documents without having been typed. This message is the result of using a trojanized third-party Mac-compatible keyboard with this "joke" hard-coded into the keyboard ROM. It's not a virus; it cannot infect anything. The only cure is to replace the keyboard. (Be polite but firm with the dealer if the keyboard was sold to you as a new one!)

The EICAR Installation Test File

The EICAR test file is not a virus (it doesn't replicate). It's a neat piece of PC assembler code carefully constructed so that it can be typed in with a plain text editor. If the program is actually executed on a real or emulated PC, it displays the text "EICAR-STANDARD-ANTIVIRUS-TEST-FILE!" It doesn't execute on a Mac (unless you're running it under some form of PC emulator), but commercial Mac scanners now detect the EICAR code as a test virus, and will alert accordingly (as will nearly all PC scanners, of course).

To make use of the EICAR test string, type or copy and paste the following text into a test file.

```
X5O!P%@AP[4\PZX54(P^)7CC)7}$EICAR-STANDARD-ANTIVIRUS-TEST-FILE!$H+H*
```

An article by Paul Ducklin of Sophos explains the EICAR test file: http://www.eicar.org/anti_virus_test_file.htm.

Information Resources

Information on Mac virus issues is, to say the least, somewhat sparse.

Mac-Related Newsgroups

Virus-related threads crop up from time to time on these groups:

> comp.sys.mac.apps
>
> comp.sys.mac.comm
>
> comp.sys.mac.misc
>
> comp.sys.mac.system

Mac-related topics are addressed occasionally on alt.comp.virus and other virus-specific newsgroups.

Books

The diskette included with the second edition of Robert Slade's *Guide to Computer Viruses* (Springer Verlag, 1996) contained most of the Mac-related information available at the University of Hamburg. The book also contains a reasonable quantity of Mac-friendly information, but is now out of print. The diskette included a copy of Disinfectant 3.6, which is now obsolete—3.7.1 was the final release.

Very few books primarily about computer viruses deal at any length with Mac viruses. Some general books on the Mac touch on the subject, but few, if any, add anything useful. Some of the *Totally Witless User's Guide to...* books dealing with security in general include information on PC *and* Mac viruses. Unfortunately, the quality of virus-related information in such publications is generally low.

Several people have been misled by some editions of David Pogue's *Dummies* books into thinking that Mac Virus is a source of anti-virus software. It was not, and is not: however, the "Viruses and the Macintosh" FAQ includes URLs for commercial software and for some shareware and freeware products. Listing in the FAQ doesn't constitute an endorsement of any sort, of course.

Pogue has also claimed several times that no virus causes damage on the Mac except AutoStart. This is seriously misleading. While it's unusual to find Mac-specific viruses in the field currently apart from AutoStart and, occasionally, SevenDust, others certainly exist and can cause damage. In fact, all viruses entail a certain amount of damage, even those with no intentionally damaging payload. And, of course, Mac users who use Microsoft Office applications continue to be vulnerable to the macro viruses that prey on those applications.

Mac OS in a Nutshell, by Rita Lewis and Bill Fishman (O'Reilly and Associates, 2000), is a decent general resource that includes reasonably accurate virus information.

Bigelow's Virus Troubleshooting Pocket Reference (McGraw-Hill Professional Publishing, 2000), by Ken Dunham, includes some Mac-specific information. Unfortunately, it's not always an accurate resource.

Sad Macs, Bombs and Other Disasters by Ted Landau (Peachpit Press, 2000) isn't particularly good on viruses, but is an excellent resource for general troubleshooting. You can find information at http://www.macfixit.com/sadmacs3promo.html.

Inside Macintosh (Addison-Wesley, 1994) is essential reading for Mac programmers. It provides umpteen volumes of fairly low-level information. It's possible to download volumes in Acrobat, and in some cases other formats, from http://devworld.apple.com/, where you can also order hardcopy and CD versions.

The Power Macintosh Emergency Handbook (Apple Computer) is well worth a look, and you may be able to find it at ftp://ftp.info.apple.com/.

Web Sites

Many major vendors have a virus information database online on their web sites. Symantec (http://www.symantec.com/, http://www.sarc.com/), Network Associates (http://www.nai.com/), and Sophos (http://www.sophos.com/) include Macintosh virus information.

Susan Lesch's Mac Virus site closed down on 5th September, 1999, but the site as it was at that time is archived at http://www.sherpasoft.org.uk and http://www.icsa.net. The URL http://www.mac virus.com/ now points to the Mac Virus II site at http://www.sherpasoft.org.uk, maintained by Harley.

The virus information database there is essentially the one reproduced here: http://www.sherpasoft.org.uk/MacVirus/reference/viruses.html.
Some additional sites to check out include the following:

▶ MacFixIt "Troubleshooting for the Macintosh": http://www.macfixit.com/

▶ The MacInTouch home page (info and services): http://www.macintouch.com/

▶ MacWEEK.com (which has run MacInTouch columns about the AutoStart worms): http://macweek.zdnet.com/
As of 5th March, 2001, the zdnet site consolidated into MacCentral at http://maccentral.macworld.com/

▶ *Macworld* magazine: http//www.macworld.com/
Strangely, this is different from the MacCentral site at macworld.com mentioned in the MacWEEK.com description.

▶ TidBITS (which has done many good articles on Mac/macro virus issues): http://www.tidbits.com/

Virus Bulletin

The expensive (but, for the professional, essential) periodical *Virus Bulletin* includes Mac-specific information from time to time. However, if you have no interest in PC issues, you probably won't consider it worth the expense. You can contact *Virus Bulletin* as follows:

> Virus Bulletin, Ltd.
> The Pentagon
> Abingdon
> OX14 3YP
> England
> +44 1235 555139
> http://www.virusbtn.com/

The proceedings of the 1997 *Virus Bulletin* conference contained a paper by Harley that, despite its obsolescence, is probably still the definitive paper on Macintosh viruses, since no one else that we are aware of has addressed the same area. Contact *Virus Bulletin* for further information on the annual conference and on obtaining the proceedings. The paper can also be found (by permission of *Virus Bulletin*) at Harley's web site, http://www.sherpasoft.org.uk/MacSupporters/, and at http://www.icsa.net/.

Macro Virus Information Resources

The University of Hamburg Virus Test Center's Macro Virus List was the definitive listing of macro viruses. It included all known macro viruses—some found only in zoo collections and research labs, some in the wild. The list doesn't include information on individual viruses apart from name and platform, and is irregularly maintained. You can find the list at the following sites:

ftp://agn-www.informatik.uni-hamburg.de/pub/texts/macro/

http://agn-www.informatik.uni-hamburg.de/vtc/eng.htm

The usual anti-virus vendor web sites usually include macro information.

Richard Martin put together an FAQ on the subject of Word viruses. It's well out of date, though, and was always inaccurate in some respects. A copy of what we believe to have been the last released version is available at SherpaSoft web site:

http://www.sherpasoft.org.uk/anti-virus/wordvirus.FAQ

Other Virus Resources

You can find excellent pages on HyperCard viruses at HyperActive Software's web site. The site provides information on HyperCard infectors, a link to Bill Swagerty's free Vaccine utility for detecting and cleaning them, a note on false positives reported by commercial software, inoculation, and a free HyperCard virus detection service.

http://www.hyperactivesw.com/Virus1.html

Virus Test Center, Hamburg: AntiVirus Catalog/CARObase

ftp://ftp.informatik.uni-hamburg.de/pub/virus/texts/catalog/
ftp://ftp.informatik.uni-hamburg.de/pub/virus/texts/carobase/
ftp://ftp.informatik.uni-hamburg.de/pub/virus/texts/viruses/

These links may be out of date; if they don't work, try the following:

ftp://agn-www.informatik.uni-hamburg.de/vtc/

INFO-MAC HyperArchive

http://hyperarchive.lcs.mit.edu/HyperArchive/Abstracts/vir/HyperArchive.html

Kevin Harris's Virus Reference was last updated 31st August, 1995. This HyperCard stack requires HyperCard 2.1 or later.

ftp://mirrors.aol.com/pub/info-mac/vir/virus-reference-216-hc.hqx

You might think Apple would have some useful information on its web sites. Unfortunately, most of the virus-related material that we have found there has been inaccurate and/or outdated.

http://www.apple.com/

Mac Troubleshooting

Here are a few steps that it might be appropriate to try if virus scanning with an up-to-date anti-virus scanner finds nothing:

▶ Rebuilding the desktop is by no means a cure-all, but rarely does any harm. It may be worth disabling extensions when you do this, especially if the operation doesn't seem to be completed successfully.

▶ To disable extensions, restart the machine with the SHIFT key held down until you see an "Extensions Off" message. If you're rebuilding the desktop, release the SHIFT key and hold down the COMMAND key (the key with the Apple outline icon) and OPTIONS (ALT) key until the program requests that you confirm that you want to rebuild.

▶ Disabling extensions is also a good starting point for tracking down an extensions conflict. If booting without extensions appears to bypass the problem, try removing extensions with Extensions Manager (system 7.5). Remove one extension at a time, and replace it before removing the next one and booting with that one removed. Remember that if removing one stops the problem, it's still worth putting it back and trying all the others to see if you can find the one creating the conflict.

▶ Extensions Manager also lets you disable system control panels. If you don't have Extensions Manager, try Now Utilities or Conflict Catcher.

▶ Parameter RAM (PRAM) contains system information, notably the settings for a number of system control panels. "Zapping" PRAM returns possibly corrupt PRAM data to default values. A problem with date and time is likely a symptom of corrupted PRAM (but could be a symptom of a corrupted system file). With system 7, hold down COMMAND-OPTION-P-R at bootup until the Mac beeps and restarts. You may have to restore changes to some Control Panels before your system works properly. If the reset values aren't retained, you may need to replace the battery.

Questions Received at Mac Virus

Here's a sample of some of the mail enquiries received since Mac Virus II opened.

I have heard rumours that an AS analogue of the I Love You worm could be manufactured easily. Is this a real threat?

It's possible. AppleScript Trojans are rare, but not unknown. There are very few languages in which it's impossible to write self-replicative code. Whether it's likely is a bigger question. AS has some of the "advantages" of Microsoft's macro languages, in that it's easy and freely available. However, Mac OS isn't blessed with the same intrinsic security holes that Windows 9x and NT have. On the other hand, the constant trickle of HyperCard infectors might tell us something. A number of Mac users are known to have received VBS/Lovelet, succumbed to the social engineering of the subject/message, and attempted to open it. They've been saved from their own gullibility only by the fact that Mac OS doesn't support the Windows Script Host.

This might also be a good time to mention a phenomenon I sometimes call Wormhausen-by-Proxy Syndrome. It goes something like this: PC-user A is infected with a PC-specific worm, which mails itself out to (among other people) Mac-user B. B tries to open the message, but can't because Macs don't normally run PC-specific programs, so B asks PC-user C to open it. Now C is infected with the worm.

What could be done preventively?

Beware of geeks bearing gifts. Treat compiled scripts and other executables with suspicion, whatever their source. Don't assume that mail from a given account was sent with the knowledge and intent of the person who uses that account. Bear in mind that you are far likelier to receive an infected object from an innocent friend, relative, or colleague than from a hacker with a cutlass between his teeth. Use commercial anti-virus software (and keep it updated), but don't assume it will protect you from *everything*.

[Do you have] any suggestions on where to get free virus protection software? I've got the WM.Cap.A virus. When I'm ready to buy virus protection software for my Mac, which one do you recommend?

I know of no free Mac software that disinfects/protects against Word/Excel or other Microsoft Office macro viruses, or Cap specifically. For that, you need either a generic tool like Padgett Petersen's MacroList, or commercial anti-virus software.

How can I obtain the latest list of all viruses to scan in my computer? And how can I tell which ones I have already?

Do you mean an informational list of all viruses, or the latest virus definitions for anti-virus software? I'm assuming you mean the latter, since a comprehensive list of all known viruses wouldn't be very helpful to you, even if there was such a thing.

You get definitions updates from the vendor who supplied your anti-virus software. If you tell me which software that is, and which version, I can, hopefully, give you specific information on that particular program.

Virex 6.*x* and Norton Anti-Virus can be configured to fetch the latest updates from the vendor's web site automatically. The program then updates its internal database so that it can recognize the latest viruses.

Sophos for Mac and F-Secure for Mac are a little different, since the whole program is updated monthly, rather than just the internal database. However, both can be updated from the vendor's web site.

As for checking the date of the last update, that depends on which program you're using.

Hello. I may have a virus. Just tonight most of the fonts on the web pages on my iMac seem corrupted—lots of "dingbat" characters and squares instead of text. For example, nothing on your web site was readable. I just clicked at random and happened to hit your email link. Can you advise?

This doesn't sound like any Mac virus I'm aware of, though it wouldn't do any harm to run an up-to-date scanner over the system. I don't know which browser you're using, but the chances are that it has a font preferences option; in Navigator, it's probably under the Edit menu, in Preferences, depending on the version. It sounds likely that the default fonts have changed, especially if the problem seems to be restricted to your browser.

I just nailed a possible SevenDust with Agax (my Virex 6.1 missed it). However, I'm no longer able to start up with extensions off; holding SHIFT down at start-up isn't working. Any suggestions or URLs you'd recommend?

This query was not mailed only to me, and several people responded. I don't feel it appropriate to quote their answers, but several points came up in the ensuing discussion that are worth alluding to:

1. The problem turned out to be mechanical (faulty keyboard).

2. This isn't a characteristic effect of either SevenDust or the Agax anti-virus program.

3. There probably wasn't a SevenDust infection. The Agax message that this enquirer saw was a little misleading, though not actually incorrect. Since the program was unable to read the file in question because of file corruption, it flagged it as possibly infected. John Dalgliesh, the author of Agax, who contributed a lot more to this discussion than I did, has indicated that this minor blemish was subsequently corrected.

I think of WM/Cap as a PC virus, in any case, so I can't see how a Mac version Word document can have it. I may be wrong about that; it may be that an original document was written on a PC with the virus and that it is still infecting the document but can't infect other Word documents on my hard drive (of which there are hundreds) because they were originated on Mac. Is that possible?

Like many macro viruses, WM/Cap thrives (depending on the variant) on Macs that use Word 6.*x*. Few of such viruses can deliver their payload (if any) on the Mac, but most of them can infect on a Mac. Cap has no payload, by the way.

Originating a document on a Mac doesn't of itself offer any protection. If you're using a Mac version of Word earlier or later than 6.*x*, though, I wouldn't expect Cap to be able to infect. Due to bugs in the original code, it's also possible for a Cap variant to be noninfective.

I'm genuinely puzzled, particularly because here in Washington, DC, I'm sending files between my Mac at home and my office where I work on a PC; however, my office's firewall never detects a problem.

Firewalls don't necessarily pick up virus problems at all. That isn't their primary function, and many don't include anti-virus capabilities at all. This isn't necessarily a bad thing, but that's a long and different discussion.

I do not have an anti-virus program but will buy one. Can you tell me what the best program for a Mac is?

Virex, Norton for Mac, or Sophos for Mac are all good products; you can get evaluation copies of any or all three from their web sites (www.nai.com, www.symantec.com, and www.sophos.com). There are free AutoStart AV programs, but it may be safer to go with a commercial program. F-Secure (www.f-secure.com) also has a commercial scanner, but it scans *only* for macro viruses and AutoStart.

(I'm being accused of sending out infected files.) HELP! Where can I find anti-virus software for my Mac. Yours is the only site that I can find at the moment for Macs. Any help will help.

You don't say which virus you're accused of spreading. If it's a macro virus, you need commercial anti-virus software; there's no freeware scanner for Mac that detects macro viruses. However, you can get evaluation copies of Virex, Norton Anti-Virus, or Sophos from their respective web sites (www.nai.com, www.symantec.com, and www.sophos.com).

Actually, there is no comprehensive freeware anti-virus software for the Mac; the freeware that exists is either obsolete, restricted in the range of threats it detects, or for time-limited evaluation only.

Hi. I would like to know whether the "I Love You" virus can affect a Mac. Thank you for your quick response to us.

VBS/Lovelet is a Visual Basic Script. It relies on the presence of the Windows Script Host, which is present only in (some versions and configurations of) Windows. Obviously, Macs don't usually have this, and therefore the script can't be executed (run). However, if the Mac is running a PC-emulation package such as SoftWindows or Virtual PC with a vulnerable version or configuration of Windows installed, it is possible for VBS scripts to be executed within that environment.

Much the same applies to other high-profile VBS viruses. However, you should be cautious about passing on attachments received from others; Mac users have a long history of passing on to others various viruses and worms that don't actually work on Macs. Some Mac anti-virus packages are unhelpful here, since they don't detect *any* PC-specific viruses.

Certain viruses (KAK, BubbleBoy) pose an additional problem in that they aren't contained in attachments, but are embedded in the body of the actual message. (This is actually rather easy to do inconspicuously, now that so many mail programs read HTML as well as plain text messages.)

Social Engineering

IN THIS CHAPTER:

This appendix is based on David Harley's Social Engineering FAQ. This FAQ is still in draft form and is not currently available on the World Wide Web. It derives from a number of previous discussions in this area, including:

▶ A presentation delivered to the 1997 SANS conference in New Orleans

▶ A paper presented to EICAR at the 1998 conference in Munich

▶ An article on hoaxes printed in the EICAR journal in 1997

▶ An FAQ on email abuse

This appendix does not present the full FAQ; it does not, for instance, include all of the material on good password practice, a topic which does not seem particularly relevant to a book on viruses. It doesn't include discussion of social engineering in the context of malware, since such a discussion would cover much the same ground as Chapter 15. The appendix will, however, give you some useful background for the social engineering references in the main text.

Chapter 15 includes a number of definitions of *social engineering* that are also cited in the full version of the FAQ. However, the working definition that this appendix uses is as follows: psychological manipulation of an individual or set of individuals to produce a desired effect on their behaviour.

IT Security

This appendix applies the classic tripod model of information security:

▶ **Confidentiality/Privacy**   Information should be available only to those who are entitled to it.

▶ **Integrity**   Information should be protected against accidental or deliberate but inappropriate modification.

▶ **Availability**   Information should be available to those who are entitled to it when they need it.

Social engineering is most often thought of as an attack on confidentiality (password stealing). However, psychological manipulation can also be used as an attack on integrity, either directly or indirectly. Indirect attacks include password stealing as a means of gaining unauthorized access so as to effect unauthorized modification. A direct attack would include persuading or conning a *mark* (a victim or target) into introducing an inappropriate modification. It can also be used as an attack on availability—for instance, dissuading the mark from using a legitimate resource can be as effective a denial of service (DoS) attack as flooding the target organization's Internet gateway with "bad" packets.

What the Intruder Wants to Know

Who "owns" the target machines/systems?

▶ Is the organization academic, commercial, high-security commercial (banks, for instance), or military? The type of organization will not only affect the desirability of the information that the intruder can steal from it, but the sort of psychological manipulation that is most likely to succeed in that environment. Academic environments are likely to be receptive to laissez-faire information sharing, whereas military environments tend to be rigidly hierarchical, so that an authoritarian persona may be more appropriate.

▶ Different units/divisions may be receptive to quite different approaches according to their differing mindsets:

   ▶ Human Resources, Finance, and similar departments will tend to be secretive.

   ▶ Public Relations will want to give away as much (favourable) information as possible.

   ▶ Research units will vary according to whether they're academically focused or more concerned with trade secrets and patents. (In real life, academics may be very concerned with patents.)

▶ Are the administrators competent? Friendly or authoritarian? Do they have exploitable personal weaknesses? Can they be bullied, seduced, or sidestepped?

▶ How about the user population? Are they computer-literate? Is there a high rate of turnover? Is the culture of the organization security-literate? Are the users deferential to authority figures (such as systems administrators)?

What sort of hardware, networks, and operating systems are in use? Are they systems with known weaknesses? Intruders tend to hate VMS, like some flavours of UNIX, and love NT, which may or may not reflect the actual comparative vulnerability of each platform. Is it likely that the administrators keep up with all the current security patches? Are there configuration quirks worth looking out for?

The social engineer may ask questions such as the following: How do I get access? Is there dial-in access? If I have one voice, fax, or modem number, what do I access if I dial some numbers close to it (*xxx-xxx*1, *xxx-xxx*2, etc.)? Will the switchboard put me through to one of the following?

► Human Resources. "What jobs are available?" (Would applying for one get me access to anything interesting?)

► Public Relations. "What can you tell me about the organization and your current projects?" (Are you worth further snooping?)

► Security. "Are you interested in staff or products such as XYZ?" ("Ah, so you're already using ABC...")

► Switchboard. "Who do I need to talk to about.....?" (Switchboard operators rarely do significant security screening.)

► Sales/Marketing. "What current products are you selling?" (What do you have that is worth stealing?)

► Help Desk. "Give me my password".

People Hacking

People may be as good a resource as any database. Here are some ways of tapping that resource.

Shouldersurfing

This usually means standing where you can watch someone type in sensitive data such as passwords, usernames, PINs, phone card numbers, and so on. Even seeing what kind of hand-held authentication device employees use may be of some use to a black hat.

NOTE

Black hat *is common security/hacker slang for a bad guy. The term stems from the Old West stereotype that the good guys wear white Stetsons while the bandits wear black hats.*

Eavesdropping/Surveillance

Hackers use a variety of methods to conduct surveillance:

▶ Using electronics: sniffers, vampire taps, directional microphones, phone taps, and so on.

▶ "Being there"—around the corner, at the next table, or in the reception area— at the right time.

▶ "Being invisible"—temps, cleaners, janitors, electricians, telco (telephone company) engineers, contractors, messengers, couriers, and similar workers tend to be overlooked by professionals. Moral: check out strangers (politely and cautiously).

Inappropriate Access

Unauthorized access and social engineering go together like ham and eggs:

▶ Unsecured servers (those with physical access to the hardware, unsecured system files, weak logins, and so on).

▶ Unsecured portable equipment.

▶ Unsecured visual access. (People who administer servers shouldn't live in glass houses, let alone throw stones.)

▶ Unsecured physical access—tailgating (following an authorized person through a locked door or turnstile, for example), insecure reception areas, shared keypad codes, and so on.

Being Sociable

Socializing creates opportunities to gather information:

▶ After-hours activities, such as chats down the pub, in newsgroups, or in chatrooms

▶ In the course of business, including social chat during business calls

Phone Phonies

People are accustomed to some freedom in responding to callers claiming to be conducting surveys, journalistic enquiries, or sales cold-calling, and may give away valuable organizational information. There are also fraudulent phone-related activities such as stealing service (conning a connection), slamming (changing providers without the knowledge or consent of the consumer), credit card fraud, and so on.

Dumpster Diving

For every firm that shreds everything, there are a dozen that don't. Skips (dumpsters), waste baskets, recycling bins, and such are often rich sources of organizational information, classified information, obsolete media, and even hardware.

Electronic Leftovers

Systems provide a lot of electronic "waste" that can yield valuable information:

▶ Disk, file, print, spool, and terminal buffers are often left untidied and unflushed.

▶ "Deleted" files are often still accessible to someone with even a bare minimum of technical knowledge or basic recovery tools.

▶ Deleted material within files is often still available: Microsoft Word files can, under some circumstances, not only contain long-discarded material (any application that allows multiple levels of "Undo" when the user is editing data may have this vulnerability), but may also contain material picked up randomly from other locations on the system.

▶ If you have physical access to a PC, there's a good chance you can retrieve something interesting if, for instance, the owner hasn't logged out of a network connection.

Targeting the Help Desk

The Help Desk is often a highly rewarding target for social engineering, such as:

▶ Asking for, begging for, or demanding a password or other access

▶ Playing the new, forgetful, demanding, or wheedling customer

▶ Playing the victim of a demanding but forgetful manager ("If he doesn't get *xxx,* I'll lose my job".)

▶ Playing the authority figure

- ▶ Applying good cop/bad cop teamwork
- ▶ Posing as a Help Desk/support person needing information (such as a password) in order to solve a system problem

Attacks on the Help Desk

Many Help Desk customers expect too much, too little, or sometimes both from support staff. However, such expectations cut two ways. Consider the standard support jokes and apocrypha about dumb users: photocopied diskettes; memoranda stapled to floppies; CD trays used as cupholders; "I pressed F1 an hour ago and no one's been back to me yet".

IT staff have low expectations with respect to the expertise of customers, who may have a very narrow, focused view of the technology on which they rely; it isn't necessarily difficult to convince an IT staff member that you need help or reminders regarding a very basic operation. It's often quite easy to persuade someone who can change your password to do so, if he or she has no particular reason to doubt your credentials, and if the organization has no strict policy on verifying password requests.

Do I Need to Disclose My Password?

If anyone asks you for your password as an aid to solving a system problem, verify the request to the best of your ability. A systems administrator is usually a highly privileged individual. He or she probably doesn't have an easy way to ascertain your current password, but probably doesn't need it: a systems administrator can access your account, email, and files using administrator/supervisor privileges. He or she can even use a utility such as *su* to act as you on the system. In such instances, the systems administrator can change your password temporarily, then let you change it back or to something personally meaningful afterwards.

Wouldn't I Notice Unwarranted Interest in Security Issues?

Not necessarily. One recommended technique for intruders is to learn to back off from exciting suspicion. Social engineers try not to pump you for information: they piece together information from a variety of sources, or ask you for just enough to get them a step nearer to free access.

How Big Is the Risk?

The degree of risk that your system faces depends on the source of the risk:

▶ From external hackers? It depends on how high-profile you are, and how well protected.

▶ From internal sources? Most sources indicate that 60 to 90 percent of breaches are internal, though most of those breaches will probably be accidental (user error) or acts of God rather than malicious. Also, the claimed level of internal breaches has shifted downward over the years, the study by CSI and the FBI at http://www.gocsi.com being a case in point. Nevertheless, a significant proportion of recorded incidents will be "planted" intruders, disgruntled or socially engineered employees, or even employees future-proofing (with time bombs or other logic bombs) in case they're suddenly "severed".

What Are the Solutions?

User education is the key solution. You can't turn every customer into a computer-literate user, let alone a security expert. But you can persuade customers to think more in terms of security—after all, security affects them, their data, and their job prospects. The better that you as a security person understand the issues, the better able you are to determine a customer's weak spots. The same principle applies to the social engineer, too, however. Generally, educating customers in this area is very similar to teaching people how to avoid con artists in nontechnical situations and taking normal precautions to protect your house, money, or children—"Don't get in a car with strangers" is a good example of the type of lesson that you need to teach. The trick is to get people to regard electronic interactions with the same caution as they apply to their offline transactions:

▶ Think code of ethics. Computer ethics remains unexplored territory for most people. Even (especially?) computer scientists tend to be lacking in ethical training. Formulate a code and make clear the costs to any individual who breaches it.

▶ Think policy. You can't expect too much of general education, but if you tie it to specific, easily available policies, you give your customers less to remember, and fewer excuses for forgetting. Specify not only what's forbidden, but some of the reasons for the restrictions.

▶ Think procedures. Give your users guidelines on how to use anti-virus software, select good passwords, practice access control, apply encryption tools, and so on.

▶ Think diagnosis. Teach users how to spot anomalies. Make sure they know what to report, and to whom. Logging and analysis are vital.

▶ Think draconian, where appropriate:

    ▶ Don't talk to strangers.

    ▶ Don't give away inappropriate information to nonstrangers.

    ▶ Query unaccompanied or unbadged visitors.

    ▶ Don't share passwords, login details, PINs, or similar information.

Help Desk and other IT units have special privileges and vulnerabilities. Educate, educate, educate. "People hackers" tend to work on their victims' respect for authority, desire to be helpful, and desire to be unhelpful, or even downright antisocial. One of those options will cover most employees.

New employees are an easy mark, because they know enough to make them worth employing, but don't know most of the people with whom they're going to work. Moral: build your defences into induction procedures. On the other hand, posing as a new employee gives the wannabe hacker credence and leverage as someone who doesn't know something; conversely, it would seem very suspicious if a seasoned employee lacked basic knowledge of the company's system and procedures.

Don't have too much trust in trust (to paraphrase Ken Thompson). Known (or perceived to be known) coworkers often aren't questioned about their actions and movements—especially IT staff. "I'm from IT. I need to check something on your PC/account. Give me your password. Give me ten minutes unobserved. Give me a file on a floppy. Let me install this utility. Let me use your phone. Let me read your mail". Non-IT staff, especially "invisible" people (described earlier in this appendix), are also dangerous, though. Getting a job as a janitor is a well-known hacker resource. As janitor, you get to:

▶ Take away trash (which you can then sift through)

▶ Go into offices when no one is there

- ▶ Fiddle with electronics
- ▶ "Clean" and even disassemble/reassemble phones, allowing for serious surveillance
- ▶ Shouldersurf
- ▶ Steal hardware, paperwork, media, personal possessions, and so on

Good Password Practice

The sad fact is that static passwords are a superficially cheap but brain-damaged solution to a very difficult problem (access control). One-time passwords are much more secure, but have other disadvantages—chiefly expense and inconvenience. Biometric systems are still expensive to install and maintain.

Why Do Password Practices Matter?

Good password practices are critical for the following reasons:

- ▶ The most common form of attack on a corporate system is password guessing.
- ▶ On most systems, most untrusted services are protected primarily by passwords rather than more glamorous methodologies such as smart cards, biometric systems, hand-held authentication, and so on.
- ▶ Insecure passwording, whether engendered by bad systems practice or bad user practice, may endanger data in breach-of-data-protection legislation, contractual obligation, or corporate policy.
- ▶ CERT (Computer Emergency Response Team) states that "80% of all network security problems [are] generated by [a] bad password".

Passwords: Good Systems Enforcement Practice

Password enforcement is a trade-off between paranoia and practicality. The tighter the restrictions, the more pressure on the user to evade restrictions as far as possible so that he or she can get on with the job. Keep the following in mind as you set your restrictions:

- ▶ Buffers that store login keystrokes are a security risk.
- ▶ Unlimited attempts to access a passworded system should not be allowed. Limitations should also apply to dial-in access.

► Where a login attempt threshold has been set, breaches should be audited. The user should be notified at the next successful login, and encouraged to report anomalies.

► Each user should have only one account unless there's a very good reason for making an exception.

► First-time users should receive a unique password (not a default password, least of all an easy guess such as *password, abc123*, or, worst of all, a null password) and be forced to change it at the first login.

► When assigning passwords, using random patterns is preferable to using the same word as the account name or using a password that derives from some other easily guessed formula.

► Passwords shouldn't be given or changed on the strength of an unverified phone call. Ringing back to a trusted phone number or mailing to a trusted individual is better than nothing, but certainly isn't as secure as requiring a user to report in person with verifiable identification.

► A classic password attack technique is to take advantage of an accessible /etc/passwd and play with the password field to apply guessing techniques offline. Shadow password files and dummy password files are recommended.

► Password aging is optimal, in principle. However, it pressures the user into evasive strategies, such as:

    ► Recycling passwords on systems that allow it. (Sometimes this strategy is just a matter of changing the password a given number of times until the system accepts the one that has just timed out.)

    ► Using the same password on a number of systems and changing them all at the same time. This strategy is subject to the same objection that is often made to single sign-on: breaking one password gives an intruder everything.

    ► Writing the password down and leaving it somewhere accessible and therefore insecure (worst case: on a yellow stickie on the monitor).

Best Practice

Don't share passwords unless there's a formal protocol set up to allow it. More than one person sharing an account is a major threat to security (except under *very* controlled conditions); at the very least, it presents difficulties in tracking problems, even where no malicious intent is suspected. Unless clearance in writing has been obtained from an appropriate person (normally the system manager or equivalent for the relevant system rather than the head of a client unit), such practice may be regarded as a breach of discipline.

Other rules of thumb for good password practice include the following:

▶ Integrity of shared data can be compromised (through overwriting by incorrect versions, inadequate file or record locking, or accidental deletion) unless sharing is properly organized.

▶ The more people with access, the greater the risk of accidental or deliberate extension of access to intruders.

▶ The more people with access, the easier cracking the password is likely to be.

▶ Any breach of security on one networked computer is likely to compromise security on the *whole* of the network.

▶ Attacks on computer systems can come from inside as well as outside.

▶ If an attack is traced to a particular account, the holder of that account will be a prime suspect.

Be aware of the social engineering approach to cracking passwords: the quickest route to appropriating a password (especially a shared one) can be via a phone call and a bluff. Don't disclose passwords to anyone whose identity you can't verify, or whose right or need to know is in doubt.

Beware of any request for your password, especially one sent by mail or generated by any program, from whatever apparent source. (The request could have been planted.)

Where Do I Get Further Information?

Here are some good sources for more detailed information on social engineering:

▶ *The NCSA Guide to Enterprise Security: Protecting Information Assets,* by Michel Kabay (McGraw-Hill, 1999)

▶ Web search for one or several articles by Ira Winkler

▶ *Halting the Hacker,* by Donald L. Pipkin (Prentice Hall, 1996)

▶ *Bandits on the Information Superhighway*, by Daniel J. Barrett (O'Reilly and Associates, 1996)

Glossary

ActiveX   A Microsoft system that allows active programming content to be placed in web pages and email messages. ActiveX is tied to a certificate system that may alert users to the presence of active content, but has no other restrictions on the scope of program activity.

activity blocker   *See* behaviour blocker.

activity monitor   A type of antiviral software that checks for signs of suspicious activity, such as attempts to rewrite program files, format disks, modify the boot sector or NORMAL.DOT, and so on. *See also* behaviour blocker. Sometimes called behaviour monitor.

alias   An alternative name for a virus. As there is no absolute naming convention for viruses, some have a number of aliases, according to the vendor and product used. Unfortunately, this can result in considerable confusion.

ANSI bomb   Use of certain codes (escape sequences, usually embedded in text files or email messages) that remap keys on the keyboard to commands such as DELETE or FORMAT.
    ANSI (the American National Standards Institute) is a short form that refers to the ANSI screen formatting rules. Many early MS-DOS programs relied on these rules, and required the use of the ANSI.SYS file, which also allowed keyboard remapping. The use of ANSI.SYS is very rare today.

antiviral   Generally, a shortened term for antiviral software or systems of all types.

Apology   Apology or Apology.B is an alias for the MTX or Matrix Worm.

AppleScript   A scripting language available on recent models of Macintosh (to some extent, a replacement for HyperCard). Some AppleScript Trojans and an AppleScript worm are known to exist at the time of this writing.

archive   A file that contains a number of related files, usually in a compressed format to reduce file size and transmission (upload or download) time on electronic bulletin boards. Most software that is distributed as shareware is distributed as an archive which contains all related programs, as well as documentation and possibly data files. Archived files, because of the compression, appear to be encrypted, and therefore infected files inside archives may not be detected by scanning software. *See also* compressed executable, self-extracting archive.

authentication The use of some kind of system to ensure that a file or message which purports to come from a given individual or company actually does. Many authentication systems are now looking toward public key encryption, and the calculation of a check based upon the contents of the file or message as well as a password or key. *See also* change detection.

AV An abbreviation used to distinguish the antiviral research community (AV) from those who call themselves "virus researchers" but who are primarily interested in writing and exchanging viral programs (VX). Also an abbreviation for antiviral software. *See also* VX.

AVIEN Anti-Virus Information Exchange Network: includes a number of mailing lists by which systems administrators and others share information on new malware and related security issues. (www.avien.org)

backdoor A function built in to a program or system to allow unusually high, or even full, access to the system either without an account or from a normally restricted account. This practice has legitimate uses in program development. The backdoor is sometimes left in a fully developed system either by design or accident. Sometimes called trapdoor. *See* RAT (remote access tools).

bacterium A specialized form of viral program that does not attach to a specific file. The use of this term is fairly obscure and rarely seen.

bait An infection target of initially known characteristics. The term is usually used in reference to a file. To trap file infectors that insist on larger files, a string of null characters of arbitrary length is often used as padding. Floppy disks are used as bait for boot-sector viral programs, but the term is not often used to refer to such disks. Another name for bait files is goat or sacrificial goat files.

behaviour blocker Similar to an activity monitor, a behaviour blocker not only alerts a user to unusual or dangerous computer operations, but actually restricts them. Sometimes called operation restrictor, activity blocker, behaviour blocker. *See also* activity monitor.

behaviour monitor   *See* activity monitor.

benign   A somewhat careless adjective often used to describe a viral code that appears not to be intentionally malicious in that it does not carry an obviously damaging payload code section. Since viral programs may cause problems simply by using system resources or modifying files, many experts are of the opinion that a "good" virus is impossible.

BIOS   Basic input/output system. The initial programming, stored in ROM (read-only memory), that is used to boot the widely used IBM-compatible family of computers that is based on Intel 80*x*86 family processors. Most of these computers are used with the MS-DOS operating system, but the BIOS programming is sufficient for some viral programs that can therefore infect machines that do not run MS-DOS. Some computers now use EEPROM (electrically erasable programmable read-only memory), and some viruses and Trojans now try to cause damage by erasing or writing garbage to such "flash" BIOS. Otherwise, however, a virus cannot infect or corrupt BIOS.

black hat   A community or individual who either attempts to break into computer systems without prior authorization or who explores security primarily from an "attack" perspective. The term originates from old American Western genre movies, where the "good guys" always wore white hats and the "bad guys" always wore black. *See also* white hat.

boot sector   The first sector on a hard disk. Most microcomputers allow "booting" from a floppy disk, and therefore automatically look for the first sector on a floppy disk and run any program found there. On an MS-DOS/BIOS computer with a hard disk, the first physical sector on the hard disk is the master boot record (*see* MBR), and the boot sector is the first sector on the "logical" disk partition.

boot-sector virus   *See* BSV.

Brain   Almost certainly the first virus written in the MS-DOS computing environment that became widespread among normal computer users. Brain is an example of a "strict" boot-sector infector, and the earliest known use of "stealth" virus programming. The virus is sometimes referred to as Brain (C) or (C) Brain due to the presence of the string "(C) 1986 Brain" in the body of the virus.

BS5750   The British standard for quality management on which ISO 9000 is based.

BS7799   A British standard consisting of a code of practice for information security management, and a specification for information security management systems. BS7799 is the basis for ISO standard 17799.

BSI   Boot-sector infector (*see* BSV). Also an acronym for the British Standards Institute, the body from which BS7799 (ISO17799) and BS5750 (ISO 9000) originated.

BSV   A boot-sector virus, sometimes known as a boot-sector infector (BSI). A virus that replaces the original boot sector on a floppy disk. A "strict" BSV infects only the boot sector regardless of whether the target is a hard disk or a floppy diskette. Sometimes a virus attacks the first physical sector of the disk, regardless of disk type; in this case, it attacks the master boot record on hard disks and is known as a BSV of MBR type.

CERT   Computer Emergency Response Team. (www.cert.org)

change detection   Antiviral software that looks for changes in the computer system. A virus must change something, and it is assumed that program files, disk system areas, and certain areas of memory should not change. This software is often referred to as integrity-checking software, but it does not necessarily protect the integrity of data, nor does it always assess the reasons for a possibly valid change. Change detection using strong encryption is sometimes also known as authentication software. *See* authentication.

checksum   In its strictest form, a calculation based upon adding up all the bytes in a file or message. This calculation is used in change-detection systems. The term is sometimes carelessly used to refer to all forms of change detection or authentication that rely on some form of calculation based upon file content, such as cyclic redundancy checking. *See also* CRC.

CHRISTMA EXEC   A specific example of a viral type of email message, the earliest known script email virus. It was written using the REXX scripting language. This message was released in December 1987. The user was asked to type "CHRISTMA" in order to generate an electronic Christmas card, but was not told that the program also made, and mailed, copies of itself during the display. (Within the virus research community, the form CHRISTMA EXEC is used almost universally. The more correct form is CHRISTMA exec, since REXX scripts were referred to as execs to distinguish them from the earlier EXEC language in IBM mainframes.)

CIAC   Computer Incident Advisory Capability. (www.ciac.org/ciac)

cluster virus   *See* link virus.

CMOS   Complementary metal oxide semiconductor. A technology that is used in a form of memory that can be held in the computer, while the main power is off, with low-power battery backup. CMOS memory is used in MS-DOS/BIOS computers to hold small tables of information regarding the basic hardware of the system. Since the memory is maintained while the power is off, there is a myth that viral programs can hide in the CMOS. The assertion is false, since CMOS memory is too small, and the contents are never executed as a program. Also, when the battery power fails, the computer is temporarily unusable. This is often attributed, falsely, to viral activity. CMOS is often confused with BIOS firmware.

code   In computer terminology, either human (source) or machine (object) readable programming or fragments thereof. Since viral programs, before they attach to a host program, are not complete programs, they are often referred to as code to distinguish them from programs, which are complete in themselves.

Code Red   A worm that takes advantage of a vulnerability in unpatched Microsoft IIS servers.

commercial software   Programs that are sold either directly from the manufacturer or through normal retail channels, as opposed to shareware. Users are often told to "buy only commercial" as a defence against viral infections. In fact, there is very little risk of obtaining viral infections from shareware, and there are many known instances of viral programs infecting commercial software.

companion virus   A type of viral program that does not actually attach to another program, but which interposes itself into the chain of command, so that the virus is executed before the infected program. Most often, the virus does this by using a similar name and the rules of program precedence to associate itself with a regular program. Also referred to as a spawning virus.

compressed executable   A program file that has been compressed to save disk space, and which automatically returns to executable form when invoked. Because compression appears to be a form of encryption, programs that are infected before being compressed may hide the infection from scanning software. *See also* archive, self-extracting archive.

compressed file   *See* file compression.

computer viral program   Rob Slade's own invention. In an attempt to avoid the fights over what constitutes a "true" virus, he uses the term viral to refer to self-reproducing programs regardless of other distinctions. So far, he's gotten away with it.

Concept (WM/Concept)   Probably the first Microsoft Word macro virus, and certainly the first macro virus (apart from Macintosh Hypercard infectors) to be successful in the wild.

core wars   A computer game in which two or more programs attempt to destroy each other inside a simulated computer. Originally played with real programs in the earliest timesharing computers and inspired by the operations of rogue programs. Often discussed in connection with the "battle" between malicious software and protective software developers. Core Wars is now a standardized game using a simulated machine language called Redstone code (or redcode). Red Code and Core Red are sometimes seen as synonyms for the Code Red worm, but this probably derives from typographical errors. There is no relationship between Redstone code and any form of the Code Red worm.

crab   Originally a prank program on Macintosh and Atari computers that erased the screen display by having graphical crabs eat it. An obscure usage refers to malicious software that erases screen displays. (There are very few examples of such software.)

cracker   Common synonym for hacker. The term is particularly associated with password "cracking" (gaining unauthorized access). The cracker "cracks" copy-protected programs, allowing easy installation of illegal copies. White hat hackers hold crackers in disdain.

CRC   Cyclic redundancy check. A version of change detection that calculates the data in a file or message as a matrix. This calculation can detect multiple or subtle changes that ordinary checksum calculations miss. CRC is also used extensively in data communications for ensuring the integrity of file transfers. *See also* checksum.

DAME   Dark Avenger's Mutation Engine. *See* MtE.

Dark Avenger   The pseudonym of a Bulgarian virus writer thought to be responsible for the "Eddie" family of viral programs (among others) and the polymorphic code known as the MtE. The pseudonym has probably been used by more than one individual.

date bomb   *See* time bomb.

DDoS   *See* distributed denial of service.

denial of service (DoS)   A form of malicious attack, particularly suited to viral programs, where no data is actually erased or corrupted but where system resources are occupied to the extent that normal service is restricted. The CHRISTMA EXEC did not corrupt data, but occupied mail links to the point where normal transfers could not take place. The Internet Worm did not erase files, but multiple copies of the process eventually meant that almost all processing was devoted to the Worm. Modern Internet DoS attacks typically try to flood a machine with synchronization requests from nonexistent addresses. DoS is not to be confused with DOS, which stands for disk operating system, and particularly the MS-DOS operating system and its variants.

disinfection   The action of removing a virus from an infected system or object, or disabling the virus without fully removing it. Because of various actions a virus may take, it is not always possible to completely restore a system to a state identical to that present prior to infection. Also, because of disagreements, particularly between vendors, as to what constitutes disinfection, deletion of the infected object is generally considered to be the best form of disinfection.

disk compression   Real-time compression and decompression of files on a disk in order to increase disk space effectively. Disk compression programs typically promise to "double" the size of the hard disk. Because disk compression works by creating a "virtual disk" that is actually a large file, scanning a compressed disk without the compression software running will typically hide viruses from a scanner.

distributed denial of service (DDoS)   A form of network DoS (denial of service) attack that uses backdoor agent, client, or zombie software on a number of machines. A master computer will attempt to control a number of machines and coordinate an attack on a target. The master computer never contacts the target directly, and the large number of zombie machines multiplies the force of the attack. *See* zombie, denial of service (DoS).

DLL   Dynamic link library. An executable file containing routines that can be accessed by one or more Windows executables.

DoS *See* denial of service.

DOS Disk operating system. Often used as shorthand for MS-DOS or PC-DOS, but not strictly correctly.

dropper Usually a program that installs a virus but is not itself viral (that is, itdoesn't replicate).

EICAR European Institute for Computer Anti-virus Research. The EICAR test file is a .COM file that can be used to test whether anti-virus software is active.

encryption A change to a message or file such that the appearance of the data is changed and cannot be recognized as the original without proper processing. Encryption is also a side effect of the file compression process. Polymorphism is a deliberate version of encryption used in viral programs to make it harder for virus scanners to recognize their presence. However, encryption is most often used to password-protect files, disks, mail messages, and so on. Also, the act of placing a coffin in a mausoleum.

exploit In security terms, an attack that uses a specific instance of a vulnerability or loophole. The Love Bug worm could be said to be an exploit of the fact that Windows 32-bit (Win32) systems use only the final filename extension as an indicator of file type, and the default installation of Windows Script Host with Windows 98, Windows 2000, and Internet Explorer 5 and higher. Sometimes the slang term "sploit" is used.

exposure In security terms, a synonym for exploit, and also the level of risk from a specific threat or vulnerability. For example, users of Microsoft software and Microsoft Windows operating systems have, generally, a higher exposure to virus infection, due to the number of possible viruses for those platforms, and the built-in functionality that virus writers can utilize.

false negative One of two types of "false" reports from antiviral software. When such software reports no viral activity or presence when a virus is in fact present, that report is a false negative. References to false negatives are usually made only in technical reports. Most people simply refer to antiviral software "missing" a virus. A false negative is more generally known in the security community as a false acceptance or a Type II error.

false positive   The second kind of false report that antiviral software can make. If the software reports the activity or presence of a virus when there is, in fact, no virus, that report is a false positive. The term has come to be very widely used among those who know about viral and antiviral programs. Very few use the analogous term, false alarm. A false positive is more generally known in the security community as a false rejection or a Type I error. The acronym FP is also sometimes used.

FAQ   An information document (from Frequently Asked Questions).

FAT (File Allocation Table)   In the MS-DOS operating system, the area of system information on the disk that refers to the physical areas of the disk which are taken up by files or portions of files. Certain viral programs are said to "take over" a file pointer without affecting directory information by manipulating FAT information. This is not quite accurate, and most researchers tend to prefer the use of the term *system virus* or *infector*.

FDISK /MBR   An MS-DOS command (usually undocumented) that is sometimes recommended as a means of disinfecting boot-sector viruses without anti-virus software. However, in some circumstances, this command can result in the loss of data and disk access.

file compression   A form of encryption performed on files to minimize the space they take on disk. File compression is generally done manually, on a file-by-file basis, as opposed to the automated disk compression. As a form of encryption, file compression may hide virus infections in compressed files. Superior antiviral programs can now scan inside normally compressed files, sometimes even inside nested compressed files (those that contain compressed files inside compressed files). However, scanning inside compressed or archived files is not always reliable.

file infector   A virus that attaches itself to, or associates itself with, a file, usually a program file. File infectors most often append or prepend themselves to regular program files, or overwrite program code. File infectors may also insert themselves into free space within the program that exists in portable executable (PE) files, or even in the middle of files, though this is not as common. The file infector class is often also used to refer to programs that do not physically attach to files but associate themselves with program filenames. The term is not usually applied to macro viruses, even though these do, in a sense, infect files. *See* system infector, companion virus.

freeware   Software to which the author or developer still retains copyright (unlike public domain), but for which there is no charge (unlike shareware or commercial software). There are sometimes restrictions on the use or distribution of freeware. *See* commercial software, open source, pubic domain, shareware.

ftp   File transfer protocol. The protocol used to copy files between computers on the Internet. ftp (almost always written in lowercase) has nothing to do with viral programs or data security at all; it has just come to be such a common term among those who work on the Internet that we have used it in the book a number of times without ever defining it. It is often used as a verb, as in "Where do I find the latest copy of DISKSECURE?" "Oh, you can ftp it from urvax". A computer set up to provide files for all callers from anywhere on the Internet is known as an ftp site. Anonymous ftp sites usually allow connection for download of software without requiring an account on the system, but have to some extent been supplanted by web sites.

generic antiviral software   Activity-monitoring and change-detection antiviral software. Such software is considered generic because it looks for suggestions of viral activity rather than specific virus signatures. Heuristic scanners are often also considered generic, because they can be viewed as a special case of activity monitors. *See* activity monitor, change detection, heuristic.

generic disinfection   The use of heuristic rather than virus-specific techniques for disinfection.

generic scan string   A virus scan string that matches more than one virus. The usefulness of generic scan strings is sometimes questioned, but they can detect an unknown virus very effectively. *See* signature.

germ   A viral program that does not directly attach to programs. *See* bacterium. The term is sometimes used to describe a generation-zero virus, one that has not yet infected its first sample.

Ghost Positive   Detection by a virus scanner of viral traces which are reported as a full-blown viral infection, usually as a result of incomplete disinfection by another product.

goat   *See* bait.

grey hat   An individual who is not quite a black hat (virus writer, cracker, vandal, or such), but not altogether a white hat either. Some "ethical hackers" and people who write both viruses and anti-virus software could be said to belong to this group.

hacker   Originally, someone who had or was on the way to acquiring an unusual degree of skill in various aspects of computer use. Now the term is used almost exclusively to refer to computer vandals, people who break into systems, and so on. Often the term is used in the phrase "hackers and virus writers", not altogether appropriately, as the two groups are not necessarily closely related, and virus-writers are not particularly admired by old-time or criminal hackers. Old-time hackers prefer to refer to computer vandals and criminals as crackers, but the equation of hacking with criminal is now firmly embedded in the popular and media consciousness.

heterogeneous virus transmission   The phenomenon where a virus finds its way into an environment in which it cannot be executed (for example, a Windows virus on UNIX server or a Macintosh virus on a PC), but can be passed on to another vulnerable system passively instead of by self-replication. Peter Radatti probably coined the term.

heuristic   In antiviral terms, the examination of program code for functions known to be associated with viral activity. (While no single activity is proof positive that a virus is present, the presence of a number of such activities is taken to suggest a likely infection.) In most cases, a heuristic is similar to activity monitoring, but without the actual execution of the program; in other cases, code is run under some type of emulation. There is also, as of this writing, a single case of a heuristic disinfection program that attempts to remove viral infections by examining unknown code.

hoax   A message warning about a non-existent virus. A hoax generally asks the reader to forward the message to everyone possible, thus becoming a virus, of a sort, itself. *See* metavirus.

Hybris   An infective program that most specialists would probably classify as a worm, since it sends copies of itself as email attachments. Hybris will generally come in a message with a coy indication that the attachment is pornography. The attachment is often named with an .SCR extension. The extension is traditionally used to indicate screensavers, but the file format is the same as for any normal executable Windows program. The notable feature of Hybris is that, when active, it checks for replacement and upgrade modules on the alt.comp.virus newsgroup. Other viruses, such as Love Bug, have attempted to establish such a modular extension function, but Hybris has extended the concept further and used an anonymous communications facility.

IDS   Intrusion Detection System. An automated process auditing activity and alerting operators to patterns indicating unauthorized penetration or attack.

infection   The transmission of a virus into a computer system, and execution of the replicative code. An infection, on a given system, does not take place until a virus has become active, reproduced, or made a change to the system. A user or system may receive a virus as a file transfer, a virus-infected piece of software, or an email attachment, and not necessarily become infected. So long as a user does not invoke the virus, or a worm does not find a specific vulnerability to exploit, the infected file may remain dormant on the system without infecting the system itself. However, a system may also be considered infected if the virus has either placed itself in a situation such that the operating system will activate it during a common occurrence (such as booting the system) or if a user is likely to call an infected, and commonly used, program.

integrity checker   *See* change detection, authentication.

intended   Code intended to be a virus, but incapable of replicating.

Internet Worm   An infamous worm, also known as the UNIX Worm after the operating system it used, or the Morris Worm after the author, or, very specifically, the Internet/Morris/UNIX Worm. Launched in November 1988, it spread to some 3,000–4,000 machines connected to the Internet, wasting CPU cycles and clogging mail spools. It affected mail traffic (in particular) throughout the Internet for a few days and was probably the viral program most widely known to the general public before Melissa and the Love Bug.

Jerusalem   One of the earliest MS-DOS file infectors known to be in the wild. Discovered and probably written in Israel, Jerusalem was originally known as the Israeli virus, and has also been called PLO, Friday the 13th, and 1813. The infector is widely used as a template for the development of variant viral strains.

joke   In the anti-virus context, this refers to joke programs rather than to funny stories. May include totally harmless programs, such as CokeGift, but some jokes may have some adverse psychological effect, such as pretending to format the hard disk.

kit   A program used to produce viral code from a menu or a list of characteristics. Use of a virus kit involves no skill on the part of the user. Fortunately, most virus kits produce easily identifiable code. Packages of antiviral utilities are sometimes referred to as tool kits.

LAN   Local area network.

latent virus   Any virus in an environment in which it cannot execute and self-replicate.

Lehigh   One of the first MS-DOS viral programs. Lehigh only infected copies of the COMMAND.COM program. The virus is thought to have been isolated to the campus of Lehigh University, where it was discovered, but most researchers and VX boards have copies. The limited use of bootable MS-DOS diskettes makes it unlikely that the virus would successfully spread if re-released.

link virus   A term that is not used very widely and is defined in a variety of ways. Amiga and Atari users talk about a link virus as a file infector. Some others use the term to refer to system or FAT viral programs. The term link may also refer to the activity or process by which a virus that does not attach to a program file becomes active when the program is called, sometimes by changing the pointer from the file directory to a different disk cluster.

logic bomb   A section of code, preprogrammed into a larger program, that waits for some trigger event to perform some damaging function. Logic bombs do not reproduce and so are not viral, but a virus may contain a logic bomb as a payload. Logic bombs that trigger at preprogrammed times are sometimes known as time bombs.

Love Bug   A script email virus that used Outlook and Windows Script Host. The virus spread itself as an email with an attachment called LOVE-LETTER-FOR-YOU.TXT.vbs. The filename was an interesting piece of social engineering, in that people were supposed to notice the .TXT extension and think the file was only a text file, and obviously were not supposed to notice the .vbs extension, the file's actual extension, which identifies the file as a script.

MacMag   An early Macintosh virus known also as Brandow, after the instigator (the publisher of *MacMag*), and Peace, after the message payload. MacMag has the dubious distinction of being the first virus known to have infected commercial software.

macro virus   A virus that attacks a macro, which is a small piece of programming in a simple language, used to perform a simple, repetitive function. Microsoft's WordBasic and VBA macro languages can include macros in data files, and have more than enough functionality to write complete viruses. Existing macro viruses are usually application-specific, rather than operating system (OS)-specific.

malicious virus   A virus known to carry an intentionally damaging payload that will erase or corrupt files or data. Many antiviral researchers feel that all viral programs carry the potential for unintentional damage since all viral programs change the target environment. *See also* benign.

malignant   In medicine (especially oncology), the antonym of benign. The adjective is rarely used in computer virology, except as an alternative to malicious, which is usually used in a less specific sense.

malware   Generally, all forms of malicious or damaging software, including viral programs, Trojan horses, logic bombs, and the like. It is generally taken to include so-called benign viruses that have no intentionally damaging payload.

Matrix   *See* MTX.

MBR   Master boot record. The "physical first" sector on the hard disk. The MBR contains information about the hard disk structure and operating system to use on BIOS/Intel computers. The MBR is a target for a certain class of boot-sector-infecting viral programs. *See* BSV.

Melissa   A Word macro virus that also used functions in the Outlook email program in order to spread itself very successfully and quickly.

meme, memetic   A unit of cultural transmission, or a unit of imitation. The term, coined by Richard Dawkins, is abbreviated from mimeme, so as to sound more like gene. As examples of memes, Dawkins cites tunes, ideas, catchphrases, and so on. The science (or pseudoscience) of memetics has grown out of this coining. In the context of security, it is usually applied in terms of virus and other hoaxes, chain letters, and so on.

memory-resident   *See* resident.

metavirus   Usually, a virus hoax, but sometimes, more loosely, a chain letter.

Michelangelo   A descendent of the Stoned boot-sector/MBR virus. Michelangelo carries a damaging payload that triggers when the computer is booted on 6th March, the birthdate of the Renaissance painter and sculptor. First discovered in early 1991, the virus gained notoriety during the "Michelangelo scare" leading up to March 1992. Although considered by many to have been media hype, the attention generated did disclose many thousands of infections prior to 6th March that were disinfected and therefore never triggered.

MtE   The most widely used abbreviation for the "mutation engine" written by the virus author known as Dark Avenger. Not a virus itself, this section of code can be attached to any virus, giving the virus polymorphic features. The code is also known, less widely, as DAME. *See* polymorphism.

MTX (Matrix, Apology)   A bipolar worm/virus that reproduces both by sending itself as an email message and by infecting program files. MTX will take control of the Internet connection of an infected machine, and seeks to bar access to many antiviral web sites.

multipartite   Traditionally, a viral program that will infect both boot sectors/MBRs and files. The term is now sometimes used to refer to a virus that will infect more than one type of object, or that reproduces in multiple ways.

Navidad   A mail-aware virus. The first version made restarting difficult because a bug in the code caused a Registry entry to point to a non-existent file. A subsequent version corrected this bug.

NLM   NetWare-loadable module. A system of programs that is specific to LAN servers using Novell network operating systems. A number of commercial antiviral vendors make a NetWare-specific NLM scanner available for NetWare server and workstation protection.

NOP   A null directive in an assembler program that doesn't actually do anything specific when it is executed.

NOS   Network operating system.

NSA   National Security Agency. (www.nsa.org)

nVIR   An early Macintosh virus, the source code for which was inadvertently published electronically. Shortly thereafter, two versions were found in the wild.

opcode   In assembly language, the part of an instruction or directive that identifies the specific operation to be performed.

open source   A software development philosophy based on the premise that the source code for software must be made available to the user, and that restrictions cannot be made on the user's modification of the code, so long as the user is also bound by the same proviso. There are some disagreements about the precise use of the term open source, but it is generally seen as being akin (but not equal) to both public domain software and freeware. However, open source software is also seen as a viable commercial model. *See also* commercial software, freeware, public domain, shareware.

operation restrictor   Synonym for behaviour blocker.

overwriting virus   A file virus that overwrites part of a file with itself.

payload   The code in a viral program that is not concerned with reproduction or detection avoidance. The payload is often a message, but is sometimes code to corrupt or erase data. Reference to damaging payload is not to code causing physical destruction of the computer or parts thereof, but to corruption or erasure of files or data.

PGP   Pretty Good Privacy. An encryption and authentication public key system held in high regard by the online community. It exists in both freeware and commercial versions.

phreak   An individual who is interested in breaking into or otherwise manipulating the telephone system. These people are referred to (and refer to themselves) as phone phreaks, using the punning variant spelling. This is generally shortened to phreaks in common usage.

polymorphism   Techniques that use some system of changing the "form" of the virus on each infection to try to avoid detection by signature-scanning software. Less sophisticated systems are sometimes referred to as self-encrypting. Strictly speaking, encryption is not the only way in which to "morph", and an encrypted virus is not necessarily polymorphic.

Ponzi Scheme   A fraudulent scheme somewhat akin to a pyramid scheme, apparently named after its inventor.

prank   Software that appears to cause problems or damage, but which, in fact, does not. In a sense, this software is the inverse of the Trojan horse. Books are being published that describe how to create pranks, and programs are now being sold that perform these "stupid computer tricks". A prank may cause heart problems, but no erasure of data. (However, sometimes drawing a hard and fast line between pranks and malware is difficult. Pranks generally cause some denial of service, but hopefully only for a short time.)

Prepender   A file infector that attaches to the beginning of the infected file.

public domain   A legal term that carries the same meaning in regard to software that it does in the field of literature. Software in the public domain may be used by anyone, for any purpose, in any manner, without restriction. This term is often used carelessly to refer to freeware, which requires no payment, but for which the author still assumes copyright and control, and shareware, which does, in fact, require payment for continued use. *See also* commerical software, freeware, open source, shareware.

public key encryption   An encryption and authentication system that allows at least one "key" to be made publicly available. This system allows anyone to read the material with the public key, but does not allow alteration of the message without detection. The major advantage in the public key concept is in key management and in the secure interaction between large numbers of users.

rabbit   A program that generates multiple copies of itself without attaching to other programs. Generally, this type of attack is a denial of service based upon excessive use of disk or memory space or CPU cycles. Usage of the term is rare.

RAT (Remote Access Tools)   Tools that allow access to, and control over, a desktop computer (normally considered to be a single user machine) from a remote site. More specifically, Remote Access Tools are designed to be installed on a machine, and they allow a remote attacker control over the machine, and provide a backdoor for other operations. Back Orifice is an example of a RAT. The acronym is sometimes used as a short form of Remote Access Trojan, although the two usages are not altogether synonymous. *See also* backdoor.

Registry   *See* Windows Registry.

replicate   In general, to copy or reproduce. In virus research, the term replicate, or sometimes reproduce, is often used to distinguish the clandestine copying action done by a virus from the normal and deliberate duplication performed by the user. Some people seem to prefer the term self-replicate, which has the advantage of clarifying the distinction between active viral replication and passive duplication by user action, as opposed to the execution of viral code. The term does, however, sidestep the issues of meme viruses and worms that rely on social engineering to trick the victim into executing code.

resident   A program that stays in the memory of the computer while other programs are running, waiting for a specific trigger event. "Accessory" software is often of this type, as is activity-monitoring and "resident" scanning software. Viral programs often attempt to "go resident", and so this is one of the functions that an activity monitor may check. Also known as memory-resident and, in MS-DOS circles, TSR. The Windows equivalent is a VxD or NT service. On a Macintosh, the equivalent would be a control panel or system extension.

rogue   A program that, because of a bug in programming, interferes with normal system operation. The damage caused by a rogue is unintentional. The term is used primarily in mainframe circles and is now relatively rarely used.

ROM   Read-only memory. A static memory type used to hold programming, regardless of power conditions. ROM is primarily used for the bootstrap programming for microcomputers. Until recently, this memory has been non-writeable in normal operation, and thus safe from viral attacks, but this has changed with the use of "flash" EEPROMs.

rootkit   A suite of trojanized system applications substituted for the untrojanized originals to enable an intruder to gain access with administrator privileges.

RTF   Rich Text Format. A file format wherein complex formatting information is embedded as text tags readable by most word processors. Sometimes preferred for document exchange because, unlike Word documents, RTF documents don't support VBA macros. However, there are circumstances in which an RTF document can be a virus transmission vector.

RTFM   Read The Friendly Manual. A less polite adjective is sometimes used.

salami   An apocryphal story of a program that takes advantage of very active systems to make incremental changes. The usual tale is of a banking system that syphons fractions of a penny at a time into the programmer's account. In spite of the lack of evidence for the existence of attacks of this type, increasing numbers of security books make reference to salami slicing.

scanner   1) A program that reads the contents of a file looking for code known to exist in specific viral programs. Also referred to as known virus scanning (KVS). 2) In network situations, a program that examines the configurations of computers and network systems, looking for security vulnerabilities. Both defenders and attackers can use this type of program. SATAN (Security Administrators Tool for Analysing Networks) is an example of this type of scanner.

Scores   A Macintosh virus that seems to have been written with intent to cause problems for a specific company and software program. Because one of the most widely published reports of infection was from an office at NASA, the virus has also been referred to as NASA.

self-extracting archive   An archive that is stored in program format (that is, as an .EXE file) and which contains the code necessary to do the "de-archiving". The archive is popular with neophyte BBS and Internet users because it does not require separate de-archiving programs, but it presents a number of potential security vulnerabilities.

shareware   Software that is distributed widely, usually on bulletin boards and networks. Users are encouraged to "try before they buy", but users who continue to use the software are supposed to pay for the programs. The honour system of distribution reduces overhead costs, and shareware is generally cheaper than commercial software. *See also* commercial software, freeware, open source, public domain.

shell scrap object   A Microsoft file format that may include executable content (and indeed practically anything). The shell scrap file extensions, .SHS and .SHB, will not display in normal Windows file dialogue boxes unless a change is made to the Registry.

shrink wrap   The plastic film used to protect the packaging of commercial software. Shrinkwrapped software is often used as a synonym for commercial software. Many people feel that shrink wrap is some kind of protection, guarantee, or warranty. It isn't.

signature   Sequence of bytes recognized by an anti-virus scanner or intrusion-detection system as suggesting the presence of a known virus or other malicious code. This sequence is an arbitrarily chosen value: there is no guarantee that two products will use the same string. Use of the term signature implies a literal (invariant) string, but many viruses cannot be detected using fixed strings, so anti-virus scanners use a variety of techniques for detection, including wildcard detection and algorithmic techniques. The more flexible term scanstring is, therefore, usually preferred by anti-virus researchers.

social engineering   A nontechnical means of breaking security, involving conning people into telling you passwords, getting them to run programs they shouldn't, and so forth. Basically, social engineering is a fancy name for fraud.

spawning virus   *See* companion virus.

sploit   Slang usage for exploit.

Stages of Life   A script email virus/worm notable for a variable message and for the use of the .SHS file extension, making it harder to spot in Windows.

stealth   Various technologies used by viral programs to avoid detection on disk. At least one virus has been named Stealth by its author, but the term properly refers to the technology, and not a particular virus.

Stoned   An extremely "successful" MS-DOS virus, in terms of the number of copies made and systems infected. A BSV of MBR type, it has, like most successful viral programs, been used as a template for numerous other viral strains.

system infector   A virus that redirects system pointers and information in order to "infect" a file without actually changing the infected program file. This is a type of stealth technology. In MS-DOS, system infectors are often referred to as FAT viruses. *See also* link virus.

template   A file used by Microsoft Word as a pattern for new documents. By default, new documents are patterned on the global template NORMAL.DOT. Traditionally, templates are named (on PCs) with a .DOT extension, while documents have a .DOC extension, but either file can actually have any extension, or none. In older Word versions, a Word document cannot contain a macro, but a template file can contain data. Therefore, .DOC files infected with macro viruses are templates, not documents. This does not apply in later versions, where documents can contain macros without being templates. Users, of course, cannot easily tell the difference, unless they're specifically looking for indicators such as the appearance of the icon. Even these indicators do not tell you for sure that a given file is not a template, or does not contain macros.

threat   In security terms, a possibility of an attack or loss of confidentiality or availability due to an inherent aspect of the system. For example, viruses are an ongoing threat for computer operations because they use only the normal functions that other programs require.

time bomb   A term sometimes used to refer to a logic bomb that triggers on a time event. A logic bomb that triggers on a specific date is sometimes referred to as a date bomb.

TOAST   An acronym first used by Padgett Peterson to refer to antiviral software that makes extravagant claims, or for which a company spends more on advertising than it does on development. The origin was a product that advertised itself as, "The Only Antivirus Software That Won't Be Obsolete By The Time You Finish Reading This Ad".

TPE   Trident Polymorphic Engine. Another example of the "mutation engine" type of functionality but from a different source. *See* MtE.

trapdoor   *See* backdoor.

trigger   In regard to viruses and other malware, the event, or the code waiting for an event, that stimulates the activity of the payload. In special cases, the term may also refer to the event or code that causes reproduction or replication of the virus, if the virus does not seek out suitable targets upon activation.

Trojan horse   A program that either pretends to have, or is described as having, a (beneficial) set of features, but which, either instead or in addition, contains a damaging payload. Most frequently the usage is shortened to Trojan. There is little agreement on whether the term Trojan horse should be capitalized, or how, but the most common usage tends to be Trojan horse and trojan or Trojan. Trojan generally refers to a name brand prophylactic.

TSR   Terminate and Stay Resident. *See* resident.

tunnelling   Techniques that involve tracing the system interrupts to the final programming. Tunnelling is used by both viral and antiviral programs to detect or disable opposing programs.

upconvert   A virus written in WordBasic when it migrates (intentionally or otherwise) to VBA. An upconverted viral macro may or may not be a viable virus after conversion.

VBA   Visual Basic for Applications. The scripting and macro language in current Microsoft Office products that allows macro viruses to operate. The first generation of Word viruses, however, was written in the closely related WordBasic dialect.

VBScript   Visual Basic Script. A scripting language similar to Visual Basic for Applications, used by a number of virus/worm authors.

viral   Having the features of a virus, particularly self-reproduction. *See* replicate.

virus   A final definition has not yet been agreed upon by all researchers. A common definition is, "a program that modifies other programs to contain a possibly altered version of itself". This definition is generally attributed to Fred Cohen, although Cohen's actual definition is in mathematical form. Another possible definition is, "an entity that uses the resources of the host (system or computer) to reproduce itself and spread, without informed operator action".

vulnerability   In security terms, the possibility of an exploit or exposure to a threat, specific to a given platform. For example, while many word processing programs contain the ability to create macro programming, Microsoft Word has a specific vulnerability to viruses because of the inclusion of macro programming in the same file that contains the data.

VX   An abbreviated reference to the virus exchange community; those people who consider it proper and right to write, share, and release viral programs, including those with damaging payloads. The term was probably coined as vx by Sarah Gordon, who has done extensive studies of the virus-exchange and security-breaking communities and who has an aversion to using the SHIFT key. Capitalization is not consistent, and vX may also be acceptable.

warhead   A synonym for payload.

white hat   An individual who attempts to explore security solely from the perspective of defence. The security community—in an attempt to avoid debates about "good" hackers versus "bad" hackers versus "crackers" versus phone phreaks versus virus writers versus VXers—has taken to using this term. The term originates from old American Western genre movies, where the "good guys" always wore white hats. *See also* black hat.

wild, in the   A jargon reference to those viral programs that have been released into, and have successfully spread in, the general computer user community and environment. It is used to distinguish those viral programs that are written and tested in a controlled research environment, without escaping, from those that are uncontrolled "in the wild".

Wild, In the (ItW)   A specific reference to those viruses formally mentioned in the WildList. The capitalization is in distinction to viruses found in the wild but not mentioned in the WildList.

WildList   A list of viruses and some worms reported as being currently in the wild, aggregated by the WildList Organization on the basis of suitably qualified expert reporters. The WildList proper consists of viruses that have been reported by at least two qualified reporters. The supplemental list consists of viruses that have been reported by one qualified reporter. The WildList is, at present, almost entirely PC-centric. Similar lists for Trojans and for Macintosh malware are under development.

Windows Registry   A database holding system start-up, configuration, security, and file-association information in Microsoft Windows 9*x,* Me, NT, and 2000 systems. This is the central repository of all such information, replacing the old CONFIG.SYS, AUTOEXEC.BAT, and .INI files (although those files do still exist, and are sometimes used). The Registry is an enormous object, often holding megabytes of data, and difficult to search. It is now being used to start viruses at boot time, without placing the viruses in identifiable start-up directories. Viruses affecting the Registry can be seen as system infectors, although changing the Registry is much easier than the programming that the old MS-DOS system infectors had to use.

Windows Script Host (WSH)   A utility that runs scripting languages such as Visual Basic Script (VBScript) on certain Windows systems in a way somewhat similar to DOS batch files, but with more versatility. The Love Bug virus (a.k.a. LoveLetter) was a Windows script virus using VBScript; it relied on the presence of WSH, which may be installed on all versions of Windows since Windows 95. Many organizations disable WSH to reduce the impact from VBScript malware.

worm   A self-reproducing program that is often distinguished from a virus in that it copies itself without being attached to a program file, or by spreading actively over computer networks, particularly via email. Many researchers regard worms as a special case or subset of viruses.

Worm   "The" worm, the Internet/Morris/UNIX Worm of November 1988. *See* Internet Worm.

zombie   A specialized type of backdoor or remote-access program designed as the agent component of a DDoS (distributed denial of service) network. Once a zombie is installed on a computer, it identifies itself to a master computer, and then waits for instructions from the master computer. After receiving instructions from the master computer, a number of zombie machines will send attack packets to a target computer. *See also* backdoor, DDoS, RAT.

zoo   Jargon term for a set of viral programs of known characteristics used to test antiviral software. Zoo viruses are often regarded as antonymous to "in the wild" viruses.

Index

INTERNATIONAL CONTACT INFORMATION

AUSTRALIA
McGraw-Hill Book Company Australia Pty. Ltd.
TEL +61-2-9417-9899
FAX +61-2-9417-5687
http://www.mcgraw-hill.com.au
books-it_sydney@mcgraw-hill.com

CANADA
McGraw-Hill Ryerson Ltd.
TEL +905-430-5000
FAX +905-430-5020
http://www.mcgrawhill.ca

**GREECE, MIDDLE EAST,
NORTHERN AFRICA**
McGraw-Hill Hellas
TEL +30-1-656-0990-3-4
FAX +30-1-654-5525

MEXICO (Also serving Latin America)
McGraw-Hill Interamericana Editores S.A. de C.V.
TEL +525-117-1583
FAX +525-117-1589
http://www.mcgraw-hill.com.mx
fernando_castellanos@mcgraw-hill.com

SINGAPORE (Serving Asia)
McGraw-Hill Book Company
TEL +65-863-1580
FAX +65-862-3354
http://www.mcgraw-hill.com.sg
mghasia@mcgraw-hill.com

SOUTH AFRICA
McGraw-Hill South Africa
TEL +27-11-622-7512
FAX +27-11-622-9045
robyn_swanepoel@mcgraw-hill.com

**UNITED KINGDOM & EUROPE
(Excluding Southern Europe)**
McGraw-Hill Education Europe
TEL +44-1-628-502500
FAX +44-1-628-770224
http://www.mcgraw-hill.co.uk
computing_neurope@mcgraw-hill.com

ALL OTHER INQUIRIES Contact:
Osborne/McGraw-Hill
TEL +1-510-549-6600
FAX +1-510-883-7600
http://www.osborne.com
omg_international@mcgraw-hill.com